Handbook of Research on Emotional and Behavioral Disorders

The *Handbook of Research on Emotional and Behavioral Disorders* explores the factors necessary for successful implementation of interventions that foster productive relationships and ecologies to establish, reinforce, and sustain adaptive patterns of emotional and behavioral functioning across childhood and into adulthood.

Although there has been a concerted focus on developing evidence-based programs and practices to support the needs of children and youth with emotional and behavioral disorders, there has been less emphasis on the developmental, social, and environmental factors that impact the implementation and effectiveness of these approaches. Chapters from leading experts tackle this complexity by drawing on a range of disciplines and perspectives including special education; mental health services; school, clinical, and community psychology; social work; developmental psychology and psychopathology; and prevention science.

An essential resource for scholars and students interested in emotional and behavioral disorders, this volume crafts an essential framework to promote developmentally meaningful strategies for children and youth with even the most adverse experiences and intensive support needs.

Thomas W. Farmer is Professor and Chair of the Department of Psychology in Education at the University of Pittsburgh.

Maureen A. Conroy is Co-Director of the Anita Zucker Center for Excellence in Early Childhood Studies, and the Anita Zucker Endowed Professor of Early Childhood Studies at the University of Florida.

Elizabeth M.Z. Farmer is Professor and Dean of the School of Social Work at the University of Pittsburgh.

Kevin S. Sutherland is Professor of Counseling and Special Education at Virginia Commonwealth University.

Handbook of Research on Emotional and Behavioral Disorders

Interdisciplinary Developmental Perspectives on Children and Youth

Edited by Thomas W. Farmer, Maureen A. Conroy, Elizabeth M.Z. Farmer, and Kevin S. Sutherland

NEW YORK AND LONDON

First published 2020
by Routledge
52 Vanderbilt Avenue, New York, NY 10017

and by Routledge
2 Park Square, Milton Park, Abingdon, Oxon, OX14 4RN

Routledge is an imprint of the Taylor & Francis Group, an informa business

© 2020 Taylor & Francis

The right of Thomas W. Farmer, Maureen A. Conroy, Elizabeth M.Z. Farmer, and Kevin S. Sutherland to be identified as the authors of the editorial material, and of the authors for their individual chapters, has been asserted in accordance with sections 77 and 78 of the Copyright, Designs and Patents Act 1988.

All rights reserved. No part of this book may be reprinted or reproduced or utilised in any form or by any electronic, mechanical, or other means, now known or hereafter invented, including photocopying and recording, or in any information storage or retrieval system, without permission in writing from the publishers.

Trademark notice: Product or corporate names may be trademarks or registered trademarks, and are used only for identification and explanation without intent to infringe.

Library of Congress Cataloging-in-Publication Data
A catalog record for this title has been requested

ISBN: 978-1-138-32070-3 (hbk)
ISBN: 978-1-138-32071-0 (pbk)
ISBN: 978-0-429-45310-6 (ebk)

Typeset in Baskerville
by Swales & Willis, Exeter, Devon, UK

Contents

List of Figures	ix
List of Tables	x

PART 1
Developmental Processes and Timing   1

1 The Development, Prevention, and Treatment of Emotional and Behavioral
   Disorders: An Interdisciplinary Developmental Systems Perspective   3
   THOMAS W. FARMER, LISA GATZKE-KOPP, AND SHAWN J. LATENDRESSE

2 The Epidemiology of Childhood Emotional and Behavioral Disorders   23
   HEATHER RINGEISEN, LEYLA STAMBAUGH, AND DALIA KHOURY

3 Prevention and Intervention in Preschool and Early
   Elementary School Years   35
   MAUREEN A. CONROY, REBECCA BULOTSKY-SHEARER, CHELSEA MORRIS,
   AND ALLYSE A. HETRICK

4 Developmental Processes and Emotional and Behavioral Disorders during
   the Middle and High School Years   50
   MOLLY DAWES, KEVIN S. SUTHERLAND, TERRI SULLIVAN, AND JENNIFER HARRIST

5 The Transition to Adulthood: A Critical Developmental Period within a
   Changing Social-Contextual Landscape   65
   KATHRYN SABELLA, MARYANN DAVIS, AND MICHELLE R. MUNSON

PART 2
Targeting Social Processes and Environmental Ecologies   81

6 Interaction-Centered Model of Language and Behavioral Development   83
   JASON C. CHOW, JENNIFER E. CUNNINGHAM, AND ERIN STEHLE WALLACE

vi *Contents*

7 Peer to Peer Support: Innovative Strategies for Families of Youth
with Emotional/Behavioral Disorders — 96
KRISTIN DUPPONG HURLEY, AL DUCHNOWSKI, KRISTA KUTASH, AND
JENNIFER FARLEY

8 The Family Check-Up: Building on Family Strengths
to Promote Child Wellbeing — 111
ANNE M. GILL AND DANIEL S. SHAW

9 Classroom Peer Ecologies and Cultures, and Students with EBD:
Social Dynamics as Setting Events for Intervention — 125
JILL V. HAMM, KRISTEN L. GRANGER, AND RICHARD A. VAN ACKER

10 Implementation of Violence Prevention Programs — 140
TERRI N. SULLIVAN, KATHERINE M. ROSS, MEGAN M. CARLSON,
STEPHANIE A. HITTI, AND KATHRYN L. BEHRHORST

11 Interventions for Youth Who Experience Trauma and Adversity — 153
ELIZABETH A. MILLER AND DAVID J. KOLKO

12 Strengthening Social Processes to Support Youth with Emotional and
Behavioral Difficulties: An Ecological, Public Health Approach in
Afterschool Programs — 167
ELISE CAPPELLA, STACY L. FRAZIER, EMILIE P. SMITH, AND SOPHIA H. J. HWANG

PART 3
Selected Effective Programs and Practices — 183

13 The Family Check-Up for Elementary and Middle School Youth and
Families Emotional/Behavioral Disorders — 185
LUCIA E. CARDENAS, JORDAN M. MATULIS, AND ELIZABETH A. STORMSHAK

14 Multi-Tiered Systems of Support — 200
LEE KERN, KENT McINTOSH, COLLEEN E. COMMISSO, AND SEAN C. AUSTIN

15 BEST in CLASS: A Tier-2 Program for Children with and
at Risk for Emotional/Behavioral Disorders — 214
KEVIN S. SUTHERLAND, MAUREEN A. CONROY, AND KRISTEN GRANGER

16 An Adaptive, Correlated Constraints Model of Classroom Management:
The Behavioral, Academic, and Social Engagement (BASE) Program — 227
THOMAS W. FARMER, JILL HAMM, DAVID LEE, BRITTANY STERRETT, KAREN RIZZO,
AND KATE NORWALK

Contents vii

17 Multi-Tiered Social-Emotional Learning: PATHS and Friendship
Group in the Fast Track Program 245
KAREN L. BIERMAN, MARK T. GREENBERG, AND THE CONDUCT PROBLEMS
PREVENTION RESEARCH GROUP

18 Checking the Connections between Effective Interventions for Students
with Emotional/Behavioral Disorders 261
ALLISON BRUHN, SARA MCDANIEL, AND KAY AUGUSTINE

19 Multisystemic Therapy for High-Risk Youth: Emotional/Behavioral
Disorders 276
MICHAEL R. McCART, ASHLI J. SHEIDOW, AND PHILLIPPE B. CUNNINGHAM

20 Treatment Foster Care: Providing Out-of-Home Treatment
in Community- and Family-Based Environments 290
ELIZABETH M.Z. FARMER, MAUREEN E. MURRAY, BARBARA J. BURNS,
AND ALLISON D. LITTLE

21 Residential Programs: Opportunities and Challenges in
the 21st-Century Treatment Environment 306
BETHANY R. LEE

22 Managing and Adapting Practice (MAP) 321
MICHAEL A. SOUTHAM-GEROW, JULIA R. COX, AND ABIGAIL KINNEBREW

23 Best Practices for Prescribing and Deprescribing Psychotropic
Medications for Children and Youth 341
CHRISTOPHER BELLONCI AND JONATHAN C. HUEFNER

24 The Homework, Organization, and Planning Skills (HOPS)
Intervention 356
JOSHUA M. LANGBERG, ROSANNA BREAUX, MELISSA R. DVORSKY,
STEPHEN J. MOLITOR, ZOE R. SMITH, AND ELIZAVETA BOURCHTEIN

25 The Daily Report Card Intervention: Summary of the Science
and Factors Affecting Implementation 371
JULIE SARNO OWENS, CHELSEA L. HUSTUS, AND STEVEN W. EVANS

26 Cognitive-Behavioral Prevention and Intervention Approaches
to Student Emotional and Behavioral Functioning 386
STEPHEN W. SMITH, JONI W. SPLETT, DANIEL V. POLING, AND JOSEPH W. GRAHAM

27 School-based Mental Health 400
STEVEN W. EVANS, R. ELIZABETH CAPPS, AND JULIE SARNO OWENS

viii *Contents*

PART 4
Preparing and Supporting the EBD Workforce

415

28 Leveraging Implementation Science and Practice to Support the Delivery of Evidence-Based Practices in Services for Youth with Emotional and Behavioral Disorders

417

BRYCE D. McLEOD, RACHEL KUNEMUND, SHANNON L. NEMER AND AARON R. LYON

29 Recruiting, Preparing, and Retaining a Diverse Emotional and Behavioral Disorders Educator Workforce

433

LARON SCOTT, CASSANDRA WILLIS, LAUREN BRUNO, KATHERINE BRENDLI, COLLEEN A. THOMA, AND ROBIN WALSH

30 Leading the Team for Youth with Emotional and Behavioral Disorders: Special Educators as Intervention Specialists

449

ELIZABETH TALBOTT, SERRA DE ARMENT, BRITTANY STERRETT, AND CHIN-CHIH CHEN

31 Professional Development to Support Service Providers of Children and Adolescents with or at Risk of Emotional and Behavioral Disorders: Issues and Innovations

462

CRISTIN M. HALL, DAVID L. LEE, RACHEL ROBERTSON, AND KAREN RIZZO

Index

479

Figures

1.1	Correlated Constraints Model of Emotional and Behavioral Adaptation	6
6.1	Interaction-centered model of language and behavioral development	84
7.1	Parent Connectors core components	101
7.2	Parent Connectors conceptual theory of change	102
8.1	The family check-up process	113
8.2	The family check-up feedback form	116
12.1	Interrelated Elements of Quality Social Processes in Afterschool Programs	173
13.1	History of FCU Research	185
15.1	BEST in CLASS Theoretical Framework	218
15.2	Adherence to and competence of delivery	222
16.1	Developmental systems/correlated constraints model of classroom/student functioning	228
19.1	Multisystemic Therapy (MST) Analytical Process	283
22.1	The evidence-based services system model	324
22.2	CARE process example: Clinical progress	327
22.3	CARE process example: Client engagement	327
22.4	The Map	328
22.5	Partial example of steps from the relaxation practice guide	332
22.6	Partial dashboard	333
22.7	MAP professional development program	334
23.1	Percentage of children aged 6–17 years prescribed medication during the past six months for emotional or behavioral difficulties, by sex and age group, and race and Hispanic origin: United States, 2011–2012	342
23.2	Psychotropic medication discontinuation and disruptive behavior for case example (with starting dosages and dosage reductions over time)	351
25.1	Sample Daily Report Card	377
28.1	Conceptual model of implementation science	420
30.1	Knowledge and skills of special educators within the collaborative care model	451

Tables

1.1	The Tiered Systems of Adaptive Support (TSAS) Framework	16
2.1	Characteristics of large epidemiological studies and estimates of childhood EBDs	26
2.2	Prevalence of specific emotional and behavioral disorders in three large-scale epidemiological studies	27
2.3	Disorder-specific severity of specific past 12-month DSM-IV emotional and behavioral disorders: Results from the National Comorbidity Survey-Adolescent Supplement	28
3.1	Overview of SEL Intervention Programs	36
11.1	Overview of Evidence-based Treatments for Trauma	156
12.1	Interrelated Elements of Quality Social Processes in Afterschool Programs with Example Measures and Strategies	172
14.1	Teaching Matrix	204
15.1	BEST in CLASS practices and definitions	219
16.1	The BASE Classroom Management Model for Adapting Supports for Students with EBD	230
22.1	PWEBS search for depression, level 2, treatment families	330
22.2	PWEBS search for depression, level 2, African-American only, treatment families	330
22.3	PWEBS search for depression, level 2, treatment practices (partial)	331
22.4	PWEBS search for depression, level 2, African-American only, treatment practices (partial)	331
24.1	HOPS Session Components	360
24.2	Efficacy Studies of the HOPS Intervention	362
28.1	Descriptions of implementation strategies and outcomes	421
29.1	Description of Information	437

Part 1

Developmental Processes and Timing

1 The Development, Prevention, and Treatment of Emotional and Behavioral Disorders

An Interdisciplinary Developmental Systems Perspective

Thomas W. Farmer, Lisa Gatzke-Kopp, and Shawn J. Latendresse

Introduction

The purpose of this volume is to provide a broad view of children and adolescents who experience, or are at risk of, emotional and behavioral disorders (EBD) at some point during their development. We are purposefully wide reaching and inclusive in our focus, as youth with EBD and the services they need represent an extensive continuum. This continuum necessitates understanding the linkages and supports required for youth with potential risk to youth who manifest disorder and who are at risk for chronic and serious difficulties across the lifecourse.

The term EBD refers to a range of characteristics and patterns of behavior. Depending on the scope, definition, and measurement frame, prevalence estimates of EBD vary widely. For instance, rates for youth who experience an emotional or behavioral problem at some point in childhood and adolescence have been estimated to range from 4% to 40% (Forness, Freeman, Paparella, Kauffman, & Walker, 2012). In a recent review of rates of children's mental health service use, Ringeisen and colleagues found a similar range and conclude that single prevalence estimates may not be realistic (Ringeisen et al., 2018). They suggest estimates are needed for different developmental periods (e.g., infancy, childhood, adolescence) that focus on both the presence of a mental disorder and impaired functioning. Despite higher estimates of prevalence, only ~1% of students receive special education services for EBD (NCES, 2019). In recent years, schools are increasingly providing mental health services within a Multi-tiered System of Support (MTSS) aimed at addressing the social, emotional, and behavioral needs of all youth (Anello et al., 2017; Atkins, Cappella, Mehta, Shernoff, & Gustafson, 2017). Still, the question remains as to whether and how we are providing comprehensive, integrated services that wrap around the complex and multifaceted needs of youth with EBD articulated in the systems of care literature (see Boothroyd, Evans, Chen, Boustead, & Blanch, 2015; Brannan, Brashears, Gyamfi, & Manteuffel, 2012; Epstein, Kutash, & Duchnowski, 1998; Garcia, Kim, Palinkas, Snowden, & Landsverk, 2016; Miller, Blau, Christopher, & Jordan, 2012; Stroul & Friedman, 1986).

Although there has been a concerted focus on developing evidence-based programs and practices to support the learning and behavioral needs of children and youth with/at risk of EBD, there has been less focus on developmental, social, and environmental factors that impact the implementation and effectiveness of these approaches. Natural developmental processes should be harnessed as an intervention ally. Youth with EBD come from a wide

4   *Thomas W. Farmer et al.*

variety of ecological contexts and are served by a complicated set of child-serving sectors and services. Many children and youth with EBD experience social and environmental ecologies that contribute to their adjustment difficulties. Additionally, the developmental timing of interventions often is not considered, which may impact the effectiveness and durability of intervention outcomes. In order to ensure positive outcomes, there needs to be a balance between the services and supports these children and youth receive, and recognition of their diverse developmental backgrounds, ecologies, and service resources that impact their responsiveness to intervention.

Development involves the transactional interplay between bio-behavioral and cognitive characteristics of the individual and the social/ecological contexts in which children and youth are embedded (Cairns & Cairns, 1994; Sameroff, 1983). To increase the effectiveness of intervention, we need to link intervention to social and ecological factors that: (a) prevent the negative reorganization of a system of positive factors that may contribute to the initiation of maladaptive patterns in children and youth who are at risk of developing EBD and (b) promote the positive reorganization of a system of negative factors that sustain maladaptive patterns in children and youth who have already developed EBD (Farmer & Farmer, 2001). The purpose of this handbook is to move beyond what we "know" is effective and focus on a complex array of factors that may contribute to the successful implementation of interventions to foster productive relationships and ecologies to establish, reinforce, and sustain adaptive patterns of emotional and behavioral functioning across childhood and into adulthood. To address this complexity, we assembled papers from researchers from a variety of disciplines and perspectives including: special education; mental health services; school, clinical, and community psychology; social work; developmental psychology and psychopathology; and prevention science. These perspectives are presented across four sections: (1) Leveraging Developmental Processes and Timing; (2) Targeting Social Processes and Environmental Ecologies; (3) Selected Effective Programs and Practices; and (4) Preparing and Supporting the EBD workforce.

To establish a common background for the chapters, the purpose of this introduction is to provide an overview of the conceptual foundations for understanding the development of EBD and how our knowledge of development can be utilized in the intervention process. First, we consider the development of EBD from a dynamic systems perspective. Then we discuss the developmental subsystems and their interplay in the prevention and treatment of EBD. Next, we discuss *developmental cascades* and *correlated constraints* perspectives as complementary models for understanding the prevention and treatment of EBD. From this backdrop we discuss Multi-tiered Systems of Support (MTSS) and Tiered Systems of Adaptive Support (TSAS) to promote positive growth and success for students with EBD. We conclude with considerations for future research, program development, and workforce training to support youth with EBD.

Developmental Systems and EBD

The Developmental Systems Framework

Children develop as an integrated whole within the contexts they experience during daily activities of living (Cairns & Cairns, 1994). Factors both within (i.e., biological, cognitive, psychological) and external to the child (i.e., cultural, ecological, sociological) are bidirectionally linked and collectively function as a dynamic system with each factor (i.e., subsystem) both influencing and being influenced by the others (Sameroff, 2000; Smith & Thelen, 2003).

As Bronfenbrenner (1996, p. xvii) suggests, development is a process of continual adaptation that involves "on one hand, individual human beings as active, holistically functioning biopsychological organisms and, on the other hand, the equally dynamic multi-level environmental systems in which they live their lives." Within this process, behavior plays a leading edge in development as it is open to rapid reorganization and serves as a conduit to link the various subsystems and their potential adaptation to each other (Cairns, 2000).

The dynamic systems perspective has important implications for understanding the functioning and (mal)adaptation of children and youth with EBD. As Hobbs (1966) proposed in his ecological framework for the treatment of children with EBD, it is helpful to view problems as not being situated in the child or the environment but in the transactions between the two. EBD involves difficulties in the processes of developmental adaptation and intervention should include a focus on supporting the positive and productive alignment between the characteristics of the child and her or his ecology (Farmer, 2013). Accordingly, it is important for researchers and interventionists in the field of EBD to understand developmental processes from early childhood to adulthood, to consider how these processes contribute to patterns of maladaptation, and to clarify how natural developmental factors and processes can be systematically utilized as an ally in intervention (Farmer & Farmer, 2001; Sameroff, 2000).

Patterns and Pathways from Birth to Adulthood

Children who experience chronic, intensive, and sustained EBD tend to have poor outcomes including academic failure, truancy, school dropout, involvement in crime and substance use, teen parenthood, and poor educational/vocational attainment (Bergman & Magnusson, 1997; Cairns & Cairns, 1994; Chen, Culhane, Metraux, Park, & Venable, 2015; Cullinan & Sabornie, 2004; Dishion & Patterson, 1998; Farmer, 1995; Lipsey & Derzon, 1998; Wagner & Newman, 2012; Walker & Sprague, 1999). Two concepts in the developmental literature are particularly useful for understanding how students with EBD have elevated levels of deleterious life experiences and inauspicious outcomes: developmental cascades and correlated constraints.

The concept of developmental cascades builds from research showing that youth with EBD tend to experience risks that exacerbate existing problems and expand the individuals' exposure to additional risk factors, leading to an accumulation of adverse outcomes over time (i.e., cumulative risk model), spreading across developmental subsystems and canalizing (i.e., creating a channel or constrained pathway) the manifestation of disorder (Masten & Cicchetti, 2010; Sameroff, 2000). For example, early childhood emotional and behavioral regulation problems are often not responsive to typical parenting approaches and may escalate into ineffective parenting responses to the child's difficulties (i.e., continuum of caretaker casualty: Sameroff, 1983) that may build into a coercive family system in which the child's problem behavior is maintained by harsh discipline accompanied by negative reinforcement (Patterson, 1982). Extending this process, a confluence model of development suggests that as they begin school, children from a coercive family system are likely to have social skills deficits and self-regulation difficulties that result in peer rejection and eventual affiliations with deviant peers who support and complement problem behavior (Coie, 1990; Dishion & Patterson, 1998).

The cascade model is sometimes interpreted as meaning that risk processes accumulate in a linear and sequential fashion and become resistant to intervention once disorder manifests (Farmer, 2013). This view is consistent with the distinction between early and late onset conduct problems and the proposition that late onset problems are temporary whereas sustained early onset problems are predictive of continuity into adulthood (Moffitt, 1993). Although the early/late onset model is descriptive of epidemiological trends, developmental research suggests that this distinction reflects a false dichotomy (Gatzke-Kopp, DuPuis, & Nix, 2013). We view the development of disorder as involving multiple risk factors operating as parallel processes with complex bidirectional transactional influences that sustain each other, but that nonetheless maintain a degree of malleability and the potential for intervention. Although early and cumulative problems can become difficult to change the longer they manifest, the concept of correlated constraints suggests that adaptation (i.e., reorganization of developmental systems and realignment of developmental trajectories) is possible across the lifecourse (Cairns & Cairns, 1994; Masten, 2001; Robins & Rutter, 1990).

The correlated constraints perspective posits that because development operates as a dynamic system with multiple subsystems bidirectionally linked to each other (see Figure 1.1), different subsystems (i.e., developmental factors) tend to be correlated in terms of their general functioning (Cairns, 2000). Problems in one domain tend to be

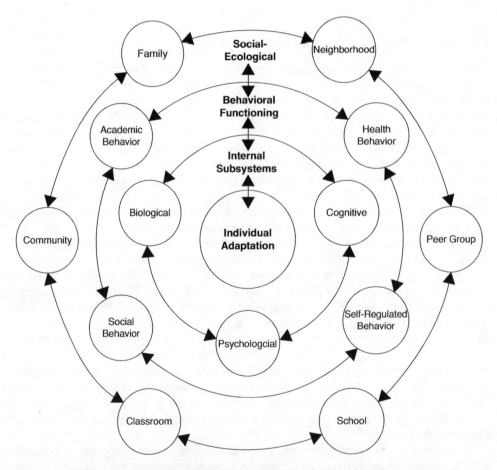

Figure 1.1 Correlated Constraints Model of Emotional and Behavioral Adaptation

associated with problems in other domains, and as problems persist they may result in increasing severity or expansion of the number of problems across domains (Farmer, Gatzke-Kopp, Lee, Dawes, & Talbott, 2016; Magnusson & Cairns, 1996). In this way, adjustment difficulties can become canalized and appear to be intractable because the individual is embedded within a system of risks. Targeting individual behavior in isolation of the contextual system of risks is likely to be unsuccessful, whereas adaptation is possible when changes in the system promote, or are supported by, changes within other subdomains in the system (Cairns, 2000). For children who have manifested EBD, intervention should be carefully coordinated to ameliorate risks and build strengths across the different domains in a systematic way that is likely to require comprehensive services that bridge the educational, mental health, health, social services, juvenile justice, and community recreational domains and agencies (Farmer & Farmer, 2001; Farmer, Farmer, Estell, & Hutchins, 2007; Sutherland, Farmer et al., 2018).

The developmental cascades and correlated constraints models are complementary rather than competing perspectives of EBD (Farmer, 2013). Both models suggest that EBD develops over time, involves multiple risks that accumulate, and reflects transactions among subsystems both within the child and the ecology. However, the cascades model focuses on the sequencing and developmental timing of the emergence of EBD while the correlated constraints model is centered on understanding how the subsystems are organized and coordinated with each other in ways that support the development and maintenance of problems. As Figure 1.1 shows, in a correlated constraints model, the development and adaptation of the individual child forms the core of a dynamic system. The inner ring is composed of the internal subsystems (i.e., biological, cognitive, psychological), the middle ring consists of domains of behavioral functioning (i.e., academic, health, self-regulation, social), and the outer ring is comprised of social-ecological subsystems (i.e., family, neighborhood, peer group, school, classroom, community).

The correlated constraints model is transactional and has the continuous potential to change, either for good or ill (Cairns, 2000). The bidirectional arrows (see Figure 1.1) within the rings indicate that at each level (i.e., internal, behavioral, social-ecological), the subsystems influence each other. Further, the bidirectional arrows spanning across the different levels or domains suggest the social-ecological, behavioral, and internal subsystems all influence each other as they co-actively contribute to development and adaptation (Gottlieb, 1996). Behavior has an important role in this model as it has the potential to rapidly reorganize in relation to other factors in the system (Cairns, 2000). However, changes in behavior may be short-lived or have little developmental impact if they are not accompanied by changes within other subsystems (Farmer, 2013). Therefore, it is important to understand how behavior problems are related to the factors in the system and how intervention can focus on systemic reorganization.

Person-oriented analysis can help clarify the development and treatment of EBD from a correlated constraints perspective and has the potential to provide new insights into what works for whom and in what situations. This approach (e.g., Latent Profile Analysis, Latent Transition Analysis, Cluster Analysis) involves identifying subtypes of youth who are characterized by configurations or patterns of variables that differentiate them from other youth (Magnusson & Cairns, 1996). Person-oriented approaches demonstrate that youth who have chronic and sustained adjustment problems are often characterized by configurations of difficulties in multiple domains and subsystems that may extend across internal, behavioral functioning, and external subsystems (Bergman & Magnusson, 1997; Cairns & Cairns, 1994; Robins & Rutter, 1990; Roeser, Eccles, & Sameroff, 2000; Roeser & Peck, 2003; Seidman &

French, 2004). Although configurations or packages of problems generally predict poor outcomes, some youth characterized by high-risk configurations go on to experience adaptive realignment of their developmental trajectories resulting in positive outcomes (Bergman, Magnusson, & El-Khouri, 2003; Cairns & Cairns, 1994; Farmer, 1995; Peck, Roeser, Zarrett, & Eccles, 2008; Robins & Rutter, 1990). Prodigal analysis, which identifies major deviations in the expected trajectories of youth with specific configurations of variables, indicates that developmental turning points often reflect natural adaptive processes that support the realignment of pathways (Cairns & Cairns, 1994; Cairns & Rodkin, 1998). This realignment has been termed the "ordinary magic" of adaptation in human development (Masten, 2001). It is incumbent upon researchers and interventionists to better understand these processes and how they may be leveraged in intervention (Farmer, 2013).

Intervention in the Context of Natural Developmental Factors and Processes

In some ways, the concept of development is simply another way of talking about the continuous activities of living and the adaptations individuals make in the moment-to-moment transactions with their ecologies (Cairns, 2000). To harness the ordinary magic of adaptation, it is essential to consider intervention through the lens of development. When not taken into consideration, developmental factors and processes may constrain or inhibit the effectiveness of intervention. Conversely, natural developmental factors and processes can also be leveraged to support and sustain intervention impact and outcomes. To effectively intervene with children with, or at risk of developing EBD, it is necessary to understand key developmental factors and processes and how they work together to affect youth functioning and the impact of intervention.

The Parts and Interplay of the Developmental System

As shown in Figure 1.1, the development and adaptation of a child involves the interplay between subsystems internal to the child, her or his behavioral functioning, and the various social and ecological contexts in which he or she develops. For the present discussion, we center our focus on internal factors (i.e., neuropsychological, social cognitive) that may become a target for multi-factored intervention along with behavioral and social-ecological factors. Other internal subsystems including biological factors (i.e., genetics, hormones) and physiological factors (e.g., general health, vision, hearing, communication) may contribute to behavioral functioning and emotional adaptation but extend beyond the focus and aims of this chapter and volume.

Internal Factors

Although innate individual differences in temperamental predispositions are clearly evident in young children, emotional development is a dynamic transaction of endogenous developmental processes and exogenous input that continues from infancy into adulthood. Emotions serve to internally guide behavioral decisions as well as communication with others in social and interpersonal contexts. Successful social development requires the ability to recognize and regulate one's own emotions, as well as recognize and react to the emotional expressions of others. Three primary and interrelated domains of biopsychological functioning that support emotional development may contribute to the development of EBD and serve as targets for intervention; emotion recognition, emotional arousal and regulation, and feedback learning.

The ability to recognize emotional expressions and experiences in others is a requisite of empathy and foundational to social development. Emotion recognition develops experientially, beginning in infancy. Studies have shown that exposure to maltreatment in infancy is associated with greater neural allocation of attention to facial expressions of emotion in children as young as 15 months old (Curtis & Cicchetti, 2013). Heightened sensitivity to facial expressions of negative affect is also evident in adults who experienced maltreatment in childhood (Van Harmelen et al., 2013), indicating a major organizational effect of these experiences in the neural processing of emotional cues. Different forms of EBD may be differentially associated with deficits in the ability to recognize specific emotional expressions. For instance, increased sensitivity to facial cues of negative affect relative to positive affect has been observed among adolescents higher in anxiety and depression, whereas a blunted sensitivity to facial cues of fear has been observed among adolescents higher in callous and unemotional traits (Leist & Dadds, 2009). In high threat contexts, such as homes characterized by episodes of violence, neural systems may develop to prioritize sensitivity over specificity. This hypervigilance to potential threat may serve an adaptive function in the home environment, but likely fails to serve the child well as he or she traverses other contexts. Specifically, in the classroom context, hypervigilance may lead children to over-react to non-threatening or minor provocations.

How children react once they identify or perceive a potential threat may also be shaped by early experiences. Coercive parent–child dynamics often establish contexts by which children are inadvertently reinforced for displays of intense emotional dysregulation. When a parent relents in the face of a child's tantrum, children begin to learn that they are more likely to achieve their goal through an increase in physiological arousal and emotional dysregulation than through the calm and compliant behavior the parent is seeking. Repeated over time, these exchanges can ingrain an emotional reactivity pattern in which children rapidly escalate their affective arousal in response to any perceived provocation (Beauchaine, Gatzke-Kopp, & Mead, 2007). When this style of reactivity extends beyond the family context, additional consequences may begin to manifest, such as peer rejection and frequent disciplinary consequences. Such experiences typically exacerbate the child's experience of sadness and anger, increasing their vulnerability to emotional outbursts.

The processes by which the environment shapes emotion recognition and reactivity is largely influenced by the neural mechanisms that facilitate the recognition of contingent associations (i.e. "this happened *because I* ..."), as well as the ability to respond flexibly to changes in contingencies. Even in the context of maladaptive parenting, typically developing children are often able to recognize when rule structures change across context, and may be quite capable of compliant and regulated behavior at school despite significant behavior problems at home. Indeed, manifestation of problem behaviors across contexts is a criterion for diagnosis of a behavior problem. Some researchers have proposed that ADHD is characterized, in part, by deficiencies in this system that make it more difficult for children to recognize contingent associations, particularly in environments in which many events are taking place. This framework suggests that the more temporally proximal to the desired behavior that a reinforcement is delivered, the more successful it will be in increasing the behavior (Johansen et al., 2009). For instance, laughter from peers that immediately follows misbehavior has a stronger reinforcing effect on that behavior than subsequent consequences. Furthermore, deficits in dopamine impair the ability of the brain to recognize changes in contingency structures (Gatzke-Kopp et al., 2009). As such, children with disruptive behavior problems may have an especially difficult time extinguishing a behavior, even when it consistently fails to be reinforced.Identifying targets for intervention should be developmentally informed. As children develop, endogenous processes regulating brain development and plasticity change over time, as do children's relations with the different subsystems depicted in Figure 1.1. When children are younger, targeting parental behaviors may interrupt and redirect developmental trajectories of escalating negative emotional reactivity. One intervention study targeting parents of preschool aged children diagnosed with ADHD found that reductions in negative parenting behaviors following the intervention were associated with a reduction in children's affective physiological arousal (Bell, Shader, Webster-Stratton, Reid, & Beauchaine, 2018). Consistent with the correlated constraints framework, targeting one domain for intervention (parenting) resulted in effects manifested in other domains (child's physiological regulation). Other research suggests that alternative environments may compensate for suboptimal home contexts. In particular, time spent in high quality childcare was found to mitigate the negative effects of highly chaotic home environments on children's school readiness (Berry et al., 2016).

As children become older, however, peers are elevated in the hierarchy of influence. Hormonal changes occurring during the pubertal process direct a reorganization in brain structure and function that facilitates a transition away from the family and toward the formation of strong non-familial bonds. Neuroimaging research indicates that adolescents engage different regions of the brain when completing a task in the presence of their parent versus in the presence of a peer (van Hoorn, McCormick, Rogers, Ivory, & Telzer, 2018). Specifically, peer presence is associated with increased activation in reward systems of the brain, and a greater propensity to make risky decisions (Ambrosia et al., 2018). Peer presence also appears to enhance mechanisms of feedback learning, potentially prioritizing learning that takes place in peer contexts (Kessler, Hewig, Weichold, Silbereisen, & Miltner, 2017). Similarly, experiences of peer rejection are associated with dampened sensitivity to rewards, consistent with that observed in depression (Ethridge, Sandre, Dirks, & Weinberg, 2018).

Social cognitive factors form an important internal subsystem for understanding the social development and adaptation of children and youth with EBD. The concept of social cognitions refers to how children perceive and understand their social world. This includes the ways youth take in information about peers and the social contexts in which they are engaged, the ways they use such information to guide their behavior and interactions with others, and the types of goals, beliefs, and values that may serve as motivating factors in their interchanges with others (Dawes, 2017; Lochman & Dodge, 1994). Students with EBD tend to have social cognitive difficulties that include poor social problem-solving, attributional biases (i.e., expecting the acts of others are intentionally harmful), poor perspective-taking skills (i.e., difficulty understanding the point of view of others), and antisocial goals that strain their relationships with others (Erdley & Asher, 1999; Lochman, Powell, Boxmeyer, & Jimenez-Camargo, 2011). These social cognitive difficulties may reflect difficulties in other internal subsystems (i.e., self-regulatory processing, language processing) and they may also involve the contributions of the child's experiences in the social ecology that may elicit and reinforce their problematic ways of thinking about processing social information. Therefore, although interventions should focus on the problematic social cognitive skills of students with EBD and explicit strategies to foster their social competence, a dynamic systems perspective suggests that it is also helpful to bolster such efforts with complementary ecological interventions that address social dynamic factors in the peer ecology (Bierman, 2004; Farmer, Talbott et al., 2018; Trach, Lee, & Hymel, 2018).

Behavioral Factors

Behavior involves the actions and interactions of individuals. In many respects, behavior operates as a conduit between the functional capacity and proclivities of the internal subsystems of the child and the demands, resources, and constraints of the social-ecology (Cairns, 2000; Farmer, Gatzke-Kopp, et al., 2016). Behavioral frameworks are often used as the foundation for intervention for students with EBD in school settings and tend to center on clarifying the antecedents and consequences that evoke and reinforce specific behaviors (Horner, Sugai, & Anderson, 2010). Yet, the behavior of students with EBD tends to be multi-determined and cannot be readily attributed to a single factor or series of consequences in the environment (Wehby, Symons, & Shores, 1995). It is helpful to identify setting events (i.e., ecological and interactional factors) that may create the conditions for behavior in particular settings even though the actual setting events themselves may occur in a different context (Farmer, Talbott, et al., 2018; Shores & Wehby, 1999). An additional consideration is that the behavior of children tends to become synchronized with the behavior of others and interventions may need to include not only a focus on changing the behavior of the focal student but also a focus on the synchronous interchanges of others that may shape, support, and maintain the focal child's behavior (Cairns & Cairns, 1994; Farmer, Talbott, et al., 2018; Kornienko, Dishion, & Ha, 2018; Patterson, 1982).

Social-Ecological Factors

Social-ecological factors include the various, often overlapping contexts in which a child is embedded and that contribute instrumental and emotional support as well as opportunities for socialization and identity development (Bronfenbrenner, 1996; Cairns & Cairns, 1994; Hobbs, 1966; Trach et al., 2018). These contexts include the family, neighborhood, community, school, classroom, and peer group. The social ecology also includes linkages among these subsystem components, the concept of culture and societal rules, and the culture, values, and beliefs that children and youth develop in their interactions and relationships with each other (Corsaro & Eder, 1990; Eccles & Roeser, 2011; Youniss, 1980). An important aspect of the social-ecology is that it can both activate and reinforce the behaviors and interactions of the child and, in this way, it engages and contributes to how internal subsystems are expressed in development (Cairns, 2000; Sameroff, 1983; Smith & Thelen, 2003).

Interchanges across Developmental Factors

The concept of interchanges has an important role in a dynamic systems model of development. Because children develop as an integrated whole with the various factors being bidirectionally linked, there is a potential for ongoing transactional exchange among the factors as they impact each other as well as the child's functioning (Cairns, 2000; Sameroff, 2000; Smith & Thelen, 2003). This means the developmental factors may change in relation to each other in ways that promote their alignment (Magnusson & Cairns, 1996). Further, behavior can serve as a leading edge in development by rapidly reorganizing in relation to changes in a factor within the system and may serve to foster changes in other factors in the system (Cairns, 2000). When the factors are in alignment and change in the system is organized around positive factors the child is likely to experience productive adaptation and growth (Cairns & Cairns, 1994; Roeser & Peck, 2003; Peck et al., 2008). However, when

12   *Thomas W. Farmer et al.*

transactions are associated with poor alignment and negative changes within a particular factor, the child is likely to experience maladaptation and adjustment difficulties (Dishion & Patterson, 1998; Eccles & Roeser, 2011; Sameroff, 2000). Emotional and behavioral difficulties may reflect poor alignment and problematic transactions between the characteristics and needs of the child and the characteristics and resources of the ecologies in which he or she is embedded (Farmer, Gatzke-Kopp, et al., 2016; Hobbs, 1966).

Leveraging Development in Interventions to Support Students with EBD

Developmental Processes and Intervention

Many developmental processes may contribute to or influence the development and adaptation of children with EBD. For the current discussion, transitions, social dynamics, and a sense of connection and belonging may be particularly relevant in understanding the adjustment difficulties of children with EBD and opportunities to leverage development in intervention.

Transitions

At their broadest, transitions can be viewed as moving or changing from one condition or activity to another. A range of transition types are relevant for children with EBD including developmental (e.g., early childhood, middle childhood, adolescence, adulthood), school (e.g., preschool, elementary school, middle school, high school, post-secondary), instructional (e.g., beginning class, changing activities, ending class), and placement (e.g., residential services, treatment settings, classroom settings). Many children with EBD are not comfortable with change and unpredictability and any of these various types of transitions may be difficult for them (Hobbs, 1966). Although transitions are a time of vulnerability, they are also a time of opportunity as they provide the possibility of new experiences, relationships, and roles in which the child can develop new behaviors, competencies, and beliefs that can positively realign her or his functioning (Cairns & Cairns, 1994; Eccles & Roeser, 2011; Masten, 2001). It is critical to design interventions in ways that recognize the potential risk of the transition while providing supports to align the ecology with the developmental needs of the child to establish and maintain a positive self with the skills, roles, and relationships necessary to sustain adaptive patterns (Bierman, 2004; Farmer, Gatzke-Kopp, et al., 2016; Seidman & French, 2004).

Social Dynamics

The concept of social dynamics refers to the roles, relationships, social structures, and processes of interaction that individuals use to organize themselves within social systems including classrooms and community settings (Farmer, Talbott, et al., 2018; Trach et al., 2018). Within the classroom or community, students may organize themselves into peer groups and use a variety of strategies for inclusion or exclusion in the group that often result in children affiliating with others who are similar to them in terms of behavioral characteristics, status, and roles in the peer system (Farmer, Talbott, et al., 2018). Students with EBD often develop affiliations and roles that support their coercive and problematic behavior and may engage in a process known as deviancy training where they further escalate the behavioral difficulties of each other (Cairns & Cairns, 1994;

Kornienko et al., 2018). Although many students with EBD need social skills training to help them develop more competent and prosocial behavior (Bierman, 2004; Coie, 1990), such efforts may not be effective or sustained if natural social dynamic processes are operating in ways that compete with the intervention (Farmer, 2013). Therefore, it may be productive to support social interventions with strategies that involve the management of classroom and community social dynamics in ways that help children to develop roles and relationships that evoke and reinforce prosocial skills (Cappella & Hwang, 2015; Farmer, Talbott, et al., 2018; Trach et al., 2018; van den Berg & Stoltz, 2018).

Connections, Belonging, and Positive Engagement

From infancy into adulthood, social-ecological connections including relationships with family members, involvement with neighborhood and community members and organizations, and linkages with school adults all provide important developmental supports at instrumental, behavioral, and emotional levels of adaptation (Bronfenbrenner, 1996; Cox & Paley, 2003; Eccles & Roeser, 2011; Sameroff, 1983). Yet, many children who develop chronic EBD have difficulty establishing trusting and positive relations with family members, school adults, and the broader neighborhood and community and often do not experience the types of relationships and supports that are associated with healthy emotional growth and adaptation (Hobbs, 1966; Sameroff, 2000). Further, youth with EBD are more likely to experience disruptive home and residential placements as well as trauma that can interfere with their opportunities and comfort in developing sustained relationships with others (Chen et al., 2016; Copeland et al., 2018; Sullivan et al., 2015). However, for many children and youth who experience significant adversity during their growth, a strong sense of connection and belonging including relationships with adults in the community or in school and involvement in extracurricular activities have been identified as critical supports and turning points associated with their positive adaptation (Cairns & Cairns, 1994; Masten, 2001; Peck et al., 2008). Monitoring, developing, and supporting positive connections and involvement in productive extracurricular activities can be an important component in promoting the positive adaptation and outcomes of youth with EBD (Christenson & Thurlow, 2004; Hobbs, 1966).

The Cascades Model of Intervention

As described earlier, the cascades model of the development of EBD focuses on the sequencing and accumulation of risk over time. From a developmental cascade perspective, problems often begin in early childhood and, particularly for externalizing difficulties, tend to follow a common sequence that may in some ways be attenuated for internalizing problems (Masten & Cicchetti, 2010; Sameroff, 2000). In general, significant emotional and behavioral difficulties in early childhood are expressed and maintained within a coercive family system, continue with behavioral and emotional regulation difficulties and peer relation problems at school entry, are exacerbated by increasing academic difficulties during the elementary school years, become linked with affiliations with antisocial peers or social isolation by late childhood, and are further consolidated with deviancy training and/or the withdrawal from positive and supportive relationships with adults and prosocial peers during adolescence (Coie, 1990; Dishion & Patterson, 1998; Masten & Cicchetti, 2010; Moffitt, 1993; Sameroff, 2000).

From a cascade perspective, the focus of intervention tends to center on prevention and intervening before problems spread to adjacent developmental domains or later developmental

14   *Thomas W. Farmer et al.*

stages (Mrazek & Haggerty, 1994). The goal is to intervene early in the developmental pathway to prevent the accumulation of risk while decreasing the likelihood that problems in one subsystem will trigger new problems within the subsystem or in other developmental subsystems (Conroy, 2016, Masten & Cicchetti, 2010; Reid, 1993). A key aspect of this process involves identifying common mediators in the development of disorder and identifying strategies to target these mediators with the aim of stopping the sequence and spread of the risk (Conduct Problems Prevention Research Group 1999; Masten & Cicchetti, 2010; Mrazek & Haggerty, 1994).

The Correlated Constraints Model of Intervention

A correlated constraints model of EBD focuses on the concept that developmental subsystems are organized in a dynamic system and bidirectionally linked to each other to co-actively contribute to the functioning and adaptation of the child. As shown in Figure 1.1, the core of the system is the functioning and adaptation of the child. This is surrounded by subsystems internal to the child (i.e., biological, cognitive, psychological). The internal subsystems are surrounded by the child's behavior. Generally, there are four forms of behavior that are critical to a child's functioning and development: academic, self-regulation, social, and health. In turn, the child's behavior links to both the internal subsystems and the social ecological subsystems (i.e., family, peer group, neighborhood, school, community, culture) that compose the outer ring of the system.

The correlated constraints perspective of intervention is not focused on the sequence of the development of disorder, though issues and understanding of developmental timing are reflected in this model. Rather, the focus is on three critical and complementary concerns: (1) *Does the problem behavior reflect difficulty or contributions from a particular subsystem?*, (2) *Do the other domains reflect strengths or adequate functioning and are they at risk of developing problems because of the difficulty in the other subsystem?*, and (3) *Do all or most of the subsystems have difficulties that contribute to the problem behavior and to difficulties in the other subsystems?*

From a correlated constraints perspective, the focus of intervention will depend on how these three questions are answered. If the problem behavior is primarily linked to one subsystem and domain of functioning (e.g., academic, self-regulation, social) then intervention should focus on the subsystem and the domain of functioning where the problems are manifested with an eye toward monitoring other subsystems and domains for the potential development of problems. If other subsystems and domains of functioning show risk for emerging problems then intervention should extend beyond the immediate problem and include a systematic focus on strengthening the other subsystems and domains with the goal of preventing the negative reorganization of the developmental system (Farmer & Farmer, 2001). However, if the behavior problem reflects a developmental system organized around problems and risks across multiple subsystems and domains, then the focus of intervention moves from prevention to treatment and should center on identifying intervention leverage points and the systematic reorganization of the developmental system by building strengths in the subdomains that are most responsive to intervention, with the goal of supporting positive behavior change and the eventual adaptation of the entire system (Farmer et al., 2007; Maggin, Wehby, Farmer, & Brooks, 2016; Sutherland, Farmer et al., 2018. The focus is not on bringing behavior under control but rather changing the behavior and critical subsystems in a coordinated fashion that ultimately result in the developmental system being aligned around positive factors and strengths in ways that naturally support adaptive patterns (Farmer, 2013; Farmer, Farmer, & Brooks, 2010).

Models and Goals of Support for Students with EBD

The MTSS Framework

The Individuals with Disability Education Act (IDEA) includes mandates for providing both instructional and behavioral supports for disabilities in general education classrooms. In response to these mandates, Response to Intervention (RTI) models were developed to support students who have diverse instructional support needs (Fuchs, Fuchs, & Stecker, 2010) and Positive Behavioral Interventions and Supports (PBIS) were established to support students who have diverse behavioral and emotional support needs (Horner et al., 2010). Both models use a three-tiered framework with Tier 1 (primary intervention) involving strategies that are meant to support all children, Tier 2 (secondary intervention) involving small group strategies designed for youth who are not responsive to Tier 1 supports, and Tier 3 (tertiary intervention) involving strategies that are individualized for students with intensive needs that are not responsive to Tier 1 and Tier 2 supports. RTI and MTSS each involve a response to intervention framework in which strategies move from less intensive (i.e., Tier 1) to more intensive strategies (Tier 2 and Tier 3) when intervention is not effective. In recent years the RTI and PBIS frameworks have been merged into Multi-tiered Systems of Support (MTSS) to promote the delivery of support for diverse learners in general education classrooms. The MTSS framework is integrated across the academic, behavioral, and social domains and focuses on the provision of increasingly intensive services to students who are not responsive to evidence-based practices (EBPs) within a less intensive tier (Lane, Carter, Jenkins, Dwiggins, & Germer, 2015).

The Tiered Systems of Adaptive Support (TSAS) Framework

The MTSS model is a welcome framework for integrating academic, behavioral, and social supports for children and for linking interventions to the intensity of children's needs. However, the response to intervention aspect of MTSS essentially involves using an intervention until it is clear that it is not working for the child and then moving to a more intensive one. This framework does not capitalize on our knowledge of developmental factors and processes, and it does not provide a systematic guide for adapting practice elements of evidence-based programs to the characteristics of the child, the ecology, and specific developmental strengths and needs. We propose that MTSS can be adapted or complemented by a Tiered System of Adaptive Supports (TSAS) that involves understanding the various developmental factors and processes that are operating for a child as a system of correlated constraints (see Figure 1.1) and adapting strategies accordingly both within and across tiers. The TSAS model is outlined in Table 1.1. The emphasis is on aligning the characteristics of the student with the features of the ecology to foster growth and adaptation in each. This model can serve as a progress monitoring framework by assessing and clarifying how changes in various factors and processes change in relation to each other and the behavioral adaptation of the child.

Understanding and Reframing Success for Youth with EBD

Often, the success of intervention and the corresponding success of students with EBD is thought to be demonstrated by the absence of problems, the reduction of discipline referrals, and a decrease in exclusionary punishment (Horner et al., 2010; Steinberg & Knitzer, 1992).

Table 1.1 The Tiered Systems of Adaptive Support (TSAS) Framework

Tier	Aims	Strategies
Tier 1: *Universal Supports & Adaptations*	• Recognize that all children need social, emotional, and behavioral supports during routine daily functioning and that their needs can change from day-to-day or moment-to-moment • Create routine and adaptable supports for the common-place aspects of daily functioning • Universal supports do not need to be one-size fits all; can be adapted to address functional needs that are individualized but serve a common purpose	• Like curb cuts in sidewalks and voice instructions at crosswalks, develop common social, emotional, and behavioral supports for daily functioning in child caring contexts to support all children when needed regardless of risk status • Supports for routine social emotional and behavioral functioning can be adapted to the characteristics of the child and the context. For example, all students should have a routine to start class and following one's own routine to start class would be universal. But different students can have different routines that reflect their needs and capacities
Tier 2: *Selected Supports & Adaptations*	• Create a screening and progress monitoring system that includes person-oriented approaches to identify youth who are at risk for the negative reorganization of their developmental system • Establish a comprehensive, multi-factored and multi-agency delivery framework to prevent the negative reorganization of the developmental system of youth who manifest risk in a single subsystem	• Use screening, person-oriented, and observational assessments to identify students who are at risk as well as corresponding intervention leverage points • Ameliorate risk in the subdomain where difficulties are manifested • Develop and promote strengths in the subdomain of difficulty • Monitor risks and strengths in other subdomains; intervene to support strengths while preventing risk from developing in the other subdomains
Tier 3: *Targeted Supports & Adaptations*	• Create a screening and progress monitoring system that includes person-oriented approaches to identify youth who manifest correlated risk/problems across multiple subsystems in their developmental system • Establish a comprehensive, multi-factored and multi-agency delivery framework to promote the positive reorganization of a correlated system of problems across multiple domains that reflect the manifestation of EBD	• Identify how factors in the system are organized to collectively contribute to a student's manifestation of EBD • Ameliorate risk in each domain and determine how different malleable factors can be changed in relation to each other • Identity potential leverage points to promote strengths that bolster against risk • Monitor how interventions impact across subdomains & how correlated constraints impact intervention effectiveness • Promote both natural and agency supports to foster developmental reorganization with a goal of realigning trajectories over time

Other measures may include improvement in school grades and achievement scores on standardized tests. Although such outcomes can be important, they may not be effective indicators of the adaptation of students with EBD nor predictive of long-term outcomes such as high school completion, educational attainment, vocational attainment, and adult mental health. In some cases, improvement in behavior may reflect behavioral control in the setting or adults' hesitancy to make discipline referrals or use specific discipline practices (i.e., suspension, expulsion) because of policy considerations rather than meaningful changes in the child's behavior and her or his emotional adjustment that reflects positive developmental adaptation.

A focus on developmental factors (i.e., subsystems) and processes can be important for coordinating multi-factored intervention by generating information about risk and resilience, clarifying how the child adapts in relation to intervention efforts, guiding systematic adjustment of strategies as factors change within the developmental system, monitoring risk and protective factors, and aligning patterns or trajectories of adaptation toward adolescent and adult outcomes of interest. For some children and youth with social histories of extensive adversity and intensive intervention needs, the goal may not be so much the prevention of emotional and behavioral problems as it is helping the child manage her or his difficulties while establishing natural and professional supports to foster adaptation and adjustment as the child transitions through childhood, adolescence, and into adulthood (Farmer, 1995, 2013).

Considerations for the Future

One of the most encouraging aspects of the complexity of dynamic systems and the development of EBD is that it gives us a variety of opportunities to foster the positive adaptation of children regardless of the intensity of their difficulties or chronicity of their problems. There is a strong need for prevention and early intervention (Conroy, 2016). However, when problems are manifested all is not lost and it is critical that researchers and interventionists work to use the ordinary magic of development and adaptation in the intervention process (Farmer, 2013). As research and intervention development moves forward, there is a need to link developmental cascade and correlated constraint perspectives with the aim of creating a support framework that seamlessly merges prevention and treatment efforts. In particular, it is necessary to leverage our understanding of development not only to prevent disorder but to provide treatment for children who have manifested EBD. Such efforts should focus not only on improving the emotional and behavioral functioning of the child but also on aligning factors in the family, school, peer, and community contexts in ways that provide natural supports and promote the development of strengths in the child that foster her or his ongoing adaptation and positive outcomes (Farmer & Farmer, 2001; Masten & Cicchetti, 2010; Trach et al., 2018).

Linking current efforts of MTSS, school mental health, and systems of care perspectives is a good start. However, we believe extending or refocusing MTSS to include or complement Tiered Systems of Adaptive Supports (TSAS) is necessary to ensure we move beyond iteratively using more intensive interventions in the search for an effective strategy when children do not respond to less intensive strategies (Sutherland, Farmer, Kunemund, & Sterrett, 2018). Instead, we can use current and emerging knowledge of developmental factors and processes to better tailor interventions to specific subtypes of youth identified via person-oriented analytic methods (Bergman & Magnusson, 1997;

Cairns & Cairns, 1994; Farmer, Gatzke-Kopp, et al., 2016). From this vantage, we can link practice elements (i.e., kernels) of evidenced based programs to elements of the developmental processes that are most likely to foster adaptation in students with specific configurations and patterns of difficulty (Chorpita & Daleiden, 2009; Cohen-Vogel, Cannata, Rutledge, & Socol, 2016; Dishion, 2011; Farmer, Hamm, et al., 2018; Sutherland, Conroy, McLeod, Kunemund, & McKnight, 2019). To do this effectively, there is a need to train and prepare a workforce that understands the developmental systems framework and the interplay across different service sectors (Farmer, Talbott, et al., 2018). Clearly, there is much work to do, but we believe that all the pieces are there and are reflected in this volume. There is much to work from and there is much that has already been accomplished. As the field moves forward, interdisciplinary efforts that leverage our knowledge of the development of EBD and natural processes of human adaptation and resilience should help us to regularly support ordinary magic in children and youth with the most adverse experiences and intensive support needs.

Authors' Note

This research was supported by grants from the Institute of Education Sciences (R305A040056; R305A120812; R305L030162; R305A160398). The views expressed in this paper are those of the authors and do not reflect the view of the granting agency.

References

Ambrosia, M., Eckstrand, K. L., Morgan, J. K., Allen, N. B., Jones, N. P., Sheeber, L., … Forbes, E. E. (2018). Temptations of friends: Adolescent's neural and behavioral responses to best friends predict risky behavior. *Social Cognitive and Affective Neuroscience, 13*, 483–491.

Anello, V., Weist, M., Eber, L., Barrett, S., Cashman, J., Rosser, M., & Bazyk, S. (2017). Readiness for positive behavioral interventions and supports and school mental health interconnection: Preliminary development of a stakeholder survey. *Journal of Emotional and Behavioral Disorders, 25*, 82–95.

Atkins, M. S., Cappella, E., Mehta, T., Shernoff, E., & Gustafson, E. (2017). Schooling and children's mental health: Realigning resources to reduce disparities and advance public health. *Annual Review of Clinical Psychology, 13*, 123–147. Doi: 10.1146/annurev-clinpsy-032816-045234

Beauchaine, T. P., Gatzke-Kopp, L. M., & Mead, H. K. (2007). Polyvagal theory and developmental psychopathology: Emotion dysregulation and conduct problems from preschool to adolescence. *Biological Psychology, 74*, 174–184.

Bell, Z., Shader, T., Webster-Stratton, C., Reid, M. J., & Beauchaine, T. P. (2018). Improvements in negative parenting mediate changes in children's autonomic responding following a preschool intervention for ADHD. *Clinical Psychological Science, 6*, 134–144.

Bergman, L. R., & Magnusson, D. (1997). A person-oriented approach in research on developmental psychopathology. *Developmental Psychopathology, 9*, 291–319.

Bergman, L. R., Magnusson, D., & El-Khouri, B. M. (2003). *Studying individual development in an interindividual context: A person-oriented approach. Vol. 4 of Paths through life.* Mahwah, NJ: Erlbaum.

Berry, D., Blair, C., Willoughby, M., Garrett-Peters, P., Vernon-Feagans, L., & Mills-Koonce, R. (2016). The family life investigators. Household chaos and children's cognitive and socio-emotional development in early childhood: Does childcare play a buffering role? *Early Child Research Quarterly, 34*, 115–127.

Bierman, K. L. (2004). *Peer rejection: Developmental processes and intervention strategies: The Guildford series on social and emotional development.* New York: Guilford Press.

Boothroyd, R. A., Evans, M. E., Chen, H.-J., Boustead, R., & Blanch, A. K. (2015). An exploratory study of conflict and its management in systems of care for children with mental, emotional, or behavioral problems and their families. *Journal of Behavioral Health Services & Research, 42*, 310–323.

Brannan, A. M., Brashears, F., Gyamfi, P., & Manteuffel, B. (2012). Implementation and development of federally-funded systems of care over time. *American Journal of Community Psychology, 49*, 476–482.

Bronfenbrenner, U. (1996). Foreword. In R. B. Cairns, G. H. Elder, & E. J. Costello (Eds.), *Developmental science* (pp. ix–xvii). New York: Cambridge University Press.

Cairns, R. B. (2000). Developmental science: Three audacious implications. In L. R. Bergman, R. B. Cairns, L.-G. Nilsson, & L. Nystedt (Eds.), *Developmental science and the holistic approach* (pp. 49–62). Mahwah, NJ: LEA.

Cairns, R. B., & Cairns, B. D. (1994). *Lifelines and risks: Pathways of youth in our time.* New York, NY: Harvester Wheatsheaf.

Cairns, R. B., & Rodkin, P. C. (1998). Phenomena regained: From configurations to pathways. In R. B. Cairns & L. R. Bergman (Eds.), *Methods and models for studying the individual* (pp. 245–265). Thousand Oaks, CA: Sage Publications, Inc.

Cappella, E., & Hwang, S. H. J. (2015). Peer contexts in schools: Avenues toward behavioral health in early adolescence. *Behavioral Medicine, 41*, 80–89.

Chen, C.-C., Culhane, D. P., Metraux, S., Park, Y.-M., & Venable, J. (2015). The heterogeneity of truancy among urban middle school students: A latent class growth analysis. *Journal of Child and Family Studies.* doi:10.1007/s10826-015-0295-3

Chen, C.-C., Culhane, D. P., Metraux, S., Park, Y.-M., Venable, J. C., & Burnett, T. C. (2016). They're not all at home: Residential placements of early adolescents in special education. *Journal of Emotional and Behavioral Disorders.* doi:10.1177/1063426615625603

Chorpita, B. F., & Daleiden, E. L. (2009). Mapping evidence-based treatments for children and adolescents: Application of the distillation and matching model to 615 treatments from 322 randomized trials. *Journal of Consulting and Clinical Psychology, 77*, 566–579.

Christenson, S. L., & Thurlow, M. L. (2004). School dropouts: Prevention considerations, interventions, and challenges. *Current Directions in Psychological Science, 13*, 36–39.

Cohen-Vogel, L., Cannata, M., Rutledge, S. A., & Socol, A. R. (2016). A model of continuous improvement in high schools: A process for research, innovation design, implementation, and scale. *Teachers College Record, 118*, 1–26.

Coie, J. D. (1990). Toward a theory of peer rejection. In S. R. Asher & J. D. Coie (Eds.), *Peer rejection in childhood* (pp. 365–399). New York: Cambridge University Press.

Copeland, W. E., Shanahan, L., Hinesley, J., Chan, R. F., Aberg, K. A., Fairbank, J. A., ... Costello, J. (2018). Association of childhood trauma exposure with adult psychiatric disorders and functional outcomes. *JAMA Network Open, 1*(7): e184493.

Corsaro, W. A., & Eder, D. (1990). Children's peer cultures. *Annual Review of Sociology, 16*, 197–220.

Cox, M. J., & Paley, B. (2003). Understanding families as systems. *Current Directions in Psychological Science, 12*, 193–196.

Cullinan, D., & Sabornie, E. J. (2004). Characteristics of emotional disturbance in middle and high school students. *Journal of Emotional and Behavioral Disorders, 12*, 157–167.

Curtis, J. W., & Cicchetti, D. (2013). Affective facial expression processing in 15-month-old infants who have experienced maltreatment: An event-related potential study. *Child Maltreatment, 18*, 140–154.

Dawes, M. (2017). Early adolescents' social goals and school adjustment. *Social Psychology of Education, 20*, 299–328.

Dishion, T. (2011). Promoting academic competence and behavioral health in public schools: A strategy of systematic concatenation of empirically based intervention principles. *School Psychology Review, 40*, 590–597.

Dishion, T. J., & Patterson, G. R. (1998). The timing and severity of antisocial behavior: Three hypotheses within an ecological framework. In D. M. Stoff, J. Breiling, & J. D. Maser (Eds.), *Handbook of antisocial behavior* (pp. 205–217). New York: John Wiley and Sons.

Eccles, J. S., & Roeser, R. W. (2011). Schools as developmental contexts during adolescence. *Journal of Research on Adolescence, 21*, 225–241.

Epstein, M. H., Kutash, K., & Duchnowski, A. (Eds.). (1998). *Outcomes for children and youth with behavioral and emotional disorders and their families: Programs & evaluation best practices.* Austin, TX: PRO-ED.

Erdley, C. A., & Asher, S. R. (1999). A social goals perspective on children's social competence. *Journal of Emotional and Behavioral Disorders, 7*, 156–167.

Ethridge, P., Sandre, A., Dirks, M. A., & Weinberg, A. (2018). Past-year relational victimization is associated with a blunted neural response to rewards in emerging adults. *Social Cognitive and Affective Neuroscience, 13*, 1259–1267.

Farmer, E. M. Z. (1995). Extremity of externalizing behavior and young adult outcomes. *Journal of Child Psychology and Psychiatry, 36*, 617–632.

Farmer, T. W. (2013). When universal approaches and prevention services are not enough: The importance of understanding the stigmatization of special education for students with EBD. *Behavioral Disorders, 39*, 32–42.

Farmer, T. W., & Farmer, E. M. Z. (2001). Developmental science, systems of care, and prevention of emotional and behavioral problems in youth. *American Journal of Orthopsychiatry, 71*, 171–181.

Farmer, T. W., Farmer, E. M. Z., & Brooks, D. S. (2010). Recasting the ecological and developmental roots of intervention for students with emotional and behavioral problems: The promise of strength-based perspectives. *Exceptionality, 18*, 53–57.

Farmer, T. W., Farmer, E. M. Z., Estell, D., & Hutchins, B. C. (2007). The developmental dynamics of aggression and the prevention of school violence. *Journal of Emotional and Behavioral Disorders, 15*, 197–208.

Farmer, T. W., Gatzke-Kopp, L. M., Lee, D. L., Dawes, M., & Talbott, E. (2016). Research and policy on disability: linking special education to developmental science. *Policy Insights from the Behavioral and Brain Sciences, 3*, 138–145.

Farmer, T. W., Hamm, J. V., Lee, D. L., Sterrett, B., Rizzo, K., & Hoffman, A. (2018). Directed consultation and supported professionalism: Promoting adaptive evidence-based practices in rural schools. *Rural Special Education Quarterly, 37*, 164–175.

Farmer, T. W., Talbott, B., Dawes, M., Huber, H. B., Brooks, D. S., & Powers, E. (2018). Social dynamics management: What is it and why is it important for intervention? *Journal of Emotional and Behavioral Disorders, 26*, 1–10.

Forness, S. R., Freeman, S. F. N., Paparella, T., Kauffman, J. M., & Walker, H. M. (2012). Special education implications of point and cumulative prevalence for children with emotional or behavioral disorders. *Journal of Emotional and Behavioral Disorders, 20*, 4–18.

Fuchs, D., Fuchs, L. S., & Stecker, P. M. (2010). The "blurring" of special education in a new continuum of general education placements and services. *Exceptional Children, 76*, 301–323.

Garcia, A. R., Kim, M., Palinkas, L. A., Snowden, L., & Landsverk, J. (2016). Socio-contextual determinants of research evidence use in public-youth systems of care. *Administration and Policy in Mental Health and Mental Health Services, 43*, 569–578.

Gatzke-Kopp, L. M., Beauchaine, T. P., Shannon, K. E., Chipman, J., Fleming, A. P., Crowell, S. E., … Aylward, E. (2009). Neurological correlates of reward responding in adolescents with conduct disorder and/or attention-deficit/hyperactivity disorder. *Journal of Abnormal Psychology, 118*, 203–213.

Gatzke-Kopp, L. M., DuPuis, D., & Nix, R. L. (2013). Social and biological changes during adolescence that precipitate the onset of antisocial behavior. In W. O'Donohue, L. Benuto, & L. Woodward Tolle (Eds.), *Handbook of adolescent health psychology* (pp. 447–462). New York, NY: Springer Publishers.

Gottlieb, G. (1996). Developmental psychobiology theory. In R. B. Cairns, G. H. Elder, & E. J. Costello (Eds.), *Developmental science* (pp. 63–77). Cambridge, UK: Cambridge University Press.

Hobbs, N. (1966). Helping disturbed children: Psychological and ecological strategies. *American Psychologist, 21*, 1105–1115.

Horner, R. H., Sugai, G., & Anderson, C. M. (2010). Examining the evidence base for school-wide positive behavior support. *Focus on Exceptional Children, 42*, 1–14.

Johansen, E. B., Killeen, P. R., Russell, V. A., Tripp, G., Wickens, J. R., Tannock, R., … Sagvolden, T. (2009). Origins of altered reinforcement effects in ADHD. *Behavioral and Brain Functions, 5*, 1–15.

Kessler, L., Hewig, J., Weichold, K., Silbereisen, R. K., & Miltner, W. H. (2017). Feedback negativity and decision-making behavior in the balloon analogue risk task (BART) in adolescents is modulated by peer presence. *Psychophysiology, 54*, 260–269.

Kornienko, O., Dishion, T. J., & Ha, T. (2018). Peer network dynamics and the amplification of antisocial to violent behavior among young adolescents in public middle schools. *Journal of Emotional and Behavioral Disorders, 26*, 21–30.

Lane, K. L., Carter, E. W., Jenkins, A., Dwiggins, L., & Germer, K. (2015). Supporting comprehensive, integrated, three-tiered models of prevention in schools: Administrators perspectives. *Journal of Positive Behavior Interventions, 17*, 209–222.

Leist, T., & Dadds, M. R. (2009). Adolescents' ability to read different emotional faces relates to their history of maltreatment and type of psychopathology. *Clinical Child Psychology and Psychiatry, 14*, 237–250.

Lipsey, M. W., & Derzon, J. H. (1998). Predictors of violent or serious delinquency in adolescence and early adulthood: A synthesis of longitudinal research. In R. Loeber & D. P. Farrington (Eds.), *Serious & violent juvenile offenders: Risk factors and successful interventions* (pp. 86–105). Thousand Oaks, CA: Sage.

Lochman, J. E., & Dodge, K. A. (1994). Social cognitive processes of severely violent, moderately aggressive, and nonaggressive boys. *Journal of Consulting and Clinical Psychology, 62*, 366–374.

Lochman, J. E., Powell, N. P., Boxmeyer, C. L., & Jimenez-Camargo, L. (2011). Cognitive-behavioral therapy for externalizing disorders in children and adolescents. *Child and Adolescent Psychiatric Clinics of North America, 20*, 305–318.

Maggin, D. M., Wehby, J. H., Farmer, T. W., & Brooks, D. S. (2016). Intensive interventions for students with emotional and behavioral disorders: Issues, theory, and future directions. *Journal of Emotional and Behavioral Disorders, 24*, 127–137.

Magnusson, D., & Cairns, R. B. (1996). Developmental science: Toward a unified framework. In R. B. Cairns, G. H. Elder, & E. J. Costello (Eds.), *Developmental science* (pp. 7–30). Cambridge, UK: Cambridge University Press.

Masten, A. S. (2001). Ordinary magic: Resilience processes in development. *American Psychologist, 56*, 227–238.

Masten, A. S., & Cicchetti, D. (2010). Developmental cascades. *Development and Psychopathology, 22*, 491–495.

Miller, B. D., Blau, G. M., Christopher, O. T., & Jordan, P. E. (2012). Sustaining and expanding systems of care for children, youth and families across America. *American Journal of Community Psychology, 49*, 566–579.

Moffitt, T. E. (1993). Adolescence-limited and life-course-persistent antisocial behavior: A developmental taxonomy. *Psychological Review, 100*, 674–701.

Mrazek, P. J., & Haggerty, R. J. (Eds.), (1994). *Reducing risks for mental disorders: Frontiers for preventive intervention research.* Washington DC: Institute of Medicine, National Academy Press.

NCES. (2019). *The condition of education 2019. U.S. Department of Education.* Washington, DC: National Center for Education Statistics.

Patterson, G. R. (1982). *The coercive family process.* Eugene, OR: Castilia.

Peck, S. C., Roeser, R. W., Zarrett, N., & Eccles, J. S. (2008). Exploring the roles of extracurricular activity quantity and quality in the educational resilience of vulnerable adolescents: Variable- and patterned-centered approaches. *Journal of Social Issues, 64*, 135–155.

Reid, J. B. (1993). Prevention of conduct disorder before and after school entry: Relating interventions to developmental findings. *Development and Psychopathology, 5*, 243–262.

Ringeisen, H., Stambaugh, L., Bose, J., Casanueva, C., Hedden, S., Avenevoli, S., … West, J. (2018). Measurement of childhood serious emotional disturbance: State of the science and issues for consideration. *Journal of Emotional and Behavioral Disorders, 25*, 195–210.

Robins, L., & Rutter, M. (Eds.). (1990). *Straight and devious pathways from childhood to adulthood.* Cambridge: Cambridge University Press.

Roeser, R. W., Eccles, J. S., & Sameroff, A. J. (2000). School as a context of early adolescents' academic and social-emotional development: A summary of research findings. *The Elementary School Journal, 100*, 443–471.

Roeser, R. W., & Peck, S. C. (2003). Patterns and pathways of educational achievement across adolescence: A holistic-developmental perspective. *New Directions for Child and Adolescent Development, 101*, 39–62.

Sameroff, A. (1983). Developmental systems: Context and evolution. In P. H. Mussen & W. Kessen (Eds.), *Handbook of child psychology: Vol. 1. History, theory, and methods* (4th ed., pp. 237–294). New York: Wiley.

Sameroff, A. J. (2000). Developmental systems and psychopathology. *Development and Psychopathology, 12*, 297–312.

Seidman, E., & French, S. E. (2004). Developmental trajectories and ecological transitions: A two-step procedure to aid in the choice of prevention and promotion interventions. *Development and Psychopathology, SI: Transition from Adolescence to Adulthood, 16*, 1141–1159.

Shores, R. E., & Wehby, J. H. (1999). Analyzing the classroom social behavior of students with EBD. *Journal of Emotional and Behavioral Disorders, 7*, 194–199.

Smith, L. B., & Thelen, E. (2003). Development as a dynamic system. *Trends in Cognitive Sciences, 7*, 343–348.

Steinberg, Z., & Knitzer, J. (1992). Classrooms for emotionally and behaviorally disturbed students: Facing the challenge. *Behavioral Disorders, 17*, 145–156.

Stroul, B., & Friedman, R. M. (1986). *A system of care for children and adolescents with severe emotional disturbances.* Washington, DC: Georgetown University Child Development Center, National Technical Assistance Center for Children's Mental Health.

Sullivan, T. N., Sutherland, K. S., Lotze, G. M., Helms, S. W., Wright, S. A., & Ulmer, L. J. (2015). Problem situations experienced by urban middle school students with high incidence disabilities that impact emotional and behavioral adjustment. *Journal of Emotional and Behavioral Disorders, 23*, 101–114.

Sutherland, K. S., Conroy, M. A., McLeod, B. D., Kunemund, R., & McKnight, K. (2019). Common practice elements for improving social, emotional, and behavioral outcomes of young elementary school students. *Journal of Emotional and Behavioral Disorders, 27*, 76–85.

Sutherland, K. S., Farmer, T. W., Kunemund, R. L., & Sterrett, B. I. (2018). Learning, behavioral, and social difficulties within MTSS: A dynamic perspective of intervention intensification. In N. D. Young, K. Bonanno-Sotiropoulos, & T. A. Citro (Eds.), *Paving the pathway for educational success: Effective classroom interventions for students with learning disabilities* (pp. 15–32). New York: Rowman & Littlefield.

Trach, J., Lee, M., & Hymel, S. (2018). A social-ecological approach to addressing emotional and behavioral problems in schools: Focusing on group processes and social dynamics. *Journal of Emotional and Behavioral Disorders, 26*, 11–20.

van den Berg, Y. H. M., & Stoltz, S. (2018). Enhancing social inclusion of children with externalizing problems through classroom seating arrangements: A randomized control trial. *Journal of Emotional and Behavioral Disorders, 26*, 31–41.

Van Harmelen, A.-L., van Tol, M.-J., Demenescu, L. R., van der Wee, N. J., Veltman, D. J., Aleman, A., ... Elzinga, B. M. (2013). Enhanced amygdala reactivity to emotional faces in adults reporting childhood emotional maltreatment. *Social Cognitive and Affective Neuroscience, 8*, 362–369.

van Hoorn, J., McCormick, E. M., Rogers, C. R., Ivory, S. L., & Telzer, E. H. (2018). Differential effects of parent and peer presence on neural correlates of risk taking in adolescence. *Social Cognitive and Affective Neuroscience, 13*, 945–955.

Wagner, M., & Newman, L. (2012). Longitudinal transition outcomes of youth with emotional disturbances. *Psychiatric Rehabilitation Journal, 35*, 199–208.

Walker, H. M., & Sprague, J. R. (1999). The path to school failure, delinquency, and violence: Causal factors and some potential solutions. *Intervention in School and Clinic, 35*, 67–73.

Wehby, J. H., Symons, F. J., & Shores, R. E. (1995). A descriptive analysis of aggressive behavior in classrooms for children with emotional and behavioral disorders. *Behavioral Disorders, 20*, 87–105.

Youniss, J. (1980). *Parents and peers in social development: A Sullivan-Piaget perspective.* Chicago: University of Chicago Press.

2 The Epidemiology of Childhood Emotional and Behavioral Disorders

Heather Ringeisen, Leyla Stambaugh, and Dalia Khoury

Children's emotional and behavioral health disorders (EBDs) are common. It is estimated that up to 17.1 million children and adolescents in the United States will be diagnosed with an EBD before the age of 18 (Merikangas, He, Burstein, et al., 2010), equating to approximately one out of every five children. Emotional and behavioral health disorders negatively impact a child's day-to-day life, making it difficult to learn (e.g., Breslau et al., 2009), make and sustain friendships (e.g., Alsaker Françoise & Perren 2009), and successfully transition to adult responsibilities such as educational attainment and employment (e.g., Gibb, Fergusson, & Horwood, 2010). Unfortunately, children with EBDs often do not receive treatment (e.g., Costello, He, Sampson, Kessler, & Merikangas, 2014), leaving many children and families suffering without appropriate and timely services. Untreated childhood EBDs are particularly problematic when one considers the persistence of childhood problems into adulthood. Fifty percent of all adult mental health disorders begin before the age of 15, and 75% before the age of 24 (Kessler et al., 2005). High levels of unmet need for childhood EBD treatment exist despite evidence that suggests common childhood emotional problems, particularly anxiety and depression, can be prevented, treated or even ameliorated (Bayer et al., 2009; Cuijpers, Van Straten, & Smit, 2005; Merry, McDowell, Hetrick, Bir, & Muller, 2004). For these reasons, there are national and international calls to action to improve mental health treatment for children and adolescents and to reduce the negative impact of childhood EBDs in adulthood (New Freedom Commission Report, 2003; World Health Organization, 2012).

Children's EBDs manifest as significant changes in the way that a child or adolescent behaves or handles their emotions that also cause problems with daily living at home, in school, with friends, or in the community. Childhood EBDs are diagnosed using guidance from the American Psychiatric Association's Diagnostic and Statistical Manual, fifth edition (APA, 2013). Common childhood EBDs include anxiety disorders (i.e., generalized anxiety disorder, panic disorder, obsessive-compulsive disorder (OCD), and post-traumatic stress disorder (PTSD)), mood disorders (i.e., major depression, dysthymia, bipolar disorder), and behavior disorders (i.e., oppositional-defiant disorder (ODD), conduct disorder (CD), attention-deficit/hyperactivity disorder (ADHD)). Anxiety and mood disorders are sometimes described as "internalizing" disorders, with symptoms composed largely of internal states. Behavior disorders are sometimes described as "externalizing" disorders, with symptoms that often involve external, visible behaviors. Reports and publications will use different terms to describe EBDs, including the more general term "mental disorders" or the more specific term "serious emotional disturbance" (SED). SED describes the presence of an emotional or behavioral disorder that results in substantial functional

24   *Heather Ringeisen et al.*

impairment that interferes with or limits a child's ability to perform day-to-day activities. In this book, and specifically within this chapter, authors will use the term EBD or EBDs with functional impairment.

The goals of this chapter are twofold: to explore the prevalence of various childhood EBDs, and to explore the likelihood of children with EBDs to receive different types of treatment and services. Prevalence estimates will be drawn from large-scale epidemiological studies and ongoing national surveys in order to best approximate EBDs for children across the United States. The population focus will be school-age children and adolescents (approximately 8–17 years) representing ages typically included in available national study samples.

National Epidemiological Studies and Ongoing Surveillance Efforts

Four large-scale epidemiological datasets have been used to produce prevalence estimates of specific childhood EBDs and treatment use in the United States. These studies include a supplemental study to the National Health and Nutrition Examination Survey (NHANES) (Merikangas, He, Brody, et al., 2010), the National Comorbidity Survey Adolescent Cohort (NCS-A) (Kessler, Avenevoli, Costello, Georgiades, et al., 2012) and the NCS-A school sample (Green et al., 2015; Li, Green, Kessler, & Zaslavsky, 2010), Methods for the Epidemiology of Child and Adolescent Mental Disorders (MECA) (Lahey et al., 1996; Shaffer et al., 1996), and the Great Smoky Mountains Study of Youth (GSMS) (Costello, Angold, Burns, Stangl et al., 1996). Methodology across these four studies include the administration of interviews to children, adolescents, and their parents designed to directly assess DSM-concordant EBDs. Due to their methodological rigor and thorough diagnostic assessments, these four studies are considered the most accurate and reliable sources of data for estimating the prevalence of childhood EBDs in the United States. Unfortunately, none of these studies are part of an ongoing annual or semi-annual surveillance process, and are thereby outdated. The most recent of the four studies, the NHANES special study, collected data in 2004. In this chapter we will focus on estimates generated from the three most recent efforts—the NHANES special study, the NCS-A, and GSMS, excluding the MECA study.

In addition to the national epidemiological studies, there are four ongoing national surveillance efforts in the United States that include indicators relevant to understanding the prevalence of childhood EBDs and their treatment. However, these ongoing national surveys are not well-suited to provide specific comprehensive estimates of disorders as they do not include diagnostic interviews. Instead, these surveys include parent reports of a child's diagnosed EBD condition, screening measures for EBDs, measures of functional impairment, or questions that ask about childhood EBD treatment use. The value of these large-scale surveys is that they are conducted every year with relatively consistent measures of childhood mental health and treatment included within each survey. Consequently, this survey data is helpful in examining trends over time in childhood EBDs and mental health treatment use. Some of these national surveys even allow the production of state-specific estimates. Recent publications summarizing the prevalence of EBDs or mental health treatment use have used data from the following national surveys: the National Health Interview Survey (NHIS; Visser et al., 2014), Medical Expenditure Panel Survey (MEPS; Olfson, Druss, & Marcus, 2015), National Survey of Children's Health (NSCH; Whitney & Peterson, 2019), and the National Survey on Drug Use and Health (NSDUH; Mojtabai, Olfson, & Han, 2016).

National Prevalence of Childhood EBDs

National epidemiological studies indicate that anywhere from 13% to more than 40% of U.S. children meet criteria for having a current or past year EBD diagnosis (Costello, Angold, Burns, Stangl et al., 1996; Kessler, Avenevoli, Costello, Georgiades et al., 2012; Merikangas, He, Brody, et al., 2010). Between 7% and 11% of children meet criteria for an EBD that results in severe problems functioning at home, in school, with peers or in the community (Costello, Angold, Burns, Erkanli et al., 1996; Kessler, Avenevoli, Costello, Green et al., 2012; Merikangas, He, Brody, et al., 2010). Estimates of the prevalence of childhood EBDs vary dramatically depending upon individual study methods and sample composition. Characteristics of these three national epidemiological studies (NHANES special study, NCS-A, and GSMS) as well as their resulting prevalence estimates are summarized in Table 2.1. Estimates across these studies cannot be directly compared to one another because of study methodological differences. The studies include different disorders and different numbers of disorders, different assessment methods, types of informants, time reference periods used to estimate disorder prevalence (e.g., past 12 months versus past 3 months), and various definitions of severe functional impairments. For example, the NHANES study measured only a small number of disorders, included only one informant per disorder (child or parent), and thus yielded lower estimates of any EBD, as well as specific EBDs, than did the NCS-A and GSMS studies. The NCS-A, meanwhile, included a much more comprehensive assessment of DSM-IV disorders (APA, 1994), including substance use and dependence. The NCS-A also included a less stringent consideration of functional impairment in the assessment of past year EBD prevalence. Child age also varies across study samples. The NCS-A sample only included adolescents, while the NHANES and GSMS studies included children down to the age of eight. Regardless of study methodological differences, the NHANES, NCS-S, and GSMS studies provide rich information on the prevalence of specific types of EBD diagnoses, impairment associated with specific disorders, as well as common demographic correlates that are associated with disorders.

Large-scale epidemiological studies show that childhood internalizing and externalizing disorders are equally common, with some studies even finding that emotional/internalizing disorders (i.e., anxiety, depression) are more common than behavioral/externalizing disorders (i.e., ADHD, CD, ODD). This may be particularly true among adolescents. The NCS-A found that the past year prevalence of any anxiety disorder among children 13–17 years old was 24.9%, any behavior disorder 16.3%, and any mood disorder 10.0% (Kessler, Avenevoli, Costello, Georgiades et al., 2012). While the ranking of the most common, specific types of EBDs varies from study to study, there is general consistency in the most common disorders (see Table 2.2). In both the NCS-A (Kessler, Avenevoli, Costello, Georgiades et al., 2012) and GSMS (Costello, Angold, Burns, Stangl et al., 1996), anxiety disorders have the highest prevalence rates of all measured EBDs. Behavior disorders such as conduct disorder, ODD, and ADHD are the next most common types of EBDs, followed by mood disorders. National estimates of the prevalence of any anxiety disorder have especially large variation across studies, dependent upon whether specific phobias, social phobias, separation anxiety disorder, and PTSD were among the types of anxiety disorders assessed. In the NHANES special study, which included a younger sample than the NCS-A and GSMS, the most common disorder was ADHD, followed by major depression. This study found a particularly low prevalence of anxiety disorders and did not include assessment of specific phobias, social phobia, PTSD, and separation anxiety disorder.

Table 2.1 Characteristics of large epidemiological studies and estimates of childhood EBDs

Survey	Age range[1]	Sample size	Most recent year fielded	Type of assessment	Disorders included	Prevalence of any EBD (% ± SE)	Prevalence of any EBD with serious impairment (% ± SE)
NHANES (special study)	8 to 15	3,042	2004	Child or parent interview (DISC-IV, DSM-IV)	MD, dysthymia, GAD, panic, ADHD, CD, eating disorder	13.1% ± 0.9 (past 12 months)	11.3% ± 0.9 (past 12 months)
NCS-A	13 to 17	6,483[2] (adolescent/ parent pairs)	2002	Child and parent interview (CIDI-A; DMS-IV)	MD, dysthymia, bipolar disorder, GAD, panic, phobias, separation anxiety, PTSD, ADHD, CD, ODD, eating disorder, substance use disorders	40.3 ± 1.2 (past 12 months)	8.0% ± 1.3 (past 12 months)
GSMS	9 to 13 (baseline age)	1,420	1999	Child and parent interview (CAPA; DSM III-R)	MD, dysthymia, bipolar disorder, mania, depression NOS, GAD, panic, phobias, separation anxiety, PTSD, OCD, ADHD, CD, ODD, eating disorders, psychosis, elimination disorders, trichotillomania, substance use disorders	20.3% ± 1.7 (past 3 months)	6.8% (past 3 months)

Sources: Merikangas, K. R., He, J. P., Brody, D., Fisher, P. W., Bourdon, K., & Koretz, D. S. (2010). Prevalence and treatment of mental disorders among US children in the 2001–2004 NHANES. *Pediatrics*, *125*(1), 75–81. Costello, E. J., Angold, A., Burns, B. J., et al. (1996). The Great Smoky Mountains Study of Youth: Goals, design, methods, and the prevalence of DSM-III-R disorders. *Archives of General Psychiatry*, *53*, 1129–1136.

Note. CAPA = Child and Adolescent Psychiatric Assessment; CIDI-A = Composite International Diagnostic Interview Adolescent; DISC-IV = Diagnostic Interview Schedule for Children Version IV; DSM = Diagnostic and Statistical Manual of Mental Disorders; GSMS = Great Smoky Mountains Study of Youth; NCS-A = National Comorbidity Survey Adolescent Supplement; NHANES = National Health and Nutrition Examination Survey.

1 Several of these studies included respondents older than 17 years. The purpose of this table is to show coverage for children and youths from birth to 17 years old.
2 The NCS-A included a larger adolescent-only sample; however, the household study of SED included only the adolescent–parent paired data.

Table 2.2 Prevalence of specific emotional and behavioral disorders in three large-scale epidemiological studies

Emotional or Behavioral Disorder	Prevalence, % (SE)		
	NCS-A (past 12 months, DSM-V)	NHANES special study (past 12 months, DSM-V)	GSMS (past 3 months; DSM-IIIR)
Mood Disorders			
Major depression	8.2 (.8)	2.7 (.6)	–*
Dysthymia	Included in estimate with depression	1.0 (.3)	–
Bipolar disorder	2.1 (.2)	NA	–
Depression, not otherwise specified	NA	NA	1.45 (.46)
Any mood/depressive disorder	10.0 (.8)	3.7 (.6)	1.52 (.46)
Anxiety Disorders			
Agoraphobia	1.8 (.2)	NA	–
Generalized anxiety disorder	1.1 (.2)	.3 (.1)	1.67 (.61)
Social phobia (social anxiety)	8.2 (.4)	NA	.58 (.32)
Specific phobia (simple phobia)	15.8 (.8)	NA	.27 (.10)
Panic disorder	1.9 (.2)	.4 (.1)	–
Post-traumatic stress disorder	3.9 (.4)	NA	–
Separation anxiety disorder	1.6 (.2)	NA	3.49 (.75)
Obsessive-compulsive disorder	NA	NA	.17 (.08)
Any anxiety disorder	24.9 (.9)	.7 (.2)	5.69 (.96)
Behavior Disorders			
Attention-deficit/hyperactivity disorder	6.5 (.5)	8.6 (.7)	1.94 (.39)
Oppositional-defiant disorder	8.3 (.7)	NA	2.75 (.41)
Conduct disorder	5.4 (.8)	2.1 (.3)	3.32 (.64)
Eating disorders	2.8 (.2)	.1 (.1)	–
Any behavior disorder	16.3 (1.1)	NA	6.56 (.81)

* Assessed within the study, but too rare to generate a reliable estimate. NA=not assessed within study or estimate not available in publication. DSM = Diagnostic and Statistical Manual of Mental Disorders; GSMS = Great Smoky Mountains Study of Youth; NCS-A = National Comorbidity Survey Adolescent Supplement; NHANES = National Health and Nutrition Examination Survey.

Sources: Merikangas, K. R., He, J. P., Brody, D., Fisher, P. W., Bourdon, K., & Koretz, D. S. (2010). Prevalence and treatment of mental disorders among US children in the 2001–2004 NHANES. *Pediatrics, 125*(1), 75–81. Costello, E. J., Angold, A., Burns, B. J., et al. (1996). The Great Smoky Mountains Study of Youth: Goals, design, methods, and the prevalence of DSM-III-R disorders. *Archives of General Psychiatry, 53*, 1129–1136. Kessler, R. C., Avenevoli, S., Costello, E. J., Georgiades, K., Green, J. G., Gruber, M. J., … Merikangas, K. R. (2012). Prevalence, persistence and sociodemographic correlates of DSM-IV disorders in the national comorbidity survey replication adolescent supplement. *Archives of General Psychiatry, 69*(4), 372–380.

28   *Heather Ringeisen et al.*

The overarching prevalence of childhood EBDs decreases substantially when requirements for serious impairment are included along with the results of a diagnostic assessment. This is the most dramatic when considering results of the NCS-A: 42.6% of adolescents in the NCS-A met symptoms criteria for the past 12-month prevalence of any EBD, but only 8% met criteria for an EBD that resulted in functional impairment that substantially interfered with the child's role or functioning in family, school or community activities (Kessler, Avenevoli, Costello, Green et al., 2012). Behavior and mood disorders result in a higher likelihood of serious functional impairment than anxiety disorders. More than one third of behavior and mood disorders result in serious functional impairment compared to 18% of anxiety disorders (see Table 2.3). And, having more than one disorder significantly increases the functional impact of EBDs on adolescents' day-to-day functioning (Kessler, Avenevoli, Costello, Green et al., 2012).

Socio-demographic features are associated with the prevalence of EBDs, particularly gender and age. The impacts of gender and age vary dependent upon the type of EBD being considered. Boys tend to be at higher risk for any psychiatric disorder across studies, but this is primarily due to their increased rates of behavioral disorders (Costello, Angold, Burns, Stangl et al., 1996). For example, Merikangas, He, Brody, et al. (2010) found that the

Table 2.3 Disorder-specific severity of specific past 12-month DSM-IV emotional and behavioral disorders: Results from the National Comorbidity Survey-Adolescent Supplement

DSM-IV Disorder	Functional Impairment Severity Distribution, % (SE)		
	Serious	Moderate	Mild
Mood Disorders			
Major depressive episode/dysthymia	35.6 (5.2)	31.0 (6.4)	33.4 (6.7)
Bipolar disorder	30.5 (5.8)	26.5 (12.1)	43.1 (10.7)
Any mood disorder	32.4 (4.5)	29.8 (7.4)	37.8 (7.7)
Anxiety Disorders			
Agoraphobia	22.1 (7.4)	25.9 (15.5)	52.0 (15.9)
Generalized anxiety disorder	32.0 (8.6)	21.0 (8.9)	47.1 (9.0)
Social phobia	23.9 (5.1)	23.8 (9.3)	52.3 (9.0)
Specific phobia	19.6 (5.1)	16.8 (11.6)	63.7 (10.6)
Panic disorder	35.4 (12.6)	21.2 (10.3)	43.4 (10.9)
Post-traumatic stress disorder	27.7 (7.0)	23.8 (11.1)	48.5 (10.4)
Separation anxiety disorder	25.0 (8.1)	25.5 (8.9)	49.5 (10.9)
Any anxiety disorder	18.4 (3.4)	19.6 (10.3)	62.0 (9.6)
Behavior Disorders			
Attention-deficit/hyperactivity disorder	35.4 (8.2)	40.6 (14.0)	24.0 (10.6)
Oppositional-defiant disorder	43.8 (7.8)	24.3 (6.8)	31.9 (8.9)
Conduct disorder	59.8 (8.4)	21.1 (9.4)	19.2 (8.6)
Eating disorders	27.5 (10.0)	26.0 (15.1)	46.5 (16.6)
Any behavior disorder	33.6 (5.1)	30.2 (9.4)	36.2 (9.6)

Source: Kessler, R. C., Avenevoli, S., Costello, J., Green, J. G., Gruber, M. J., McLaughlin, K. A., Petukhova, M., Sampson, N. A., Zaslavsky, A. M., & Merikangas, K. R. (2012). Severity of 12-month DSM-IV disorders in the National Comorbidity Survey Replication Adolescent Supplement. *Archives of General Psychiatry, 69*(4), 381–389.

prevalence rate of ADHD among boys was twice that of girls. Meanwhile, adolescent girls have higher rates of mood, anxiety, and eating disorders than boys (Kessler, Avenevoli, Costello, Georgiades et al., 2012). With regards to age, generally, EBDs have a slightly higher prevalence among older children. Rates of conduct disorder and mood disorders, particularly major depressive disorder, are higher in adolescents than school-age children; whereas ADHD is slightly more common in school-age children (Merikangas, He, Brody, et al., 2010). Differences in prevalence by age group are consistent with findings around the age of EBD onset. Results from the NCS-A show a median age of onset for anxiety disorders of six years, followed by 11 years for behavior disorders, and 13 years for mood disorders (Merikangas, He, Burstein, et al., 2010). Findings around differences in EBD prevalence by race/ethnicity and income are not consistent across studies.

Trends in the Prevalence of EBDs

Given the study-specific differences in child age groups and methodologies, there is no way to track trends across studies in the prevalence of specific childhood EBDs over time in the United States. However, individual, annual, national surveys that ask parents about specific EBD diagnoses in their children can help examine changes over time. A 2013 article in the *Morbidity and Mortality Weekly Report* summarized current surveillance efforts designed to capture indicators of children's behavioral health in national surveys from 2005 to 2011 (CDC, 2013). Available national indicators included parent-reported child diagnoses such as ADHD, major depressive episode (MDE), as well as the prevalence of substance abuse and suicide. A few recent studies find that the prevalence of certain childhood EBDs may be increasing. For example, a study using 2003 to 2011 data from the National Survey of Children's Health documented the increasing prevalence of parent-reported ADHD over that time period (Visser et al., 2014). Mojtabai et al. (2016) similarly used data from the National Survey on Drug Use and Health (NSDUH) to demonstrate a statistically significant increase in the 12-month prevalence of MDE among adolescents from 2005 to 2014. While the prevalence of certain disorders such as ADHD and MDE may be increasing, a study using Medical Expenditure Panel Survey (MEPS) data from 1998 to 2012 found decreases in the number of children (aged six to 17 years) with severe functional impairment related to mental health problems (Olfson et al., 2015). These findings highlight the utility of consistently measuring the prevalence of childhood behavioral health indicators over time. Unfortunately, national surveillance efforts only capture a few EBDs rendering it challenging to draw implications from this limited data.

Prevalence of Treatment Use

While prevalence estimates of specific EBDs vary from study to study, estimates of the proportion of children with EBDs who received treatment in the past year is starkly consistent. Across large-scale national epidemiological studies, half or fewer of all children meeting the diagnostic threshold for an EBD receive treatment (Costello et al., 2014; Katoaka, Zhang & Wells, 2002; Merikangas, He, Brody, et al., 2010). More specifically, 45% of adolescents with EBDs in the NCS-A received some form of professional services (Costello et al., 2014); only 50.6% of children and adolescents in the NHANES study with disorders reported past year service use (Merikangas, He, Brody, et al., 2010). Despite public concerns about the overmedication of children, findings about children's use of psychotropic medications also show high levels of unmet need. Data from the NCS-A demonstrate that only 14% of adolescents with an EBD report being treated with a psychotropic medication in the past year (Merikangas, He, Rapoport, Vitiello, & Olfson, 2013). Less than 2.5% of adolescents not meeting diagnostic criteria for an EBD reported psychotropic medication use; and most of these "non-EBD" cases showed evidence of emotional or behavioral health problems or impairment. The levels of mental health treatment described by these large-scale national studies fail to portray the full extent of unmet need for children's mental health services. Epidemiological studies set a very low threshold for "treatment receipt," often defining this construct as a child or parent reporting *at least* one mental health treatment or visit in the past year. So, while at best half of children with EBDs received some treatment in the past year, even more children likely do not receive adequate treatment.

Treatment results from these large-scale epidemiological studies stem from data that is more than a decade outdated. However, a more recent study examining results from the 2016 National Survey of Children's Health (NSCH) finds strikingly similar results (Whitney & Peterson, 2019). The NSCH includes parent reports of child depression, anxiety, and ADHD diagnoses. If parents report a diagnosis, they are then asked if their child received any treatment or counseling from a mental health professional in the past year. Only half of the estimated 7.7 million children described as having a depression, anxiety, or ADHD diagnosis in the 2016 NSCH received mental health treatment in the past year (Whitney & Peterson, 2019). Findings across these national studies directly point to the drastic need for greater recognition and treatment of child and adolescent EBDs across the United States.

Some childhood EBDs are more likely to receive treatment than others. In general, children with externalizing behavior problems are much more likely to have received treatment in the past year than children with internalizing conditions, particularly anxiety. For example, the NHANES special study showed that children 9–17 years with ADHD (47.7%) and conduct disorder (46.4%) had the highest treatment rates, while generalized anxiety disorder and panic disorder had the lowest (32.2%). With an adolescent-only sample, the NCS-A findings showed that youth with ADHD were the most likely to receive treatment (73.8%), followed by those with CD (73.4%), ODD (71.0%), major depressive disorder or dysthymia (62.1%) and PTSD (60.2%). Adolescents with anxiety disorder were the least likely to have received any treatment in the past year (41.4%). In both studies, a higher level of impairment was consistently associated with a greater likelihood of treatment receipt.

Child characteristics do have some influence on treatment use. Older age is associated with a higher likelihood of treatment use among children with EBDs (Katoaka, Zhang & Wells, 2002). Merikangas and colleagues (2010) found that young adolescents (ages 12–15) were more likely to use mental health services than children aged eight to 11, even when analyses controlled for mental health need. However, throughout adolescence, treatment access may not be consistently high. In fact, later in adolescence, treatment use may decline. Ringeisen et al. (2016) found that outpatient, inpatient, and school-based service use increased from age 12 to14 years, and then either declined (outpatient mental health and school-based services) or remained level (hospitalizations) from age 15 to 17. The decline was particularly apparent for school-based services, where service use decreased from 14.5% at age 13 to 9.6% at age 17. Other socio-demographic correlates, including gender and even insurance status, are not consistently associated with service use across studies. And even when found, these associations appear to differ by age, type of service use, and diagnosis.

Children and adolescents receive mental health services from mental health specialty (outpatient or inpatient mental health treatment) as well as non-mental health specialty (schools, pediatric primary care, juvenile justice) settings. Adolescents with EBDs often are more likely or just as likely to receive some mental health services in a school setting as they are to receive services provided by specialty mental health providers (Burns, Costello & Angold, 1995; Costello et al., 2014). During childhood, schools are a particularly critical point of access for mental health services and for the early identification of mental health problems (Farmer, Burns, Phillips, Angold, & Costello, 2003). This is particularly true for elementary and middle school-age children, but also for adolescents. The latest data from the NSDUH continue to show that high-school-age adolescents are almost equally likely to use specialty mental health services as they are to use school-based services (SAMHSA, 2019). These data illustrate the settings in which adolescents (12–17 years) report having received mental health services in the past year (SAMHSA, 2019):

- 3.9 million (16.0% of all U.S. adolescents) received mental health services in a specialty mental health setting (inpatient or outpatient care);
- 3.4 million (14.2% of all U.S. adolescents) received mental health services in an education setting;
- 767,000 (3.1% of all U.S. adolescents) received mental health services in a general medical setting;
- 94,000 (0.4% of all U.S. adolescents) received mental health services in a child welfare setting; and
- 48,000 (0.2% of all U.S. adolescents) received mental health services in a juvenile justice setting.

Children, adolescents and their families can receive mental health services across multiple settings. Unfortunately, despite these multiple potential avenues for service receipt, most children with EBDs are not identified as needing help by the professionals within these settings. Far too many children receive no treatment or very limited service supports for their mental health problems.

Trends in Treatment

Overarching rates of mental health treatment receipt among children and adolescents in the United States do appear to be gradually increasing. Olfson et al. (2015) analyzed data from the MEPS from 1996 to 2012. The percentage of children aged six to 17 years who received any outpatient mental health service increased from 9.2% (1996–1998) to 13.3% (2010–2012). Similar increases were found in children's use of psychotropic medications, which increased from 5.5% (1996–1998) to 8.9% (2010–2012). NSDUH data from 2009–2018 also show an increase in adolescents' (aged 12 to 17 years) report of services received in specialty mental health settings (12.0% in 2009 to 16.0% in 2018) as well as the proportion of adolescents who reported receipt of mental health services in an education setting (12.1% in 2009 to 14.2% in 2018; SAMHSA, 2019).

Unfortunately, increasing rates of treatment may simply coincide with increasing rates of childhood EBDs and associated impairments. Even those studies that find an increasing trend in mental health treatment use continue to find high levels of unmet need among those with mental health problems. For example, despite their observation of an increase in MDE among adolescents in the past decade, Mojtabai et al. (2016) did not find a commensurate increase in the proportion of adolescents with past 12-month MDE who received mental health counseling or treatment for their depression. And, similarly, despite Olfson et al.'s (2015) finding of increased treatment use since 1996, fewer than half of children with severe functional impairment in the 2010–2012 MEPS survey received mental health services in the past year. The national surveys that include annual data on child or adolescent mental health treatment use do not also include specific measures of childhood EBDs. The MEPS survey only includes a measure of mental health functional impairment (no information on EBD diagnoses); and the NSDUH only includes a measure of adolescent MDE (no other EBD diagnoses). Despite these limitations, these surveys showing current trends in mental health service and psychotropic medication use may suggest little progress in narrowing the mental health treatment gap associated with child and adolescent EBDs.

Conclusion

Approximately one in five children and adolescents meet diagnostic criteria for an EBD, but only half of those children receive even limited treatment to help manage the symptoms and functional impairments associated with their disorder. Ongoing surveillance efforts suggest that the rates of childhood EBDs across the United States may be increasing. Unfortunately, these surveillance efforts do not similarly suggest improvements in the consistently high levels of unmet treatment needs for children diagnosed with EBDs. Children are part of a complicated service system in which treatment and preventive services may be offered at home, in school and in other community settings. These settings include, but are not limited to, specialty mental health service systems. Integrating successful interventions into traditional mental health service systems as well as into children's natural home, school, and community environments is challenging. Knowledge gained about effective interventions and their successful implementation within complex systems needs to be applied to make improvements in the children's mental health service system infrastructure in the United States. Only this type of work holds promise to improve the well-being of children with EBDs and to begin to close the long-standing gap between these children's mental health needs and their receipt of effective, timely, and appropriate treatment and services.

References

Alsaker Françoise, D., & Perren, S. (2009). Depressive symptoms from kindergarten to early school age: Longitudinal associations with social skills deficits and peer victimization. *Child and Adolescent Psychiatry and Mental Health, 3*(1), 28.

American Psychiatric Association. (1994). *Diagnostic and statistical manual of mental disorders* (4th ed.). Washington, DC: Author.

American Psychiatric Association. (2013). *Diagnostic and statistical manual of mental disorders* (5th ed.). Arlington, VA: American Psychiatric Publishing.

Bayer, J., Hiscock, H., Scalzo, K., Mathers, M., Mcdonald, M., Morris, A., … Wake, M. (2009). Systematic review of preventive interventions for children's mental health: What would work in Australian contexts? *Australian and New Zealand Journal of Psychiatry, 43*(8), 695–710.

Breslau, J., Miller, E., Breslau, N., Bohnert, K., Lucia, V., & Schweitzer, J. (2009). The impact of early behavior disturbances on academic achievement in high school. *Pediatrics, 123*(6), 1472–1476. doi:10.1542/peds.2008-1406

Burns, B. J., Costello, E. J., Angold, A., Tweed, D., Stangl, D., Farmer, E. M., & Erkanli, A. (1995). Children's mental health service use across service sectors. *Health Affairs (Project Hope), 14*(3), 147–159.

Centers for Disease Control and Prevention. (2013). Mental health surveillance among children: United States, 2005–2011. *Morbidity and Mortality Weekly Report, 62*(Suppl 2), 1–35.

Costello, E., He, J., Sampson, N., Kessler, R., & Merikangas, K. (2014). Services for adolescents with psychiatric disorders: 12-month data from the National Comorbidity Survey-Adolescent. *Psychiatric Services (Washington, D.C.), 65*(3), 359–366.

Costello, E. J., Angold, A., Burns, B. J., Erkanli, A., Stangl, D. K., & Tweed, D. L. (1996). The Great Smoky Mountains Study of Youth: Functional impairment and serious emotional disturbance. *Archives of General Psychiatry, 53*(12), 1137–1143. doi:10.1001/archpsyc.1996.01830120077013

Costello, E. J., Angold, A., Burns, B. J., Stangl, D. K., Tweed, D. L., Erkanli, A., & Worthman, C. M. (1996). The Great Smoky Mountains Study of Youth: Goals, design, methods, and the prevalence of DSM-III-R disorders. *Arch Gen Psychiatry, 53*(12), 1129–1136. doi:10.1001/archpsyc.1996.01830120067012

Cuijpers, P., Van Straten, A., & Smit, F. (2005). Preventing the incidence of new cases of mental disorders: A meta-analytic review. *The Journal of Nervous and Mental Disease, 193*(2), 119–125.

Farmer, E., Burns, B., Phillips, S., Angold, A., & Costello, E. (2003). Pathways into and through mental health services for children and adolescents. *Psychiatric Services, 54*(1), 60–66.

Gibb, S., Fergusson, D., & Horwood, L. (2010). Burden of psychiatric disorder in young adulthood and life outcomes at age 30. *The British Journal of Psychiatry, 197*(2), 122–127.

Green, J. G., Alegria, M., Kessler, R. C., McLaughlin, K. A., Gruber, M. J., Sampson, N. A., & Zaslavsky, A. M. (2015). Neighborhood sociodemographic predictors of serious emotional disturbance (SED) in schools: Demonstrating a small area estimation method in the National Comorbidity Survey (NCS-A) Adolescent Supplement. *Administration and Policy in Mental Health and Mental Health Services Research, 42*(1), 111–120. doi:10.1007/s10488-014-0550-8

Katoaka, S. H., Zhang, L., & Wells, K. B. (2002). Unmet need for mental health care among U.S. children: Variation by ethnicity and insurance status. *American Journal of Psychiatry, 159*(9), 1548–1555.

Kessler, R. C., Avenevoli, S., Costello, E. J., Georgiades, K., Green, J. G., Gruber, M. J., & Merikangas, K. R. (2012). Prevalence, persistence and sociodemographic correlates of dsm-iv disorders in the national comorbidity survey replication adolescent supplement. *Archives of General Psychiatry, 69*(4), 372–380.

Kessler, R. C., Avenevoli, S., Costello, J., Green, J. G., Gruber, M. J., McLaughlin, K. A., ... Merikangas, K. R. (2012). Severity of 12-month DSM-IV disorders in the National Comorbidity Survey Replication Adolescent Supplement. *Archives of General Psychiatry, 69*(4), 381–389. doi:10.1001/archgenpsychiatry.2011.1603

Kessler, R. C., Berglund, P., Demler, O., Jin, R., Merikangas, K. R., & Walters, E. E. (2005). Lifetime prevalence and age-of-onset distributions of DSM-IV disorders in the national comorbidity survey replication. *Archives of General Psychiatry, 62*(6), 593–602. doi:10.1001/archpsyc.62.6.593

Li, F., Green, J. G., Kessler, R. C., & Zaslavsky, A. M. (2010). Estimating prevalence of serious emotional disturbance in schools using a brief screening scale. *International Journal of Methods in Psychiatric Research, 19*, 88–98. doi:10.1002/mpr.315

Merikangas, K., He, J., Burstein, M., Swanson, S., Avenevoli, S., Cui, L., ... Swendsen, J. (2010). Lifetime prevalence of mental disorders in U.S. adolescents: Results from the National Comorbidity Survey Replication–Adolescent Supplement (NCS-A). *Journal of the American Academy of Child & Adolescent Psychiatry, 49*(10), 980–989.

Merikangas, K., He, J., Rapoport, J., Vitiello, B., & Olfson, M. (2013). Medication use in US youth with mental disorders. *JAMA Pediatrics, 167*(2), 141–148.

Merikangas, K. R., He, J. P., Brody, D., Fisher, P. W., Bourdon, K., & Koretz, D. S. (2010). Prevalence and treatment of mental disorders among US children in the 2001–2004 NHANES. *Pediatrics, 125*(1), 75–81. doi:10.1542/peds.2008-2598

Merry, S., McDowell, H., Hetrick, S., Bir, J., & Muller, N. (2004). Psychological and/or educational interventions for the prevention of depression in children and adolescents. *The Cochrane Database of Systematic Reviews, 2*(1), CD003380.

Mojtabai, R., Olfson, M., & Han, B. (2016). National trends in the prevalence and treatment of depression in adolescents and young adults. *Pediatrics, 138*(6), pii: e20161878.

Lahey, B. B. et al. (1996). The NIMH methods for the epidemiology of child and adolescent mental disorders (MECA) study: Background and methodology. *Journal of the American Academy of Child and Adolescent Psychiatry, 35*(7), 855–864.

Olfson, M., Druss, B. G., & Marcus, S. C. (2015). Trends in mental health care among children and adolescents. *New England Journal of Medicine, 373*(11), 1079. doi:10.1056/NEJMc1507642

Ringeisen, H., Miller, S., Munoz, B., Rohloff, H., Hedden, S. L., & Colpe, L. J. (2016). Mental health service use in adolescence: Findings from the National Survey on Drug Use and Health. *Psychiatric Services, 67*(7), 787–789.

Shaffer, D., Fisher, P., Dulcan, M. K., Davies, M., Piacentini, J., SchwabStone, M. E., … Regier, D. A. (1996). The NIMH Diagnostic Interview Schedule for Children Version 2.3 (DISC-2.3): Description, acceptability, prevalence rates, and performance in the MECA study. *Journal of the American Academy of Child and Adolescent Psychiatry, 35*(7), 865–877. doi:10.1097/00004583-199607000-00012

Substance Abuse and Mental Health Services Administration. (2019). *Key substance use and mental health indicators in the United States: Results from the 2018 National Survey on Drug Use and Health* (HHS Publication No. PEP19-5068, NSDUH Series H-54). Rockville, MD: Author. Retrieved from www.samhsa.gov/data/

United States. President's New Freedom Commission on Mental Health. (2003). *Achieving the promise: Transforming mental health care in America: Final report.* Rockville, MD: President's New Freedom Commission on Mental Health.

Visser, S. N., Danielson, M. L., Bitsko, R. H., Holbrook, J. R., Kogan, M. D., Ghandour, R. M., … Blumberg, S. J. (2014). Trends in the parent-report of health care provider-diagnosed and medicated attention-deficit/hyperactivity disorder: United States, 2003–2011. *Journal of the American Academy of Child and Adolescent Psychiatry, 53*(1), 34–46. e32. doi:10.1016/j.jaac.2013.09.001

Whitney, D. G., & Peterson, M. D. (2019). US national and state-level prevalence of mental health disorders and disparities of mental health care use in children. *JAMA Pediatrics, 173*(4), 389–391. doi:10.1001/jamapediatrics.2018.5399

World Health Organization. (2012). *Adolescent mental health: Mapping actions of nongovernmental organizations and other international development organizations.* Geneva: Author.

3 Prevention and Intervention in Preschool and Early Elementary School Years

Maureen A. Conroy, Rebecca Bulotsky-Shearer, Chelsea Morris, and Allyse A. Hetrick

Introduction

Although diagnosing an emotional and behavioral disorder (EBD) is challenging, and often does not occur until after entering school, many children begin to show early signs of social-emotional learning (SEL) delays or behavioral concerns in their toddler and preschool years (Briggs-Gowan & Carter, 2008). These children have difficulty regulating their emotions and lack social problem-solving skills as well as demonstrate communication delays, which may lead to increased behavioral challenges (e.g., aggression, defiance, disruption) (Blair & Raver, 2012; Chow & Wehby, 2018; Qi & Kaiser, 2003). Additionally, they are at risk for a host of negative outcomes including poor school readiness, negative student–teacher relationships, peer rejection, and academic failure (e.g., see Brennan, Shaw, Dishion, & Wilson, 2012; Bulotsky-Shearer, Bell, & Dominguez, 2012; Pianta & Stuhlman, 2004). Experiencing negative outcomes during early childhood may increase the likelihood of longer-term negative consequences as children age (e.g., gaps in or failure of academic achievement or the development of significant clinical EBD) (Campbell, Spieker, Burchinal, & Poe, 2006; Forness et al., 1998; Lamont & Council on School Health, 2013; Skiba et al., 2014). Further, discipline data suggest that young children who are unable to negotiate social, emotional, and behavioral expectations early in their schooling are at risk of suspension or expulsion, resulting in a loss of valuable foundational opportunities for growth and learning (Losen & Gillespie, 2012).

Fortunately, preventive classroom-based intervention programs that address the SEL and behavioral needs of young children are available (for examples, see Table 3.1 below). These classroom-based interventions can provide young children at risk for EBD access to high quality learning opportunities, including positive interactions with their teachers and engagement in daily learning activities that support the development of school readiness skills (e.g., Mashburn & Pianta, 2006; Sutherland et al., 2018). In this chapter, we provide a brief overview of the developmental characteristics and developmental considerations of young children with SEL difficulties. We also provide an integrative review of evidence-based preventive interventions and practices designed to ameliorate SEL delays and behavioral concerns of young children. Finally, we propose directions for further research and practice.

Overview of SEL Delays and Behavioral Challenges

Social and emotional and milestones emerge before kindergarten (Halle, Hair, Burchinal, Anderson, & Zaslow, 2012). Developing skills in this area require children to understand

Table 3.1 Overview of SEL Intervention Programs

Program	Authors	Overall Purpose	Target Population & Age	Delivery Setting
Pyramid Model for Supporting Social Emotional Competence in Infants and Young Children	Fox, Dunlap, Hemmeter, Joseph, and Strain (2003)	Multi-tiered system of supports focused on the intentional teaching of social-emotional skills to support nurturing and responsive caregiving relationships, high-quality environments, targeted social emotional needs, and intensive intervention	Children ages 0–5	classroom-based
PK-PATHS	Domitrovich, Cortes, and Greenberg (2007)	Comprehensive curriculum intended to enhance social competence and prevent or reduce behavior and emotional problems, with emphasis on emotional awareness and self-regulation	Preschool and kindergarten children ages 3–6 years old	classroom-based
LOOK	Downer et al. (2018)	Data-derived, video-based early childhood mental health consultation model intended to increase teacher effective implementation of classroom-based strategies to increase positive engagement and decrease negative engagement	Preschool age children ages 3–5 with problem behavior	classroom-based
Banking Time	Pianta & Hamre (2001), Driscoll and Pianta (2010)	Dyadic intervention designed to promote supportive teacher–child relationships	Preschool age children ages 3–5 with problem behavior	classroom-based (but pull-out within)
BEST in CLASS	Conroy & Sutherland (2008), Conroy et al. (2019), Sutherland et al. (2018)	Tier 2 intervention designed to enhance teachers use of effective instructional practices and promote positive teacher–child relationships and decrease problem behaviors	Children PK-2nd grade with problem behavior	classroom-based
Incredible Years Classroom Management Training (TCM) for Teachers	Webster-Stratton (2001)	One of three components of a multifaceted, and developmentally based curricula for parents, teachers, and children to promote emotional and social competence and to prevent, reduce, and treat aggression and emotional problems	Children ages 4–8 (infant programs are currently undergoing evaluation; studies for children at risk and for children with ODD have been positive)	classroom-based

Table 3.1 (Cont.)

	Group Size	Change Agent	Program Components	Practice Elements Included
Pyramid Model for Supporting Social Emotional Competence in Infants and Young Children	universal large group; targeted small group; intensive individual	teachers	state and program capacity-building framework, professional development materials, practice-based coaching materials; resources available for leaders, trainers & coaches, educators & families, and community partners	emotion regulation, problem-solving, social skills, promoting behavioral competence, praise, rehearsal, modeling, OTR, rules, instructive feedback, narrating, choices, differential reinforcement, supportive listening, monitoring, precorrection, Premack statements, scaffolding, visual cueing
PK-PATHS	universal large group or small group lessons	teachers	teacher training, manuals, program curriculum, intervention materials	emotion regulation, instructive feedback, modeling, OTR, praise, problem-solving, rules, scaffolding, social skills, tangible reinforcement, promoting teacher–child relationship
LOOK	Universal, small group, or individual implemented during any daily activity	teachers	on-line learning modules, assessment reporting system, evidence-based strategy resources, guided video review embedded within practice-based coaching (or mental health consultation) cycles	emotion regulation, problem-solving, social skills, promoting behavioral competence, promoting teacher–child relationship, praise, tangible reinforcement, rehearsal, modeling, OTR, rules, instructive feedback, choices, ignoring, differential reinforcement, Premack statements, visual cues
Banking Time	1:1 teacher and child	teachers	teacher manual and guidelines for implementation	emotion regulation, narrating, promoting teacher–child relationship
BEST in CLASS	large or small group implemented during any daily activity	teachers	teacher workshop, teacher training, practice-based coaching materials, family communication materials	Pre-K – rules, precorrection, OTR, praise, instructive feedback, error correction Elementary – rules, precorrection, OTR, promoting teacher–child relationship, praise, emotion regulation
Incredible Years Classroom Management Training (TCM) for Teachers	Large or small group or 1:1 lessons	teachers	video modeling for group discussion, problem-solving, and sharing of ideas; parent training components; peer teacher coaching; facilitator manuals, books, take-home assignments, and handouts; goal-setting and self-reflective learning materials	active supervision, choices, emotion regulation, error correction, Premack statements, ignoring, instructive feedback, modeling, OTR, praise, precorrection, problem-solving, promoting behavioral competence, rules, scaffolding, social skills, supportive listening, tangible reinforcement, time-out

38 Maureen A. Conroy et al.

their own feelings and feelings of others, regulate and express emotions, and build positive relationships (Denham & Weissberg, 2004). In general, when children have difficulties reaching the milestones associated with appropriate social and emotional skill development, their behaviors are seen as challenging or problematic. Concerns are most often categorized as externalizing behaviors or internalizing behaviors, and there is well-known comorbidity between the two (Gilliom & Shaw, 2004). Externalizing behaviors are those that are disruptive or harmful to others (e.g., overactivity, opposition, aggression) while internalizing behavior is described as anxious (e.g. worry, solitary, distress, fear) or withdrawn (Campbell, 2006).

Prevalence of SEL Delays in Young Children

Due to their age and developmental levels, an accurate assessment of the prevalence of young children SEL delays or behavioral concerns is difficult to ascertain; however, existing estimates are startling (Carter et al., 2010; Keenan & Wakschlag, 2002; Ringeisen et al., 2017). Infant and toddler rates of problem behavior have been reported as high as 32% (Briggs-Gowan & Carter, 2008) while others have estimated that, in kindergarten, the prevalence of problem behavior is 14% (Montes, Lotyczewski, Halterman, & Hightower, 2012). Of note, the prevalence in young children can also vary greatly between contexts. For example, De Los Reyes and Kazdin (2005) found that 29.4% of preschool-age children displayed problem behavior in parent-only settings, while only 8.8% of preschool-age children displayed problem behavior across both parent and teacher settings. Thus, the clinical recognition of behavior has, historically, used multiple informants to evaluate children's behavior and provide a more comprehensive view of the child (De Los Reyes & Kazdin, 2005).

Understanding the prevalence of SEL delays and behavioral difficulties in young children requires a holistic view of predictors, as the causes are likely a complex interaction of biological (e.g., temperament) and environmental (e.g., family structure, school experiences) factors (for a discussion see Farmer, Gatzke-Kopp, & Latendresse, 2020). For instance, parental or family characteristics such as low socio-economic status, living in rural poverty, harsher parenting styles, high levels of family hardship, and maternal depression may be associated with behavior problems (Feldman, Hancock, Rielly, Minnes, & Cairns, 2000; Ingoldsby et al., 2006). Also, early childhood adversity, such as maltreatment and neglect, is gaining widespread attention as a predictor of externalizing and internalizing behavior problems and decreased school engagement (Bethell, Newacheck, Hawes, & Halfon, 2014; Hunt, Slack, & Berger, 2017).

Prevalence and Socio-economic Status

One population that is considered vulnerable and warrants specific attention is children who live in low-income households or households at or below the poverty line. Over 11 million children under age six are currently living in households at or below the poverty line (i.e., low income, poor, or deep poverty; National Center for Children in Poverty, 2016), giving rise to the attention needed to intervene early in social, emotional, and behavioral challenges that might occur in this population. When young children live in low-income households or households at or below the poverty line, the prevalence of problem behavior could be as high as 30% (Qi & Kaiser, 2003). Statistics from research conducted in Head Start, a program largely serving children who live in low-income households, indicates that between 23% and

33% of their students demonstrate chronic problem behaviors (Del'Homme, Sinclair, Kasari, & Sigman, 1994; Kaiser, Hancock, Cai, Michael, & Hester, 2000; Qi & Kaiser, 2003).

Living at or below the poverty line may be related to distinct disadvantages that link to SEL difficulties and behavioral concerns in comparison to children who grow up in middle-or higher-income households (Yoshikawa, Aber, & Beardslee, 2012). For example, by age three, children who live in poor households are exposed to considerably fewer words and have fewer linguistically complex exchanges with their caregivers when compared to children who come from higher income families (Fernald, Marchman, & Weisleder, 2013; Hart & Risley, 1995). These early, less multifaceted experiences result in gaps in their knowledge and skills and have been found to have lasting detrimental effects on children's future performance in school and beyond (Hart & Risley, 2003). Additionally when compared to those children who live in more financially stable households, children living in poverty can experience multiple daily stressors that may lead to differences in executive functioning and self-regulatory skills needed for successful social, emotional, and behavioral adjustment (Blair & Raver, 2012).

Context and Identification of Problem Behavior

Recommended practice in early childhood suggests that identification of SEL difficulties and interventions to address them should be guided by a developmental and contextual under-standing of children's behavior (Neisworth & Bagnato, 2004). Therefore, the context in which behavior occurs should be considered when discussing the prevalence, characteristics, and factors leading to suspected SEL delays and behavioral concerns (for a discussion, see Trach, Lee, & Hymel, 2018). Some behaviors are perceived as problematic because of the context in which they occur and the social and cultural expectations of others (Bayat, 2015) and are influenced by the group dynamics of peers and classroom settings (Trach et al., 2018). For example, inability to pay attention, work independently, or follow classroom rules become concerning in school, because these are behaviors that are considered critical for success in that environment (Lane, Stanton-Chapman, Roorbach Jamison, & Phillips, 2007).

In a dynamic, transactional model examining children's behavior in context, behavior problems are best understood as a mismatch between the demands of the classroom social or learning environment (cognitive, social, behavioral, or regulatory) and the child's developmental capacities (Bulotsky-Shearer, Fantuzzo, & McDermott, 2008; Vitiello, Booren, Downer, & Williford, 2012). Addressing children's SEL skills through this develop-mental, ecological approach ensures repeated learning opportunities in early childhood activities throughout the day (Powell, Burchinal, File, & Kontos, 2008). This approach considers within-classroom ecology and the contexts in which children develop beyond the classroom. Rather than viewing problem behavior as a deficit within the child, emphasis shifts to adjusting the demands of the context to match better the developmental capacities of the child.

SEL, Behavior, and the Teacher–child Relationship

Interactions and relationships between children and their teachers that are low in conflict and high in responsivity and warmth may lead to better social-emotional outcomes for young children (e.g., Garner, Mahatmya, Moses, & Bolt, 2014). Conversely, when school-aged children have conflictual relationships with teachers, described as "resistance and dishar-mony/discordance and negativity" (Pianta, Hamre, & Stuhlman, 2003), they are at greater risk of demonstrating problem behaviors (Meehan, Hughes, & Cavell, 2003). Children

40 *Maureen A. Conroy et al.*

experiencing these conflictual relationships often develop coercive and negative interaction patterns with the adults in their lives (Gunter & Coutinho, 1997; Patterson, Reid, & Dishion, 1992). As a result, they experience less instruction provided by their teachers and ongoing and intensifying negative coercive interactions with adults, which are associated with negative outcomes in school and beyond (Doumen, Verschueren, Buyse, Germeijs, & Luyckx, 2008; Raver & Knitzer, 2002). Relatedly, the teacher–child relationship may fuel the labeling of behavior as appropriate and manageable in some children, but considered challenging and problematic in others based on implicit, or unconscious, bias of culturally and socially desirable behaviors which places children at risk for being perceived as having problem behavior based on their gender, racial, and socio-economic backgrounds (Cyphert, 2014; Gilliam, 2016).

Summary

Although estimates vary and are influenced by a number of contextual factors, the prevalence of young children at risk for or with EBD is a public health concern. Significant SEL delays and behavioral concerns are detrimental to children's overall achievement and school success. Additionally, if not addressed early, young children's SEL delays negatively impact their future success in life. Fortunately, preventative early intervention programs and practices that can support young children's SEL development are available. In the next section, we review developmental considerations and adaptations.

SEL Adaptations and Developmental Considerations

Given the unique characteristics of young children with SEL delays and behavioral concerns that place them at risk for EBD, there is an increased focus on effective ways to proactively address these concerns through targeted interventions that support children to develop social, emotional, and behavioral skills. Adaptations are made that consider children's unique developmental needs, for example, adapting content of social emotional skills so it is developmentally appropriate, and embedded in activities in naturalistic settings, and daily routines. During the first five years of a child's life, development is more malleable (Denham & Weissberg, 2004; Tominey & McClelland, 2011), which makes practices focused on the SEL delays and behavioral concerns of young children distinct from those programs focused on older children and youth who have established an EBD. For example, once a child has been diagnosed with an EBD, intensive individualized interventions with a licensed therapist often occur in a specialized setting (e.g., mental health clinic or hospital) to reduce clinical symptoms. Whereas, interventions addressing early risk signs of EBD in younger children are embedded within proximal settings in which children spend most of their day, such as the home and early care and education settings. Additionally, interventions are more likely to be implemented by authentic change agents most proximal to the child, such as their teachers or caregivers (Bronfenbrenner & Morris, 1998; Downer, Booren, Lima, Luckner, & Pianta, 2010).

Early childhood and early elementary school classrooms are ideal contexts for the implementation of intervention programs and practices and many researchers have developed and adapted effective programs and practices so that they can be implemented by teachers with fidelity within classrooms. Using job-embedded professional development strategies, such as practice-based coaching (Snyder, Hemmeter, & Fox, 2015) or behavioral consultation support (Sheridan & Kratochwill, 2007), teachers become the mechanism for delivering the intervention and children have opportunities to learn and practice SEL and behavioral skills within naturally occurring daily learning activities or social interactions in the classroom (e.g., see Conroy et al., 2019; Downer et al., 2018; Hemmeter, Hardy, Schnitz, Adams, & Kinder, 2015; Hemmeter, Snyder, Fox, & Algina, 2016).

Implementation of intervention programs and practices within classrooms often consider both broader foundational classroom supports for children's SEL and behavioral skills, as well as individual children's developmental profile of strengths and needs. For example, interventions that promote social problem-solving skills or emotion regulation might be provided by the teacher through scripted stories during a large group instructional time (e.g., Promoting Alternative Thinking Strategies (PATHS), Domitrovich et al., 2007; Incredible Years, Webster-Stratton, 2001). Alternatively, teachers can learn to modify classroom transitions and routines that support positive engagement for all children and preventatively reduce problem behaviors (e.g., Teaching Pyramid; Fox et al., 2003; Hemmeter et al., 2016).

Additionally, providing direct instruction to children during large group time through puppet play, visual cues, or other game-like activities can promote social skills or emotion vocabulary. Early childhood teachers might use a picture book or photos to illustrate and help children to identify and label emotions or use a puppet to illustrate in a story about how a child might feel scared to make new friends at a new school. In the Pyramid Model, the story about "Tucker the turtle" is used along with a puppet to teach children self-regulation strategies when feeling angry or upset. For individual children with behavioral concerns, more focused practices (e.g., using specific praise or reinforcement or cues and visuals) could be implemented to adapt classroom activities to reduce problem behavior and increase successful learning and engagement (e.g., Learning to Objectively Observe Kids (LOOK); Downer et al., 2018; Behavioral, Emotional, and Social Training: Competent Learners Achieving School Success (BEST in CLASS); Conroy et al., 2019; Sutherland et al., 2018). In addition, for children with persistent problem behavior, individualized behavior plans can be created and implemented by teaching staff and mental health professionals once a functional behavioral assessment has helped better identify classroom setting antecedents or consequences of behavior, and the reason why children are displaying behavior problems (Fox et al., 2003).

A final adaptation for interventions with young children is the inclusion of families in the intervention process. In many early childhood programs, parents are valued as their child's first teacher and, for example in Head Start, the Performance Standards mandate "maximum feasible participation" of parents in all aspects of the program (U.S. Department of Health and Human Services, U.S. Department of Education, 2016). Young children who have behavioral challenges often lack the cognitive or communication skills to articulate complex behavioral or regulatory challenges, and instead communicate through their behavior and emotional displays in the classroom settings (Campbell, 2006). Teachers need caregivers' input, including relevant developmental history and information about children's adjustment in the home setting, to develop an effective approach for addressing problem behavior in the classroom setting. In a recent meta-analysis conducted by Sheridan, Smith, Kim, Beretvas, and Park (2019) on family–school interventions and children's social-emotional functioning, school-based interventions that included the family had positive impacts on children's SEL competence and behavior. Additional factors that played a critical role in the effectiveness of interventions were communication, collaboration, and relationships between teachers and family members and structural elements, such as interventions that included behavioral supports or home–school involvement. For example, when teachers and caregivers work together to share information about children's success and challenges and problem solve

42 *Maureen A. Conroy et al.*

strategies that work, communication improves and, as a result, improves children's SEL and behavioral outcomes (Sheridan et al., 2019).

In summary, each year a number of young children with SEL delays and behavior concerns enter early childhood and early elementary classroom settings. A host of developmental and environmental factors contribute to their SEL difficulties and behavioral needs; however, a key to their future success is addressing SEL needs early to prevent further difficulties that have long-term consequences. Early childhood classrooms are ideal contexts to address their SEL needs. Through embedded learning opportunities throughout the day, teachers can implement interventions and practices to prevent and remediate SEL difficulties and behavioral concerns. Additionally, teachers can work with children's families to help them learn how to provide learning opportunities at home. In the following section, we review several preventive classroom-based programs that focus on development of social, emotional, and behavioral skills of young children at risk for SEL difficulties or EBD.

Overview of Interventions and Practices

One goal of this chapter is to provide an overview of preventive interventions designed to address the SEL needs of young children with SEL delays and behavioral concerns. A comprehensive review of the literature is beyond the scope of the chapter; therefore, we systematically selected a sample of preventive intervention programs and provide an overview of the goals of the program and effective components. All programs selected met the following criteria: (1) listed as an evidence-based program on a national registry or resource (e.g., Substance Abuse and Mental Health Services Association (SAMSHA) National Registry, National Center on Quality Teaching and Learning: Social Emotional Preschool Curriculum Consumer Report, Blueprints for Healthy Youth Development, Collaborative for Academic, Social, and Emotional Learning (CASEL), Institute of Education Sciences What Works Clearinghouse or funded by Institute of Education Sciences National Center for Education Research or National Center for Special Education Research; (2) preventive (i.e., included Tier 1 or 2 practices) intervention program designed to address the SEL needs of children (birth to 8 years old) who are at risk for SEL delays or EBD; and (3) delivered in a school-based setting by early childhood providers. Each program is described in Table 3.1 including the overall purpose of the program, target population and age range, delivery setting, group size, change agent, program components, and instructional practices or practice elements (see Table 3.1).

As seen in Table 3.1, several commonalities are apparent among this selected sample of evidence-based preventive intervention programs. As indicated earlier, we targeted programs that were delivered within a school setting; however, consistently across the targeted programs, the delivery setting is primarily embedded within the classroom with a teacher targeted as the change agent. Not surprising, within the classroom setting, most of these programs target more individualized strategies for young children who have been systematically identified as needing Tier 2 practices or are at risk for EBD. Three of the programs (i.e., Teaching Pyramid, PK-PATHS, LOOK) include curriculum focused on a Tier 1 level and prevention of SEL difficulties. In addition, each program has demonstrated effectiveness with preschool-age populations, with the majority extending into kindergarten or early elementary grades (i.e., Teaching Pyramid, PK-PATHS, BEST in CLASS, Incredible Years). Further, several of these intervention programs include a component of teacher coaching as a means to enhance teachers' use of evidenced-based practices (i.e., Teaching Pyramid, LOOK, BEST in CLASS, Incredible Years). With regard to the practice elements (identified based on the definitions provided by McLeod et al., 2017), several are used consistently across all of these programs: emotion regulation, praise, opportunities to respond, rules, and instructive feedback.

While there are many commonalities across these programs, there are also important differences. The Teaching Pyramid is the only program that provides a three-tiered, multi-system of support. LOOK provides both Tier 1 and 2 practices, which support the needs of target children who demonstrate problem behaviors as well as all children in the classroom. The remainder of the programs focus solely on practices delivered at a Tier 1 or Tier 2 level. Interestingly, most of the programs deliver intervention during naturally occurring classroom-based activities and routines; however, Banking Time is delivered by the teacher in a one-to-one pull-out setting with the child. With the exception of LOOK, professional development activities for the majority of the programs are delivered in person. Finally, all programs focus on development of teacher–child relationships, but Incredible Years is the only program that has a strong focus on training families to implement preventive practices.

Considerations and Future Directions

As discussed in this chapter, early preventive efforts to reduce young children's behavioral challenges and improve their SEL skills are important and can lead to long-term benefits. Fortunately, evidence-based intervention programs and practices exist to address their SEL and behavioral needs. Although research has documented the efficacy of these programs, there is a need for further research to ensure that on-going intervention efforts continue to be sensitive to the changing needs of children, families, and practitioners. In this section, we discuss several areas of consideration for future research and practice including expansion of comprehensive supports, increased cultural sensitivity, and scaling up and sustainability.

Comprehensive Supports

One key consideration underlying intervention programs and practices for young children with SEL delays or behavioral concerns centers largely on tiered, comprehensive support. As evidenced by the successes of many of the programs mentioned in this chapter, tiered and targeted implementation allows for a wide reach of program effectiveness. Namely, the universal preventive focus of Tier 1 interventions is a national priority to promote the mental health and social-emotional well-being of young children (New Freedom Commission on Mental Health, 2003). Additionally, having multiple pathways of support prior to referral to special education services and supports for an EBD eliminates a "wait to fail" environment for children. Similarly, comprehensive intervention encourages thinking about what works, for whom, in what context, under what conditions prior to labeling, diagnosis requests, and intensive special education evaluations. This requires greater service interventions (e.g., school psychologists, mental health counselors, social workers) to be integrated into the system of service delivery and a transdisciplinary approach to provide a coordinated comprehensive system of care.

Culturally Sensitive Intervention

The perspective of what constitutes appropriate behavior varies considerably across cultures. Consistent with the example of considering the classroom ecology, one priority of program implementation is increasing cultural congruence and partnership between the child's home and school, a cornerstone of responsive practices. Developing culturally relevant practices encourages program implementers to respond to each child's strengths and needs (Copple & Bredekamp, 2009) and better understand a child's thoughts, feelings, or internal state (DeBernardis, Hayes, & Fryling, 2014). In this way, teacher–child relationships improve and behavior biases are lessened, both well-known influences on discipline practices in early childhood settings (Gilliam, Maupin, Reyes, Accavitti, & Shic, 2016). As such, organizations that routinely make recommendations and policy announcements for responding to problem behavior should reinforce approaches that emphasize the interconnected aspects of the classroom, school, home, and community in a holistic way (Morris, 2017).

Scaling up Intervention

As the field continues to develop and rigorously test the efficacy of innovative SEL programs and practices for young children, scalability and sustainability are critical considerations. Implementation/prevention science and public health fields provide excellent models to consider to broaden the reach and impact of innovative SEL programs within early childhood programs and systems (Halle, Metz, & Martinez-Beck, 2013). Researchers spend multiple years to develop interventions, such as the ones reviewed in this chapter, tailored to meet the developmental needs of young children within the natural contexts where supports reach them directly. The efficacy of these interventions is tested carefully within highly controlled studies to determine the causal impact of the intervention on practitioner practice and children's outcomes (Institute for Education Sciences, 2012). Following efficacy trials, the next step of research is to determine whether these innovative interventions be scaled up to reach more children and families. A number of factors influence the scalability of interventions including the competence of the personnel delivering the intervention. Although the interventions described in this chapter are manualized, during efficacy trials they are implemented with a high degree of expertise, technical assistance, and fidelity.

Scaling up an intervention in an authentic setting can be challenging. Teachers need to be taught the knowledge and skills to implement the intervention with adherence and competence. Additionally, the coaches working with teachers in these authentic settings need to have the knowledge and skills to support teachers in their implementation. As we consider the factors discussed in this chapter that influence children's SEL and behavioral challenges (e.g., culture, socio-economic status, context) and the complexity of authentic early childhood classrooms, we recommend adapting the intervention to match the characteristics of the context in which it is implemented and the inclusion of intervention specialists to ensure delivery with fidelity (for a discussion, see Talbot and colleagues, this edition).

When considering scaling up an intervention, the following factors should be considered: (1) training and supports needed for school-based coaches or intervention specialists and teachers to implement the intervention with the fidelity needed to produce positive outcomes for children and families; (2) leadership, policy, and program-wide supports needed to ensure the intervention implementation is sustained; (3) adaptations to ensure that the intervention is a contextual fit with the program, teachers, and children and families and can address the needs of the authentic setting; and (4) measurement of implementation fidelity to ensure that supports are provided within the program to implementers when needed. The Pyramid Model is an excellent example of an intervention where at state- and district-levels, program-wide supports have been developed (Smith et al., 2018). In this way, existing expertise of staff within programs can be nurtured, leveraged, and strengthened to support scalability and sustainability. However, much more research is needed if the reach of innovation of SEL interventions is to be broadened and the promise of change for children with SEL difficulties and behavioral challenges is sustained in the longer term.

Conclusion

In summary, this chapter has provided an overview of the characteristics of young children who have SEL delays and behavioral concerns, placing them at future risk for EBD. As discussed, behavioral warning signs appear early and have long-term consequences. However, when targeted, developmentally appropriate intervention occurs early, these behavior patterns can be ameliorated and the negative consequences can be prevented. Evidence-based interventions are available for implementation in classroom settings by practitioners, but not surprisingly, many young children and their families do not have access to these interventions. One important next step in research and practice is scaling-up interventions, including adaptations to match the cultural context of children, families, and communities as well as developing community-based coordinated systems of care that can provide early identification and comprehensive supports that can lead to prevention of EBD in young children.

Author Note

This research was supported by grants from the U.S. Department of Education, Institute for Education Sciences (R305A150246; R324A160158). The opinions expressed by the authors are not necessarily reflective of the position of or endorsed by the U.S. Department of Education.

References

Bayat, M. (2015). *Addressing challenging behaviors and mental health issues in early childhood*. New York, NY: Routledge.

Bethell, C. D., Newacheck, P., Hawes, E., & Halfon, N. (2014). Adverse childhood experiences: Assessing the impact on health and school engagement and the mitigating role of resilience. *Health Affairs, 33*, 2106–2115. doi:10.1377/hlthaff.2014.0914

Blair, C., & Raver, C. C. (2012). Child development in the context of adversity: Experiential canalization of brain and behavior. *American Psychologist, 67*, 309–318. doi:10.1037/a0027493

Brennan, L. M., Shaw, D. S., Dishion, T. J., & Wilson, M. (2012). Longitudinal predictors of school-age academic achievement: Unique contributions of toddler-age aggression, oppositionality, inattention, and hyperactivity. *Journal of Abnormal Child Psychology, 40*, 1289–1300. doi:10.1007/s10802-012-9639-2

Briggs-Gowan, M. J., & Carter, A. S. (2008). Social-emotional screening status in early childhood predicts elementary school outcomes. *Pediatrics, 121*(5), 957–962. doi:10.1542/peds.2007-1948

Bronfenbrenner, U., & Morris, P. A. (1998). The ecology of developmental processes. In W. Damon (Ed.), *Handbook of child psychology: Theoretical models of human development* (Vol. 1, 5th ed., pp. 993–1028). New York: John Wiley.

Bulotsky-Shearer, R., Fantuzzo, J. W., & McDermott, P. A. (2008). An investigation of classroom situational dimensions of emotional and behavioral adjustment and cognitive and social outcomes for Head Start children. *Developmental Psychology, 44*, 139–154. doi:10.1037/0012-1649.44.1.139

Bulotsky-Shearer, R. J., Bell, E. R., & Dominguez, X. (2012). Latent profiles of problem behavior within learning, peer, and teacher contexts: Identifying subgroups of children at academic risk across the preschool year. *Journal of School Psychology, 50*, 775–798. doi:10.1016/j.jsp.2012.08.001

46 *Maureen A. Conroy et al.*

Campbell, S. B. (2006). *Behavior problems in preschool children: Clinical and developmental issues.* New York: Guilford.

Campbell, S. B., Spieker, S., Burchinal, M., & Poe, M. D.; NICHD Early Child Care Research Network. (2006). Trajectories of aggression from toddlerhood to age 9 predict academic and social functioning through age 12. *Journal of Child Psychology and Psychiatry, 47,* 791–800. doi:10.1111/j.1469-7610.2006.01636.x

Carter, A. S., Wagmiller, R. J., Gray, S. O., McCarthy, K. J., Horwitz, S. M., & Briggs-Gowan, M. J. (2010). Prevalence of DSM-IV disorder in a representative, healthy birth cohort at school entry: Sociodemographic risks and social adaptation. *Journal of the American Academy of Child & Adolescent Psychiatry, 49,* 686–689. doi:10.1016/j.jaac.2010.03.018

Chow, J. C., & Wehby, J. H. (2018). Associations between language and problem behavior: A systematic review and correlational meta-analysis. *Educational Psychology Review, 30,* 61–82. doi:10.1007/s10648-016-9385-z

Conroy, M. A., & Sutherland, K. S. (2008). Promoting social, emotional, and behavioral competence in young high-risk children: A preventative classroom-based early intervention model. Unpublished document, Virigina Commonwealth University, Richmond, VA.

Conroy, M. A., Sutherland, K. S., Algina, J. J., Ladwig, C., Werch, B., Martinez, J., ... Gyure, M. (2019). BEST in CLASS: A professional development intervention fostering high quality classroom experiences for young children with problem behavior. *School Psychology Review, 48,* 38–45.

Copple, C., & Bredekamp, S. (2009). *Developmentally appropriate practice in early childhood programs serving children from birth through age 8* (3rd ed.). Washington, DC: NAEYC.

Cyphert, A. (2014). Addressing radical disparities in preschool suspension and expulsion rates. *Tennessee Law Review, 82,* 893–936.

De Los Reyes, A., & Kazdin, A. E. (2005). Informant discrepancies in the assessment of childhood psychopathology: A critical review, theoretical framework, and recommendations for further study. *Psychological Bulletin, 131,* 483–509. doi:10.1037/0033-2909.131.4.483

DeBernardis, G. M., Hayes, L. J., & Fryling, M. J. (2014). Perspective taking as a continuum. *The Psychological Record, 64*(1), 123–131. doi:10.1007/s40732-014-0008-0

Del'Homme, M. A., Sinclair, E., Kasari, C., & Sigman, M. (1994). Preschool children with behavioral problems: Observation in instructional and free play contexts. *Behavioral Disorders, 19,* 221–232. doi:10.1177/019874299401900301

Denham, S. A., & Weissberg, R. P. (2004). Social-emotional learning in early childhood. In E. Chesebrough, P. King, M. Bloom, T. Gullotta, & M. Bloom (Eds.), *A blueprint for promotion of prosocial behavior in early childhood* (pp. 13–50). New York: Kluwer Academic/Plenum.

Domitrovich, C. E., Cortes, R. C., & Greenberg, M. T. (2007). Improving young children's social and emotional competence: A randomized trial of the preschool "PATHS" curriculum. *Journal of Primary Prevention, 28,* 67–91. doi:10.1007/s10935-007-0081-0

Doumen, S., Verschueren, K., Buyse, E., Germeijs, V., & Luyckx, K. (2008). Reciprocal relations between teacher-child conflict and aggressive behavior in kindergarten: A three-wave longitudinal study. *Journal of Clinical Child & Adolescent Psychology, 37,* 588–599. doi:10.1080/15374410802148079

Downer, J. T., Booren, L. M., Lima, O. K., Luckner, A. E., & Pianta, R. C. (2010). The Individualized Classroom Assessment Scoring System (inCLASS): Preliminary reliability and validity of a system for observing preschoolers' competence in classroom interactions. *Early Childhood Research Quarterly, 25,* 1–16. doi:10.1016/j.ecresq.2009.08.004

Downer, J. T., Williford, A. P., Bulotsky-Shearer, R. J., Vitiello, V. E., Bouza, J., Reilly, S., & Lhospital, A. (2018). Using data-driven, video-based early childhood consultation with teachers to reduce children's challenging behaviors and improve engagement in preschool classrooms. *School Mental Health, 10,* 226–242. doi:10.1007/s12310-017-9237-0

Driscoll, K. C., & Pianta, R. C. (2010). Banking Time in Head Start: Early efficacy of an intervention designed to promote supportive teacher-child relationships. *Early Education and Development, 21,* 38–64. doi:10.1080/10409280802657449

Farmer, T., Gatzke-Kopp, L., & Latendresse, S. (2020). The development, prevention, and treatment of emotional and behavioral disorders. An interdisciplinary developmental systems perspective.

In T. Farmer, M. A. Conroy, E. Farmer, & K. Sutherland (Eds.), *Handbook of research on emotional and behavioral disorders: Interdisciplinary developmental perspectives on children and youth* (pp. 3–22). New York: Rutledge.

Feldman, M. A., Hancock, C. L., Rielly, N., Minnes, P., & Cairns, C. (2000). Behavior problems in young children with or at risk for developmental delay. *Journal of Child and Family Studies, 9*, 247–261. doi:10.1023/A:1009427306

Fernald, A., Marchman, V. A., & Weisleder, A. (2013). SES differences in language processing skill and vocabulary are evident at 18 months. *Developmental Science, 16*, 234–248. doi:10.1111/desc.12019

Forness, S. R., Cluett, S. E., Ramey, C. T., Ramey, S. L., Zima, B. T., Hsu, C., ... MacMillan, D. L. (1998). Special education identification of Head Start children with emotional and behavioral disorders in second grade. *Journal of Emotional and Behavioral Disorders, 6*, 194–204. doi:10.1177/106342669800600401

Fox, L., Dunlap, G., Hemmeter, M. L., Joseph, G. E., & Strain, P. S. (2003). The teaching pyramid: A model for supporting social competence and preventing challenging behavior in young children. *Young Children, 58*, 48–52.

Garner, P. W., Mahatmya, D., Moses, L. K., & Bolt, E. N. (2014). Associations of preschool type and teacher-child relational quality with young children's social-emotional competence. *Early Education and Development, 25*, 399–420. doi:10.1080/10409289.2013.801706

Gilliam, W. (2016). Early childhood expulsions and suspensions undermine our nation's most promising agent of opportunity and social justice [Issue Brief]. *Robert Wood Johnson Foundation.* Retrieved from http://bma.issuelab.org/resources/25852/25852.pdf

Gilliam, W. S., Maupin, A. N., Reyes, C. R., Accavitti, M., & Shic, F. (2016). *Do early educators' implicit biases regarding sex and race relate to behavior expectations and recommendations of preschool expulsions and suspensions?* Connecticut: Yale Child Study Center. Retrieved from https://medicine.yale.edu/childstudy/zigler/publications/Preschool%20Implicit%20Bias%20Policy%20Brief_final_9_26_276766_5379_v1.pdf

Gilliom, M., & Shaw, D. S. (2004). Codevelopment of externalizing and internalizing problems in early childhood. *Development and Psychopathology, 16*, 313–333. doi:10.1017/S0954579404044530

Gunter, P., & Coutinho, M. (1997). Negative reinforcement in classrooms: What we're beginning to learn. *Teacher Education and Special Education, 20*, 249–264. doi:10.1177/088840649702000306

Halle, T., Hair, E., Burchinal, M., Anderson, R., & Zaslow, M. (2012). In the running for successful outcomes: Exploring the evidence for thresholds of school readiness. (Research Report). Retrieved from U.S. Department of Health and Human Services, Office of the Assistant Secretary for Planning and Evaluation website: https://aspe.hhs.gov/pdf-report/running-successful-outcomes-exploring-evidence-thresholds-school-readiness-technical-report

Halle, T., Metz, A., & Martinez-Beck, I. (2013). *Applying implementation science in early childhood programs and systems.* Baltimore: Brookes.

Hart, B., & Risley, T. R. (1995). *Meaningful differences in the everyday experience of young American children.* Baltimore: Brookes.

Hart, B., & Risley, T. R. (2003). The early catastrophe: The 30 million word gap by age 3. *American Educator, 27*, 4–9.

Hemmeter, M. L., Hardy, J. K., Schnitz, A. G., Adams, J. M., & Kinder, K. A. (2015). Effects of training and coaching with performance feedback on teachers' use of Pyramid Model practices. *Topics in Early Childhood Special Education, 35*, 144–156. doi:10.1177/0271121415594924

Hemmeter, M. L., Snyder, P. A., Fox, L., & Algina, J. (2016). Evaluating the implementation of the Pyramid Model for promoting social-emotional competence in early childhood classrooms. *Topics in Early Childhood Special Education, 36*, 133–146. doi:10.1177/0271121416653386

Hunt, T. K., Slack, K. S., & Berger, L. M. (2017). Adverse childhood experiences and behavioral problems in middle childhood. *Child Abuse & Neglect, 67*, 391–402. doi:10.1016/j.chiabu.2016.11.005

Ingoldsby, E. M., Shaw, D. S., Winslow, E., Schonberg, M., Gilliom, M., & Criss, M. M. (2006). Neighborhood disadvantage, parent-child conflict, neighborhood peer relationships, and early anti-social behavior problem trajectories. *Journal of Abnormal Child Psychology, 34*, 293–309. doi:10.1007/s10802-006-9026-y

48　*Maureen A. Conroy et al.*

Institute for Education Sciences. (2012). 2012 National Board for Education Sciences Annual Report Briefing Material for Board Members: NCER Goal Structure. Retrieved 1/11/19 from https://ies.ed.gov/director/board/briefing/pdf/2012_briefing_material.pdf

Kaiser, A. P., Hancock, T. B., Cai, X., Michael, E., & Hester, P. P. (2000). Parent-reported behavioral problems and language delays in boys and girls enrolled in Head Start classrooms. *Behavioral Disorders, 26,* 26–41. doi:10.1177/019874290002600104

Keenan, K., & Wakschlag, L. S. (2002). Can a valid diagnosis of disruptive behavior be made in preschool children? *American Journal of Psychiatry, 159,* 351–358. Retrieved from www.ncbi.nlm.nih.gov/pubmed/11869995

Lamont, J. H., & Council on School Health. (2013). Policy statement: Out-of-school suspension and expulsion. *Pediatrics,* e1000–e1007. doi:10.1542/peds.2012-3932

Lane, K. L., Stanton-Chapman, T., Roorbach Jamison, K., & Phillips, A. (2007). Teacher and parent expectations of preschoolers' behavior: Social skills necessary for success. *Topics in Early Childhood Special Education, 27,* 86–97. doi:10.1177/02711214070270020401

Losen, D., & Gillespie, J. (2012). Opportunities suspended: The disparate impact of disciplinary exclusion from school. *Civil Rights Project, UCLA.* Retrieved from: http://civilrightsproject.ucla.edu/resources/projects/center-for-civil-rights-remedies/school-to-prison-folder/federal-reports/upcoming-ccrr-research/losen-gillespie-opportunity-suspended-2012.pdf

Mashburn, A. J., & Pianta, R. C. (2006). Social relationships and school readiness. *Early Education and Development, 17,* 151–176. doi:10.1207/s15566935eed1701_7

McLeod, B. D., Sutherland, K. S., Martinez, R. G., Conroy, M. A., Snyder, P. A., & Southam-Gerow, M. A. (2017). Identifying common practice elements to improve social, emotional, and behavioral outcomes of young children in early childhood classrooms. *Prevention Science, 18*(2), 204–213. doi:10.1007/s11121-016-0703-y

Meehan, B. T., Hughes, J. N., & Cavell, T. A. (2003). Teacher–student relationships as compensatory resources for aggressive children. *Child Development, 74,* 1145–1157. doi:10.1111/1467-8624.00598

Montes, G., Lotyczewski, B. S., Halterman, J. S., & Hightower, A. D. (2012). School readiness among children with behavior problems at entrance into kindergarten: Results from a U.S. national study. *European Journal of Pediatrics, 171,* 541–548. doi:10.1007/s00431-011-1605-4

Morris, C. T. (2017). Preventing the preschool-to-prison pipeline: Examining preschool discipline policy recommendations. *Roosevelt House Faculty Journal.* Retrieved from www.roosevelthouse.hunter.cuny.edu/?forum-post=preventing-preschool-prison-pipeline-recommendations-policy-practice

National Center for Children in Poverty. (2016). Basic facts about low income children: Children under 18 years. Retrieved from www.nccp.org/publications/pub_1194.html

Neisworth, J. T., & Bagnato, S. J. (2004). The mismeasure of young children: The authentic assessment alternative. *Infants & Young Children, 17,* 198–212.

New Freedom Commission on Mental Health. (2003). Achieving the promise: Transforming mental health in America. Retrieved from https://govinfo.library.unt.edu/mentalhealthcommission/reports/reports.htm

Patterson, G. R., Reid, J. B., & Dishion, T. J. (1992). *A social interactional approach. Vol. 4. Antisocial boys.* Eugene, OR: Castalia.

Pianta, R. C., & Hamre, B.K. (2001). *Banking Time: Pre-K manual.* Charlottesville, VA: The Center for Advanced Study of Teaching and Learing at the University of Virginia.

Pianta, R. C., Hamre, B., & Stuhlman, M. (2003). Relationships between teachers and children. In W. M. Reynolds, G. E. Miller, & I. B. Weiner (Eds.), *Handbook of psychology* (pp. 199–234). Hoboken, NJ: John Wiley & Sons, Inc.

Pianta, R. C., & Stuhlman, M. W. (2004). Teacher-child relationships and children's success in the first years of school. *School Psychology Review, 33,* 444–458.

Powell, D. R., Burchinal, M. R., File, N., & Kontos, S. (2008). An eco-behavioral analysis of children's engagement in urban public school preschool classrooms. *Early Childhood Research Quarterly, 23,* 108–123. doi:10.1016/j.ecresq.2007.04.001

Qi, C. H., & Kaiser, A. P. (2003). Behavior problems of preschool children from low-income families: Review of the literature. *Topics in Early Childhood Special Education, 23*, 188–216. doi:10.1177/02711214030230040201

Raver, C. C., & Knitzer, J. (2002). *Ready to enter: What research tells policymakers about strategies to promote social and emotional school readiness among three- and four-year-olds.* St. Louis: Federal Reserve Bank of St Louis. Retrieved from http://proxy.library.vcu.edu/login?url=http://search.proquest.com.proxy.library.vcu.edu/docview/1698411792?accountid=14780

Ringeisen, H., Stambaugh, L., Bose, J., Casanueva, C., Hedden, S., Avenevoli, S., ... West, J. (2017). Measurement of childhood serious emotional disturbance: State of the science and issues for consideration. *Journal of Emotional and Behavioral Disorders, 25*, 195–210. doi:10.1177/1063426616675165

Sheridan, S. M., & Kratochwill, T. R. (2008). *Conjoint behavioral consultation: Promoting family–school connections and interventions.* New York: Springer.

Sheridan, S. M., Smith, T. E., Kim, E. M., Beretvas, S. N., & Park, S. (2019). A meta-analysis of family-school interventions and children's social-emotional functioning: Moderators and components of efficacy. doi:10.3102/0034654318825437

Skiba, R. J., Chung, C., Trachok, M., Baker, T. L., Sheya, A., & Hughes, R. L. (2014). Parsing disciplinary disproportionality: Contributions of infraction, student, and school characteristics to out-of-school suspension and expulsion. *American Education Research Journal, 51*, 640–670. doi:10.3102/0002831214541670

Smith, B. J., Fox, L., Strain, P., Binder, D. P., Bovey, T., Jones, A., ... Danaher, J. (2018). *Statewide implementation guide.* Retrieved from http://ectacenter.org/sig

Snyder, P. A., Hemmeter, M. L., & Fox, L. (2015). Supporting implementation of evidence-based practices through practice-based coaching. *Topics in Early Childhood Special Education, 35*, 133–143. doi:10.1177/0271121415594925

Sutherland, K. S., Conroy, M. A., Algina, J., Ladwig, C., Jessee, G., & Gyure, M. (2018). Reducing child problem behaviors and improving teacher-child interactions and relationships: A randomized controlled trial of BEST in CLASS. *Early Childhood Research Quarterly, 42*, 31–43. doi:10.1016/j.ecresq.2017.08.001

Tominey, S. L., & McClelland, M. M. (2011). Red light, purple light: Findings from a randomized trial using circle time games to improve behavioral self-regulation in preschool. *Early Education & Development, 22*(3), 489–519. doi:10.1080/10409289.2011.574258

Trach, J., Lee, M., & Hymel, S. (2018). A social-ecological approach to addressing emotional and behavioral problems in schools: Focusing on group processes and social dynamics. *Journal of Emotional and Behavioral Disorders, 26*, 11–20. doi:10.1177/1063426617742346

U. S. Department of Health and Human Services, U. S. Department of Education. (2016). *Policy statement on expulsion and suspension policies in early childhood settings.* Retrieved from www2.ed.gov/policy/gen/guid/school-discipline/policy-statement-ece-expulsions-suspensions.pdf

Vitiello, V. E., Booren, L. M., Downer, J. T., & Williford, A. P. (2012). Variation in children's classroom engagement throughout a day in preschool: Relations to classroom and child factors. *Early Childhood Research Quarterly, 27*(2), 210–220. doi:10.1016/j.ecresq.2011.08.005

Webster-Stratton, C. (2001). *The Incredible Years: Parents, teachers and children training series.* Seattle, WA: Leader's Guide.

Yoshikawa, H., Aber, J. L., & Beardslee, W. R. (2012). The effects of poverty on the mental, emotional, and behavioral health of children and youth: Implications for prevention. *American Psychologist, 67*(4), 272. doi:10.1037/a0028015

4 Developmental Processes and Emotional and Behavioral Disorders during the Middle and High School Years

Molly Dawes, Kevin S. Sutherland, Terri Sullivan, and Jennifer Harrist

Typically spanning the middle and high school years (ages 12–18), adolescence is a time of tremendous change for youth across multiple domains including changes in the cognitive and emotional demands of school as well as changes in their peer relationships and the general school environment. Navigating and positively adapting to these changes can be challenging for all youth but it may be particularly difficult for youth with, or at risk for, emotional and behavioral disorders (EBD). Youth with EBD exhibit difficulties in regulating their emotions, difficulties displaying appropriate types of behavior, and experience challenging social interactions, all of which interfere with their development (Kauffman & Landrum, 2012). The inclusion of EBD as one of the 13 disability categories under the 2004 reauthorization of the Individuals with Disabilities Act (IDEA, 2004) means that youth with EBD are entitled to additional support and services to aid in their functioning and adaptation which has spurred ongoing research on their experiences and needs.

A common theme found in research on youth with EBD is that they can experience risk across multiple domains including psychobiological factors, cognitive and academic problems, problems in social information processing, family processes, problematic peer relations, school instruction and disciplinary practices, and ecological difficulties (Farmer & Farmer, 2001). Given that youth with EBD may experience challenges in multiple domains, reducing risk in one domain alone may not be enough. Rather, multiple factors may need to be addressed in order to promote reorganization of their system of constraints, meaning the dynamic interactions between the individual's internal domains (e.g., cognitive, emotional functioning) and his or her external domains (e.g., family and peer ecologies; Farmer & Farmer, 2001; Maggin, Wehby, Farmer, & Brooks, 2016; Magnusson & Cairns, 1996), around positive instead of negative factors. Efforts in this direction have highlighted the need to identify possible developmental processes and transitions that can be used and harnessed as leverage points to influence adjustment in multiple domains (Farmer & Farmer, 2001; Maggin et al., 2016). In this sense, developmental transitions can be viewed as "prevention windows" (Masten, 2004) and developmental processes can be seen as allies in the intervention process such that developmental tasks, changes, and transitions can be opportunities to help realign and reorganize the internal and external subsystems for youth with EBD in ways that promote adaptation and positive adjustment (Farmer & Farmer, 2001).

What better time during the lifespan to attempt system reorganization than during the adolescent developmental period when there is a remarkable confluence of changes across internal and external domains? Because adolescent experiences can have lifelong implications for health and well-being (e.g., McDougall & Vaillancourt, 2015), it behooves us to take advantage of the opportunity to promote positive change during the middle and high school years to reduce the risk for maladaptive outcomes. While some have characterized this period as a time of stress, others see it as a period of opportunity characterized by heightened flexibility and heightened potential (Steinberg, 2014). In the spirit of viewing adolescence as a period of opportunity, this chapter's overarching goal is to identify the major developmental changes and tasks that occur during adolescence that can be harnessed to promote positive outcomes for all youth, but especially for those with EBD.

Accordingly, we first describe relevant normative developmental changes youth experience during the middle and high school years as well as adolescent-specific developmental tasks. Next, we discuss how the developmental science perspective provides a useful framework for understanding how the changes in youth's internal (e.g., cognitive, affective) and external (e.g., peer context) subsystems converge and interact to impact developmental trajectories. We then turn our attention to a discussion of the contextual experiences of youth with EBD during the middle and high school years. Finally, we end with a discussion on how understanding normative developmental processes can help us promote system reorganization for youth with EBD such that they experience more positive adjustment outcomes across multiple domains.

Normative Developmental Changes and Tasks during the Middle and High School Years

During adolescence, youth experience dramatic changes to numerous internal and external factors. Knowledge of the stage-salient developmental tasks and skills that should be mastered can inform our approaches to identifying and supporting youth who experience challenges adjusting to these changes. In the following sections, we first discuss internal domains that undergo rapid change during the middle and high school years including cognitive, emotional, psychological, and behavioral domains. Second, given that development unfolds within contexts that are person-specific, we discuss several changes to external factors such as changes in youth's relationships with family and peers and changes to their school environment that can influence youth's development. Lastly, we discuss the key developmental tasks adolescents seek to attain during the middle and high school years.

Changes to Internal Factors

The transition into adolescence is heralded by significant biological changes (i.e., puberty) in conjunction with extensive changes to neural networks in the brain and hormonal systems that unfold across adolescence (e.g., Smetana, Campione-Barr, & Metzger, 2006). We focus in this chapter on factors that are often targets of interventions: changing youth's thoughts (i.e., cognitions), their emotions, (e.g., emotional regulation), their psychological symptoms (e.g., anxiety), and their behavior. Although we discuss these changes separately, it is vital to understand that these systems operate as interconnected domains and functioning in one domain can influence functioning in another (e.g., Cairns, 2000).

Cognitive Changes

There are several significant cognitive changes that occur during early adolescence that continue throughout this developmental period including improvements in reasoning ability (e.g., the ability to use general principles to make specific conclusions), ability to think abstractly, and improvements in executive functioning skills (e.g., planning, problem solving, attention, decision making; Steinberg, 2005). Improvements in executive functioning skills

52   *Molly Dawes et al.*

allow adolescents to engage in more goal-setting and pursuit processes which are considered to be a fundamental part of the development of their identify or self-concept (see reviews by Massey, Gebhardt, & Garnefski, 2008). As part of this process, youth select goals that are meaningful for them, direct their behavior in pursuit of those goals, and evaluate whether or not their behavior helped them achieve their goal. The focus on education goals tends to increase into middle adolescence (age 15) before declining in later adolescence (see Massey et al., 2008). Adolescents also endorse a variety of social goals including the goal to be popular among peers, which increases as youth begin middle school (see Dawes, 2017). Understanding what goals adolescents pursue can help explain the behavioral patterns we see and should therefore be considered when trying to understand adolescent functioning.

Emotional Changes

Studies demonstrate more emotional distress and more negative emotional reactions during adolescence (particularly for girls, see review by Rudolph, 2002). For example, one longitudinal study found that youth report increasingly negative emotional states (e.g., unhappy, angry) across early adolescence but the trend levels out later in adolescence (Larson, Moneta, Richards, & Wilson, 2002). This research suggests it is developmentally normative for middle school youth to report more negative emotions but it is reasonable to expect the downward trend to stop in high school. At the same time, it is reasonable to expect middle and high school youth to have better emotion regulation skills such as improved ability to monitor, evaluate, and modify emotional reactions (Thompson, 1994). These emotional skills require several high-level cognitive processes including perspective taking skills and inhibitory control which likewise improve during adolescence (Steinberg, 2005). Altogether, while the middle and high school years can be described as a time of increased emotional distress and negative emotional reactivity for some youth, there are also improvements in emotion regulations skills.

Psychological Changes

Unfortunately for youth, there is a marked rise in the prevalence and intensity of psychopathology during the middle and high school years. Specifically, studies have revealed that anxiety disorders, mood disorders such as depression, and substance use disorders increase across the adolescent developmental period (Costello, Copeland, & Angold, 2011). The outcomes associated with adolescent psychopathology, including self-harm and suicide, are cause for grave concern (Nock et al., 2013). What is particularly troubling is that mental health problems, particularly internalizing problems, often go unnoticed or underreported by youth which hamstrings efforts to effectively intervene and provide support (Merikangas et al., 2011). Collectively, this suggests that the middle and high school years may be a particularly vulnerable time for the development of psychological problems in youth.

Behavioral Changes

Behaviorally, the middle and high school years can be seen as a paradox with improvements in some behavioral tendencies while other risk behaviors emerge. For example, adolescents are better able than their younger counterparts to engage in behavioral inhibition, meaning they are less likely to behave impulsively, which is a change attributed in part to their growing cognitive capacities (e.g., Casey, Jones, & Somerville, 2011; Steinberg, 2008). One example of this is that by this developmental period, it is expected that youth will use less reactive aggression, meaning they will not lash out in response to provocation as much as would be expected by a younger child. However, this does not mean that aggression ceases. Indeed, some youth increase their use of antisocial behaviors (including aggression) specifically during adolescence (i.e., adolescence-limited path; Moffitt, 1993). In fact, adolescents are more likely to engage in proactive (i.e., planned) acts of aggression such as bullying that can become increasingly covert (e.g., Olweus, 1994) as their cognitive capacities expand to accommodate more planned behavior over more reactionary aggressive behavior.

Simultaneously, this developmental period is also typified by an increase in risk-taking behavior, particularly during middle adolescence when youth are between the ages of 14 and 17. During this time, there is an increase in reward-seeking behavior such as binge drinking, reckless driving, unprotected sex, or criminal behavior which carries significant risks for positive outcome (e.g., Steinberg, 2008). At the same time these reward-seeking tendencies increase, youth's cognitive control systems (i.e., prefrontal cortex) are still developing, meaning their ability to self-regulate behavior in the face of competing inputs is still somewhat immature (Casey et al., 2011; Steinberg, 2008). In sum, middle and high school youth are better able to control their behavioral impulses compared to younger children but high schoolers especially are more likely to engage in risk behavior that can significantly impact their developmental trajectories across the lifespan.

Changes to External Factors: Relationships and Context

In addition to the multitude of internal changes experienced by youth during middle and high school, they also experience dramatic changes to their relationships and contexts that can influence their developmental trajectories (e.g., Smetana et al., 2006). Bronfenbrenner's (1979) social ecological model organizes an individual's context into a series of nested systems that can influence child development. The microsystem, consisting of youth's family, peers, and the classroom and school setting, is closest to the child and therefore assumed to have the most influence on child outcomes. The interaction between two or more microsystems, such as when parents interact with their child's teacher at school, is referred to as the mesosystem. Bronfenbrenner proposed two additional systems, the exosystem (e.g., industry) and macrosystem (e.g., cultural norms) but for this chapter, we constrain our discussion to key features of the microsystem including the family, peers, and school environment.

Most often, the social-ecological model is used to illustrate how one's context can influence development in a uni-directional way. However, Bronfenbrenner's (1979) model accounted for the possibility of a bidirectional influence between nested levels such that influence can happen in both a top-down (e.g., microsystem to individual) and a bottom-up (e.g., individual to microsystem) fashion (see also transactional model as part of developmental systems theory; Sameroff, 2000). The basic assumption of bidirectional influence is that youth are shaped by their environment as they simultaneously shape their own environment. Consider the following example: students who are not as engaged may be reprimanded by the teacher which may increase the amount of noncompliance from the student which can then cause teachers to avoid interacting with that student (Sutherland & Oswald, 2005). A robust presentation of the transactional processes that can impact youth's adjustment in middle and high school is beyond the scope of this chapter but it is important to acknowledge the possibility of bidirectional influence between an individual and his or her context.

The next sections discuss a few of the major contextual changes that occur during the middle and high school years that are relevant for our understanding of youth's adjustment.

54 *Molly Dawes et al.*

Specifically, we discuss (1) changes to family relationships and the family context, (2) changes to peer relationships and the peer context, and (3) changes to student–teacher relationships and the classroom and school context. Each of these contexts is critical to consider in efforts to promote positive outcomes for all youth, but especially for students with EBD.

Family Relationships and Family Context

One common stereotype about the adolescent developmental period is that it is a time of extreme conflict between parents and children. While some research suggests that frequent, intense, and angry fights are not typical during adolescence (see Steinberg, 2001 for discussion), other research has demonstrated that the number of conflicts and how frequently they occur peaks in early adolescence before declining, whereas the intensity of conflict increases across early and middle adolescence (Laursen, Coy, & Collins, 1998). However, even as the number and intensity of conflicts increase, many youth report positive relationships with their parents during adolescence (Steinberg, 2001). That said, parents do perceive the childrearing stage of adolescence to be particularly challenging and difficult (Buchanan et al., 1990) which is likely due to the challenges inherent in maintaining warmth and responsiveness while also keeping consistent rules for a teenager who begins to question rules more and seek greater autonomy and independence from adults. Regardless, compared to later childhood, early adolescents spend less time with their parents, instead preferring to spend more time with peers (Larson, 2001).

Peers Relationships and Peer Context

Peers become progressively more important to adolescents during the middle and high school years. Adolescents' experiences with their peers range from interactions to relationships (e.g., friendships), to peer groups, each of which provides a rich and influential context for development (Rubin, Bukowski, & Laursen, 2011; Ryan, 2001; Smetana et al., 2006). It is developmentally normative for youth to seek acceptance from their peers (such as through friendships or membership in a peer group) and to initiate dating relationships that initially occur within the peer group context and tend to have short duration and less stability during early adolescence (Connolly & McIsaac, 2009; Sullivan, 1953). Because of their increased importance to youth during this developmental period, peers can have tremendous influence over youth's thoughts and behaviors through processes of peer selection (pick peers to associate with those who are similar to them) or peer socialization (peers become more similar over time; Smetana et al., 2006). Such influence can yield negative and positive outcomes. On the negative side, research has demonstrated peer influence on depression (via co-rumination, see Rose, 2002), antisocial behavior, and aggression (Dishion & Tipsord, 2011). On the positive side, peers can positively influence achievement and motivation (Ryan, 2001).

Regrettably, one all too common peer experience is involvement in bullying and/or victimization (Gladden, Vivolo-Kantor, Hamburger, & Kumpkin, 2014). One study found that 29.9% of 6th through 10th graders were moderately (i.e., sometimes) to frequently (i.e., weekly) involved in bullying either as victims, bullies, or bully-victims with differential outcomes associated with each type of involvement (Nansel et al., 2001). Longitudinal research highlights the determinantal adult outcomes of involvement in peer victimization which underscores the need to reduce students' risk for involvement and support those who are involved to mitigate the negative consequences associated with this specific peer experience (e.g., McDougall & Vaillancourt, 2015). Understanding risk for involvement in peer victimization requires examination of youth's social roles and reputations, relationships, peer group memberships, and positions in the social status hierarchy (e.g., peer social dynamics; Farmer & Xie, 2007). All told, a comprehensive understanding of adolescents' development during the middle and high school years would be incomplete without assessing their peer relationships and the peer context.

Relationships with Teachers and School Context

School contexts have a significant influence on adolescent development (Wentzel, 2015). Unlike the structural arrangement of elementary schools where teachers who share the same students are organized to work together, most middle and high schools are configured by content area. Further, instead of staying in self-contained classrooms taught by one teacher, students often travel to different classrooms and are taught by numerous teachers (Barber & Olsen, 2004). As a result of these structural differences, not to mention the developmental changes adolescents are undergoing whereby peer relations are becoming more salient, it may be difficult for teachers to develop relationships as readily as they can in earlier grades. Indeed, students perceive less support and less respect from teachers during the middle and high school years (Barber & Olsen, 2004) which can be a barrier to the development of warm, supportive relationships with teachers that are associated with youth's adjustment at school (Hamre & Pianta, 2001).

Developmental Tasks for Adolescents

As youth navigate these changes to their internal and external domains, they are also trying to attain age-specific developmental tasks related to their individual needs and social expectations (Havighurst, 1948). Whether or not youth have attained salient developmental tasks serves as a benchmark for understanding their adaptation to life (e.g., Seiffge-Krenke, Kiuru, & Nurmi, 2010). Havighurst (1948) proposed several developmental tasks that have been added to and edited over the years (Seiffge-Krenke et al., 2010), yielding the following ten adolescent-specific tasks, including: (1) achieving autonomy from parents/guardians, (2) developing friendships with peers, (3) being integrated into a peer group, (4) developing romantic relationships, (5) developing a value system, (6) establishing one's personal identity, (7) demonstrating socially responsible behavior, (8) accepting one's body, (9) adopting a gender role, and (10) preparing for a future career. Attainment of these developmental tasks requires coordination across multiple internal domains of functioning such as the cognitive domain (e.g., ability to set goals) and behavioral domain (e.g., ability to enact behaviors to achieve task-relevant goals), all of which are navigated in increasingly complex environments such as the peer and school contexts.

Changes to internal domains and the context can impact youth's attainment of these developmental tasks. On the other hand, attainment of developmental tasks can influence further functioning in both the external and internal domains. For instance, in a recent meta-analysis by Pinquart and Pfeiffer (2018), the authors found that initial psychological symptoms (e.g., depression) predicted lower attainment of seven of the ten developmental tasks: body acceptance, friendship, peer group membership, identity development, showing socially responsible behavior, career preparation, and developing a value system. Conversely, higher levels of initial attainment of those same seven developmental tasks predicted lower psychological symptoms over time, meaning that youth who are able to achieve salient expectations

56 Molly Dawes et al.

for their age do not experience mental distress to the same extent as those adolescents struggling to attain developmental tasks (Pinquart & Pfeiffer, 2018). Interestingly, higher psychological symptoms predicted greater attainment of romantic or sexual relationships and higher attainment of those same relationships predicted greater psychological symptoms over time, indicating unique risk for those adolescents involved in dating relationships at an earlier age. Altogether, the evidence suggests a bidirectional relationship between psychological symptoms and the attainment of developmental tasks such that psychological symptoms impede youth's ability to achieve some age-salient tasks and lower attainment of some developmental tasks can increase youth's psychological distress (Pinquart & Pfeiffer, 2018). Given that the attainment of developmental tasks in adolescence can hinder the attainment of salient expectations in later developmental periods such as young adulthood, it is worth understanding whether youth are making progress toward achieving these expectations during middle and high school and how best to support them in their efforts to do so (Seiffge-Krenke et al., 2010).

Considering Changes and Tasks in Combination: Developmental Science Perspective

While it may be tempting to determine which factor is the primary driver of functioning and adaptation, the reality is that development is much more complex than that. A useful framework for organizing and understanding this complexity is the developmental science perspective (e.g., Cairns, 2000) which posits that individuals operate as an integrated whole and development is the result of dynamic interrelations among subsystems within the individual (e.g., biological, cognitive, emotional) and subsystems outside the individual (e.g., family context, school environment; see also Magnusson & Cairns, 1996). Put simply, we are not products of our thoughts and emotions solely, nor are we exclusive products of our family or school contexts. Instead, as alluded to above, it is the interactions between multiple bidirectional factors, such as emotions and family dynamics, that drive development. One illustrative example of this phenomenon is the increase in risky behavior during adolescence that is largely influenced by the presence of peers as youth seek to gain peer approval for their risk-taking behaviors at a time when their cognitive capacities are still developing (Steinberg, 2008). Thus, it is necessary to consider how the peer context interacts with individual's cognitive capacities to understand their behavior.

The developmental science construct of correlated constraints may be particularly useful for our understanding of the functioning and adaption of youth with EBD during their middle and high school years. The notion of correlated constraints is based on the idea that developmental factors mutually influence one another and work as a system to promote continuity in behavior (Magnusson & Cairns, 1996). Systems of correlated constraints can be arranged around positive (e.g., parental support, high quality school) or negative factors (e.g., coercive relationships with family members, unsafe neighborhood; Cairns & Cairns, 1994; Farmer & Farmer, 2001). When risk is introduced into a system of positive factors, the system can decrease the negative impact of the risk and continue to promote a positive developmental trajectory. Applied to the adolescent developmental period, if a student struggles academically after the transition to middle school when academic demands increase, this risk may be mitigated by supportive parents, academically motivated peers, or positive student–teacher relationships. When risk is introduced into a system consisting of negative factors, the correlated constraints can lead to problematic adjustment patterns and maintain behavioral difficulties (Cairns & Cairns, 1994; Farmer & Farmer, 2001). For a student with EBD who may have contentious family processes, problematic peer relationships, or cognitive difficulties, the risk to his or her system of negative correlated constraints caused by the transition to middle school can exacerbate and sustain difficulties for that youth, leading to problematic developmental trajectories.

Rooted at the core of the developmental science perspective is that humans have the capacity to adapt, reorganize, and grow (Cairns, 2000; Magnusson & Cairns, 1996). This viewpoint is particularly important to keep in mind when we think about youth with EBD. Using developmental science as a conceptual guide, "EBD should not be viewed as a condition inherent in the child that unfolds overtime in a distinct and unwavering manner" (Farmer, Sutherland, et al., 2016, p. 175). Rather, it is useful to consider how youth's correlated constraints, consisting of both internal and external factors, either confers or reduces risk for problematic outcomes. With this understanding that problems are not inherent to the child and that all youth have the capacity to change, a fruitful path forward is to consider the strategies that will prompt reorganization of the system of correlated constraints in ways that promote positive outcomes for youth with EBD. Toward that end, knowledge of developmentally normative tasks and experiences can be utilized as an ally in the process to promote the realignment of several factors toward more positive developmental pathways (Farmer & Farmer, 2001). The following sections will discuss the experiences of youth with EBD that should be taken into account to better understand their functioning and identify points across development that can be leveraged for positive change.

The Middle and High School Years for Youth with EBD

Recent reports indicate that the number of students with EBD served in special education is below 1% (U.S. Department of Education, National Center for Education Statistics, 2019). However, a recent review of both point and cumulative prevalence rates of youth with EBD suggest that the numbers are higher and many youth are under-identified in schools (Lloyd, Bruhn, Sutherland, & Bradshaw, 2019). For instance, Forness and colleagues (2012) concluded that at one point in time, as many as 12% of youth have an EBD. Further, they identified a cumulative percentage of approximately 38% of students having EBD at some point in their K-12 experience (Forness et al., 2012).

As discussed above, adolescents typically improve their executive functioning skills, emotion regulation skills, and behavioral inhibition and control skills during the middle and high school years. However, youth with EBD or who are at risk for developing EBD may exhibit a wide range of difficulties across their internal domains such as impulsivity, attention problems, problems with social information processing (e.g., problems interpreting intentions), language and communication difficulties, and emotional and behavioral challenges such as externalizing and internalizing problems (Farmer & Farmer, 2001; Lane, Carter, Pierson, & Glaeser, 2006; Wagner, Kutash, Duchnowski, Epstein, & Sumi, 2005). Rather than focus on the diverse challenges youth with EBD may experience within their internal domains, we discuss several key contextual experiences for youth with EBD that should be considered as part of youth's correlated constraints.

Family Context Experiences for Youth with EBD

Research suggests that youth with EBD frequently experience a complex array of family-related risk factors (e.g., residential instability, family adversity, lack of financial support) that hamper their development and future success (e.g., Cairns & Cairns, 1994). One critical

58 *Molly Dawes et al.*

consideration for youth with EBD is that they have elevated rates for being removed or served out of their home environment including placement in residential programs in the mental health, juvenile justice, and child welfare systems (Chen et al., 2016). Youth with EBD had the highest rates of involvement with any system at 32.1% (Chen et al., 2016) and of those involved in out-of-home placements, 21.2% were involved in one system and 10.9% were involved in two or more systems with the highest involvement being with the juvenile justice services, then mental health, then child welfare. These out-of-home placements heighten students' risks across the emotional, behavioral, and psychosocial domains (Chen et al., 2016) and point to the importance of coordinated services and supports within systems of care (Farmer & Farmer, 2001).

Peer Context Experiences for Youth with EBD

The existing body of research on the peer relations of students with EBD suggest that many of them struggle to gain peer acceptance and experience problematic peer interactions as exemplified by their increased risk for peer rejection and involvement in peer victimization (e.g., Farmer, Pearl, & Van Acker, 1996; Rose, Simpson, & Moss, 2015). For instance, in a study of 14,000 middle and high school students, including youth with and without disabilities, Rose and colleagues (2015) found that students with EBD reported higher rates of victimization and aggression as compared to youth in several other disability categories and those without disabilities. The negative outcomes associated with victimization (e.g., McDougall & Vaillancourt, 2015) underscore the critical need to identify supports for those involved to mitigate negative consequences as well as identify factors associated with increased risk for involvement.

For example, youth's ability to garner acceptance from peers and their risk for victimization involvement is influenced by their social skills (Rose et al., 2015) and the opportunity to utilize those skills with peers (Farmer et al., 1996). Consider that how youth interpret social cues will influence how they make bids for friendships. If there is a deficit in social information processing, such as a hostile attribution bias, they may have poor relationships with peers. Efforts to ameliorate negative peer experiences (rejection, victimization) have resulted in the creation of numerous social skills training programs to teach youth the requisite skills they need for positive interactions with peers. However, the impact of social skills training programs on students' social competences has been modest (Maag, 2006) and they are likely insufficient on their own to help students develop their social competences (e.g., Farmer, Farmer, & Brooks, 2010). This is because social skills training alone does not address the peer social dynamics that can constrain students' peer opportunities and their ability to use new skills with their peers (Farmer & Xie, 2007). From a developmental science perspective, it is imperative we assess the dynamic interactions between youth's social skills and their peer interaction patterns, relationships, and affiliations to fully understand the social functioning of youth with EBD (Farmer et al., 1996).

School Context Experiences for Youth with EBD

The secondary school years are particularly problematic for youth with EBD. School discipline practices can significantly impact EBD students' adjustment at school. Students with EBD are more likely to cause classroom disruptions which increase their risk for discipline-related referrals compared to their classroom peers (Lane, Wehby, & Barton-Arwood, 2005). These youth also experience higher rates of suspensions or expulsions. In

Developmental during Middle and High School 59

fact, youth with EBD had the highest rates (44%) of these harsh disciplinary practices in 2001–2002 according to the National Longitudinal Transition Study-2 (NLTS2), a rate that is considerably higher than the suspension/expulsion rate of 13% for youth with EBD in the mid-1980s (Wagner, Newman, & Cameto, 2004). Unfortunately, youth with EBD are less likely to complete school than youth in other disabilities areas. For example, youth with EBD had the highest dropout rate (35%) among all disability categories during the 2014–2015 school year (National Center for Education Statistics, 2019).

Interactions and relationships with teachers may be particularly salient for students with EBD as research suggests that students with learning and behavior problems receive fewer learning opportunities than their typically developing peers (Sutherland & Oswald, 2005). Youth who are already struggling academically and socially may fall even further behind which can lead to coercive interactions with teachers and other adults in school. To illustrate, Hirn and Scott (2014) found that high school students without challenging behavior were engaged about 18% more of the time than students with challenging behaviors, while teachers provided twice the rate of negative feedback to students with challenging behavior in comparison to their peers without challenging behavior. These types of coercive interactions may contribute to conflictual teacher–student relationships, contributing to even poorer adjustment later in school and life (Hamre & Pianta, 2001).

Another critical consideration for adjustment in the classroom is that many teachers of students with EBD lack the training needed to effectively support these youth (Whelan & Simpson, 1996). There is wide recognition of the shortage of certified teachers for students with EBD (see Lloyd et al., 2019 for discussion). Of those that are certified, some have emergency certification status which has important implications for how they manage their classrooms which in turn can influence how students with EBD function and adapt at school (e.g., Sutherland, Denny, & Gunter, 2005). This means that it is possible that students with EBD may be in classrooms with teachers whose certification status is in question. Even for those teachers who are fully licensed, there is some concern that they are not receiving the training they need in evidenced-based practices (Freeman, Simonsen, Briere, & MacSuga-Gage, 2014). Indeed, many general education teachers may lack the knowledge or skills in how best to deliver evidence-based practices or know how to adjust and adapt their approaches to intensify efforts throughout the intervention process (Fuchs & Fuchs, 2015). This lack of requisite skills is highly concerning, especially given the reliance on classroom teachers to deliver Tier 1 interventions shown to be effective for students with EBD or those who are at risk for EBD (see Lloyd et al., 2019 for discussion). Imagine the challenges and barriers to effective implementation and sustainability if the teacher who is expected to provide the intervention is ill-equipped to do so.

Using Developmental Processes in System Reorganization for Youth

For youth with a system of negative correlated constraints, it is essential that we capitalize on the opportunity for reorganization during the middle and high school years as a system of negative factors may consolidate in later adolescence and be difficult to shift, jeopardizing the likelihood for successful outcomes across the lifespan. Indeed, the high school years represent our last chance to intervene before youth transition from school to adult life (Lane et al., 2006).

What might system reorganization look like and what are some specific developmental processes that can be harnessed to help promote system reorganization? The first step should be assessing youth's system of correlated constraints and their strengths in order to align intervention efforts with their particular needs as well as promote existing capabilities in line with a strengths-based perspective (Farmer et al., 2010). The second step would be to use the knowledge of key developmental tasks, changes, or processes as potential leverage points in the intervention process. For example, a youth's struggle to make new friends in class following the transition to middle school can jeopardize his or her ability to attain the developmental task of gaining friendships and integrating into a peer group. To help in this endeavor, a teacher who is attuned to the peer relations and dynamics in the classroom can help set up social interactions and opportunities with prosocial, academically oriented peers who are similar to the youth in question in some way (e.g., same interests or hobbies), all of which can have a cascading effect on other domains such as more positive peer experiences, reduced likelihood of being victimized, and even increased interest in school (Hamm, Farmer, Dadisman, Gravelle, & Murray, 2011). Further, knowing that middle and high school youth increasingly seek autonomy across this developmental period, restructuring school and classroom opportunities in ways that allow for more choice can help youth achieve autonomy and establish their own personal identity which may in turn increase academic motivation (which can decrease during these school years) and improve perceptions of teacher and school support. Such positive perceptions may in turn improve youth's relationship with teachers which is critical for students' long-term academic achievement (Hamre & Pianta, 2001). Such efforts in the external domains can be coupled with efforts to realign any problems in internal domains such as cognitive appraisals of situations, emotional regulation skills, and mental health concerns. Combining and coordinating these efforts across domains may seem daunting, but it is exactly this type of holistic, whole-child approach – addressing multiple systems simultaneously – that will ultimately lead to positive trajectories across the lifespan (Cairns, 2000; Magnusson & Cairns, 1996).

What does this mean for interventions for students with EBD? The developmental science perspective suggests that lock-step interventions comprised of evidence-based practices that teachers can pull off the shelf may have limited success and limited capacity to make lasting change on the factors or processes that are sustaining difficulties for students with EBD (Farmer, Gatzke-Kopp, Lee, Dawes, & Talbott, 2016; Farmer, Sutherland, et al., 2016). It also highlights some limitations in multi-tiered systems of support based on the reliance on response to treatment in the determining intervention choices (Horner, Sugai, & Anderson, 2010). Although it is important for youth with EBD to receive interventions of the correct intensity to adequately address their presenting risk factors, it is those presenting risk and protective factors, across internal and external domains, and the way their interactions inform developmental processes that should drive needs assessment and intervention planning and implementation for youth with EBD. It is our belief that knowledge about key developmental tasks and contextual changes during the middle and high school years should be used in interventions tailored to the specific challenges faced by youth with EBD during this developmental stage. In this sense, developmental processes can be harnessed as opportunities to help realign and reorganize the internal and external subsystems for youth with EBD in ways that promote adaptation and positive adjustment (Farmer & Farmer, 2001).

References

Barber, B. K., & Olsen, J. A. (2004). Assessing the transitions to middle and high school. *Journal of Adolescent Research, 19*, 3–30.

Bronfenbrenner, U. (1979). *The ecology of human development: Experiments by nature and design.* Cambridge, MA: Harvard University Press.

Buchanan, C. M., Eccles, J. S., Flanagan, C., Midgley, C., Feldlaufer, H., & Harold, R. D. (1990). Parents' and teachers' beliefs about adolescents: Effects of sex and experience. *Journal of Youth and Adolescence, 19*, 363–394.

Cairns, R. B. (2000). Developmental science: Three audacious implications. In L. R. Bergman, R. B. Cairns, L.-G. Nilsson, & L. Nystedt (Eds.), *Developmental science and the holistic approach* (pp. 49–62). Mahwah, NJ: Erlbaum.

Cairns, R. B., & Cairns, B. D. (1994). *Lifelines and risks: Pathways of youth in our time.* New York: Cambridge University Press.

Casey, B. J., Jones, R. M., & Somerville, L. H. (2011). Braking and accelerating of the adolescent brain. *Journal of Research on Adolescence, 21*, 21–33.

Chen, C. C., Culhane, D. P., Metraux, S., Park, J. M., Venable, J. C., & Burnett, T. C. (2016). They're not all at home: Residential placements of early adolescents in special education. *Journal of Emotional and Behavioral Disorders, 24*, 247–256.

Connolly, J. A., & McIsaac, C. (2009). Romantic relationships in adolescence. In R. M. Lerner & L. Steinberg (Eds.), *Handbook of adolescent psychology: Contextual influences on adolescent development* (pp. 104–151). Hoboken, NJ: John Wiley & Sons.

Costello, E. J., Copeland, W., & Angold, A. (2011). Trends in psychopathology across the adolescent years: What changes when children become adolescents, and when adolescents become adults? *Journal of Child Psychology and Psychiatry, 52*, 1015–1025.

Dawes, M. (2017). Early adolescents' social goals and school adjustment. *Social Psychology of Education, 20*, 299–328.

Dishion, T. J., & Tipsord, J. M. (2011). Peer contagion in child and adolescent social and emotional development. *Annual Review of Psychology, 62*, 189–214.

Farmer, T. W., & Farmer, E. M. (2001). Developmental science, systems of care, and prevention of emotional and behavioral problems in youth. *American Journal of Orthopsychiatry, 71*(2), 171–181.

Farmer, T. W., Farmer, E. M., & Brooks, D. S. (2010). Recasting the ecological and developmental roots of intervention for students with emotional and behavior problems: The promise of strength-based perspectives. *Exceptionality, 18*, 53–57.

Farmer, T. W., Gatzke-Kopp, L. M., Lee, D. L., Dawes, M., & Talbott, E. (2016). Research and policy on disability: Linking special education to developmental science. *Policy Insights from the Behavioral and Brain Sciences, 3*, 138–145.

Farmer, T. W., Pearl, R., & Van Acker, R. M. (1996). Expanding the social skills deficit framework: A developmental synthesis perspective, classroom social networks, and implications for the social growth of students with disabilities. *The Journal of Special Education, 30*, 232–256.

Farmer, T. W., Sutherland, K. S., Talbott, E., Brooks, D. S., Norwalk, K., & Huneke, M. (2016). Special educators as intervention specialists: Dynamic systems and the complexity of intensifying intervention for students with emotional and behavioral disorders. *Journal of Emotional and Behavioral Disorders, 24*, 173–186.

Farmer, T. W., & Xie, H. (2007). Aggression and school social dynamics: The good, the bad, and the ordinary. *Journal of School Psychology, 45*, 461–478.

Forness, S. R., Freeman, S. F., Paparella, T., Kauffman, J. M., & Walker, H. M. (2012). Special education implications of point and cumulative prevalence for children with emotional or behavioral disorders. *Journal of Emotional and Behavioral Disorders, 20*, 4–18.

Freeman, J., Simonsen, B., Briere, D. E., & MacSuga-Gage, A. S. (2014). Pre-service teacher training in classroom management: A review of state accreditation policy and teacher preparation programs. *Teacher Education and Special Education, 37*, 106–120.

Fuchs, D., & Fuchs, L. S. (2015). Rethinking service delivery for students with significant learning problems: Developing and implementing intensive interventions. *Remedial and Special Education, 36*, 105–111.

Gladden, R. M., Vivolo-Kantor, A. M., Hamburger, M. E., & Lumpkin, C. D. (2014). *Bullying surveillance among youths: Uniform definitions for public health and recommended data elements, Version 1.0.* Atlanta, GA: National Center for Injury Prevention and Control, Centers for Disease Control and Prevention, and U. S. Department of Education.

Hamm, J. V., Farmer, T. W., Dadisman, K., Gravelle, M., & Murray, A. R. (2011). Teachers' attunement to students' peer group affiliations as a source of improved student experiences of the school social–affective context following the middle school transition. *Journal of Applied Developmental Psychology*, *32*(5), 267–277.

Hamre, B. K., & Pianta, R. C. (2001). Early teacher–child relationships and the trajectory of children's school outcomes through eighth grade. *Child Development*, *72*, 625–638.

Havighurst, R. J. (1972). *Developmental tasks and education* (3rd ed.). New York: McKay.

Hirn, R. G., & Scott, T. M. (2014). Descriptive analysis of teacher instructional practices and student engagement among adolescents with and without challenging behavior. *Education and Treatment of Children*, *37*, 589–610.

Horner, R. H., Sugai, G., & Anderson, C. M. (2010). Examining the evidence base for school-wide positive behavior support. *Focus on Exceptional Children*, *42*, 1–14.

Individuals with Disabilities Education Act, 20 U.S.C. § 1400 (2004).

Kauffman, J. M., & Landrum, T. J. (2012). *Characteristics of emotional and behavioural disorders of children and youth* (10th ed.). Upper Saddle River, NJ: Pearson Education.

Lane, K. L., Carter, E. W., Pierson, M. R., & Glaeser, B. C. (2006). Academic, social, and behavioral characteristics of high school students with emotional disturbances or learning disabilities. *Journal of Emotional and Behavioral Disorders*, *14*, 108–117.

Lane, K. L., Wehby, J., & Barton-Arwood, S. M. (2005). Students with and at risk for emotional and behavioral disorders: Meeting their social and academic needs. *Preventing School Failure*, *49*, 6–9.

Larson, R. W. (2001). How US children and adolescents spend time: What it does (and doesn't) tell us about their development. *Current Directions in Psychological Science*, *10*, 160–164.

Larson, R. W., Moneta, G., Richards, M. H., & Wilson, S. (2002). Continuity, stability, and change in daily emotional experience across adolescence. *Child Development*, *73*, 1151–1165.

Laursen, B., Coy, K. C., & Collins, W. A. (1998). Reconsidering changes in parent-child conflict across adolescence: A meta-analysis. *Child Development*, *69*, 817–832.

Lloyd, B. P., Bruhn, A. L., Sutherland, K. S., & Bradshaw, C. P. (2019). Progress and priorities in research to improve outcomes for students with or at risk for emotional and behavioral disorders. *Behavioral Disorders*, *44*, 85–96.

Maag, J. W. (2006). Social skills training for students with emotional and behavioral disorders: A review of reviews. *Behavioral Disorders*, *32*, 4–17.

Maggin, D. M., Wehby, J. H., Farmer, T. W., & Brooks, D. S. (2016). Intensive interventions for students with emotional and behavioral disorders: Issues, theory, and future directions. *Journal of Emotional and Behavioral Disorders*, *24*, 127–137.

Magnusson, D., & Cairns, R. B. (1996). Developmental science: Toward a unified framework. In R. B. Cairns, G. H. Elder, Jr., & E. J. Costello (Eds.), *Cambridge studies in social and emotional development. Developmental science* (pp. 7–30). New York, NY: Cambridge University Press.

Massey, E. K., Gebhardt, W. A., & Garnefski, N. (2008). Adolescent goal content and pursuit: A review of the literature from the past 16 years. *Developmental Review*, *28*, 421–460.

Masten, A. S. (2004). Regulatory processes, risk, and resilience in adolescent development. *Annals of the New York Academy of Sciences*, *1021*, 310–319.

McDougall, P., & Vaillancourt, T. (2015). Long-term adult outcomes of peer victimization in childhood and adolescence: Pathways to adjustment and maladjustment. *American Psychologist*, *70*, 300–310.

Merikangas, K., He, J., Burstein, M., Swendsen, J., Avenevoli, S., Case, B., & Olfson, M. (2011). Service utilization for lifetime mental disorders in U.S. adolescents: Results of the National Comorbidity Survey-Adolescent Supplement (NCS-A). *Journal of the American Academy of Child and Adolescent Psychiatry*, *50*, 32–45.

Moffitt, T. E. (1993). Life-course-persistent and adolescence-limited antisocial behavior: A developmental taxonomy. *Psychological Review*, *100*, 674–701.

Nansel, T. R., Overpeck, M., Pilla, R. S., Ruan, W. J., Simons-Morton, B., & Scheidt, P. (2001). Bullying behaviors among US youth: Prevalence and association with psychosocial adjustment. *JAMA, 285,* 2094–2100.

National Center for Education Statistics. (2019). *The condition of education 2019.* Washington, DC: U.S. Department of Education.

Nock, M. K., Green, J. G., Hwang, I., McLaughlin, K. A., Sampson, N. A., Zaslavsky, A. M., & Kessler, R. C. (2013). Prevalence, correlates, and treatment of lifetime suicidal behavior among adolescents: Results from the National Comorbidity Survey Replication Adolescent Supplement. *JAMA Psychiatry, 70*(3), 300–310.

Olweus, D. (1994). Bullying at school: Basic facts and effects of a school based intervention program. *Journal of Child Psychology and Psychiatry, 35,* 1171–1190.

Pinquart, M., & Pfeiffer, J. P. (2018). Longitudinal associations of the attainment of developmental tasks with psychological symptoms in adolescence: A meta-analysis. *Journal of Research on Adolescence.* Advance online publication.

Rose, A. J. (2002). Co-rumination in the friendships of girls and boys. *Child Development, 73,* 1830–1843.

Rose, C. A., Simpson, C. G., & Moss, A. (2015). The bullying dynamic: Prevalence of involvement among a large-scale sample of middle and high school youth with and without disabilities. *Psychology in the Schools, 52,* 515–531.

Rubin, K. H., Bukowski, W. M., & Laursen, B. (Eds.). (2011). *Handbook of peer interactions, relationships, and groups.* New York: Guilford Press.

Rudolph, K. D. (2002). Gender differences in emotional responses to interpersonal stress during adolescence. *Journal of Adolescent Health, 30,* 3–13.

Ryan, A. M. (2001). The peer group as a context for the development of young adolescent motivation and achievement. *Child Development, 72,* 1135–1150.

Sameroff, A. (2000). Developmental systems and psychopathology. *Development and Psychopathology, 12*(3), 297–312.

Seiffge-Krenke, I., Kiuru, N., & Nurmi, J. E. (2010). Adolescents as "producers of their own development": Correlates and consequences of the importance and attainment of developmental tasks. *European Journal of Developmental Psychology, 7,* 479–510.

Smetana, J. G., Campione-Barr, N., & Metzger, A. (2006). Adolescent development in interpersonal and societal contexts. *Annual Review of Psychology, 57,* 255–284.

Steinberg, L. (2001). We know some things: Parent–adolescent relationships in retrospect and prospect. *Journal of Research on Adolescence, 11,* 1–19.

Steinberg, L. (2005). Cognitive and affective development in adolescence. *Trends in Cognitive Sciences, 9,* 69–74.

Steinberg, L. (2008). A social neuroscience perspective on adolescent risk-taking. *Developmental Review, 28,* 78–106.

Steinberg, L. (2014). *Age of opportunity: Lessons from the new science of adolescence.* Boston, MA: Houghton Mifflin Harcourt.

Sullivan, H. S. (1953). *Interpersonal theory of personality.* New York, NY: Norton.

Sutherland, K. S., Denny, R. K., & Gunter, P. L. (2005). Teachers of students with emotional and behavioral disorders reported professional development needs: Differences between fully licensed and emergency-licensed teachers. *Preventing School Failure: Alternative Education for Children and Youth, 49,* 41–46.

Sutherland, K. S., & Oswald, D. P. (2005). The relationship between teacher and student behavior in classrooms for students with emotional and behavioral disorders: Transactional processes. *Journal of Child and Family Studies, 14,* 1–14.

Thompson, R. A. (1994). Emotion regulation: A theme in search of definition. *Monographs of the Society for Research in Child Development, 59,* 25–52.

Wagner, M., Kutash, K., Duchnowski, A. J., Epstein, M. H., & Sumi, W. C. (2005). The children and youth we serve: A national picture of the characteristics of students with emotional disturbances receiving special education. *Journal of Emotional and Behavioral Disorders, 13,* 79–96.

U.S. Department of Education, National Center for Education Statistics. (2019). *Digest of education statistics, 2017* (NCES 2018–070). Retrieved from https://nces.ed.gov/fastfacts/display.asp?id=64

Wagner, M., Newman, L., & Cameto, R. (2004). *Changes over time in the secondary school experiences of students with disabilities.* A report of findings from the National Longitudinal Transition Study (NLTS) and the National Longitudinal Transition Study-2 (NLTS2). Menlo Park, CA: SRI International.

Wentzel, K. R. (2015). Socialization in school settings. In J. E. Grusec & P. D. Hastings (Eds.), *Handbook of socialization: Theory and research* (pp. 251–275). New York, NY: Guilford Press.

Whelan, R. J., & Simpson, R. L. (1996). Preparation of personnel for students with emotional and behavioral disorders: Perspectives on a research foundation for future practice. *Behavioral Disorders, 22*, 49–54.

5 The Transition to Adulthood

A Critical Developmental Period within a Changing Social-Contextual Landscape

Kathryn Sabella, Maryann Davis, and Michelle R. Munson

Young Adulthood: A Unique Developmental and Social Life Stage

A recent report (Institute of Medicine, 2015) describes young adulthood as a period of life that is "unique," "pivotal," and "critical." In the U.S., young adults are expected to make several role transitions which include completing education and training, obtaining employment, leaving home, forming a romantic partnership, and heading or contributing to a household (Schulenberg & Schoon, 2012; Shanahan, 2000). Youth are expected to make these role transitions while moving from the safety net of adults making decisions for them and carrying the responsibility for those decisions, to making decisions for themselves and being responsible for their own decisions. For success in "self-determination," youth need to learn a great deal through practice and experimentation, all while their brains are still maturing.

Cognitive and Social-Emotional Development in Young Adulthood

Cognitive development refers to the ability to think, reason, and understand. Typical cognitive development during adolescence and young adulthood involves the evolution from (1) more concrete to more abstract thinking; (2) more singular to more multidimensional thoughts; and (3) increasing ability for self-reflection and self-awareness. Young adults are increasingly able to consider multiple abstract ideas simultaneously which helps them plan for the future, put themselves in other's "shoes," and more carefully consider "if/then" situations. Executive functioning, the capacities needed to plan, initiate, and regulate goal-directed behavior necessary for adaptive functioning, is also one of the most important areas of cognitive development in adolescence and young adulthood (Breiner et al., 2018; Cohen et al., 2016).

Social-emotional development includes the adolescent's experience, expression, and management of emotions and the ability to establish positive and rewarding relationships with others. Adolescent social-emotional development is marked by the growing importance of peer relations, relationships that are more complex, and expanding social networks. Sexuality also becomes central in adolescence and young adulthood, introducing intense physical sensations, new types of intimacy, different roles in peer groups, and important health and life considerations. Adolescence and young adulthood are also generally the ages when sexual orientation and gender identity are explored.

Brain development supports and reflects cognitive and socio-emotional development. The prefrontal cortex is the region of the brain that supports abstract reasoning and planning, executive functions, and provides control and modulation of behavior (Fuster, 2008). Essentially, the prefrontal cortex plays a major role in decision-making (Fuster, 2002; Luna, 2009).

By young adulthood, individuals can access prefrontal executive systems that support adult-level decision-making. Furthermore, the striatum, another region of the brain, provides motivational modulation of behavior through its connection to prefrontal systems (Cools, 2008). Developmental changes in the striatum peak at an even later time through adolescence than cortical regions (Raznahan et al., 2014; Sowell, Thompson, Holmes, Jernigan, & Toga, 1999; Wierenga et al., 2014). Similarly, the amygdala (also in the limbic system), which supports emotional processing, has a peak in gray matter growth in the teen years but subsequent decreasing in volume (Greimel et al., 2013; Scherf, Smyth, & Delgado, 2013). The normative heightened risk-taking seen in adolescence reflects the developmental gap between a faster-maturing subcortical reactive system (i.e. limbic) and a slower-maturing cortical regulation system. Research on neurodevelopment in young adulthood is not as extensive as in childhood and adolescence (IOM, 2015). However, in studies conducted to date, it is clear that young adult brains are still developing, particularly in the areas of cognitive control in emotional situations (Cohen et al., 2016), and self-regulation (Steinberg et al., 2018).

It is important to note that maturation in one developmental area does not necessitate maturation in all areas, yet some areas of development overlap. For example, adolescents may be able to apply logical operations to school work long before they are able to apply them to personal problem-solving. Moreover, individuals develop at different rates all within their own unique social context. Ecological approaches, which focus on understanding interactions among developing persons, the contexts of development, and the processes that account for development (Bronfenbrenner & Morris, 1998), dominate developmental research.

The Social-Contextual Landscape of Young Adulthood

The cognitive and brain development that young adults experience has not changed dramatically across generations, but their social functioning has (Steinberg, 2013). Social and behavioral scientists frequently discuss social functioning in terms of five major role transitions of young adulthood – leaving home, completing school, committing to the labor market, forming a romantic partnership, and transitioning into or moving towards parenthood (Schulenberg & Schoon, 2012). During the first half of the 20th century, it was quite typical for young men and women to move in an orderly fashion from completing their schooling and living with family, to entry into work, marriage, and parenting, usually by the age of 25 (Fussell & Furstenberg, 2005).

For a host of reasons, both identified and not, in western industrial society the task of becoming functioning adults has become increasingly complicated, extended, and disorganized compared to the orderly progression typical from post-World War II into the 1960s. Many more older young adults (ages 25–35) of the "millennial" generation are living at home compared to previous generations and for longer stretches of time (Pew Research Center, 2017). More young people are working and pursuing post-secondary education at the same time (Child Trends, 2017) and the proportion of "non-traditional undergraduate" students (those older than age 24, working more than part-time, and/or raising children) compared to "traditional" undergraduates (students under 24 who pursued college immediately after secondary school, working only part-time, not married) has been increasing steadily over the last 50 years (National Center for Education Statistics, 2014). Cohabitation has become more common than marriage during young adulthood. While nearly 50% of young adults in the U.S. have cohabited by the time they turn 25, only about a quarter have married (Payne,

The Transition to Adulthood   67

2011) and many young adults are having children without being married. Taken together, the linearity of movement into adult roles has disappeared, and the age by which most young people have completed schooling, moved out of the family home, obtained steady work, married and had children has moved up to age 30 and older (Arnett, 2004; Martin, Hamilton, Osterman, Curin, & Matthews, 2013; Mathews & Hamilton, 2009; Settersten, Furstenberg, & Rumbaut, 2005).

There have also been important economic changes in the last 20 years that have contributed to some of these changing patterns. Essentially, there has been a decline in the availability of jobs requiring less education, and an increase in the number of jobs that require higher educational levels, reflecting the shift from a manufacturing-based to a service- and information-based economy (Blank, 1997; Danziger & Gottschalk, 1995; Levy, 1998). Furthermore, the value of the minimum wage has declined since the 1970s, resulting in many young people working for wages that do not cover their basic needs (Corcoran & Matsudaira, 2005).

These economic changes have put new demands on families to support their young adult children for longer periods of time so that they can obtain the education needed for higher paying jobs that support independent living (Schoeni & Ross, 2005) adding to already changing relationship dynamics within the family context. As adolescents mature into adulthood, family relationships reflect a delicate balance between the growing need for greater independence from family and the continued need for their emotional and instrumental support (Karpel & Strauss, 1983). Many cultures do influence interdependence or collectivist relationships with adult children, but generally, parent–adolescent relationships in young adulthood proceeds towards more egalitarian relationships of adult children with parents within cultural norms.

Emotional and Behavioral Disorders in Young Adulthood: Prevalence and Associated Risk Factors

Before describing the prevalence and associated risk factors of young adults with emotional behavioral disorders (EBD), it is important to acknowledge the unique challenges associated with the varying terminology that is used to describe emotional and behavioral challenges during the transition from adolescence (i.e. child) to adulthood. EBD is a term primarily used in special education. Its equivalent term in the children's mental health system is serious emotional disturbance (SED). Therefore, both EBD and SED are terms primarily applied to minors (except in the case of someone over the age of 18 who is still receiving special education services into their early twenties). The adult mental health system (ages 18 and over) uses the term serious mental illness (SMI). Increasingly, the term serious mental health condition (SMHC) is used to refer to the emotional and behavioral challenges of young adults. These varying definitions that span the transition to adulthood (age 16–25) contribute to discontinuity of care and create various policy barriers (see Davis & Koroloff, 2006 for a more detailed discussion) and also complicate the task of reporting prevalence statistics for this age group. Prevalence statistics and associated risk factors that are described below will reflect the chosen definitions and terminology of the original sources that correspond with the relevant developmental period.

Emotional and behavioral disorders (EBD) are increasingly common among young adults. In 2016 it was estimated that approximately 2 million (5.9%) young adults, ages 18–25, reported a serious mental illness in the past year (Ahrnsbrak, Bose, Hedden, Lipari, & Park-Lee, 2016). Over the last 15 years or so, prevalence rates of major depressive episodes,

68 *Kathryn Sabella et al.*

psychological distress in the last month, and suicide-related outcomes (suicidal ideation, plans, attempts, and deaths by suicide) in the last year have increased among young adults aged 18–25, faster than in any other age group (Twenge, Cooper, Joiner, Duffy, & Binau, 2019). Many experts are pointing to an increasing mental health crisis among young adults.

It is important to note that rates of EBD are not evenly distributed across all members of the population. Several risk factors are associated with a higher likelihood of EBD in young adulthood and should be taken into consideration. Social class is an important determinant of health and mental health although there are varying theories as to the exact mechanisms that cause such disparities (and are beyond the scope of this chapter). Twenty-one percent of low-income youth aged 6–17 have been found to have mental health conditions, and 57% of these youth come from households living at or below the federal poverty level (Howell, 2004). Similarly, individuals over the age of 18 living below the poverty line have higher rates of serious mental illness than those living at or above the poverty line (6.8% versus 4.3% and 3.3% respectively) (SAMHSA, 2016a). Rates of EBD also vary by race and ethnicity. Among adults over the age of 18, blacks, Hispanic, and American Indian/Alaskan Natives have some of the higher rates of serious mental illness (SAMHSA, 2016b).

Adverse life experiences, including trauma, have been associated with poorer mental health outcomes in young adulthood (Schilling, Aseltine, & Gore, 2007). Many young people with EBD have also been served in the foster care system (McMillen et al., 2005) where it is estimated that half of children and youth, up to age 14, have mental health disorders (Burns et al., 2004). Young adults who are navigating non-conforming sexual orientations and gender identities are also at increased likelihood of experiencing psychological distress and EBD. Young adults in high school who are lesbian, gay, bisexual, or unsure about their sexuality are more likely than their heterosexual peers to report persistent feelings of sadness and hopelessness, suicide attempts, injection of illegal drugs, or opioid misuse (Centers for Disease Control, 2018). While the data are harder to track, young adults who identify with a gender different from the sex they were born with are at increased risk of poor mental health outcomes due to feelings of stress, anxiety, and depression associated with how their gender identity is perceived by others (Headspace, 2018).

Developmental and Social-Contextual Considerations for Young Adults with Emotional and Behavioral Disorders

Youth and young adults with EBD often experience delays in their cognitive and social-emotional development. Prior research has suggested that adolescents and young adults with emotional and behavioral disorders can have delays in all areas of development (Davis & Vander Stoep, 1997). Current developmental theory and research highlights the influence of positive contextual conditions that are associated with successful psychosocial maturity development (Scott & Steinberg, 2008). Accordingly, young adults with EBD, especially those who lack positive adult role models (Steinberg, Chung, & Little, 2004), a role in determining their services (Collins & Steinberg, 2006; Mahoney, Larson, Eccles, & Lord, 2005), and who are involved in systems that separate them from positive peers (Brown, 2004) may be particularly vulnerable to delayed cognitive and psychosocial development.

It is also well documented that individuals with serious psychiatric conditions often have cognitive impairments that affect the skills associated with executive function (Gold & Harvey, 1993; Hutton et al., 1998; Johnson-Selfridge & Zalewski, 2001). Cognitive difficulties, including executive functioning impairments, are significantly related to poorer functional outcomes in areas such as school, work, and social relationships (Dickerson et al., 2004;

Green, Kern, & Heaton, 2004; Nuechterlein et al., 2011). Symptoms of anxiety and depression can also negatively impact one's social interactions and manifest as shyness, social awkwardness, or social isolation.

Young adults with emotional and behavioral disorders also struggle to achieve milestones of adulthood including post-secondary education, employment, and housing. In fact, mental health conditions are one of the leading causes of disability in youth and young adults within the United States (Institute of Medicine, 2015). Thirty-five percent of young adults with emotional and behavioral disorders who have been in either public mental health services or special education due to their mental health have not completed high school (U.S. Department of Education, 2017). This dropout rate is substantially higher than the dropout rate for any other disability category. Many of those who *do* graduate from high school and pursue higher education experience long delays in entering college and have high dropout rates compared to students with other disabilities (Newman et al., 2011; Salzer, Wick, & Rogers, 2008). Young adults with emotional and behavioral disorders are less likely to be employed compared to older adults with mental illness (Waghorn, Chant, & Harris, 2009) and their peers without mental illness (Frank, 1991; Newman et al., 2011; Vander Stoep et al., 2000).

Many young adults with EBD experience substance use challenges, justice system involvement, homelessness, trauma, co-occurring addictions, and foster care placement. Among young adults with serious mental health conditions, 34.9% report substance use disorder in the last year, a rate higher than any other age group (Ahrnsbrak et al., 2016). About 57–62% of state and federal prisoners aged 18–24 and 70% of young adults in local jails had symptoms of a mental health problem or received a mental health diagnosis in the last 12 months (Bureau of Justice Statistics, 2006). About one-third of homeless individuals are age 24 or younger, and within them the prevalence of psychiatric disorders is up to four times the rate of youth and young adults in the general population (Castro et al., 2014; SAMHSA, 2014). Housing challenges are especially difficult for youth and young adults with EBD who are lesbian, gay, bisexual, and transgender (LGBT) or who are transitioning from foster care (Durso & Gates, 2012; Dworsky, Dillman, Dion, Coffee-Bordon, & Rosenau, 2012).

Service and System Considerations

Despite all of these challenges, young adults often under-utilize treatment for EBD. Only about half of young adults with serious mental illness and young adults with co-occurring substance use disorders (55%) report receiving treatment for those conditions (SAMHSA, 2014). The treatment attrition (i.e., dropout or low attendance) of young adults in outpatient mental health therapy is substantially higher in young adults than mature adults over the age of 25 (Fernandez, Salem, Swift, & Ramtahal, 2015; Olfson et al., 2009; Swift & Greenberg, 2012). Treatment patterns also vary by race and ethnicity; the rates at which youth and young adults from racial and ethnic minority groups seek treatment are much lower than their white counterparts (SAMHSA, 2010).

Unmet treatment needs can be at least partially explained by the challenge of navigating the existing treatment system. It is important to note that the nature of both mental health and substance use disorders can impede individuals' abilities to advocate for themselves in the system, and for young adults, the requirement for self-advocacy is new since parents and others would have advocated for them as minors. Thus, simply providing them information about how and where to get health insurance or care, while important, also needs to be married to active and effective outreach by the health care system that is culturally appealing to help them access and complete needed treatment.

70   *Kathryn Sabella et al.*

High rates of outpatient treatment dropout in this age group may also be attributable to the currently unavoidable process young adults face that requires them cross the "age-divide" from child to adult services. Many service systems serve only children (up to age 18 or 21) or only adults (age 18 and older). And some systems that serve both age groups (e.g. public mental health and substance use systems) organize and finance their child and adult systems separately. Examples include special education (ending at age 21), foster care (typically ending at age 18 or 21), juvenile justice (typically ending at age 17 or 18), and criminal justice (starting at ages 16, 17, or 18). Medical health care settings are also typically either pediatric or adult. Within public mental health services, policies that define eligibility criteria or target populations for services are distinctly different for child and adult mental health (Davis & Koroloff, 2006), with adult criteria typically being more narrow. The youngest adults in adult behavioral health systems may still be involved with multiple child systems, and coordination between those systems is needed to ensure continuity of care. In recent years there has been increased recognition of these structural system-level issues and efforts to address at least part of them (e.g., the John H. Chafee Foster Care Program for Successful Transition to Adulthood). However, the current system remains fragmented, age-determined, and full of gaps for transition-aged youth.

Evidence-Based, Promising Practices and Future Directions of Research

Even if these systemic issues could be addressed, perhaps the most pressing barrier to quality services for youth and young adults with EBD is that there are few interventions with strong evidence of effectiveness *specifically for this age group* (GAO, 2008; IOM/NRC, 2015; Skehan & Davis, 2017). Most standards for establishing effectiveness of interventions include:

1) The need for standardization (a manual that describes the practice with some degree of specificity, standard means for training practitioners, and measures to assess the degree of practice adherence to the specified practice).
2) The need for comparison of those receiving the experimental intervention to a comparable group that is not receiving the intervention.
3) A sample size large enough to provide enough statistical power that a moderate effect size can be detected.

Furthermore, when it comes to establishing the effectiveness of interventions specifically for young adults, providers and researchers must also consider the age group addressed in the research. Evidence-based practices for adolescents can be assumed to be effective for the youngest of youth and young adults (i.e. the adolescent ages included in the research), but should not be assumed effective for youth and young adults beyond the ages in the research (e.g. studies include 14–18 year olds but there is no evidence for 19–26 year olds). Similarly, studies of "adults" (e.g., 18–55 year olds) do not establish evidence in young adults unless either the average age of the participants falls within the young adult age range, or the sample size of young adults is large enough to detect a moderate effect size in an age comparison of the outcomes in young vs older adults in the sample.

From the perspective of these guidelines, there are only a few interventions with substantial evidence of efficacy for improving behavioral health outcomes, including functional outcomes, specifically for young adults. First, **motivational interviewing strategies** and techniques have evidence of efficacy with young adults for several specific conditions, including postpartum depression (Grote et al., 2009), social anxiety disorder (Buckner & Schmidt, 2009), and substance use (Acuff et al., 2019; Monti et al., 2007; Murphy et al., 2012). Motivational interviewing (MI) techniques use conversational approaches to help people identify their readiness, willingness, and ability to change and to make use of their own change-talk. This approach, combined with the principles of MI (express empathy, roll with resistance, develop discrepancy, and support self-efficacy) and a person-centered approach is not only effective but also well-received by young adults (Naar-King & Suarez, 2011).

Second, **Coordinated Specialty Care (CSC)**, a team-based multifaceted approach, has demonstrated efficacy and evidence for improving outcomes of young adults with schizophrenia-spectrum first episode psychosis (Kane et al., 2016). CSC is a recovery-oriented approach that emphasizes shared decision-making between the client, the treatment team, and the family (when applicable). Coordinated specialty services offered during or shortly after a first episode of psychosis that provide continuity of specialized care for up to five years post-psychosis onset have been shown to help reduce the effects of psychosis mostly among young adults up to their mid-twenties (Craig et al., 2004; Norman et al., 2011; Petersen et al., 2005).

Third, **Individual Placement and Supports (IPS)** helps people with psychiatric conditions achieve competitive employment. IPS clients work with an employment specialist who coordinates their efforts with those of the clinical team. The evidence base for the effectiveness of IPS with older adults is well established (Bond, Drake, & Becker, 2008; Knapp et al., 2013). IPS has also been found to produce better employment outcomes in young adults compared to those who do not receive IPS (Bond, Drake, & Campbell, 2012). However, among those who received IPS, the average number of hours worked per week was less than 20 and over an 18-month period most young adults were unemployed more weeks than they were employed. Two IPS versions for those with early psychosis (Killackey, Jackson, & McGorry, 2008; Nuechterlein et al., 2008) have integrated supported education with supported employment and produced better employment outcomes for those young adults compared to standard services in America (Baksheev, Allott, Jackson, McGorry, & Killackey, 2012; Killackey, Jackson, & McGorry, 2008).

Promising Practices and Approaches

Given the lack of evidence-based practices specifically for young adults with emotional and behavioral disorders, providers have had to rely on the use of several promising practices that meet some criteria for being an evidence-based intervention. Many promising practices share characteristics and commonalities that, taken together, illustrate promising *approaches* to more developmentally appropriate and culturally appealing practices for young adults with emotional and behavioral disorders. These approaches, and examples of specific promising practices that are in development, are outlined below.

Use of Young Adult Peers

Generally speaking, a peer provider is someone who uses his or her own lived experience of mental health challenges to help clients take action towards their recovery and become more involved in their own health treatment and decisions. Peer providers partner with the treatment team to provide services to young adults, educate staff on the recovery process, and serve as role models to young adults. Peer roles (e.g. peer specialist, peer provider, peer mentor) in the U.S. are considered a profession, accompanied by practice guidelines and codes of ethics, and in many states are Medicaid reimbursable. Federal partners and community-based providers are increasingly recognizing the need for age-tailored peer roles. Young Adult Peers build upon adult peer and family peer initiatives in adult and children's mental health systems but are distinct in that they address young adult issues (transition from child to adult service systems, typical functional outcomes such as school and work) in a culturally appealing way.

Preliminary research has shown that young adults endorse the flexibility and authenticity of working with near-age young adult peers and that they particularly value the community-based interactions, feeling understood, and forming a bond with these mentors (Klodnick et al., 2015). Research has also shown that clients working with young adult peers report improvements in hope, self-determination, and mental health (Geenan et al., 2015). Furthermore, young adult peers can strengthen engagement of young adults with emotional and behavioral disorders with treatment and some evidence shows they may improve overall satisfaction with and participation in treatment planning (Radigan, Wang, Chen, & Xiang, 2014; Walker & Gowen, 2011).

There are several young adult peer worker models and interventions being utilized across the country with a variety of peer role responsibilities, principles, and curricula. The **Peer Academic Support for Success (PASS)** approach utilizes Junior/Senior college students as academic coaches to support Freshmen/Sophomore college students with mental health conditions that interfere with academic success. Although not required, many coaches have their own lived-experience or have close friends and family members with lived experience. Coaches work from an extensive curriculum that covers skills and exercises to support academic success, such as wellness approaches to reducing stress, time-management skills, self-advocacy, and emotional resiliency. Coaches also provide informational support, strategies for requesting accommodation from faculty, and identification of campus resources. PASS is currently in development and is undergoing a pilot clinical trial. The research is conducted in partnership with young adults with lived experience at the Learning and Working Rehabilitation Research and Training Center at University of Massachusetts Medical School (Transitions ACR, 2019).

The Young Adult Engagement Project, also known as **Just Do You**, is a meta-intervention (an intervention discussing evidence-based interventions) that provides young adults an orientation to mental health services alongside a young-adult set of intervention strategies designed to address empirically identified barriers to engagement for this population (Munson et al., 2016a). Just Do You was designed in partnership with young adults living with serious mental health conditions with a series of pilot studies. The program is co-facilitated by a licensed clinician and a person with lived experience (peer mentor) and uses technology-based interventions, music and creative arts to engage young adults in mental health conversations on typical professional services, trust, aspects of recovery, stigma and management of disclosure, and addressing fear, anger, and hopelessness. The intervention is manualized, has shown feasibility and acceptability (Munson et al., 2016a) and is currently being tested in an efficacy trial in the adult mental health system with young adults who are all poor, marginalized and have used public systems of care during childhood.

Wraparound and Multi-Component Interventions

Wraparound is a widely implemented and well-established comprehensive team approach for planning and providing individualized, community-based care for children and adolescents with emotional and behavioral disorders who are typically involved in family-serving systems. A Wraparound care coordinator is responsible for ensuring that team members (e.g. family members, teachers) effectively collaborate to develop, implement, and monitor an individualized plan of care that coordinates services and supports for the child/youth and family. The principles of wraparound are likely to be effective with slightly older clients (i.e. 18–25). However, research focusing on the experiences of older youth in Wraparound indicates that they may not be active participants in the team, actively contributing to decisions and conversations, and in turn are less satisfied than other stakeholders regarding their Wraparound experiences (Walker & Schutte, 2005). In short, Wraparound for young adults needs to be youth-guided and as a result be more developmentally appropriate, culturally appealing, and lead to increased engagement.

Two young adult adaptations to Wraparound are being utilized in communities around the country. The first, **Achieve My Plan (AMP)**, was designed to increase providers' capacity for working with young people to promote their acquisition of self-determination skills, ensure that care/treatment is based on their perspectives and priorities, and highlight and build on strengths in meaningful ways (Walker, Seibel, & Jackson, 2017). Findings from a randomized study of AMP showed that young people (aged 12–18) who received Wraparound with the AMP enhancement participated more – and in a more active and self-determined manner – with their teams relative to youth who received "as usual" Wraparound. They also rated their alliance with their Wraparound teams significantly higher and adult team members in the AMP enhancement group rated team meetings as being more productive and "better than usual." Another adaptation of Wrapround involves embedding the **Transition to Independence Process (TIP) Model**™ framework, an evidence-supported practice, to existing wraparound services. In the TIP Model™, young people, in conjunction with key individuals in their life (e.g. parents, an older sister, girlfriend), are encouraged to explore their interests and futures as related to several transition domains (e.g. employment and career, education, community–life functioning). The TIP Model™ is operationalized through seven guidelines that drive practice-level activities with young people to provide the delivery of coordinated, non-stigmatizing, trauma-informed, developmentally appropriate, appealing supports and services to them.

Cornerstone is a multi-component intervention for transition-age youth that is manualized and has shown feasibility, acceptability, and limited efficacy-testing outcomes among youth. Cornerstone bridges the clinic and the community and seamlessly integrates evidence-based practices, such as navigation, trauma-focused cognitive-behavioral therapy, and mentorship, along with coordination of medication management by a hybrid team of a licensed social worker and a person with lived experience (Munson et al., 2016b). Cornerstone is currently being tested in a small randomized trial in an adolescent mental health clinic in a low-resourced community where participants come from families who are all poor or near poor.

Multisystemic Therapy for Emerging Adults (MST-EA) (for 16–26 year olds) is an adaptation of the well-established and effective intervention Multisystemic Therapy, which reduces delinquency in juveniles (ages 12–17; Henggeler, Schoenwald, Borduin, Rowland, & Cunningham, 1998). The goals of MST-EA treatment are to reduce criminal behaviors and recidivism, reduce mental health and substance use disorders symptoms, help youth develop an effective social network (a "family of choice") for adulthood, increase functioning in school, work, and independent living, and if applicable, teach parenting skills. MST-EA blends cognitive behavioral therapy, behavioral interventions, motivational interviewing, affective education, and extensive skill building to address the array of issues associated with the

74 *Kathryn Sabella et al.*

emerging adult's mental health symptoms, antisocial behavior, and other problems. The emerging adult collaborates with the therapist in designing the treatment plan that will be carried out over approximately 7–8 months (services generally range from 6 to 12 months depending on client needs). MST-EA treatment is delivered in the home or wherever the emerging adult prefers. Therapists are readily available 24/7 to emerging adults and their social network to address emergencies and remove barriers to treatment. MST-EA also includes paraprofessional "Coaches" who help teach concrete life skills and engage clients in prosocial activities and MST-EA therapists engage psychiatric and physical health professionals to coordinate effective health care. Preliminary findings from a small feasibility open trial are promising (Davis, Sheidow, & McCart, 2015); those enrolled in MST-EA had significant reductions in charges, symptoms, and association with antisocial peers. An additional pilot randomization controlled trial within the MST-EA open trial indicated that MST-EA treated youth whose vocational supports were embedded within MST-EA treatment had much higher likelihoods of engaging in school or work after treatment than those whose vocational supports were sought from the state vocational rehabilitation system (Davis, Sheidow, McCart, & Perrault, 2018).

Integrated Supported Employment and Supported Education

It is typical and age-appropriate for young adults to pursue both employment and education or training in the years following high school, either contemporaneously or in turn. Several providers have begun delivering supported education services in conjunction with supported employment services. One new research initiative, **Helping Youth on the Path to Employment** (HYPE: https://umassmed.edu/hype) was recently developed and manualized in partnership with young adults with lived experience. HYPE is a comprehensive career development approach that fully complements the normative vocational development of young adults (aged 18–30), which could include a combination of work, post-secondary schooling, or training. A HYPE Career Specialist works with young adults in community-based settings for up to one year to support them in identifying their education, training, and employment goals, developing the skills and capacities to pursue those goals, and provides strategic and ongoing support in the pursuit of those goals. HYPE is currently undergoing a large randomized clinical trial at the Transitions to Adulthood Center for Research (https://umassmed.edu/TransitionsACR).

Conclusion and Future Directions

Young adulthood is a unique developmental and social-contextual period that requires age-tailored interventions to improve the outcomes of young adults with emotional and behavioral disorders. There are well-documented risks and poor outcomes during this period for youth with emotional and behavioral disorders. Despite these fairly long-standing and compelling data on the challenges and problematic outcomes, there are very few evidence-based practices to effectively serve youth with emotional and behavioral disorders during this critical period.

The lack of evidence-based practices specifically for this population points to the urgent need for researchers to develop and rigorously test new interventions that effectively improve the emotional, behavioral, and functional outcomes of young adults with emotional and behavioral disorders. This mission can be accomplished in several ways. Researchers and practitioners need to partner to establish the efficacy and effectiveness of promising practices that are already being implemented across the country. Promising practices such as comprehensive models (e.g. wrap-around, supported education and employment interventions, and young adult peer mentor models) need further standardization and they need to be tested in randomized control trials with a sufficient sample of young adults. In other cases, established interventions that have shown to be effective in adolescents or adults need to be tested with a sufficient sample of young adults, perhaps after adapting them to be more culturally appealing and developmentally appropriate (Institute of Medicine and National Research Council, 2015). Interventions, both existing and new, also need to be tested with young adults from diverse and/or disadvantaged backgrounds to ensure they are culturally and linguistically competent.

However, evidence-based interventions will not necessarily solve the challenge of low engagement of young adults in mental health services. Systemic barriers also need to be simultaneously addressed by improving coordination and collaboration between multiple child- and adult-serving systems that young adults are likely to encounter. The period of development and life course experiences covered during the transition to adulthood are challenging even under the most supportive conditions in the contemporary world. There is a tremendous need to improve system- and treatment-level factors that can provide effective supports for youth who are simultaneously navigating the multiple transitions that youth much accomplish during this period with the additional complexities of addressing and managing mental health conditions and challenges.

References

Acuff, S. F., Voss, A. T., Dennhardt, A. A., Borsari, B., Martens, M. P., & Murphy, J. G. (2019). Brief motivational interventions are associated with reductions in alcohol-induced blackouts among heavy drinking college students. *Alcoholism: Clinical and Experimental Research, 43*, 988–996. doi:10.1111/acer.14019

Ahrnsbrak, R., Bose, J., Hedden, S. L., Lipari, R. N., & Park-Lee, E. (2016). Center for behavioral health statistics and quality, substance abuse and mental health services administration (SAMHSA). Key substance use and mental health indicators in the United States: Results from the 2016 National Survey on Drug Use and Health (HHS Publication No. SMA 17-5044, NSDUH Series H-52). Retrieved September 8, 2018 from www.samhsa.gov/data/sites/default/files/NSDUH-FFR1-2016/NSDUH-FFR1-2016.htm

Arnett, J. J. (2004). *Emerging adulthood: The winding road from the late teens through the twenties.* New York: Oxford University Press.

Baksheev, G. N., Allott, K., Jackson, H. J., McGorry, P. D., & Killackey, E. (2012). Predictors of vocational recovery among young people with first-episode psychosis: Findings from a randomized controlled trial. *Psychiatric Rehabilitation Journal, 35*(6), 421–427.

Blanco, C., Okuda, M., Wright, C., Hasin, D. S., Grant, B. F., Liu, S. M., & Olfson, M. (2008). Mental health of college students and their non–college-attending peers: Results from the national epidemiologic study on alcohol and related conditions. *Archives of General Psychiatry, 65*(12), 1429–1437.

Blank, R. (1997). *It takes a nation.* Princeton, NJ: Princeton University Press.

Bond, G., Drake, R., & Campbell, K. (2012). The effectiveness of the individual placement and support model of supported employment for young adults: Results from four randomized controlled trials. *Early Intervention in Psychiatry, 6*(Suppl. 1), 30.

Bond, G. R., Drake, R. E., & Becker, D. R. (2008). An update on randomized controlled trials of evidence-based supported employment. *Psychiatric Rehabilitation Journal, 31*(4), 280–290.

Breiner, K., Li, A., Cohen, A. O., Steinberg, L., Bonnie, R. J., Scott, E. S., … Galván, A. (2018). Combined effects of peer presence, social cues, and rewards on cognitive control in adolescents. *Developmental Psychobiology, 60*, 292–302. doi:10.1002/dev.21599

Bronfenbrenner, U., & Morris, P. (1998). The ecology of developmental processes. In R. M. Lerner (Ed.), *Theorectical models of human development* (5th ed., pp. 993–1028). New York: Wiley. Handbook of Child Psychology; Vol. 1.

76 *Kathryn Sabella et al.*

Brown, B. B. (2004). Adolescents' relationships with peers. *Handbook of Adolescent Psychology, 2*, 363–394.

Buckner, J. D., & Schmidt, N. B. (2009). A randomized pilot study of motivation enhancement therapy to increase utilization of cognitive-behavioral therapy for social anxiety. *Behaviour Research and Therapy, 47*(8), 710–715.

Bureau of Justice Statistics. (2006). Bureau of justice statistics special report: Mental health problems of prison and jail inmates. Office of Justice Programs. Retrieved October 23, 2018 from www.bjs.gov/content/pub/pdf/mhppji.pdf

Burns, B. J., Phillips, S. D., Wagner, H. R., Barth, R. P., Kolko, D. J., Campbell, Y., & Landsverk, J. (2004). Mental health need and access to mental health services by youths involved with child welfare: A national survey. *Journal of the American Academy of Child & Adolescent Psychiatry, 43*(8), 960–970.

Castro, A. L., Gustafson, E. L., Ford, A. E., Edidin, J. P., Smith, D. L., Hunter, S. J., & Karnik, N. S. (2014). Psychiatric disorders, high-risk behaviors, and chronicity of episodes among predominantly African American homeless Chicago youth. *Journal of Health Care for the Poor and Underserved, 25*(3), 1201.

Centers for Disease Control. (2018). Youth risk behavior survey: Data summary and trends report, 2007–2017. Retrieved September 8, 2018 from www.cdc.gov/healthyyouth/data/yrbs/pdf/trendsreport.pdf

Child Trends. (2017). Trends in youth employment. Retrieved October 22, 2018 from www.childtrends.org/indicators/youth-employment

Cohen, A. O., Breiner, K., Steinberg, L., Bonnie, R. J., Scott, E. S., Taylor-Thompson, K., … Casey, B. J. (2016). When is an adolescent an adult? Assessing cognitive control in emotional and nonemotional contexts. *Psychological Science, 27*(4), 549–562.

Collins, W. A., & Steinberg, L. (2006). Adolescent development in interpersonal context. In N. Eisenberg, W. Damon, &R. M. Lerner (Eds.), *Handbook of child psychology: Social, emotional, and personality development* (pp. 1003–1067). Hoboken, NJ: John Wiley & Sons Inc.

Cools, R. (2008). Role of dopamine in the motivational and cognitive control of behavior. *The Neuroscientist, 14*(4), 381–395.

Corcoran, M., & Matsudaira, J. (2005). Is it getting harder to get ahead? Economic attainment in early adulthood for two cohorts. In R. A. Setterson, Jr, F. K. Furstenberg, Jr, & R. G. Rumbaut (Eds.), *On the frontier of adulthood: Theory, research, and public policy* (pp. 356–395). Chicago, IL: The University of Chicago Press.

Craig, T., Garety, P., Power, P., Rahaman, N., Colbert, S., Fornells-Ambrojo, M., & Dunn, G. (2004). The Lambeth Early Onset (LEO) team: Randomised controlled trial of the effectiveness of specialized care for early psychosis. *British Medical Journal, 329*, 1067–1071.

Danziger, S., & Gottschalk, P. (1995). *America unequal.* New York: Russell Sage Foundation.

Davis, M., & Koroloff, N. (2006). The great divide: How public mental health policy fails young adults. In W. H. Fisher (Ed.), *Community based mental health services for children and adolescents* (Vol. 14, pp. 53–74). Oxford, UK: Elsevier Sciences.

Davis, M., Sheidow, A., McCart, M., & Perrault, R. (2018). Vocational coaches for justice-involved emerging adults. *Psychiatric Rehabilitation Journal, 41*(4), 266–276. doi:10.1037/prj0000323

Davis, M., Sheidow, A. J., & McCart, M. R. (2015). Reducing recidivism and symptoms in emerging adults with serious mental health conditions and justice system involvement. *Journal of Behavioral Health Services and Research, 42*(2), 172–190. doi:10.1007/s11414-014-9425-8

Davis, M., & Vander Stoep, A. (1997). The transition to adulthood among children and adolescents who have serious emotional disturbance part I: Developmental transitions. *Journal of Mental Health Administration, 24*(4), 400–427.

Dickerson, F., Boronow, J. J., Stallings, C., Origoni, A. E., Cole, S. K., & Yolken, R. H. (2004). Cognitive functioning in schizophrenia and bipolar disorder: Comparison of performance on the repeatable battery for the assessment of neuropsychological status. *Psychiatry Research, 129*(1), 45–53.

Durso, L. E., & Gates, G. J. (2012). *Serving our youth: Findings from a national survey of service providers working with lesbian, gay, bisexual, and transgender youth who are homeless or at risk of becoming homeless.* Los Angeles, CA: The Williams Institute with True Colors Fund and The Palette Fund. Rerieved from http://williamsinstitute.law.ucla.edu/wp-content/uploads/Durso-Gates-LGBT-Homeless-Youth-Survey-July-2012.pdf

Dworsky, A., Dillman, K. N., Dion, M. R., Coffee-Borden, B., & Rosenau, M. (2012). *Housing for youth aging out of foster care: A review of the literature and program typology.* United States Department of Housing and

Urban Development, Office of Policy Development and Research. Retrieved from www.huduser.gov/portal/publications/pdf/HousingFosterCare_LiteratureReview_0412_v2.pdf

Fernandez, E., Salem, D., Swift, J. K., & Ramtahal, N. (2015). Meta-analysis of dropout from cognitive behavioral therapy: Magnitude, timing, and moderators. *Journal of Consulting and Clinical Psychology*, *83*(6), 1108.

Frank, A. R. (1991). Transition of adolescents with behavioral disorders – Is it successful? *Behavioral Disorders*, *16*(3), 180–191.

Fussell, E., & Furstenberg, E. (2005). The transition to adulthood during the 20th century: Race, nativity and gender. In R. Settersten, F. Frustenberg, & R. Rumbaut (Eds.), *On the frontier of adulthood: Theory, research, and public policy* (pp. 29–75). Chicago, IL: The University of Chicago Press.

Fuster, J. M. (2002). Frontal lobe and cognitive development. *Journal of Neurocytology*, *31*(3–5), 373–385.

Fuster, J. M. (2008). *The prefrontal cortex* (4th ed.). Oxford, UK: Elsevier Ltd.

Geenan, S., Powers, L. E., Phillips, L. A., Nelson, M., McKenna, J., Winges-Yanez, N., ... Swank, P. (2015). Better futures: A randomized field test of a model for supporting young people in foster care with mental health challenges to participate in higher education. *The Journal of Behavioral Health Services and Research*, *42*(2), 150–171.

Gold, J. M., & Harvey, P. D. (1993). Cognitive deficits in schizophrenia. *Psychiatric Clinics North America*, *16*(2), 295–312.

Government Accountability Office (GAO), U.S. (2008). *Young adults with serious mental illness: Some states and federal agencies are taking steps to address their transition challenges*. No. 08–678. Washington, DC: GAO Publication.

Green, M. F., Kern, R. S., & Heaton, R. K. (2004). Longitudinal studies of cognition and functional outcome in schizophrenia: Implications for MATRICS. *Schizophrenia Research*, *72*(1), 41–51.

Greimel, E., Nehrkorn, B., Schulte-Rüther, M., Fink, G. R., Nickl-Jockschat, T., Herpertz-Dahlmann, B., ... Eickhoff, S. B. (2013). Changes in grey matter development in autism spectrum disorder. *Brain Structure and Function*, *218*(4), 929–942.

Grote, N. K., Swartz, H. A., Geibel, S. L., Zuckoff, A., Houck, P. R., & Frank, E. (2009). A randomized controlled trial of culturally relevant, brief interpersonal psychotherapy for perinatal depression. *Psychiatric Services*, *60*(3), 313–321.

Headspace National Youth Mental Health Foundation (Australia). (2018). Gender identity and mental health. Retrieved September 8, 2018 from www.headspace.org.au/young-people/gender-identity-and-mental-health/

Henggeler, S. W., Schoenwald, S. K., Borduin, C. M., Rowland, M. D., & Cunningham, P. E. (1998). *Mulstisystemic treatment of antisocial behavior in children and adolescents*. New York, NY: Guilford Press.

Howell, E. M. (2004). Access to children's mental health services under Medicaid and SCHIP. Urban Institute. Retrieved 1/26/2020 from www.urban.org/sites/default/files/publication/57751/311053-Access-to-Children-s-Mental-Health-Services-under-Medicaid-and-SCHIP.PDF.

Hutton, S. B., Puri, B. K., Duncan, L. J., Robbins, T. W., Barnes, T. R. E., & Joyce, E. M. (1998). Executive function in first-episode schizophrenia. *Psychological Medicine*, *28*(2), 463–473.

Institute of Medicine and National Research Council. (2015). *Investing in the health and well-being of young adults*. Washington, DC: The National Academies Press. doi:10.17226/18869

Johnson-Selfridge, M., & Zalewski, C. (2001). Moderator variables of executive functioning in schizophrenia: Meta-analytic findings. *Schizophrenia Bulletin*, *27*(2), 305–316. doi:10.1093/oxfordjournals.schbul.a006876

Kane, J. M., Robinson, D. G., Schooler, N. R., Mueser, K. T., Penn, D. L., Rosenheck, R. A., ... Heinssen, R. K. (2016). Comprehensive versus usual community care for first-episode psychosis: 2-year outcomes from the NIMH RAISE early treatment program. *The American Journal of Psychiatry*, *173*, 362–372. doi:10.1176/appi.ajp

Karpel, M., & Strauss, E. (1983). *Family evaluation*. New York: Gardner Press.

Kessler, R. C., Berglund, P., Demler, O., Jin, R., Merikangas, K. R., & Walters, E. E. (2005). Lifetime prevalence and age-of-onset distributions of DSM-IV disorders in the National Comorbidity Survey Replication. *Archives of General Psychiatry*, *62*(6), 593–602.

78 *Kathryn Sabella et al.*

Killackey, E., Jackson, H. J., & McGorry, P. D. (2008). Vocational intervention in first- episode psychosis: Individual placement and support v. treatment as usual. *The British Journal of Psychiatry, 193*(2), 114–120.

Klodnick, V. V., Sabella, K., Brenner, C. J., Krzos, I. M., Ellison, M. L., Kaiser, S. M., … Fagan, M. A. (2015). Perspectives of young emerging adults with serious mental health conditions on vocational peer mentors. *Journal of Emotional and Behavioral Disorders, 23*(4), 226–237.

Knapp, M., Patel, A., Curran, C., Latimer, E., Catty, J., Becker, T., & Lauber, C. (2013). Supported employment: Cost effectiveness across six European sites. *World Psychiatry, 12*(1), 60–68.

Levy, F. (1998). *The new dollars and dreams.* New York: Russell Sage Foundation.

Luna, B. (2009). Developmental changes in cognitive control through adolescence. *Advances in Child Development and behavior, 37*, 233–278.

Mahoney, J. L., Larson, R. W., Eccles, J. S., & Lord, H. (2005). Organized activities as developmental contexts for children and adolescents. In J. L. Mahoney, R. W. Larson, & J. S. Eccles (Eds.), *Organized activities as contexts of development: Extracurricular activities, after-school and community programs* (pp. 3–22). Mahwah, NJ: Lawrence Erlbaum Associates, Inc.

Martin, J., Hamilton, B., Osterman, M., Curin, S., & Matthews, T. J. (2013). *Births: Final data for 2012.* Washington, DC: Department of Health and Human Services.

Mathews, T. J., & Hamilton, B. E. (2009). Delayed childbearing: More women are having their first child later in life. *NCHS Data Brief, 21*, 1–8.

McMillen, J. C., Zima, B. T., Scott, L. D., Auslander, W. F., Munson, M. R., Ollie, M. T., & Spitznagel, E. L. (2005). Prevalence of psychiatric disorders among older youths in the foster care system. *Journal of the American Academy of Child & Adolescent Psychiatry, 44*(1), 88–95.

Monti, P. M., Barnett, N. P., Colby, S. M., Gwaltney, C. J., Spirito, A., Rohsenow, D. J., & Woolard, R. (2007). Motivational interviewing versus feedback only in emergency care for young adult problem drinking. *Addiction, 102*, 1234–1243. doi:10.1111/j.1360-0443.2007.01878.x

Mortimer, J. T., Zimmer-Gembeck, M. J., Holmes, M., & Shanahan, M. J. (2002). The process of occupational decision making: Patterns during the transition to adulthood. *Journal of Vocational Behavior, 61*, 439–465.

Munson, M. R., Cole, A., Jaccard, J., Kranke, D., Farkas, K., & Frese, F. J. (2016a). An engagement intervention for young adults with serious mental health conditions. *The Journal of Behavioral Health Services & Research, 43*(4), 542–563.

Munson, M. R., Cole, A., Stanhope, V., Marcus, S. C., McKay, M., Jaccard, J., & Ben-David, S. (2016b). Cornerstone program for transition-age youth with serious mental illness: Study protocol for a randomized controlled trial. *Trials, 17*(1), 537.

Murphy, J. G., Dennhardt, A. A., Skidmore, J. R., Borsari, B., Barnett, N. P., Colby, S. M., & Martens, M. P. (2012). A randomized controlled trial of a behavioral economic supplement to brief motivational interventions for college drinking. *Journal of Consulting and Clinical Psychology, 80*, 876–886. doi:10.1037/a0028763

Naar-King, S., & Suarez, M. (2011). *Motivational interviewing with adolescents and young adults.* New York: Guilford Press.

National Center for Education Statistics. (2014). *Digest of education statistics: 2014.* Institute of Education Sciences. Retrieved October 22, 2018 from https://nces.ed.gov/programs/digest/d14/ch_3.asp

Newman, L., Wagner, M., Knokey, A. M., Marder, C., Nagle, K., Shaver, D., … Schwarting, M. (2011). *The post-high school outcomes of young adults with disabilities up to 8 years after high school.* A Report from the National Longitudinal Transition Study-2 (NLTS2) (NCSER 2011-3005). Menlo Park, CA: SRI International.

Norman, R., Merchana, R., Malla, A., Windell, D., Harricharan, R., & Northcott, S. (2011). Symptom and functional recovery outcomes for a 5 year early intervention program for psychosis. *Schizophrenia Research, 129*(2–3), 111–115.

Nuechterlein, K. H., Subotnik, K. L., Green, M. F., Ventura, J., Asarnow, R. F., Gitlin, M. J., … Mintz, J. (2011). Neurocognitive predictors of work outcome in recent-onset schizophrenia. *Schizophrenia Bulletin, 37*(Suppl_2), S33–S40.

Nuechterlein, K. H., Subotnik, K. L., Turner, L. R., Ventura, J., Becker, D. R., & Drake, R. E. (2008). Individual placement and support for individuals with recent-onset schizophrenia: Integrating supported education and supported employment. *Psychiatric Rehabilitation Journal, 31*(4), 340–349.

Olfson, M., Mojtabai, R., Sampson, N. A., Hwang, I., Druss, B., Wang, P. S., ... Kessler, R. C. (2009). Dropout from outpatient mental health care in the United States. *Psychiatric Services, 60*(7), 898–907.

Patel, V., Flisher, A. J., Hetrick, S., & McGorry, P. (2007). Mental health of young people: A global public-health challenge. *Lancet, 369*(9569), 1302–1313.

Payne, K. K. (2011). FP-11-08 on the road to adulthood: Forming families. National Center for Family and Marriage Research Family Profiles, 12. Retrieved January 26, 2020 from https://scholarworks.bgsu.edu/ncfmr_family_profiles/12

Petersen, L., Jeppesen, P., Thorup, A., Abel, M. B., Øhlenschlæger, J., Christensen, T. Ø., ... Nordentoft, M. (2005). A randomized multicenter trial of integrated versus standard treatment for patients with a first episode of psychotic illness. *British Medical Journal, 331*, 602–608.

Pew Research Center. (2017). *Fact tank news in the numbers: It's becoming more common for young adults to live at home – And for longer stretches.* Pew Research Center. Retrieved October 23, 18 from http://pewrsr.ch/2pdI0mq

Radigan, M., Wang, R., Chen, Y., & Xiang, J. (2014). Youth and caregiver access to peer advocates and satisfaction with mental health services. *Community Mental Health Journal, 50*(8), 915–921.

Raznahan, A., Shaw, P. W., Lerch, J. P., Clasen, L. S., Greenstein, D., Berman, R., ... Giedd, J. N. (2014). Longitudinal four-dimensional mapping of subcortical anatomy in human development. *Proceedings of the National Academy of Sciences of the United States of America, 111*(4), 1592–1597.

Salzer, M. S., Wick, L. C., & Rogers, J. A. (2008). Familiarity with and use of accommodations and supports among postsecondary students with mental illnesses. *Psychiatric Services, 59*(4), 370–375.

Scherf, K. S., Smyth, J. M., & Delgado, M. R. (2013). The amygdala: An agent of change in adolescent neural networks. *Hormones and Behavior, 64*(2), 298–313.

Schilling, E. A., Aseltine, R. H., & Gore, S. (2007). Adverse childhood experiences and mental health in young adults: A longitudinal survey. *BMC Public Health, 7*, 30–40.

Schoeni, R. F., & Ross, K. E. (2005). Material assistance from families during the transition to adulthood. In R. A. Settersten, Jr., F. K. Furstenberg, Jr, & R. G. Rumbaut (Eds.), *On the frontier of adulthood: Theory, research, and public policy* (pp. 396–453). Chicago, IL: The University of Chicago Press.

Schulenberg, J., & Schoon, I. (2012). The transition to adulthood across time and space: Overview of special section. *Longitudinal and Life Course Studies, 3*(2), 164.

Scott, E. S., & Steinberg, L. (2008). Adolescent development and the regulation of youth crime. *The Future of Children, 18*(2), 15–33.

Settersten, R. A., Jr., Frustenberg, F. F., & Rumbaut, R. G. (Eds.). (2005). *On the frontier of adulthood: Theory, research, and public policy.* Chicago, IL: The University of Chicago Press.

Shanahan, M. J. (2000). Pathways to adulthood in changing societies: Variability and mechanisms in life course perspective. *Annual Review of Sociology, 26*(1), 667–692.

Skehan, B., & Davis, M. (2017). Aligning mental health treatments with the developmental stage and needs of late adolescents and young adults. *Child and Adolescent Psychiatric Clinics, 26*(2), 177–190.

Sowell, E. R., Thompson, P. M., Holmes, C. J., Jernigan, T. L., & Toga, A. W. (1999). In vivo evidence for post-adolescent brain maturation in frontal and striatal regions. *Nature Neuroscience, 2*(10), 859–861.

Steinberg, L. (2013). *Psychological development in young adulthood.* Presentation at IOM/NRC Workshop on Improving the Health, Safety, and Well-Being of Young Adults, Washington, DC.

Steinberg, L., Chung, H. L., & Little, M. (2004). Reentry of young offenders from the justice system: A developmental perspective. *Youth Violence and Juvenile Justice, 2*(1), 21–38.

Steinberg, L., Icenogle, G., Shulman, E. P., Breiner, K., Chein, J., Bacchini, D., ... Takash, H. M. S. (2018). Around the world, adolescence is a time of heightened sensation seeking and immature self-regulation. *Developmental Science, 21*(2), e12532.

Substance Abuse and Mental Health Services Administration. (2010). *1 in 7 Hispanic/Latino young adults experienced serious psychological distress in the past year* [Press Release]. Retrieved September 8, 2018 from www.samhsa.gov/newsroom/press-announcements/201007080245-1

Substance Abuse and Mental Health Services Administration. (2016a). *The CBHSQ report: Serious mental illness among adults below the poverty line*. Results from the 2013 National Survey on Drug Use and Health: Summary of National Findings, NSDUH Series H-48, HHS Publication No. (SMA) 14-4863. Rockville, MD: Substance Abuse and Mental Health Services Administration. Retrieved September 31, 2018 from www.samhsa.gov/data/sites/default/files/report_2720/Spotlight-2720.html

Substance Abuse and Mental Health Services Administration. (2016b). *2016 NSDUH: Race and ethnicity summary sheets*. Rockville, MD: Substance Abuse and Mental Health Services Administration. Retrieved September 31, 2018 from www.samhsa.gov/data/report/2016-nsduh-race-and-ethnicity-summary-sheets

Swift, J. K., & Greenberg, R. P. (2012). Premature discontinuation in adult psychotherapy: A meta-analysis. *Journal of Consulting and Clinical Psychology, 80*(4), 547.

Transitions ACR. (2019, April 23–24). Navigating the ups and downs to caps and gowns: Creating a path to academic success for college students with mental health conditions. In *NARRTC Conference*. Retrieved August 5, 2019 from https://umassmed.edu/contentassets/7cf9562c1c6141be81839c97e43e7f3d/2019-narrtc/final_narrtc-slides-for-pass_6.4.19.pdf

Twenge, J. M., Cooper, A. B., Joiner, T. E., Duffy, M. E., & Binau, S. G. (2019). Age, period, and cohort trends in mood disorder indicators and suicide-related outcomes in a nationally representative dataset, 2005–2017. *Journal of Abnormal Psychology, 128*(3), 185–199.

U.S. Department of Education, Office of Special Education and Rehabilitative Science. Office of Special Education Programs. (2017). 39th annual report to congress on the implementation of the individuals with disabilities education act, 2017. Retrieved from www2.ed.gov/about/reports/annual/osep/2017/parts-b-c/39th-arc-for-idea.pdf

Vander Stoep, A., Beresford, S. A. A., Weiss, N. S., McKnight, B., Cauce, A. M., & Cohen, P. (2000). Community-based study of the transition to adulthood for adolescents with psychiatric disorder. *American Journal of Epidemiology, 152*(4), 352–362.

Waghorn, G., Chant, D., & Harris, M. G. (2009). The stability of correlates of labour force activity. *Acta Psychiatrica Scandinavica, 119*(5), 393–405.

Walker, J. S., & Gowen, L. K. (2011). *Community-based approaches for supporting positive development in youth and young adults with serious mental health conditions*. Portland, OR: Research and Training Center for Pathways to Positive Futures, Portland State University.

Walker, J. S., Seibel, C. L., & Jackson, S. (2017). Increasing youths' participation in team-based treatment planning: The achieve my plan enhancement for wraparound. *Journal of Child and Family Studies, 26*(8), 2090–2100.

Wierenga, L., Langen, M., Ambrosino, S., van Dijk, S., Oranje, B., & Durston, S. (2014). Typical development of basal ganglia, hippocampus, amygdala and cerebellum from age 7 to 24. *NeuroImage, 96*, 67–72.

Part 2

Targeting Social Processes and Environmental Ecologies

6 Interaction-Centered Model of Language and Behavioral Development

Jason C. Chow, Jennifer E. Cunningham, and Erin Stehle Wallace

Language is a central skill to success in educational and social environments. It has been well established that children's language skills when they enter formal schooling predict academic achievement and social development in school (Chow, Ekholm, & Coleman, 2018; Duncan et al., 2007). Further, language ability remains relatively stable over the course of development (Bornstein, Hahn, Putnick, & Pearson, 2018), and unfortunately children who have delayed language skills are at substantially higher risk of facing lifelong challenges. For example, children who are diagnosed with language impairments in school face substantial vocational barriers when they enter the workforce (Conti-Ramsden, Durkin, Toseeb, Botting, & Pickles, 2018), and these individuals are more likely to report higher alcohol use, have contact with law enforcement, and exhibit aggressive behavior (Winstanley, Webb, & Conti-Ramsden, 2018). Thus, a concerted effort aimed at preventing these long-term and pervasive consequences that stem from early language difficulty is a public health issue. Fortunately, there are several language-based classroom practices that are linked to improvements in classroom behavior as well as general language skills and overall achievement. In this chapter, we (1) review the current literature on the associations between language skills and problem behavior and how behavior problems interfere with classroom success, (2) present a model that outlines key preventative mechanisms aimed at the prevention and remediation of language delays and challenging classroom behavior, and (3) discuss implications and recommendations for research and current practice.

Associations between Language Skills and Behavior Problems

It is well-established that language ability significantly predicts later behavioral functioning. More specifically, delays in early language ability predict later externalizing and internalizing behavior problems, attention problems, and social anxiety, as well as children's mental health trajectories (Bao, Brownlie, & Beitchman, 2016; Brownlie, Bao, & Beitchman, 2016; Chow, 2018; Law, Rush, Clegg, Peters, & Roulstone, 2015; Petersen et al., 2013). Given that the mental health of children and youth in our nation is a priority, a focus on the adverse effects of delayed language skills on social and behavioral functioning is timely (Law & Levickis, 2018). To effectively educate and support the academic and social-emotional development of all children in classrooms, specific attention to practices teachers can use to support children and youth who are at high risk for poor outcomes must receive increased attention.

There is a growing body of literature that has identified language and communicative ability as an important factor in the development of maladaptive classroom behavior (Chow & Wehby, 2018; Yew & O'Kearney, 2013). Children with emotional and behavioral disorders (EBD) often present low and clinically significant language performance (Benner, Nelson, &

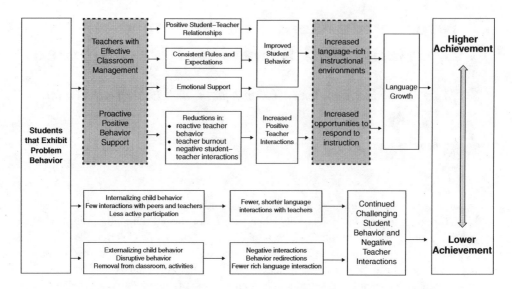

Figure 6.1 Interaction-centered model of language and behavioral development

Epstein, 2002; Chow & Hollo, 2018; Chow & Wehby, 2017), and these language deficits are often under-identified (Hollo, Wehby, & Oliver, 2014), which carries important implications for researchers and practitioners alike. If children with EBD who also have clinically significant language problems are regularly going through school without their problems addressed, it is likely that their educational performance will continue to suffer regardless of the success of behavioral interventions.

Researchers argue that the relation between behavior and language is likely reciprocal in nature, in that children who have delayed language are more likely to exhibit problem behaviors with peers and adults because of their limited ability to express emotions and regulate their environment using appropriate communication (Rescorla, Ross, & McClure, 2007; Roben, Cole, & Armstrong, 2013). These behaviors may influence children's interactions with their teachers in a way that limits their exposure to complex language as well as opportunities to practice and use more complex language themselves (Hollo & Chow, 2015; Qi, Kaiser, Milan, & Hancock, 2006).

Teacher Language-Based Practices

The theoretical model presented in Figure 6.1 represents (1) the pathway by which problem behavior in the classroom negatively impacts achievement (bottom panel) and (2) the mechanisms by which teacher practices could ameliorate this negative relationship in the classroom (top panel). In this model, effective classroom management and proactive positive behavior support provide an environment that allows teachers to increase the language-rich environments and opportunities to respond to instruction for their students. Following Chow et al. (2018), we situate this integrative model within an ecological-transactional framework to contextualize our understanding of how language skills and problematic classroom behavior interact with each other within dynamic educational environments. The ecological model (Bronfenbrenner, 1994) views child development within a set of interrelated systems which are inseparable from learning and social-emotional development (Burns, Warmbold-Brann, & Zaslofsky, 2015; Chow & Wehby, 2018; Sutherland, Conroy, Abrams, & Vo, 2010). The transactional model (Sameroff, 2009) describes how language and communication skills may influence how children behave specific to both the interactions and the relationships they have with their teachers. The ecological-transactional framework emphasizes the dynamic relations between language skills and classroom behavior that highlights both the unique dyadic relationships and interactions individual students have with their teachers, and the integrated, nested systems of classroom learning environments. That is, the unique transactions that comprise individual teacher–student relationships may influence the overall ecology of the classroom, particularly in relationships where conflict, negative interactions, and problem behavior are present.

Why Does Problematic Behavior Interfere with Classroom Success?

Problem behavior interferes with student learning and these problem behaviors may influence the ways teachers interact with children in the classroom. Subsequently, teacher–child interactions may influence the rate of language learning in the preschool years, which ultimately impacts later academic engagement and achievement (Pentimonti et al., 2017; Perry, VandeKamp, Mercer, & Nordby, 2002). Problem behavior in the classroom can be broadly categorized as either internalizing or externalizing behaviors. Children with internalizing behavior problems are more likely to be anxious and withdrawn from social situations with peers and adults, whereas children with externalizing behaviors are more likely to exhibit aggressive behaviors towards others (Baker, Grant, & Morlock, 2008). Both internalizing and externalizing problem behaviors negatively impact a student's ability to succeed, but they are associated with different types of language deficits (Hollo, Chow, & Wehby, 2018) and their expression may have differential influence on a child's interactions with their teachers. To illustrate, the topography of problem behavior a child exhibits differentially influences the type of interactions with adults and peers in the classroom. For example, because children who have internalizing problems are more withdrawn or anxious, they may be less likely to initiate to peers and adults and participate actively in the classroom (Hymel, Rubin, Rowden, & LeMare, 1990). Conversely, children with externalizing, disruptive classroom behaviors may be more likely to engage in negative interactions with others in the classroom (Shores et al., 1993). In turn, the manifestations of each of these types of problem behavior is predicted to change the quantity and quality of language interactions (Qi et al., 2006). Within our model, both types of problem behavior in classrooms are likely to reduce the amount of high quality language that the child is exposed to and has the opportunity to practice, which ultimately decelerates language growth.

Mechanisms to Prevent Problem Behavior and Improve Achievement

The top panel of the model emphasizes two malleable dimensions of teacher practice that, in conjunction, promote positive behavior and language development: (1) effective classroom management, and (2) language-rich instructional environments. Moreover, the active integration of these dimensions can lead to reciprocal improvement and maximize the delivery and impact of language-rich instructional practices. While children who present persistent problem behaviors in the classroom also struggle with language and communication, there are some promising language and literacy practices that may support the improvement of classroom behavior as well as language growth. In theory, improving early language skills will not only improve later literacy skills, but may have the potential to alter the trajectory of maladaptive behavioral development, given that higher language skills predict concurrent and future behavior (Chow et al., 2018). Therefore, our model emphasizes that a direct relation between the amount of high quality language and communication directed at or involving an individual child will be significantly predictive of that child's growth in language, and in turn, their academic performance.

Effective Classroom Management

We argue that effective classroom management helps to "set the stage" for positive child–teacher relationships, and a higher dosage of language learning opportunities within ongoing classroom activities and conversations. Proactive positive behavior support is preventive in nature, consistent and predictable, and framed in a positive manner. Features of classrooms with effective management practices in place include (a) positive behavioral expectations that are explicitly taught and modeled; (b) consistent and specific positive feedback for prosocial behavior and meeting behavior expectations; (c) organization of physical and temporal classroom environment to maximize engagement and increase independence; (d) explicit instruction on important prosocial skills to foster emotional regulation, friendship, and independent social problem solving; and (e) individualized supports for children with persistent problem behavior (Hemmeter, Fox, Jack, & Broyles, 2007; Hemmeter, Ostrosky, & Fox, 2006). These features are designed and can be tailored to support children's engagement and on-task behavior, independence, and social-emotional competence.

By employing effective classroom management practices, teachers can dedicate less of their time to responding to problem behavior, redirecting, and re-engaging children, and more time forming positive relationships and engaging in play and conversation with children. That is, teacher–child interactions that are primarily focused on the behavior problems of a child are less likely to include the types of conversational and instructional interactions that foster language development. Positive teacher–child interactions are also essential, as children with lower language skills exhibit higher rates of problem behavior in classrooms where teachers provide lower levels of emotional support (Qi, Zieher, Lee Van Horn, Bulotsky-Shearer, & Carta, 2019). Without effective classroom management practices in place to support child behavior and engagement, a teachers' ability to leverage naturally occurring opportunities and conversations throughout the day as opportunities to teach and model language may be limited.

Because classroom management is a top concern for practicing teachers (Greenberg, Putman, & Walsh, 2014), classroom management strategies are an important skill for teachers to master because they positively and preventatively support appropriate behavior, influence teacher–child relationships, and promote positive academic and social outcomes (Chow & Gilmour, 2016; Maggin, Pustejovsky, & Johnson, 2017; Simonsen, Fairbanks, Briesch, Myers, & Sugai, 2008). Thus, effective classroom management is central to our model, and can provide the necessary setting to effectively integrate supplemental language-rich interactions and practices into children's daily learning environments.

Language-rich Instructional Environments

Classroom management and behavior support practices that foster engagement and positive teacher–child relationships serve as an important foundation for learning; however, these practices alone are not sufficient to support child language development. Paired with systematic and intentional language practices, the strategies outlined in the previous section can be leveraged to maximize child outcomes, and further support engagement and relationships. More specifically, the use of high-quality language support strategies can facilitate conversations and interactions between teachers and children that are positive, engaging, and capitalize on child interests, which could act to foster positive relationships. The use of such strategies can enhance children's skill and confidence in communication with others, which can bolster their ability to more successfully navigate the classroom environment in their interactions with peers and adults.

Positive teacher–child relationships marked by closeness and warm affect play a key role in children's overall development (Sabol & Pianta, 2012). There is evidence that teacher–child relationships in early elementary school are strongly tied to both academic and social-emotional and behavioral outcomes in children, and that the quality of those early relationships is predictive of future outcomes extending into middle school (Hamre & Pianta, 2010). Specifically, teacher–child relationships characterized as negative and marked by conflict were a significant predictor of poorer academic achievement and behavioral outcomes (Hamre & Pianta, 2001); whereas positive, close teacher–child relationships are predictive of stronger social skills and fewer reports of challenging behavior (Pianta, Steinberg, & Rollins, 1995). Teacher–child relationships can also be viewed as a potential protective mechanism, which can ameliorate the effects of other factors that place children at risk for delayed social, behavioral, and even academic growth (Sabol & Pianta, 2012). Relationships are built through positive, child-focused interactions between teachers and children in the classroom (Sabol & Pianta, 2012), and these relationships predict child behavior – particularly for younger children (Lei, Cui, & Chiu, 2016).

Communication and interaction-based strategies

In a recent analysis of the dimensions of the language learning environment in preschool classrooms, Justice and colleagues (2018) reported that teacher communication facilitating behaviors were the strongest predictor of child vocabulary development. In this study, the communication facilitation behaviors analyzed included (1) warm affect and looking expectantly to encourage conversation; (2) maintaining a slow pace to give children time to participate; (3) eliciting child contributions and extending conversations using open-ended questions; and (4) encouraging and supporting talk among peers (Justice, Jiang, & Strasser, 2018). Because delayed vocabulary is associated with the development of problem behaviors (Chow & Wehby, 2018; Henrichs et al., 2013), increased use of teacher communication facilitating behaviors that increase child vocabulary is likely to support not only language development but also reductions in behavior problems.

Researchers have repeatedly demonstrated that one of the most important behaviors adults can do to facilitate language growth is to *respond contingently* to children's vocal initiations (Hoff & Naigles, 2002; Tamis-Lemonda, 2002). Teachers' responsiveness to children's initiations contributes to their language learning in early care and education environments in their early childhood years (Cabell, Justice, McGinty, DeCoster, & Forston, 2015; Giralometto & Weitzman, 2002). This interaction between teachers and children is of particular importance because vocabulary growth is associated with positive developmental trajectories of behavior (Westrupp et al., 2019). Another important consideration in facilitating quality conversations in the classroom is the provision of wait time, to allow children to be active participants. Particularly after being asked a question, it is key to for the teacher to pause and allow children to think and provide a response before following up immediately with a follow-up question or comment (Hindman, Wasik, & Bradley, 2019; Wasik & Hindman, 2018). Provision of wait time can have positive impacts on child contributions to conversations, and thus increase opportunities to practice and receive feedback on language use (Hanna, 1977; Wasik & Hindman, 2018).

The evidence supporting these communication and interaction based strategies highlights the importance of creating a context in which teachers and children can engage in extended, back and forth positive and productive exchanges. These exchanges afford children the opportunity to be exposed to adult models of more complex language, and provide teachers with the opportunity to use strategies (described below) to elicit language from children. This feedback loop that occurs between adults and children during ongoing conversations is key to language development (Adamson, Kaiser, Tamis-LaMonda, Owen, & Dimitrova, 2019), and thus these foundational strategies for encouraging children to be active participants in conversations are essential to facilitating language in the classroom. Because the association between conversation and children's vocabulary development is well established (Cabell et al., 2015), engaging in conversations with teachers provides young children the opportunity to learn novel words and thus, expand their vocabulary (Christ & Wang, 2010). Furthermore, early childhood teachers who engaged in more multi-turn and child-initiated conversations with children provided significantly more opportunities for their children to practice semantically contingent talk, which may play a critical role in increasing children's vocabulary learning (Cabell et al., 2015). Children who engage in conversations are more likely to increase in their vocabulary because they are provided the opportunity to learn and use novel words. Increasing child language production through language-rich interactions not only provides children with more exposure to language modeling, but it reduces the opportunities for children to engage in behavior problems.

Linguistic input

Not only is global responsiveness to child communication important for language growth, *how* adults respond is important as well. Responses that contain semantically related information or an expansion of a child's utterance are associated with positive child language gains (Wasik, Bond, & Hindman, 2006; Wasik & Hindman, 2011). Expansions and recasts of child language are components of several evidence-based language and communication interventions (Camarata, Nelson, & Camarata, 1994; Cleave, Becker, Curran, Van Horne, & Fey, 2015; Nelson, Camarata, Welsh, Butkovsky, & Camarata, 1996; Roberts & Kaiser, 2015). The vocabulary and sentence structures that adults model for children are essential components of high quality language interactions (Hart & Risley, 1995; Hoff, 2003; Huttenlocher, Vasilyeva, Cymerman, & Levine, 2002). Adults who model diverse vocabulary and complex sentence structures have a more positive impact on child language development (Hoff, 2003; Ruston & Schwanenflugel, 2010). For example, Hadley and colleagues (2016) reported that the diversity of parents' noun phrase subjects used in conversations during play was a strong predictor of children's sentence diversity. Syntax development is strongly tied to children's academic achievement and reading ability (Catts, Fey, Zhang, Tomblin, 2001) and children's exposure to adult input that includes models of complex syntax is predictive of growth in child language development (Huttenlocher et al., 2002).

These relations between adult input and child language are not only noted in the growth of child language skills over time, but also within conversational and instructional interactions. Justice, McGinty, Zucker, Cabell, and Piasta (2013) reported that within teacher–child interactions, children's utterances were more likely to be syntactically complex immediately following a teacher utterance that contained complex syntax. This relation was found to be bi-directional, such that instances of teachers use of complex syntax was more likely to occur following a child utterance that contained complex syntax. These findings support the assertion that it is not just the nature of the linguistic input, but also the dyadic and dynamic interactions between adults and children that facilitate language growth (Chow et al., 2018; Justice et al., 2013). This is particularly important in the context of an interaction-centered model of language and behavioral development, as language interactions and behavioral interactions both provide opportunities to support positive, productive child outcomes in both domains. Thus, one way to enhance child language growth and comprehension can be to respond to child initiations with comments and extensions that add syntactic or semantic complexity. Caregiver use of inferential language has also been found to influence growth in comprehension as well as vocabulary outcomes in children, and child-directed speech predicts vocabulary development (Golinkoff, Can, Soderstrom, & Hirsh-Pasek, 2015; Hindman et al., 2008; Rowe, 2008). Teachers' language may play similar supportive roles in child language development in the classroom. Using such strategies supports teachers and children in engaging in longer exchanges, which can act as important feedback loops and opportunities to model complex language that is linked to the child's interests and focus. As teachers provide more opportunities for children to engage in language interactions, they reduce the opportunities for children with EBD to disengage from instruction. This is important, as language skills predict general engagement in students with EBD, and providing more opportunities to actively respond to teacher instruction buffers the negative impacts low language skills have on the classroom performance of children with EBD (Chow & Wehby, 2017).

Elicitation of child language

Finally, in creating a high quality language environment in the classroom, teachers must consider not only what they model in conversations, but what strategies they can use to elicit child language to provide opportunities for children to practice essential language skills. An important strategy for extending conversations and eliciting child language is the use of open-ended questions, in which children are expected to respond with answers more complex than a single word or a yes/no response (Wasik & Hindman, 2013, 2018). By using strategies that elicit language from children, teachers can engage children in longer conversations in which they have increased opportunities to respond to child language with feedback and models of increasingly complex and sophisticated language.

Teachers must also have strategies for engaging children in complex thought and language use during instructional activities, in a way that is sensitive to individual child needs (Pentimonti et al., 2017). In their analysis of early childhood teachers' use of scaffolding strategies during language and literacy lessons, Pentimonti and colleagues reported that teachers' use of three scaffolding strategies were predictive of child vocabulary gains: (1) generalizing (asking children to connect the instructional content to other experiences outside the current context); (2) reasoning (asking children to explain why something happened); and (3) predicting (asking children to predict an outcome). The use of such strategies can support longer conversational exchanges, as well as providing opportunity to model and elicit inferential or decontextualized language. In conversations with children in the classroom, teachers should consider how to balance literal talk (labeling, describing, etc.) and inferential

90 *Jason C. Chow et al.*

talk (synthesizing, predicting, hypothesizing), both in the language they model, and in the types of questions and scaffolds they use to elicit child language (Sembiante, Dynia, Kaderavek, & Justice, 2017).

The use of these strategies provides conversational support for children, which increases the likelihood of multi-turn conversations occurring (Pentimonti et al., 2017). The more conversations that occur, the more exposure children have to complex language, diversity of vocabulary, and novel words, which can improve vocabulary development and oral language which are both associated with higher academic engagement and lower rates of aggression in children with EBD (Chow & Wehby, 2017).

Next Steps for Research

We acknowledge much of the language practices research to date has been conducted in early childhood classrooms, while research in the area of EBD has focused more on school-age children. Future research should prospectively examine the nature of the co-development and support of language and behavior across multiple age bands including preschool- and school-age populations. Future research should examine the role that individual child characteristics and teachers' perceptions of child skill play in predicting the provision of language support to individual children. This research should specifically target children with or at risk for EBD, as much of the current literature focuses on children with or at risk for language delays. Based on the theoretical model presented in this chapter, we hypothesize that children who exhibit internalizing and externalizing behavior problems are less likely to participate in and benefit from frequent, quality language interactions, as compared to their typically developing peers who exhibit appropriate on-task behavior. Understanding how teachers differentially distribute their language support across children may be another critical piece in understanding the lack of child effects found in many language-focused professional development interventions, particularly in classrooms serving children from low-income backgrounds where the prevalence of delays in language and prosocial development may be high (Qi & Kaiser, 2004). This information could not only inform our understanding of the underlying mechanism of the relationship between challenging behavior and decelerated achievement, but also support the development of professional development models that emphasize differential language facilitation strategies based on learner profiles. Tailoring an intervention in ways that support teachers in identifying child learner characteristics could help to maximize the effects of professional development models, and empower teachers to provide differentiated instruction to all learners in their classroom.

The field must also pay careful attention to the measurement of language and behavior. This is essential for research, because measure selection has a direct influence on how consumers interpret intervention effectiveness. Proximal measures that are aligned with intervention are known to be associated with larger effect sizes than those of more distal measures (Cheung & Slavin, 2016; Hill, Bloom, Black, & Lipsey, 2008; Taylor et al., 2018). We recommend careful, prospective measure selection relative to the purposes of the study design and included outcome constructs. This may be particularly important in language and behavior research, because teachers of children with EBD underestimate their students' language skills (Chow & Hollo, 2018). Further, child language skills predict directly observed behavior problems in classrooms, but they do not predict teacher ratings of the same behaviors (Chow & Wehby, 2017). While this example presents discrepancies between teacher ratings and direct assessment (of both language and behavior), additional facets of concern include but are not limited to those involving rater (parent, teacher, peer), measure characteristics (e.g., alignment with intervention, norm-referenced), reliability, and appropriateness for the study sample.

We also must consider the ways in which we measure the language learning opportunities of individual children in the classroom, including interactions with peers, teachers, observational learning, and engagement in academic tasks and learning opportunities. Certain domains have relied heavily on single measures of a construct. For example, the Student–Teacher Relationship Scale (Pianta, 2001) is the predominant measure in the study of teacher–child relationships, and the field will benefit from additional measures to better inform the precision of the measurement of the construct as well as the sensitivity of a construct in which intervention aims to change. In addition, we rely heavily on rating scales of behavior (see Chow et al., 2018; Curtis, Frey, Watson, Hampton, & Roberts, 2018), and due to the qualitative differences between rating a child's general behavior and directly observing them in classrooms, discussions around how research captures the nature of problem behavior must be included in our work. Careful consideration of the environmental factors in research that is framed in classroom ecological systems should be central to research as well, which includes teacher (e.g., attitudes, attributions, self-efficacy, burnout) and classroom (e.g., adversity, organizational variables) and school factors (e.g., administrative support, resources).

Concluding Remarks

Taken together, teacher practices can positively influence child behavior and engagement in the classroom setting, enhance teacher–child relationships, and provide the foundation for a high quality language learning environment. By intentionally and systematically applying these practices in the classroom, teachers can effectively interrupt the cyclical development of challenging behavior and decelerated language learning and academic achievement. Considering the strong association that exists between children's prosocial development and academic achievement, teachers and practitioners should consider how to approach these two domains of development together in a systematic and complementary way, as opposed to addressing them in isolation. Professional development models should consider the influence that these variables have on the learning context within a classroom, and provide foundational support when needed to teachers both within and across domains in a way that maximizes effects for teachers, and subsequently the children they serve.

References

Adamson, L. B., Kaiser, A. P., Tamis-LaMonda, C. S., Owen, M. T., & Dimitrova, N. (2019). The developmental landscape of early parent-focused language intervention. *Early Childhood Research Quarterly*. doi:10.1016/j.ecresq.2018.11.005

Baker, J. A., Grant, S., & Morlock, L. (2008). The teacher-student relationship as a developmental context for children with internalizing or externalizing behavior problems. *School Psychology Quarterly*, *23*, 3–15. doi:10.1037/1045-3830.23.1.3

Bao, L., Brownlie, E. B., & Beitchman, J. H. (2016). Mental health trajectories from adolescence to adulthood: Language disorder and other childhood and adolescent risk factors. *Development and Psychopathology*, *28*, 489–504. doi:10.1017/S0954579415001054

Benner, G. J., Nelson, J. R., & Epstein, M. H. (2002). Language skills of children with EBD: A literature review. *Journal of Emotional and Behavioral Disorders*, *10*, 43–56. doi:10.1177/106342660201000105

Bornstein, M. H., Hahn, C. S., Putnick, D. L., & Pearson, R. M. (2018). Stability of core language skill from infancy to adolescence in typical and atypical development. *Science Advances*, *4*, 11. doi:10.1126/sciadv.aat7422

Bronfenbrenner, U. (1994). Ecological models of human development. *Readings on the Development of Children*, *2*, 37–43.

Brownlie, E. B., Bao, L., & Beitchman, J. (2016). Childhood language disorder and social anxiety in early adulthood. *Journal of Abnormal Child Psychology*, *44*, 1061–1070. doi:10.1007/s10802-015-0097-5

Burns, M. K., Warmbold-Brann, K., & Zaslofsky, A. F. (2015). Ecological systems theory in school psychology review. *School Psychology Review*, *44*, 249–261. doi:10.17105/spr-15-0092.1

Cabell, S. Q., Justice, L. M., McGinty, A. S., DeCoster, J., & Forston, L. D. (2015). Teacher–child conversations in preschool classrooms: Contributions to children's vocabulary development. *Early Childhood Research Quarterly*, *30*, 80–92. doi:10.1016/j.ecresq.2014.09.004

Camarata, S. M., Nelson, K. E., & Camarata, M. N. (1994). Comparison of conversational-recasting and imitative procedures for training grammatical structures in children with specific language impairment. *Journal of Speech and Hearing Research*, *37*, 1414–1423. doi:10.1044/jshr.3706.1414

Catts, H. W., Fey, M. E., Zhang, X., & Tomblin, J. B. (2001). Estimating the risk of future reading difficulties in kindergarten children. *Language, Speech, and Hearing Services in Schools*, *32*, 38–50. doi:10.1044/0161-1461(2001/004)

Cheung, A. C., & Slavin, R. E. (2016). How methodological features affect effect sizes in education. *Educational Researcher*, *45*, 283–292. doi:10.3102/0013189X16656615

Chow, J. C. (2018). Comorbid language and behavior problems: Development, frameworks, and intervention. *School Psychology Quarterly*, *33*, 356–360. doi:10.1037/spq0000270

Chow, J. C., Ekholm, E., & Coleman, H. (2018). Does oral language underpin the development of later behavior problems? A longitudinal meta-analysis. *School Psychology Quarterly*, *33*, 337–349. doi:10.1037/spq0000255

Chow, J. C., & Gilmour, A. F. (2016). Designing and implementing group contingencies in the classroom: A teacher's guide. *TEACHING Exceptional Children*, *48*, 137–143. doi:10.1177/0040059918757945

Chow, J. C., & Hollo, A. (2018). Language ability of students with emotional disturbance: Discrepancies between teacher ratings and direct assessment. *Assessment for Effective Intervention*, *43*, 90–95. doi:10.1177/1534508417702063

Chow, J. C., & Wehby, J. H. (2017). Profiles of problem behavior in children with varying language ability. *Journal of Emotional and Behavioral Disorders*. doi:10.1177/1063426617733714

Chow, J. C., & Wehby, J. H. (2018). Associations between language and problem behavior: A systematic review and correlational meta-analysis. *Educational Psychology Review*, *30*, 61–82. doi:10.1007/s10648-016-9385-z

Christ, T., & Wang, X. C. (2010). Bridging the vocabulary gap: What the research tells us about vocabulary instruction in early childhood. *Young Children*, *65*(4), 84–91.

Cleave, P., Becker, S., Curran, M., Van Horne, A., & Fey, M. (2015). The efficacy of recasts in language intervention: A systematic review and meta-analysis. *American Journal of Speech-Language Pathology*, *24*, 237–255. doi:10.1044/2015_AJSLP-14-0105

Conti-Ramsden, G., Durkin, K., Toseeb, U., Botting, N., & Pickles, A. (2018). Education and employment outcomes of young adults with a history of developmental language disorder. *International Journal of Language & Communication Disorders*, *53*, 237–255. doi:10.1111/1460-6984.12338

Curtis, P. R., Frey, J. R., Watson, C. D., Hampton, L. H., & Roberts, M. Y. (2018). Language disorders and problem behaviors: A meta-analysis. *Pediatrics*, *142*, 2. doi:10.1542/peds.2017-3551

Duncan, G. J., Dowsett, C. J., Claessens, A., Magnuson, K., Huston, A. C., Klebanov, P., … Sexton, H. (2007). School readiness and later achievement. *Developmental Psychology*, *43*, 1428–1446. doi:10.1037/0012-1649.43.6.1428

Girolametto, L., & Weitzman, E. (2002). Responsiveness of child care providers in interactions with toddlers and preschoolers. *Language, Speech, and Hearing Services in Schools*, *33*(4), 268–281.

Golinkoff, R. M., Can, D. D., Soderstrom, M., & Hirsh-Pasek, K. (2015). (Baby) talk to me: The social context of infant-directed speech and its effects on early language acquisition. *Current Directions in Psychological Science*, *24*, 339–344. doi:10.1177/0963721415595345

Greenberg, J., Putman, H., & Walsh, K. (2014). *Training our future teachers: Classroom management*. Washington, DC: National Council on Teacher Quality.

Hadley, P. A., Rispoli, M., & Hsu, N. (2016). Toddlers' verb lexicon diversity and grammatical outcomes. *Language, Speech, and Hearing Services in Schools, 47*, 44–58. doi:10.1044/2015_LSHSS-15-0018

Hamre, B., & Pianta, R. (2001). Early teacher–Child relationships and the trajectory of children's school outcomes through eighth grade. *Child Development, 72*, 625–638. doi:10.1111/1467-8624.00301

Hamre, B. K., & Pianta, R. (2010). Classroom environments and developmental processes: Conceptualization, measurement, & improvement. In J. L. Meece & J. S. Eccles (Eds.), *Handbook of research on schools, schooling and human development* (pp. 25–41). New York: Routledge. doi:10.3102/0013189X09332374

Hanna, G. P. (1977). The effect of wait time on the quality of response of first grade children. Thesis submitted for the Master's degree, University of Kansas, Lawrence, KA.

Hart, B., & Risley, T. R. (1995). *Meaningful differences in the everyday experience of young American children.* Paul H Brookes Publishing.

Hemmeter, M. L., Fox, L., Jack, S., & Broyles, L. (2007). A program-wide model of positive behavior support in early childhood settings. *Journal of Early Intervention, 29*, 337–355. doi:10.1177/105381510702900405

Hemmeter, M. L., Ostrosky, M., & Fox, L. (2006). Social and emotional foundations for early learning: A conceptual model for intervention. *School Psychology Review, 35*, 583–601.

Henrichs, J., Rescorla, L., Donkersloot, C., Schenk, J. J., Raat, H., Jaddoe, V. W., … Tiemeier, H. (2013). Early vocabulary delay and behavioral/emotional problems in early childhood: The generation R study. *Journal of speech, language, and Hearing Research, 56*, 553–566. doi:10.1044/1092-4388(2012/11-0169)

Hill, C. J., Bloom, H. S., Black, A. R., & Lipsey, M. W. (2008). Empirical benchmarks for interpreting effect sizes in research. *Child Development Perspectives, 2*, 172–177. doi:10.1111/j.1750-8606.2008.00061.x

Hindman, A., & Wasik, B. (2008). Head start teachers' beliefs about language and literacy instruction. *Early Childhood Research Quarterly, 23*, 479–492. doi:10.1016/j.ecresq.2008.06.002

Hindman, A., Wasik, B., & Bradley, D. (2019). How classroom conversations unfold: Exploring teacher–child exchanges during shared book reading. *Early Education and Development.* doi:10.1080/10409289.2018.1556009

Hoff, E. (2003). The specificity of environmental influence: Socioeconomic status affects early vocabulary development via maternal speech. *Child Development, 74*, 1368–1378. doi:10.1111/1467-8624.00612

Hoff, E., & Naigles, L. (2002). How children use input to acquire a lexicon. *Child Development, 73*(2), 418–433.

Hollo, A., & Chow, J. (2015). Communicative functions of problem behavior for students with high-incidence disabilities. *Beyond Behavior, 24*, 23–30. doi:10.1177/107429561502400304

Hollo, A., Chow, J. C., & Wehby, J. H. (2018). Profiles of language and behavior in students with emotional disturbance. *Behavioral Disorders.* doi:10.1177/0198742918804803

Hollo, A., Wehby, J. H., & Oliver, R. M. (2014). Unidentified language deficits in children with emotional and behavioral disorders: A meta-analysis. *Exceptional Children, 80*, 169–186. doi:10.1177/001440291408000203

Huttenlocher, J., Vasilyeva, M., Cymerman, E., & Levine, S. (2002). Language input and child syntax. *Cognitive Psychology, 45*, 337–374. doi:10.1016/S0010-0285(02)00500-5

Hymel, S., Rubin, K. H., Rowden, L., & LeMare, L. (1990). Children's peer relationships: Longitudinal prediction of internalizing and externalizing problems from middle to late childhood. *Child Development, 61*, 2004–2021. doi:10.1111/j.1467-8624.1990.tb03582.x

Justice, L. M., Jiang, H., & Strasser, K. (2018). Linguistic environment of preschool classrooms: What dimensions support children's language growth? *Early Childhood Research Quarterly, 42*, 79–92. doi:10.1016/j.ecresq.2017.09.003

Justice, L. M., McGinty, A. S., Zucker, T., Cabell, S. Q., & Piasta, S. B. (2013). Bi-directional dynamics underlie the complexity of talk in teacher–child play-based conversations in classrooms serving at-risk pupils. *Early Childhood Research Quarterly, 28*, 496–508. doi:10.1016/j.ecresq.2013.02.005

Law, J., & Levickis, P. (2018). Early language development must be a public health priority. *Journal of Health Visiting, 6*, 586–589. doi:10.12968/johv.2018.6.12.586

Law, J., Rush, R., Clegg, J., Peters, T., & Roulstone, S. (2015). The role of pragmatics in mediating the relationship between social disadvantage and adolescent behavior. *Journal of Developmental & Behavioral Pediatrics, 36*, 389–398. doi:10.1097/DBP.0000000000000180

Lei, H., Cui, Y., & Chiu, M. M. (2016). Affective teacher-student relationships and students' externalizing behavior problems: A meta-analysis. *Frontiers in Psychology, 7*, 1–12. doi:10.3389/fpsyg.2016.01311

Maggin, D. M., Pustejovsky, J. E., & Johnson, A. H. (2017). A meta-analysis of school-based group contingency interventions for students with challenging behavior: An update. *Remedial and Special Education, 38*, 353–370. doi:10.1177/0741932517716900

Nelson, K. E., Camarata, S. M., Welsh, J., Butkovsky, L., & Camarata, M. (1996). Effects of imitative and conversational recasting treatment on the acquisition of grammar in children with specific language impairment and younger language- normal children. *Journal of Speech and Hearing Research, 39*, 850–859. doi:10.1044/jshr.3904.850

Pentimonti, J. M., Justice, L. M., Yeomans-Maldonado, G., McGinty, A. S., Slocum, L., & O'Connell, A. (2017). Teachers' use of high-and low-support scaffolding strategies to differentiate language instruction in high-risk/economically disadvantaged settings. *Journal of Early Intervention, 39*, 125–146. doi:10.1177/1053815117700865

Perry, N. E., VandeKamp, K. O., Mercer, L. K., & Nordby, C. J. (2002). Investigating teacher-student interactions that foster self-regulated learning. *Educational Psychologist, 37*(1), 5–15. doi:10.1207/S15326985EP3701_2

Petersen, I. T., Bates, J. E., D'onofrio, B. M., Coyne, C. A., Lansford, J. E., Dodge, K. A., … Van Hulle, C. A. (2013). Language ability predicts the development of behavior problems in children. *Journal of Abnormal Psychology, 122*, 542–557. doi:10.1037/a0031963

Pianta, R. C. (2001). *Student-teacher relationship scale*. Lutz, FL: Psychological Assessment Resources, Inc.

Pianta, R. C., Steinberg, M. S., & Rollins, K. B. (1995). The first two years of school: Teacher-child relationships and deflections in children's classroom adjustment. *Development and Psychopathology, 7*, 295–312. doi:10.1017/S0954579400006519

Qi, C. H., & Kaiser, A. P. (2004). Problem behaviors of low-income children with language delays: An observation study. *Journal of speech, language, and Hearing Research, 47*, 595–609. doi:10.1044/1092-4388 (2004/046)

Qi, C. H., Kaiser, A. P., Milan, S., & Hancock, T. (2006). Language performance of low-income African American and European American preschool children on the PPVT–III. *language, speech, and Hearing Services in Schools, 37*, 5–16. doi:10.1044/0161-1461(2006/002

Qi, C. H., Zieher, A., Lee Van Horn, M., Bulotsky-Shearer, R., & Carta, J. (2019). Language skills, behaviour problems, and classroom emotional support among preschool children from low-income families. *Early Child Development and Care*. doi:10.1080/03004430.2019.1570504

Rescorla, L., Ross, G. S., & McClure, S. (2007). Language delay and behavioral/emotional problems in toddlers: Findings from two developmental clinics. *Journal of Speech, Language, and Hearing Research, 50*, 1063–1078. doi:10.1044/1092-4388(2007/074)

Roben, C. K., Cole, P. M., & Armstrong, L. M. (2013). Longitudinal relations among language skills, anger expression, and regulatory strategies in early childhood. *Child Development, 84*, 891–905. doi:10.1111/cdev.12027

Roberts, M., & Kaiser, A. (2015). Early intervention for toddlers with language delays: A randomized controlled trial. *Pediatrics, 135*, 686–693. doi:10.1542/peds.2014-2134

Rowe, M. L. (2008). Child-directed speech: Relation to socioeconomic status, knowledge of child development and child vocabulary skill. *Journal of Child Language, 35*, 185–205. doi:10.1017/S0305000907008343

Ruston, H. P., & Schwanenflugel, P. J. (2010). Effects of a conversation intervention on the expressive vocabulary development of prekindergarten children. *Language, Speech, and Hearing Services in Schools, 413*, 303–313. doi:10.1044/0161-1461(2009/08-0100)

Sabol, T. J., & Pianta, R. C. (2012). Patterns of school readiness forecast achievement and socioemotional development at the end of elementary school. *Child Development, 83*, 282–299. doi:10.1111/j.1467-8624.2011.01678.x

Sameroff, A. (2009). The transactional model. In A. Sameroff (Ed.), *The transactional model of development: How children and contexts shape each other* (pp. 3–21). Washington, DC: American Psychological Association. doi:10.1037/11877-000

Sembiante, S., Dynia, J., Kaderavek, J., & Justice, L. (2017). Teachers' literal and inferential talk in early childhood and special education classrooms. *Early Education and Development, 29*, 14–30. doi:10.1080/10409289.2017.1362916

Shores, R. E., Jack, S. L., Gunter, P. L., Ellis, D. N., DeBriere, T. J., & Wehby, J. H. (1993). Classroom interactions of children with behavior disorders. *Journal of Emotional and Behavioral Disorders, 1*, 27–39.

Simonsen, B., Fairbanks, S., Briesch, A., Myers, D., & Sugai, G. (2008). Evidence-based practices in classroom management: Considerations for research to practice. *Education and Treatment of Children, 31*, 351–380.

Sutherland, K. S., Conroy, M., Abrams, L., & Vo, A. (2010). Improving interactions between teachers and young children with problem behavior: A strengths-based approach. *Exceptionality, 18*, 70–81. doi:10.1080/09362831003673101

Tamis-LeMonda, C. S., & Bornstein, M. H. (2002). Maternal responsiveness and early language acquisition. *Advances in Child Development and Behavior, 29*(C), 89–127.

Taylor, J. A., Kowalski, S. M., Polanin, J. R., Askinas, K., Stuhlsatz, M. A., Wilson, C. D., … Wilson, S. J. (2018). Investigating science education effect sizes: Implications for power analyses and programmatic decisions. *AERA Open, 4*. doi:10.1177/2332858418791991

Wasik, B. A., Bond, M. A., & Hindman, A. (2006). The effects of a language and literacy intervention on head start children and teachers. *Journal of Educational Psychology, 98*, 63–74. doi:10.1037/0022-0663.98.1.63

Wasik, B. A., & Hindman, A. H. (2011). Improving vocabulary and pre-literacy skills of at-risk preschoolers through teacher professional development. *Journal of Educational Psychology, 103*, 455–469. doi:10.1037/a0023067

Wasik, B. A., & Hindman, A. H. (2013). Open-ended prompts: Fostering conversations with children. *The Reading Teacher, 67*, 302–311.

Wasik, B. A., & Hindman, A. H. (2018). Increasing preschoolers' vocabulary development through a streamlined teacher professional development intervention. *Early Childhood Research Quarterly*. doi:10.1016/j.ecresq.2018.11.001

Westrupp, E. M., Reilly, S., McKean, C., Law, J., Mensah, F., & Nicholson, J. M. (2019). Vocabulary development and trajectories of behavioral and emotional difficulties via academic ability and peer problems. *Child Development*, 1–18.

Winstanley, M., Webb, R. T., & Conti-Ramsden, G. (2018). More or less likely to offend? Young adults with a history of identified developmental language disorders. *International Journal of Language & Communication Disorders, 53*, 256–270. doi:10.1111/1460-6984.12339

Yew, S. G. K., & O'Kearney, R. (2013). Emotional and behavioural outcomes later in childhood and adolescence for children with specific language impairments: Meta-analyses of controlled prospective studies. *Journal of Child Psychology and Psychiatry, 54*, 516–524. doi:10.1111/jcpp.12009

7 Peer to Peer Support

Innovative Strategies for Families of Youth
with Emotional/Behavioral Disorders

*Kristin Duppong Hurley, Al Duchnowski, Krista Kutash, and
Jennifer Farley*

The Family Movement

Currently available peer support programs for families with a child who has emotional or behavioral disorders (EBD) have their roots in the family arm of the disability movement. Historically, families of children who had diverse physical and cognitive impairments began to meet informally to support each other and advocate for services in parts of Europe, Canada, and the United States as early as the 1940s. These families provided support to each other and advocated for a greater role in partnering with service providers in determining the nature and structure of the programs that were offered to their children. Over time, organizations began to form, focused on specific disabilities such as cognitive and intellectual impairment.

Progress in the area of children's mental health was much slower compared to other disability groups. It was not until 1979 that a group of parents met around a kitchen table to establish what became the National Alliance for Mental Illness (NAMI). The founders of NAMI had adult children with severe mental illness, which became the focus of their efforts. It was not until a few years later that NAMI developed a full range of support programs for families of children of any age. The Federation of Families for Children's Mental Health (FFCMH) is another family organization that has played an important role in the development of peer support. A grassroots organization, the FFCMH was founded in 1986 by a dozen parents of children who had EBD, meeting in the basement of a very active parent advocate in Virginia. Today, both organizations have a national presence providing peer support, advocacy, and family education programs in all 50 states. They are joined by many regional groups that are family-run and devoted to family advocacy and support.

The development of family empowerment and peer support for parents of children who have EBD is embedded in the overall effort to improve the children's mental health system. In 1982, Jane Knitzer published the results of her landmark study *Unclaimed Children* (Knitzer & Olson, 1982), in which she examined the actions of the multiple agencies charged with serving children who have EBD and their families. She declared the system a failure. Parents found themselves in a revolving door going from agency to agency seeking help for their child. Knitzer's study was a contributing factor to federal efforts that began a series of grants to states to improve mental health services for children and support for their families. This funding initiative led to the development of the System of Care (Stroul & Friedman, 1994), a coordinated effort comprising all the agencies involved in meeting the needs of children who have EBD and their families. A guiding principle of the System of

Care was that services would be child-centered and family-focused. Parents were to be accepted as equal decision-making partners in every step of the development of a treatment plan for their child. This was a parallel to the requirement for parent participation in the development of the Individual Educational Plan (IEP) for children who received special education services at school. The federal agencies of Education and Mental Health serve children who have EBD and their families, and both have recognized the value of family voice and have worked to strengthen the family movement through mandates and tangible support.

Stigma, Blame, and Caregiver Strain

In spite of these positive advances, the number of families who became active participants in and benefited from the family movement was marginal. For example, parents of children who have EBD and who are served in special education programs are the least likely to attend and participate in their child's IEP meeting compared to parents of children who have other disabilities (Wagner, Kutash, Duchnowski, Epstein, & Sumi, 2005). As mandates and funding for parent advocacy and support increased in the mental health field, researchers began to examine issues related to the characteristics of families and their potential lack of involvement in services intended to help their children (Kutash, Duchnowski, Green, & Ferron, 2011). Evidence began to emerge that supported the contentions of advocacy groups, such as NAMI and the FFCMH, that parents of children who have EBD feel blamed for their child's behavior and that there is a powerful stigma attached to mental illness. The feeling of blame and stigma leads to disengagement and social isolation on the part of these families and may result in fewer treatment outcomes due to reduced engagement on the part of the parent (Kutash, Duchnowski, Green, & Ferron, 2011).

Another factor serving as a barrier to engagement for families of children who have EBD is caregiver strain. While all families who have a child with a disability experience some level of strain, the impact on families who have a child with EBD has been identified as a serious challenge (Brannan & Heflinger, 2006). The family's coping mechanisms and strategies are often pushed to their limit. The negative effects of high levels of strain are manifested in several domains of family life. For example, families of children with emotional and behavioral challenges may have higher rates of marital discord (Wymbs, Pelham, Molina, & Gnagy, 2008), as well as economic issues related to finding and maintaining quality childcare and dealing with frequent interruptions to their employment while supporting their child (Rosenzweig, Brennan, & Ogilvie, 2002). In a survey of parents of children with emotional and behavioral needs, Rosenzweig and Huffstutter (2004) found that nearly half of parents had, at one point in time, quit their job to care for their child and nearly a third of parents had been fired due to care responsibilities disrupting work.

While the family movement offers hope to families in terms of more effective services for their children and a greater role in determining the nature of these services, there are potent barriers facing families in attempting to participate in this process. Stigma, feelings of blame, and high levels of strain associated with caring for a child who has EBD can facilitate social isolation and reduce the ability of parents to experience optimal treatment for their child. Peer support programs such as Parent Connectors, described in this chapter, can offer targeted support that aims to diminish the effects of stigma, blame, and caregiver strain. In an effort to increase the availability of such evidence-based practices, leaders in the family movement continue to press to have their voices heard. An important development in this effort has been the concept of family-driven care.

98 *Kristin Duppong Hurley et al.*

Family-Driven Care

The concept of family-driven care has been most clearly explicated by Osher and her colleagues (Osher, Osher, & Blau, 2008). They have presented a strategic framework aimed at achieving the type of services originally envisioned in the System of Care principle of child-centered and family-focused, articulated with extensive input by families. Their original framework is a work in progress and continues to be refined especially through efforts of the FFCMH. They provide the following definition of family-driven care:

> Family-driven means families have a primary decision-making role in the care of their own children as well as the policies and procedures governing care for all children in their community, state, tribe, territory and nation. This includes choosing supports, services and providers; setting goals; designing and implementing programs; monitoring outcomes; participating in funding decisions; and determining the effectiveness of all efforts to promote the mental health and wellbeing of children and youth.
>
> (Osher, Osher, Blau, 2008, p. 44)

Osher and colleagues also developed ten guiding principles for family-driven care that provide additional guidance. These principles emphasize shared decision making (Principle 2) between (a) families and youth, who make informed choices (Principle 1), advocate for systems change (Principle 3), and engage in family-run organizations (Principle 5) to provide peer support (Principle 4), (b) providers and administrators who change to family-driven practices (Principle 6 and 7) which are culturally and linguistically responsive (Principle 10), and (c) communities that remove discrimination and stigma (Principle 8) and embrace diversity (Principle 9). (Osher, Osher, & Blau, 2008). The principles of family driven care are clearly ambitious. Families, along with the mental health community, are challenged to continue efforts aimed at achieving their implementation.

Parent-to-Parent Family Support Services for Children with EBD

The interest in supporting families of youth with emotional and behavioral needs has expanded recently, and comprehensive research reviews have been conducted (Hoagwood, 2005; Hoagwood et al., 2010; Kuhn & Laird, 2014; Robbins et al., 2008). These reviews concluded that there were not enough experimental studies to support the effectiveness of family-based support for youth with behavioral challenges and that more research is needed. They also found that rigorous research methods were most likely to be used in assessing the effectiveness of clinician-led programs (which often include parenting strategies), rather than peer-led or co-led (clinician and peer) programs. Yet, there were several findings that provide key information related to the family support process. First, family self-efficacy and empowerment can be improved through provision of family support. These efforts have been associated with numerous improved outcomes, including service initiation and completion, increased understanding of the youth's condition and relevant services, satisfaction, and youth functioning at discharge (Bickman Heflinger, Northrup, Sonnichsen, & Schilling, 1998; Kutash, Garraza, et al., 2013). Additionally, mental health symptoms in caregivers, including depression, anxiety, and strain from caregiving, have been reduced through parent support programs (Ireys, Chernoff, DeVet, & Kim, 2001; Ireys & Sakwa, 2006; Preyde & Ardal, 2003).

Grassroots efforts to provide parent-to-parent approaches of providing support to families of youth with EBD are often supported by local chapters of national family groups. A recent study of peer organizations in New York found that a large number of peer advocates were providing support, and had done so for up to 20 years (Acri, Craig, & Adler, 2018). Yet, little research has been conducted on such practices, and what does exist related to peer support includes mostly pre-post designs and is not as robust as professionally provided family support (Acri et al., 2018; Hoagwood et al., 2010; Kuhn & Laird, 2014). However, national studies of children with mental health issues found that about 33% of families reported using parent-to-parent family support services (Gyamfi et al., 2009). Hoagwood and colleagues (2010) found that these programs were likely to provide parents with a combination of the following supports: advocacy, emotional support, information, skill building, and connections to community resources. Yet, an exploratory study of the provision of family-to-family support indicated that these services may differ in terms of eligibility, processes, or content (Wisdom, Olin, Shorter, Burton, & Hoagwood, 2011). The majority of peer family support programs are delivered to groups of parents, but they also are delivered one-on-one, either in-person or on the phone. While these one-on-one interventions are not as common as peer-led small groups, research indicates they provide improved outcomes for families, demonstrated with more comprehensive research designs (January et al., 2016; Kutash, Duchnowski, Green et al., 2011; Kutash, Duchnowski et al., 2013; Olin et al., 2015).

One such intervention is the Parent Engagement and Empowerment Program model, which prepares Family Peer Advocates to provide family-to-family support (Olin et al., 2010; Rodriguez et al., 2011). The model's underlying framework, Parents as Agents of Change, draws on the combination of the Principles of Parent Support and the Unified Theory of Behavior Change to achieve parent empowerment (Hoagwood et al., 2018; Olin et al., 2010; Rodriguez et al., 2011). The training program builds Family Peer Advocate knowledge of mental health disorders, processes, and services as well as skills and strategies for building relationships and engaging families in children's mental health services. The model employs a 40-hour manualized training, co-facilitated by a Family Peer Advocate and a mental health clinician, which is followed by bi-weekly consultation calls for six months. Research indicates that the program supports Family Peer Advocates to develop skills and implement strategies to empower families and maintain those skills for six months after training, when trained directly or through a train-the-trainer model (Hoagwood et al., 2018; Rodriguez et al., 2011).

While focusing on parent support around community-based resources for youth with emotional and behavioral needs is essential, it is also important to recognize the parent's role in school-related services for their child. Both the Individuals with Disabilities Education Improvement Act (IDEIA, 2004) and the more recent Every Student Succeeds Act (ESSA, 2015) stress parental involvement as an important element in improving educational outcomes for children. Parental involvement has been effective in improving academic outcomes, and is supported by an extensive empirical base, including three meta-analyses synthesizing the results of 118 studies and producing findings that include moderate to large effect sizes (Fan & Chen, 2001; Jeynes, 2005, 2007). However, findings from large national studies indicate that, compared to peers who either have other types of disabilities or no disabilities, students with EBD are the least likely to have families who are involved in their education (Duppong Hurley, Lambert, & Huscroft-D'Angelo, 2019; Wagner et al., 2006, 2005). Yet, for families of youth with emotional and behavioral needs parental involvement is complex. Studies also find high reports of involvement in areas such as parental confidence in their ability to help with homework and attending parent–teacher conferences (Duppong Hurley, Lambert, & Huscroft-D'Angelo, 2019; Wagner et al., 2006).

While many schools offer activities to bring parents to the school, educators need to think about strategies to support parental involvement in their child's education at home as well as

100 *Kristin Duppong Hurley et al.*

ways to increase parental educational expectations of their children (Newman, 2005). However, few schools offer support to families of students with disabilities to increase parental involvement (Duchnowski et al., 2013; Schiller et al., 2003; Wagner et al., 2005). Research with parents of children from other disability categories (i.e., intellectual disability, autism, chronic health conditions) demonstrates that both access to information about services for their child and support from other parents provides them with a sense of hope, empowerment, belonging, reduction in isolation, and the skills necessary to advocate for their child (Douglas, Redley, & Ottmann, 2016; Law, King, Stewart, & King, 2002; Solomon, Pistrang, & Barker, 2001). Given that youth spend a large portion of their time in schools and many receive considerable emotional and behavioral supports from schools, it seems essential that effective family support interventions encompass services provided to youth both in school and in community settings. To date, research on parent-to-parent support for students identified with EBD that contains both educational and mental health components includes only Parent Connectors, which has focused primarily on middle school students (e.g., Kutash, Duchnowski, Green et al., 2011). In order to better understand the theoretical underpinnings of peer-to-peer support models, we will explore the Parent Connectors program as an example of potential supports that could be built for the families of youth with EBD.

Theoretical Foundations and Core Components of Parent Connectors

Parent Connectors is the only school-focused, parent-to-parent support intervention developed to assist families of middle-school youth with EBD that has been found efficacious in reducing caregiver strain, increasing use of school-based resources, and reducing school suspensions (Kutash, Duchnowski, Green, et al., 2011, 2013). Parent Connectors is an innovative, theory-based, parent-to-parent support intervention delivered via weekly phone calls from a parent of a child with EBD. The objective of Parent Connectors is to (1) provide emotional support, (2) improve positive attitudes towards school and mental health services, (3) support understanding school special education and emotional/behavioral services, and (4) provide instrumental support to identify and meet basic family needs (see Figure 7.1). The conceptual framework of Parent Connectors is built upon two well-developed and empirically supported theoretical models, the Model of Family Stress and the Theory of Planned Behavior.

Family Stress Model

The Double ABCX Model of Family Stress draws upon concepts of stress, both psychological and physiological, as well as research on family stress, adaption, and coping (e.g., Brannan, Heflinger, & Foster, 2003; Heflinger, Northrup, Sonnichsen, & Brannan, 1998; McCubbin & Patterson, 1983). There are several stressors that have been identified as being common in families with children who have EBD such as the child's disruptive behavior and poor functioning in school, strain on family relationships, financial difficulties, and challenges in obtaining services (Heflinger et al., 1998; Resch et al., 2010). According to the family stress model, these stressors are processed by parents through their perceptions of available resources, potentially leading to high levels of caregiver strain, which can impact both family and child use of services (Green, Lambert, & Duppong Hurley, 2019; Kutash, Cross, Madias, Duchnowski, & Green, 2012). Importantly, high levels of caregiver strain have been found to have an impact on the manner in which parents seek and obtain services for their

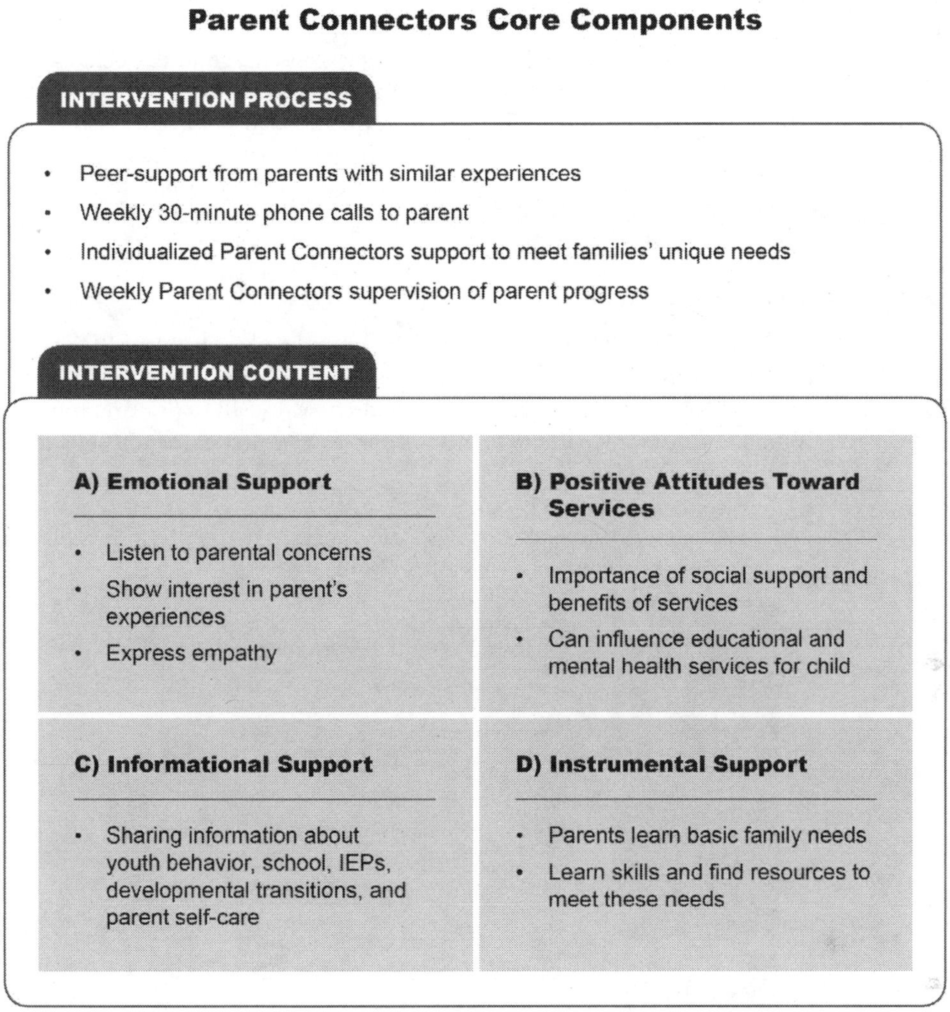

Parent Connectors Core Components

INTERVENTION PROCESS

- Peer-support from parents with similar experiences
- Weekly 30-minute phone calls to parent
- Individualized Parent Connectors support to meet families' unique needs
- Weekly Parent Connectors supervision of parent progress

INTERVENTION CONTENT

A) Emotional Support

- Listen to parental concerns
- Show interest in parent's experiences
- Express empathy

B) Positive Attitudes Toward Services

- Importance of social support and benefits of services
- Can influence educational and mental health services for child

C) Informational Support

- Sharing information about youth behavior, school, IEPs, developmental transitions, and parent self-care

D) Instrumental Support

- Parents learn basic family needs
- Learn skills and find resources to meet these needs

Figure 7.1 Parent Connectors core components

children, with highly strained parents accessing highly restrictive and more costly services for their children (e.g., residential care; Brannan et al., 2003; Farmer, Burns, Angold, & Costello, 1997). Thus, a goal of Parent Connectors is to reduce caregiver strain and facilitate the development of skills and attitudes that promote effective partnerships with teachers and counselors.

Theory of Planned Behavior

Another guide for Parent Connector's theory of change is the Theory of Planned Behavior (TPB), which predicts behaviors perceived to require specific resources, skills, or opportunities not readily, nor consistently, available (Ajzen, 1991). The theory proposes that a person's attitudes towards (a) the benefit of engaging in the behavior, (b) the social norms and pressures surrounding the behavior, and (c) the person's perceived behavioral control over performing the behavior, predict the individual's willingness to engage in the behavior. The predictive validity of the TPB is supported by several studies (Armitage & Conner, 2001; Godin & Kok, 1996). In response to the TPB model, key components of *Parent Connectors* were designed to (a) facilitate the development of positive expected benefits resulting from parents engaging with teachers and (b) increase the perception that parents can positively influence the education and support programs of their children.

Parent Connectors Logic Model

The theoretical framework for Parent Connectors, based upon the Double ABCX Family Stress model and the Theory of Planned Behavior, is graphically presented in Figure 7.2. Parent Connectors (PCs) are veteran parents of children with EBD who are trained to conduct weekly phone calls with parents to deliver the core processes of the intervention

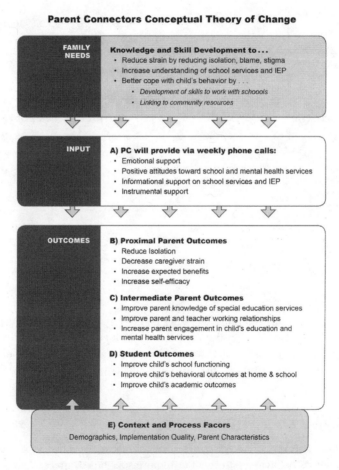

Figure 7.2 Parent Connectors conceptual theory of change

(Figure 7.2. A). These core components are designed to improve proximal parent outcomes regarding self-efficacy, expected benefits, and caregiver strain (Figure 7.2. B). Specifically, PCs reduce caregiver strain by providing emotional support, facilitating parents' engagement in activities to promote success, and linking them to instrumental supports. Accordingly, parents begin to see that they can influence their child's educational and mental health services (Heflinger et al., 1998; Kutash, Duchnowski, Green, & Ferron, 2011). The promotion of positive attitudes toward engagement in school and the mental health system result in parents' continued growth in self-efficacy. They overcome negative social pressures to see the benefit of engagement for their child as well as for themselves. Parents increase self-efficacy by learning skills and information to become better partners with teachers and mental health services providers. Caregiver strain can be further reduced and self-efficacy increased when community resources provide access to basic needs services to assist the child. The acquisition of these proximal parent outcomes is the central focus of the intervention (Figure 7.2. B) and may be considered the active ingredients necessary to affect the intended intermediate outcomes. Acquisition of these new skills and information result in improved intermediate parental outcomes (Figure 7.2. C), such as productive partnering between parents, educators, and mental health professions, resulting in increased parental engagement in their child's educational and mental health services and a better understanding of special education services. In turn, these changes are expected to influence student outcomes (Figure 7.2. D), such as improved child school functioning (e.g., increased attendance), better behavior at home and school, and improved academic achievement. Further, a variety of context and process factors (e.g., demographic variables, parent characteristics, quality of program implementation) likely influence the efficacy of the intervention (Figure 7.2. E). A positive impact on outcomes is anticipated when the intervention is implemented with fidelity to the program model.

Core Intervention Components

Parent Connectors' core components are each linked to the TPB and Family Stress Double ABCX models. The objective is to use weekly 30–60 minute phone calls, by a PC (a trained peer who also has a child with EBD) to provide support, information, and skill-building (Ireys & Sakwa, 2006; Kutash, Duchnowski, Green, & Ferron, 2011; McKay, Stoewe, McCadam, & Gonzales, 1998). During the school year, the four core components delivered include (a) provision of emotional support, (b) promotion of benefits of actions and positive expectations, (c) provision of informational support, and (d) instrumental support (see Figure 7.1).

The PCs, by sharing their experiences, *provide emotional support* to reduce feelings of isolation and strain in the parent. The PC may also address any negative pressure and social influence that prevents the parent's positive engagement with both the education and mental health systems. The *benefits of being an engaged parent* are promoted by the PC and attitudes are encouraged that reflect a feeling that the parent can have some influence over their child's education. The skills needed to achieve these attitudes and expectations are role-played, modeled, and evaluated during the weekly calls. Parents of children who have EBD often do not have important *information about the child's education program and mental health services* in an easily accessible format. The PC provides information about the IEP, mental health professionals, and school-based services that are part of the IEP. Finally, many parents experience economic and environmental risk factors that may be aided by *instrumental support* commonly provided by community agencies. Links to these agencies are often complicated and a PC can offer valuable assistance in accessing needed community services.

Core Topics and Strategies Used during PC Calls

On each weekly call, PCs are trained to focus on a few topics ranging from parent blame and stigma, parent communication with the school, child behavior and academics, child's IEP, mental health services, and community resources. PCs are also trained to use a variety of specific strategies with parents, including to provide emotional support, share their experiences, discuss expected benefits of engagement with services, encourage parents to see they have influence over their child's services, identify parent's social supports, provide information support, and problem solve with the parent. These topics and strategies are reflected in the Family Contact Log which PCs are trained to complete following each call. PCs are not expected to cover all topics or use all strategies on each call, but rather to individualize the calls to the immediate needs of the family. The focus of the calls is on providing parent-to-parent support to help promote positive engagement in school and community mental health services available for a child with EBD. This is accomplished by PCs sharing their experiences, something that can only be provided by another parent with a similar lived experience. It is important to note that PCs are not trained to provide parent training or case management typically provided by professionals (e.g., Family Check-up; Dishion et al., 2014). Rather, the goal is for the PC to encourage the parent to be an effective partner with school and mental health professionals, knowledgeable about special education and emotional/behavioral services, and a skilled advocate for their child.

Recruitment and Training of PCs

As described in the Parent Connectors Administration Manual (Duchnowski & Kutash, 2018) the program begins with recruiting and interviewing peers to serve as PCs. While schools can recruit their own PCs, we have found partnering with local family support agencies to be an excellent source for identifying veteran parents. Once hired, a manualized training program is implemented for the PCs that includes 24 hours of initial training, by a certified Parent Connectors Trainer and a former Parent Connector. During the training, PCs participate in extensive team building, didactic sessions, role playing, and share their personal experiences. The training emphasizes that PCs give support, not therapy, and provide resources, not intervention, to the family. PCs are coached to emphasize the parent's role in encouraging the participation of their youth in the education and counseling services that are offered to them in school, to attend school regularly, and to be engaged in learning. The content of the training ensures that PCs are prepared to implement the intervention's four components (see Figure 7.1). Booster training sessions are provided throughout the year to expand skill sets. It is recommended that PCs who work about 15 hours a week are assigned approximately 10–15 families to contact each week for a phone conversation lasting approximately 30 to 60 minutes. PCs are also expected to engage in ongoing assessments of fidelity of implementations of the program.

Supervision

PCs are supervised and supported by a Parent Connector Coach, who also monitors the fidelity of implementation of the program. The PC Coach is a professional who holds a master's degree (e.g., social worker, psychologist) and has extensive experience with children who have EBD and their families. The PC Coach could be recruited from a variety of sources such as a school-employed social worker or a psychologist providing services to students at the schools. A 6-hour manualized training is implemented for the PC Coach to develop understanding of the program model and competency in assessing fidelity and providing support and supervision for the PCs. The PC Coach meets weekly as a group for two hours with the PCs to review the content of each parent contact for that week and to share experiences. During these meetings, fidelity data are discussed using the weekly Family Contact Log, including the number and duration of calls made to each family, as well as the topics of conversation. PCs also discuss ways to tailor conversations for specific family needs and to problem-solve solutions to difficulties. The PC Coach also routinely collaborates with the Program Administrator(s), which could be a school administrator or a director of a local family agency, which hires and supervises the PCs. The PC Coach ensures that the fidelity data are entered weekly and that the weekly/quarterly implementation reports are run and shared with Program Administrators, appropriate school administrators, and the Parent Connectors Training team.

Randomized Studies of Parent Connectors

To date, three U.S. Department of Education funded studies (Duchnowski, 2004 (CFDA 84.324C); Duppong Hurley, 2013 (R324A130180); Duchnowki, 2009 (R324A090049)) have been conducted on Parent Connectors. The initial development study included 115 families of middle school students with EBD (see Kutash, Duchnowski, Green and Ferron, 2011). For the Parent Connectors condition, engagement in the intervention was high; 70% were engaged with their PC. Pre-post changes between the Parent Connectors and a comparison condition revealed increases in both family empowerment and efficacy with the education and mental health systems for the PC condition. The students of participating families experienced an increase (corresponding to a medium effect size) in the number of school-based mental health services they received, attended almost a month more of school, and increased their reading achievement. Exploratory analyses also indicated that the positive effects of program participation were greater for those parents who exhibited the highest levels of caregiver strain at pre-test.

The second study explored the theoretical underpinnings of Parent Connectors, developed a theory of change, and conducted a small randomized clinical trial. This trial included 128 families of middle school students with EBD. Of the 66 families in the treatment condition, 88% were engaged. A psychometrically sound fidelity implementation system was designed for this study (Kutash et al., 2012). Students whose parents had a PC had fewer school suspensions and received a significantly greater amount of school-based mental health services than the comparison group. Examination of the subgroup of highly strained parents revealed that parents who participated in Parent Connectors experienced greater improvements than the comparison group. For proximal parent outcomes, parents in the treatment condition had significantly higher scores at posttest than the comparison group regarding expected benefit, and trended towards improved outcomes for mitigating social norms, decreasing strain, and increased self-efficacy. With regard to student outcomes, for the high-strain parents, youth in the treatment condition received significantly more minutes of school-based mental health services and students had better emotional functioning than those in the comparison group (see Kutash, Duchnowski, Green & Ferron, 2013). We also found that parents with high stress participated in significantly more phone calls than caregivers with less stress (Duppong Hurley, January, & Lambert, 2017). A third study is currently being conducted to examine the efficacy of Parent Connectors with over 300 middle school students with EBD.

Peer-to-peer support for families of youth with EBD provides an important avenue to reach families struggling with high levels of stigma and blame surrounding their child's mental health. Participants in our studies report that teachers or other family members may be judgmental and not fully understand their situation or child's diagnosis, which can lead to increased feelings of stigma and isolation. However, the support of a peer whose child has similar behavioral challenges is different. We have found that parents are highly receptive to peer-to-peer support, and find the idea that they are not alone in their journey to support their child to be reassuring. In Parent Connectors post-program surveys, 95% of participants discussed the importance of shared experience, making it the most prominent theme identified. Shared experienced not only reduced feelings of stigma and isolation, but created an environment for honest and authentic communication. Furthermore, having another parent—who has walked the same road—to provide encouragement and helpful strategies can help remove barriers to engaging in educational and mental health supports. Parents report being open to and appreciating the informational supports, resources, problem-solving, and strategies provided to them through peer-to-peer support. The results of these initial studies are encouraging on two fronts. The adoption and implementation of models such as Parent Connectors within the community is realistic. Secondly, the results indicate improved outcomes for the families of children with EBD.

Pressing Issues and New Directions for Peer-to-Peer Family Support

While providing peer-to-peer support for families of youth with EBD is a promising practice, many issues have yet to be addressed. One important factor surrounding peer support is funding models. In 2014, 31 states allowed Medicaid to finance family and peer support through certified peer specialists (Ostow, Steinwachs, Leaf, & Naeger, 2017). Peer support is recognized as a growing and essential field, yet what states specifically fund and at what reimbursement rates remains highly variable. For example, some states support peer-support only for adults, while others allow reimbursement also for peer-support for the families of youth with EBD. Along with funding is the related issue of where peer-support services for families of youth with EBD are located within the service system. Some efforts to embed peer-support specialists into multidisciplinary mental health teams has experienced difficulties with role clarifications (Kutash, Acri et al., 2014). Currently, many peer specialists are located in free-standing family-serving agencies often affiliated with national organizations such as NAMI and FFCMH, which also provide access to training and certification material to members. So, other agencies such as schools, child welfare, or juvenile justice agencies wishing to provide peer-support may wish to partner with these family-serving agencies to meet the needs of families of youth with EBD.

With additional funding possibilities for peer-support for families with EBD, increased attention is being directed toward understanding how to best implement, train, disseminate, and customize peer-support programs. A key aspect of this research needs to help provide guidance on how to best match families to peer-support services of different intensity and format (e.g. small groups, online support, one-on-one support). Along with this are questions regarding frequency and duration, such as how long peer-to-peer supports should be offered to families. These sorts of factors encompass a broad field of implementation and dissemination questions regarding how peer-to-peer support services are delivered and what aspects are the most helpful to families during different developmental stages with their child. The creation of a continuum of access of peer-support ranging from informal to formal services with scaffolding to help families move in and out of more formal support structures would be ideal. In recent years, technology has been emerging as a way that might be able to help scaffold peer-support services. Technology can influence both formal and informal support with online support groups, messaging forums, social communities (e.g. Facebook) as well as phone calls and text messaging. Future efforts exploring how to tailor technology to deliver effective peer-to-peer support (such as incorporating HIPPA compliant peer-support texting apps) hold considerable promise, and could help reach many more families in need.

One of the inherent strengths of the peer-support model is the incredible ease of customization for diverse and unique populations. For example, the way Parent Connectors is trained and delivered remains largely constant regardless of use with middle school youth or elementary age youth, or whether the youth are identified with EBD or it is used in more of a prevention approach with youth at risk for EBD (January et al., 2016). We are beginning to explore any adaptations that might be needed to implement with other diverse populations. But, as the primary method to reach families is by sharing the experiences of parents, this approach is highly flexible to be implemented with a range of diverse populations and settings, such as recent immigrants, families entering juvenile justice or child welfare settings (Gopalan, Acri, Lalayants, Hooley, & Einbinder, 2014).

Finally, peer to peer support for families of youth with EBD needs to keep focused on outcomes that are within their scope of reach. By providing peer support, these interventions are attempting to accomplish goals such as reducing caregiver strain, improving parental attitudes towards school and community services for youth with EBD, increasing parental knowledge about EBD, reducing parental shame and stigma, and improving the child's use and access of necessary supports. However, funders are often also interested in additional layers of outcomes, such as improvements in the child's mental health and academic functioning. Typically, these more distal outcomes are beyond the direct influence of peer-support programs. In essence, peer support is primarily an engagement intervention designed to help increase the uptake of other supports in the community. If the other services are mediocre or ineffective, then the impact on distal outcomes could be rather negligible despite an effective peer-support model. Research to examine the effect of pairing peer-support with other evidence-based models of family services could be a highly effective combination.

The provision of peer support has been a key grassroots effort for many years as friends and neighbors have helped to support each other through difficult times. With the development of manualized and research-supported peer-support interventions, we are now embarking on a new frontier to discover ways to provide effective, high-quality, customizable peer support that can be delivered to all families of youth with EBD in an affordable manner whenever needed. By helping parents to shed the stigma of blame and shame, and walking with them—as equal partners—peer-support can help parents be effective advocates for their children with EBD and, together, can reshape the future of our at risk children.

Author Note

The research was supported by grants from the U.S. Department of Education, Institute for Education Sciences (R324A130180; R324B160033). The opinions expressed by the authors are not necessarily reflective of the position of or endorsed by the U.S. Department of Education.

References

Acri, M., Craig, N., & Adler, J. (2018). An examination of peer-delivered parenting skills programs across New York State. *Community Mental Health Journal.* doi:10.1007/s10597-018-0269-1.

Ajzen, I. (1991). The theory of planned behavior. *Organizational Behavior and Human Decision Processes, 50,* 179–211.

Armitage, C., & Conner, M. (2001). Efficacy of the theory of planned behaviour: A meta-analytic review. *British Journal of Social Psychology, 40,* 471–499.

Bickman, L., Heflinger, C. A., Northrup, D., Sonnichsen, S., & Schilling, S. (1998). Long term outcomes to family caregiver empowerment. *Journal of Child and Family Studies, 7*(3), 269–282.

Brannan, A. M., & Heflinger, C. A. (2006). Caregiver, child, family, and service system contributors to caregiver strain in two child mental health service systems. *The Journal of Behavioral Health Services & Research, 33*(4), 408–422.

Brannan, A. M., Heflinger, C. A., & Foster, E. M. (2003). The role of caregiver strain and other family variables in determining children's use of mental health services. *Journal of Emotional and Behavioral Disorders, 11,* 77–91. doi:10.1177/106342660301100202

Dishion, T. J., Brennan, L. M., Shaw, D. S., McEachern, A. D., Wilson, M. N., & Jo, B. (2014). Prevention of problem behavior through annual family check-ups in early childhood: Intervention effects from home to early elementary school. *Journal of Abnormal Child Psychology, 42,* 343–354.

Douglas, T., Redley, B., & Ottmann, G. (2016). The first year: The support needs of parents caring for a child with an intellectual disability. *Journal of Advanced Nursing, 72,* 2738–2749.

Duchnowski, A. (2004). An empirical investigation of the effectiveness of parent support groups. U.D. Department of Education, Office of Special Education Programs (OSEP) – Model Development Project. (CFDA 84.324C).

Duchnowski, A. (2009). Parent connectors: A parent support program to improve outcomes for students who have emotional disturbances. U.S. Department of Education Institute for Educational Sciences. (#R324A090049).

Duchnowski, A., & Kutash, K. (2018). *Parent connectors: Agency administrators manual.* Lincoln, NE: University of Nebraska - Lincoln.

Duchnowski, A. J., Kutash, K., Green, A. L., Ferron, J. M., Wagner, M., & Vengrofski, B. (2013). Parent support services for families of children with emotional disturbances served in elementary school special education settings: Examination of data from the special education elementary longitudinal study. *Journal of Disability Policy Studies, 24*(1), 36–52. doi:10.1177/1044207312460889

Duppong Hurley, K. (2013). Parent connectors: An efficacy study of peer-support for parents of middle-school youth with emotional disorders. U.S. Department of Education Institute for Educational Sciences. (#R324A130180).

Duppong Hurley, K., January, S.-A.-A., & Lambert, M. C. (2017). Using caregiver strain to predict participation in a peer-support intervention for parents of children with emotional or behavioral needs. *Journal of Emotional and Behavioral Disorders, 25,* 170–177.

Duppong Hurley, K. L., Lambert, M. C., & Huscroft D'Angelo, J. N. (2019). Comparing a framework for conceptualizing parental involvement in education between students at risk of emotional and behavioral issues and students without disabilities. *Journal of Emotional and Behavioral Disorders, 27*(2), 67–75.

Elementary and Secondary Education Act of 1965, 20 U.S.C. §§ 6301-7981 (2015).

Fan, X., & Chen, M. (2001). Parental involvement and students' academic achievement: A meta-analysis. *Educational Psychology Review, 13,* 1–22.

Farmer, E. M. Z., Burns, B. J., Angold, A., & Costello, E. J. (1997). Impact of children's mental health problems on families: Effects on services. *Journal of Emotional and Behavioral Disorders, 5,* 230–238.

Godin, G., & Kok, G. (1996). The theory of planned behavior: A review of its applications to health-related behaviors. *American Journal of Health Promotion, 11,* 87–98.

Gopalan, G., Acri, M., Lalayants, M., Hooley, C., & Einbinder, E. (2014). Child welfare involved caregiver perceptions of family support in child mental health treatment. *Journal of Family Strengths, 14,* 1–25.

Green, A. L., Lambert, M. C., & Duppong Hurley, K. (2019). Measuring activation in parents of youth with emotional and behavioral disorders. *The Journal of Behavioral Health Services & Research, 46*(2), 306–318.

Gyamfi, P., Walrath, C., Burns, B., Stephens, R., Geng, Y., & Stambaugh, L. (2009). Family education and support services in systems of care. *Journal of Emotional and Behavioral Disorders, 18*, 14–26.

Heflinger, C., Northrup, D., Sonnichsen, S., & Brannan, A. (1998). Including a family focus in research on community-based services for children with serious emotional disturbance: Experiences from the Fort Bragg evaluation project. In M. Epstein, K. Kutash, & A. Duchnowski (Eds.), *Outcomes for children and youth with emotional and behavioral disorders and their families: Programs and evaluation best practices* (pp. 261–293). Austin, TX: Pro-Ed.

Hoagwood, K. (2005). Family-based services in children's mental health: A research review and synthesis. *The Journal of Child Psychology and Psychiatry, 46*(7), 690–713.

Hoagwood, K., Olin, S., Storfer-Isser, A., Kuppinger, A., Shorter, P., Wang, N., ... Horwitz, S. (2018). Evaluation of a train-the-trainers model for family peer advocates in children's mental health. *Journal of Child and Family Studies, 27*, 1130–1136.

Hoagwood, K. E., Cavaleri, M. A., Olin, S. S., Burns, B. J., Slaton, E., Gruttadaro, D., & Hughes, R. (2010). Family support in children's mental health: A review and synthesis. *Clinical Child and Family Psychology Review, 13*(1), 1–45.

Individuals with Disabilities Education Improvement Act, 20 U.S.C. § 1400 et seq. (2004). Retrieved from https://sites.ed.gov/idea/statute-chapter-33

Ireys, H., & Sakwa, D. D. (2006). Building family-to-family support programs: Rationale, goals, and challenges. *Focal Point, 20*(1), 10–14.

Ireys, H. T., Chernoff, R., DeVet, K. A., & Kim, Y. (2001). Maternal outcomes of a randomized controlled trial of a community-based support program for families of children with chronic illnesses. *Archives of Pediatrics & Adolescent Medicine, 155*(7), 771–777.

January, S.-A.-A., Duppong Hurley, K., Stevens, A. L., Kutash, K., Duchnowski, A. J., & Pereda, N. (2016). Evaluation of a community-based peer-to-peer support program for parents of at risk youth with emotional and behavioral difficulties. *Journal of Child and Family Studies, 25*, 836–844.

Jeynes, W. (2005). A meta-analysis of the relation of parental involvement to urban elementary school student academic achievement. *Urban Education, 40*, 237–269.

Jeynes, W. (2007). The relationship between parental involvement and urban secondary school student academic achievement: A meta-analysis. *Urban Education, 42*, 82–110.

Knitzer, J., & Olson, L. (1982). *Unclaimed children: The failure of public responsibility to children and adolescents in need of mental health services.* Washington, DC: Children's Defense Fund.

Kuhn, E., & Laird, R. (2014). Family support programs and adolescent mental health: Review of evidence. *Adolescent health, medicine, and Therapeutics, 5*, 127–142.

Kutash, K., Acri, M., Pollock, M., Armusewicz, K., Olin, S. C. S., & Hoagwood, K. E. (2014). Quality indicators for multidisciplinary team functioning in community-based children's mental health services. *Administration and Policy in Mental Health and Mental Health Services Research, 41*(1), 55–68.

Kutash, K., Cross, B., Madias, A., Duchnowski, A. J., & Green, A. L. (2012). Description of a fidelity implementation system: An example from a community-based children's mental health program. *Journal of Child and Family Studies, 21*, 1028–1040.

Kutash, K., Duchnowski, A. J., Green, A. L., & Ferron, J. (2013). Effectiveness of the parent connectors program: Results from a randomized controlled trial. *School Mental Health, 5*, 192–208.

Kutash, K., Duchnowski, A. J., Green, A. L., & Ferron, J. M. (2011). Supporting parents who have youth with emotional disturbances through a parent-to-parent support program: A proof of concept study using random assignment. *Administration and Policy in Mental Health, 38*, 412–427.

Kutash, K., Garraza, L. G., Ferron, J. M., Duchnowski, A. J., Walrath, C., & Green, A. L. (2013). The relationship between family education and support services and parent and child outcomes over time. *Journal of Emotional and Behavioral Disorders, 21*, 264–276.

Law, M., King, S., Stewart, D., & King, G. (2002). The perceived effects of parent-led support groups for parents of children with disabilities. *Physical & Occupational Therapy in Pediatrics, 21*(2–3), 29–48.

McCubbin, H., & Patterson, J. (1983). The family stress process: The double ABCX Model of adjustment and adaptation. *Marriage and Family Review, 6*(1–2), 7–37.

McKay, M., Stoewe, J., McCadam, K., & Gonzales, J. (1998). Increasing access to child mental health services for urban children and their caregivers. *Health and Social Work, 23*, 9–15.

Newman, L. (2005). *Family involvement in the educational development of youth with disabilities: A special topic report of findings from the national longitudinal transition study-2 (NLTS2).* Menlo Park, CA: SRI International.

Olin, S. S., Hoagwood, K., Rodriguez, J., Ramos, B., Burton, G., Penn, M., … Jensen, P. (2010). The application of behavior change theory to family-based services: Improving parent empowerment in children's mental health. *Journal of Child and Family Studies, 19*, 462–470.

Olin, S. S., Shen, S., Rodriguez, J., Radigan, M., Burton, G., & Hoagwood, K. E. (2015). Parent depression and anger in peer-delivered parent support services. *Journal of Child and Family Studies, 24*, 3383–3395.

Osher, T. W., Osher, D., & Blau, G. M. (2008). Families matter. In T. Gullotta & G. Blau (Eds.), *Family influences on childhood behavior and development* (pp. 57–80). New York, NY: Routledge.

Ostow, L., Steinwachs, D., Leaf, P., & Naeger, S. (2017). Medicaid reimbursement of mental health peer-run organizations: Results of a national survey. *Admiration and Policy in Mental Health and Mental Health Services, 44*, 501–5121.

Preyde, M., & Ardal, F. (2003). Effectiveness of a parent "buddy" program for mothers of very preterm infants in a neonatal intensive care unit. *Canadian Medical Association Journal, 168*, 969–973.

Resch, A., Mireles, G., Benz, M. R., Grenweldge, C., Peterson, R., & Zhang, D. (2010). Giving parents a voice: A qualitative study of the challenges experienced by parents of children with disabilities. *Rehabilitation Psychology, 55*, 139–150.

Robbins, V., Johnston, J., Barnett, H., Hobstetter, W., Kutash, K., Duchnowski, A. J., & Annis, S. (2008). *Parent to parent: A synthesis of the emerging literature.* Tampa, FL: University of South Florida, The Louis de la Parte Florida Mental Health Institute, Department of Child & Family Studies.

Rodriguez, J., Olin, S. S., Hoagwood, K., Shen, S., Burton, G., Radigan, M., & Jensen, P. (2011). The development and evaluation of a parent empowerment program for family peer advocates. *Journal of Child and Family Studies, 20*, 397–405.

Rosenzweig, J., Brennan, E., & Ogilvie, A. M. (2002). Work-family fit: Voices of parents of children with emotional and behavioral disorders. *Social Work, 47*, 415–424.

Rosenzweig, J. M., & Huffstutter, K. J. (2004). Disclosure and reciprocity: On the job strategies for taking care of business and family. *Focal Point: A National Bulletin on Family Support and Children's Mental Health, 18*(1), 4–7.

Schiller, E., Burnaska, K., Cohen, G., Douglas, Z., Fiore, T., & Glazier, R. (2003). *The study of state and local implementation and impact of the individuals with disabilities education act: Final interim report (1999–2000 school year).* Bethesda, MD: Abt Associates.

Solomon, M., Pistrang, N., & Barker, C. (2001). The benefits of mutual support groups for parents of children with disabilities. *American Journal of Community Psychology, 29*, 113–132.

Stroul, B. A., & Friedman, R. M. (1994). *A system of care for children and youth with severe emotional disturbances.* Washington, DC: Georgetown University, CASSP Technical Assistance Center.

Wagner, M., Friend, M., Bursuck, W. D., Kutash, K., Duchnowski, A. J., Sumi, W. C., & Epstein, M. H. (2006). Educating students with emotional disturbance: A national perspective on school programs and services. *Journal of Emotional and Behavioral Disorders, 14*, 12–30.

Wagner, M., Kutash, K., Duchnowski, A. J., Epstein, M. H., & Sumi, W. C. (2005). The children and youth we serve: A national picture of the characteristics of students with emotional disturbances receiving special education. *Journal of Emotional and Behavioral Disorders, 13*, 79–96.

Wisdom, J., Olin, S., Shorter, P., Burton, G., & Hoagwood, K. (2011). Family peer advocates: A pilot study of the content and process of service provision. *Journal of Child and Family Studies, 20*, 833–843.

Wymbs, B., Pelham, W., Molina, B., & Gnagy, E. (2008). Mother and adolescent reports of interparental discord among parents of adolescents with and without attention-deficit/hyperactivity disorder. *Journal of Emotional and Behavioral Disorders, 16*(1), 29–41.

8 The Family Check-Up
Building on Family Strengths to Promote Child Wellbeing

Anne M. Gill and Daniel S. Shaw

The demand for evidence-based intervention models that promote child wellbeing and healthy patterns of social and emotional development has led to a burgeoning awareness about best practices. The purpose of this chapter will be to highlight many of the established best practices for promoting healthy child development and family functioning through the lens of the Family Check-Up Model, an evidence-based program for the prevention and treatment of child behavioral and emotional problems (Dishion et al., 2008; Reuben, Shaw, Brennan, Dishion, & Wilson, 2015; Shaw et al., 2016, 2019; Shaw, Dishion, Supplee, Gardner, & Arnds, 2006; Shelleby et al., 2012).

Countless studies demonstrate the importance of ecology and family when treating problem behavior and promoting positive outcomes for children (Forgatch & Patterson, 2010; Stormshak et al., 2011; Weisz & Kazdin, 2010; Zisser & Eyberg, 2010). More than two decades of research demonstrates the effectiveness of early home, pediatric, and community based interventions to promote positive child outcomes via improvement in parenting practices (Dishion et al., 2008; Dishion & Kavanagh, 2003; Weisz & Kazdin, 2010). Additionally, recent research demonstrates that improvements in early caregiving quality facilitate healthy brain development and link to long-term positive child outcomes across a range of domains, among them: language development and academic achievement, cognitive functioning, emotion regulation, and social skills (Brennan et al., 2013; Chang, Shaw, Dishion, Gardner, & Wilson, 2014; Fisher, Frenkel, Noll, Berry, & Yockelson, 2016; Mendelsohn, Cates, Weisleder, Berkule, & Dreyer, 2013). Often described as two-generation programs, these models promote healthy child development by improving parenting practices and thus address the important link between parental caregiving and child wellbeing.

The Family Check-Up: Theoretical Underpinnings

Family Check-Up Model developer Tom Dishion and others posit a "Cascade Model" (Dishion, Ha, & Véronneau, 2012; Dodge, Greenberg, Malone, & CPPRGroup, 2008; Haller, Handley, Chassin, & Bountress, 2010; Sitnick, Shaw, & Hyde, 2014) to describe the process by which problems in early childhood, such as the child's poor emotion regulation and aggressive behavior, can initiate a cascade of effects that predict a negative trajectory over time. Masten and Cicchetti (2010) discuss the hypothesis that "developmental cascades alter the course of development" (p. 491), a point echoed by others (Shaw & Gilliam, 2017; Shaw & Gross, 2008; Sitnick et al., 2017), who have identified early predictors of later antisocial behavior. For instance, before a child is 3 years old, parenting quality, maternal depression, and other family stressors (e.g., parenting hassles, low parental social support) are some of the best predictors of persistent trajectories of antisocial behavior from ages 2 to

17 (Shaw & Gilliam, 2017; Shaw & Gross, 2008). Focusing only on child factors, as early as ages 2–3, impairments with emotion regulation and elevated levels of oppositional and aggressive behavior are consistent predictors of adolescent and young adult antisocial behavior (Shaw & Gilliam, 2017). These developmental cascades operate with bidirectional child and parent factors interacting with ecological stressors (such as poverty and neighborhood dangerousness). Looking outside the family context, the intra- and inter-personal factors in the social (peer) environment can potentiate negative behavior patterns in these cascades (Dishion et al., 2008; Sitnick et al., 2017). The highly complex interplay among these factors is one of the reasons that behavioral interventions should be designed to address the complexity of children's lives. The identification of early problems, ecological factors, and/or skills deficits (in child or parent) associated with the initiation of a negative developmental cascade can be a cue for intervention. Ideally, effective strategies to modify the course of the negative trajectory can begin early and serve the function of preventing maladaptive child outcomes.

Throughout childhood, the presence of positive family factors, such as warmth in family relationships, effective communication, appropriate use of positive behavior support, and low levels of parent–child conflict, can have a strong countervailing impact on these negative developmental cascades (Masten & Reed, 2002; Stouthamer-Loeber, Loeber, Wei, Farrington, & Wikström, 2002). It behooves us as a field to identify and effectively apply evidence-based models of intervention to interrupt negative patterns and to foster the presence of supportive, resilient, and engaged parenting practices that have the power to promote positive futures for children.

Over the past two decades, the field of prevention science has seen a tremendous increase in knowledge about best practices for promoting child development and social, emotional, and behavioral health (Becker et al., 2015; Chorpita & Daleiden, 2009). Most of these programs describe the important role of parenting quality for promoting child wellbeing and offer intervention strategies designed to improve caregiving quality. Across models of effective intervention, better outcomes for child development, wellbeing, and behavior are observed when interventions include the following components (Becker et al., 2015; Filene, Kaminski, Valle, & Cachat, 2013; Landry, Smith, Swank, & Guttentag, 2008; Mendelsohn et al., 2013), presented here in list format for ease of reference:

- Teach developmental norms and appropriate expectations.
- Provide instruction and practice (rehearsal/role play) for behavior management techniques and responsive and sensitive parenting practices.
- Build a caring, trusting relationship with family.
- Provide learning materials – such as toys and books.
- Use video review and video feedback of parent–child interactions.
- Address parental substance use and mental health.
- Include problem-solving components.
- Include assessment practices.
- Match clients and interventionist on race and ethnicity.

The Family Check-Up (FCU) incorporates most of the aforementioned components in a stepwise fashion. In addition to these critical components, the FCU adds (1) a clear emphasis on parent, child, and family strengths, (2) attention to motivational enhancement, and (3) an ecological and multi-method assessment of parent and child wellbeing and relationship functioning. In this way, the FCU expands on the existing literature about best practices and offers a powerful method of effective intervention, in part, because of its capacity to address the complexity of children's ecologies. Additionally, the FCU stands apart from many other interventions because it can be offered as a stand-alone intervention or as a precursor or enhancement to other evidence-based interventions.

The Family Check-Up Model

The FCU Model is a strength-based, brief intervention designed to promote child wellbeing and to prevent problem behavior by addressing and supporting improvements in parenting practices and ecological stressors. The FCU consists of three key steps: the Initial Interview, a Child and Family Assessment, and a Feedback Session, each of which takes about 60 minutes to complete (see Figure 8.1). The FCU was originally designed as a home visitation model, however, it can be offered in any community, pediatric, or clinic setting. The home visitation approach is designed to remove obstacles to treatment for families experiencing high levels of adversity where issues such as transportation, extreme poverty, and household chaos may prevent them from presenting at a community clinic.

The FCU begins with an Initial Interview. This Initial Interview offers parent(s) (or caregiver(s); for clarity, this author will use the term parent throughout) and provider a chance to "get to know each other" and to begin establishing the relational and procedural frame for the intervention process. The FCU Initial Interview differs from a standard intake assessment or clinical interview, as it offers a more relaxed frame for a highly strength-based conversation, *and* the provider makes a concerted effort to link issues that arise to impacts on caregiving quality and child wellbeing. This initial interview begins building a collaboration between provider and parent where both members have the opportunity to ask questions and share information. In addition to the good clinical practice of exploring issues and patterns around the presenting problem and family structure, the provider also asks about enjoyable family activities and strengths in parenting, child, and family domains. This balanced focus on problems *and* areas of positive functioning encourages parent and provider alike to consider ways in which the family already possesses the skills they need – or early precursors of those

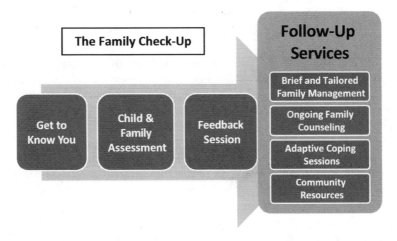

Figure 8.1 The family check-up process

skills – to make the changes they desire. This Initial Interview also carefully weaves in best practices designed to enhance engagement (Kazdin & Krouse, 1983), including: providing a rationale for engaging in the FCU; explaining the length, number, and frequency of sessions; and describing, without the use of jargon, the likelihood for success based on outcomes from the scientific literature. At the completion of this Initial Interview, the provider and parent discuss the next step: the Child and Family Assessment.

The Child and Family Assessment incorporates an ecological approach, acknowledging that children are embedded within relationships and contexts that can provide useful data for case conceptualization and tailoring the intervention phase of the process. The FCU assessment is a multi-method and multi-informant process comprised of both standard and unique questionnaires as well as video-based observation of parent–child interaction. Congruent with the model, the assessment includes indices of child behavioral, emotional, and social functioning, and developmental milestones; indices of parent functioning, wellbeing, mental health, trauma, and substance use, stress and parenting stress; as well as an assessment of caregiving quality in four key areas: positive behavior support, limit setting, monitoring and supervision, and parent–child relationship quality. Providers select an assessment battery that matches the developmental stage of the child, from 1 month to 17 years, with questionnaires and parent–child interaction tasks changing accordingly. The ecological assessment of child and family wellbeing and functioning is a step that sets the FCU apart from many other parent skills training models. The aim of this assessment is twofold: to gather as much information as possible to create a thorough understanding of the child's ecology for both provider and parent, and to increase motivation on the part of the parent to engage in the subsequent steps of the FCU.

Yet another unique feature of the FCU assessment process is the inclusion of videotaped observation of parent–child interactions. This component of the FCU Model is incredibly valuable for providers and parents alike as it brings to life the dynamics of the parent–child relationship and communication patterns. Parent–child interaction tasks are tailored to the developmental age of the child; for example, toddlers and parents engage in a series of play tasks, a clean-up task, and teaching tasks, while adolescents and their parents participate in a series of structured conversations about relevant topics (e.g., parental monitoring of youth activities). Observational tasks are selected to elicit core components of parent–child interaction, including the parent's use of positive behavior support, limit-setting skills, communication patterns, problem-solving skills, and child's level of cooperation, emotion regulation, and attentional focus. The observational assessment serves multiple purposes: (1) it provides parents with the opportunity to interact one-on-one with their child; (2) it demonstrates important information about the dynamics of parent–child interaction along factors that predict child outcomes; and (3) video clips selected from observational assessment are utilized in the Feedback Session of the FCU to give parents the opportunity to directly observe their interactions with their child.

Completing the assessment is an important investment of family time that elucidates much regarding child and family processes, strengths, motivation, ecology, and challenges. An assessment that invites parents to report on their own and their child's wellbeing and functioning begins to promote the parent's capacity for self-reflection about the relationships among their own wellbeing, parenting, and their child's wellbeing. In fact, after the completion of the assessment, parents frequently remark that they want to try something new or make a change in their behavior based on ideas generated through the assessment process itself. In this way, the assessment serves as a springboard for the next step of the FCU: the Feedback Session.

The Feedback Session is the third step in the FCU and is comprised of two phases: the preparation phase, referred to as the case conceptualization, and the in-person Feedback Session with the parent. It is important not to short-change the value of the case conceptualization process, which is an intermediary step between the FCU assessment and Feedback. The case conceptualization phase involves non-direct time on the part of the provider. During this process, the provider is holding the family in mind: Their strengths and resilience, challenges and concerns, their narrative and broader ecology, and even their expressed strivings for improvement. It is the job of the provider to synthesize all of the information gathered from the Initial Interview, the questionnaires from involved caregivers (parents and day care or school teachers), and the observational tasks. This critical step allows the provider to begin to "connect the dots" among the various strengths and stressors within a given family system. With the case conceptualization, the provider crafts a cohesive and accurate reflection of child and family functioning that can be presented in a way that is accessible and motivating for the parent. The task of the provider is to integrate and synthesize data from the various sources into a set of messages that the parent can make meaningful use of in the service of promoting their child's wellbeing.

The Feedback Session itself is the powerhouse of the FCU Model. During the Feedback Session, parent and provider have a collaborative and fact-based conversation about child and family strengths, challenges, and desire for growth and change. The Feedback Session typically lasts between 60 and 90 minutes, depending on the complexity of the family system and the issues the parent is willing to address. The provider presents information to the parent using a Child and Family Feedback Form, which is tailored to reflect the domains assessed and determined to be important for this particular family. This feedback form serves as a guide for the conversation, and serves the purpose of facilitating a "big picture" understanding for the parent about the broad ecology of their family. Presenting family and child strengths and challenges in this format also allows the provider to more easily demonstrate links between areas of functioning, for example, the link between a mother's significant depressive symptomatology and her limited ability to effectively set limits around her child's misbehavior. See an example in Figure 8.2.

The Feedback Session: Structure and Process

In addition to the use of the feedback form to guide the conversation, the Feedback Session incorporates a set of core components, which form a standard structure designed to enhance parent engagement and understanding. The components are as follows:

1. Parent Self-Assessment.
2. Explaining and orienting the family to the structure and process of the Feedback Session.
3. Sharing feedback based on questionnaires, observations, and interviews in a collaborative manner that supports exploration of strengths and problem areas.
4. Checking-in with parent(s) to determine "fit" and accuracy of feedback information.
5. Using video clips selected from the videotaped interaction tasks to highlight parent strengths and provide opportunities for parent self-reflection about parent–child relationship, communication patterns, and child behaviour.
6. Incorporating research to punctuate strengths and highlight areas of concern.
7. Using motivational enhancement strategies.
8. Summarizing the conversation to facilitate goal-setting.
9. Setting parent-driven goals for child and family.
10. Reviewing and discussing a menu of service options.

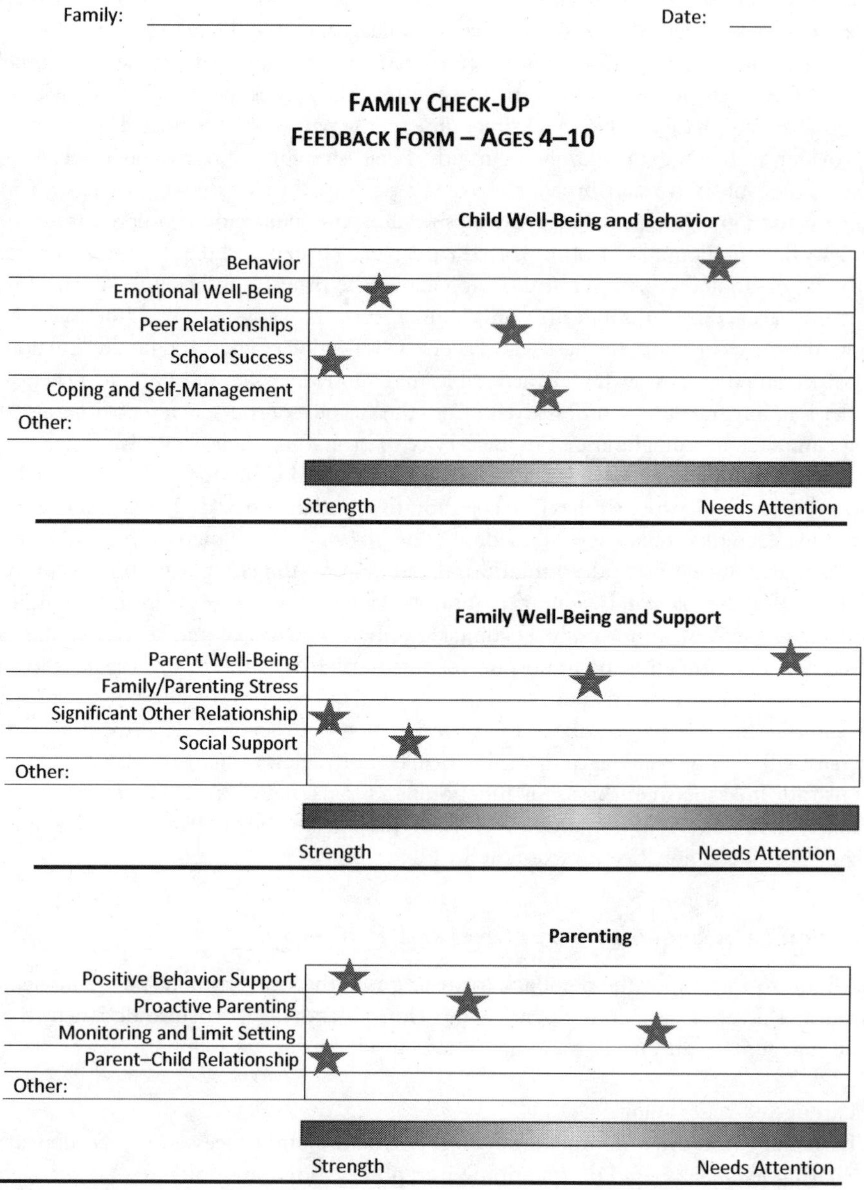

116 *Anne M. Gill and Daniel S. Shaw*

Family: _____   Date: ____

FAMILY CHECK-UP
FEEDBACK FORM – AGES 4–10

Child Well-Being and Behavior

	Strength ———————————— Needs Attention
Behavior	★ (needs attention)
Emotional Well-Being	★ (strength)
Peer Relationships	★ (middle)
School Success	★ (strength)
Coping and Self-Management	★ (middle)
Other:	

Strength — Needs Attention

Family Well-Being and Support

	Strength ———————————— Needs Attention
Parent Well-Being	★ (needs attention)
Family/Parenting Stress	★ (middle)
Significant Other Relationship	★ (strength)
Social Support	★ (strength)
Other:	

Strength — Needs Attention

Parenting

	Strength ———————————— Needs Attention
Positive Behavior Support	★ (strength)
Proactive Parenting	★ (middle)
Monitoring and Limit Setting	★ (needs attention)
Parent–Child Relationship	★ (strength)
Other:	

Strength — Needs Attention

Figure 8.2 The family check-up feedback form

The "Parent Self-Assessment" component occurs at the very beginning of the Feedback Session to convey to the parent that they have a voice in this process and that their opinions matter. Here, the provider poses a question to the parent about what they learned about their child and as a parent by participating in the first two steps of the FCU. Parents vary in their ability to respond and responses offer another window into understanding their perspective about themselves and their child. For example, the self-assessment question often reveals helpful information about the developmental appropriateness of parents' expectations for their child and a "hot topic" or emerging crisis that will need management throughout the session. Once the value of the parent's voice is established, provider and parent(s) are primed to delve into the process of exploring the narrative created in the case conceptualization process.

The provider then spends time explaining the Feedback Session structure and process. This orientation to the process helps to build the rationale for engagement. It also clarifies for the parent that the true focus of the Feedback Session is discovering how to best support their child's optimal development and wellbeing. Provider and parent form a working alliance which places the child's wellbeing at the center of the conversation.

Delivering feedback across all domains explores and reveals how each influences child wellbeing and invites parents to reflect on where they are and where they want to be as a parent as well as what they want for their child. Ambivalence is welcomed and explored as an essential part of the change process and as a method for increasing understanding about facilitators and barriers to change. It is important to note that the Feedback Session is primarily conversational. Each domain provides a fact-based springboard for conversation and exploration to inquire about successes and challenges, and to assess whether the current information fits with the parent's perceptions about their child and family. Examples from the research literature are also incorporated in an accessible way to inform parents about where their child falls according to culturally relevant norms and also to highlight the value of protective factors. The strategic use of research can educate a parent regarding the risk that early problem behavior has on the child's future development (recall developmental cascades) and can also promote the hopeful message that change is possible – intervening early can make a difference for their child.

Importantly, and, consistent with best practices, this feedback conversation weaves in video examples of parent–child interaction. Carefully selected clips from the observational assessment are used to highlight parent strengths, and, when sensitively and thoughtfully applied, can offer the opportunity to examine missed opportunities in the parent–child interaction. This direct transfer of information, unfiltered through the provider's subjective language and experience is very powerful for parents. Based on personal clinical and supervisory experience, the sharing of video-based feedback is often *the* point in the Feedback Session when the parent leans in, when affect brightens, conversations expand, and a palpable enhancement in the working alliance between provider and parent develops. We believe it is much more powerful for a parent to *observe directly* the impact that their praise and involvement has on their child's affect, body language, and attention than having their provider tell them that these factors are important for their child's social and emotional wellbeing.

After reviewing all of the domains on the feedback form and linking areas of functioning, clarifying strengths and problem areas, the provider has an important task: to provide a motivating and accurate summary of the conversation. The Feedback Session covers a wide range of areas, and the provider will have been listening carefully to parent motivation and readiness for change as well as any expression of change talk. When these expressions occur, the provider references these moments in the summary. It may sound something like this, "When we were talking about Julian's temper tantrums, you mentioned you'd like to find a way to prevent them, to feel more in charge; it sounds like you might be willing to talk about strategies on this issue." It is the provider's job to track parent statements and "aha" moments during the feedback session and to remind the parent about these motivational moments prior to inviting the parent to set goals.

The final step of the Feedback Session is setting parent-driven goals. There is considerable emphasis in the field on setting concrete, reasonable, and measurable goals for treatment, which is certainly important; however, at this stage of the FCU, the aim is to promote the parent's voice and engagement in subsequent steps. Parents are often able to articulate value-based and broad-based changes they would like to see in their child's behavior, their own parenting, and/or their living circumstances. At the end of the Feedback Session, the provider is concerned with amplifying motivation for a continued working relationship in which the parent feels that their voice and priorities have been heard and valued. Parent-articulated goals are noted with minimal interpretation or revision (other than to add a positive reframe for negatively stated goals) and then the range of follow-up options is reviewed.

The final step in the FCU Feedback Session is to present parents with a menu of service options. This menu is tailored according to the services and referrals available to a provider/agency and is discussed with the aim of educating parents about the options available and appropriate for them. Follow-up services after the Feedback Session can take many forms, including meeting with their FCU provider for weekly sessions targeting child behavior problems or parent mental health issues, to twice-monthly individualized parent skills training, to group therapy or psychiatric referral, naming just a few options. It is important to present parents with the range of intervention options based on the Feedback Session conversation, along with some clinically informed recommendations for parents to consider. Over the years, parents have told us that this experience of feeling that they had a choice in the amount and type of follow-up service was meaningful for them. So often, in service systems, the type and frequency of services is predetermined or assumed. The FCU is not a one-size-fits-all type of program and affords parents and providers alike the opportunity to select the service that fits best for them at any given point in time. Typically, about one third of parents choose ongoing weekly or every other week sessions with their provider, another third choose to meet for an additional 2–3 sessions on a focused parent skills domain, and the final third choose to address their goals on their own or with another service provider with whom they are already involved.

In terms of follow-up services in the domain of parenting, the FCU is most commonly implemented along with its companion parent-skills training program, called Everyday Parenting (Dishion, Stormshak, & Kavanagh, 2012). The Everyday Parenting (EDP) program is empirically informed and based on best practices in the field. The EDP contains skills-training components common to all evidence-based parenting programs: Positive Behavior Support, Effective Limit Setting and Monitoring, Proactive Parenting, and Family Relationships and Communication. These sessions follow an established structure, beginning with creating a collaborative set and an agenda for each session, the inclusion of tracking and assessment components, consistent use of experiential practice including role play activities with careful coaching, and the opportunity for parent self-assessment and self-reflection.

Outcomes and Empirical Support

The Family Check-Up has robust empirical support across the developmental span of childhood along a range of outcomes that are critical for promoting positive outcomes for children. Multiple randomized controlled trials (RCTs) have demonstrated long-term effects of the FCU, with these trials typically initiated either in early childhood (age 2–3) or early adolescence (age 10–13). In addition to its association with positive outcomes for children, the FCU also has demonstrated significant improvements for parents in both caregiving and wellbeing domains, both of which are associated with improvements in child wellbeing and have been found to mediate the effects of the positive effects of the FCU on child outcomes. Based on this volume's focus on school-age children and adolescents, our discussion of outcomes focuses on intervention trials initiated in early childhood for which follow-ups have been conducted during the school-age period and adolescence.

FCU and Outcomes in Early Childhood

Two RCTs of the FCU initiated during the toddler period have demonstrated significant improvements in child disruptive behavior at preschool (Dishion et al., 2008; Shaw, Dishion, Supplee, Gardner, & Arnds, 2006) and in one trial, through the school-age period (Shaw et al., 2016) and adolescence (Shaw et al., 2019). Similar positive effects have been demonstrated for child emotional problems, beginning in the preschool period (Shaw et al., 2009), but continuing through school-age (Reuben et al., 2015), and adolescence (Connell et al., 2019). Importantly, these improvements have persisted from 2 to 12 years and were based on reports by observers, parents, and teachers. Additionally, the FCU has been consistently associated with improvements in multiple facets of children's self-regulation, including emotion regulation (Shelleby et al., 2012) and inhibitory control (Chang, Shaw, Dishion, Gardner, & Wilson, 2014; Chang, Shaw, Dishion, Gardner, & Wilson, 2015), both of which have been linked to children's later behavioral and academic functioning. Participation in the FCU is also associated with increases in early language development (Lunkenheimer et al., 2008) and academic achievement at school-age (Brennan et al., 2013). Importantly, in many of these studies, intervention effects have been mediated by improvements either in caregiving skills (Brennan et al., 2013; Dishion et al., 2008; Lunkenheimer et al., 2008), maternal depression (Reuben et al., 2015; Shaw et al., 2009), or early child self-regulation skills (Chang et al., 2015; Connell et al., 2019), all targeted mechanisms thought to underlie the effects of the FCU in early childhood.

Considerations for Application and Implementation

The FCU was originally developed by Thomas Dishion at University of Oregon in the 1990s where he conducted the first in a series of RCTs applying the FCU with children in middle school (Dishion, Kavanagh, Schneiger, Nelson, & Kaufman, 2002). Since that time, the FCU has been adapted across the developmental span of childhood, from birth through age 17, and across a range of service delivery platforms and systems, methods, and presenting problems. Examples of service delivery platforms and systems utilizing the FCU include: pediatric and hospital-based clinics, community and social service agencies, schools, Early Head Start and Head Start programs, Early Intervention, and Nutritional Supplement Program for Women, Infants, and Children (WIC). While a more detailed description highlighting key adaptations and implementations follows, the range of FCU applications includes: the FCU as an enhancement to other evidence-based universal or targeted service programs such as Video Interaction Project (VIP; Cates et al., 2018; Positive Behavior Interventions and Support [PBIS]; Pennsylvania Training and Technical Assistance Network), telehealth and online versions (Stormshak et al., 2019), applications specific for the school environment, including threat assessments (Moore, 2019), and applications for specific child and family issues, among them: pediatric obesity (Smith et al., 2018), parental opioid use and associated perinatal opioid exposure (Shaw, Morris, & Mendelsohn, 2019), conduct problems (Shaw, Dishion, Supplee, Gardner, & Arnds, 2006), and teen substance use

(Dishion, Nelson, & Kavanagh, 2003) and health behaviors (Rofey, McMakin, Shaw, & Dahl, 2013). As noted, the FCU is highly flexible and thus able to target a range of clinical issues within various contexts. This transportability across contexts and issues is something unique to the FCU – the model was designed to be tailored to the individual family ecology, and there is a parallel process with the ecology of various service systems and processes.

Applications for School-Age Children: Positive Family Support and the Family Check-Up Online

The FCU is effective for families with children of all ages and can be offered to children exhibiting problems in the home and/or the school environment. Families may seek assistance through the school or through a community behavioral health clinic and providers trained in the FCU can apply the model in its original format to address the needs of families and children. To maximize integration with the school environment and to reach families with limited access to services, two adaptations of the FCU are noteworthy: Positive Family Support and The Family Check-Up Online.

Positive Family Support (PFS) is an adaptation of the FCU designed specifically for the school environment (Stormshak et al., 2011). The PFS version of the FCU is evidence-based and includes universal, selected, and individualized (targeted) components designed to promote positive home-to-school connections and communication. PFS providers collaborate with families and school personnel to improve student behavior, to improve communication between family and school about behavioral expectations, and to offer instruction to families regarding evidence-based strategies to improve youth behavior, wellbeing, and educational performance. Additionally, PFS can be integrated with a school's current Multi-Tiered System of Supports (MTSS), such as Positive Behavioral Interventions and Support (PBIS) and Response to Intervention (RtI), by adding a family component at each level of support. The highest level of support, for students experiencing the greatest level of behavioral disruption, includes offering the three sessions of the FCU, followed by Everyday Parenting sessions.

Another exciting area currently under development by Beth Stormshak at the University of Oregon is the adaptation of FCU for web-based service delivery. Dr. Stormshak has developed The FCU Online – an eHealth tool for prevention and intervention with at risk youth in middle school (Stormshak et al., 2019). This application offers families with limited access to traditional services the opportunity to complete the FCU online. The online version of the FCU incorporates questionnaire assessments, video examples, and interactive tasks designed to enhance parent engagement. A recent trial offered families the opportunity to complete the FCU online-only or online with guided telephone support from a trained FCU provider. Results indicated that reductions in child emotional problems and enhanced parenting confidence at a three-month post-test were greater when the online FCU was accompanied with the telephone-based coaching support (Stormshak et al., 2019).

Applications in Pediatrics: The Use of Screening Tools and Integration with Universal Interventions

Yet another important application has been the work of colleagues Daniel Shaw, Debra Bogen, Alan Mendlesohn, and Pamela Morris to make two significant service delivery adaptations: (1) to embed the FCU within the pediatric platform and (2) to integrate the

FCU into a tiered platform of services by combining FCU with a universal intervention, Video Interaction Project (VIP, Mendelsohn et al., 2013; Shaw, Morris, Mendelsohn, 2019). Across the United States, there is momentum to co-locate behavioral health and pediatric services. Parents see pediatric clinics as a trusted source for care and information; pediatric clinics are also settings with which families are familiar and where parents may have a long-term relationship with a provider/pediatrician. These factors can facilitate engagement in, and trust of, services and are part of what has driven the decision to integrate the FCU within pediatric clinics.

Key issues with co-location of behavioral health within pediatrics include identifying families most in need of a service and burden to both families and clinics. The integration of FCU with VIP has presented the opportunity to test a tiered system of service provision. FCU and VIP share similar goals of enhancing parenting quality and utilize similar components (video-based feedback), which allows them to work well in tandem. Currently, a two-site randomized controlled trial is underway that offers all families assigned to the treatment group the opportunity to participate in VIP, the universal intervention (Shaw, Morris, et al., 2019). To determine eligibility and need for higher intensity services (the FCU), all families complete a screening assessment at repeated intervals to identify elevated risk in domains known to be both predictive of child outcomes as addressable using the FCU (e.g., maternal depression, parenting stress, level of child behavior problems, lack of parental social support). When families report elevated levels of risk, they also are offered the FCU as a home visitation program. Families who decide to receive the FCU continue to participate in the VIP program as they normally would.

Next Steps and Conclusion

This chapter offered an overview of the core components of the FCU, emphasizing best practices for prevention and treatment services for children with emotional and behavioral problems. As a model, the FCU pays special attention to the critical role that parenting quality plays in child wellbeing. The FCU incorporates an ecological frame to assess and intervene in a collaborative and parent-driven process that enhances child and family functioning.

With the wealth of knowledge on best practices and common elements, new frontiers seem to be those related to implementation and adaptation. As noted in this chapter, this can involve implementing evidence-based programs within a range of service delivery systems and adapting model components to address specific issues and areas of concern. The FCU, designed with tailoring in mind from its inception, is a particularly adaptable model and has already been applied across a range of settings and presenting problems.

References

Becker, K. D., Lee, B. R., Daleiden, E. L., Lindsey, M., Brandt, N. E., & Chorpita, B. F. (2015). The common elements of engagement in children's mental health services: Which elements for which outcomes? *Journal of Clinical Child & Adolescent Psychology, 44*(1), 30–43.

Brennan, L. M., Shelleby, E., Shaw, D. S., Dishion, T. J., Gardner, F., & Wilson, M. N. (2013). Indirect effects of the family check-up on school-age academic achievement through improvements in parenting in early childhood. *Journal of Educational Psychology, 105*(762–773), PMC38500059. doi:10.1037/a0032096

Cates, C. B., Weisleder, A., Johnson, S. B., Seery, A. M., Canfield, C. F., Huberman, H., ... & Mendelsohn, A. L. (2018). Enhancing parent talk, reading, and play in primary care: Sustained impacts of the Video Interaction Project. *The Journal of Pediatrics, 199*, 49–56.

Chang, H., Shaw, D. S., Dishion, T. J., Gardner, F., & Wilson, M. N. (2014). Direct and indirect effects of the family check-up on self-regulation from toddlerhood to early school-age. *Journal of Abnormal Child Psychology*, *42*(7), 1117–1128.

Chang, H., Shaw, D. S., Dishion, T. J., Gardner, F. & Wilson, M. N. (2015), Proactive parenting and children's effortful control: Mediating role of language and indirect intervention effects. Social Development, 24, 206–223. doi:10.1111/sode.12069.

Chorpita, B. F., & Daleiden, E. L. (2009). Mapping evidence-based treatments for children and adolescents: Application of the distillation and matching model to 615 treatments from 322 randomized trials. *Journal of Consulting and Clinical Psychology*, *77*(3), 566.

Connell, A. M., Shaw, D., Wilson, M., Danzo, S., Weaver-Krug, C., Lemery-Chalfant, K., & Dishion, T. J. (2019). Indirect effects of the early childhood family check-up on adolescent suicide risk: The mediating role of inhibitory control. *Development and Psychopathology*, *31*(5), 1901–1910.

Dishion, T. J., Connell, A. M., Weaver, C. M., Shaw, D. S., Gardner, F., & Wilson, M. N. (2008). The family check-up with high-risk indigent families: Preventing problem behavior by increasing parents' positive behavior support in early childhood. *Child Development*, *79*(5), 1395–1414.

Dishion, T. J., Ha, T., & Véronneau, M. H. (2012). An ecological analysis of the effects of deviant peer clustering on sexual promiscuity, problem behavior, and childbearing from early adolescence to adulthood: An enhancement of the life history framework. *Developmental Psychology*, *48*(3), 703.

Dishion, T. J., & Kavanagh, K. (2003). *Intervening in adolescent problem behavior: A family-centered approach.* New York, NY: Guilford Press.

Dishion, T. J., Kavanagh, K., Schneiger, A., Nelson, S., & Kaufman, N. K. (2002). Preventing early adolescent substance use: A family-centered strategy for the public middle school. *Prevention Science*, *3*(3), 191–201.

Dishion, T. J., Nelson, N. E., & Kavanagh, K. (2003). The Family Check-Up with high-risk young adolescents: Preventing early-onset substance use by parent monitoring. *Behavior Therapy*, *34*, 553–571.

Dishion, T. J., Stormshak, E. A., & Kavanagh, K. A. (2012). *Everyday parenting: A professional's guide to building family management skills.* Champaign, IL: Research Press.

Dodge, K. A., Greenberg, M. T., & Malone, P. S. Conduct Problems Prevention Research Group. (2008). Testing an idealized dynamic cascade model of the development of serious violence in adolescence. *Child Development*, *79*(6), 1907–1927.

Filene, J. H., Kaminski, J. W., Valle, L. A., & Cachat, P. (2013). Components associated with home visiting program outcomes: A meta-analysis. *Pediatrics*, *132*(Supplement 2), S100–S109.

Fisher, P. A., Frenkel, T. I., Noll, L. K., Berry, M., & Yockelson, M. (2016). Promoting healthy child development via a two-generation translational neuroscience framework: The filming interactions to nurture development video coaching program. *Child Development Perspectives*, *10*(4), 251–256.

Forgatch, M. S., & Patterson, G. R. (2010). Parent management training Oregon model: An intervention for antisocial behavior in children and adolescents. In J. Weisz & A. Kazdin (Eds.), *Evidence-based psychotherapies for children and adolescents* (2nd ed., pp. 159–178). New York: The Guilford Press.

Haller, M., Handley, E., Chassin, L., & Bountress, K. (2010). Developmental cascades: Linking adolescent substance use, affiliation with substance use promoting peers, and academic achievement to adult substance use disorders. *Development and Psychopathology*, *22*(4), 899–916.

Kazdin, A. E., & Krouse, R. (1983). The impact of variations in treatment rationales on expectancies for therapeutic change. *Behavior Therapy*, *14*(5), 657–671.

Landry, S. H., Smith, K. E., Swank, P. R., & Guttentag, C. (2008). A responsive parenting intervention: The optimal timing across early childhood for impacting maternal behaviors and child outcomes. *Developmental Psychology*, *44*(5), 1335.

Lunkenheimer, E. S., Dishion, T. J., Shaw, D. S., Connell, A., Gardner, F., Wilson, M. N., & Skuban, E. M. (2008). Collateral benefits of the family check up on early childhood school readiness: Indirect effects of parents' positive behavior support. *Developmental Psychology*, *44*, 1737–1752.

Masten, A. S., & Cicchetti, D. (2010). Developmental cascades. *Development and Psychopathology*, *22*(3), 491–495.

Masten, A. S., & Reed, M. J. (2002). Resilience in development. In C. R. Snyder & S. J. López (Eds.), *Handbook of positive psychology* (pp. 117–131). New York: Oxford University Press.

Mendelsohn, A. L., Cates, C. B., Weisleder, A., Berkule, S. B., & Dreyer, B. P. (2013). Promotion of early school readiness using pediatric primary care as an innovative platform. *Zero to Three, 34*(1), 29–40.

Moore, K. (2019, August). Increasing the ecological validity and pragmatic usefulness of threat assessments by using structured family assessments: The family check-up as an example. Presented at the Family Check-Up Retreat in Pittsburgh, PA.

Reuben, J., Shaw, D. S., Brennan, L. M., Dishion, T. J., & Wilson, M. N. (2015). A family-based intervention for improving children's emotional problems through effects on maternal depression. *Journal of Consulting and Clinical Psychology, 83*, 1142–1148.

Rofey, D. L., McMakin, D. L., Shaw, D., & Dahl, R. E. (2013). Self-regulation of sleep, emotion, and weight during adolescence: Implications for translational research and practice. *Clinical and Translational Science, 6*(3), 238–243.

Shaw, D. S., Dishion, T. J., Connell, A., Wilson, M. N., & Gardner, F. (2009). Improvements in maternal depression as a mediator of intervention effects on early child problem behavior. *Development and Psychopathology, 21*(417–439), PMC2770003. doi:10.1017/s0954579409000236

Shaw, D. S., Dishion, T. J., Supplee, L. H., Gardner, F., & Arnds, K. (2006). A family-centered approach to the prevention of early-onset antisocial behavior: Two-year effects of the family check-up in early childhood. *Journal of Consulting and Clinical Psychology, 74*, 1–9. Lead article.

Shaw, D. S., Galán, C., Lemery-Chalfant, K., Dishion, T. J., Elam, K. K., Wilson, M. N., & Gardner, F. (2019). Trajectories and predictors of children's early-starting conduct problems: Child, family, genetic, and intervention effects. *Development and Psychopathology, 31*(5), 1911–1921.

Shaw, D. S., & Gilliam, M. (2017). Early childhood predictors of low-income boys antisocial behavior from middle childhood through early adulthood. *Infant Mental Health Journal, 38*(1), 68–82.

Shaw, D. S., & Gross, H. (2008). Early childhood and the development of delinquency: What we have learned from recent longitudinal research. In A. Lieberman (Ed.), *The long view of crime: A synthesis of longitudinal research* (pp. 79–127). New York: Springer.

Shaw, D. S., Morris, P. A., & Mendelsohn, A. L. (2019, September). Smart beginnings. Retrieved from www.ppcl.pitt.edu/our-research/smart-beginnings

Shaw, D. S., Sitnick, S., Brennan, L. M., Choe, D. E., Dishion, T. J., Wilson, M. N., & Gardner, F. (2016). The long-term effectiveness of the Family Check-Up on school-age conduct problems: Moderation by neighborhood deprivation. *Development and Psychopathology, 28*, 1471–1487, PMC26646197, doi:10.1017/S0954579415001212

Shelleby, E. C., Shaw, D. S., Cheong, J., Chang, H., Gardner, F., Dishion, T. J., & Wilson, M. N. (2012). Behavioral control in at-risk toddlers: The influence of the family check-up. *Journal of Clinical Child and Adolescent Psychology, 41*(288–301), PMC3409090. doi:10.1080/15374416.2012.664814

Sitnick, S. L., Shaw, D. S., & Hyde, L. W. (2014). Precursors of adolescent substance use from early childhood and early adolescence: Testing a developmental cascade model. *Development and Psychopathology, 26*(1), 125–140.

Sitnick, S. L., Shaw, D. S., Weaver, C. M., Shelleby, E. C., Choe, D. E., Reuben, J. D., … Taraban, L. (2017). Early childhood predictors of severe youth violence in low-income male adolescents. *Child Development, 88*(1), 27–40.

Smith, J. D., Berkel, C., Rudo-Stern, J., Montaño, Z., St George, S., Prado, G., … Dishion, T. J. (2018). The Family Check-Up 4 Health (FCU4Health): Applying implementation science frameworks to the process of adapting an evidence-based parenting program for prevention of pediatric obesity and excess weight gain in primary care. *Frontiers in Public Health, 6*, 293.

Stormshak, E. A., Connell, A. M., Véronneau, M. H., Myers, M. W., Dishion, T. J., Kavanagh, K., & Caruthers, A. S. (2011). An ecological approach to interventions with high-risk students in schools: Using the family check-up to motivate parents' positive behavior support. *Child Development, 82*, 209–255.

Stormshak, E. A., Seeley, J. R., Caruthers, A. S., Cardenas, L., Moore, K. J., Tyler, M. S., … Danaher, B. (2019). Evaluating the efficacy of the family check-up online: A school-based, ehealth model for the prevention of problem behavior during the middle school years. *Development and Psychopathology, 31*(5), 1873–1886.

Stouthamer-Loeber, M., Loeber, R., Wei, E., Farrington, D. P., & Wikström, P. O. H. (2002). Risk and promotive effects in the explanation of persistent serious delinquency in boys. *Journal of Consulting and Clinical Psychology, 70*(1), 111.

Weisz, J., & Kazdin, A. (Eds.). (2010). *Evidence-based psychotherapies for children and adolescents* (2nd ed.). New York: The Guilford Press.

Zisser, A., & Eyberg, S. M. (2010). Parent-child interaction therapy and the treatment of disruptive behavior disorders. In J. Weisz & A. Kazdin (Eds.), *Evidence-based psychotherapies for children and adolescents* (2nd ed., pp. 179–193). New York: The Guilford Press.

9 Classroom Peer Ecologies and Cultures, and Students with EBD

Social Dynamics as Setting Events for Intervention

Jill V. Hamm, Kristen L. Granger, and Richard A. Van Acker

Introduction

Emotional and behavioral disorders (EBD) are prevalent in a meaningful proportion of students, making this disorder a common experience present in most classrooms in the United States (Ringeisen et al., 2018). Students with and at risk for EBD experience significant difficulties with adjustment at school, including social difficulties, facing barriers in forming and maintaining high quality peer relationships given their low social competence, limited social skills, and often aggressive and disruptive behaviors (Powers & Bierman, 2013). At the same time, the broader context of classroom social dynamics sets the stage for the peer relationships and social experiences of students with or at risk for EBD. Although students' own behavior contributes to both peer experiences and classroom social dynamics, their behavior is occasioned by on-going roles, relationships, norms, and setting events that in turn influence the classroom peer ecology. Teachers guide the social experiences of all students; their intentional and unintentional practices can contribute to classroom social dynamics that promote healthy relationships and social adjustment of students with and at risk for EBD. Understanding the nature of this interplay of individual student, teacher, and classroom social dynamics supports insight into potential malleable factors and leverage points to improve the social adjustment and experiences of students with or at risk for EBD.

Peer Experiences of Students with or at Risk for EBD

In general, interpersonal challenges are a key characteristic of EBD. For instance, approximately 48% of students identified with EBD are rated by their teachers and parents as having social skills at or below the 16th percentile (NTLS–2, 2006). Peer difficulties in this population of students occur early – externalizing behavior problems are highly stable throughout the early elementary school period and contribute to experiences of peer rejection (Sturaro, Van Lier, Cuijpers, & Koot, 2011). Peer relationship difficulties that develop in elementary school often continue into adolescence and without intervention can remain a significant source of impairment through adulthood (Henricsson & Rydell, 2006).

Although social skills deficits are a contributing factor, the peer experiences of students with or at risk for EBD are differentiated by configurations of problem behavior, social roles and relationships with peers, and academic behaviors. Research findings based on person-oriented analyses identify typologies or profiles of students based on co-occurrences of adjustment across academic, behavioral, and social domains. Studies across grade levels have consistently identified five typologies of students: *Model* (above-average academic and social adjustment, and below-average internalizing and externalizing behaviors); *Average* (average levels of academic and social adjustment and internalizing behaviors, and below-average externalizing behaviors); *Tough* (above-average externalizing behaviors and popularity with peers; average academic and social adjustment; and below-average internalizing behaviors); *Troubled* (above-average levels of externalizing and internalizing behaviors; below-average levels of academic and social adjustment); and *Passive* (above-average levels of internalizing; below-average levels of externalizing behaviors and social and academic adjustment). Students with or at risk for EBD can be found in any typology, but are overrepresented as Troubled and Passive, and underrepresented as Model students (Chen et al., 2019; Farmer, Hall, Weiss, Petrin, Meece, & Moorhr, 2011; Farmer, Rodkin, Pearl, & Van Acker, 1999).

Research findings based on person-centered analyses reveal important distinctions in the role of problem behavior across students with or at risk for EBD. Students in different typologies may share specific problem behaviors, but these behaviors serve different functions in the context of the other behaviors typical of the student. For instance, students in both Tough and Troubled typologies exhibit high levels of aggression, but aggressive behavior likely serves different purposes in the context of other aspects of these students' adaptation. Students characterized as Tough are popular and influential with peers, and are likely to use their aggression to dominate classmates and maintain their high social status. Moreover, youth in this typology are perceived by peers to be socially skilled, not lacking in social skills (e.g., Farmer, Estell, Bishop, O'Neal, & Cairns, 2003). In contrast, students characterized as Troubled tend to be socially isolated from peers and to exhibit poor adjustment overall. These students are not leaders with peers, but are more likely to be both bullies and victims. Indeed, Chen et al. (2019) found that sixth grade boys in Troubled, but not Tough or other typologies, were the least likely to report that they would protect peers who were bullied, perceived less peer protection from bullying, and were the most likely of students in all typologies to encourage bullying. Students characterized as both Troubled and Passive exhibit high levels of internalizing behaviors and are at risk for victimization, but only those in the Troubled typology are also likely to bully peers.

Thus, social skills deficits are only one component of difficult peer relationships, and are, in fact, not the primary concern for all students with or at risk for EBD. Behaviors such as aggression that are unequivocally viewed as problematic by adults may serve desirable social functions for students, and may be reinforced by sources other than the teacher. Understanding the peer experiences of students with or at risk for EBD requires attending to the classroom peer ecology: to the social processes among students within a classroom; and the structural, relational, and normative dimensions of classrooms that shape and are shaped by the behaviors and peer relations of any individual student. From this perspective, students with or at risk for EBD can both contribute to and be victims of classrooms in which problem behavior is normative and drives the peer culture (Farmer et al., 2013).

Classroom Peer Ecologies

Within and across formal and informal settings at school, students experience an array of social dynamics within *peer ecologies*. Peer ecologies comprise two major relational systems: a system of interpersonal relationships (i.e., peer group affiliations, friendships), and a social status system that reflects individual students' social standing (i.e., peer acceptance, popularity, disliking) within the larger collective of students (Rodkin & Ryan, 2012). A variety of social processes occur among groups of students within classrooms and schools, which directly contribute to and maintain the interpersonal relationships and social status of individual students, including students with and at risk for EBD.

Individual students participate in the peer ecology by forming and maintaining peer relationships and by positioning themselves in the peer social structure, but these relational systems also develop a larger *peer culture*, which affects and is affected by individual students and their relationships and behaviors. Peer cultures reflect the norms, activities, and values of the peer ecology, particularly with respect to aggression, prosociality, and academic effort and achievement (Hamm, Hoffman, & Farmer, 2012). Peer cultures can be evidenced by the norms that characterize peer groups, by the behavioral characteristics of students who occupy key social roles (e.g., popularity), as well as by the distribution of social status (e.g., popularity, peer acceptance). Peer cultures are also reflected in the structure of the relational system, particularly in terms of access to desirable social status. Peer ecologies in which desirable social status such as popularity is open to all students are egalitarian; when social status is limited to a select few the peer ecology is hierarchical. These aspects of peer cultures directly contribute to and maintain the interpersonal relationships and social status of individual students, including students with and at risk for EBD.

Classroom peer ecologies and peer cultures also indirectly influence the peer relationships of students with or at risk for EBD, as *setting events* for behaviors that influence students' peer relationships (e.g., aggression or social withdrawal; Farmer et al., 2018; Van den Berg & Stolz, 2018). Setting events include interpersonal interactions or social events that can influence the relation between a trigger (i.e., a direct antecedent to a student's behavior) and the resulting behavior. For example, a teacher's verbal reprimands can serve as a trigger for student withdrawal and/or for the display of student aggression (Van Acker, Grant, & Henry, 1996). While triggers are antecedent events that typically occur immediately prior to the display of behavior, setting events typically occur earlier to or concurrent with the behavior and moderate the behavior displayed. For example, a successful social interaction, such as a group of popular students inviting an aggressive, disliked classmate to sit with them at lunch, may positively moderate that student's response to a verbal reprimand from a teacher later that afternoon, allowing the student to accept and respond positively to the reprimand rather than becoming defiant. In this way, the social dynamics of the classroom can serve as setting events that moderate both student behaviors that affect peer relationships, and the effectiveness of behavioral interventions (Farmer, Reinke, & Brooks, 2014).

Classroom Social Dynamics and Peer Relationships of Students with or at Risk for EBD

Through bi-directional interactions among students with or at risk for EBD, and their peers whose behaviors do not put them at risk for EBD, student behaviors and relationships evolve and adapt to fit in with the broader classroom peer ecology and culture. In turn, these naturally occurring social dynamics within classrooms, including group-level social processes, and the emergence and maintenance of relationship structures and norms, contribute to the peer relations of students with or at risk for EBD.

Group-Level Social Processes

Social processes between individual students with or at risk for EBD, and groups of peers, can yield problematic as well as productive relationships. Selection and synchrony can lead students to affiliate with peers similar to themselves in peer groups (selection) and to coordinate their behavior to align with their peer group affiliates (synchrony; Farmer, Hamm, Dawes, Barko-Alva, & Cross, 2019). For example, Farmer and Hollowell (1994) demonstrated that boys with EBD associated with peers who also engaged in high levels of aggression and low levels of cooperation, leadership, and academic performance (i.e., selection). Further, Light and Dishion (2007) reported significant peer influence on behavior, showing that over time adolescents increased their levels of antisocial behavior to become similar to their best friends (i.e., synchrony). In the context of behaviors associated with emotional and behavior disorders (e.g., disruptive behavior, emotional regulation difficulties), peer influence may manifest through deviancy training; a process by which peers reinforce delinquent or aggressive behavior (Dishion & Dodge, 2005). Indeed, Kellam and colleagues (1998) demonstrated that aggressive boys in classrooms with a low proportion of aggressive children exhibited significantly fewer behavior problems six years later than aggressive boys in classrooms with a high proportion of aggressive students. If students with or at risk for EBD associate with peers who display challenging behaviors, they are at increased risk for developing normative beliefs that support the display of aggression and antisocial behavior (Farmer & Hollowell, 1994).

Importantly, however, through their influence over peers and affiliations with other popular-aggressive and popular classmates (e.g., Farmer et al., 2003; Robertson et al., 2010), students with or at risk for EBD who are popular-aggressive (i.e., students in the Tough typology) are likely a source, not victim, of norms favoring aggression. And, not all students who exhibit high levels of aggression affiliate with peer groups comprising classmates high in aggression or social isolation. For example, competent-aggressive students can have social networks as large as those of less aggressive children. These findings demonstrate that the profiles of these peer groups are highly diverse, and suggest that the affiliations of aggressive-popular children are not restricted to aggressive peers (Estell, Cairns, Farmer, & Cairns, 2002). Understanding the interplay between individual student characteristics and the peer context is important as this relation may help to explain the persistence of norms favoring aggression within a classroom.

Particularly relevant to the poor peer relationships for students with or at risk for EBD are social processes engaged in by classmates to exclude or maintain low status of peers with aversive behaviors (Mikami & Normand, 2015). Reputation bias, which refers to the phenomenon in which students' perceptions and interpretations of classmates' behavior depend on their liking of the classmate (Hymel, 1986), is particularly concerning for students with or at risk for EBD, who have a higher prevalence of being disliked by peers. For instance, pre- and early adolescents are more likely to exclude peers who exhibit hyperactive behaviors compared to low academic performance; moreover, children and adolescents maintain negative attitudes toward peers with attention-deficit/hyperactivity disorder (ADHD) and depression, with particularly negative views among early adolescents compared with children, and for ADHD compared with depression (Bellanca & Pote, 2013). In addition to reputation bias, students' attributions for their peers' behaviors influence social relationships. Peers interpret the negative behavior of disliked classmates as stable and under their own control, whereas they interpret the same negative behavior if enacted by liked classmates as unstable and not under their control (Hymel, 1986). And pre- and early adolescents are more likely to believe that peers who exhibit hyperactive behaviors should be able to control their behavior (Gasser, Malti, & Buholzer, 2014). It is important to note that studies of attitudes toward classmates with or at risk for EBD and reputation bias have tended to focus on elementary school children, but reputation bias was found to perpetuate rejection for disliked high school students, as well (Hymel, 1986).

Taken together, these findings suggest that some students with highly disruptive behaviors are disliked and vulnerable to reputation bias, which means that they are not given the benefit of the doubt by peers when they engage in negative – or even ambiguous – behaviors. Moreover, classmates do not integrate these peers into their peer relationships (Mikami & Normand, 2015). An exception to these findings is that if students who frequently exhibit aggression have a peer who provides support during and following intervention, the focal students' peer status improves (Bierman, 1986). This exception may reflect that children and adolescents maintain more favorable attitudes toward peers with ADHD and depression if they interact with those peers (Bellanca & Pote, 2013). Finally, although the results of these studies follow the perspective that students who are rejected by peers are socially marginalized and that reputation bias perpetuates that marginalization, it is also the case that highly aggressive students who are rejected also enjoy influence over peers as well as affiliations with influential peers (Farmer, Hall, Leung, Estell, & Brooks, 2011).

In sum, attention to the interplay of individual student characteristics, such as aggressive or hyperactive behavior, with features of the peer ecology provides critical insight into the variable experiences of students with or at risk for EBD. Considerations of structural and normative dimensions of the classroom peer ecology further help to explain why students who exhibit disruptive, defiant, and aggressive behavior may enjoy high peer status including popularity and well-connected peer group affiliations in some classrooms but may experience peer rejection in others.

Classroom Hierarchical Structure

Results of several studies reveal that the extent to which the overall classroom peer ecology is hierarchical, versus egalitarian, contributes to the social status of students who exhibit high levels of aggression, and who may be at risk for EBD. In a hierarchical classroom, the most powerful and influential social ties and social status roles, such as popularity, are distributed among only a small number of students. In egalitarian classrooms, there are many social ties among children and desirable social status is accessible to more students. Although students on the whole are more productive and have better social adjustment in egalitarian classrooms, students, particularly boys, who exhibit higher levels of aggression tend to enjoy high peer status in hierarchical, compared to egalitarian classrooms (Garandeau, Ahn, & Rodkin, 2011). Moreover, boys who exhibited high levels of aggression early in the school year lost social status across the year in egalitarian classrooms (Ahn & Rodkin, 2014). In classrooms in which the social hierarchy is ambiguous, aggression may become more common perhaps because students become more tolerant of aggression as a way to promote their own status to avoid feeling socially vulnerable (e.g., Adler & Adler, 1995; Evans & Eder, 1993). The authors of these studies have argued that aggression thrives on power imbalances; because the strongest and most powerful social ties are concentrated among only a few students, students who have distinctly low social status and who lack social ties to peers are easy social targets for classmates who exhibit aggression. Students who are prone to aggressive behaviors can maintain their own social status by victimizing more vulnerable classmates. Students are generally motivated to have social ties, particularly to prominent classmates, and tend to avoid behaviors, such as helping out a victimized and lower-status classmate, if that behavior would potentially jeopardize their own status.

Classroom Normative Context

Classroom norms are a key dimension of the classroom peer culture, reflecting the expected and accepted behaviors and dispositions of a group of students such as a class. Different types and focal points of classroom norms have been investigated for their contribution to the peer relationships of students with or at risk for EBD; we summarize findings from a few studies to illustrate particular norms that educators should be aware of, for how they provide a context for peer acceptance and social status, as well as serve as potential setting events for students with or at risk for EBD.

130   *Jill V. Hamm et al.*

Results from studies of elementary school students underscore the importance of classroom *descriptive norms,* which reflect the typical behaviors of members of the class. Classrooms in which students average high achievement and social competence, and low incidences of aggression are generally beneficial for students as a whole, but can have a social cost for students with or at risk for EBD. In one study, first graders with emotional difficulties were more likely to be harassed by peers in classrooms in which high social competence was normative (Leadbeater, Hoglund, & Woods, 2003). In a different study, first graders who evidenced high levels of aggression were rejected by peers only in classrooms in which aggression was not normative (Stormshak, Bierman, Bruschi, Dodge, & Coie, 1999). Chang (2004) demonstrated similar findings for Chinese seventh graders, in which students perceived by peers to be highly aggressive enjoyed greater peer acceptance in classrooms in which aggressive behaviors were normative. A similar pattern emerged, in which students perceived by peers to evidence social withdrawal were more socially accepted in classrooms in which socially withdrawn behaviors were more prevalent. Researchers have interpreted these findings as a function of fit, or similarity between the child and the setting, in which the presence of seemingly undesirable characteristics such as aggression interfere with peer acceptance only when the behaviors deviate from what is typical among the larger group of students (e.g., Bellmore, Witkow, Graham, & Juvonen, 2004). Classroom norms that favor aggression may also function as a setting event; students who fall into the Tough typology (i.e., popular-aggressive youth), in particular, will likely socially thrive in classrooms with norms favoring aggression and will be loath to change their behavior at the risk of losing peer influence.

It is noteworthy that findings are not consistent across studies. For instance, among late elementary school children, the average level of aggression in the class was not associated with peer rejection of students who evidenced aggressive behaviors, although these students were more likely to be rejected in classrooms with norms toward high achievement (Garandeau et al., 2011). Although this possibility requires longitudinal study, developmental changes in the acceptability of aggressive and disruptive behavior may yield different effects of classroom norms as children move into adolescence. For instance, Galvan, Spatzier, and Juvonen (2011) found that students who exhibited disruptive behaviors tended to be viewed as cool by middle schoolers compared to late elementary schoolers, and in a study of elementary schools, fifth graders who exhibited high levels of aggression were more popular and more liked than were fourth graders who exhibited aggressive behaviors (Garandeau et al., 2011). As a result, adolescent students who are highly aggressive with peers and disruptive to the class may enjoy social dominance over peers, and their prestige may be pronounced in classrooms in which disruptive behavior is not the norm (Jonkmann, Trautwein, & Ludtke, 2009).

In a very different line of research, classroom norms for sympathy and inclusion are relevant to the peer relations of students who exhibit hyperactive behaviors. Findings are based on students' responses to hypothetical scenarios, and involve perceptions of classmates' views rather than actual behaviors and attitudes, but reveal that late elementary students' intentions to include hyperactive peers in activities that their behavior would disrupt, such as social interactions, are influenced by their perceptions that classmates would be sympathetic toward and include these peers (Gasser, Grutter, & Torchetti, 2018). In a different study of 6, 9, and 12 year olds, these authors found that classroom norms that emphasized competition did not differentiate hypothetical treatment of peers whose behaviors were disruptive to classroom functioning, but did reveal that the oldest students differentiated exclusion of peers with disabilities based on the potential of the disability to disrupt the activity (Gasser et al., 2014). In a later study, although students still anticipated that they would exclude peers who exhibited hyperactive behaviors from both social and academic activities, they took a more differentiated view in sixth versus fifth grade, of the potential for the peers' disability to interrupt the activity by excluding hyperactive, but not low-achieving peers from social activities (Gasser, Grütter, Torchetti, & Buholzer, 2017). These findings are intriguing because they suggest that students improve in their ability to coordinate an understanding of the nature of peers' disabilities with the potential impact on the flow of common classroom activities when evaluating how to interact with peers who have or are at risk for EBD.

In summary, when structural aspects of classroom peer ecologies and normative features of peer cultures are taken into consideration, a nuanced picture of peer relationships emerges with important implications for intervention with students with or at risk for EBD. It is noteworthy that the presence of classroom features that enable these students to gain high social status tends to be associated with problematic adjustment for most students. That is, these are structural features that teachers would be encouraged to take steps to avoid in their classrooms. The features that favor aggression – hierarchical structure and norms – may serve as setting events that both encourage aggressive behavior, and impede the effectiveness of teachers' efforts to address aggressive behavior. In contrast, students in classrooms with an egalitarian structure or norms that favor academic engagement may support teachers' efforts to intervene with classmates' aggression. We discuss these possibilities more fully in a subsequent section.

Teachers and Peer Ecologies

Students construct their peer ecologies through interactions with one another, but teachers lay the foundation and provide on-going guidance for the opportunities that students have for interaction, and how they view and treat one another. Teachers' role in the peer ecology has been characterized as the "invisible hand"; although they may engage in intentional and overt practices to influence their students' relationships or the peer culture, their practices often have a covert or even unintentional impact (Farmer, Lines, & Hamm, 2011). For example, teachers may use seating charts and group assignments with the explicit intention of encouraging or discouraging particular relationships among students, or they can engage in these same practices without an awareness that these assignments shape students' dispositions toward or relationships with one another. They may openly express their intentions for managing peer relationships, or they may keep those objectives to themselves. Indeed, the impact of certain practices or their own beliefs about students' peer relations and classroom social dynamics may be invisible to teachers themselves; for instance, by publicly and angrily punishing students who are disruptive, they may inadvertently fuel the dislike for that student maintained by the rest of the class.

Critical to understanding teachers' role is recognition that, although classroom social dynamics may actively support or neutrally coexist with the teacher's aims, they may also undermine the best intentions of the teacher. For instance, a hierarchical structure or norms that support aggression likely serve as setting events that exacerbate the display of aggression from students who are already aggressive with peers, but may also interfere with the teacher's efforts to intervene with the individual student. These coexisting dynamic social systems influence one another bi-directionally, and classroom and behavior management is enhanced when educators consider the academic and behavioral characteristics of their students as well as the classroom peer ecology and peer culture within which both students and staff function (Farmer et al., 2016).

Teacher Affect and Knowledge

Teachers can contribute to the classroom peer ecology, and to the relationships of individual students through diverse means, but their overt treatment of students with or at risk for EBD;

their own tolerance of aggression, and their attunement to social groups and to which students have a peer reputation for being aggressive, are specifically relevant to the peer relations of students with or at risk for EBD. Several studies reveal ways in which teachers' interactions with students who exhibit aggression, disruption, and defiance, which put them at risk for EBD, shape peers' liking or disliking of these students. To illustrate, Hughes and Im (2016) found that elementary school children who were perceived to be in frequent conflict with the teacher were more likely to be disliked, but that dislike was attenuated by teachers' warmth and low levels of conflict. In another study, when students perceived that teachers were more frequently in conflict with students in general, levels of student aggression were higher (Hendrickx, Mainhard, Boor-Klip, Cillessen, & Brekelmans, 2016). Multiple studies of elementary grades classrooms document that teacher liking and disliking contributes to classmates' liking and disliking of highly aggressive peers (Chang et al., 2007; Hendrickx, Mainhard, Boor-Klip, Cillessen, & Brekelmans, 2017). Middle schoolers' rejection of class-mates who were characterized as antisocial and disruptive intensified when teachers maintained negative attitudes toward aggression (Chang, 2003). However, in both studies by Chang and colleagues, teachers' dispositions softened the negative impact of students' aggression on classmates' rejection. Middle schoolers were less likely to reject an aggressive classmate if teachers were more tolerant of aggression (Chang, 2003) and elementary students were less likely to reject an antisocial and disruptive classmate if teachers were highly authoritative (Chang et al., 2007). The influence of teachers' liking or tolerance of aggression may diminish as students progress through adolescence, however; Engels and colleagues (2016) found that high school teachers' affect toward students with low levels of behavioral engagement was not associated with their likeability or popularity with classmates. Developmental differences in teacher influence over the social status of students with disruptive classroom behaviors may reflect both improvements to students' processing of social information with age and a greater array of social experiences to draw on as they evaluate classmates (Chang et al., 2007). Moreover, as students move into adolescence, they orient more toward peer rather than teacher regard, and the social value of teacher-endorsed behaviors such as helping and engaging in academic tasks diminishes in favor of disruptive and aggressive behaviors (Galvan et al., 2011). Explanations for this trend require further investigation, but the findings underscore that at least throughout elementary and into middle school students take social cues from teachers' interactions with classmates regarding the extent to which they accept or like classmates who exhibit higher levels of aggression or disruptive behavior.

Teachers' attunement to, or awareness of the peer relationships of their students has garnered recent attention, with findings that in general, all students benefit socially and affectively from teachers' accurate understanding of peer group affiliations and peer reputations (e.g., Hamm, Farmer, Dadisman, Gravelle, & Murray, 2011; Norwalk, Hamm, Farmer, & Barnes, 2016). Unfortunately, regardless of grade level taught, teachers vary significantly in their attunement and maintain surprisingly low accuracy in perceiving their students' relationships (e.g., Hamm et al., 2011); attunement to students who have a peer reputation for aggression is no exception (Ahn & Rodkin, 2014). In a study of late elementary grades, teachers were especially unlikely to recognize the students identified by classmates as highly aggressive if these students were also popular or socially integrated (Dawes et al., 2017). The authors speculated that these students may experience a "halo effect" that diverts teachers' attention away from their aggressive behavior with peers. However, a concern with teachers' inaccurate perception is that there is tacit acceptance of aggression by the teacher; middle school students who exhibit aggression with peers are less likely to experience peer rejection when their teachers are more tolerant of aggression (Chang et al., 2007). Moreover, students may emulate the behaviors of popular classmates, which means that additional students may initiate or engage with aggression. Together, these act as setting events that can encourage classroom norms that favor aggression, which may perpetuate the high status of students with aggression at the expense of positive developmental outcomes for the class as a whole. Indeed, when teachers are more attuned to the students who have a peer reputation for aggression, those students lose social status across the school year (Ahn & Rodkin, 2014). It is noteworthy that teachers also failed to identify students who had a peer reputation for aggression if those students were also perceived by classmates to be shy and withdrawn. Inattention to students who exhibit both internalizing and externalizing behaviors to peers is a missed opportunity to support students who may be at strong risk for EBD.

In summary, social processes, structures, and norms within classroom peer ecologies strongly influence the peer experiences of children with or at risk for EBD, but they are highly receptive to teachers' influence – whether unintentional or intentional. A growing body of intervention research has revealed key leverage points for teachers to improve aspects of classroom peer ecologies to re-shape the peer relationships of students with and at risk for EBD.

Evidence-Based Interventions Targeting Teachers' Management of Classroom Social Dynamics: Serving Students with or at Risk for EBD

Interventions that span the three levels included in the Multi-tiered System of Support (MTSS) framework help teachers manage their classrooms in ways that support productive peer relationships in general, and simultaneously provide targeted support to students with and at risk for EBD. Reflecting the findings from a classroom social dynamics perspective and the corresponding research studies above, we emphasize that efforts to improve the peer relationships of students with or at risk for EBD should focus not simply on "fixing" individual students, but rather on helping teachers create and support a peer ecology that promotes productive social dynamics for all students while simultaneously enhancing the social skills and behavior of students who need extra support (e.g., students with and at risk for EBD). These combined efforts may promote peer acceptance and healthy relationships for not only socially vulnerable youth but all students in the classroom.

Universal prevention strategies help teachers move the classroom peer system toward a healthier and more productive culture (e.g., egalitarian social structure, devaluation of peer aggression). However, research findings make it clear that doing so may jeopardize the social status and peer relationships specifically of students with or at risk for EBD. That is, functioning in these changed classroom contexts may be problematic for students with or at risk for EBD who may have benefited from a peer ecology that valued and rewarded aggression and disruptive behaviors. To illustrate, as the classroom peer culture shifts to be less tolerant of aggression and less hierarchically structured, students who previously exhibited elevated levels of disruptive and aggressive behavior but enjoyed high social status (perhaps as a result of their aggressive behaviors) will become less influential, less liked, and less tied to their peers through friendship – or potentially, overtly rejected by peers. Similarly, students who previously exhibited elevated levels of disruptive and aggressive behavior but were rejected by their peers may be likely to experience continued peer rejection. Without the necessary skills to succeed in a healthier peer culture these students may continue to experience poor social outcomes. An understanding of the potential of universal interventions that have demonstrated success in improving peer ecologies and peer cultures helps to establish how social dynamics can be transformed as setting events for the entire classroom or grade level – but it is essential that teachers understand that improving aspects of the classroom peer ecology is initially likely to result in diminished social status, at minimum, for students with or at risk for EBD. Thus, attunement to students' relationships and an understanding of ways to supplement universal approaches with targeted interventions is vital for successful classroom adjustment of students with or at risk for EBD.

We review the findings from a few universal (tier 1) and combined universal and targeted (tier 2) interventions that demonstrate how teachers can change aspects of classroom peer ecologies and peer cultures that support problematic behaviors for all students, but especially for those with or at risk for EBD. These interventions target specific features of the peer ecology and have documented success changing both the overall classroom peer ecology, and supporting peer relationships for students with or at risk for EBD. We highlight findings from studies carefully designed to capitalize on the power of social dynamics to support healthy behavior and relationships for students with or at risk for EBD, while attending to the implications of altering these social dynamics for classmates who are naturally well-adjusted.

Universal intervention programs can improve multiple aspects of peer ecologies in ways that support or have the potential to support students with or at risk for EBD. To illustrate, the Supporting Early Adolescent Learning and Social Success (SEALS) program (Farmer et al., 2013), an instantiation of the BASE Model (see Farmer, Hamm et al., this volume) was developed to address the known social, behavioral, and academic challenges experienced by students as they transition into early adolescence, and middle school, specifically. Rather than trying to fix students who may be at particular risk for adjustment difficulties in this transition, in concert with classroom management and instructional strategies, the SEALS model targets teachers' attunement to social dynamics, and provides support for implementing evidence-based strategies to support a productive and supportive peer ecology.

The SEALS model has been tested in randomized controlled trials of rural and metropolitan schools across the U.S. In rural schools, the peer culture became more supportive of effort and achievement, and less supportive of aggression in schools implementing the SEALS program (Farmer, Hamm, Chen, & Irvin, 2014; Hamm, Farmer, Lambert, & Gravelle, 2014; Hamm et al., 2010). When classroom and peer group norms favor productive behaviors and low levels of aggression, aggressive students are less likely to attain influential and prominent status. One study of SEALS versus control schools revealed that students at risk for EBD due to high levels of aggression affiliated with more academically productive peers and were less likely to affiliate with peers identified as bullies or victims (Farmer et al., 2010). Thus, participating in the SEALS professional development training helped teachers alter classroom peer norms as setting events that improved students' affiliative patterns.

One of the means through which the SEALS program may have its effects is through teachers' attunement and social dynamics management practices. In rural schools, SEALS teachers maintained greater attunement to students' peer group affiliations at the beginning of the school year, than did comparison teachers (Farmer, Hall, Petrin, Hamm, & Dadisman, 2010; Hamm et al., 2011). Evaluation of the efficacy of the SEALS program in metropolitan middle schools is underway, but indicates that SEALS teachers more adeptly manage classroom social dynamics, and are less likely to use classroom management practices that involve negative and disruptive behavioral feedback (Motoca et al., 2014). Given that students are more likely to be disliked or rejected by classmates when they are in frequent conflict with teachers or it appears that teachers dislike them (e.g., Chang et al., 2007; Hughes & Im, 2016), teachers' capacity to redirect behavior in positive and supportive ways may minimize negative peer reactions to students with disruptive behavior, thus altering the setting events that could otherwise exacerbate problematic peer relationships for students with or at risk for EBD.

Other intervention approaches are intended to help teachers create inclusive classroom norms. As an example, Making Socially Accepting Inclusive Classrooms (MOSAIC) helps teachers to develop warm relationships and to engage in positive interactions with all students, and to support socially competent behaviors of students with ADHD. Teachers are encouraged to publicly recognize the socially valued strengths of all children, but particularly those with ADHD; and to publicly recognize children who offer social acceptance to classmates with ADHD. Teachers also learn how to establish class-wide rules for social inclusion. These practices are supplemented by a class-wide management system and daily social skills training. Comparison classrooms experienced the management system and social skills training, but not the professional development for teachers focused on students' peer relations and the peer ecology. In one randomized controlled study, elementary students with ADHD in MOSAIC classrooms enjoyed greater social preference and more reciprocated friendships than did students with ADHD in control classrooms (Mikami et al., 2013). Typically developing students, but especially those with elevated levels of disruptive behavior, benefited as well, receiving fewer negative peer nominations and negative social interactions, and more reciprocated friendships in MOSAIC versus control classrooms (Mikami, Reuland, Griggs, & Jia, 2013).

When responding to the behavior of students with intensive needs, educators often select empirically validated interventions based solely on the individual characteristics of target students and overlook how naturally occurring peer processes in the classroom directly and indirectly influence specific student behavior. A more efficacious approach is to select an intervention that not only addresses target students' undesired behavior, but that also takes advantage of social dynamics within the peer ecology to facilitate social opportunities that will allow the student to observe and emulate desirable behavior that will be naturally supported within the setting (Farmer et al., 2018). In such an intervention focused on late elementary classrooms and teachers, Van den Berg and Stolz (2018) sought to improve classroom behaviors and peer acceptance for students exhibiting externalizing behaviors (target children), by using a classroom seating chart informed by the classroom relational structure. Based on findings that students adjust their behavior to be similar to peer affiliates and that lower social status improves when students affiliate with higher status peers, in randomly assigned intervention classrooms, "peer buddies" who exhibited low levels of aggression, high levels of prosocial behavior, and who were liked by classmates, were seated next to target children for approximately ten weeks. In control classes, target students were seated next to a randomly assigned classmate. Target children became more liked when their seatmate was a prosocial and broadly liked peer buddy rather than a randomly assigned classmate, and when they were disliked by classmates initially.

This intervention was attentive to naturally occurring relational structures and social processes as setting events in the classroom in several thoughtful ways. The potential for reputation bias was reduced by the assignment of target students to sit by a prosocial and high status peer, which improved the social status of disliked target children with that classmate. The researchers also anticipated that sitting next to a disruptive peer could lead the peer buddy to engage in more disruptive behavior, given the ease with which classroom defiance can spread among students who are both socially and physically connected (McFarland, 2001), and that this assignment could compromise the peer buddy's high status. Peer buddies exhibited low levels of peer aggression, in addition to high levels of prosocial behaviors and likeability, reflecting attention to research findings that during late childhood, liked children can exhibit both prosocial and aggressive behaviors with peers (e.g., Garandeau et al., 2011). The level of aggressive behavior of peer buddies (as well as randomly assigned peers) was robust to the influence of target children, but their prosociality increased.

Interventions, such as van den Berg and Stolz's, are successful through and benefit from changing the peer culture and classroom context as setting events to devalue and detach aggressive behaviors from social rewards while simultaneously helping target students respond in ways that will gain peer esteem. However, educators should consider that popular-aggressive (i.e., Tough) children may pose a challenge for improving the classroom peer culture. When popular-aggressive students maintain and value high social status there is little incentive to decrease negative peer behaviors (Garandeau et al., 2011). This may be particularly relevant for teachers of older students, who are more willing to violate normative behavior for status benefits than are younger students (LaFontana & Cillessen, 2010). Van den Berg and Stolz (2018) were careful to avoid target students who had high social status as well as high levels of aggression. This approach is further supported as teachers may overlook aggression if enacted by students with high social status (Dawes et al., 2017) without training to recognize the co-occurrence of these behaviors. Thus, the effects of the simple use of seating charts could potentially be enhanced through professional development to enhance teacher attunement.

Conclusion

Students who have or are at risk for EBD are likely to experience difficult peer relationships. These difficulties may stem in part from individual and interpersonal social skills deficits but, from a social dynamics perspective, likely reflect a complex interplay between individual characteristics, the classroom peer ecology and culture, teaching practices, and developmental changes in students. As such, improving social outcomes for students becomes less a matter of fixing individual students and more a matter of educators understanding and guiding the classroom social environment so that students' social interactions and relationships function as setting events that occasion productive behavioral and relational outcomes for all students. To date, several interventions support students from a social dynamics perspective and highlight ways that teachers can create and support a peer ecology that promotes productive social dynamics for all students while simultaneously enhancing the social skills and behavior of students who need extra support. Given the high prevalence of students displaying symptoms of EBD or who are at risk for EBD, it is critically important for researchers and practitioners to continue investigating classroom and school social dynamics that may be leveraged to promote positive social trajectories for this population of students and their peers.

References

Adler, P. A., & Adler, P. (1995). Dynamics of inclusion and exclusion in preadolescent cliques. *Social Psychology Quarterly, 58*(3), 145–165.

Ahn, H.-J., & Rodkin, P. C. (2014). Classroom-level predictors of the social status of aggression: Friendship centralization, friendship density, teacher–student attunement, and gender. *Journal of Educational Psychology, 106*, 1144–1155.

Bellanca, F., & Pote, H. (2013). Children's attitudes towards ADHD, depression and learning disabilities. *Journal of Research in Special Educational Needs, 13*(4), 234–241.

Bellmore, A. D., Witkow, M. R., Graham, S., & Juvonen, J. (2004). Beyond the individual: The impact of ethnic context and classroom behavioral norms on victims' adjustment. *Developmental Psychology, 40*(6), 1159–1172.

Bierman, K. (1986). Process of change during social skills training with preadolescents and its relation to treatment outcome. *Child Development, 57*, 230–240.

Chang, L. (2003). Variable effects of children's aggression, social withdrawal, and prosocial leadership as functions of teacher beliefs and behaviors. *Child Development, 74*, 535–548.

Chang, L. (2004). The role of classrooms in contextualizing the relations of children's social behaviors to peer acceptance. *Developmental Psychology, 40*, 691–702.

Chang, L., Liu, H., Fung, K. Y., Wang, Y., Wen, Z., Li, H., & Farver, J. (2007). The mediating and moderating effects of teacher preference on the relations between children's social behaviors and peer acceptance. *Merrill Palmer Quarterly, 53*, 603–630.

Chen, C. C., Farmer, T. W., Hamm, J. V., Brooks, D. S., Lee, D. L., Norwalk, K., Lambert, K., Dawes, M., Sterrett, B., & Rizzo, K. (2019). Emotional and behavioral risk configurations, students with disabilities, and perceptions of the middle school ecology. *Journal of Emotional and Behavioral Disorders, https://doi-org.libproxy.lib.unc.edu/10.1177/1063426619866829.*

Dawes, M., Chen, C. C., Zumbrunn, S. K., Mehtaji, M., Farmer, T. W., & Hamm, J. V. (2017). Teacher attunement to peer-nominated aggressors. *Aggressive Behavior, 43*(3), 263–272.

Dishion, T. J., & Dodge, K. A. (2005). Peer contagion in interventions for children and adolescents: Moving towards an understanding of the ecology and dynamics of change. *Journal of Abnormal Child Psychology, 33*, 395–400.

Engels, M. C., Colpin, H., Van Leeuwen, K., Bijttebier, P., Van Den Noortgate, W., Claes, S., Goossens, L., & Verschueren, K. (2016). Behavioral engagement, peer status, and teacher–Student relationships in adolescence: A longitudinal study on reciprocal influences. *Journal of Youth and Adolescence, 45*(6), 1192–1207.

Estell, D. B., Cairns, R. B., Farmer, T. W., & Cairns, B. D. (2002). Aggression in inner-city early elementary classrooms: Individual and peer-group configurations. *Merrill-Palmer Quarterly, 48*, 52–76.

Evans, C., & Eder, D. (1993). "No exit": Processes of social isolation in the middle school. *Journal of Contemporary Ethnography, 22*, 139–170.

Farmer, T. W., Dawes, M., Hamm, J. V., Lee, D. L., Mehtaji, M., Hoffman, A. S., & Brooks, D. S. (2018). Classroom social dynamics: Why the invisible hand matters for special education. *Remedial and Special Education, 39*, 177–192.

Farmer, T. W., Estell, D., Bishop, J., O'Neal, K., Cairns, B.D. (2003). Rejected bullies or popular leaders? The social relations of aggressive subtypes of African American early adolescents.

Farmer, T. W., Hall, C. M., Leung, M.-C., Estell, D. B., & Brooks, D. S. (2011). Social prominence and the heterogeneity of rejected status in late elementary school. *School Psychology Quarterly, 26*, 260–274.

Farmer, T. W., Hall, C. M., Petrin, R. A., Hamm, J. V., & Dadisman, K. (2010). Evaluating the impact of a multicomponent intervention model on teachers' awareness of social networks at the beginning of middle school in rural communities. *School Psychology Quarterly, 95*, 94–106.

Farmer, T. W., Hall, C. M., Weiss, M. P., Petrin, R., Meece, J., & Moohr, M. (2011). The school adjustment of rural adolescents with and without disabilities: Variable and person-centered approaches. *Journal of Child and Family Studies, 20*, 78–88. https://doi-org.libproxy.lib.unc.edu/10.1007/s10826-010-9379-2

Farmer, T. W., Hamm, J. L., Petrin, R. A., Robertson, D. L., Murray, R. A., Meece, J. L., & Brooks, D. S. (2010). Creating supportive classroom contexts for academically and behaviorally at-risk youth during the transition to middle school: A strength-based perspective. *Exceptionality, 18*, 94–106.

Farmer, T. W., Hamm, J. V., Chen, C. C., & Irvin, M. (2014, April). Promoting socially supportive middle level contexts during the era of high-stakes testing: Reducing the popularity of aggression. *Paper presented at the Society for Research on Child Development Special Topic Meeting: Strengthening Connections Among Child and Family Research*, Policy and Practice, Arlington, VA.

Farmer, T. W., Hamm, J. V., Dawes, M., Barko-Alva, K., & Cross, J. (2019). Promoting inclusive communities in diverse classrooms: Teacher attunement and social dynamics management. *Educational Psychologist, 54*, 286–305.

Farmer, T. W., Hamm, J. V., Lane, K. L., Lee, D., Sutherland, K. S., Hall, C. M., & Murray, R. A. (2013). Conceptual foundations and components of a contextual intervention to promote student engagement during early adolescence: The Supporting Early Adolescent Learning and Social Success (SEALS) model. *Journal of Educational and Psychological Consultation, 23,* 115–139.

Farmer, T. W., & Hollowell, J. L. (1994). Social networks in mainstream classrooms: Social affiliations and behavioral characteristics of students with emotional and behavioral disorders. *Journal of Emotional and Behavioral Disorders, 2,* 143–155.

Farmer, T. W., Lines, M. A., & Hamm, J. V. (2011). Revealing the invisible hand: The role of teachers in children's peer experiences. *Journal of Applied Developmental Psychology, 32,* 247–256.

Farmer, T. W., Pearl, R., & VanAcker, R. (1996). Expanding the social skills deficit framework: A developmental synthesis perspective, classroom social networks, and implications for the social growth of students with disabilities. *Journal of Special Education, 30,* 232–256.

Farmer, T. W., Reinke, W., & Brooks, D. S. (2014). Managing classrooms and challenging behavior: Theoretical considerations and critical issues. *Journal of Emotional and Behavioral Disorders, 22,* 67–73.

Galvan, A., Spatzier, A., & Juvonen, J. (2011). Perceived norms and social values to capture school culture in elementary and middle school. *Journal of Applied Developmental Psychology, 32,* 436–453.

Garandeau, C. F., Ahn, H.-J., & Rodkin, P. C. (2011). The social status of aggressive students across contexts: The role of classroom status hierarchy, academic achievement, and grade. *Developmental Psychology, 47*(6), 1699–1710.

Gasser, L., Grutter, J., & Torchetti, L. (2018). Inclusive classroom norms, children's sympathy, and intended inclusion toward students with hyperactive behavior. *Journal of School Psychology, 71,* 72–84.

Gasser, L., Grütter, J., Torchetti, L., & Buholzer, A. (2017). Competitive classroom norms and exclusion of children with academic and behavior difficulties. *Journal of Applied Developmental Psychology, 49,* 1–11.

Gasser, L., Malti, T., & Buholzer, A. (2014). Swiss children's moral and psychological judgments about inclusion and exclusion of children with disabilities. *Child Development, 85*(2), 532–548.

Hamm, J. V., Farmer, T. W., Dadisman, K., Gravelle, M., & Murray, A. R. (2011). Teachers' attunement to students' peer group affiliations as a source of improved student experiences of the school social–affective context following the middle school transition. *Journal of Applied Developmental Psychology, 32*(5), 267–277.

Hamm, J. V., Farmer, T. W., Lambert, K., & Gravelle, M. (2014). Enhancing peer cultures of academic effort and achievement in early adolescence: Promotive effects of the SEALS intervention. *Developmental Psychology, 50*(1), 216–228.

Hamm, J. V., Farmer, T. W., Robertson, D., Dadisman, K. A., Murray, A., Meece, J. L., & Song, S. (2010). Effects of a developmentally based intervention with teachers on Native American and White early adolescents' schooling adjustment in rural settings. *Journal of Experimental Education, 78*(3), 343–377.

Hamm, J. V., Hoffman, A., & Farmer, T. W. (2012). Peer cultures of academic success in adolescence: Why they matter and what teachers can do to promote them. In A. Ryan & G. Ladd (Eds.), *Peer relationships and adjustment at school.* New York, NY: IAP, 219–250.

Hendrickx, M., Mainhard, T. M., Boor-Klip, H. J., Cillessen, A. N., & Brekelmans, M. (2016). Social dynamics in the classroom: Teacher support and conflict in the peer ecology. *Teaching and Teacher Education, 53,* 30–40.

Hendrickx, M., Mainhard, T. M., Boor-Klip, H. J., Cillessen, A. N., & Brekelmans, M. (2017). Teacher liking as an affective filter for the association between student behavior and peer status. *Contemporary Educational Psychology, 49,* 250–262.

Henricsson, L., & Rydell, A. M. (2006). Children with behavior problems: The influence of social competence and social relations on problem stability, school achievement and peer acceptance across the first six years of school. *Infant and Child Development, 15,* 347–366.

Hughes, J. N., & Im, M. (2016). Teacher-student relationships and peer disliking and liking across grades 1–4. *Child Development, 87,* 593–611.

Hymel, S. (1986). Interpretations of peer behavior: Affective bias in childhood and adolescence. *Child Development, 57*(2), 431–445.

Jonkmann, K., Trautwein, U., & Ludtke, O. (2009). Social dominance in adolescence: The moderating role of the classroom context and behavioral heterogeneity. *Child Development, 80*, 338–355.

Kellam, S. G., Ling, X., Merisca, R., Brown, C. H., & Ialongo, N. (1998). The effect of the level of aggression in the first grade classroom on the course and malleability of aggressive behavior into middle school. *Development and Psychopathology, 10*, 165–185.

LaFontana, K. M., & Cillessen, A. H. N. (2010). Developmental changes in the priority of perceived status in childhood and adolescence. *Social Development, 19*(1), 130–147.

Leadbeater, B., Hoglund, W., & Woods, T. (2003). Changing contents? The effects of a primary prevention program on classroom levels of peer relational and physical victimization. *Journal of Community Psychology, 31*(4), 397–418.

Light, J. M., & Dishion, T. J. (2007). Early adolescent antisocial behavior and peer rejection: A dynamic test of a developmental process. *New Directions for Child and Adolescent Development, 118*, 77–89.

McFarland, D. A. (2001). Student resistance: How the formal and informal organizations of classrooms facilitate everyday forms of student defiance. *American Journal of Sociology, 107*, 612–678.

Mikami, A. Y., Griggs, M. S., Lerner, M. D., Emeh, C. C., Reuland, M. M., Jack, A., & Anthony, M. R. (2013). A randomized trial of a classroom intervention to increase peers' social inclusion of children with attention-deficit/hyperactivity disorder. *Journal of Consulting and Clinical Psychology, 81*(1), 100–112.

Mikami, A. Y., & Normand, S. (2015). The importance of social contextual factors in peer relationships of children with ADHD. *Current Developmental Disorders Reports, 2*, 30–37.

Mikami, A. Y., Reuland, M. M., Griggs, S., & Jia, M. (2013). Collateral effects of a peer relationship intervention for children with ADHD on typically developing classmates. *School Psychology Review, 42*(4), 458–476.

Motoca, L., Farmer, T. W., Hamm, J. V., Byun, S.-Y., Lee, D., Brooks, D. S., … Moohr, M. (2014). Directed consultation, the SEALS Model, and teachers' classroom management. *Journal of Emotional of Behavioral Disorders, 22*, 119–129.

National Longitudinal Transition Study–2. (2006). *The social adjustment of elementary and middle school students with disabilities.* Washington, DC: U.S. Department of Education, Institute for Educational Sciences.

Norwalk, K. E., Hamm, J. V., Farmer, T. W., & Barnes, K. (2016). Improving the school context of early adolescence through teacher attunement to victimization: Effects on school belonging. *Journal of Early Adolescence, 36*, 989–1009.

Powers, C. J., & Bierman, K. L. (2013). The multifaceted impact of peer relations on aggressive–disruptive behavior in elementary school. *Developmental Psychology, 49*, 1174–1186.

Ringeisen, H., Stambaugh, L., Bose, J., Casanueva, C., Hedden, S., Avenevoli, S., Blau, G, Canino, G., Carter, A., Colpe, L., Copeland, W., Fisher, P.W., Kaufman, J., Merikangas, K., Narrow, W., Strout, B., & West, J. (2018). Measurement of childhood serious emotional disturbance: State of the science and issues for consideration. *Journal of Emotional and Behavioral Disorders, 25*, 195–210.

Robertson, D., Farmer, T. W., Crowther, A., Duncan, T., Fraser, M., Day, S. H., & Dadisman, K. (2010). Interpersonal competence configurations and peer relations in early elementary classrooms: Perceived popular and unpopular aggressive subtypes. *International Journal of Behavioral Development, 34*, 73–87.

Rodkin, P. C., & Ryan, A. M. (2012). Child and adolescent peer relations in educational context. In K. R. Harris, S. Graham, & T. Urdan (Eds.), *Handbook of educational psychology: Individual differences, cultural variations, and contextual factors* (Vol. 2, pp. 363–389). Washington, DC: APA. doi:10.1037/13274-015

Stormshak, E. A., Bierman, K. L., Bruschi, C., Dodge, K. A., & Coie, J. D.; The Conduct Disorders Prevention Group. (1999). The relation between behavior problems and peer preference in different classroom contexts. *Child Development, 70*(1), 169–182.

Sturaro, C., Van Lier, P. A., Cuijpers, P., & Koot, H. M. (2011). The role of peer relationships in the development of early school-age externalizing problems. *Child Development, 82*, 758–765.

Van Acker, R., Grant, S., & Henry, D. (1996). Teacher and student behavior as a function of risk for aggression. *Education and Treatment of Children, 19*(3), 316–334.

Van den Berg, Y. H. M., & Stolz, S. (2018). Enhancing social inclusion of children with externalizing problems through classroom seating arrangements: A randomized control trial. *Journal of Emotional and Behavioral Disorders, 26*(1), 31–41.

10 Implementation of Violence Prevention Programs

Terri N. Sullivan, Katherine M. Ross, Megan M. Carlson, Stephanie A. Hitti, and Kathryn L. Behrhorst

In the U.S., the public school system is the primary entity mandated by the Individuals with Disabilities Education Act (PL 105–17; IDEA, 1997) to provide interventions and supports for youth with or at risk for emotional/behavioral disorders (EBD). Ideally, the right combination of interventions and supports that target a youth's ecological and individual risk factors will promote socio-emotional, behavioral, and academic competencies that contribute to successful outcomes in these areas across adolescence and into adulthood. Many youth with EBD receive services in schools that use multi-tiered systems of support (MTSS) (Horner, Sugai, & Anderson, 2010). MTSS generally comprises three levels of support including: (a) Tier 1 – universal prevention approaches designed for all students, (b) Tier 2 – selective programs for youth who have a risk factor(s) that increases their chances for developmental challenges, and (c) Tier 3 – indicated programs for youth who have many associated risk factors or meet the criteria for a disability (Farmer, Farmer, Estell, & Hutchins, 2007).

The identification of risk factors targeted by interventions at each tier of MTSS along with the content and delivery of these interventions can help to determine their potential to support comprehensive treatment plans for youth with EBD. These youth have experienced limited progress when compared to youth in other disability categories in areas including academic achievement, graduation rates, and gaining and keeping employment (Kern, 2015; Mayer, Lochman, & Van Acker, 2005). Additionally, the long-term outcomes for youth with EBD include a higher likelihood of involvement with the justice, mental health, and welfare systems (e.g., Mayer, Lochman & Van Acker, 2005). These statistics show the importance of understanding the potential advantages and drawbacks of the range of services available to youth with EBD within a school based on their individual profiles of risk.

The current chapter focuses on the potential benefits and challenges of addressing some ecological and individual risk factors for youth with or at risk for EBD through school-based youth violence prevention programs. We first discuss the prevalence of and risk factors associated with youth violence. We then briefly review how some risk factors for youth violence exposure may be manifested in the ecologies and characteristics of youth with or at risk for EBD. Next, we discuss MTSS and the developmental science perspective and identify risk factors for youth violence addressed by prevention programs and their potential relevance for youth with or at risk for EBD. Lastly, we discuss the research needed to evaluate the potential benefit of these prevention approaches and implementation considerations that may impact the significance of these programs for this population.

Prevalence of Youth Violence and Risk Factors

Youth violence is the use of intentional acts or threats of physical aggression or power by youths to hurt another person(s). Various behaviors fit into the larger umbrella of youth violence, for example, bullying, threats of violence in person or via social media, relational aggression, and fighting (David-Ferdon & Simon, 2014). Youth violence is prevalent and occurs across peer, family, school, and community ecologies in rural, suburban, and urban contexts. Over 1,000 youth are seen in U.S. emergency departments daily as a result of physical assault (David-Ferdon et al., 2016). Further, national survey data showed that within a 12-month period, 19% of high school students were bullied on school grounds and 24% were in a physical fight (Kann et al., 2018). Youth violence has negative consequences including physical injury, psychosocial maladjustment, and social and academic difficulties (Kann et al., 2018).

Ecological risk factors for youth violence occur within community, family, school, and peer contexts. At the community level, neighborhoods characterized by high concentrations of poverty, isolation from economic opportunities, and disorganization place youth at risk for violence exposure (Elliott, Wilson, Huizinga, Elliott, & Ranking, 1996; Sampson, Raudenbush, & Earls, 1997). Residents may experience low levels of social cohesion, which can be due to safety concerns, and high levels of mobility and family disruption that also represent risk factors (Elliott et al., 1996). Some family risk factors include parental discipline practices that are absent, severe, or inconsistent and low levels of parental warmth and attachment (David-Ferdon et al., 2016; Mercy, Butchart, Farrington, & Cerda, 2002). Low levels of parental involvement and monitoring of youths' activities and difficulties with family management and conflict also increase levels of risk. Additional risk factors include parental history of drug abuse, criminal activity, and barriers in attaining high levels of education (Farrington, Gaffney, & Ttofi, 2017; Kashani, Jones, Bumby, & Thomas, 1999; Mercy et al., 2002). In the school environment, poor school climate (e.g., characterized by low quality relationships and negative interactions between students and with their teachers), poor discipline practices, safety monitoring and classroom management, and school norms that support aggression are risk factors (Olweus & Limber, 2007). In the peer context, some risk factors include relationships with peers who support aggression, gang involvement, and rejection by prosocial peers (Farrington, Gaffney, & Ttofi, 2017; Mercy et al., 2002; Olweus & Limber, 2007).

A number of individual risk factors for youth violence have been identified. These include psychobiological, social cognitive, and social behavioral risk factors. Some psychobiological risk factors include distractibility, hyperactivity, and impulsivity (Mercy et al., 2002). Social cognitive risk factors include challenges in social-cognitive information processing (e.g., hostile attribution biases, beliefs supporting aggression, and difficulties in social problem-solving), cognitive functioning and learning, and difficulties with academic achievement. Social behavioral risk factors include emotion dysregulation, difficulties with behavioral control, low involvement in prosocial activities, low bonding and commitment to school, low school attendance, and school failure (e.g., repeating grades) (Farrington, Gaffney & Ttofi, 2017; Mercy et al., 2002). Individual risk factors for youth violence also include a history of: (a) aggression which may start in early childhood, (b) emotional problems, (c) exposure to violent victimization, and (d) substance use (Farrington, Gaffney, & Ttofi, 2017; Kashani et al., 1999; Mercy et al., 2002). Overall, these risk factors highlight challenges that are often interrelated and may build one upon the other to create ongoing maladaptive behavior patterns.

Ecological and Individual Risk Factors for EBD

Some studies suggest that youth with EBD are overrepresented as victims and/or aggressors compared to their peers without disabilities and youth represented in other disability categories (Rose, Monda-Amaya, & Espelage, 2011; Rose, Simpson, & Moss, 2015). Studies have shown that youth with disabilities experienced higher rates of victimization, and in some instances, engaged in higher rates of aggression, especially in the face of chronic victimization (Rose et al., 2011). Rose and colleagues (2015) extended this work to examine patterns of victimization and aggression among youth with EBD. Among sixth to twelfth graders with and without disabilities, youth with EBD reported higher levels of relational victimization and combined experiences of victimization and aggression as compared to youth without disabilities and youth in other disability categories (Rose et al., 2015). These findings indicated that youth with EBD may struggle with both peer victimization and aggression (which may occur in reaction to victimization experiences) (Rose et al., 2011).

Risk factors for youth violence exposure may occur in ecologies and/or be represented in the characteristics of youth with or at risk for EBD. Key individual risk factors include struggles with social skills, emotion regulation, social-cognitive information processing, and executive functioning skills which contribute to difficulties in learning, interpersonal relationships, and the development and maintenance of adaptive behavior patterns (Crews et al., 2007; Lane, Carter, Pierson, & Glaeser, 2006). Youth with or at risk for EBD may experience social rejection and peer victimization and associate with peers who reinforce aggression (Farmer & Farmer, 2001; Rose et al., 2011). Some family risk factors include parenting practices that are harsh or inconsistent and attachment difficulties between parent and child (Farmer & Farmer, 2001). In the school ecology, youth may experience risk factors including ineffective classroom and school management and discipline practices, poor school climate (e.g., poor quality student–student and student–teacher relationships), and school norms supporting aggression (Farmer & Farmer, 2001). Lastly, youth with EBD are overrepresented in high burden neighborhoods characterized by economic disadvantage (Wagner et al., 2005).

MTSS

MTSS offers a systematic strategy for addressing risk factors for youth with or at risk for EBD by providing services based on their level of current risk. Tier 1 universal prevention approaches support developmental processes expected to be attained during specific time-frames (e.g., during early adolescence in middle school) and are provided to all students (e.g., in a grade or school). Students who exhibit a risk factor(s) that could lead to developmental challenges (e.g., a behavior problem) in spite of exposure to Tier 1 supports may receive more intensive and selective Tier 2 supports such as a small group intervention. Students who manifest many ongoing risk factors (e.g., youth with or at risk for EBD) may receive individualized Tier 3 supports. An aspect of MTSS is to assess response to intervention, and in response to failure at a lower level of support (i.e., Tier 1), move to increasingly more intensive interventions (Horner et al., 2010).

Another approach in assessing needs and intervening with youth with or at risk for EBD stems from developmental science and highlights the need to consider human development as an ongoing process that unfolds through continual interactions between internal (e.g., psychobiological factors) and external (e.g., socio-ecological factors) developmental subsystems (Farmer, 2013; Farmer, Gatzke-Kopp, Lee, Dawes, & Talbott, 2016). The developmental subsystems reflect interrelated constraints which may be positive and mitigate risk or negative and exacerbate risk for developmental challenges (Farmer & Farmer, 2001). Because constraints are correlated, it is essential to consider an individual's overall pattern of constraints, the degree to which they are negative or positive, and how they relate to each another across internal and external developmental subsystems (Farmer & Farmer, 2001). For individuals who exhibit multiple negative constraints, the entire system may need to be reorganized to introduce positive constraints across subsystems in order to promote adaptive development (Farmer & Farmer, 2001).

For youth with or at risk for EBD, it is critical to take into account each individual's profile of risk factors across internal and external subsystems and to match this profile to interventions and supports across ecologies. Youth have varying characteristics and strengths that present different patterns of assets and challenges (Farmer, Gatzke-Kopp, et al., 2016). Violence prevention programs are clearly not sufficient to mitigate the combination of presenting factors for this population. However, these programs do address some risk factors by promoting individual social skills development and enhancing school climate (CASEL, 2015; Olweus & Limber, 2007). School-based violence prevention programs tend to fall within two broad categories including social-emotional learning (SEL) programs and school environment interventions (although there is some overlap). In this section, we describe these programs and identify risk factors for youth violence addressed by them that may be relevant for youth with or at risk for EBD.

Risk Factors at the Individual Level

Youth with or at risk for EBD experience individual risk factors reflecting difficulties in social, emotional, and behavioral competencies. Universal school-based violence prevention programs following the SEL model (CASEL, 2015) target some of these individual risk factors (e.g., challenges in social problem-solving, emotion regulation, and behavioral control). The SEL model is comprised of five competencies including self-awareness, self-management, responsible decision-making, social awareness, and relationship skills (CASEL, 2015). Self-awareness is the ability to perceive how your own cognitions and emotions impact behavior. Self-management is the adaptive regulation of cognitions, emotions, and behavior across situations and contexts. Responsible decision-making is the ability to solve problems by effectively weighing choices, potential consequences, and the impact of decisions on yourself and others. Social awareness is the ability to recognize and appreciate others' perspectives, cultures, and social norms, and relationships skills address those abilities (e.g., cooperation and listening) needed to build and maintain healthy relationships (CASEL, 2015).

SEL programs may be delivered via several approaches that include: (1) teacher instructional practices that foster students' social skills development (e.g., High Scope Educational Approach; Schweinhart, Barnes, & Weikart, 1993), (2) direct student instruction on social skills (e.g., Second Step: Committee for Children, 2008), and (3) the integration of skill instruction with academic content (e.g., Steps to Respect; Frey et al., 2005) (CASEL, 2015). The first target is direct skills instruction with youth (approaches 2 and 3 above). The second target is the teacher; either through improving teaching practices, teacher mental health, and/or student-teacher relationships (approach 1).

Risk Factors in the School and Peer Ecology

Some risk factors for youth violence that are manifested in the peer and school ecologies for students with or at risk for EBD include poor quality student–student and student–teacher relationships, ineffective classroom and school management and discipline practices, and school norms and social hierarchies that support aggression (Farmer & Farmer, 2001). School environment interventions that address these types of risk factors include anti-bullying programs such as Steps to Respect (Frey et al., 2005), the Olweus Bullying Prevention Program (OBPP; Olweus & Limber, 2007) and the KiVa program (Salmivalli, Poskiparta, Ahtola, & Haataja, 2013). Some mechanisms to mitigate these risk factors are encouraging school norms supporting prosocial behavior, setting and consistently reinforcing school-wide behavior expectations and rules, and improving interpersonal relationships at school (e.g., Olweus & Limber, 2007). These programs are led by school staff and use universal approaches and targeted strategies (e.g., support groups and individual interventions for aggressors and victims). Some anti-bullying programs, such as Steps to Respect, include both an SEL curriculum and school environment components (e.g., increasing student awareness and reporting of bullying behaviors). Other programs such as the OBPP and KiVa more narrowly address social and emotional skills to promote empathy for victims of bullying behavior (Olweus & Limber, 2007; Salmivalli et al., 2013). In addition, the content and delivery mechanisms for a number of SEL programs address the quality of student–student and student–teacher relationships (CASEL, 2015).

Some components of school environment interventions (e.g., increasing awareness of bullying behaviors and social hierarchies that support aggression, and fostering empathy for victims) are reinforced in the classroom via lessons, role plays, and group activities and discussions (Olweus & Limber, 2007; Salmivalli et al., 2013). For example, teacher-led class meetings are used to teach students about peer roles and group dynamics that encourage or discourage peer aggression. In OBPP, students learn about the bullying circle and peer roles that contribute to or disrupt incidents of bullying behavior. The OBPP and the KiVa programs use "participant role approaches" where students are encouraged to take on the role of defenders and intervene in bullying situations to support students who are being victimized (Olweus & Limber, 2007; Salmivalli et al., 2013, p. 81).

These types of programs may benefit youth with or at risk for EBD. A large body of research suggests positive relationships with teachers foster prosocial relationships with peers, academic engagement, and behavioral competencies (Murray & Pianta, 2006; Pianta, Hamre, & Allen, 2012). Youth with or at risk for EBD may have a history of difficulties in forming positive student–teacher relationships starting early in their school career that perpetuate across primary and secondary school (Sutherland & Oswald, 2005). Teacher training for SEL programs often includes a developmental understanding of social and emotional skills for youth, with an emphasis on increasing teacher awareness and creating realistic expectations for student behavior in the classroom.

SEL programs provide youth the opportunity to practice skills with typically developing peers which may reinforce these skills and help students to generalize them outside the classroom. These programs may give youth with or at risk for EBD opportunities for positive interactions with prosocial classmates, modeling and reinforcing prosocial behaviors in dyadic interactions that may be less likely to form naturally (Farmer & Hollowell, 1994; Xie, Cairns, & Cairns, 1999). Both positive peer and student–teacher relationships are associated with decreased behavioral problems for youth with EBD (Murray & Greenberg, 2006).

Consistent expectations and consequences for behavior across school contexts (e.g., classrooms, cafeterias, hallways, and buses) may create an environment that is more predictable and addresses some negative constraints for youth with or at risk for EBD. Generalized behavioral expectations increase the likelihood that teachers and peers are modeling positive behaviors and that school personnel recognize and reinforce positive behaviors. School environment interventions also provide a process for mobilizing school staff to monitor the school environment and increase student safety by intervening in incidents involving student aggression (Olweus & Limber, 2007). At the classroom-level, interventions such as the Good Behavior Game (GBG) offer additional structure and support for students with or at risk for EBD that may foster an environment which enhances prosocial and learning behaviors (Rubow, Vollmer, & Joslyn, 2018). In conclusion, youth struggling with emotional and behavioral regulation may benefit from a surrounding ecology that (1) prioritizes social and emotional skills in addition to academic skills, (2) supports, recognizes, and rewards prosocial behavior at the individual level, and (3) supports prosocial interactions between students, teachers, administrators, and other school staff (CASEL, 2015).

Risk Factors in Family and Community Ecologies

Although SEL programs are predominantly delivered in the classroom, some incorporate a family component with activities such as parent–child homework assignments and presentation of the SEL program for parents (Committee for Children, 2008). A few SEL programs include a community component in which students participate in activities with community organizations such as local recreation centers (CASEL, 2015). Similarly, school environment interventions such as OBPP incorporate a parent engagement component that includes strategies such as informing parents about the program, including them on the school-level program coordinating committee, connecting them with their child's teachers and school staff, and providing strategies to generalize skills learned in OBPP to the home environment. Additionally, OBPP includes a community component where community organizations may adopt the school intervention's anti-bullying messages and prevention strategies (Olweus & Limber, 2007).

These activities address some risk factors for youth violence that may be found in the family or community ecologies for youth with or at risk for EBD. In the family context, the focus on parent engagement may increase parents' involvement and connection with their child's school activities and school more generally. Program aspects may also provide parents some strategies for addressing academic and/or behavior issues at home that are consistent with those used at school. In the community context, participation in community activities could foster increased involvement in prosocial activities. These types of activities also represent potential transactional leverage points between ecologies that ideally could be explored to determine how to maximize their benefit for youth with or at risk for EBD (e.g., exploring how to turn participation in an activity with a community organization into ongoing activities and relationships within this organization).

Research Needs

Research on universal violence prevention approaches that specifically focus on youth with EBD is needed to understand the degree to which SEL programs and school environment interventions successfully address risk factors at the individual-level and in peer and school ecologies. Additionally, research could identify shortcomings to address ways to modify interventions for youth with or at risk for EBD. Studies have assessed the efficacy of SEL programs for youth with disabilities including EBD; however, students were collapsed across several disability categories into one group for these analyses (Espelage, Rose, & Polanin, 2015, 2016; Kam, Greenberg, & Kusche, 2004; Sullivan, Sutherland, Farrell, & Taylor, 2015). Three studies tested the efficacy of Second Step (Espelage et al., 2015, 2016; Sullivan et al., 2015), a curriculum that addresses emotion regulation, empathy, communication, and problem-solving skills to enhance decision-making and relationship management (Committee for Children, 2008). Middle school students with disabilities (e.g., learning disabilities, mild intellectual disabilities, and EBD) who participated in Second Step reported lower frequencies of relational victimization (Sullivan et al., 2015) and bullying perpetration (Espelage et al., 2015), and higher levels of willingness to intervene in bullying situations and improvements in grades (Espelage et al., 2016) as compared to youth with disabilities in the control condition. However, no significant differences between control and intervention groups were found for measures of teacher-reported empathy, caring, and emotion regulation or student-reported school belongingness (Espelage et al., 2016; Sullivan et al., 2015). Thus, Second Step positively impacted some behavioral and academic outcomes, but did not produce improvements in more proximal SEL outcomes for youth with disabilities.

The efficacy of the Promoting Alternative Thinking Strategies curriculum (PATHS: Conduct Problems Prevention Research Group, 1999) was examined among 113 first through third graders with learning disabilities, mild intellectual disabilities, EBD, and physical or other health impairments in 18 special education classrooms with classroom-level assignment to the intervention or control condition (Kam, Greenberg, & Kusche, 2004). The PATHS curriculum provides skill instruction in problem-solving, self-control, and emotion regulation. Two years post-intervention, growth curve analyses showed decreased trajectories of externalizing behaviors for students in the intervention condition but increased trajectories of externalizing behaviors for youth in the control condition (Kam et al., 2004).

Another study compared the efficacy of the Second Step program (Committee for Children, 2008) combined with the OBPP (Olweus & Limber, 2007) to the OBPP only, and included subgroup analyses for youth with high-incidence disabilities (Sullivan, Sutherland, Farrell, Taylor, & Doyle, 2017). Randomization occurred at the classroom-level with seven classrooms assigned to the combined intervention and seven assigned to the OBBP alone condition. Disability status moderated intervention effects such that greater increases in teacher-reported social skills were found for students in the combined versus the OBPP alone condition. This is one of the only studies in which increased social skills emerged as an outcome for youth with disabilities; however, in contrast to other studies (Espelage et al., 2015, 2016), specific effects on self- or teacher-reported aggression were not found.

Considering school environment interventions, to our knowledge, there have been no evaluations of the efficacy of only school environment interventions (i.e., OBPP and KiVa) for youth with disabilities. However, studies have evaluated the effectiveness of the GBG for youth with EBD (e.g., Pennington & McComas, 2017; Rubow et al., 2018). In a study of early adolescents with EBD in two classrooms at an alternative school, GBG decreased disruptive and aggressive behavior and increased teacher praise (Rubow et al., 2018). Although Pennington and McComas (2017) noted similar behavioral results for the GBG among three eight-year-old students who were at risk or met the criteria for EBD, their findings showed little evidence of generalizability of these positive results when the GBG trial ended. The authors found that students with or at risk for EBD needed the structure of the GBG to demonstrate behavioral improvements and that without it they did not show improvement.

Current evaluations of SEL programs and school environment interventions at the classroom level show some improvements for youth with disabilities in behavioral and academic outcomes (e.g., Espelage et al., 2015, 2016) and for social competencies when these approaches are combined (Sullivan et al., 2017). One classroom management strategy, the GBG, was specifically evaluated for youth with EBD, who showed improvements in behavioral competencies. More research is needed to better understand patterns of social skill acquisition for youth with EBD in the context of SEL programs and to identify the underlying mechanism by which the combined SEL and school environment intervention promoted improvements in socio-emotional competencies among youth with disabilities including EBD.

Implementation Considerations

Selection of Universal Prevention Programs

There are a number of evidence-based SEL programs and school environment interventions available to schools. These two types of programs prioritize some different risk factors (e.g., individual social skills versus school norms for aggression) (CASEL, 2015; Olweus & Limber, 2007). School environment interventions can introduce positive constraints that decrease the likelihood of aggression for youth with or at risk for EBD by promoting a school climate with rigorous supervision, clear behavioral expectations that are consistently reinforced, and parental engagement (Olweus & Limber, 2007). There is evidence that when combined with a school environment intervention, SEL curricula improved social skills for middle school students with high incidence of disabilities (Sullivan et al., 2017) whereas SEL programs alone showed no or more limited outcomes in this area (Espelage et al., 2015, 2016; Kam et al., 2004).

Inevitably, the selection of a specific universal violence prevention program will address some risk factors but leave gaps in covering others. In this case, a logical next step may be the combination of programs to cover a larger domain of risk factors across ecological contexts. However, for teachers, there is a finite amount of time and energy available to invest in prevention efforts (e.g., training, lesson preparation and delivery, and coordination of school-level components) before becoming overburdened (Hughes, Cavell, Meehan, Zhang, & Collie, 2005). Thus, determining the feasibility of implementing multiple violence prevention programs and relative time and effort that each program will require from teachers is one key aspect in the selection of programs. Ultimately, the prioritization and selection of a universal school-based prevention program(s) requires the identification of risk factors for aggression among students in the school ecology and understanding of how these factors operate and impact student progress in academic, social, and behavioral domains (Farmer et al., 2007).

Assessing the Efficacy of Universal Violence Prevention Programs in Real Time

We know little about the actual benefits of universal violence prevention programs for youth with EBD. Aside from case studies of the efficacy of the GBG (Pennington & McComas, 2017; Rubow et al., 2018), most research has not specifically studied how these programs benefit youth with EBD (e.g., Sullivan et al., 2015). Further, most studies evaluating SEL programs for youth with disabilities have focused on changes in outcomes from pre-test to post-test and/or follow-up (Espelage et al., 2015, 2016; Kam et al., 2004; Sullivan et al., 2015). These analyses provide little information on students' skill acquisition over the course of curriculum implementation.

Sutherland and colleagues (2008) noted that one promising approach to learn more about skill acquisition during program delivery is a curriculum-based measure (CBM) for SEL curricula. CBMs can be used to monitor individual student progress in the attainment of social skills at specific points during SEL program implementation (Sutherland et al., 2008). Similar to CBMs that teachers use to check student progress in basic academic areas, this methodology can be used to assess the degree to which social skills are mastered (e.g., assessing improvement on risk factors after units addressing these factors are presented). The ability to assess ongoing progress in skill acquisition could inform curriculum modifications and highlight areas where additional practice or remediation is needed in real time. For SEL programs implemented in the general education classroom, this individual-level data may provide opportunities for general education teachers to collaborate with special education teachers and/or instructional assistants involved in the implementation of individual interventions for youth with EBD to synchronize efforts around areas of risk.

Teachers' Effectiveness in Managing Classroom Social Dynamics

Assessments of changes in socio-emotional competencies for youth with disabilities after receiving SEL programs showed few improvements in this area (Espelage et al., 2015, 2016; Kam et al., 2004; Sullivan et al., 2015). One reason for this may be that programs focused on social skills instruction are not addressing classroom social dynamics (Farmer et al., 2007). Trach, Lee, and Hymel (2018) highlight that although universal violence prevention programs may provide opportunities to practice social skills with peers (e.g., group activities and role plays), there is a need for teachers to understand and manage the behavioral and social dynamics occurring in the classroom for these program aspects to be most effective.

The Supporting Early Adolescents' Learning and Social Success (SEALS) program includes teacher training in "academic engagement enhancement" (e.g., classroom strategies such as small group activities to engage at risk students), "competence engagement behavior management" (e.g., strategies to encourage positive behavior and relationships), and "social dynamics management" (e.g., understanding students' roles, peer group structures, and social hierarchies) (Farmer et al., 2010, pp. 96–97). This training could enhance the delivery of SEL and school environment intervention components for youth with EBD. Training teachers to manage challenging classroom behaviors in a way that promotes prosocial interactions may improve student–teacher relationships and could increase students' receptivity to SEL or teacher-led components of school environment interventions. In addition, the teacher's knowledge of social dynamics in the classroom could facilitate peer selection for small group activities, role plays, and discussions, and the management of these activities in ways that enhance the skills being taught. Teachers may also be able to capitalize on student roles in the classroom and peer group dynamics to reinforce and help to generalize the skills learned in these programs.

Further, teachers' understanding of social dynamics in the classroom may help to counter unintended effects of school environment interventions. Garandeau, Lee, and Salmivalli (2018) examined the plight of stable victims (i.e., those whose victimization status did not improve as a result of intervention) after the implementation of the KiVa program across two successive years for elementary school students. Stable victims in classrooms where the proportion of stable victims had decreased experienced higher levels of anxiety, depression, and were less popular with classmates as compared to stable victims in classrooms where the proportion of stable victims had stayed constant or increased. The authors suggested that being with peers who were now not victims decreased stable victims' self-regard and that peers who were now not victimized may not want to jeopardize their new status by affiliating with stable victims. In this context, teachers may be able to help students who remain vulnerable by managing the classroom social dynamics.

Prevention and Intervention Strategies for Youth with EBD

As schools may adopt a set of programs to provide supports at the universal, selective, and indicated levels, the additive and synergistic nature of universal violence prevention programs should be assessed in the context of selective and indicated interventions. It is important to understand the risk and protective processes addressed by a specific universal program and its relevance for youth with EBD. A universal program may add to selective and indicated interventions by addressing unique risk or protective processes that provide specific skills or enhance environmental contexts in ways that promote socio-emotional, behavioral, and academic competencies for youth with EBD. These programs may also address risk and protective processes that overlap with selective and indicated interventions but do so in a way that complements and adds to these interventions.

Some universal violence prevention strategies are designed as components of more complex programs that integrate universal, selective, and/or indicated components such as the OBPP and KiVa (Olweus & Limber, 2007; Salmivalli et al., 2013). The overall load of prevention and intervention strategies should be considered for youth with EBD and strategies prioritized as needed. For example, if a student with EBD experiences peer victimization, should this be addressed through the selective or indicated components of school environment interventions or through other selective or indicated supports that the youth may already have in place? The effectiveness of the selective and indicated supports may vary depending on the degree to which school staff know students and are familiar with their history, needs, and areas of risk and resilience. Overall, it is important to understand the efficacy of each intervention and support for youth with EBD and how they work alone and in combination to determine best strategies to implement and when to modify them.

School environment interventions focus on changing school-level norms to support active intervention in situations where a student is being victimized (e.g., Olweus & Limber, 2007). This relies in part on students' comfort in disclosing incidents of witnessed or experienced violence to their teachers. This is important as middle school students' perceptions of teacher awareness of violence occurring at school, their encouragement for students to report these incidents, and students' comfort in making these reports predicted higher quality student–teacher relationships over a six-month timeframe (Behrhorst, Sullivan, & Sutherland, 2019). Youth with EBD may experience lower levels of trust and confidence in their relationships with teachers and thus could be less likely to confide in them about incidents involving aggression at school.

Conclusion

The areas of interrelated risk for youth with EBD are complex, experienced across constantly interacting individual and ecological domains (e.g., family, school, peer, and community ecologies), and fluctuate with changes in development, circumstances, and stressors (Farmer, Sutherland, et al., 2016). Based on the individualized needs of youth with EBD, universal violence prevention programs may be implemented within the context of these needs. We need to understand more about the degree to which universal violence prevention programs that address risk factors which are relevant for youth with or at risk for EBD are actually benefitting them. The assessment of youths' progress in real time could help teachers capitalize on programs or components of programs that are working, understand and address barriers to participation or progress, and ultimately make determinations about how and to what degree these programs can address a particular risk factor(s) present for students with or at risk for EBD.

References

Behrhorst, K., Sullivan, T. N., & Sutherland, K. S. (2019). Influence of school climate and awareness and reporting of violence on student aggression and victimization in middle school. *Journal of Early Adolescence*. Advance online publication. https://doi-org.proxy.library.vcu.edu/10.1177/0272431619870616.

Collaborative for Academic, Social, and Emotional Learning. (2015). Effective social and emotional learning programs: Middle and high school edition. Retrieved from https://casel.org/middle-and-high-school-edition-casel-guide

Committee for Children. (2008). *Second step: Student success through prevention program*. Seattle, WA: Author.

Conduct Problems Prevention Research Group. (1999). Initial impact of the fast track prevention trial for conduct problems II: Classroom effects. *Journal of Consulting and Clinical Psychology, 67*, 648–657. doi:10.1037/0022-006X.67.5.648

Crews, S. D., Bender, H., Cook, C. R., Gresham, F. M., Kern, L., & Vanderwood, M. (2007). Risk and protective factors of emotional and/or behavioral disorders in children and adolescents: A mega-analytic synthesis. *Behavioral Disorders, 32*(2), 64–77.

David-Ferdon, C., & Simon, T. R. (2014). *Preventing youth violence: Opportunities for action*. Atlanta, GA: National Center for Injury Prevention and Control, Centers for Disease Control and Prevention.

David-Ferdon, C., Vivolo-Kantor, A. M., Dahlberg, L. L., Marshall, K. J., Rainford, N., & Hall, J. E. (2016). *A comprehensive technical package for the prevention of youth violence and associated risk behaviors*. Atlanta, GA: National Center for Injury Prevention and Control, Centers for Disease Control and Prevention.

Elliott, D. S., Wilson, W. J., Huizinga, D., Elliott, A. C., & Ranking, B. (1996). The effects of neighborhood disadvantage on youth development. *Journal of Research in Crime and Delinquency, 33*, 389–426.

Espelage, D. L., Rose, C. A., & Polanin, J. R. (2015). Socio-emotional learning program to reduce bullying, fighting, and victimization among middle school students with disabilities. *Remedial and Special Education*, 299–311. doi:10.1177/074193251564564

Espelage, D. L., Rose, C. A., & Polanin, J. R. (2016). Social-emotional learning program to promote prosocial and academic skills among middle school students with disabilities. *Remedial and Special Education, 37*(6), 323–332. doi:10.1177/0741932515627475

Farmer, T. W. (2013). When universal approaches and prevention services are not enough: The importance of understanding the stigmatization of special education for students with EBD. A response to Kauffman and Badar. *Behavioral Disorders, 39*(1), 32–42. doi:10.1177/019874291303900105

Farmer, T. W., & Farmer, E. M. (2001). Developmental science, systems of care, and prevention of emotional and behavioral problems in youth. *American Journal of Orthopsychiatry, 71*(2), 171–181. doi:10.1037/0002-9432.71.2.171

Farmer, T. W., Farmer, E. M. Z., Estell, D. B., & Hutchins, B. C. (2007). The developmental dynamics of aggression and the prevention of school violence. *Journal of Emotional and Behavioral Disorders, 15*, 197–208. doi:10.1177/10634266070150040201

Farmer, T. W., Gatzke-Kopp, L. M., Lee, D. L., Dawes, M., & Talbott, E. (2016). Research and policy on disability: Linking special education to developmental science. *Policy Insights from the Behavioral and Brain Sciences, 3*(1), 138–145. doi:10.1177/2372732215624217

Farmer, T. W., Hamm, J. V., Petrin, R. A., Robertson, D., Murray, R. A., Meece, J. L., & Brooks, D. S. (2010). Supporting early adolescent learning and social strengths: Promoting productive contexts for students at-risk for EBD during the transition to middle school. *Exceptionality, 18*(2), 94–102. doi:10.1080/09362831003673192

Farmer, T. W., & Hollowell, J. H. (1994). Social networks in mainstream classrooms: Social affiliations and behavioral characteristics of students with EBD. *Journal of Emotional and Behavioral Disorder, 2*(3), 143–155.

Farmer, T. W., Sutherland, K. S., Talbott, E., Brooks, D. S., Norwalk, K., & Huneke, M. (2016). Special educators as intervention specialists: Dynamic systems and the complexity of intensifying interventions for students with emotional and behavioral disorders. *Journal of Emotional and Behavioral Disorders, 24*(3), 173–186. doi:10.1177/1063426616650166

Farrington, D. P., Gaffney, H., & Ttofi, M. M. (2017). Systematic reviews of explanatory risk factors of violence, offending, and delinquency. *Aggression and Violent Behavior, 33*, 24–36.

Frey, K. S., Hirschstein, M. K., Snell, J. L., Van Schoiack Edstrom, L., MacKenzie, E. P., & Broderick, C. J. (2005). Reducing playground bullying and supporting beliefs: An experimental trial of the steps to respect program. *Developmental Psychology, 41*, 479–491. doi:10.1037/0012-1649.41.3.479

Garandeau, C. F., Lee, I. A., & Salmivalli, C. (2018). Decreases in the proportion of bullying victims in the classroom: Effects on the adjustment of remaining victims. *International Journal of Behavioral Development, 42* (1), 64–72. doi:10.1177/0165025416667492

Horner, R. H., Sugai, G., & Anderson, C. M. (2010). Examining the evidence base for school-wide positive behavior support. *Focus on Exceptional Children, 42*(8), 1–14.

Hughes, J. N., Cavell, T. A., Meehan, B. T., Zhang, D., & Collie, C. (2005). Adverse school context moderates the outcomes of selective interventions for aggressive children. *Journal of Consulting and Clinical Psychology, 73*, 731–736. doi:10.1037/0022-006X.73.4.731

Individuals with Disabilities Education Act of 1997, Pub. L. No. 105-17, 20 U.S.C. § 1400, 111 Stat. 37.

Kam, C., Greenberg, M. T., & Kusche, C. A. (2004). Sustained effects of the PATHS curriculum on the social and psychological adjustment of children in special education. *Journal of Emotional and Behavioral Disorders, 12*, 66–78. doi:10.1177/10634266040120020101

Kann, L., McManus, T., Harris, W. A., Shanklin, S. L., Flint, K. H., Queen, B., & Ethier, K. A. (2018). Youth risk behavior survey – United States. Morbidity and mortality weekly report. *Surveillance Summaries, 67*(8), 1–114.

Kashani, J. H., Jones, M. R., Bumby, K. M., & Thomas, L. A. (1999). Youth violence: Psychosocial risk factors, treatment, prevention, and recommendations. *Journal of Emotional and Behavioral Disorders, 7*, 200–210. doi:10.1177/106342669900700402

Kern, L. (2015). Addressing the needs of students with social, emotional, and behavioral problems: Reflections and visions. *Remedial and Special Education, 36*, 24–27. doi:10.11177/0741932514554104

Lane, K. L., Carter, E. W., Pierson, M. R., & Glaeser, B. C. (2006). Academic, social, and behavioral characteristics of high school students with emotional disturbances or learning disabilities. *Journal of Emotional and Behavioral Disorders, 14*, 108–117. doi:10.1177/10634266060140020101

Mayer, M., Lochman, J., & Van Acker, R. (2005). Introduction to the special issue: Cognitive-behavioral interventions with students with EBD. *Behavioral Disorders, 30*, 197–212. doi:10.1177/019874290503000306

Mercy, J., Butchart, A., Farrington, D., & Cerda, M. (2002). Youth violence. In E. Krug, L. L. Dahlberg, J. A. Mercy, A. B. Zwi, & R. Lozano, *World report on violence and health* (pp. 25–56). Geneva, Switzerland: World Health Organization.

Murray, C., & Greenberg, M. T. (2006). Examining the importance of social relationships and social contexts in the lives of children with high-incidence disabilities. *Journal of Special Education, 39*, 220–233.

Murray, C., & Pianta, R. C. (2006). The importance of teacher–student relationships for adolescents with high incidence disabilities. *Theory into Practice, 46*(2), 105–112.

Olweus, D., & Limber, S. P. (2007). *Olweus Bullying Prevention Program: Teacher guide*. Center City, MN: Hazelden.

Pennington, B., & McComas, J. J. (2017). Effects of the good behavior game across classroom contexts. *Journal of Applied Behavioral Analysis, 50*, 176–180. doi:10.1002/jaba.357

Pianta, R. C., Hamre, B., & Allen, J. (2012). Teacher-student relationships and engagement: Conceptualizing, measuring, and improving the capacity of classroom interactions. In S. Christenson, A. Reschly, & C. Wylie (Eds.), *Handbook of research on student engagement* (pp. 365–386). Boston, MA: Springer.

Rose, C., Monda-Amaya, L., & Espelage, D. (2011). Bullying perpetration and victimization in special education: A review of the literature. *Remedial and Special Education, 32*, 114–130. doi:10.1177/0741932510361247

Rose, C., Simpson, C. G., & Moss, A. (2015). The bullying dynamic: Prevalence of involvement among a large-scale sample of middle and high school youth with and without disabilities. *Psychology in the Schools, 52*(5), 515–531. doi:10.1002/pits21840

Rubow, C. C., Vollmer, T. R., & Joslyn, P. R. (2018). Effects of the good behavior game on student and teacher behavior in an alternative school. *Journal of Applied Behavior Analysis, 51*, 382–392. doi:10.1002/jaba.455

Salmivalli, C., Poskiparta, E., Ahtola, A., & Haataja, A. (2013). The implementation and effectiveness of the KiVa antibullying program in Finland. *European Psychologist, 18*, 79–88. doi:10.1027/1016-9040/a00014

Sampson, R. J., Raudenbush, S. W., & Earls, F. (1997). Neighborhoods and violent crime: A multilevel study of collective efficacy. *Science, 277*, 918–924. doi:10.1126science.277.5328.918

Schweinhart, L. J., Barnes, H. V., & Weikart, D. P. (1993). *Significant benefits: The HighScope Perry Preschool Study through age 27 (Monographs of the HighScope Educational Research Foundation, 10)*. Ypsilanti, MI: HighScope Press.

Sullivan, T. N., Sutherland, K. S., Farrell, A. D., & Taylor, K. A. (2015). An evaluation of second step: What are the benefits for youth with and without disabilities? *Remedial and Special Education, 36*(5), 286–298. doi:10.1177/0741932515575616

Sullivan, T. N., Sutherland, K. S., Farrell, A. D., Taylor, K. A., & Doyle, S. T. (2017). Evaluation of violence prevention approaches among early adolescents: Moderating effects of disability status and gender. *Journal of Child and Family Studies, 26*(4), 1151–1163. doi:10/1007/s10826-016-0629-9

Sutherland, K. S., & Oswald, D. P. (2005). The relationship between teacher and student behavior in classrooms for students with emotional and behavioral disorders: Transactional processes. *Journal of Child and Family Studies, 14*(1), 1–14. doi:10.1007/s10826-005-1106z

Sutherland, K. S., Wright, S. A., & Sullivan, T. N. (2008). *Measuring social competence skill acquisition using curriculum-based measures: Development of measures and initial findings*. Paper presented at the 32nd annual Severe Behavior Disorders of Children and Youth Conference, Tempe, AZ.

Trach, J., Lee, M., & Hymel, S. (2018). A social-ecological approach to addressing emotional and behavioral problems in schools: Focusing on group processes and social dynamics. *Journal of Emotional and Behavioral Disorders, 26*(1), 11–20. doi:10.1177/1063426617742346

Wagner, M., Friend, M., Bursuck, W. D., Kutash, K., Duchnowski, A. J., Sumi, W. C., & Espstein, M. H. (2005). Educating students with emotional disturbances: A national perspective on school programs and services. *Journal of Emotional and Behavioral Disorder, 14*(1), 12–30. doi:10.1177/10634266060140010201

Xie, H., Cairns, R., & Cairns, B. D. (1999). Social networks and configurations in inner-city schools: Aggression, popularity, and implications for students with EBD. *Journal of Emotional and Behavioral Disorders, 7*(3), 147–155. doi:10.1177/106342669900700303

11 Interventions for Youth Who Experience Trauma and Adversity

Elizabeth A. Miller and David J. Kolko

Introduction

This chapter provides an overview of the influence of trauma and adversity on youth mental health and describes current approaches to treatment and prevention. It reviews the prevalence and consequences of childhood trauma and adversity, evidence-based treatments for youth who experience trauma, and systemic approaches to addressing trauma and adversity, including trauma-informed care and universal screening. The chapter closes with a discussion of strategies for preventing childhood trauma and adversity.

Traumatic experiences are events that individuals perceive as threatening their life or safety, such as physical assault, sexual assault, natural disasters, and serious motor vehicle collisions (American Psychiatric Association, 2013). Trauma refers to lasting negative effects on functioning and well-being following a traumatic event (Substance Abuse and Mental Health Services Administration, 2014). Trauma is also popularly used to refer not only to traumatic experiences and their sequelae, but also to other adverse experiences and psychosocial stressors that do not involve an immediate threat to life or safety. Examples of adverse experiences include child neglect, caregiver substance abuse or mental illness, incarceration of a caregiver, divorce, and bullying.

Prevalence and Consequences of Childhood Trauma and Adversity

Over the past few decades, several forces have converged to drive forward attention to childhood trauma and adversity. One is increasing awareness of the prevalence and impact of traumatic experiences among children and adolescents (hereafter referred to as youth), both in the general population and in systems serving youth (e.g., mental health, child welfare). The most recent National Survey of Children's Exposure to Violence, a population survey of youth in the United States, found that in the past year, 37% of youth experienced physical assault (most commonly from siblings and peers), 15% of youth experienced child maltreatment, and 25% witnessed violence in their family or community (Finkelhor, Turner, Shattuck, & Hamby, 2015). Polyvictimization was common, with 40% of youth experiencing more than one type of direct victimization (Finkelhor et al., 2015). Rates are higher in at risk samples; for example, approximately 75% of youth referred to child welfare reported two or more experiences of victimization (Kolko et al., 2010).

As a group, youth who experience trauma and adversity are at increased risk for developing emotional and behavioral disorders (EBD), including internalizing disorders (e.g., depression, generalized anxiety disorder) and externalizing disorders (e.g., oppositional defiant disorder, substance use disorders) (Chen et al., 2010; Evans, Davies, & DiLillo, 2008; Fowler, Tompsett,

Braciszewski, Jacques-Tiura, & Baltes, 2009; Hillberg, Hamilton-Giachritsis, & Dixon, 2011; Norman et al., 2012). Some youth may develop posttraumatic stress disorder (PTSD), the diagnosis of which requires identification of a specific traumatic experience (i.e., an event experienced as threatening to life or safety). Among youth exposed to potentially traumatic experiences, a relatively small group of youth develop PTSD, a slightly larger group exhibit elevated symptoms, and the majority are resilient (Kolko et al., 2010; Miller-Graff & Howell, 2015; Self-Brown, Lai, Thompson, McGill, & Kelley, 2013). In a national survey of adolescents, more than half (62%) had experienced a potentially traumatic event in their lifetime, yet only 5% met criteria for PTSD (McLaughlin et al., 2013). However, rates in populations exposed to chronic and ongoing trauma (e.g., refugee children, youth exposed to war) are often much higher, averaging close to 50% and as high as 87% (Attanayake et al., 2009).

Another key driver of attention to child trauma and adversity has been the accumulation and dissemination of research on the impact of adverse childhood experiences (ACES) on adult mental and physical health (Felitti et al., 1998). ACES include multiple types of adversity – child abuse (i.e., physical, sexual, and emotional abuse; witnessing violence), neglect (i.e., physical and emotional), and household dysfunction (i.e., mental illness, substance abuse, and incarceration within the household; parental separation or divorce).

Research on ACES has clearly established two crucial facts. First, many youth experience a high number of ACES. Half or more of individuals report at least one ACE, with a significant minority (estimates from 6 to 20%) reporting four or more (Cronholm et al., 2015; Felitti et al., 1998; Gilbert et al., 2015; Wade et al., 2016). Second, ACES confer significant risk for mental health, physical health, relationships, and independent functioning across the lifespan. Higher ACE scores have been associated with increased risk for a multitude of problems, including depression and suicide attempts, substance use problems, sexual risk behaviors, intimate partner violence perpetration, smoking, obesity, and cardiovascular disease (Anda et al., 2005; Felitti et al., 1998; Gilbert et al., 2015; Wade et al., 2016).

The development and dissemination of ACES research has been influential in increasing public awareness of the prevalence and impact of ACES and driving efforts to prevent ACES and ameliorate their negative effects. However, we must remain mindful of its limitations as we consider how best to apply this information (Finkelhor, 2018). The consequences of trauma and adversity are multifaceted and heterogeneous, with individuals' outcomes affected more strongly by an accumulation of risk factors and absence of protective factors than by any one risk factor (Huston & Bentley, 2010).

In summary, the past few decades have seen great increases in attention to the prevalence and impact of traumatic and adverse experiences in childhood. Increasing awareness has galvanized clinicians, institutions, policymakers, and society as a whole to develop better ways to serve youth who have experienced trauma and adversity.

Treatment for Youth Who Experience Trauma and Adversity

Evidence-Based Treatments

Because adverse and traumatic experiences are associated with a broad range of psychopathology, effective treatments for youth who experience trauma and adversity include interventions that specifically target symptoms of posttraumatic stress as well as interventions that target other outcomes. Evidence-based assessment is needed to match youth with appropriate treatments and monitor progress throughout treatment. Ongoing assessment has been found to increase the impact of psychotherapy generally (Bickman, Kelley, Breda, de

Andrade, & Riemer, 2011) and has been identified as a key component in interventions designed to address youth trauma exposure (Ai, Foster, Pecora, Delaney, & Rodriguez, 2013).

Well-established psychosocial treatments (i.e., with strong research support) for youth exposed to traumatic events include individual cognitive-behavioral therapy (CBT) with caregiver involvement, individual CBT, and group CBT (Dorsey et al., 2017; Gutermann et al., 2016; Leenarts, Diehle, Doreleijers, Jansma, & Lindauer, 2013). The most frequently tested model of CBT with caregiver involvement for youth who experience trauma is Trauma-Focused Cognitive Behavior Therapy (TF-CBT). TF-CBT is a phased and component-based approach designed to treat youth who have experienced an identifiable traumatic event and are exhibiting symptoms of posttraumatic stress, depression, anxiety, and/or behavior problems (see Cohen & Mannarino, 2015). Treatment phases are (1) stabilization, (2) trauma narration and processing, and (3) integration and consolidation; caregivers are actively involved in all phases. Components are specified by the acronym PRAC-TICE: Psychoeducation, Parenting, Relaxation, Affect modulation, Cognitive coping, Trauma narrative and processing, In vivo exposure, Conjoint caregiver-child sessions, and Enhancing safety. Gradual exposure (i.e., increasing exposure to trauma reminders) is essential and occurs throughout the course of treatment (Cohen & Mannarino, 2015). TF-CBT has been tested in more than 20 randomized controlled trials and has consistently demonstrated effectiveness in reducing PTSD symptoms, symptoms of depression and anxiety, and externalizing behaviors, with benefits sustained over time (Cary & McMillen, 2012; Cohen, Deblinger, Mannarino, & Steer, 2004; Deblinger, Beld, & Glickmans, 2012; Gutermann et al., 2016). Meta-analytic findings indicate TF-CBT has large effects on PTSD and depression symptoms relative to no treatment ($g = -1.48$ and $g = -0.78$, respectively) and small-to-medium effects relative to alternative treatments ($g = -0.28$ and $g = -0.25$, respectively) (Lenz & Hollenbaugh, 2015).

Other specific well-established treatment models include individual and group variants of TF-CBT, adapted versions of adult treatments (e.g., Prolonged Exposure for Adolescents), and Cognitive-Behavioral Intervention for Trauma in Schools (CBITS) (Dorsey et al., 2017). Probably efficacious treatments (i.e., moderate research support, not yet considered well-established) include group CBT with caregiver involvement and Eye Movement Desensitization and Reprocessing (EMDR) (Dorsey et al., 2017). Many evidence-based treatments utilize a phased approach (i.e., beginning with psychoeducation and skill-building and progressing to exposure) and share common elements, including psychoeducation about trauma, emotion regulation and coping strategies, problem-solving skills, cognitive processing, and imaginal and/or in vivo exposure to feared stimuli (Dorsey et al., 2017; Leenarts et al., 2013). Exposure to trauma reminders is thought to be a crucial process through which trauma-related fears are reduced. There is some evidence that individual treatments and those involving caregivers are more effective than group treatments or those without caregiver involvement (Gutermann et al., 2016).

Additional treatments that may be appropriate for youth with adverse and traumatic experiences include those focused on child physical abuse or exposure to physical aggression, family dysfunction, negative parenting practices, and/or youth behavior problems. Table 11.1 lists relevant examples, including Alternatives for Families: A Cognitive Behavioral Therapy (Kolko, Herschell, Baumann, Hart, & Wisniewski, 2018; Kolko, Simonich, & Loiterstein, 2014), Child–Parent Psychotherapy (Lieberman, Ghosh Ippen, & Hernandez Dimmler, 2019; Lieberman, Van Horn, & Ghosh Ippen, 2005), Multidimensional Treatment Foster Care (Smith & Chamberlain, 2010), Multisystemic Therapy for Child Abuse and Neglect (Swenson, Schaeffer, Henggeler, Faldowski, & Mayhew, 2010), and Parent–Child Interaction Therapy (Chaffin, Funderburk, Bard, Valle, & Gurwitch, 2011; Eisenstadt, Eyberg, McNeil, Newcomb, & Funderburk, 1993; Kennedy, Kim, Tripodi, Brown, & Gowdy, 2016).

156 *Elizabeth A. Miller and David J. Kolko*

Table 11.1 Overview of Evidence-based Treatments for Trauma

Treatment Name	Age Range	Target Population	Treatment Outcomes
Alternatives for Families: A Cognitive Behavioral Therapy (AF-CBT)	5–17	Families with heightened conflict, coercion, or aggression, including child physical abuse, and/or youth behavior problems	Reductions in family conflict and dysfunction, risk for physical abuse, youth behavior problems, PTSD symptoms
Child–Parent Psychotherapy (CPP)	0–5	Infants, toddlers, and preschoolers exposed to adversity and trauma	Reductions in youth behavioral and emotional problems and maternal distress
Multidimensional Treatment Foster Care (MTFC)	3–18.	Youth in out-of-home placement with chronic antisocial behavior, emotional disturbance, and/or delinquency	Reductions in youth behavior problems, delinquency and criminal justice involvement, and placement instability
Multisystemic Therapy for Child Abuse and Neglect (MST-CAN)	6–17	Families involved with the child welfare system due to physical abuse and/or neglect	Reductions in youth mental health symptoms, parenting behaviors associated with maltreatment, and the likelihood of out-of-home placement
Parent–Child Interaction Therapy (PCIT)	2–7	Young children with behavior problems and/or parent–child relationship problems	Reductions in youth behavior problems, parent stress, parent–youth conflict, and physical abuse recidivism

Unfortunately, implementation of evidence-based treatments in community settings is an ongoing challenge, and many youth do not have access to evidence-based treatments. Methods for efficient and effective implementation of evidence-based practices (Proctor et al., 2009; Williams & Beidas, 2019) and policy and funding changes to support large-scale system transformations are vital (Aarons et al., 2016; Beidas, Stewart, et al., 2016; Regan et al., 2017).

Treatment Considerations

Treatment engagement, attendance, and adherence are crucial to improving outcomes for youth who experience trauma and adversity. Unfortunately, populations at greater risk for trauma and adversity, including youth living in poverty and ethnic/racial minority youth, are also less likely to engage in treatment (Baker-Ericzén, Jenkins, & Haine-Schlagel, 2012; Huey & Polo, 2010; McKay & Bannon, 2004; Miller, Southam-Gerow, & Allin, 2008; Schnitzer, 1996). Engagement barriers include logistical barriers (e.g., time off work, childcare, transportation), as well as perceptual barriers (e.g., perceived effectiveness of treatment, stigma) (Gopalan et al., 2010; McKay & Bannon, 2004). Barriers are especially high for youth who experience trauma and those with disruptive behavior problems (Gopalan et al., 2010). Adding preparatory or continuous enhancement strategies (e.g., orientation letter, brief motivational intervention) to treatment can increase engagement (Gopalan et al., 2010; Ingoldsby, 2010; Nock & Kazdin, 2005). Increased implementation of evidence-based engagement strategies can facilitate treatment engagement and ultimately improve youth mental health outcomes (Ingoldsby, 2010; McKay et al., 2004).

In addition to impairing treatment engagement, trauma and adversity may negatively affect treatment response for youth with EBD. For example, maltreatment history has been associated with poorer course of depression (e.g., more recurrent and persistent episodes) and diminished response to treatment (Lewis et al., 2010; Nanni, Uher, & Danese, 2012). Youth with EBD are also at increased risk for experiencing or re-experiencing trauma and adversity, which may worsen existing EBD and/or lead to additional mental health problems. Compared to youth without EBD, youth with EBD are at increased risk for child abuse and neglect, peer victimization, physical violence, and sexual victimization (Jones et al., 2012; Sullivan, 2009; Sullivan & Knutson, 2000; Turner, Vanderminden, Finkelhor, Hamby, & Shattuck, 2011).

Clinicians should be aware of the increased risk for victimization among youth with EBD and engage in ongoing assessment to identify and address any new experiences of victimization during treatment. Treatment should also include attention to preventing victimization. Some treatment approaches, such as TF-CBT and AF-CBT, include an explicit focus on safety and preventing re-victimization, while other approaches rely on clinicians to judge when safety should be addressed in treatment. Given high rates of victimization for youth with EBD, safety planning and skills are appropriate to include in treatment for all youth.

Transforming Systems to Address Trauma and Adversity

Trauma-Informed Care

One response to increasing awareness of trauma and adversity is the concept of trauma-informed care. Trauma-informed care incorporates an understanding of trauma and its impact into all aspects of organizational functioning and is distinct from trauma-specific interventions. The Substance Abuse and Mental Health Services Administration (SAMHSA) defines a trauma-informed organization or system as one that

> realizes the widespread impact of trauma and understands potential paths for recovery; recognizes the signs and symptoms of trauma in clients, families, staff, and others involved with the system; and responds by fully integrating knowledge about trauma into policies, procedures, and practices, and seeks to actively resist re-traumatization.
>
> (SAMHSA, 2014, p. 9)

Specific principles are: (1) safety, (2) trustworthiness and transparency, (3) peer support, (4) collaboration and mutuality, (5) empowerment, voice, and choice, and (6) cultural, historical, and gender issues (SAMHSA, 2014).

Trauma-informed trainings and initiatives to transform systems into trauma-informed systems are now ubiquitous (e.g., Bartlett et al., 2016; Beidas, Adams, et al., 2016; Kerns et al., 2016; Lang, Campbell, Shanley, Crusto, & Connell, 2016). The increasing awareness of children's experiences of trauma and adversity is heartening, as is the enthusiasm for efforts to improve the quality of care. However, poor operationalization of trauma-informed principles makes it difficult to determine when institutions, organizations, or individual providers are actually delivering trauma-informed care. The aforementioned SAMHSA definition and principles are essentially principles of good care, not specific to trauma, which should characterize all systems-level responses. Importantly, evidence for the benefits of trauma-informed care has not kept pace with the proliferation of trauma-informed trainings and initiatives. The challenge for the trauma-informed care movement is to demonstrate that the substantial investments made in trauma-informed care actually improve the lives of youth (Berliner & Kolko, 2016).

Trauma-informed care initiatives typically include multiple layers of activities, including increasing awareness, enhancing cross-system collaboration, establishing routine screening, and increasing access to trauma-specific evidence-based treatments. These initiatives may help raise the general quality of care in child-serving systems by encouraging professionals to be more empathic and understanding and more attuned to how services are delivered, whether youth have been affected by trauma or not (Berliner & Kolko, 2016). Increasing awareness of trauma is typically a first step toward trauma-informed care, but even just increasing awareness requires evidence to identify the most important pieces of information to be shared and consideration of possible iatrogenic effects. For example, awareness training focused solely on the prevalence and negative impact of trauma may inadvertently lead to decreased hope and expectations for change. It is just as important to convey that most youth are resilient and do not have persisting general or trauma-related problems (Bell, Romano, & Flynn, 2015; Miller-Graff & Howell, 2015). There is little downside to brief awareness training, but without good evidence that increasing awareness benefits youth and families, organizations must thoughtfully consider how to best utilize their limited resources. Awareness of trauma is important, but so is awareness of other topics (e.g., family strengths and stressors, racism and discrimination, child development).

For organizations aiming to become more trauma-informed, awareness training alone is insufficient and should not be considered a substitute for changing practices to improve identification, assessment, and linkage to effective services (Berliner & Kolko, 2016). If trauma-informed care is intended to produce changes in practice, then it is important to carefully conceptualize, operationalize, and measure the intended outcomes. Documenting specific system-level and individual-level practice changes and their impact on trauma-affected youth and their families would greatly strengthen the case for trauma-informed care. Similarly, strengthening coordination across systems is a common goal of trauma-informed care initiatives; this concept must be operationalized in terms of both the general principle of better case coordination and the trauma-informed aspect of increased identification and linkage to trauma-specific services. Given that more services and more time spent coordinating may not always be the most beneficial use of scarce professional and organizational resources, approaches that are more parsimonious and focused may be warranted (Berliner et al., 2015).

The concept of trauma-informed care has created movement toward a highly desirable goal – that all youth who have experienced trauma receive a warm and caring response from knowledgeable professionals. To capitalize on the potential of this movement to improve outcomes for youth, systems must work to ensure that youth who experience trauma are not only recognized, but also receive effective care. Two logical ways to achieve this goal are to make routine screening for trauma exposure and impact a priority in child welfare and mental health systems and to increase the availability of effective trauma-specific treatments (Berliner & Kolko, 2016). These practices must remain the central target of trauma-informed care efforts if the movement is to be a meaningful one for youth and families affected by trauma.

Screening for Adverse and Traumatic Experiences

Awareness of the impact of ACES on child development has led to a push for universal screening for ACES in pediatric primary care (Purewal et al., 2016). Early detection is intended to lead to tailored interventions to prevent or ameliorate negative consequences on physical and mental health (Purewal et al., 2016). Although we recommend screening for trauma exposure and impact in child welfare and mental health systems, the benefits of ACES screening in the broader population (e.g., in primary care or schools) are less clear.

Finkelhor (2018) raises three essential cautions regarding ACE screening in healthcare. First, for screening to have a demonstrable impact on outcomes, there must be strong links to effective interventions to mitigate risk. Unfortunately, there are no evidence-based interventions for ACES, largely because they have heterogeneous effects on outcomes. A high ACE score indicates that an individual is at risk for a range of poor outcomes, but provides no information about an individual's current functioning or needs. Proponents of screening suggest that normalization and psychoeducation about the impact of ACEs may positively impact outcomes (Dube, 2018; Machtinger, Cuca, Khanna, Rose, & Kimberg, 2015), but there is no evidence yet to support this hypothesis.

A second caution is that ACE screening may have costly and iatrogenic effects (Finkelhor, 2018). For example, screening could be perceived as intrusive or uncomfortable, youth or caregiver awareness of the negative consequences of ACES could lead to demoralization and hopelessness, and systems may be overburdened by mandated reporting requirements. Perhaps more likely, ACE screening may result in overuse of referrals to mental health treatment for individuals with high ACE scores, even in the absence of significant mental health symptoms. Research is needed to assess both the benefits and costs of ACE screening before widespread implementation.

Lastly, ACE screening should not take the place of screening for specific symptoms or problems for which effective treatments exist (Finkelhor, 2018). Systems seeking to improve the ways in which they care for individuals who have experienced trauma and adversity through screening will be better served by screening for trauma impact, rather than exposure. Given that trauma has a heterogeneous impact, systems may choose to screen broadly (e.g., mental health symptoms) or prioritize screening for problems commonly associated with child adversity and trauma for which effective interventions exist (e.g., depression, Siu & U.S. Preventative Services Task Force, 2016; sexual risk behaviors, LeFevre & U.S. Preventative Services Task Force, 2014; substance use, Curry et al., 2018; Moyer & U.S. Preventative Services Task Force, 2013).

Prevention of Childhood Trauma and Adversity

Ultimately, the most effective way to reduce the individual and societal burdens associated with childhood trauma and adversity is to prevent youth from experiencing trauma and adversity. Considerable efforts have focused on preventing child abuse and neglect through reduction of associated family risk factors. Home visiting programs for families with young children, such as Nurse–Family Partnership (Olds, Henderson, Chamberlin, & Tatelbaum, 1986), SafeCare (Chaffin, Hecht, Bard, Silovsky, & Beasley, 2012), Healthy Families America (Duggan et al., 2004; DuMont et al., 2008), and others have been shown to reduce maltreatment and associated risk factors (see Avellar & Supplee, 2013). The federal government has made substantial investments in home visiting through the Maternal, Infant, and Early Childhood Home Visiting Program, greatly expanding the reach of these programs. However, implementation is fraught with challenges and family engagement is often low, limiting their impact (Alonso-Marsden et al., 2013; Damashek, Doughty, Ware, & Silovsky, 2011; Donelan-McCall, Eckenrode, & Olds, 2009).

SEEK (A Safe Environment for Every Kid) is a universal prevention program delivered through pediatric primary care. It aims to promote children's health, development, and safety by addressing common psychosocial adversities associated with increased risk for maltreatment that also have direct negative impacts on children's development, such as parental depression, substance abuse, intimate partner violence, and food and housing insecurity (Dubowitz, Feigelman, Lane, & Kim, 2009; Dubowitz, Lane, Semiatin, & Magder, 2012). Pediatric primary care professionals are trained to use a questionnaire to screen for the targeted problems, follow algorithms that help address the targeted problems briefly and efficiently, and provide guidance and adjunctive caregiver handouts during well-child visits. Findings from two randomized controlled trials indicate the SEEK model is a cost-effective strategy for reducing child maltreatment and feasible for large-scale implementation (Dubowitz et al., 2009, 2012; Eismann, Theuerling, Maguire, Hente, & Shapiro, 2019).

Comprehensive prevention of childhood trauma and adversity must include not only family-level preventative services, but community and societal changes to create healthy, safe, and developmentally supportive environments for all youth. Unfortunately, policies to promote child well-being often take low priority in the United States, which remains the only country that has not ratified the United Nations Convention on the Rights of the Child. In 2017, 9% of the federal budget was spent on youth, in contrast to 45% spent on retirement and health benefits for adults (Isaacs et al., 2018).

One way to prevent childhood trauma and adversity is through policies that provide families with more resources. For example, paid family leave, expansions of the Earned Income Tax Credit, and increases in minimum wage have all been linked to declines in child maltreatment (Berger, Font, Slack, & Waldfogel, 2017; Klevens, Luo, Xu, Peterson, & Latzman, 2016; Raissian & Bullinger, 2017). Additional strategies to reduce child trauma and adversity and promote well-being include, among others, increasing access to and affordability of high-quality childcare and early childhood education (Mersky, Topitzes, & Reynolds, 2011; Reynolds & Robertson, 2003; Zhai, Waldfogel, & Brooks-Gunn, 2013), reducing the use of exclusionary discipline in schools (Skiba, Arredondo, & Williams, 2014), and reforming the criminal justice system to minimize parental separations and incarceration-related stressors (Day, 2007; Mapson, 2013). Lastly, policies that directly create trauma and adversity for youth, such as the Trump administration's immigration policies separating youth (including young children) from caregivers and placing youth in inhumane detention conditions (Wood, 2018), must be adamantly opposed. Only through prioritizing the needs and well-being of youth can we hope to ease the individual and societal burdens associated with childhood trauma and adversity.

Summary and Conclusions

This chapter has provided a brief overview of the impact of trauma and adversity on youth mental health and evidence-based approaches to prevention and treatment. Although childhood trauma and adversity are all too common and increase risk for EBDs, there is substantial evidence highlighting the clinical benefits of family-focused interventions for youth who experience trauma and adversity. Continued rigorous research is needed to further develop effective methods to identify and treat the sequelae of trauma and adversity and improve implementation of evidence-based practices in community settings. Increasing awareness of the prevalence and impact of childhood trauma and adversity has motivated widespread efforts to transform systems and change policies to better meet the needs of youth. Changes in policies and practices must be grounded in research evidence and rigorously evaluated to realize the potential of this movement to prevent childhood trauma and adversity and promote child well-being.

References

Aarons, G. A., Green, A. E., Trott, E., Willging, C. E., Torres, E. M., Ehrhart, M. G., & Roesch, S. C. (2016). The roles of system and organizational leadership in system-wide evidence-based intervention sustainment: A mixed-method study. *Administration and Policy in Mental Health and Mental Health Services Research, 43*, 991–1008. doi:10.1007/s10488-016-0751-4

Ai, A. L., Foster, L. J. J., Pecora, P. J., Delaney, N., & Rodriguez, W. (2013). Reshaping child welfare's response to trauma: Assessment, evidence-based intervention, and new research perspectives. *Research on Social Work Practice, 23*, 651–668. doi:10.1177/1049731513491835

Alonso-Marsden, S., Dodge, K. A., O'Donnell, K. J., Murphy, R. A., Sato, J. M., & Christopoulos, C. (2013). Family risk as a predictor of initial engagement and follow-through in a universal nurse home visiting program to prevent child maltreatment. *Child Abuse & Neglect, 37*, 555–565. doi:https://doi.org/10.1016/j.chiabu.2013.03.012

American Psychiatric Association. (2013). *Diagnostic and statistical manual of mental disorders* (5th ed.). Washington, DC: American Psychiatric Publishing.

Anda, R. F., Felitti, V. J., Bremner, J. D., Walker, J. D., Whitfield, C., Perry, B. D., … Giles, W. H. (2005). The enduring effects of abuse and related adverse experiences in childhood. *European Archives of Psychiatry and Clinical Neuroscience, 256*, 174–186. doi:10.1007/s00406-005-0624-4

Attanayake, V., McKay, R., Joffres, M., Singh, S., Burkle, F., & Mills, E. (2009). Prevalence of mental disorders among children exposed to war: A systematic review of 7,920 children. *Medicine, Conflict, and Survival, 25*, 4–19. 10.1080/13623690802568913

Avellar, S. A., & Supplee, L. H. (2013). Effectiveness of home visiting in improving child health and reducing child maltreatment. *Pediatrics, 132*, S90–S99. doi:10.1542/peds.2013-1021G

Baker-Ericzén, M. J., Jenkins, M. M., & Haine-Schlagel, R. (2012). Therapist, parent, and youth perspectives of treatment barriers to family-focused community outpatient mental health services. *Journal of Child and Family Studies, 22*, 854–868. doi:10.1007/s10826-012-9644-7

Bartlett, J. D., Barto, B., Griffin, J. L., Fraser, J. G., Hodgdon, H., & Bodian, R. (2016). Trauma-informed care in the Massachusetts Child Trauma Project. *Child Maltreatment, 21*, 101–112. doi:10.1177/1077559515615700

Beidas, R. S., Adams, D. R., Kratz, H. E., Jackson, K., Berkowitz, S., Zinny, A., … Evans, A., Jr. (2016). Lessons learned while building a trauma-informed public behavioral health system in the City of Philadelphia. *Evaluation and Program Planning, 59*, 21–32. doi:10.1016/j.evalprogplan.2016.07.004

Beidas, R. S., Stewart, R. E., Adams, D. R., Fernandez, T., Lustbader, S., Powell, B. J., … Barg, F. K. (2016). A multi-level examination of stakeholder perspectives of implementation of evidence-based practices in a large urban publicly-funded mental health system. *Administration and Policy in Mental Health and Mental Health Services Research, 43*, 893–908. doi:10.1007/s10488-015-0705-2

Bell, T., Romano, E., & Flynn, R. J. (2015). Profiles and predictors of behavioral resilience among children in child welfare. *Child Abuse & Neglect, 48*, 92–103. doi:10.1016/j.chiabu.2015.04.018

Berliner, L., Fitzgerald, M. M., Dorsey, S., Chaffin, M., Ondersma, S. J., & Wilson, C. (2015). Report of the APSAC task force on evidence-based service planning guidelines for child welfare. *Child Maltreatment, 20*, 6–16. doi:10.1177/1077559514562066

Berliner, L., & Kolko, D. J. (2016). Trauma informed care: A commentary and critique. *Child Maltreatment, 21*, 168–172. doi:10.1177/1077559516643785

Bickman, L., Kelley, S. D., Breda, C., de Andrade, A. R., & Riemer, M. (2011). Effects of routine feedback to clinicians on mental health outcomes of youths: Results of a randomized trial. *Psychiatric Services, 62*, 1423–1429. doi:10.1176/appi.ps.002052011

Cary, C. E., & McMillen, J. C. (2012). The data behind the dissemination: A systematic review of trauma-focused cognitive behavioral therapy for use with children and youth. *Children and Youth Services Review, 34*, 748–757. doi:10.1016/j.childyouth.2012.01.003

Chaffin, M., Funderburk, B., Bard, D., Valle, L. A., & Gurwitch, R. (2011). A combined motivation and parent–child interaction therapy package reduces child welfare recidivism in a randomized dismantling field trial. *Journal of Consulting and Clinical Psychology, 79*, 84–95. doi:10.1037/a0021227

Chaffin, M., Hecht, D., Bard, D., Silovsky, J. F., & Beasley, W. H. (2012). A statewide trial of the SafeCare home-based services model with parents in child protective services. *Pediatrics*, *129*, 509–515. doi:10.1542/peds.2011-1840

Chen, L. P., Murad, M. H., Paras, M. L., Colbenson, K. M., Sattler, A. L., Goranson, E. N., … Zirakzadeh, A. (2010). Sexual abuse and lifetime diagnosis of psychiatric disorders: Systematic review and meta-analysis. *Mayo Clinic Proceedings*, *85*, 618–629. doi:10.4065/mcp.2009.0583

Cohen, J. A., Deblinger, E., Mannarino, A. P., & Steer, R. A. (2004). A multisite, randomized controlled trial for children with sexual abuse–related PTSD symptoms. *Journal of the American Academy of Child & Adolescent Psychiatry*, *43*, 393–402. doi:10.1097/00004583-200404000-00005

Cohen, J. A., & Mannarino, A. P. (2015). Trauma-focused cognitive behavior therapy for traumatized children and families. *Child and Adolescent Psychiatric Clinics of North America*, *24*, 557–570. doi:10.1016/j.chc.2015.02.005

Cronholm, P. F., Forke, C. M., Wade, R., Bair-Merritt, M. H., Davis, M., Harkins-Schwarz, M., … Fein, J. A. (2015). Adverse childhood experiences. *American Journal of Preventive Medicine*, *49*, 354–361. doi:10.1016/j.amepre.2015.02.001

Curry, S. J., Krist, A. H., Owens, D. K., Barry, M. J., Caughey, A. B., Davidson, K. W., … Wong, J. B. (2018). Screening and behavioral counseling interventions to reduce unhealthy alcohol use in adolescents and adults: U.S. Preventive Services Task Force recommendation statement. *JAMA*, *320*, 1899–1909. doi:10.1001/jama.2018.16789

Damashek, A., Doughty, D., Ware, L., & Silovsky, J. (2011). Predictors of client engagement and attrition in home-based child maltreatment prevention services. *Child Maltreatment*, *16*, 9–20. doi:10.1177/1077559510388507

Day, R. D. (2007). The G.I. Bill of the 21st century: Mass incarceration and how crime is paying. *Applied Developmental Science*, *11*, 249–253. doi:10.1080/10888690701762183

Deblinger, E., Beld, L. E., & Glickmans, A. R. (2012). Trauma-focused therapy for children who have experienced sexual abuse. In P. C. Kendall (Ed.), *Child and adolescent therapy: Cognitive-behavioral procedures* (pp. 345–375). New York, NY: Guilford.

Donelan-McCall, N., Eckenrode, J., & Olds, D. L. (2009). Home visiting for the prevention of child maltreatment: Lessons learned during the past 20 years. *Pediatric Clinics of North America*, *56*, 389–403. doi:10.1016/j.pcl.2009.01.002

Dorsey, S., McLaughlin, K. A., Kerns, S. E. U., Harrison, J. P., Lambert, H. K., Briggs, E. C., … Amaya-Jackson, L. (2017). Evidence base update for psychosocial treatments for children and adolescents exposed to traumatic events. *Journal of Clinical Child & Adolescent Psychology*, *46*, 303–330. doi:10.1080/15374416.2016.1220309

Dube, S. R. (2018). Continuing conversations about adverse childhood experiences (ACEs) screening: A public health perspective. *Child Abuse & Neglect*, *85*, 180–184. doi:10.1016/j.chiabu.2018.03.007

Dubowitz, H., Feigelman, S., Lane, W., & Kim, J. (2009). Pediatric primary care to help prevent child maltreatment: The Safe Environment for Every Kid (SEEK) model. *Pediatrics*, *123*, 858–864. doi:10.1542/peds.2008-1376

Dubowitz, H., Lane, W. G., Semiatin, J. N., & Magder, L. S. (2012). The SEEK model of pediatric primary care: Can child maltreatment be prevented in a low-risk population? *Academic Pediatrics*, *12*, 259–268. doi:10.1016/j.acap.2012.03.005

Duggan, A., McFarlane, E., Fuddy, L., Burrell, L., Higman, S. M., Windham, A., & Sia, C. (2004). Randomized trial of a statewide home visiting program: Impact in preventing child abuse and neglect. *Child Abuse & Neglect*, *28*, 597–622. doi:10.1016/j.chiabu.2003.08.007

DuMont, K., Mitchell-Herzfeld, S., Greene, R., Lee, E., Lowenfels, A., Rodriguez, M., & Dorabawila, V. (2008). Healthy Families New York (HFNY) randomized trial: Effects on early child abuse and neglect. *Child Abuse & Neglect*, *32*, 295–315. doi:10.1016/j.chiabu.2007.07.007

Eisenstadt, T. H., Eyberg, S., McNeil, C. B., Newcomb, K., & Funderburk, B. (1993). Parent-child interaction therapy with behavior problem children: Relative effectiveness of two stages and overall treatment outcome. *Journal of Clinical Child Psychology*, *22*, 42–51. doi:10.1207/s15374424jccp2201_4

Eismann, E. A., Theuerling, J., Maguire, S., Hente, E. A., & Shapiro, R. A. (2019). Integration of the Safe Environment for Every Kid (SEEK) model across primary care settings. *Clinical Pediatrics, 58*, 166–176. doi:10.1177/0009922818809481

Evans, S. E., Davies, C., & DiLillo, D. (2008). Exposure to domestic violence: A meta-analysis of child and adolescent outcomes. *Aggression and Violent Behavior, 13*, 131–140. doi:10.1016/j.avb.2008.02.005

Felitti, V. J., Anda, R. F., Nordenberg, D., Williamson, D. F., Spitz, A. M., Edwards, V., ... Marks, J. S. (1998). Relationship of childhood abuse and household dysfunction to many of the leading causes of death in adults: The Adverse Childhood Experiences (ACE) study. *American Journal of Preventive Medicine, 14*, 245–258. doi:10.1016/S0749-3797(98)00017-8

Finkelhor, D. (2018). Screening for adverse childhood experiences (ACEs): Cautions and suggestions. *Child Abuse & Neglect, 85*, 174–179. doi:https://doi.org/10.1016/j.chiabu.2017.07.016

Finkelhor, D., Turner, H. A., Shattuck, A., & Hamby, S. L. (2015). Prevalence of childhood exposure to violence, crime, and abuse: Results from the National Survey of Children's Exposure to Violence. *JAMA Pediatrics, 169*, 746. doi:10.1001/jamapediatrics.2015.0676

Fowler, P. J., Tompsett, C. J., Braciszewski, J. M., Jacques-Tiura, A. J., & Baltes, B. B. (2009). Community violence: A meta-analysis on the effect of exposure and mental health outcomes of children and adolescents. *Development and Psychopathology, 21*, 227–259. doi:10.1017/S0954579409000145

Gilbert, L. K., Breiding, M. J., Merrick, M. T., Thompson, W. W., Ford, D. C., Dhingra, S. S., & Parks, S. E. (2015). Childhood adversity and adult chronic disease: An update from ten states and the District of Columbia, 2010. *American Journal of Preventive Medicine, 48*, 345–349. doi:10.1016/j.amepre.2014.09.006

Gopalan, G., Goldstein, L., Klingenstein, K., Sicher, C., Blake, C., & McKay, M. M. (2010). Engaging families into child mental health treatment: Updates and special considerations. *Journal of the Canadian Academy of Child and Adolescent Psychiatry, 19*, 182–196.

Gutermann, J., Schreiber, F., Matulis, S., Schwartzkopff, L., Deppe, J., & Steil, R. (2016). Psychological treatments for symptoms of posttraumatic stress disorder in children, adolescents, and young adults: A meta-analysis. *Clinical Child and Family Psychology Review, 19*, 77–93. doi:10.1007/s10567-016-0202-5

Hillberg, T., Hamilton-Giachritsis, C., & Dixon, L. (2011). Review of meta-analyses on the association between child sexual abuse and adult mental health difficulties: A systematic approach. *Trauma, Violence, & Abuse, 12*, 38–49. doi:10.1177/1524838010386812

Huey, S. J., & Polo, A. J. (2010). Assessing the effects of evidence-based psychotherapies with ethnic minority youths. In J. R. Weisz & A. E. Kazdin (Eds.), *Evidence-based psychotherapies for children and youth* (2nd ed., pp. 451–465). New York, NY: Guilford Press.

Huston, A. C., & Bentley, A. C. (2010). Human development in societal context. *Annual Review of Psychology, 61*, 411–437. doi:10.1146/annurev.psych.093008.100442

Ingoldsby, E. M. (2010). Review of interventions to improve family engagement and retention in parent and child mental health programs. *Journal of Child and Family Studies, 19*, 629–645. doi:10.1007/s10826-009-9350-2

Isaacs, J. B., Lou, C., Hahn, H., Hong, A., Quakenbush, C., & Steuerle, C. E. (2018). *Kids' share 2018: Report on federal expenditures on children through 2017 and future projections.* Washington, DC: Urban Institute.

Jones, L., Bellis, M. A., Wood, S., Hughes, K., McCoy, E., Eckley, L., ... Officer, A. (2012). Prevalence and risk of violence against children with disabilities: A systematic review and meta-analysis of observational studies. *Lancet, 380*, 899–907. doi:10.1016/S0140-6736(12)60692-8

Klevens, J., Luo, F., Xu, L., Peterson, C., & Latzman, N. E. (2016). Paid family leave's effect on hospital admissions for pediatric abusive head trauma. *Injury Prevention, 22*, 442–445. doi:10.1136/injuryprev-2015-041702

Kennedy, S. C., Kim, J. S., Tripodi, S. J., Brown, S. M., & Gowdy, G. (2016). Does parent–child interaction therapy reduce future physical abuse? A meta-analysis. *Research on Social Work Practice, 26*, 147–156. doi:10.1177/1049731514543024

Kerns, S. E. U., Pullmann, M. D., Negrete, A., Uomoto, J. A., Berliner, L., Shogren, D., ... Putnam, B. (2016). Development and implementation of a child welfare workforce strategy to build a trauma-informed system of support for foster care. *Child Maltreatment, 21*, 135–146. doi:10.1177/1077559516633307

Kolko, D. J., Herschell, A. D., Baumann, B. L., Hart, J. A., & Wisniewski, S. R. (2018). AF-CBT for families experiencing physical aggression or abuse served by the mental health or child welfare system: An effectiveness trial. *Child Maltreatment, 23*, 319–333. doi:10.1177/1077559518781068

Kolko, D. J., Hurlburt, M. S., Zhang, J., Barth, R. P., Leslie, L. K., & Burns, B. J. (2010). Posttraumatic stress symptoms in children and adolescents referred for child welfare investigation: A national sample of in-home and out-of-home care. *Child Maltreatment, 15*, 48–63. doi:10.1177/1077559509337892

Kolko, D. J., Simonich, H., & Loiterstein, A. (2014). Alternatives for families: A cognitive behavioral therapy: An overview and a case example. In S. Timmer & A. Urquiza (Eds.), *Evidence-based approaches for the treatment of maltreated children* (pp. 187–212). New York, NY: Springer.

Lang, J. M., Campbell, K., Shanley, P., Crusto, C. A., & Connell, C. M. (2016). Building capacity for trauma-informed care in the child welfare system: Initial results of a statewide implementation. *Child Maltreatment, 21*, 113–124. doi:10.1177/1077559516635273

Leenarts, L. E. W., Diehle, J., Doreleijers, T. A. H., Jansma, E. P., & Lindauer, R. J. L. (2013). Evidence-based treatments for children with trauma-related psychopathology as a result of childhood maltreatment: A systematic review. *European Child & Adolescent Psychiatry, 22*, 269–283. doi:10.1007/s00787-012-0367-5

LeFevre, M. L.; U.S. Preventative Services Task Force. (2014). Behavioral counseling interventions to prevent sexually transmitted infections: U.S. Preventive Services Task Force recommendation statement. *Annals of Internal Medicine, 161*, 894–901. doi:10.7326/M14-1965

Lenz, A. S., & Hollenbaugh, K. M. (2015). Meta-analysis of trauma-focused cognitive behavioral therapy for treating PTSD and co-occurring depression among children and adolescents. *Counseling Outcome Research and Evaluation, 6*, 18–32. doi:10.1177/2150137815573790

Lewis, C. C., Simons, A. D., Nguyen, L. J., Murakami, J. L., Reid, M. W., Silva, S. G., & March, J. S. (2010). Impact of childhood trauma on treatment outcome in the Treatment for Adolescents with Depression Study (TADS). *Adolescent Psychiatry, 49*, 132–140.

Lieberman, A. F., Ghosh Ippen, C., & Hernandez Dimmler, M. (2019). Child-parent psychotherapy. In V. G. Carrión (Ed.), *Assessing and treating youth exposed to traumatic stress* (pp. 223–237). Washington, DC: American Psychiatric Association Publishing.

Lieberman, A. F., Van Horn, P., & Ghosh Ippen, C. (2005). Toward evidence-based treatment: Child-parent psychotherapy with preschoolers exposed to marital violence. *Journal of the American Academy of Child & Adolescent Psychiatry, 44*, 1241–1248. doi:10.1097/01.chi.0000181047.59702.58

Machtinger, E. L., Cuca, Y. P., Khanna, N., Rose, C. D., & Kimberg, L. S. (2015). From treatment to healing: The promise of trauma-informed primary care. *Women's Health Issues, 25*, 193–197. doi:10.1016/j.whi.2015.03.008

Mapson, A. (2013). From prison to parenting. *Journal of Human Behavior in the Social Environment, 23*, 171–177. doi:10.1080/10911359.2013.747402

McKay, M. M., & Bannon, W. M., Jr. (2004). Engaging families in child mental health services. *Child and Adolescent Psychiatric Clinics of North America, 13*, 905–921. doi:10.1016/j.chc.2004.04.001

McKay, M. M., Hibbert, R., Hoagwood, K., Rodriguez, J., Murray, L., Legerski, J., & Fernandez, D. (2004). Integrating evidence-based engagement interventions into "real world" child mental health settings. *Brief Treatment and Crisis Intervention, 4*, 177–186. doi:10.1093/brief-treatment/mhh014

McLaughlin, K. A., Koenen, K. C., Hill, E. D., Petukhova, M., Sampson, N. A., Zaslavsky, A. M., & Kessler, R. C. (2013). Trauma exposure and posttraumatic stress disorder in a national sample of adolescents. *Journal of the American Academy of Child & Adolescent Psychiatry, 52*, 815–830.e14. doi:10.1016/j.jaac.2013.05.011

Mersky, J. P., Topitzes, J. D., & Reynolds, A. J. (2011). Maltreatment prevention through early childhood intervention: A confirmatory evaluation of the Chicago Child–Parent Center preschool program. *Children and Youth Services Review, 33*, 1454–1463. doi:10.1016/j.childyouth.2011.04.022

Miller, L. M., Southam-Gerow, M. A., & Allin, R. B. (2008). Who stays in treatment? *Child & Youth Care Forum, 37*, 153–170.

Miller-Graff, L. E., & Howell, K. H. (2015). Posttraumatic stress symptom trajectories among children exposed to violence. *Journal of Traumatic Stress, 28*, 17–24. doi:10.1002/jts.21989

Moyer, V. A.; U.S. Preventative Services Task Force. (2013). Primary care interventions to prevent tobacco use in children and adolescents: U.S. Preventive Services Task Force recommendation statement. *Annals of Internal Medicine, 159*, 552–557.

Nanni, V., Uher, R., & Danese, A. (2012). Childhood maltreatment predicts unfavorable course of illness and treatment outcome in depression: A meta-analysis. *American Journal of Psychiatry, 169*, 141–151.

Nock, M. K., & Kazdin, A. E. (2005). Randomized controlled trial of a brief intervention for increasing participation in parent management training. *Journal of Consulting and Clinical Psychology, 73*, 872–879. doi:10.1037/0022-006X.73.5.872

Norman, R. E., Byambaa, M., De, R., Butchart, A., Scott, J., & Vos, T. (2012). The long-term health consequences of child physical abuse, emotional abuse, and neglect: A systematic review and meta-analysis. *PLOS Medicine, 9*, e1001349. doi:10.1371/journal.pmed.1001349

Olds, D. L., Henderson, C. R., Chamberlin, R., & Tatelbaum, R. (1986). Preventing child abuse and neglect: A randomized trial of nurse home visitation. *Pediatrics, 78*, 65–78.

Proctor, E. K., Landsverk, J., Aarons, G., Chambers, D., Glisson, C., & Mittman, B. (2009). Implementation research in mental health services: An emerging science with conceptual, methodological, and training challenges. *Administration and Policy in Mental Health and Mental Health Services Research, 36*, 24–34. doi:10.1007/s10488-008-0197-4

Purewal, S. K., Bucci, M., Wang, L. G., Koita, K., Marques, S. S., Oh, D., … Berry, T. (2016). Screening for adverse childhood experiences (ACEs) in an integrated pediatric care model. *Zero to Three, 36*, 10–17.

Raissian, K. M., & Bullinger, L. R. (2017). Money matters: Does the minimum wage affect child maltreatment rates? *Children and Youth Services Review, 72*, 60–70. doi:10.1016/j.childyouth.2016.09.033

Regan, J., Lau, A. S., Barnett, M., Stadnick, N., Hamilton, A., Pesanti, K., … Brookman-Frazee, L. (2017). Agency responses to a system-driven implementation of multiple evidence-based practices in children's mental health services. *BMC Health Services Research, 17*, 671. doi:10.1186/s12913-017-2613-5

Reynolds, A. J., & Robertson, D. L. (2003). School–Based early intervention and later child maltreatment in the Chicago Longitudinal Study. *Child Development, 74*, 3–26. doi:10.1111/1467-8624.00518

Schnitzer, P. K. (1996). They Don't Come In! *American Journal of Orthopsychiatry, 66*, 572–582.

Self-Brown, S., Lai, B. S., Thompson, J. E., McGill, T., & Kelley, M. L. (2013). Posttraumatic stress disorder symptom trajectories in Hurricane Katrina affected youth. *Journal of Affective Disorders, 147*, 198–204. doi:10.1016/j.jad.2012.11.002

Siu, A. L., & U.S. Preventative Services Task Force. (2016). Screening for depression in children and adolescents: U.S. Preventive Services Task Force recommendation statement. *Annals of Internal Medicine, 164*, 360–366. doi:10.7326/M15-2957

Skiba, R. J., Arredondo, M. I., & Williams, N. T. (2014). More than a metaphor: The contribution of exclusionary discipline to a school-to-prison pipeline. *Equity & Excellence in Education, 47*, 546–564. doi:10.1080/10665684.2014.958965

Smith, D. K., & Chamberlain, P. (2010). Multidimensional treatment foster care for adolescents: Processes and outcomes. In J. R. Weisz & A. E. Kazdin (Eds.), *Evidence-based psychotherapies for children and adolescents* (2nd ed., pp. 243–258). New York, NY: Guilford Press.

Substance Abuse and Mental Health Services Administration. (2014). *SAMHSA's concept of trauma and guidance for a trauma-informed approach (HS publication no. (SMA) 14-4884).* Rockville, MD: Substance Abuse and Mental Health Services Administration.

Sullivan, P. M. (2009). Violence exposure among children with disabilities. *Clinical Child and Family Psychology Review, 12*, 196–216. doi:10.1007/s10567-009-0056-1

Sullivan, P. M., & Knutson, J. F. (2000). Maltreatment and disabilities: A population-based epidemiological study. *Child Abuse & Neglect, 24*, 1257–1273. doi:10.1016/S0145-2134(00)00190-3

Swenson, C. C., Schaeffer, C. M., Henggeler, S. W., Faldowski, R., & Mayhew, A. M. (2010). Multisystemic therapy for child abuse and neglect: A randomized effectiveness trial. *Journal of Family Psychology, 24*, 497–507. doi:10.1037/a0020324

Turner, H. A., Vanderminden, J., Finkelhor, D., Hamby, S., & Shattuck, A. (2011). Disability and victimization in a national sample of children and youth. *Child Maltreatment, 16*, 275–286. doi:10.1177/1077559511427178

166 *Elizabeth A. Miller and David J. Kolko*

Wade, R., Cronholm, P. F., Fein, J. A., Forke, C. M., Davis, M. B., Harkins-Schwarz, M., … Bair-Merritt, M. H. (2016). Household and community-level adverse childhood experiences and adult health outcomes in a diverse urban population. *Child Abuse & Neglect, 52,* 135–145. doi:10.1016/j.chiabu.2015.11.021

Williams, N. J., & Beidas, R. S. (2019). Annual research review: The state of implementation science in child psychology and psychiatry: A review and suggestions to advance the field. *Journal of Child Psychology and Psychiatry, 60,* 430–450. doi:10.1111/jcpp.12960

Wood, L. C. N. (2018). Impact of punitive immigration policies, parent-child separation and child detention on the mental health and development of children. *BMJ Paediatrics Open, 2.* doi:10.1136/bmjpo-2018-000338

Zhai, F., Waldfogel, J., & Brooks-Gunn, J. (2013). Estimating the effects of head start on parenting and child maltreatment. *Children and Youth Services Review, 35,* 1119–1129. doi:10.1016/j.childyouth.2011.03.008

12 Strengthening Social Processes to Support Youth with Emotional and Behavioral Difficulties

An Ecological, Public Health Approach in Afterschool Programs

Elise Cappella, Stacy L. Frazier, Emilie P. Smith, and Sophia H. J. Hwang

Children ages five to 13 spend up to three hours each weekday in out-of-school, out-of-home activities (McCombs, Whitaker, & Yoo, 2017). The number of hours and types of activities vary by economic, social, and cultural factors at family and community levels. Yet, for low-income families, reliance on subsidized afterschool care for their school-age children is common. Nearly one in four U.S. families has a school-age child enrolled in afterschool care; the proportion is higher for Latino and African-American children (Afterschool Alliance, 2014a, 2014b). These lower- or no-cost programs serve as the afterschool counterpart to public schools for families requiring safe, supervised care when the school day ends but a caregiver is not home.

Time spent out of school may be especially pivotal for the trajectories of youth with, or at risk for, emotional and/or behavioral disorders (EBD).[1] Unstructured, unsupervised time after school exposes youth to opportunities for risk-taking, including substance use, sexual experimentation, and delinquency (Osgood, Anderson, & Shaffer, 2005). These situations are difficult to navigate in safe and healthy ways but may be particularly challenging for youth with EBD due to poor regulation, coping, and/or social-cognitive skills. Notably, children with EBD are more likely to become disruptive or inattentive in settings that lack organization and safety, even when an adult is present (Brophy, 1983; Epstein, Atkins, Cullinan, Kutash, & Weaver, 2008); thus, access to organized, safe settings may mitigate risk for young adolescents with EBD during out-of-school hours.

Parents report satisfaction with programs that provide a safe and supervised setting for their child to complete homework (Afterschool Alliance, 2014a). However, many ASPs aim to provide more than homework help by targeting multiple domains of youth development (Durlak, Weissberg, & Pachan, 2010; Pierce, Bolt, & Vandell, 2010; Yohalem & Wilson-Ahlstrom, 2010). Unlike schools, which face pressure to improve academic performance, many ASPs can prioritize social-emotional learning, civic engagement, lifestyle behaviors, athletic or artistic competence, or life skills – alongside academic enrichment (Catalano, Berglund, Ryan, Lonczak, & Hawkins, 2004; Smith, Akiva, McGovern, & Peck, 2014). High-quality ASPs, defined by the presence of structural elements and social processes that meet children's needs (Tseng & Seidman, 2007) and organized, active, focused, and intentional practices (Durlak et al., 2010), benefit children's psychosocial and academic adjustment (Niehaus, Rudasill, & Adelson, 2012; Pierce et al., 2010; Smith, Osgood, Oh, & Caldwell, 2018).

168   *Elise Cappella et al.*

Youth with EBD may stand to benefit uniquely from high-quality ASPs. The ecological framework for EBD, introduced by Hobbs (1966) and expanded by Farmer, Farmer, and Brooks (2010), suggests that behavior develops within the context of social settings and adult and peer relationships; therefore, treatment is most meaningful during the "daily activities of living" and when it focuses on building relationships and nurturing strengths (Farmer et al., 2010, p. 54). Quality afterschool programs with clear structure, strengths-based activities, and positive, productive relationships may offer the "re-education" during the afterschool hours to shift maladaptive behaviors (Hobbs, 1966), thereby counteracting substandard, or even adverse, day school experiences (Mahoney, Parente, & Zigler, 2010).

Yet, getting to quality is challenging. Historically, afterschool research has relied on transporting evidence-based interventions designed for day school to the afterschool setting. Although some efforts are promising (e.g., Smith, Wise et al., 2014), implementation and sustainment challenges abound (Lyon, Frazier, Mehta, Atkins, & Weisbach, 2011). Afterschool programs differ from day schools in student attendance, workforce characteristics, and staff support. In addition, ASPs themselves vary widely in their composition, mission, policies, and procedures, which may explain not only variation in implementation but also mixed findings regarding the benefits of ASPs for children's academic, health, and behavior trajectories (Frazier et al., 2019; James-Burdumy, Dynarski, & Deke, 2007).

Challenges may be greater in ASPs that serve a high proportion of youth with EBD, in particular, without accompanying strategies or resources to meet their needs. Behavioral disruption and emotional dysregulation impede program delivery, thereby reducing benefits for all children (i.e., due to interrupted programming) and disruptive children (i.e., due to removal from activities). Moreover, some children require additional support to manage their emotional or behavioral symptoms. Without the benefit of specialized training or assistance, ASP staff may struggle to implement targeted supports (for select youth) along-side universal practices (for all youth). Finally, given the range of contexts and communities in which ASPs operate, a "one-size-fits-all" approach for strengthening ASPs is inappropriate, insensitive, and ineffective (Greene, Lee, Constance, & Hynes, 2013; Sheldon, Arbreton, Hopkins, & Grossman, 2010).

Mitigating challenges and promoting sustainability of evidence-based practices have been a recent focus of research-practice partnerships (RPPs) among universities and youth-serving organizations (see Lerner & Simon, 2014). Partners consider how to strategically allocate and activate existing resources toward successful implementation of evidence-based practices and sustainment of quality improvement. Public health approaches that advocate promotion and prevention *prior* to intervention and treatment (Atkins, Cappella, Shernoff, Mehta, & Gustafson, 2017; Nastasi, 2004) are expanding to ASPs, such that universal interventions to facilitate health and wellness are supplemented by targeted strategies to minimize disruption, maximize engagement, and enhance child functioning prior to referral to more intensive services. Universal approaches hold promise for afterschool, given limited time and resources and the unique structure and settings of ASPs. "One-size-fits-all" curricula have been supplemented or replaced by empirically supported "behavioral kernels" (Embry, 2002; Embry & Biglan, 2008) – small, potent strategies that can be implemented in ASPs with economical levels of training – that match the strengths, needs, and cultures of the setting (Cappella, Reinke, & Hoagwood, 2011; Frazier et al., 2019). Many of these research efforts begin with RPPs and reflect a blend of local and scholarly knowledge to establish "proof of concept." Yet, missing are larger-scale studies to establish effectiveness or generalizability to the broader population of ASPs serving youth with EBD. Thus, substantial gaps remain between what we *know* at the local level and what we *do* at scale to strengthen social processes and enhance outcomes for youth with EBD.

In this chapter, we are guided by systems theory of social processes (Tseng & Seidman, 2007) and public health principles (Nastasi, 2004), prevention and implementation science (Embry & Biglan, 2008; Wandersman et al., 2008), and mental health research (Atkins et al., 2017) to provide a framework for understanding and enhancing social processes in ASPs for youth with EBD.[2] Social processes are the interpersonal interactions that create safe, supportive, and enriching environments and opportunities for the development of youth competence. Our goal is to (a) synthesize evidence on high-quality ASPs for elementary and middle school children with EBD, (b) discuss the common elements of quality ASPs, and (c) present exemplar partnerships working to improve social processes and impact outcomes for youth with EBD. We end with research and practice recommendations to increase the likelihood that more ASPs will achieve their potential to enhance the positive developmental trajectories for youth with EBD.

Importance of Afterschool Programs for Children with EBD

Childhood and early adolescence are key periods for the development of social-emotional skills and academic behaviors. Social-emotional learning (SEL) involves "how students think and feel about themselves, get along with others, and regulate their attention and behavior" (Cappella, Blair, & Aber, 2016, p. 1). Academic behaviors involve executive functions such as organization and planning as well as behavioral engagement (attendance, participation). Youth with EBD demonstrate early deficits in social-emotional skills and academic behaviors (Walker & Sprague, 1999), which can trigger developmental cascades (Masten & Cicchetti, 2010) that manifest in persistent social problems (Coie & Dodge, 1998; Prinstein & La Greca, 2004) and academic underachievement (Nelson, Benner, Lane, & Smith, 2004). Associations between EBD and maladaptive outcomes are stronger for youth of color and youth living in neighborhoods of concentrated poverty, in part due to inadequate access to school and community-based mental health services (Garland et al., 2005; Merikangas et al., 2011), limited or low quality education and prevention/promotion programs (Cappella, Frazier, Atkins, Schoenwald, & Glisson, 2008), and other inequities (e.g., discrimination, neighborhood risk). Long-term, youth with EBD are more likely than their peers to leave school early and to face difficulties as young adults (e.g., unemployment, substance use, criminal justice system involvement; Erskine et al., 2016).

Schools have been the primary context for SEL and other programs to promote social-emotional competence and academic behaviors among youth (Boustani et al., 2014). Universal SEL programs have, on average, moderate positive effects on social-emotional competencies and small positive effects on academic outcomes (Durlak, Weissberg, Dymnicki, Taylor, & Schellinger, 2011), with some evidence of greater impact for students with social-behavioral difficulties (Wilson, Gottfredson, & Najaka, 2001). Impact, though, depends on fit with the student population and school context, and the extent to which programs are adopted, implemented, and sustained (Elias, Zins, Graczyk, & Weissberg, 2003). In addition, public schools are tasked with improving achievement in core academic subjects, with underperforming and low-income schools facing the greatest pressure to improve academic outcomes (Kim & Sunderman, 2005). Hence, schools that serve more students with EBD may be least likely to have the resources, abilities, or incentives to implement universal prevention or SEL programs though research has shown that leadership can result in positive changes for this population (Greenberg, Domitrovich, Weissberg, & Durlak, 2017). In addition, schools inadvertently limit opportunities for the very peer interactions that may enhance social skills and academic behaviors. They may do so through use of didactic lectures and individual seatwork rather than collaborative, peer-assisted approaches that may improve social skills and academic performance (Rohrbeck, Ginsburg-Block, Fantuzzo, & Miller, 2003; Sutherland & Snyder, 2007; Sutherland, Wehby, & Gunter, 2000). In addition, youth are often sorted into homogenous groups by prior achievement, disability, or language status – though mixed groups increase the performance of lower-performing students with no deleterious effects on more skilled students (Gamoran, 2009) – thereby restricting opportunities for social and academic learning via diverse and/or more advanced peers (Bandura, 1977; Vygotsky, 1987).

ASPs may be better positioned than schools to promote SEL and academic behaviors for youth living in under-resourced neighborhoods, many of whom spend up to 15 hours per week in publicly-funded ASPs (Afterschool Alliance, 2014a). In the absence of accountability pressures, ASPs enjoy more freedom than day schools to explicitly focus on positive youth development – including social-emotional learning – as it relates to school, relationship, and life success (Catalano et al., 2004; Smith & Bradshaw, 2017; Smith, Osgood, Caldwell, Hynes, & Perkins, 2013). For example, some ASPs offer sports, recreation, and arts/music programming that is inherently SEL-promoting (Payton et al., 2008) and others incorporate explicit activities or curriculum related to peer leadership, civic engagement, service learning, risk prevention, and promotion of life skills (Frazier, Mehta, Atkins, Hur, & Rusch, 2013; Smith et al., 2013). ASPs integrate youth across ages and grades, and incorporate diverse instructional modalities to inspire peer interactions and mastery-building opportunities for all youth, including those with EBD who otherwise may struggle to remain attentive during traditional instruction (Bollmer, Milich, Harris, & Maras, 2005).

Elements of Effective Afterschool Programs for Children with EBD

Findings regarding the benefits of ASP programming have been equivocal, pointing to differences in program quality. For instance, a randomized trial evaluating middle school ASPs detected no positive effects on youth outcomes (Gottfredson, Cross, Wilson, Rorie, & Connell, 2010), and an evaluation of 21st century Community Learning Centers found a negative impact of ASP enrollment on behavior, though this study included no controls for program quality or youth participation (James-Burdumy et al., 2007). Notably, *high-quality ASPs* show consistent positive effects for youth across multiple populations and settings (Durlak et al., 2010; Smith et al., 2018; Smith, Witherspoon, & Osgood, 2017). For instance, in longitudinal correlational studies and meta-analyses of experimental and quasi-experimental designs, attendance in well-organized ASPs is associated with subsequent improvement in academic performance, test scores, and/or social confidence among youth at risk for school failure (Lauer et al., 2006) and in large national samples (Vandell, Lee, Whitaker, & Pierce, 2018). A propensity score matching study indicated that a large sample of urban youth with academic risk benefited from school-based afterschool programming in their third grade reading achievement (Baker, Kamata,

Wright, Farmer, & Nippert, 2019). In a small sample of third to eighth grade youth of color attending free, urban ASPs, quality classrooms positively predicted oral reading skills and academic engagement across one year, an association that was greater for students with social-behavioral problems (Cappella, Hwang, Kieffer, & Yates, 2018). Thus, high-quality ASPs benefit youth – and these benefits are pronounced for students facing socioeconomic disadvantage and academic or behavioral difficulties.

Historically, definitions of quality have included both structural and process elements (Halpern, 1999). Yet, the bioecological model (Bronfenbrenner & Morris, 2007) and systems theory of social processes (Tseng & Seidman, 2007) suggest social processes (relationships, interactions) have the most direct and powerful influence on development, given their direct proximity to youth. The literature points to four elements of process quality (Table 12.1): (1) safe and organized environment (Vandell, Reisner, & Pierce, 2007), (2) engaging, relevant, and interactive activities (Mahoney, Parente, & Lord, 2007), (3) warm social climate via reciprocal interactions (Rhodes, 2004), and (4) sensitive and responsive instruction toward skill development (Little, 2007). We posit that these interconnected, complementary elements must be consistently present for youth to experience positive developmental trajectories (Figure 12.1).

A *safe and organized environment* with appropriate structure and supervision provides a necessary foundation for high-quality ASPs (e.g., space, funding, staff; Mahoney et al., 2010). Specifically, afterschool staff work to ensure that their setting provides consistent routines and positive expectations, clear and equitable consequences for misbehavior, and calm, productive spaces in which youth are emotionally and physically safe (Little, 2007; National Research Council – Institute of Medicine: NRC-IOM, 2002). In a national study of low-income, racially/ethnically diverse youth, those who participate regularly in ASPs with appropriate structure and low chaos, as measured by observations using the Promising Practices Rating Scale (PPRS; Vandell et al., 2005/2012), had improved grades and behavior in comparison to youth in programs with low levels of supervision (Vandell et al., 2007). Other research suggests that safety and organization are particularly critical for targeted subgroups of youth, such as those with EBD and/or elevated adverse childhood experiences, who may be triggered by, and exhibit dysregulation in, disorganized spaces (Nadeem et al., 2014).

A safe and organized environment is necessary but insufficient; high-quality ASPs offer *engaging, relevant, and interactive activities* that are relevant and appealing with opportunities for leadership, autonomy, and cooperation. Programs with these characteristics yield greater youth engagement and skill development than those dedicated to homework (Durlak et al., 2010; Lauer et al., 2006; Yohalem & Wilson-Ahlstrom, 2010). Empirical findings from a longitudinal, correlational study of elementary-age youth in urban, school-based ASPs indicate that afterschool engagement may, in fact, transfer into higher motivation and social competence during the school day (Mahoney et al., 2007). Little research has been conducted on the potentially unique importance of quality activities for young people with EBD, though theory and related work suggest that varied, active, and collaborative instructional formats on topics of interest and relevance enable youth with attentional problems to stay engaged (Steiner, Sheldrick, Frenette, Rene, & Perrin, 2014; Wentzel & Watkins, 2002).

A *warm social climate* is a core element of ASP quality centering on positive, trusting and supportive relationships with and between adults and youth. Interpersonal connections may help to facilitate sense of belonging (NRC-IOM, 2002), and may be especially salient for youth with EBD who struggle to form connections in day school (Mikami, Griggs, Reuland, & Gregory, 2012; Xie, Cairns, & Cairns, 1999). The After-School Environment Scale

Table 12.1 Interrelated Elements of Quality Social Processes in Afterschool Programs with Example Measures and Strategies

Element	Definition	Instruments Measuring Elements of Quality	Strategies to Promote Elements of Quality
Safe and organized environment	Appropriate structure and adult supervision supported by policies, regulations, and practice. This includes physical space, program size, and resources alongside consistent routines, clear rules and consequences, and effective behavior management.	• Promising Practices Rating Scale (PPRS; Vandell et al., 2005/2012) • School-Age Care Environment Rating Scale (SACERS; Harms, Jacobs, & White, 2013) • After-School Environment Scale (ASES; Rosenthal & Vandell, 1996) • Observational Record of the Caregiving Environment (NICHD ECCRN, 1996)	• Good Behavior Game • Short, Soft, Close, Calm • Cool Down Strategies • SPARKS for cooperative physical games • Cooperative Learning Strategies • Daily Mood Monitoring • Positive Peer Reporting • Individual or Reciprocal Peer Tutoring • Daily Report Cards
Engaging and interactive activities	Programming and practices that foster meaningful, appealing, and active learning for diverse youth (e.g., ages, abilities, cultures, interests). This includes opportunities for leadership, cooperation, and autonomy.		
Warm social climate via supportive interactions	Positive, warm, and supportive interactions and relationships between adults and youth, and among youth toward a sense of belonging and connectedness.		
Sensitive and responsive instruction to build skills	Staff recognize youth strengths and needs, and individualize lessons to bolster strengths and address needs. Staff employ effective strategies to cultivate academic, social, and behavioral skills in youth.		

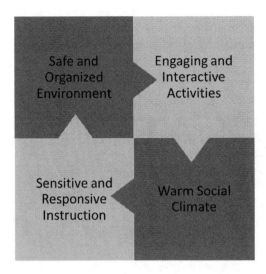

Figure 12.1 Interrelated Elements of Quality Social Processes in Afterschool Programs

(ASES; Rosenthal & Vandell, 1996) measures social climate from the perspective of youth (e.g., emotional support, autonomy, peer affiliation). Positive associations between ASES scores and day school academic and prosocial behavior were found in a predominately low-income, racially/ethnically diverse sample of middle school youth across four states (Kataoka & Vandell, 2013). Although the proportion of youth with EBD in this sample is not known, prior work reveals the potential for positive bonding, relationships, and social climate in ASPs to reduce challenging behaviors (Stewart, 2003) and internalizing and externalizing problems (Pierce, Hamm, & Vandell, 1999). ASPs with positive social climate have youth with greater social skills, initiative, and behavioral adjustment (Gottfredson et al., 2010).

Sensitive and responsive instruction, the final element of high-quality ASPs, is achieved by staff who not only state learning goals and scaffold lessons but also recognize and acknowledge youth strengths and challenges, individualize instruction, and exhibit patience (Durlak et al., 2010). In essence, they employ a "youth as partner" mentality (NRC-IOM, 2002) toward fostering academic, social, and/or behavioral skills. In one study, youth with staff who engaged in genuine, reciprocal conversations and supported students with affection and enthusiasm had higher reading and math grades than youth who had less engaged and supportive staff (Pierce et al., 2010). In addition, improved social skills among the second graders in this trial was moderated by gender, with even greater gains for boys (Pierce et al., 2010). Concrete examples of sensitive and responsive instruction, including strategies to support emotion regulation and decrease bullying and victimization (Garner & Hinton, 2010), will be discussed in the following section.

Taken together, these interrelated and complementary elements of ASPs characterize a high-quality youth development setting. There is great promise in understanding how universal supports may be implemented in the afterschool context; small effects for over 10 million students in ASPs (Afterschool Alliance, 2014a) would have a meaningful, cumulative impact. Given this promise, researchers and practitioners should work together to

174   *Elise Cappella et al.*

understand how to leverage existing routines and resources, infuse evidence-based kernels and strategies into ASPs, and evaluate outcomes with rigor to ensure that benefits are accessible for all youth enrolled in publicly funded afterschool programs.

Applications of Theory and Empirical Evidence to Afterschool Practice

Robust findings on the indicators and benefits of high-quality ASPs have led to research-practice partnerships (RPPs: Coburn & Penuel, 2016) for enhancing ASP quality and youth outcomes. Partnered research between university researchers and practice/policy professionals aims to produce rigorous, actionable knowledge to improve youth-serving systems and thereby short- and long-term youth trajectories (Tseng, Easton, & Supplee, 2017). Funded by foundations and federal agencies, RPPs have strengthened education research over the last decade, leading to the adoption of more culturally responsive, system-embedded programming informed by local knowledge and empirical evidence (Noam & Rosenbaum Tillinger, 2004). Partnered approaches may be particularly important within complex social environments where low-income, public ASPs are often situated. The work within RPPs is informed by prevention and intervention science *and* considers the unique characteristics of each ASP, differentiating recommendations to align with each ASP's mission, routines, resources, needs, and challenges. In this way, RPPs explicitly seek to leverage what is unique and promising about afterschool contexts broadly – and about each program individually.

RPPs seek to enhance ASP capacity to implement evidence-based strategies to meet both universal goals and the targeted needs of children with EBD. Afterschool RPPs explicitly focus on strengthening social processes by examining and promoting: (1) structure and organization via clear rules and consistent routines that minimize chaos and encourage autonomy, (2) engaging activities that utilize sports, arts, nature, and recreation to encourage physical activity and social negotiation, (3) healthy peer relationships and adult partnerships with nurturing social interactions, and (4) diverse instructional strategies that leverage staff expertise and diverse peer groups to inspire learning, enrichment, cognitive growth, and skill mastery. Examples of effective universal programs are SPARKS for cooperative games (Sportime, 2007), Fit2Play for physical activity (Messiah et al., 2016), PAX Good Behavior Game (GBG) for engagement (Smith et al., 2018), and SAFE (sequenced, active, focused, and explicit) skills training for social-emotional learning (Durlak et al., 2010).

Children with EBD may benefit most from structured and engaging universal programs that enhance overall program quality via their influence on social processes. Yet, these children also remain at risk for disrupting activities, straining already-stressed staff and resources, and diminishing benefits (Frazier et al., 2013). Targeted interventions that build specific skills or remediate deficits via academic (e.g., tutoring), social (e.g., peer buddies), or behavioral (e.g., daily report card) supports (Frazier, Cappella, & Atkins, 2007) may be key – but remain rare in ASPs, which likely reflects the additional resources required for the part-time, under-resourced staff to learn and implement them. Below are three RPPs that focus on quality social processes in ASPs, via universal and targeted strategies, to benefit youth with and without EBD.

Project NAFASI. Project NAFASI (Kiswahili for Opportunity; Nurturing All Families through After School Improvement) involves Frazier and colleagues' collaboration with county park districts and community-based ASPs in two metropolitan regions. Long-standing partnerships with frontline staff and program directors informed an evidence-based approach to workforce support (Frazier et al., 2019) that embraces elements from mental health and prevention science (Boustani et al., 2014). NAFASI prioritizes social interactions and skills to mitigate risk and promote resilience for youth in under-resourced communities. Specifically, NAFASI leverages and infuses teachable moments during natural afterschool routines to practice and promote emotion literacy, effective communication, and problem solving. For example, *huddles* are recommended before and after sports or recreation activities, "pre-game" to introduce and practice discrete skills (e.g., emotion recognition, problem-solving) and "post-game" to reflect on use and increase generalizability to other settings. *Mood monitoring* is infused into staff routines of taking attendance. Before afterschool activities begin, staff invite children to privately indicate how they feel via a "Mood Cup" (or mood wheel, emoji box). During attendance, staff check in briefly with children who disclose feeling angry or sad to express compassion, demonstrate and practice relaxation (e.g., Mindful Minute; 4-2-8 breaths), and encourage activity engagement. Daily documentation enables staff to identify children whose chronic negative mood may warrant a referral for more intensive services, thus leveraging ASP as a gateway to mental health care.

Staff training and support around these "kernels of influence" (Embry & Biglan, 2008) include technology-facilitated didactic approaches (http://nafasipartners.fiu.edu); large and small group in-person trainings with demonstrations, practice, and feedback; and in-vivo, on-site modeling, co-facilitation, and coaching. Frazier and colleagues have used online, in-person, and real-time formats to introduce Huddles and Mood Cups to over 100 staff at ~20 park-based ASPs for elementary and middle school youth over two cities and three years. Despite some implementation challenges, staff express high enthusiasm, several have applied modifications, and efforts are ongoing to systemize and expand their routine use. Notable in NAFASI is the infusion of empirically supported kernels aligned with the four social process elements of quality and the opportunity to serve youth with universal, targeted, and intensive needs. They serve both research and practice functions; are low-cost and low-burden with potential for high reach; easy to infuse and modify for local needs; and incorporate mental health and social-emotional principles without over-extending the role or expectations for staff.

LEGACY Together. Smith and colleagues illustrate the "science migration" of Paxis Institute's Good Behavior Game (PAXGBG) through the LEGACY Together (Leading, Educating, Guiding a Community of Youth) Afterschool Project (Smith, Wise et al., 2014, 2018). This project involves 76 programs and over 1,000 youth throughout urban, suburban, and rural Pennsylvania and Georgia. LEGACY Together illustrates the application of implementation science to inform evidence-based intervention for behavior management in community ASPs.

This project draws upon a settings framework by focusing on ASP norms and social processes to prevent problem behavior and promote positive youth development (Tseng & Seidman, 2007). Given the importance of youth engagement and agency, quality social relationships, and shared behavioral norms (Table 12.1), researchers partnered with afterschool staff and youth using PAXGBG to develop a shared vision of the program and practices that encouraged self-regulation and "co-regulation" using a common language and symbolism. The cooperative game involves periods of "stop and go" in which heterogeneous teams of youth self-regulate in order to "win" activity prizes for low levels of collective off-task behaviors (Kellam et al., 2008). Critical to the success of this initiative was a prevention support system (Wandersman et al., 2008) of coaching and technical assistance informed by rapid data collection and feedback to enhance implementation (Becker, Bradshaw, Domitrovich, & Ialongo, 2013).

176 *Elise Cappella et al.*

LEGACY Together research suggests that when PAXGBG is implemented well, youth benefit. In high implementation programs, youth reported less hyperactivity and more positive youth development (Smith et al., 2018). These results held across diverse ASPs serving urban and suburban youth from varied socioeconomic and ethnic-racial backgrounds. High-quality settings were related to positive youth development (competence, connection, and caring) for all youth and, especially for African-American youth, supportive relationships were related to cultural values of respect for adults (Smith et al., 2017). This work demonstrates that strengthening settings-level processes can be helpful in enhancing program quality and positive youth development.

ACROSS: Advancing Collaborative Research in Out-of-School Settings. Cappella, Hwang, and colleagues at NYU's Institute for Human Development and Social Change launched an RPP in 2014 with a large place-based, multiservice organization, Good Shepherd Services, which serves over 4,000 elementary and middle school students in more than 20 afterschool programs in low-income neighborhoods each year. The partnership aims to increase knowledge of and inform changes to ASP professional development to strengthen workforce skills, improve program quality, and impact youth outcomes. Additional goals are to build capacity to engage in ongoing research to advance science and practice. The partnership principles outlined by Tseng and colleagues (2017) – mutualism, sustained collaboration, and trust – frame the work. Specific partnered efforts have included: (a) descriptive research on afterschool social processes and youth social-emotional and academic outcomes, (b) development of a peer network intervention to enhance the social integration of disconnected youth, including youth with EBD, and (c) practical measurement to assess social-emotional skills and inform program improvements.

The RPP focuses on realistic and effective ways to improve afterschool process quality and improve social-emotional and academic development of youth. In one research project, youth with social-behavioral difficulties demonstrated academic benefits when enrolled in afterschool classrooms with high-quality social processes (Cappella et al., 2018). This work informed a research brief aimed at informing future studies and a practice brief integrated into workforce training (https://steinhardt.nyu.edu/ihdsc/connect/across). Within this project, the team applied an implementation science framework to existing coaching of afterschool staff to improve implementation of practical, cooperative strategies (e.g., turn-and-talk, think-pair-share; Peterson & Taylor, 2012; Raba, 2017) within academic and social-emotional learning activities. Lastly, the partnered team has refined data collection efforts and added new tools to assess program, staff, and youth needs, and begun to match evidence-based strategies to those needs.

Conclusions and Recommendations for Future Research and Practice

Low-income youth spend substantial time in subsidized afterschool programs that provide a supervised space during risky out-of-school hours. A rich empirical literature indicates that high-quality ASPs – with safe, engaging, sensitive, and warm interactions – promote positive social-emotional, behavioral, and academic development. Aligned with strengths-based, developmentally responsive, ecological intervention that emphasizes the role of supportive, non-traditional education to foster skills and strengths among youth with EBD (Farmer et al., 2010), high-quality ASPs represent a critical opportunity to support youth learning and development. Moreover, given the education, health, and economic consequences of inadequate prevention and intervention for youth facing disadvantage, it is incumbent upon the research, policy, and practice communities to unite around ASPs as a primary context for investment and study. We recommend the following next steps for research and practice:

1. Conduct rigorous empirical research on the methods for and impacts of scaling up the *processes* identified in "proof of concept" studies: e.g., systematic selection, refinement, and use of evidence-based universal strategies to promote quality social processes that enhance the strengths and respond to the needs of diverse ASP contexts;
2. Through iterative, partnered research, and extending evidence in education, mental health, and prevention science, identify feasible, targeted strategies that are relevant to the diverse contexts and populations of ASPs, complement universal strategies, and contribute to enhancing academic and social behaviors among youth with EBD;
3. Systematically explore in large-scale, longitudinal studies the heterogeneity in ASP effects not only by examining program-level differences in structural or social processes but also by exploring child-level differences in presence, level, and type of EBD;
4. Advocate for additional resources to enhance social processes in afterschool settings while maximizing existing resources by studying in small-scale field experiments the best methods to strengthen afterschool educators' ability to use universal behavioral kernels with fidelity and flexibility – given their low cost and high potential for reward.

Author Note

The research described was funded, in part, by the William T. Grant Foundation [#8529], Wallace Foundation [#20080489]; National Institute for Drug Abuse [#R01 DA025187]; and Institute of Education Sciences, U.S. Department of Education, through R305B140037 to New York University. The opinions expressed by the authors do not necessarily reflect the opinions of the funding agencies. We are grateful to the afterschool organizations, educators, families, and youth who participated in this research.

Notes

1 For the purposes of this chapter, EBD refers to a broad range of children who experience emotional and behavioral disorders and difficulties, including children without a classification or diagnosis. The aim is to capture the broader group of youth who face challenges in domains relevant to school outcomes; e.g., peer relationships, self-regulation, and behavioral engagement.
2 Our focus is free or low-cost ASPs that meet consistently across the school year, involve heterogeneous groups of youth, and have broad rather than specialized goals for skill development. These programs are often subsidized by public agencies and/or private organizations and situated in schools, parks, or community centers.

References

Afterschool Alliance. (2014a). America after 3PM: Afterschool programs in demand. Retrieved from www.afterschoolalliance.org/documents/aa3pm-2014/aa3pm_national_report.pdf
Afterschool Alliance. (2014b). America after 3PM special report: Afterschool in communities of concentrated poverty. Retrieved from www.afterschoolalliance.org/AA3PM/Concentrated_Poverty.pdf

Atkins, M. S., Cappella, E., Shernoff, E. S., Mehta, T. G., & Gustafson, E. L. (2017). Schooling and children's mental health: Realigning resources to reduce disparities and advance public health. *Annual Review of Clinical Psychology, 13*(1), 123–147.

Baker, S. K., Kamata, A., Wright, A., Farmer, D., & Nippert, R. (2019). Using propensity score matching to estimate treatment effects of afterschool programs on third-grade reading outcomes. *Journal of Community Psychology, 47*(1), 117–134.

Bandura, A. (1977). Self-efficacy: Toward a unifying theory of behavioral change. *Psychological Review, 84* (2), 191–215.

Becker, K. D., Bradshaw, C. P., Domitrovich, C., & Ialongo, N. S. (2013). Coaching teachers to improve implementation of the Good Behavior Game. *Administration and Policy in Mental Health, 40*(6), 482–493.

Bollmer, J. M., Milich, R., Harris, M. J., & Maras, M. A. (2005). A friend in need: The role of friendship quality as a protective factor in peer victimization and bullying. *Journal of Interpersonal Violence, 20*(6), 701–712.

Boustani, M. M., Frazier, S. L., Becker, K. D., Bechor, M., Dinizulu, S. M., Hedemann, E. R., … Pasalich, D. S. (2014). Common elements of adolescent prevention programs: Minimizing burden while maximizing reach. *Administration and Policy in Mental Health and Mental Health Services Research, 42*(2), 209–219.

Bronfenbrenner, U., & Morris, P. A. (2007). The bioecological model of human development. In W. Damon & R. M. Lerner (Eds.), *Handbook of child psychology* (pp. 793–828). Hoboken, NJ: John Wiley & Sons, Inc.

Brophy, J. E. (1983). Classroom organization and management. *The Elementary School Journal, 83*(4), 265–285.

Cappella, E., Blair, C., & Aber, J. L. (2016). Outcomes beyond test scores—What is social-emotional learning? Preparing students for school and life success. Retrieved from https://steinhardt.nyu.edu/e/i2/edsolutions/201609/2SELOutcomesBeyondTestScores.pdf

Cappella, E., Frazier, S. L., Atkins, M. S., Schoenwald, S. K., & Glisson, C. (2008). Enhancing schools' capacity to support children in poverty: An ecological model of school-based mental health services. *Administration and Policy in Mental Health and Mental Health Services Research, 35*(5), 395–409.

Cappella, E., Hwang, S. H. J., Kieffer, M. J., & Yates, M. (2018). Classroom practices and academic outcomes in urban afterschool programs: Alleviating social-behavioral risk. *Journal of Emotional and Behavioral Disorders, 26*(1), 42–51.

Cappella, E., Reinke, W. M., & Hoagwood, K. E. (2011). Advancing intervention research in school psychology: Finding the balance between process and outcome for social and behavioral interventions. *School Psychology Review, 40*(4), 455–464.

Catalano, R. F., Berglund, M. L., Ryan, J. A., Lonczak, H. S., & Hawkins, J. D. (2004). Positive youth development in the United States: Research findings on evaluations of positive youth development programs. *The Annals of the American Academy of Political and Social Science, 591*(1), 98–124.

Coburn, C. E., & Penuel, W. R. (2016). Research–Practice partnerships in education: Outcomes, dynamics, and open questions. *Educational Researcher, 45*(1), 48–54.

Coie, J. D., & Dodge, K. A. (1998). Aggression and antisocial behavior. In W. Damon & N. Eisenberg (Eds.), *Handbook of child psychology* (pp. 779–862). Hoboken, NJ: John Wiley & Sons, Inc.

Durlak, J. A., Weissberg, R. P., Dymnicki, A. B., Taylor, R. D., & Schellinger, K. B. (2011). The impact of enhancing students' social and emotional learning: A meta-analysis of school-based universal interventions. *Child Development, 82*(1), 405–432.

Durlak, J. A., Weissberg, R. P., & Pachan, M. (2010). A meta-analysis of after-school programs that seek to promote personal and social skills in children and adolescents. *American Journal of Community Psychology, 45* (3–4), 294–309.

Elias, M. J., Zins, J. E., Graczyk, P. A., & Weissberg, R. P. (2003). Implementation, sustainability, and scaling up of social-emotional and academic innovations in public schools. *School Psychology Review, 32*(3), 303–319.

Embry, D. D. (2002). The Good Behavior Game: A best practice candidate as a universal behavioral vaccine. *Clinical Child and Family Psychology Review, 5*(4), 273–297.

Embry, D. D., & Biglan, A. (2008). Evidence-based kernels: Fundamental units of behavioral influence. *Clinical Child and Family Psychology Review, 11*(3), 75–113.

Epstein, M., Atkins, M., Cullinan, D., Kutash, K., & Weaver, R. (2008). Reducing behavior problems in the elementary school classroom: A practice guide. Retrieved from https://files.eric.ed.gov/fulltext/ED502720.pdf

Erskine, H. E., Norman, R. E., Ferrari, A. J., Chan, G. C., Copeland, W. E., Whiteford, H. A., & Scott, J. G. (2016). Long-term outcomes of attention-deficit/hyperactivity disorder and conduct disorder: A systematic review and meta-analysis. *Journal of the American Academy of Child & Adolescent Psychiatry, 55*(10), 841–850.

Farmer, T. W., Farmer, E. M. Z., & Brooks, D. (2010). Recasting the ecological and developmental roots of intervention for students with emotional and behavior problems: The promise of strength-based perspectives. *Exceptionality, 18*(2), 53–57. doi:10.1080/09362831003673051

Frazier, S. L., Cappella, E., & Atkins, M. S. (2007). Linking mental health and after school systems for children in urban poverty: Preventing problems, promoting possibilities. *Administration and Policy in Mental Health and Mental Health Services Research, 34*(4), 389–399.

Frazier, S. L., Chou, T., Ouellette, R. R., Helseth, S. A., Kashem, E. R., & Cromer, K. D. (2019). Workforce support for urban after-school programs: Turning obstacles into opportunities. *American Journal of Community Psychology, 0*(1–14). doi:10.1002/ajcp.12328

Frazier, S. L., Mehta, T. G., Atkins, M. C., Hur, K., & Rusch, D. (2013). Not just a walk in the park: Efficacy to effectiveness for after school programs in communities of concentrated urban poverty. *Administration and Policy in Mental Health and Mental Health Services Research, 40*(5), 406–418.

Gamoran, A. (2009). Tracking and inequality: New directions for research and practice. Retrieved from https://files.eric.ed.gov/fulltext/ED506617.pdf

Garland, A. F., Lau, A. S., Yeh, M., McCabe, K. M., Hough, R. L., & Landsverk, J. A. (2005). Racial and ethnic differences in utilization of mental health services among high-risk youths. *The American Journal of Psychiatry, 162*(7), 1336–1343.

Garner, P. W., & Hinton, T. S. (2010). Emotional display rules and emotion self-regulation: Associations with bullying and victimization in community-based after school programs. *Journal of Community & Applied Social Psychology, 20*(6), 480–496.

Gottfredson, D., Cross, A. B., Wilson, D., Rorie, M., & Connell, N. (2010). Effects of participation in after-school programs for middle school students: A randomized trial. *Journal of Research on Educational Effectiveness, 3*(3), 282–313.

Greenberg, M. T., Domitrovich, C. E., Weissberg, R. P., & Durlak, J. A. (2017). Social and emotional learning as a public health approach to education. *The Future of Children, 27*(1), 13–32.

Greene, K. M., Lee, B., Constance, N., & Hynes, K. (2013). Examining youth and program predictors of engagement in out-of-school time programs. *Journal of Youth and Adolescence, 42*(10), 1557–1572.

Halpern, R. (1999). After-school programs for low-income children: Promises and challenges. *The Future of Children, 9*(2), 81–95.

Harms, T., Jacobs, E. V., & White, D. R. (2013). *School-age care environment rating scale.* New York, NY: Teachers College Press.

Hobbs, N. J. (1966). Helping disturbed children: Psychological and ecological strategies. *American Psychologist, 21*(12), 1105–1115.

James-Burdumy, S., Dynarski, M., & Deke, J. (2007). When elementary schools stay open late: Results from the national evaluation of the 21st Century Community Learning Centers program. *Educational Evaluation and Policy Analysis, 29*(4), 296–318.

Kataoka, S., & Vandell, D. L. (2013). Quality of afterschool activities and relative change in adolescent functioning over two years. *Applied Developmental Science, 17*(3), 123–134.

Kellam, S. G., Brown, C. H., Poduska, J. M., Ialongo, N. S., Wang, W., Toyinbo, P., … Wilcox, H. C. (2008). Effects of a universal classroom behavior management program in first and second grades on young adult behavioral, psychiatric, and social outcomes. *Drug and Alcohol Dependence, 95*(Suppl. 1), S5–S28.

Kim, J. S., & Sunderman, G. L. (2005). Measuring academic proficiency under the No Child Left Behind Act: Implications for educational equity. *Educational Researcher, 34*(8), 3–13.

Lauer, P. A., Akiba, M., Wilkerson, S. B., Apthorp, H. S., Snow, D., & Martin-Glenn, M. L. (2006). Out-of-school-time programs: A meta-analysis of effects for at-risk students. *Review of Educational Research*, *76*(2), 275–313.

Lerner, R. M., & Simon, L. A. K. (2014). *University-community collaborations for the twenty-first century: Outreach scholarship for youth and families*. New York: Routledge.

Little, P. M. (2007). The quality of school-age child care in after-school settings. Retrieved from www.nccp.org/publications/pdf/text_739.pdf

Lyon, A. R., Frazier, S. L., Mehta, T., Atkins, M. S., & Weisbach, J. (2011). Easier said than done: Intervention sustainability in an urban after-school program. *Administration and Policy in Mental Health and Mental Health Services Research*, *38*(6), 504–517.

Mahoney, J. L., Parente, M. E., & Lord, H. (2007). After-school program engagement: Links to child competence and program quality and content. *The Elementary School Journal*, *107*(4), 385–404.

Mahoney, J. L., Parente, M. E., & Zigler, E. F. (2010). After-school program participation and children's development. In J. Meece & J. Eccles (Eds.), *Handbook of research on schools, schooling, and human development* (pp. 379–397). New York, NY: Wiley.

Masten, A. S., & Cicchetti, D. (2010). Developmental cascades. *Development and Psychopathology*, *22*(3), 491–495.

McCombs, J., Whitaker, A., & Yoo, P. (2017). The value of out-of-school time programs. Retrieved from www.rand.org/content/dam/rand/pubs/perspectives/PE200/PE267/RAND_PE267.pdf

Merikangas, K. R., He, J. P., Burstein, M., Swendsen, J., Avenevoli, S., Case, B., … Olfson, M. (2011). Service utilization for lifetime mental disorders in US adolescents: Results of the National Comorbidity Survey-Adolescent Supplement (NCS-A). *Journal of the American Academy of Child & Adolescent Psychiatry*, *50*(1), 32–45.

Messiah, S. E., Vidot, D., Hansen, E., Kardys, J., Sunil Matthew, M., Nardi, M., & Arheart, K. L. (2016). Impact of a park-based afterschool program replicated over five years on modifiable cardiovascular disease risk factors. *Preventive Medicine*, *95*(1), 66–73.

Mikami, A. Y., Griggs, M. S., Reuland, M. M., & Gregory, A. (2012). Teacher practices as predictors of children's classroom social preference. *Journal of School Psychology*, *50*(1), 95–111.

Nadeem, E., Jaycox, L. H., Langley, A. K., Wong, M., Kataoka, S. H., & Stein, B. D. (2014). Effects of trauma on students: Early intervention through the cognitive behavioral intervention for trauma in schools. In M. D. Weist, N. A. Lever, C. P. Bradshaw, & J. S. Owens (Eds.), *Handbook of school mental health* (pp. 145–157). Boston, MA: Springer.

Nastasi, B. K. (2004). Meeting the challenges of the future: Integrating public health and public education for mental health promotion. *Journal of Educational & Psychological Consultation*, *15*(3–4), 295–312. doi:10.1207/s1532768xjepc153&4_6

National Research Council. (2002). *Community programs to promote youth development*. Washington, DC: National Academies Press.

Nelson, J. R., Benner, G. J., Lane, K., & Smith, B. W. (2004). Academic achievement of K-12 students with emotional and behavioral disorders. *Exceptional Children*, *71*(1), 59–73.

NICHD Early Child Care Research Network. (1996). Observational record of the caregiving environment [Measurement instrument]. Retrieved from www.researchconnections.org/childcare/resources/2980

Niehaus, K., Rudasill, K. M., & Adelson, J. L. (2012). Self-efficacy, intrinsic motivation, and academic outcomes among Latino middle school students participating in an after-school program. *Hispanic Journal of Behavioral Sciences*, *34*(1), 118–136.

Noam, G. G., & Rosenbaum Tillinger, J. (2004). After-school as intermediary space: Theory and typology of partnerships. *New Directions for Youth Development*, *2004*(101), 75–113.

Osgood, D. W., Anderson, A. L., & Shaffer, J. N. (2005). Unstructured leisure in the after-school hours. In J. L. Mahoney, R. W. Larson, & J. S. Eccles (Eds.), *Organized activities as contexts of development: Extracurricular activities, after-school and community programs* (pp. 45–64). Mahwah, NJ: Lawrence Erlbaum Associates, Inc.

Payton, J., Weissberg, R. P., Durlak, J. A., Dymnicki, A. B., Taylor, R. D., Schellinger, K. B., & Pachan, M. (2008). The positive impact of social and emotional learning for kindergarten to eighth-grade students: Findings from three scientific reviews. Chicago, IL: Collaborative for Academic, Social, and Emotional Learning. Retrieved from https://files.eric.ed.gov/fulltext/ED505370.pdf

Peterson, D. S., & Taylor, B. M. (2012). Using higher order questioning to accelerate students' growth in reading. *The Reading Teacher, 65*(5), 295–304.

Pierce, K. M., Bolt, D. M., & Vandell, D. L. (2010). Specific features of after-school program quality: Associations with children's functioning in middle childhood. *American Journal of Community Psychology, 45*(3–4), 381–393.

Pierce, K. M., Hamm, J. V., & Vandell, D. L. (1999). Experiences in after-school programs and children's adjustment in first-grade classrooms. *Child Development, 70*(3), 756–767.

Prinstein, M. J., & La Greca, A. M. (2004). Childhood peer rejection and aggression as predictors of adolescent girls' externalizing and health risk behaviors: A 6-year longitudinal study. *Journal of Consulting and Clinical Psychology, 72*(1), 103–112.

Raba, A. (2017). The influence of Think-Pair-Share (TPS) on improving students' oral communication skills in EFL classrooms. *Creative Education, 8*(1), 12–23.

Rhodes, J. E. (2004). The critical ingredient: Caring youth-staff relationships in after-school settings. *New Directions for Youth Development, 2004*(101), 145–161.

Rohrbeck, C. A., Ginsburg-Block, M. D., Fantuzzo, J. W., & Miller, T. R. (2003). Peer-assisted learning interventions with elementary school students: A meta-analytic review. *Journal of Educational Psychology, 95*(2), 240–257.

Rosenthal, R., & Vandell, D. L. (1996). Quality of care at school-aged child-care programs: Regulatable features, observed experiences, child perspectives, and parent perspectives. *Child Development, 67*(5), 2434–2445.

Sheldon, J., Arbreton, A., Hopkins, L., & Grossman, J. B. (2010). Investing in success: Key strategies for building quality in after-school programs. *American Journal of Community Psychology, 45*(3–4), 394–404.

Smith, C., Akiva, T., McGovern, G., & Peck, S. C. (2014). Afterschool quality. *New Directions for Youth Development, 2014*(144), 31–44.

Smith, E. P., & Bradshaw, C. (2017). Promoting nurturing environments in afterschool settings. *Clinical Child and Family Psychology, 20*(2), 117–126.

Smith, E. P., Osgood, D. W., Caldwell, L. C., Hynes, K., & Perkins, D. F. (2013). Measuring collective efficacy among children in community-based afterschool: Pathways toward prevention and positive youth development. *American Journal of Community Psychology, 52*(1–2), 27–40.

Smith, E. P., Osgood, D. W., Oh, Y., & Caldwell, L. C. (2018). Promoting afterschool quality and positive youth development: Cluster randomized trial of the PAX Good Behavior Game. *Prevention Science, 19*(2), 159–173.

Smith, E. P., Wise, E., Rosen, H., Rosen, A., Childs, S., & McManus, M. (2014). Top-down, bottom-up, and around the jungle gym: A social exchange and networks approach to engaging afterschool programs in implementing evidence-based practices. *American Journal of Community Psychology, 53*(3–4), 491–502.

Smith, E. P., Witherspoon, D. P., & Osgood, D. W. (2017). Positive youth development among diverse racial-ethnic children: Quality afterschool contexts as developmental assets. *Child Development, 88*(4), 1063–1078.

Sportime. (2007). SPARK School Specialty. Retrieved from www.sparkpe.org

Steiner, N. J., Sheldrick, R. C., Frenette, E. C., Rene, K. M., & Perrin, E. C. (2014). Classroom behavior of participants with ADHD compared with peers: Influence of teaching format and grade level. *Journal of Applied School Psychology, 30*(3), 209–222.

Stewart, E. A. (2003). School social bonds, school climate, and school misbehavior: A multilevel analysis. *Justice Quarterly, 20*(3), 575–604.

Sutherland, K. S., & Snyder, A. (2007). Effects of reciprocal peer tutoring and self-graphing on reading fluency and classroom behavior of middle school students with emotional or behavioral disorders. *Journal of Emotional and Behavioral Disorders, 15*(2), 103–118.

Sutherland, K. S., Wehby, J. H., & Gunter, P. L. (2000). The effectiveness of cooperative learning with students with emotional and behavioral disorders: A literature review. *Behavioral Disorders, 25*(3), 225–238.

Tseng, V., Easton, J. Q., & Supplee, L. H. (2017). Research-practice partnerships: Building two-way streets of engagement. *Social Policy Report, 30*(4), 1–17.

Tseng, V., & Seidman, E. (2007). A systems framework for understanding social settings. *American Journal of Community Psychology, 39*(3–4), 217–228.

Vandell, D. L., Lee, K. T., Whitaker, A. A., & Pierce, K. M. (2018). Cumulative and differential effects of early child care and middle childhood out-of-school time on adolescent functioning. *Child Development, 00*(0), 1–16.

Vandell, D. L., Reisner, E. R., Brown, B. B., Dadisman, K., Pierce, K. M., Lee, D., & Pechman, E. M. (2005/2012). The study of promising after-school programs: Examination of intermediate outcomes in year 2. *Report to the Charles Stewart Mott Foundation.* Retrieved from http://childcare.wceruw.org/

Vandell, D. L., Reisner, E. R., & Pierce, K. M. (2007). Outcomes linked to high-quality afterschool programs: Longitudinal findings from the study of promising afterschool programs. Retrieved from https://files.eric.ed.gov/fulltext/ED499113.pdf

Vygotsky, L. S. (1987). *The collected works of L. S. Vygotsky: Problems of general psychology* (Vol. 1). New York, NY: Plenum Press.

Walker, H. M., & Sprague, J. R. (1999). The path to school failure, delinquency, and violence: Causal factors and some potential solutions. *Intervention in School and Clinic, 35*(2), 67–73.

Wandersman, A., Duffy, J., Flaspohler, P., Noonan, R., Lubell, K., Stillman, L., … Saul, J. (2008). Bridging the gap between prevention research and practice: The interactive systems framework for dissemination and implementation. *American Journal of Community Psychology, 41*(3–4), 171–181.

Wentzel, K. R., & Watkins, D. E. (2002). Peer relationships and collaborative learning as contexts for academic enablers. *School Psychology Review, 31*(3), 366–377.

Wilson, D. B., Gottfredson, D. C., & Najaka, S. S. (2001). School-based prevention of problem behaviors: A meta-analysis. *Journal of Quantitative Criminology, 17*(3), 247–272.

Xie, H., Cairns, R. B., & Cairns, B. D. (1999). Social networks and configurations in inner-city schools: Aggression, popularity, and implications for students with EBD. *Journal of Emotional and Behavioral Disorders, 7*(3), 147–155.

Yohalem, N., & Wilson-Ahlstrom, A. (2010). Inside the black box: Assessing and improving quality in youth programs. *American Journal of Community Psychology, 45*(3–4), 350–357.

Part 3

Selected Effective Programs and Practices

13 The Family Check-Up for Elementary and Middle School Youth and Families Emotional/Behavioral Disorders

Lucia E. Cardenas, Jordan M. Matulis, and Elizabeth A. Stormshak

Several decades of research on the treatment and prevention of emotional/behavioral disorders (EBD) clearly suggests that family-centered interventions are effective approaches to risk reduction and prevention of problem behavior among youth who are most vulnerable for a variety of later adjustment problems, including conduct disorder, substance abuse, depression, and high-risk behavior (CPPRG, 1999; Dishion, Kavanagh, Schneiger, Nelson, & Kaufman, 2002; Forgatch & Patterson, 2010; Kazdin, 2010; Stormshak, Fosco, & Dishion, 2010; Zisser & Eyberg, 2010). This chapter provides an overview of an ecological approach to treatment, called the Family Check-Up (FCU), that emerged from a series of intervention trials that we conducted with elementary and middle school youth (Dishion & Stormshak, 2007). Inspired by the research suggesting an integrative intervention that coordinates services across multiple domains (e.g., home, family–peer, school) for children and families is most successful, we developed the FCU for delivery in schools, community settings, and primary care. Over the past 20 years, there have been more than 15 randomized trials conducted using the FCU model, with a range of outcomes, targets, and long-term follow-up of families and youth (see Figure 13.1). The majority of these trials focused on middle school and adolescent youth, and thus will be the basis for this chapter.

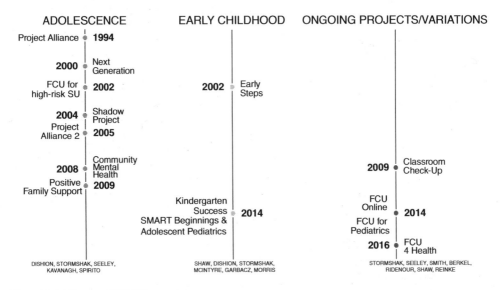

Figure 13.1 History of FCU Research

186 *Lucia E. Cardenas et al.*

In this chapter we highlight the FCU program of research focused on school-age and middle school youth, which began in 1995 with *Project Alliance* (Dishion et al., 2002), and continues today with multiple funded projects. Many of these projects build on the initial research with adolescents and middle school families (see Figure 13.1). Our chapter will highlight outcomes from these randomized trials and discuss implementation of the FCU in school settings, including barriers to effective implementation and future directions.

Emotional/Behavior Disorders (EBD)

The number of children who have mental health problems has been increasing in the past decade. The prevalence of EBD ranges from 4.3% to 11.5% across a variety of studies (Ringeisen et al., 2017), yet some reports suggest that the rate is as high as 1 in 5 children. At the same time, schools are experiencing a decrease in funding and support for students with problem behavior, and some estimates suggest that only 20% of these children receives the services they need (Biglan, Mrazek, Carnine, & Flay, 2003). Rates of EBD are a significant concern for schools, whose goals involve helping all children reach their academic potential.

It is also clear that EBD, if left untreated, may lead to a range of problem behaviors in late adolescence and adulthood, such as high-risk behavior, substance abuse, and low educational attainment (Nelson, Van Ryzin, & Dishion, 2015; Stormshak, DeGarmo, Chronister, & Caruthers, 2018; Van Ryzin, Fosco, & Dishion, 2012). Problem behavior in middle childhood is predictable from poor adjustment and risk factors in early childhood, and, even more so, from disrupted parenting and family environments (Stormshak, Bierman, McMahon, & Lengua, 2000). Early behavior problems contribute to achievement and self-regulation problems in school, which further exacerbate adjustment over time (Dishion & Patterson, 2006).

In this chapter, we review a program of research that has focused on the significant relationships in children's lives that either protect them from chronic EBD or disrupt development and may precipitate later problems, such as school failure and high-risk problem behavior. Two decades of research suggests that significant relationships with family members is either a risk or protective factor during middle school. Family management skills have a significant influence on the developmental pattern underlying adolescent problem behaviors (Fosco, Stormshak, Dishion, & Winter, 2012; Nelson et al., 2015). Ample evidence has shown that poor family management, including inconsistency, lack of supervision, and negative parenting strategies, is associated with problem behavior, which, in turn, is related to academic failure, substance use, and emotional distress into the adolescent and adult years (e.g., Dishion, Nelson, & Bullock, 2004). Positive changes in family management and parenting skills have been linked to meaningful improvements in adolescent behavior across family cultures and ethnic groups, even among adolescents who engage in risk behavior (Galambos, Barker, & Almeida, 2003; Gonzales et al., 2012; Smith, Knoble, Zerr, Dishion, & Stormshak, 2014). Clearly, improvements in parenting practices that include increasing positive behavior support in the home can disrupt the developmental chain of events that leads to risk behaviors and poor adjustment (Connell, Dishion, Yasui, & Kavanagh, 2007; Dishion, Nelson, & Kavanagh, 2003; Stormshak et al., 2018).

Historically, schools have managed these problems by identifying students who need assistance in the form of individualized education plans (IEPs) or other mandated educational planning, and then provided a child-focused, school-based intervention to support achievement and success. Educational planning usually has been provided only for the youth at highest risk.

However, less than 1% of youth get special education services for EBD (NCES, 2019). Given that youth with EBD are more likely to live in out-of-home placements, such as alternative family care, group homes, or residential treatment homes, it is particularly important to consider the usefulness of support interventions being coordinated across multiple agencies (Chen et al., 2016). These child-focused interventions are minimally successful at the school level, and can be strengthened by including families in the treatment plan (Moore, Garbacz, et al., 2016).

The Family Check-Up Model of Intervention

The Family Check-Up (FCU) is a brief, ecological, family-centered, preventive intervention found to reduce problem behaviors in children, adolescents, and young adults by targeting parenting skills and family interactions (Connell, McKillop, & Dishion, 2016; Connell, Stormshak, Dishion, Fosco, & Van Ryzin, 2018; Stormshak et al., 2010; Van Ryzin, Stormshak, & Dishion, 2012; Véronneau, Dishion, Connell, & Kavanagh, 2016). The FCU is a motivational intervention originally inspired by an alcohol and drug treatment called the Drinker's Check-Up (Miller & Rollnick, 2002). The FCU intervention integrates elements of motivational interviewing, ecological assessment, and parenting skills training to address youth's increased problem behaviors, substance use, and academic problems (Connell et al., 2018; Dishion et al., 2008).

The overall objective of the FCU is to support family and child development by helping parents recognize approaches to family management that result in decreases of the presenting child concerns. The intervention uses an ecological assessment designed to motivate family members to use enhanced parenting skills congruent to their motivation to change. Based on results of this assessment, the FCU model is individually tailored to the presenting concerns of each family (Smith, Dishion, Shaw, & Wilson, 2013). Specifically, the therapist uses motivational interviewing to promote the caregiver's motivation to change parenting skills and apply these new skills to the management of child behavior. The FCU model focuses on building upon existing parent strengths and increasing positive family management skills (Sitnick et al., 2015; Smith et al., 2013). Because the FCU is strength-based and adapted to the presenting problems of the family, it is ideally delivered at critical junctures in the child's development, such as during the transition to school or other developmental transitions, such as adolescence or young adulthood.

Theoretical Framework of the FCU

Ecological Model

The FCU is grounded in a developmental-ecological theoretical model which emphasizes the transactional dynamics between children, their caregivers, and their communities. Developmental trajectories are influenced not only by biology and temperament, but also by the environments (e.g., family, peers, and school) and the interactions between these systems of care (Bronfenbrenner, 1977; Farmer & Farmer, 2001). Consistent with a developmental, systems perspective, EBD symptoms are contextualized as being impacted by the child's interactions with their environment, such as parents, peers, and teachers (Granic & Lamey, 2002). Child and family intervention informed by an ecological approach emphasizes both the environment and the child with the goal of mitigating problem behavior and emotional difficulties. As such, treatment approaches that follow from this model suggest that combining

188   *Lucia E. Cardenas et al.*

motivation and support to enhance parenting skills can improve youth problem behaviors and emotional distress, leading to long-term positive outcomes mediated by family management skills (Stormshak et al., 2011).

Additionally, these interventions often consider the utility of linking multiple environments and systems impacting youth at home and school (Dishion & Stormshak, 2007), which is particularly salient for youth with EBD, as this population is more likely to live in out-of-home placements and to be involved in multiple service agencies including the juvenile justice system (Barrett & Katsiyannis, 2016; Chen et al., 2016).

FCU Intervention

The FCU model combines intervention targets (e.g., family-management, problem-solving skills) and behavior change principles (Dishion & Stormshak, 2007) into a brief, targeted intervention that can be adapted to a variety of service settings. The approach is unique in three ways. First, the model tailors interventions to families in order to target their presenting concerns based on the FCU assessment results. This approach allows for the recommendation of a menu of evidence-based services. By offering a variety of flexible services, parent engagement and motivation for the change process are enhanced (Dishion & Kavanagh, 2003b). Second, the FCU provides interventions during periods of critical developmental transition, such as entry into elementary school or the transition from middle school to high school (Stormshak & Dishion, 2009). Third, the FCU attends to motivation to change at several phases of the intervention (Miller & Rollnick, 2002; Stormshak & Dishion, 2009).

The FCU intervention is comprised of three stages: (a) an initial interview; (b) a multi-informant, ecological, and home-based observational session; and (c) a feedback session (Dishion & Stormshak, 2007). The intervention is grounded in the formation of a collaborative therapeutic relationship between parents and the parent consultant, who may be housed in a variety of different settings and can be in multiple professional roles (e.g., school psychologist, behavioral support specialist, or counselor). The development of rapport begins during the initial interview, when the parent consultant meets with the caregivers. The parent consultant surveys the caregivers' concerns, particularly about family issues that are salient to the overall well-being of the child (Dishion et al., 2015; Dishion & Stormshak, 2007). Additionally, the consultant examines the parents' individual motivations to change and uses motivational interviewing techniques to promote the parent's motivation to attend to their areas of growth while building on current strengths (Dishion et al., 2015).

The second stage of the FCU is a questionnaire assessment and a videotaped family interaction assessment (Stormshak & Dishion, 2009). These assessments are created to encapsulate important information about the child and family across several contexts. The written assessment includes a multi-informant questionnaire which is completed by child participants, their caregivers, and their teachers. This questionnaire measures key information to gain a broad understanding of the child and family system. Specifically, the assessment surveys how the child is impacted by various levels in their ecology, such as their family, peers, and schools (Stormshak & Dishion, 2009). The observational video assessment provides concrete data on parent–child interactions (Connell et al., 2007).

The third stage of the FCU is the feedback session. During this session, the parent consultant meets with parents to discuss the results of the ecological assessment in detail. The feedback session is intended to (a) promote motivation to change; (b) give parents information regarding areas of growth, as well as areas of family and child strength; and (c) evaluate the need for follow-up parenting support services laid out in a menu of family-centered intervention options using the Everyday Parenting curriculum (Dishion, Stormshak, & Kavanagh, 2011; Stormshak & Dishion, 2009). The menu is generated utilizing the norm-based data from the ecological assessment and is made up of potential intervention options individually tailored to meet the needs and goals of families (Smith et al., 2013; Stormshak & Dishion, 2009). After completion of the FCU, caregivers may continue to receive support based on their goals and targets, which follow directly from the assessment and feedback session (Stormshak & Dishion, 2009).

The Everyday Parenting Curriculum

The Everyday Parenting curriculum is used to guide the intervention support provided after the FCU (Stormshak & Dishion, 2009), and is a traditional parent training curriculum based on social learning theory (Forgatch & Patterson, 2010). The curriculum includes a range of parenting skills training activities, which are established, skill-building, evidence-based inter-ventions for disruptive behaviors with children (Brestan & Eyberg, 1998). Skill-building interventions engage parents and support development of their family management skills, including a focus on positive behavior support, limit-setting, monitoring, open communica-tion, and problem solving (Stormshak & Dishion, 2009). The curriculum emphasizes colla-boration and respect for cultural diversity in family management and parenting approaches (Dishion et al., 2011). Dosage varies based on parent engagement, goals, and strengths. This adapted delivery system enables parents to commit to a brief intervention, such as one session, which enhances engagement over time (Stormshak & Dishion, 2009).

The family management skills training comprises a set of family management skills that fall within four broad domains of parenting: positive behavior support, limit setting, monitoring/supervision, and problem-solving skills (Dishion et al., 2011). Proactive parenting, or preven-tion and scaffolding to reduce problem behavior, is part of the curriculum and a theme across all four domains of parenting (Dishion et al., 2011). Proactive parenting is defined as using planned strategies to surmount parenting obstacles with a de-emphasis on reactive methods of child raising (Denham et al., 2000). Together, monitoring and proactive parenting encompass *mindful parenting*, which is parenting that focuses on managing daily interactions with your child in a planful approach to parenting (Dishion et al., 2011).

The Everyday Parenting curriculum is typically conducted individually after completion of the FCU (Dishion & Stormshak, 2007). Sessions 1 through 4 of the Everyday Parenting Curriculum focus on positive behavior support. Positive behavior support is a behavior management principle that underscores the use of reinforcing and supportive parent–child interactions to foster development (Dishion et al., 2011). In this stage of the curriculum, parents learn the usefulness of tracking child behavior to identify and positively reinforce desired behavioral outcomes. Positive behavior support is based on parents' capacity to make effective requests in a clear and specific manner that does not blame the child or adolescent. As parents consistently attend to, praise, incentivize, and tangibly reward positive behaviors, desired behaviors increase over time (Dishion et al., 2011).

Effective limit-setting includes setting rules and limits that clearly communicate desired behaviors, as well as potential consequences when youth do not obey. One component of the limit setting curriculum is the SANE guidelines which outline how to respond to problem behaviors. The acronym, SANE, describes effective consequences that are Small, Avoid punishing the parent, Nonabusive to the child, and Effective. By recognizing beliefs and parenting practices that negatively impact limit-setting, parents can effectively apply

190   *Lucia E. Cardenas et al.*

consequences and reduce negative emotions. In addition to creating effective limits, parental monitoring is an essential component of limit-setting.

Monitoring refers to parents' involvement with their child and their overall knowledge of their child's day to day activities, safety, feelings, and behaviors. During childhood, parental monitoring mostly takes place in home and school settings. However, as children enter adolescence, parents must adjust strategies to effectively monitor unsupervised activities in the community and with peers (Racz & McMahon, 2011). Methods for parental monitoring include networking with the school, community, and other parents (Dishion et al., 2011).

Problem solving and communication are other dimensions of parenting addressed in the Everyday Parenting curriculum A core aspect of communication focused on during these sessions is listening skills to support parents as their roles evolve when children grow older. When children are younger, it is usual for parents to offer solutions to problems. However, for adolescents, it is useful for parents to recognize that they can learn and understand more about their child's decision-making processes through listening and active observation. The curriculum focuses on helping families navigate conflict and providing opportunities for adolescents to contribute to problem solving. In these sessions, parents learn to include their adolescent in problem solving and decision making, and to support autonomy while setting consistent limits. The problem-solving skills that are taught (e.g., using neutral problem statements, brainstorming alternative solutions) teach both adolescents and parents a process for navigating problem behaviors and family conflict. The sessions in this section of the curriculum are structured and use role-plays and integration of humor to practice skills (Dishion et al., 2011).

The Family Check-Up for Adolescence and Young Adults

Adolescence is a significant developmental stage that is characterized by many social, cognitive, and behavioral changes. Along with the physical, cognitive, and individual changes a child experiences, this transition is also accompanied by higher risk of engagement in problem behaviors, including substance use, aggression, and antisocial behaviors (Van Ryzin, Fosco, & Dishion, 2012). Furthermore, significant changes also occur in the parent–child relationship, with lower levels of communication and less time spent together (Van Heel et al., 2019; Van Ryzin, Stormshak, & Dishion, 2012). It is no surprise that problem behaviors often increase throughout this developmental period, as children explore adult behaviors and test the limits of their relationships with parents and peers. These problems, if left unattended, can lead to unhealthy behaviors that persist into adulthood. As a result, adolescence is an especially salient time to intervene and implement positive parenting practices in the family system (Dishion & Patterson, 2006; Dishion & Stormshak, 2007).

Although this time frame can be a great opportunity to intervene, it can also be a difficult time to engage in family interventions. During early adolescence years, individuals move away from parental authority to gain independence (Hadiwijaya, Klimstra, Vermunt, Branje, & Meeus, 2017). This leads to increased parent–child conflict, and often the relationship quality worsens in early adolescence (Tsai, Telzer, & Fuligni, 2013). However, this is temporary in most cases, and as individuals gain autonomy, the relationship quality between parent and child typically improves (Hadiwijaya et al., 2017). Ultimately, even though adolescents aim to individuate from their family of origin, this relationship has proven to be an influential factor throughout adolescent development in both supportive and detrimental ways. Parents continue to provide support that predicts positive outcomes for youth even into the young adult years (Stormshak, Caruthers et al., 2019). Therefore, supporting adolescents through family-centered interventions is particularly important to facilitate parent engagement and support the parent–child relationship through a time of drastic change.

Empirical Support

The FCU was originally intended as a brief approach aimed to motivate parents to monitor, supervise, and manage adolescents at high risk, specifically targeting substance use and problem behaviors (Dishion et al., 2008; Dishion & Stormshak, 2007). The FCU was developed based on a long history of developmental research suggesting that low levels of monitoring coupled with disengaged parenting during adolescence predicts problem behavior. As a result, the primary target of the FCU is enhancing parenting skills, which is hypothesized to be the key mechanism associated with improvements in child behavior over time.

The first randomized trial of the FCU was conducted in middle school, and targeted youth at high risk for EBD. The research was innovative at the time for several reasons. First, there were few interventions that integrated family support into schools. Second, the typical family interventions delivered in schools were parenting groups, which had demonstrated efficacy but low enrollment, which was a problem for dissemination and implementation. Research from the randomized prevention trial, Project Alliance 1, revealed an association with lowered substance use and a reduction in rates of depression through enhanced parent monitoring and supervision (Connell & Dishion, 2008; Dishion et al., 2003; Stormshak & Dishion, 2009). This sample was then followed into high school and young adulthood, where research continued to show significant reductions in tobacco, marijuana, and alcohol use as well as reduced risks of antisocial behavior into the adult years (Connell et al., 2016; Véronneau et al., 2016). Beyond substance use and problem behaviors, research has also demonstrated intervention effects on self-regulation, academic performance, high-risk sexual behavior, and school engagement (Caruthers, Van Ryzin, & Dishion, 2014; Connell et al., 2007; Stormshak et al., 2018). Many projects since Project Alliance 1 have also demonstrated positive outcomes with middle school youth, including teacher ratings of problem behavior, parent self-efficacy, and long-term changes in self-regulation and high-risk behavior during the young adult years (Stormshak, Caruthers et al., 2019, 2018; Stormshak, Dishion, Light, & Yasui, 2005). These projects focused on at risk or high-risk youth drawn from school populations with limited resources (high levels of free and reduced lunch, poor funding, and low attendance).

The Family Check-Up for Elementary School

The transition into kindergarten is one of the most important developmental transitions of a child's life, and early adjustment to school predicts positive long-term academic and behavioral outcomes (Hooper, Roberts, Sideris, Burchinal, & Zeisel, 2010). During this time, students encounter a wide range of academic and social experiences that pose new emotional and behavioral challenges (Hughes, 2015). Sustained attention, emotional regulation, and early literacy skills (Cadima, Doumen, Verschueren, & Buyse, 2015; Garbacz, McIntyre, Stormshak, & Kosty, 2018) are all critical elements of the successful transition to school, and predict later academic achievement (Fink, Browne, Hughes, & Gibson, 2019).

Until recently, there had not been a school-based, randomized trial of the FCU administered at school entry. In the FCU-Kindergarten study we adapted the model for school entry and tested the effects of the FCU in a randomized trial with kindergarten, first, and second grade children in low income schools (Garbacz et al., 2018). The FCU was adapted for this population in several ways. First, assessments that focused on key skills needed for a successful transition to kindergarten were collected from parents and teachers. For children, this included measures of self-regulation, sustained attention, and academic readiness skills. For parents, the assessment was tailored to measure parenting skills associated with adjustment during early childhood, such as positive parenting, family routines, school involvement, and consistency. Families were observed in a videotaped interaction engaging in a variety of developmentally appropriate tasks designed to elicit parenting skills during the transition to school, including a homework task and reading task with their child. The recordings from these interactions were then coded by therapists, and the results were used to provide feedback to parents on homework and reading skills with their children in a process consistent with the overall FCU model. Books at the developmental level of the child were provided to support reading at home, and parents in the FCU condition received support to engage with their child in reading and homework using effective parenting skills, such as positive support, creating a reading routine, and choosing books at the child's reading level.

Results of the FCU-Kindergarten model suggest that school entry is an effective point of intervention for children and families. Guided by a developmental, ecological model consistent with prior FCU research, our model is based on parenting skills as a key mediator that impacts child outcomes over time. When we examined the effect of the FCU at school entry on parenting skills, we found that the random assignment was related to improved parenting skills, especially for families with high levels of stress. Stress moderated outcomes for kindergarten families, with higher levels of stress associated with improved parenting and monitoring/family routines (Stormshak, Seeley et al., 2019). Furthermore, teachers completed ratings of child behavior each year during kindergarten, first grade, and second grade. Initial results indicated that children in the FCU treatment condition performed better on teacher report measures of emotional and behavioral problems during the first and second grade, and children with higher initial levels of emotional and behavioral problems experienced greater benefit from treatment (Garbacz et al., 2018). These outcomes were consistent, regardless of special services received by the children in school, and are consistent with prior FCU research, suggesting greater effects for children and families at higher risk (Pelham, Dishion, Tein, Shaw, & Wilson, 2017).

Next Steps and Future Directions

Although family-centered interventions show the largest effects over time for youth, multiple barriers limit schools to implement these programs (Forman, Olin, Hoagwood, Crowe, & Saka, 2009). One of the most glaring reasons that implementation efforts are unsuccessful is because of a lack of resources. Many schools face the dilemma of serving a growing population of mental health and behavioral issues with limited financial resources (Stormshak et al., 2011). These limitations often force schools to make difficult decisions about how to allocate funds, with mental health usually overlooked in the interest of academic support (Smolkowski et al., 2017).

In addition to financial strains, administrative support and staff turnover can also prevent effective implementation of these interventions. Because of limited time and resources, school personnel rarely receive adequate training in essential intervention components (Stormshak et al., 2005). This issue often leaves school staff feeling unsupported and unprepared, leaving little energy to devote to the success of family–school partnerships, compromising the quality and fidelity of the program (Dusenbury, Brannigan, Hansen, Walsh, & Falco, 2005). Furthermore, administrative turnover limits support from districts, a critical element for successful implementation in schools (Smolkowski et al., 2017). As a result, implementing family interventions can be a very difficult task to accomplish. For example, in a randomized effectiveness trial of the FCU, the FCU intervention was linked to enhanced outcomes for students, such as increased use of parental monitoring. However, despite some significant outcomes, results demonstrated that schools faced many challenges to implementation (Smolkowski et al., 2017). Obstacles limiting effective implementation of the intervention included a lack of trained staff, lack of resources, and time limitations (Fosco et al., 2014). Improvements in school implementation would likely involve fewer demands on schools, as well as improved training (Smolkowski et al., 2017). Overall, studies point to the long-term impact created by motivating parents to participate in family management (Soutullo, Smith-Bonahue, Sanders-Smith, & Navia, 2016; Stormshak et al., 2010). Thus, steps were taken to design an eHealth intervention iteration of the FCU that would overcome common implementation barriers and require minimal school resources (Danaher et al., 2018).

FCU Online: An Ehealth Model of Intervention in Schools

Increases in Internet usage as well as the wide-scale use of cell phones open up potential for mental health interventions to reach a larger part of the population. In a recent Pew Research report, it was reported that about 90% of adults currently use the Internet (Anderson, Perrin, Jiang, & Kumar, 2019). Another recent survey conducted by the Pew Research Center (2019) reported that about 96% of adults use a mobile phone (81% smartphones). Access to technology also improves participation in intervention and treatment. Ehealth interventions have been associated with higher levels of participation than traditional, in-person interventions with families (Jones, 2014).

A number of evidence-based parenting curriculums have been effectively adapted to web-based programs that are self-administered or aided by qualified human support (Cardamone-Breen et al., 2018; Enebrink, Högström, Forster, & Ghaderi, 2012; Gelatt, Adler-Baeder, & Seeley, 2010; Sourander et al., 2016; Yap et al., 2018). The participant engagement and intervention efficacy of online behavioral health treatments can be augmented by the addition of human support, such as technician-level coaches or therapists (Mohr, Cuijpers, & Lehman, 2011). These interventions have been effective in the decrease of risk outcomes in children, such as the Triple-P Online intervention (Baker, Sanders, Turner, & Morawska, 2017) and Partner in Parenting (Yap et al., 2018).

We recently developed the FCU Online and tested the model in a randomized trial with middle school families and youth. The developmental process of the FCU Online intervention was iterative and guided by focus groups with families and school staff. The eHealth intervention was tested and subsequently underwent modifications with feedback. The FCU Online program includes an online assessment and feedback process in line with the FCU model (Danaher et al., 2018). As mentioned previously, research suggests the addition of guided human support may enhance outcomes (Mohr et al., 2011). Both an online-only version and coach version of the FCU Online intervention were designed and implemented. The FCU Online-only model enables users to log into the FCU Online website to fill out the FCU assessment, receive feedback results, and use the website based on their areas of

194 *Lucia E. Cardenas et al.*

strengths and growth. The FCU Online plus coach model provides users access to the same features as the FCU Online-only model, as well as short and focused coaching calls via telephone or Skype and a feedback session.

Consistent with the tailored and adaptive model of the FCU Online, after completing the FCU assessment, the user is then provided access to targeted intervention modules based on their assessment results. The skills sessions emphasized in the FCU Online include positive parenting, setting limits, monitoring, and open communication. These targeted online interventions allow for personalized focus on areas of growth that can quickly be administered (Danaher et al., 2018). The four parenting skills sessions included on the website integrate various interactive online engagement activities that are created to motivate the parent to use the program (Danaher et al., 2018). These activities include animations and dyad videos that model skills in both the correct and incorrect ways, host videos that guide the user through the website, and interactive activities that offer opportunities to apply skill knowledge (Danaher et al., 2018). The user also has the option to received automated text messages to prompt use of the skills they learn in each skills module (Mohr, Burns, Schueller, Clarke, & Klinkman, 2013). The FCU Online website includes an online tracking tool for parents to track their use of skills presented in each module, a library that offers a variety of articles about salient topics (e.g., homework tips, cyberbullying), and a checkup summary that provides users with their overall scores on their ecological checkup assessment (Danaher et al., 2018).

In a randomized control trial of the FCU Online, participants were randomly assigned to a waitlist control, FCU Online as a web-based intervention, or FCU Online with coach support. Assignment to the FCU Online with coach support was linked with decreased emotional problems for children and enhanced parental confidence and feelings of self-efficacy three months posttest. In addition, youth who were more at risk demonstrated stronger effects than those with marginal risk (Stormshak, Seeley et al., 2019) and 37% of families who engaged in the treatment scored in the risk range on overall problem behavior. Overall, a major strength of the FCU Online is that it is flexible and can be adapted based on the resources available for schools and families. For instance, when staffing limitations in schools make the FCU Online with coach support version difficult to administer, the FCU Online version with no coach can be used instead because it does not require significant school staffing and can be delivered as a broad-based public health intervention. Additionally, the FCU Online is usable and convenient for families in both urban and rural areas because it is intended for use in the home setting (Danaher et al., 2018).

Conclusion

This chapter presents an overview of the FCU intervention for adolescents and school-age children. The FCU is an ecological, school-based, and family-centered intervention that has been shown to effectively reduce EBDs in children, adolescents, and young adults and bolster parenting and family management skills (Dishion & Kavanagh, 2003a). After an ecological assessment and focused feedback regarding the family's presenting concerns, the FCU integrates parent management training that focuses on several key aspects of parenting skills that are evidenced-based, including positive behavior support, limit setting, monitoring, and problem solving (Dishion et al., 2011). Despite the need for school-based interventions to target EBDs, schools face several obstacles with regard to implementing parenting interventions (Forman et al., 2009). Online interventions, which are more convenient and efficient in delivery for schools and families, may reduce these barriers (Feil et al., 2008; Stormshak, Seeley et al., 2019).

Author Note

This research was supported by grants from the U.S. Department of Education, Institute for Education Sciences (R305A140189; R324A180037) and from the National Institute on Drug Abuse (DA037628; DA018374) to the third author. The opinions expressed by the authors are not necessarily reflective of the position of or endorsed by the U.S. Department of Education or the National Institute on Drug Abuse.

References

Anderson, M., Perrin, A., Jiang, J., & Kumar, E. (2019, April 22). 10% of Americans don't use the internet. Who are they? Retrieved from https://pewresearch.org/fact-tank/2019/04/22/some-americans-dont-use-the-internet-who-are-they/

Baker, S., Sanders, M. R., Turner, K. M., & Morawska, A. (2017). A randomized controlled trial evaluating a low-intensity interactive online parenting intervention, Triple P online brief, with parents of children with early onset conduct problems. *Behaviour Research and Therapy, 91*, 78–90.

Barrett, D. E., & Katsiyannis, A. (2016). Juvenile offending and crime in early adulthood: A large sample analysis. *Journal of Child and Family Studies, 25*(4), 1086–1097.

Biglan, A., Mrazek, P. J., Carnine, D., & Flay, B. R. (2003). The integration of research and practice in the prevention of youth problem behaviors. *American Psychologist, 58*(6–7), 433–440.

Brestan, E. V., & Eyberg, S. M. (1998). Effective psychosocial treatments for children and adolescents with disruptive behavior disorders: 29 years, 82 studies, and 5272 kids. *Journal of Clinical Child Psychology, 27*, 179–188.

Bronfenbrenner, U. (1977). Toward an experimental ecology of human development. *American Psychologist, 32*, 513–531. doi:10.1037/0003-066X.32.7.513

Cadima, J., Doumen, S., Verschueren, K., & Buyse, E. (2015). Child engagement in the transition to school: Contributions of self-regulation, teacher–child relationships and classroom climate. *Early Childhood Research Quarterly, 32*, 1–12.

Cardamone-Breen, M. C., Jorm, A. F., Lawrence, K. A., Rapee, R. M., Mackinnon, A. J., & Yap, M. B. H. (2018). A single-session, web-based parenting intervention to prevent adolescent depression and anxiety disorders: Randomized controlled trial. *Journal of Medical Internet Research, 20*(4), e148.

Caruthers, A. S., Van Ryzin, M. J., & Dishion, T. J. (2014). Preventing high-risk sexual behavior in early adulthood with family interventions in adolescence: Outcomes and developmental processes. *Prevention Science, 15*(1), 59–69.

Chen, C. C., Culhane, D. P., Metraux, S., Park, J. M., Venable, J. C., & Burnett, T. C. (2016). They're not all at home: Residential placements of early adolescents in special education. *Journal of Emotional and Behavioral Disorders, 24*(4), 247–256.

Conduct Problems Prevention Research Group. (1999). Initial impact of the fast track prevention trial for conduct problems: I. The high-risk sample. *Journal of Consulting and Clinical Psychology, 67*(5), 631–647.

Connell, A. M., & Dishion, T. J. (2008). Reducing depression among at-risk early adolescents: Three-year effects of a family-centered intervention embedded within schools. *Journal of Family Psychology, 22*(4), 574–585.

Connell, A. M., Dishion, T. J., Yasui, M., & Kavanagh, K. (2007). An adaptive approach to family intervention: Linking engagement in family-centered intervention to reductions in adolescent problem behavior. *Journal of Consulting and Clinical Psychology, 75*(4), 568–579.

Connell, A. M., McKillop, H. N., & Dishion, T. J. (2016). Long-term effects of the family check-up in early adolescence on risk of suicide in early adulthood. *Suicide and Life-Threatening Behavior, 46*, S15–S22.

Connell, A. M., Stormshak, E., Dishion, T., Fosco, G., & Van Ryzin, M. (2018). The family check up and adolescent depression: An examination of treatment responders and non-responders. *Prevention Science, 19*(1), 16–26.

196   *Lucia E. Cardenas et al.*

Danaher, B. G., Seeley, J. R., Stormshak, E. A., Tyler, M. S., Caruthers, A. S., Moore, K. S., Cardenas, L. (2018). The Family Check-up Online program for parents of middle school students: Protocol for a Randomized Controlled Trial. *JMIR Research Protocols. JMIR Research Protocols, 7*(7), e11106.

Denham, S. A., Workman, E., Cole, P. M., Weissbrod, C., Kendziora, K. T., & Zahn-Waxler, C. (2000). Prediction of externalizing behavior problems from early to middle childhood: The role of parental socialization and emotion expression. *Development and Psychopathology, 12*(1), 23–45.

Dishion, T. J., & Kavanagh, K. (2003a). *Intervening in adolescent problem behavior: A family-centered approach.* New York, NY: Guilford Press.

Dishion, T. J., & Kavanagh, K. (2003b). The adolescent transitions program: A family-centered prevention strategy for schools. In J. B. Reid, J. J. Snyder, & G. R. Patterson (Eds.), *Antisocial behavior in children and adolescents: A developmental analysis and the Oregon model for intervention* (pp. 257–272). Washington, DC.: American Psychological Association.

Dishion, T. J., Kavanagh, K., Schneiger, A., Nelson, S., & Kaufman, N. K. (2002). Preventing early adolescent substance use: A family-centered strategy for the public middle school. *Prevention Science, 3*(3), 191–201.

Dishion, T. J., Mun, C. J., Drake, E. C., Tein, J. Y., Shaw, D. S., & Wilson, M. (2015). A transactional approach to preventing early childhood neglect: The family check-up as a public health strategy. *Development and Psychopathology, 27*(4pt2), 1647–1660.

Dishion, T. J., Nelson, S. E., & Bullock, B. M. (2004). Premature adolescent autonomy: Parent disengagement and deviant peer process in the amplification of problem behaviour. *Journal of Adolescence, 27*(5), 515–530.

Dishion, T. J., Nelson, S. E., & Kavanagh, K. (2003). The family check-up with high-risk young adolescents: Preventing early-onset substance use by parent monitoring. *Behavior Therapy, 34*(4), 553–571.

Dishion, T. J., & Patterson, G. R. (2006). The development and ecology of antisocial behavior in children and adolescents. In D. Cicchetti & D. J. Cohen (Eds.), *Developmental psychopathology: Vol. 3. Risk, disorder, and adaptation* (pp. 503–541). New York, NY: Wiley.

Dishion, T. J., Shaw, D., Connell, A., Gardner, F., Weaver, C., & Wilson, M. (2008). The family check-up with high-risk indigent families: Preventing problem behavior by increasing parents' positive behavior support in early childhood. *Child Development, 79*(5), 1395–1414.

Dishion, T. J., & Stormshak, E. A. (2007). *Intervening in children's lives: An ecological, family-centered approach to mental health care.* Washington, DC: American Psychological Association.

Dishion, T. J., Stormshak, E. A., & Kavanagh, K. (2011). *Everyday parenting: A professional's guide to building family management skills.* Champaign, IL: Research Press.

Dusenbury, L., Brannigan, R., Hansen, W. B., Walsh, J., & Falco, M. (2005). Quality of implementation: Developing measures crucial to understanding the diffusion of preventive interventions. *Health Education Research, 20,* 308–313.

Enebrink, P., Högström, J., Forster, M., & Ghaderi, A. (2012). Internet-based parent management training: A randomized controlled study. *Behaviour Research and Therapy, 50*(4), 240–249.

Farmer, T. W., & Farmer, E. M. Z. (2001). Developmental science, systems of care, and prevention of emotional and behavioral problems in youth. *American Journal of Orthopsychiatry, 71,* 171–181.

Feil, E. G., Baggett, K. M., Davis, B., Sheeber, L., Landry, S., Carta, J. J., & Buzhardt, J. (2008). Expanding the reach of preventive interventions: Development of an internet-based training for parents of infants. *Child Maltreatment, 13*(4), 334–346.

Fink, E., Browne, W. V., Hughes, C., & Gibson, J. (2019). Using a "child's-eye view" of social success to understand the importance of school readiness at the transition to formal schooling. *Social Development, 28* (1), 186–199.

Forgatch, M. S., & Patterson, G. R. (2010). Parent management training—Oregon model: An intervention for antisocial behavior in children and adolescents. In J. R. Weisz & A. E. Kazdin (Eds.), *Evidence-based psychotherapies for children and adolescents* (pp. 159–177). New York, NY: The Guilford Press.

Forman, S. G., Olin, S. S., Hoagwood, K. E., Crowe, M., & Saka, N. (2009). Evidence-based interventions in schools: Developers' views of implementation barriers and facilitators. *School Mental Health, 1*(1), 26.

Fosco, G. M., Seeley, J. R., Dishion, T. J., Smolkowski, K., Stormshak, E. A., McCarthy, D., ... Strycker, L. A. (2014). Lessons learned from scaling up the ecological approach to family interventions and treatment in middle schools. In M. Weist, N. Lever, C. Bradshaw, & J. Owens (Eds.), *Handbook of school mental health, research, training, practice, and policy* (2nd ed., pp. 237–251). New York, NY: Springer.

Fosco, G. M., Stormshak, E. A., Dishion, T. J., & Winter, C. E. (2012). Family relationships and parental monitoring during middle school as predictors of early adolescent problem behavior. *Journal of Clinical Child & Adolescent Psychology, 41*(2), 202–213.

Galambos, N. L., Barker, E. T., & Almeida, D. M. (2003). Parents do matter: Trajectories of change in externalizing and internalizing problems in early adolescence. *Child Development, 74*(2), 578–594.

Garbacz, S. A., McIntyre, L. L., Stormshak, E. A., & Kosty, D. B. (2018). The efficacy of the family check-up on children's emotional and behavior problems in early elementary school. *Journal of Emotional and Behavioral Disorders*, Advance online. doi: 1063426618806258.

Gelatt, V. A., Adler-Baeder, F., & Seeley, J. R. (2010). An interactive web-based program for stepfamilies: Development and evaluation of efficacy. *Family Relations, 59*(5), 572–586.

Gonzales, N. A., Dumka, L. E., Millsap, R. E., Gottschall, A., McClain, D. B., Wong, J. J., ... Kim, S. Y. (2012). Randomized trial of a broad preventive intervention for Mexican American adolescents. *Journal of Consulting and Clinical Psychology, 80*(1), 1–16.

Granic, I., & Lamey, A. V. (2002). Combining dynamic systems and multivariate analyses to compare the mother–child interactions of externalizing subtypes. *Journal of Abnormal Child Psychology, 30*(3), 265–283.

Hadiwijaya, H., Klimstra, T. A., Vermunt, J. K., Branje, S. J., & Meeus, W. H. (2017). On the development of harmony, turbulence, and independence in parent–adolescent relationships: A five-wave longitudinal study. *Journal of Youth and Adolescence, 46*(8), 1772–1788.

Hooper, S. R., Roberts, J., Sideris, J., Burchinal, M., & Zeisel, S. (2010). Longitudinal predictors of reading and math trajectories through middle school for African American versus Caucasian students across two samples. *Developmental Psychology, 46*(5), 1018–1029.

Hughes, C. (2015). The transition to school. *The Psychologist, 28*(9), 714–717.

Jones, D. J. (2014). Future directions in the design, development, and investigation of technology as a service delivery vehicle. *Journal of Clinical Child & Adolescent Psychology, 43*(1), 128–142.

Kazdin, A. E. (2010). Problem-solving skills training and parent management training for oppositional defiant disorder and conduct disorder. In J. R. Weisz & A. E. Kardin (Eds.), *Evidence-based Psychotherapies for Children and Adolescents* (pp. 211–226). The Guildord Press.

Miller, W. R., & Rollnick, S. (2002). *Motivational interviewing: Preparing people for change* (2nd ed.). New York, NY: Guilford Press.

Mohr, D. C., Burns, M. N., Schueller, S. M., Clarke, G., & Klinkman, M. (2013). Behavioral intervention technologies: Evidence review and recommendations for future research in mental health. *General Hospital Psychiatry, 35*(4), 332–338.

Mohr, D. C., Cuijpers, P., & Lehman, K. (2011). Supportive accountability: A model for providing human support to enhance adherence to eHealth interventions. *Journal of Medical Internet Research, 13*(1), e30.

Moore, K. J., Garbacz, S. A., Gau, J. M., Dishion, T. J., Brown, K. L., Stormshak, E. A., & Seeley, J. R. (2016). Proactive parent engagement in public schools: Using a brief strengths and needs assessment in a multiple-gating risk management strategy. *Journal of Positive Behavior Interventions, 18*(4), 230–240.

NCES. (2019). *The condition of education 2019*. Washington, DC: U.S. Department of Education, National Center for Education Statistics.

Nelson, S. E., Van Ryzin, M. J., & Dishion, T. J. (2015). Alcohol, marijuana, and tobacco use trajectories from age 12 to 24 years: Demographic correlates and young adult substance use problems. *Development and Psychopathology, 27*(1), 253–277.

Pelham, W. E., Dishion, T. J., Tein, J. Y., Shaw, D. S., & Wilson, M. N. (2017). What doesn't work for whom? Exploring heterogeneity in responsiveness to the family check-up in early childhood using a mixture model approach. *Prevention Science, 18*(8), 911–922.

Pew Research Center. (2019, June 12). *Mobile Fact Sheet* [Report]. Retrieved from www.pewinternet.org/fact-sheet/mobile/

Racz, S. J., & McMahon, R. J. (2011). The relationship between parental knowledge and monitoring and child and adolescent conduct problems: A 10-year update. *Clinical Child and Family Psychology Review, 14*, 377–398.

Ringeisen, H., Stambaugh, L., Bose, J., Casanueva, C., Hedden, S., Avenevoli, S., & West, J. (2017). Measurement of childhood serious emotional disturbance: State of the science and issues for consideration. *Journal of Emotional and Behavioral Disorders, 25*, 195–210.

Sitnick, S. L., Shaw, D. S., Gill, A., Dishion, T., Winter, C., Waller, R., … Wilson, M. (2015). Parenting and the family check-up: Changes in observed parent-child interaction following early childhood intervention. *Journal of Clinical Child & Adolescent Psychology, 44*(6), 970–984.

Smith, J. D., Dishion, T. J., Shaw, D. S., & Wilson, M. N. (2013). Indirect effects of fidelity to the family check-up on changes in parenting and early childhood problem behaviors. *Journal of Consulting and Clinical Psychology, 81*(6), 962–974.

Smith, J. D., Knoble, N. B., Zerr, A. A., Dishion, T. J., & Stormshak, E. A. (2014). Family check-up effects across diverse ethnic groups: Reducing early-adolescence antisocial behavior by reducing family conflict. *Journal of Clinical Child & Adolescent Psychology, 43*(3), 400–414.

Smolkowski, K., Seeley, J. R., Gau, J. M., Dishion, T. J., Stormshak, E. A., Moore, K. J., & Garbacz, S. A. (2017). Effectiveness evaluation of the positive family support intervention: A three-tiered public health delivery model for middle schools. *Journal of School Psychology, 62*, 103–125.

Sourander, A., McGrath, P. J., Ristkari, T., Cunningham, C., Huttunen, J., Lingley-Pottie, P., … Fossum, S. (2016). Internet-assisted parent training intervention for disruptive behavior in 4-year-old children: A randomized clinical trial. *JAMA Psychiatry, 73*(4), 378–387.

Soutullo, O. R., Smith-Bonahue, T. M., Sanders-Smith, S. C., & Navia, L. E. (2016). Discouraging partnerships? Teachers' perspectives on immigration-related barriers to family–school collaboration. *School Psychology Quarterly, 31*(2), 226–240.

Stormshak, E., Caruthers, A., Chronister, K., DeGarmo, D., Stapleton, J., Falkenstein, C., … Nash, W. (2019). Reducing risk behavior with family-centered prevention during the young adult years. *Prevention Science, 20*(3), 321–330.

Stormshak, E., DeGarmo, D., Chronister, K., & Caruthers, A. (2018). The impact of family-centered prevention on self-regulation and subsequent long-term risk in emerging adults. *Prevention Science, 19*(4), 549–558.

Stormshak, E. A., Bierman, K. L., McMahon, R. J., & Lengua, L. J. (2000). Parenting practices and child disruptive behavior problems in early elementary school. *Journal of Clinical Child Psychology, 29*(1), 17–29.

Stormshak, E. A., Connell, A. M., Véronneau, M.-H., Myers, M. W., Dishion, T. J., Kavanagh, K., & Caruthers, A. S. (2011). An ecological approach to promoting early adolescent mental health and social adaptation: Family-centered intervention in public middle schools. *Child Development, 82*, 209–225.

Stormshak, E. A., & Dishion, T. J. (2009). A school-based, family-centered intervention to prevent substance use: The family check-up. *The American Journal of Drug and Alcohol Abuse, 35*(4), 227–232.

Stormshak, E. A., Dishion, T. J., Light, J., & Yasui, M. (2005). Implementing family-centered interventions within the public middle school: Linking service delivery to change in student problem behavior. *Journal of Abnormal Child Psychology, 33*, 723–733.

Stormshak, E. A., Fosco, G. M., & Dishion, T. J. (2010). Implementing interventions with families in schools to increase youth school engagement: The family check-up model. *School Mental Health, 2*(2), 82–92.

Stormshak, E. A., Seeley, J. R., Caruthers, A. S., Cardenas, L., Moore, K. J., Tyler, M. S., … Danaher, B. (2019). Evaluating the efficacy of the family check-up online: A school-based, ehealth model for the prevention of problem behavior during the middle school years. *Development and Psychopathology, 31*(5), 1873–1886.

Tsai, K. M., Telzer, E. H., & Fuligni, A. J. (2013). Continuity and discontinuity in perceptions of family relationships from adolescence to young adulthood. *Child Development, 84*(2), 471–484.

Van Heel, M., Bijttebier, P., Claes, S., Colpin, H., Goossens, L., Van Den Noortgate, W., … Van Leeuwen, K. (2019). Measuring parenting throughout adolescence: Measurement invariance across informants, mean level, and differential continuity. *Assessment, 26*(1), 111–124.

Van Ryzin, M. J., Fosco, G. M., & Dishion, T. J. (2012). Family and peer predictors of substance use from early adolescence to early adulthood: An 11-year prospective analysis. *Addictive Behaviors, 37*(12), 1314–1324.

Van Ryzin, M. J., Stormshak, E. A., & Dishion, T. J. (2012). Engaging parents in the family check-up in middle school: Longitudinal effects on family conflict and problem behavior through the high school transition. *Journal of Adolescent Health, 50*(6), 627–633.

Véronneau, M. H., Dishion, T. J., Connell, A. M., & Kavanagh, K. (2016). A randomized, controlled trial of the family check-up model in public secondary schools: Examining links between parent engagement and substance use progressions from early adolescence to adulthood. *Journal of Consulting and Clinical Psychology, 84*(6), 526–543.

Yap, M. B. H., Mahtani, S., Rapee, R. M., Nicolas, C., Lawrence, K. A., Mackinnon, A., & Jorm, A. F. (2018). A tailored web-based intervention to improve parenting risk and protective factors for adolescent depression and anxiety problems: Postintervention findings from a randomized controlled trial. *Journal of Medical Internet Research, 20*(1), e17.

Zisser, A., & Eyberg, S. M. (2010). Parent-child interaction therapy and the treatment of disruptive behavior disorders. In J. R. Weisz & A. E. Kazdin (Eds.), *Evidence-based psychotherapies for children and adolescents* (pp. 179–193). New York, NY: The Guilford Press.

14 Multi-Tiered Systems of Support

Lee Kern, Kent McIntosh, Colleen E. Commisso, and Sean C. Austin

Over the past two decades, multi-tiered systems of support (MTSS) have emerged as important frameworks in school settings, due largely to their efficiency and effectiveness (McIntosh & Goodman, 2016). These systems are relevant across many domains within the school context, having been applied to behavior, academic, mental health, and social supports for students, as well as teacher training. For instance, Response to Intervention (RtI) is an early example that addressed academics (Fletcher & Vaughn, 2009). RtI was initially derived in response to the presumed over-identification of students as learning disabled and the accompanying belief that this over-identification was largely caused by inadequate general education instruction. The intent of RtI was to offer an alternative to the two options of general and special education by creating a continuum of appropriately intensive intervention that would prevent academic failure (Fletcher & Vaughn, 2009). Similarly, school-wide positive behavioral interventions and supports (SWPBIS) was initiated as a preventive and instructive framework to teach students appropriate behavior and diminish problem behavior. Most critical in the commencement of SWPBIS was a pattern of exceedingly punitive responses when students engaged in problem behavior (McIntosh & Goodman, 2016). As with RtI, the underlying premise of SWPBIS is that all children can be taught (academic skills and behavior), and instruction is most effective when it is delivered early with the core intention of preventing further difficulties.

For simplicity, some schools have merged systems of student support (i.e., academic, behavior, mental health), reducing the need for multiple teams (Domitrovich et al., 2010). A corollary is that this approach to blending supports addresses each student's needs in a holistic fashion. The connection between academic difficulties and behavioral concerns has been extensively documented (e.g., McIntosh, Sadler, & Brown, 2012) and the notion of jointly remediating these problems is important. That is, schools are rich with examples of students who engage in problem behaviors because they are unsuccessful with academic schoolwork. Likewise, students may fall behind academically because mental health problems, such as anxiety or depression, prevent them from completing assignments in a timely manner. When systems of support are united, a plan that comprehensively addresses all of a student's needs is most likely forthcoming.

The rationale for multi-tiered systems of support, as implied above, is to provide early, systematic, and increasingly intensive intervention to *all* students (Sugai & Horner, 2009). We emphasize *all* because universal or Tier 1 support is delivered to every student. This level of support, when applied consistently using evidence-based strategies, will greatly reduce the need for more intensive intervention, either academic or behavioral. A small number of students, approximately 15%, will require more intensive support at Tier 2, generally provided in the form of small group instruction. Accordingly, a yet smaller percentage (approximately 5%) will need intensive and individualized Tier 3 support.

When support is applied in a preventive manner, resources in a school are leveraged most effectively and efficiently (Bradshaw, Koth, Bevans, Ialongo, & Leaf, 2008; Horner, Sugai, & Anderson, 2010). Intensive and individualized Tier 3 programs that are inherently teacher demanding and therefore costly are needed for only a very small group of students. Further, all students (and staff) benefit from a common approach with research to document that it is effective. Finally, the "wait to fail" tactic that has exacerbated student challenges can be avoided.

Although the concept of multi-tiered systems of support has been applied to many domains, our intention in this chapter is to focus on SWPBIS, the system that is usually most essential for students with emotional and behavioral disabilities. Note that we embrace the movement toward integrating systems; however, a comprehensive description of more than one system is beyond the scope of a single chapter. One additional caveat is that we acknowledge there are copious programs and strategies that address school discipline and student behavior problems. We favor SWPBIS for at least three reasons. Most important is the underlying non-punitive philosophy. Second, it offers the most clearly articulated continuum of supports. Third, it is supported by a solid and growing research base, both as a comprehensive program and within each tier, with an abundance of evidence demonstrating that it is highly effective.

School-Wide Positive Behavioral Interventions and Supports

SWPBIS is firmly based on the science of applied behavior analysis, with additional emphasis on person-centered planning, as well as organizational management and implementation science (Horner, Sugai, & Fixsen, 2017). In SWPBIS, there is a focus on systems, which can be expressed in terms of various layers of the educational system (McIntosh & Goodman, 2016). Although the level of outcome is the student (i.e., impact), the level of intervention is the school (i.e., the local context), and the level of implementation is the district (i.e., the broader context).

The history of the evolution of SWPBIS is an effort to support children and youth with emotional and behavioral challenges. Providing individual supports without attending to the context is ineffective (McIntosh, Lucyshyn, Strickland-Cohen, & Horner, 2015), and the context of the school is not only the environment, but also the social networks within the school. Hence, an effective plan for individual students involves changing the social culture of the school, and changing the culture of the school involves attending to school systems, including organization and leadership, as the "host environments" for effective intervention (Kame'enui, Simmons, & Coyne, 2000). In this way, SWPBIS began as a way to focus on school-wide intervention to improve outcomes for all students.

The framework of SWPBIS has been articulated and adopted widely based on three key variables (Horner et al., 2017). First, its established effectiveness provides a preferred option for those seeking to improve student behavior outcomes quickly and visibly. Second, SWPBIS can be implemented by typical school personnel with typical educational funding, eliminating the need for external specialists or certified trainers or implementers. Third, its emphasis on systems delivery has allowed for durable and scalable implementation. These aspects have resulted in widescale adoption of SWPBIS in over 26,000 U.S. schools and in over 20 different countries.

202   *Lee Kern et al.*

SWPBIS is based on certain foundational aspects that drive intervention and implementation (McIntosh, Filter, Bennett, Ryan, & Sugai, 2010). Central to the framework is an *instructional approach to discipline,* in which the first element of behavior support is clarifying behaviors that are desired and teaching those behaviors directly. Attention to principles of instructional design is critical, including teaching through examples and non-examples and performance feedback. Another essential aspect is *environmental redesign,* the creation of physical and social environments that cue and reinforce desired behavior, as well as discourage unwanted behavior.

The *multi-tiered continuum of support* described above is also a foundational feature, as are the systems for indicating what levels of support students need, accomplished through *teaming* and *data.* Teams in SWPBIS use a problem-solving model to identify what level of support individual students need based on school data (McIntosh, Fisher, Kennedy, Craft, & Morrison, 2012), and students can be referred for Tier 2 or 3 support based on screening data or teacher nomination. Teams use progress-monitoring data to evaluate intervention responsiveness as well as reduce or remove supports when students are successful.

Finally, there is attention to *systems of implementation.* This systems focus allows SWPBIS to be a framework for implementing a range of interventions, including academic supports and those targeting other valued outcomes. In keeping with a systems-focused framework, there is an underlying assumption that implementation and the interventions selected will need to be adapted to maximize *contextual fit,* or the extent to which the intervention meets the needs of students, their families, and resources of the school system (McIntosh, Horner, & Sugai, 2009).

Research Base

A broad base of research regarding SWPBIS supports its characterization as an evidence-based practice. In addition to case studies and single-case research, multiple randomized controlled trials, conducted by both developers and independent researchers at other institutions, have found consistently positive and statistically significant effects of SWPBIS on the following outcomes: reduced rates of problem behavior, reduced bullying, reduced rates of illegal drug and alcohol use, increased rates of prosocial behavior, improved emotional regulation, improved academic achievement, improved perceptions of school safety, and improved organizational health (Bradshaw, Waasdorp, & Leaf, 2012; Horner et al., 2010; Waasdorp, Bradshaw, & Leaf, 2012). As education has increasingly moved toward the identification of evidence-based practices, several organizations and agencies have advanced criteria to determine whether a practice is evidence based (e.g., American Psychological Association, What Works Clearinghouse, Council for Exceptional Children). These standards suggest that an intervention can be rendered evidence based if it is supported by a sufficient number of research studies (e.g., at least two randomized controlled trials, five single subject studies) with documented elements of experimental control meeting predetermined standards. Because the practices differ considerably at each tier of SWPBIS, evaluations have considered evidence at each tier. In the paragraphs below, we describe intervention at each tier and research evidence.

Intervention at Tier 1 and Research Support

Tier 1 behavior instruction is intended to be accessible to all students, including those with disabilities (Horner & Sugai, 2015). Although it is common to plan support for students with emotional and behavioral disorders (EBD) on a child-by-child basis, focusing on prevention and consistency in the environment for the student body as a whole provides benefits for students who generally have Tier 3 needs as well. Within a SWPBIS framework, Tier 1 support is aimed at promoting a foundational understanding about the expectations students should have of the environment (i.e., consistency), and about what others expect of them as students (i.e., clarity).

In schools with a well-implemented Tier 1 system, students demonstrate reduced problem behavior (Horner et al., 2010). This gives students with EBD proportionally greater instances of classmates serving as prosocial behavior models, which can increase engagement and prosocial behavior among students with EBD (Ryan, Pierce, & Mooney, 2008). Tier 1 SWPBIS teams also attend to how the physical environment may improve student behaviors; giving a closer look at the layout and traffic flow of classrooms and common spaces can be a minimally invasive tool for increasing the likelihood of positive behavior. At a school-wide level, teams review data to determine any traffic bottlenecks in common areas, and subsequently designate alternative routes or adjust passing times to relieve congestion and reduce unwanted behaviors. At a classroom level, a teacher might implement Tier 1 support by rearranging her classroom to minimize the required steps students must take to gather all materials for a project or arrange desks in a way that active supervision is more available for all students from a desk.

Core practices of Tier 1 SWPBIS systems

Successful Tier 1 implementation requires that staff rely on five core SWPBIS practices:

Define Expectations

School staff must first define and come to agreement on five or fewer broad, positively stated expectations of their students (e.g., Be Safe, Be Responsible, Be Caring) that serve to promote positive behavior school-wide. Once these expectations are established, the staff must then clearly define how those expectations should be demonstrated across common areas in the school building (e.g., cafeteria, hallways, playground). Each of the broad expectations should be reflected as specific, observable behaviors in these settings, providing important distinctions for students as they move across settings. For example, the defined behavior of being responsible in the cafeteria may be that students will empty trash off their trays and place trays in red bins, but being responsible in the hallway may be to shut their locker door before going to class. Explicitly defining these differences illustrates precise behaviors for both teachers and students to reference. These expectations across settings are often outlined in a teaching matrix (See Table 14.1).

Teach Expectations

Once expected behavior is defined across settings, the next step is for staff to directly teach those expectations to students. Instruction occurs on a school-wide level, often using alternating schedules to ensure students have an opportunity to visit each setting for lessons on expected behavior. During instruction, staff often model both examples and non-examples of behavior to offer clarity on the boundaries of the expected behavior. Particularly in lower

204 *Lee Kern et al.*

Table 14.1 Teaching Matrix

	Cafeteria	Hallways	Playground
Be Safe	• Use two hands to carry tray	• Walking feet only • Keep hands and feet to self	• Keep rocks and sand on the ground
Be Responsible	• Empty tray into garbage can when finished • Then place tray in red bin	• Shut locker door before going to the classroom	• Clean up balls and toys, put in box for next class
Be Caring	• Wait your turn in line • Use kind words towards peers	• Use kind words towards peers	• Share toys with others • Use kind words towards peers

grades, staff should offer guided practice opportunities for students to demonstrate the expected behaviors with feedback from the teacher. This lesson element allows all students to both demonstrate the expected behavior with accuracy and receive positive acknowledgement from staff for meeting those expectations.

Acknowledge Desired Behavior

Acknowledgement systems are used to encourage students to demonstrate expected behaviors in the school setting. Verbal praise of expected behavior is often effective as positive reinforcement for students. Effective acknowledgement of behavior will positively praise a specific behavior the student performed and the related expectation. For example, a teacher might stop a student briefly in the hallway and say, "Richard, you walked in the hallway quietly with your hands to yourself. That is a great way to be safe in school." Research indicates that higher rates of behavior-specific praise are associated with increased academic engagement for students with EBD (Allday et al., 2012). Staff can strive for a high ratio (3:1 or greater) of positive to corrective statements. Schools may have formal acknowledgement systems in the form of tickets or tokens distributed to individual or groups of students immediately after they demonstrate an expected positive behavior. Some schools use these tokens as positive notes that students can take home to parents or even as raffle tickets or token economies for intermittent tangible rewards.

Respond to Unwanted Behaviour

Although positive acknowledgement is vital, it is important that staff have a standardized, consistent, and instructional approach when unwanted behavior occurs. School policies and procedures should reflect clear behavior definitions and a bank of mild, instructional consequences across staff (McIntosh, Girvan, Horner, & Smolkowski, 2014). Verbal redirection, reminders, and pre-corrections can be delivered early and often to support students in correcting their behavior before escalation to more intense or disruptive behaviors.

Use School-Wide Data for Decision-Making

To obtain an understanding of the health and functioning of the Tier 1 system, school teams rely on multiple sources of data to inform how to improve practices. School discipline data indicate to school staff how effective efforts have been in reducing student misbehaviors. Data about problem behavior can be broken down to analyze trends across settings/times for use by a school team in decision-making. In addition to collecting outcomes data, it is critical to assess the fidelity (i.e., quality) of implementation of the essential components of SWPBIS. The regular review and dissemination of this information to stakeholders is vital for data-based decision-making, staff buy-in, and sustained implementation (McIntosh, Ellwood, McCall, & Girvan, 2018).

Intervention at Tier 2 and Research Support

Intervention at Tier 2 is intended to provide additional support to students who do not respond to Tier 1 intervention. The three-tiered public health model applied to behavior support (Walker et al., 1996) suggests that roughly 15% of students will require more support than a strong Tier 1 system offers. To reduce labor intensity, Tier 2 interventions are generally provided either in a group format or in a systematic manner across students. This increases both their efficiency and feasibility (Anderson & Borgmeier, 2010).

For many years, Tier 2 operations and interventions were least studied among the SWPBIS tiers. However, a surge of recent research and literature reviews has heightened our understanding of both the practices at Tier 2 and their effectiveness (Bruhn, Lane, & Hirsh, 2014). In addition, conceptual papers and emerging research has articulated ways that Tier 2 interventions can be adapted to increase their effectiveness, thereby avoiding the need for intensive Tier 3 interventions for many students (Kern & Wehby, 2014). In the sections below, we briefly describe the most common Tier 2 interventions. We also describe simple adaptations to standard Tier 2 protocols to improve student responsiveness.

Check In–Check Out (CICO)

CICO, also referred to as the Behavior Education Program (BEP; Crone, Hawken, & Horner, 2010), is the most frequently used Tier 2 intervention (Bruhn et al., 2014). In this intervention, the student (a) checks in with an adult at the start of the school day to review expectations; (b) carries a daily progress report (DPR) listing school-wide expectations throughout the day in which teacher(s) rate the student's adherence to each expectation at pre-designated time intervals; (c) checks out with the adult at the end of the day who reviews teacher ratings, providing praise, reinforcement, and feedback; and (d) takes the DPR home and obtains his/her parent's signature, allowing home–school communication.

Research has documented the effectiveness of CICO for increasing appropriate classroom behavior and decreasing problem behavior (Bruhn et al., 2014). The existing research has been largely conducted with elementary age students; however, studies have demonstrated successful extensions to middle school (e.g., Hawken, Bundock, Kladis, O'Keeffe, & Barrett, 2014). Based on a recent literature review of CICO for reducing challenging behaviors (Maggin, Zurheide, Pickett, & Baillie, 2015), nine single-subject studies were identified as meeting What Works Clearinghouse (WWC) standards. Results indicated that there was sufficient evidence from the single-case research studies to categorize CICO as an evidence-based program.

Skill Groups

Social skills groups are also a common Tier 2 intervention. Social skills are typically provided in small groups matched to student concern, such as interacting appropriately with others, coping with difficult situations, and managing anger. There is an abundance of structured social skills programs commercially available, many with evidence to support their effectiveness (Interpersonal Skills Groups; Evans, Schultz, & DeMars, 2014). What Works Clearinghouse has determined that social skills instruction is an evidence-based intervention based on three randomized controlled studies meeting design standards (https://ies.ed.gov/ncee/wwc/Intervention/763).

An alternative type of small skill groups is Cognitive Behavior Therapy (CBT). CBT is commonly used for mild to moderate depression or anxiety and is the most well-researched behavioral intervention for these problems (Hilt-Panahon, Kern, & Divatia, 2007). The basic CBT process involves making the student aware of negative thoughts or feelings and teaching techniques to replace those thoughts with healthy or more pleasant thoughts. There are several structured CBT programs commercially available (e.g., Coping Cat; Kendall & Hedtke, 2006; Khanna & Kendall, 2008). Coping Cat is endorsed as an evidence-based program within the National Registry of Evidence-Based Programs and Practices (NREPP), maintained by the Substance Abuse and Mental Health Services Administration (SAMHSA). The effectiveness of Coping Cat for treating anxiety among children and adolescents has been investigated in at least 19 randomized controlled studies with mostly promising findings (Lenz, 2015).

Self-Management

Self-management is a process whereby students are provided tools and instruction to monitor their own behavior. A strength of self-management is that it teaches students to become self-reliant with respect to their behavior, rather than depending on adults to observe and provide feedback. This reduces the burden of teacher vigilance and accommodates the many situations when adults are not present. The National Center for Intensive Intervention has identified eight self-management studies with rigorous single subject experimental designs, indicating it is an evidence-based intervention (https://charts.intensiveintervention.org/chart/behavioral-intervention-chart).

Adapting Tier 2 Interventions

Recent Tier 2 research and literature reviews have suggested that approximately 25% of students receiving standard Tier 2 interventions will require more individualized support (e.g., Swoszowski, McDaniel, Jolivette, & Melius, 2013). Typically, students whose behaviors do not respond to tier 2 interventions move to Tier 3. However, because Tier 3 interventions are resource intensive, researchers and practitioners have begun to conceptualize a continuum of Tier 2 supports. Rather than applying Tier 2 interventions in a systematic and standardized manner, teams may adapt the dosage, components, or intensity of standard Tier 2 interventions based on student characteristics and school contextual factors. This enhances intervention effectiveness while avoiding the need for resource-intensive Tier 3 interventions.

Example Adaptations

A variety of adaptations have been made to CICO to address non-response to the standard protocol (see Majeika et al., 2020, for a review). Multiple studies have adapted the check-in component by using a peer mentor instead of an adult staff member (e.g., Collins, Gresham, & Dart, 2016). Other studies have adjusted the student's point goal from 80% (recommend in the CICO manual) or modified the student's point goal over time based on responsiveness (e.g., McDaniel & Bruhn, 2016). Many studies also have added components to CICO, such as a brief social skills lesson during check-in or homework planner checks during check-out (e.g., Turtura, Anderson, & Boyd, 2014). Another component of CICO that has been adapted is the Daily Progress Report (DPR). For example, some studies have changed the expectations listed on the DPR to include specific behaviors of concern related to the student or added additional components to the DPR, such as steps to request a break (e.g., Boyd & Anderson, 2013). Studies also have described adaptations to the teacher feedback component of CICO by increasing the amount of feedback provided throughout the day (e.g., half-hour intervals rather than hour) (e.g., Fairbanks, Sugai, Guardino, & Lathrop, 2007). Less frequently, the parent communication component of CICO has also been adapted by providing training to the parents about CICO or including home-based incentives for meeting CICO point goals (e.g., Turtura et al., 2014).

Similar to CICO, adaptations to social skills programs have included the use of a peer to serve as the lesson instructor or as a participant in the lesson to assist the target student(s) practicing specific skills (e.g., Blake, Wang, Cartledge, & Gardner, 2000). Other adaptations to structured social skills programs include adding or removing specific lessons/skills, altering the session length, and selecting specific lessons to address a student's skill deficits (Lane et al., 2003). Self-management has also been utilized in addition to social skills instruction where students monitor their own social behavior (e.g., Miller, Fenty, Scott, & Park, 2011).

Adaptations to self-management also have been described in the literature. One frequent approach is the addition of specific verbal or written feedback given to a student by a teacher or peer regarding the student's behavior (e.g., Ingram, Lewis-Palmer, & Sugai, 2005). For example, a teacher or peer might periodically compare scores with the student monitoring his/her behavior to determine whether the student's self-monitoring was accurate. Additional adaptations involve goal setting and providing reinforcement for various aspects of the process, such monitoring accurately or meeting a predetermined goal (e.g., Bruhn, Vogelgesang, Fernando, & Lugo, 2016).

Intervention at Tier 3 and Research Support

Tier 3 intervention is intensive and individualized, making implementation quite time consuming. For this reason, it should be restricted to a small group of students. If Tiers 1 and 2 are implemented well, fewer than 5% of students in a given school should need Tier 3 support. As we described above, the premise of a tiered system is that support is increased (movement to higher tiers) only after receipt and non-responsiveness to lower levels of support. However, nearly every school has students who have significant support needs due to disrupted family situations, mental health issues, trauma, histories of inconsistent parenting, significant difficulties with the academic or social demands of schools, and a plethora of other reasons. These students are noticeable to school staff due to the serious and intransigent nature of their behavior problems. For these students, there is high likelihood that Tiers 1 and 2 support will be insufficient and Tier 3 support should be immediately arranged. Theoretically, students with EBD warrant Tier 3

208   *Lee Kern et al.*

support since the severity of their behavior resulted in special education identification under the "ED" label. However, the precision of this label is inexact and students often retain the label despite behavioral improvements (Walker, Nishioka, Zeller, Severson, & Feil, 2000). Therefore, our best recommendation is to provide Tier 3 support unless behavior problems have abated.

Tier 3 interventions rely on information from a functional behavioral assessment (FBA; Bambara & Kern, 2005; Kern, George, & Weist, 2016; O'Neill, Albin, Storey, Horner, & Sprague, 2015). The purpose of an FBA is to identify variables in the environment that contribute to problem behavior. This includes events that occur just before problem behavior (antecedents), events that follow problem behavior (consequences), and distal events that indirectly influence problem behavior (setting events). After information is gathered it is summarized and used to formulate hypothesis statements that facilitate development of a comprehensive, multi-component support plan.

Numerous research studies have documented the effectiveness of functional behavioral assessment-based interventions. Because of the individualized nature of FBA, studies typically use single case designs. What Works Clearinghouse has judged FBA-based interventions to be evidence based (https://ies.ed.gov/ncee/wwc/Intervention/1241). Specifically, among the studies meeting design standards, eight have demonstrated reductions in problem behavior, 15 have resulted in increases in school engagement, and three have shown improvements in social-emotional development.

Issues Related to Implementation

In the systems change field, it is widely understood that simply selecting an evidence-based practice and providing training to school personnel is necessary but insufficient to achieve implementation of a practice as it was designed. It is often necessary to attend to the context of implementation, including assuring staff buy-in and building readiness for installing core features *before* initial implementation and coaching for sustained implementation *after* initial implementation.

Fortunately, there is SWPBIS research to guide implementers regarding which contextual variables are most predictive of full and durable implementation of Tier 1 systems (McIntosh et al., 2018). In general, school characteristics (e.g., school size, community SES, student body racial/ethnic makeup) have not been shown to be strong predictors of which schools will or will not implement and sustain. Instead, there are some key actions that school and district teams can take to enhance the sustainability of SWPBIS and other multi-tiered systems.

At the school level, one of the strongest predictors of sustainability is implementing as a team, as opposed to one individual being responsible for leading the efforts (McIntosh et al., 2013). That team needs administrator support, but it is team functioning that is the stronger predictor, as a single administrator leading the efforts risks abandonment when she or he moves positions. Just as important, the team needs continuous access to data (regarding fidelity and student outcomes) and needs to use these data actively for ongoing decision making. Finally, teachers who also implement positive supports in their classrooms are more likely to sustain SWPBIS overall and see improved student outcomes (Mathews, McIntosh, Frank, & May, 2014).

At the district or state level, there is another set of predictors. To implement well, school teams need access to effective training, ongoing coaching for implementation, and a network of implementing schools to share successes, barriers, and new ideas (McIntosh et al., 2013). It is also beneficial to maintain a set of local model implementing schools that potential adopters can visit and see SWPBIS in action, as well as to dispel misrules (McIntosh, Kelm, & Canizal Delabra, 2016).

SWPBIS Research Gaps and Future Directions

Although the SWPBIS research base is solid and continues to grow, there are a number of areas deserving of future study. Replications of tiered systems of support are needed across a range of settings. For example, there is comparably less research regarding effective implementation of SWPBIS in high schools and schools in urban contexts. Moreover, although there is growing evidence that SWPBIS can decrease the racial and disability discipline gaps (McIntosh Ellwood et al., 2018; McIntosh, Gion, & Bastable, 2018), such gaps are not necessarily eliminated, which would require additional and sustained commitment. For instance, although it is widely agreed that it is important to design or adapt Tier 1 systems to improve contextual fit with the values and needs of students and their families, there is little evidence indicating the most effective methods for doing so (Bastable, Falcon, Nese, & McIntosh, 2018).

In addition, although there are effective interventions at all three tiers and research examining Tier 1 systems outcomes (e.g., implementation, sustainability), there is less direction regarding how SWPBIS can be optimally implemented at Tiers 2 and 3. For instance, the ideal number of Tier 2 interventions that should be implemented in a school is unknown. Additional research is needed to determine whether a set of interventions targeting diverse challenges (e.g., social skills, anxiety/depression, attention seeking problem behavior) can adequately address the majority of problems experienced by Tier 2 students. A related challenge is selecting Tier 2 interventions a priori that are linked to student need. Future research should develop an empirically validated model of intervention selection. Further, additional research is needed to guide practitioners in making adaptations to the standard protocols of Tier 2 interventions to make them optimally effective. For instance, student characteristics (e.g., behavioral function, responsiveness to Tier 1 intervention) could be identified that predict the likelihood that a student will respond to a standard intervention or whether adaptations can be made at initiation to enhance responsiveness. Similarly, elucidating the many contextual variables (e.g., teacher willingness to implement an intervention, ease of implementation, student preference for an intervention) that contribute to both intervention integrity and intervention effectiveness will lead to greater Tier 2 success (e.g., Wehby & Kern, 2014). Research also is needed to delineate how and when students move across tiers. Systems of data-based decision making will help render tiered systems truly efficient and effective.

Finally, there is a need for models and demonstrations that seamlessly align support across multiple target areas into a single decision-making framework. For instance, an ongoing concern of schools is identifying and meeting the needs of students with internalizing problems, such as depression and anxiety. Recent models (e.g., Virginia Tiered Systems of Support; vtss-ric.org) have illustrated how academics, behavior, and social-emotional wellness can be targeted within a single framework, thereby addressing the multiple needs of school aged students.

Summary

Multi-tiered systems of support have proven to be both effective and efficient. Systems such as SWPBIS, focused on student behavior, are ideally suited for students with emerging emotional and behavioral concerns due to their preventive and instructional focus. In spite of compelling research to date illustrating effectiveness, a great deal of additional research and practical applications are needed illustrating (a) variations across diverse school settings and age groups; (b) the optimal number and type of interventions at each tier as well as strategies to adapt standard intervention protocols to enhance effectiveness; and (c) ways to seamlessly blend academic, behavioral, and mental wellness into a single framework. We believe multi-tiered systems hold much promise and as they continue to evolve, schools will be well positioned to successfully meet the diverse needs of all youth.

Author Note

This research was supported by grants from the U.S. Department of Education, Institute for Education Sciences (R324A160096, R324A1800027). The opinions expressed by the authors are not necessarily reflective of the position of or endorsed by the U.S. Department of Education.

References

Allday, R. A., Hinkson-Lee, K., Hudson, T., Neilsen-Gatti, S., Kleinke, A., & Russel, C. S. (2012). Training general educators to increase behavior-specific praise: Effects on students with EBD. *Behavioral Disorders, 37*, 87–98.

Anderson, C. M., & Borgmeier, C. (2010). Tier II interventions within the framework of school-wide positive behavior support: Essential features for design, implementation, and maintenance. *Behavior Analysis in Practice, 3*(1), 33–45.

Bambara, L. M., & Kern, L. (2005). *Designing positive behavior supports for students.* New York: Guilford Press.

Bastable, E., Falcon, S., Nese, R. N. T., & McIntosh, K. (2018). Adapting school-wide positive behavioral interventions and supports to enhance cultural responsiveness. Manuscript submitted for publication.

Blake, C., Wang, W., Cartledge, G., & Gardner, R. (2000). Middle school students with serious emotional disturbances serve as social skills trainers and reinforcers for peers with SED. *Behavioral Disorders, 25*, 280–298.

Boyd, R. J., & Anderson, C. M. (2013). Breaks are better: A tier II social behavior intervention. *Journal of Behavioral Education, 22*, 348–365. doi:10.1007/s10864-013-9184-2

Bradshaw, C. P., Koth, C. W., Bevans, K. B., Ialongo, N., & Leaf, P. J. (2008). The impact of school-wide positive behavioral interventions and supports (PBIS) on the organizational health of elementary schools. *School Psychology Quarterly, 23*(4), 462.

Bradshaw, C. P., Waasdorp, T. E., & Leaf, P. J. (2012). Effects of school-wide positive behavioral interventions and supports on child behavior problems and adjustment. *Pediatrics*, e1136–e1145. doi:10.1542/peds.2012-0243

Bruhn, A. L., Lane, K. L., & Hirsh, S. E. (2014). A review of tier 2 interventions conducted within multitiered models of behavioral prevention. *Journal of Emotional and Behavioral Disorders, 22*, 171–189. doi:10.1177/1063426613476092

Bruhn, A. L., Vogelgesang, K., Fernando, J., & Lugo, W. (2016). Using data to individualize a multicomponent, technology-based self-monitoring intervention. *Journal of Special Education Technology, 31*, 64–76. doi:10.1177/0162643416650024

Collins, T. A., Gresham, F. M., & Dart, E. H. (2016). The effects of peer-mediated check-in/check-out on the social skills of socially neglected students. *Behavior Modification, 40*(4), 568–588. doi:10.1177/0145445516643066

Crone, D. A., Hawken, L. S., & Horner, R. H. (2010). *Responding to problem behavior in schools: The behavior education program.* New York: Guilford Press.

Domitrovich, C. E., Bradshaw, C. P., Greenberg, M. T., Embry, D., Poduska, J. M., & Ialongo, N. S. (2010). Integrated models of school-based prevention: Logic and theory. *Psychology in the Schools*, *47*(1), 71–88.

Evans, S. W., Schultz, B. K., & DeMars, C. E. (2014). High school based treatment for adolescents with ADHD: Results from a pilot study examining outcomes and dosage. *School Psychology Review*, *43*, 185–202.

Fairbanks, S., Sugai, G., Guardino, D., & Lathrop, M. (2007). Response to intervention: Examining classroom behavior support in second grade. *Exceptional Children*, *73*(3), 288–310. doi:10.1177/001440290707300302

Fletcher, J. M., & Vaughn, S. (2009). Response to intervention: Preventing and remediating academic difficulties. *Child Development Perspectives*, *3*(1), 30–37.

Hawken, L. S., Bundock, K., Kladis, K., O'Keeffe, B., & Barrett, C. A. (2014). Systematic review of the check-in, check-out intervention for students at risk for emotional and behavioral disorders. *Education and Treatment of Children*, *37*, 635–658.

Hilt-Panahon, A., Kern, L., & Divatia, A. (2007). School-based interventions for students with or at-risk for depression: A review of the literature. *Advances in School Based Mental Health Promotion*, *1*, 32–41.

Horner, R. H., & Sugai, G. (2015). School-wide PBIS: An example of applied behavior analysis implemented at a scale of social importance. *Behavior Analysis in Practice*, *8*, 80–85.

Horner, R. H., Sugai, G., & Anderson, C. M. (2010). Examining the evidence base for school-wide positive behavior support. *Focus on Exceptional Children*, *42*(8), 1–14.

Horner, R. H., Sugai, G., & Fixsen, D. L. (2017). Implementing effective educational practices at scales of social importance. *Clinical Child and Family Psychology Review*, *20*, 25–35.

Ingram, K., Lewis-Palmer, T., & Sugai, G. (2005). Function-based intervention planning: Comparing the effectiveness of function-based and non-function-based intervention plans. *Journal of Positive Behavior Interventions*, *7*, 224–236. doi:10.1177/10983007050070040401

Kame'enui, E. J., Simmons, D. C., & Coyne, M. D. (2000). Schools as host environments: Toward a schoolwide reading improvement model. *Annals of Dyslexia*, *50*(1), 31–51.

Kendall, P. C., & Hedtke, K. (2006). *Coping cat workbook*. (2nd ed.). Ardmore, PA: Workbook Publishing.

Kern, L., George, M. P., & Weist, M. (2016). *Step-by-step support for students with emotional and behavioral problems: Prevention and intervention strategies*. Baltimore, MD: Paul H. Brookes.

Kern, L., & Wehby, J. (2014). Using data-based individualization to intensify behavioral interventions: Implementation example. *Teaching Exceptional Children*, *46*, 45–53.

Khanna, M., & Kendall, P. C. (2008). Computer assisted CBT for child anxiety: The coping cat CD-ROM. *Cognitive and Behavioral Practice*, *15*, 159–165.

Lane, K. L., Wehby, J., Menzies, H. M., Doukas, G. L., Munton, S. M., & Gregg, R. M. (2003). Social skills instruction for students at risk for antisocial behavior: The effects of small-group instruction. *Behavioral Disorders*, *28*, 229–248.

Lenz, A. S. (2015). Meta-analysis of the coping cat program for decreasing severity of anxiety symptoms among children and adolescents. *Journal of Child and Adolescent Counseling*, *1*, 51–65. doi:10.1080/23727810.2015.1079116

Maggin, D. M., Zurheide, J., Pickett, K. C., & Baillie, S. J. (2015). A systematic review of the check-in/check-out program for reducing student challenging behaviors. *Journal of Positive Behavior Interventions*, *17*, 197–208. doi:10.1177/1098300715573630

Majeika, C. E., Van Camp, A. M., Wehby, J. H., Kern, L., Commisso, C. E., & Gaier, K. (2020). An evaluation of adaptations made to Check-In Check-Out. *Journal of Positive Behavior Interventions*, *22*, 25–37.

Mathews, S., McIntosh, K., Frank, J. L., & May, S. L. (2014). Critical features predicting sustained implementation of school-wide positive behavior support. *Journal of Positive Behavior Interventions*, *16*, 168–178.

McDaniel, S. C., & Bruhn, A. L. (2016). Using a changing-criterion design to evaluate the effects of check-in/check-out with goal modification. *Journal of Positive Behavior Interventions*, *18*(4), 197–208. doi:10.1177/10983300715588263

McIntosh, K., Ellwood, K., McCall, L., & Girvan, E. J. (2018). Using discipline data within a PBIS framework to enhance equity in school discipline. *Intervention in School and Clinic, 53,* 146–152.

McIntosh, K., Filter, K. J., Bennett, J. L., Ryan, C., & Sugai, G. (2010). Principles of sustainable prevention: Designing scale-up of school-wide positive behavior support to promote durable systems. *Psychology in the Schools, 47,* 5–21. doi:10.1002/pits.20448

McIntosh, K., Fisher, E. S., Kennedy, K. S., Craft, C. B., & Morrison, G. M. (2012). Using office discipline referrals and school exclusion data to assess school discipline. In S. R. Jimerson, A. B. Nickerson, M. J. Mayer, & M. J. Furlong (Eds.), *Handbook of school violence and school safety: International research and practice* (2nd ed., pp. 305–315). New York: Routledge.

McIntosh, K., Gion, C., & Bastable, E. (2018). *Do schools implementing SWPBIS have decreased racial disproportionality in school discipline?* PBIS evaluation brief. Eugene, OR: OSEP TA Center on Positive Behavioral Interventions and Supports.

McIntosh, K., Girvan, E. J., Horner, R. H., & Smolkowski, K. (2014). Education not incarceration: A conceptual model for reducing racial and ethnic disproportionality in school discipline. *Journal of Applied Research on Children, 5*(2), 1–22.

McIntosh, K., & Goodman, S. (2016). *Integrated multi-tiered systems of support: Blending RTI and PBIS.* New York: Guilford Press.

McIntosh, K., Horner, R. H., & Sugai, G. (2009). Sustainability of systems-level evidence-based practices in schools: Current knowledge and future directions. In W. Sailor, G. Dunlap, G. Sugai, & R. H. Horner (Eds.), *Handbook of positive behavior support* (pp. 327–352). New York: Springer Publishing Co.

McIntosh, K., Kelm, J. L., & Canizal Delabra, A. (2016). In search of how principals change: A qualitative study of events that help and hinder administrator support for school-wide PBIS. *Journal of Positive Behavior Interventions, 18,* 100–110. doi:10.1177/1098300715599960

McIntosh, K., Lucyshyn, J. M., Strickland-Cohen, M. K., & Horner, R. H. (2015). Building supportive environments: Toward a technology for enhancing fidelity of implementation. In F. Brown, J. Anderson, & R. L. DePry (Eds.), *Individual positive behavior supports: A standards-based guide to practices in school and community-based settings* (pp. 401–415). Baltimore, MD: Brookes.

McIntosh, K., Mercer, S. H., Hume, A. E., Frank, J. L., Turri, M. G., & Mathews, S. (2013). Factors related to sustained implementation of schoolwide positive behavior support. *Exceptional Children, 79,* 293–311.

McIntosh, K., Mercer, S. H., Nese, R. N. T., Strickland-Cohen, M. K., Kittelman, A., Hoselton, R., & Horner, R. H. (2018). Factors predicting sustained implementation of a universal behavior support framework. *Educational Researcher, 47,* 307–316.

McIntosh, K., Sadler, C., & Brown, J. A. (2012). Kindergarten reading skill level and change as risk factors for chronic problem behavior. *Journal of Positive Behavior Interventions, 14,* 17–28. doi:10.1177/1098300711403153

Miller, M. A., Fenty, N., Scott, T. M., & Park, K. L. (2011). An examination of social skills instruction in the context of small-group reading. *Remedial and Special Education, 32,* 371–381. doi:10.1177/0741932510362240

O'Neill, R. E., Albin, R. W., Storey, K., Horner, R. H., & Sprague, J. R. (2015). *Functional assessment and program development.* Ontario: Nelson Education.

Ryan, J. B., Pierce, C. D., & Mooney, P. (2008). Evidence-based teaching strategies for students with EBD. *Beyond Behavior, 17*(3), 22–29.

Sugai, G., & Horner, R. H. (2009). Defining and describing schoolwide positive behavior support. In W. Sailor, G. Dunlap, G. Sugai, R. Horner, W. Sailor, G. Dunlap, & R. Horner (Eds.), *Handbook of positive behavior support* (pp. 307–326). New York, NY: Springer Publishing Co. doi:10.1007/978-0-387-09632-2_13

Swoszowski, N. C., McDaniel, S. C., Jolivette, K., & Melius, P. (2013). The effects of tier II check-in/check-out including adaptation for non-responders on the off-task behavior of elementary students in a residential setting. *Education and Treatment of Children, 36,* 63–79.

Turtura, J. E., Anderson, C. M., & Boyd, R. J. (2014). Addressing task avoidance in middle school students: Academic behavior check-in/check-out. *Journal of Positive Behavior Interventions*, *16*(3), 159–167. doi:10.1177/1098300713484063

Waasdorp, T. E., Bradshaw, C. P., & Leaf, P. J. (2012). The impact of schoolwide positive behavioral interventions and supports on bullying and peer rejection. *Archives of Pediatrics & Adolescent Medicine*, *166*, 149–156.

Walker, H. M., Horner, R. H., Sugai, G., Bullis, M., Sprague, J. R., Bricker, D., & Kaufman, M. J. (1996). Integrated approaches to preventing antisocial behavior patterns among school-age children and youth. *Journal of Emotional and Behavioral Disorders*, *4*, 194–209.

Walker, H. M., Nishioka, V. M., Zeller, R., Severson, H. H., & Feil, E. G. (2000). Causal factors and potential solutions for the persistent underidentification of students having emotional or behavioral disorders in the context of schooling. *Assessment for Effective Intervention*, *26*(1), 29–39.

Wehby, J., & Kern, L. (2014). Intensive behavior intervention: What is it, what is its evidence base, and why do we need to implement now? *Teaching Exceptional Children*, *46*, 38–44.

15 BEST in CLASS

A Tier-2 Program for Children with and at Risk for Emotional/Behavioral Disorders

Kevin S. Sutherland, Maureen A. Conroy, and Kristen Granger

Recent estimates suggest that 5% to 25% of young children exhibit problem behavior consistent with emotional/behavioral disorders (EBD; Brauner & Stephens, 2006), with the prevalence of EBD ranging from 4.3% to 11.5% across a number of studies (Ringeisen et al., 2017). While problem behaviors can range from difficulties such as attending to classroom activities and completing tasks to increasingly consequential problem behaviors (e.g., aggressive, destructive, and/or behaviors that are harmful to self and others), it is clear that the presence of EBDs has a significant impact on children's ability to fully benefit from educational experiences (Myers & Pianta, 2008). To illustrate, many children with and at risk for EBD are not prepared to succeed in school and also have difficulty in academic skills related to school success (Howes et al., 2008). Even for those students who do not exhibit early academic skill deficits, the presence of problem behaviors increases the likelihood of long-term academic and behavioral problems (Kellam, Ling, Merisca, Brown, & Ialongo, 1998; O'Connor, Dearing, & Collins, 2011; Spilt, Koomen, Thijs, & van der Leij, 2012). As such, teachers (Reinke et al., 2011) and principals (Grimes, 2018) identify addressing the social, emotional, and behavioral needs of students in preschool through elementary school as one of their most pressing needs.

The purpose of this chapter is to describe an intervention, Behavioral, Emotional, Social Skills Training: Competent Learners Achieving School Success (BEST in CLASS; Conroy et al., 2015; Sutherland et al., 2018), that trains and coaches teachers to implement evidence-based practices during ongoing classroom instruction with children (grades PK – 3) with and at risk for EBD. Below we describe the need for Tier 2 intervention programs for children with and at risk for EBD as well as the promise for programs that target improvements in teacher–child interactions. We then discuss how BEST in CLASS is designed to overcome implementation challenges via leveraging naturally occurring opportunities for intervention presented within classrooms, in particular by targeting instructional practices that teachers may already be using. Last, we describe the BEST in CLASS intervention model and share research findings from both early childhood and elementary school samples and finish with a discussion of implications for practice.

Need for Tier 2 Programs for Children with and at Risk for EBD

Multi-tiered systems of support (MTSS), which can be used to coordinate the delivery of services to individual as well as groups of children, serves as a framework for addressing the behavioral and learning needs of children in many schools (Horner, Sugai, & Anderson,

2010). A central tenet of MTSS is that standard and universal evidenced-based practices (i.e., Tier 1) are generally effective for the majority of children in classrooms (i.e., 80%). When children are not responsive to these universal practices they likely need more intensive forms of intervention (Tier 2; Cook & Odom, 2013; Danielson & Rosenquist, 2014). In turn, for children not responding to Tier 2 interventions, even more targeted and intensive intervention (Tier 3) is warranted. Given the intensive needs of children with or at risk for EBD, Tier 2 (and in some cases, Tier 3) interventions are particularly necessary to help these children learn the skills needed to successfully navigate their early school experience as well as create learning contexts that are more supportive of their specialized learning needs.

Importance of Teacher–Child Interactions and Relationships

While the topography of problem behavior in classrooms can vary greatly, both within the same child and between children, what is clear is the impact children's problem behavior has on interactions and relationships between teachers and children in the classroom. To illustrate, teachers of students with EBD frequently report low confidence in their ability to manage problem behavior (Conroy, Alter, Boyd, & Bettini, 2014). Teachers who feel less secure in their ability to manage student behaviors also report experiencing more negative attitudes and callous feelings toward their students (compared to teachers with higher behavior management efficacy; Brouwers & Tomic, 2000; Garcia-Ros, Fuentes, & Fernandez, 2015; Kokkinos, 2007). This may explain, in part, why students who exhibit problem behaviors face an increased risk for negative interactions and low quality relationships with their teachers as well as social adjustment problems (e.g., peer rejection) with peers (Hendrickx, Mainhard, Boor-Klip, Cillessen, & Brekelmans, 2016; Hughes, Im, & Wehrly, 2014). In turn, this may place children with and at risk for EBD at an increased risk for poor developmental trajectories and school failure; research suggests that the proximal nature of student–teacher interactions predicts greater growth in students' academic achievement than other more distal processes, such as the education and training of teachers (Early et al., 2006).

Both negative reinforcement (Gunter & Coutinho, 1997) and the transactional nature of social interchanges (Sutherland & Oswald, 2005) are posited as theoretical explanations for the negative interaction patterns between teachers and children with and at risk for EBD. That is, the challenges presented by children with problem behavior likely result in these children receiving lower rates of desired teacher instructional practices, which can contribute to increased likelihood of problem behavior and academic failure (Sutherland & Oswald, 2005). For instance, in classrooms where teachers struggle to manage child behavior, negative interactions between teachers and children contribute to documented low rates of positive teacher attention (e.g., academic interactions, teacher praise, and opportunities to respond) received by children with and at risk for EBD (e.g., Van Acker, Grant, & Henry, 1996; Wehby, Symons, & Shores, 1995). Unfortunately, negative interaction patterns between teachers and children tend to persist across time (Henricsson & Rydell, 2004; O'Connor, 2010), highlighting the need for interventions that improve teacher–child interactions as these interventions may be particularly relevant and helpful for children who enter school demonstrating problem behavior. Thus, interventions designed to reduce negative teacher–child interactions for young children with chronic problem behavior are necessary to improve the teaching and learning environment for both teachers and their children, and ultimately to improve child social, behavioral, and academic outcomes.

Leveraging Opportunities to Maximize Impact

While focusing on increasing the quality of teacher–child interactions is important for improving the outcomes of children with and at risk for EBD, implementation challenges exist (Domitrovich, Gest, Jones, Gill, & DeRousie, 2010; Durlak, 2010). Recognizing and overcoming implementation challenges is also important as prior work suggests social-emotional learning programs that are implemented with high quality have effect sizes up to twice as large as those implemented with low quality for a variety of outcomes, including academic skills and conduct problems (Durlak, Weissberg, Dymnicki, Taylor, & Schellinger, 2011). A number of factors have been identified (see Domitrovich et al., 2008; Durlak, 2016) that affect program implementation, and among these are several that have implications for teacher interventions targeting improving interactions with children with chronic problem behavior.

Two factors associated with program implementation that have been identified in the literature include: (1) characteristics of those implementing the program, and (2) characteristics of the program being implemented (Durlak, 2016). In regards to individuals' characteristics, factors such as perceived need for the program, self-efficacy, and possession of a minimum skill level are identified as critically important for successful implementation. For the characteristics of the program itself, factors such as compatibility of the program with a school's mission and adaptability of the program were both identified as important for program success. With these two factors in mind, programs that have a focus on enhancing teachers' use of practices already in their instructional repertoire (i.e., practices representing both academic instruction and classroom management) during ongoing classroom instruction have particular promise for impacting the learning experience of children with and at risk for EBD.

To illustrate, recent research has found that there are common practice elements, or active ingredients, within evidence-based programs targeting social, emotional, and behavioral outcomes of young children (McLeod et al., 2017) and elementary-aged children (Sutherland, Conroy, McLeod, Kunemund et al., 2019). Each of these research syntheses identified 24 practice elements common across evidence-based programs and interventions delivered by teachers, with 12 of the practices (e.g., praise, opportunities to respond) common across both targeted age ranges (i.e., preschool or elementary school) and 12 unique to each. Further, many of the practices included in these reviews have been observed in classrooms including children with and at risk for EBD (e.g., Reinke, Herman, & Stormont, 2013; Sutherland, Wehby & Yoder, 2002; Wehby et al., 1995). The identification of these practices has implications for addressing implementation challenges, as descriptive work has shown that teachers are already using many of them in their instruction with children who are at risk for or have EBD, although the extensiveness and quality of delivery of the practices remains an open question. Thus, if teachers are already using these practices they may be more likely to see the need for an intervention program comprised of these practices, and potentially demonstrate some efficacy at baseline for delivering the practices. In addition, intervention programs made up of these practices may be more likely to be compatible with a school's mission and be potentially adaptable for the needs of their children. This would help address two of the factors (i.e., characteristics of those implementing a program and characteristics of the program being implemented) associated with high quality implementation identified by Durlak (2016).

While overcoming implementation challenges is one way to increase the impact of programs and practices on the outcomes of children with and at risk for EBD, targeting improvements in teacher–child interactions also requires maximum flexibility of the practices being implemented. That is, teachers and children have multiple opportunities to interact with each other across a variety of contexts each day. Therefore, practices flexible enough to be used by teachers during various activities (e.g., one–one instruction, small or whole-class group instruction, transitions between activities, recess), when implemented with fidelity (i.e., extensively and with high quality; Sutherland, Conroy, Vo, & Ladwig, 2015), have tremendous promise at improving teacher–child interactions and ultimately improving child outcomes. BEST in CLASS, which was designed for maximum feasibility of implementation and impact, trains and coaches teachers to embed evidence-based practices during ongoing classroom instructional activities at an increased dosage, intentionality, and high quality with children with and at risk for EBD.

BEST in CLASS

BEST in CLASS (Conroy et al., 2015; Sutherland et al., 2018) is a theoretically informed Tier 2 classroom-based intervention founded upon evidence-based instructional practice elements that target the chronic problem behaviors of children with and at risk for EBD. A "value-added" model, BEST in CLASS targets increasing the dosage, quality, and intentionality of specific instructional practices delivered by teachers with focal children in the classroom who are at risk for EBD with the goals of improving teacher–child interactions and preventing and reducing the occurrence of their chronic problem behaviors. Because the professional development needs of teachers and developmental needs of children change from preschool to elementary school (see Sutherland, Conroy, McLeod, Granger et al., 2019), two versions of BEST in CLASS have been developed: one for preschool age children (BEST in CLASS – PK) and one for young elementary students (BEST in CLASS – E; Kindergarten–3rd grade). Below we describe the theoretical foundation of BEST in CLASS, followed by a description of the three BEST in CLASS components that support implementation: teacher workshop, teacher resource manual, and practice-based coaching. Next, we discuss the practices that comprise the two versions of BEST in CLASS as well as initial findings from studies examining the efficacy of the BEST in CLASS model. We finish the chapter with a discussion of implications for practice.

Theoretical Framework

The BEST in CLASS theoretical framework (see Figure 15.1) integrates three theories that capture how teacher and child behavior influences each other over time. First, behavioral theory (Skinner, 1954) is represented by the inner oval; within this oval are the three-term contingencies that represent learning interactions between teachers and children (e.g., teacher delivery of an opportunity to respond [A], child response [B], teacher feedback [C]). The larger outer oval represents Bronfenbrenner's (1979, 2005) ecological model, in this case the broader classroom context within which these teacher–child interactions occur. Finally, the arrows within the ovals represent Sameroff's (1983, 1995) transactional theory, suggesting that teacher–child interactions within classrooms influence each other in a reciprocal manner. The repeating ovals and darkening arrow represent the potential strengthening of these interaction patterns across time, a pattern that BEST in CLASS seeks to enhance in a positive manner via the increase of positive teacher–child interactions.

Teacher Workshop

The BEST in CLASS teacher workshop is comprised of didactic and interactive learning activities and is delivered via a 6-hour in-service day. The purpose of the workshop is to provide teachers with introductory knowledge and awareness of the BEST in CLASS

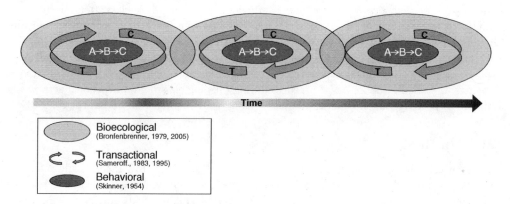

Figure 15.1 BEST in CLASS Theoretical Framework

intervention, including the practices and the practice-based coaching. Workshop topics include describing the need for early Tier-2 programs, such as BEST in CLASS, providing an overview of the BEST in CLASS practices, using video exemplars of teacher implementation of practices, knowledge check activities, and opportunities to role-play practices with coaches. During the workshop, teachers are provided with the teacher resource manual.

Teacher Resource Manual

The BEST in CLASS teacher resource manual summarizes the primary content of the training and serves as a framework for the skill acquisition and mastery that is supported by 14 weeks of manualized practice-based coaching. The manual includes detailed descriptions of the BEST in CLASS practices, implementation tips and forms that the teachers use to communicate and partner with families. Coaches refer to the teacher manual with teachers during their coaching meetings to help ensure the highest quality implementation possible.

Practice-based Coaching

The BEST in CLASS practice-based coaching model is adapted from the model developed by Snyder, Hemmeter, and Fox (2015). Trained coaches meet weekly with teachers following the teacher workshop to support implementation of the BEST in CLASS practices with focal students who have been identified as at risk for EBD (see Sutherland et al., 2015 for a detailed description of the coaching process). Coaches and teachers collaboratively plan goals and develop an action plan, using data collected from the coach's focused observation of the teacher delivering BEST in CLASS practices with focal children during classroom instructional activities. Teachers and coaches then reflect on the teachers' use of the practices and the coach provides performance feedback on the quantity and quality of the teacher's use and delivery of the practices. Coaches follow a cycle during each coaching meeting that involves facilitated instruction of the practice, collaboratively developing goals and action planning, guided practice (i.e., modeling or role-playing), teacher reflection on the use of the practice, a focused observation by the coach of the teacher using the practice, and coach's reflection and performance feedback on the teacher's use of the practice. Coaches use a variety of means to provide feedback to teachers including direct observation data, graphs

BEST in CLASS   219

of teacher implementation of the practices and child behavior, video examples from teacher's implementation, and follow-up emails and text messages summarizing the outcomes of the coaching meeting. Finally, coaches also support teachers' communication and partnerships with families of the focal children.

Overview of the BEST in CLASS Practices

BEST in CLASS – PK Practices

BEST in CLASS – PK is comprised of seven teacher learning modules that are delivered throughout the practice-based coaching. Each module is linked to one of six practices and is delivered over a 2-week period (see Table 15.1 for a description of the practices). The first module reintroduces the teacher to BEST in CLASS and includes guidelines and strategies for creating and implementing developmentally appropriate classroom *rules*, defined as behavioral expectations and activity-based routines. The second module focuses on *precorrection*

Table 15.1 BEST in CLASS practices and definitions

Practice	Definition	BEST in CLASS – PK	BEST in CLASS – E
Rules	Teacher provides intentional instruction to teach the focal child the rules and behavioral expectations of specific classroom activities	X	X
Behavior specific praise	Teacher uses verbal approval of desirable focal child behavior that specifies the behavior	X	X
Precorrection	Teacher uses statements or prompts (i.e., gestural, verbal, visual, physical) that orient the focal child to a setting or task by explaining desired behavior or correct responding *before* starting a task or entering a new setting	X	X
Opportunities to respond	Teacher uses questions or prompts (i.e., gestural, verbal, visual, physical) that seek an active, observable, and specific response from the focal child	X	X
Corrective feedback	Teacher provides corrective feedback following an incorrect response or undesirable behavior demonstrated by the focal child	X	
Instructive feedback	Teacher provides extra instructional information following a correct response or appropriate behavior of focal child	X	
Supportive relationships	Teacher engages in verbal and non-verbal behavior(s) that conveys warmth, closeness, and interest when listening to and interacting directly with the focal child		X

and teaches preventive strategies for addressing predictable social-behavioral and pre-academic errors. The third module provides information on using brisk instructional pacing including the presentation of frequent, varied, high quality social-behavioral and pre-academic *opportunities to respond* to increase engagement and reduce problem behavior. The fourth module targets the use of high quality *behavior specific praise* to reinforce appropriate child responses and behavior and promote positive teacher–child interactions. Module five focuses on using *corrective feedback* with children. That is, providing children information about what they might have done that was not correct and additional information about the correct response. *Instructive feedback*, which extends learning, is the focus of the sixth module. The final module, linking and mastery, targets helping teachers proficiently link together practices during ongoing classroom instruction.

BEST in CLASS – E Practices

BEST in CLASS – E also includes seven teacher learning modules, including five evidence-based practices that support focal students' learning and engagement. Following a brief introduction, the first module details the *home–school partnership* component. Teachers learn about the importance of forming partnerships with families of students with and at risk for EBD and are guided through the framework that supports this component of the intervention. In addition, this component is embedded in the remaining modules to support partnering with families throughout implementation. The second module focuses on helping teachers use *supportive relationships* with their focal students. Embedded in *supportive relationships* is helping teachers learn about the importance of emotion regulation and how to promote and support focal children during ongoing instruction in the classroom. The third module includes guidelines and strategies for creating and implementing developmentally appropriate classroom *rules*, context-specific expectations, and daily and activity-based routines. The fourth module focuses on *precorrection* and teaches preventive strategies for addressing predictable social-behavioral and academic errors. The fifth module targets the use of high quality *praise* to reinforce appropriate child responding and behavior and promote positive teacher–student interactions. The sixth module provides information on the presentation of frequent, varied, high quality social-behavioral and academic *opportunities to respond* to increase engagement and reduce problem behavior. The final module, linking and mastery, targets helping teachers proficiently link together practices during ongoing classroom instruction.

Several studies have examined the efficacy and influence of BEST in CLASS on a variety of teacher and child outcomes. Below we describe findings from studies examining the effects of BEST in CLASS – PK on teacher and child outcomes and will next describe findings from a study examining the effect of BEST in CLASS – E on teacher and child outcomes.

Empirical Support for BEST in CLASS

BEST in CLASS – PK

BEST in CLASS – PK has demonstrated efficacy at improving desirable teacher behaviors as well as reducing focal children's problem behaviors and increasing their desirable outcomes. Conducted with 186 teachers and 465 children, results from an efficacy trial, which employed a multi-site cluster randomized design (Spybrook & Raudenbush, 2009), indicated significant increases in teachers' use of instructional practices, self-efficacy, and overall classroom quality (Conroy et al., 2019). To illustrate, effect sizes ranged from .50 to .75 on the four subscales of the *Teacher Efficacy Beliefs Scale* (Dellinger, Bobbett, Olivier, & Ellett, 2008), and .54 to .78 on the three subscales of the *Teacher Self-Efficacy Scale* (Tschannen-Moran & Hoy, 2001). Overall classroom quality also improved in BEST in CLASS classrooms, with effect sizes of .58 for *Classroom Organization*, .47 for *Emotional Support* and .65 for *Instructional Support* as measured by the *Classroom Assessment Scoring System* (Pianta, La Paro, & Hamre, 2008).

In addition to positive effects for teachers, research has also shown reductions in problem behavior and improvements in teacher–child interactions and relationships (Sutherland et al., 2018). Improvements in observed child behavior noted in Conroy et al. (2014) are supported by teachers' reports of decreased problem behavior ($ES = -.42$ on *Social Skills Improvement System – Rating Scale* [SSIS-RS; Gresham & Elliott, 2008]) and externalizing problems ($ES = -.42$ on *Caregiver Teacher Report Form* [C-TRF; Achenbach & Rescorla, 2000]) associated with BEST in CLASS. Teacher–child relationships also improved in the BEST in CLASS condition, with effect sizes of .26 for the Closeness scale and –.29 for the Conflict scale as measured by the *Student–Teacher Relationship Scale* (Pianta & Hamre, 2001). Teacher–child interactions as measured by the *Teacher–Child Interactions Direct Observation System* (Sutherland, Conroy, Abrams, Vo & Ogston, 2013) also improved in the BEST in CLASS condition, with effects sizes of .45 and –.43 for positive and negative interactions, respectively. Finally, Conroy, Sutherland, Algina, Werch, and Ladwig (2018) investigated the clinical implications from the efficacy trial and found that 42% to 78% of children in the BEST in CLASS condition with clinical or borderline scores on the C-TRF at pretest had scores within the normal range at posttest, and 49% to 61% of the children in the BEST in CLASS condition with clinical or borderline scores on the SSIS-RS at pretest had posttest scores in the normal range. In sum, findings from research on BEST in CLASS – PK indicate positive effects across a variety of teacher and child measures.

BEST in CLASS – E

A small randomized controlled trial was conducted as part of the intervention development project in which BEST in CLASS – PK was adapted to support implementation in early elementary classrooms. Twenty-six teachers ($n = 14$ in BEST in CLASS condition) and 45 children ($n = 25$ in BEST in CLASS condition) participated in this study. Similar to the findings from the BEST in CLASS – PK study, teachers in the BEST in CLASS condition benefited from the program, with reductions in emotional exhaustion (ES = -.35) in comparison to teachers in the business-as-usual condition. Students in the BEST in CLASS condition also benefited, with an effect size for problem behavior as rated by teachers on the SSIS of –.32. Also consistent with findings from the previous work on BEST in CLASS, effect sizes of .55 and –.18 were noted for the *Closeness* and *Conflict* scales, respectively, on the STRS. In summary, findings from previous research on BEST in CLASS in both early childhood and elementary schools signal this model may be an effective intervention for improving outcomes for children with and at risk for EBD and their teachers.

Implications for Practice

Findings from studies examining the effect of BEST in CLASS on both teacher and child outcomes in preschool and elementary school suggest the efficacy and promise of the intervention for early childhood teachers and children. Findings also inform practice as it relates to Tier-2 interventions for young children and students with and at risk for EBD, and in particular to efforts to improve teacher–child interactions. Below we will focus on three unique aspects of BEST in CLASS that promote implementation and might inform other efforts for implementing teacher-delivered interventions.

First, the value-added nature of BEST in CLASS would appear to support implementation, therefore contributing to teachers' ability to implement BEST in CLASS practices at a high quality and to embed them during naturally occurring instructional activities. As mentioned earlier, many of the practices that comprise BEST in CLASS are part of typical practice delivered by teachers; BEST in CLASS trains and coaches teachers to implement these practices with identified focal children with increased frequency (adherence) and quality (competence). Figure 15.2 illustrates observed adherence and competence at pretest, posttest, and maintenance for BEST in CLASS and business-as-usual conditions in the BEST in CLASS – PK study. These data show that teachers were, to some degree, using BEST in CLASS practices at pre-test prior to training and coaching; in essence the training and coaching of BEST in CLASS resulted in increased adherence and competence of delivery of the practices. We would hypothesize therefore that teachers are better able to implement practices they are already comfortable implementing, such as those in BEST in CLASS, with fidelity via training and coaching. Leveraging these existing evidence-based practices in intervention development and implementation has promise, versus attempting to train and coach teachers in new, unfamiliar practices that may require more time and effort to master. With this in mind targeted efforts to increase teachers' use of evidence-based practices that are naturally occurring in classrooms (e.g., praise, opportunities to respond) would appear to be a promising approach to improving the outcomes of students with and at risk for EBD.

Second, BEST in CLASS targets improvements in teacher–child interactions by increasing teachers' use and competence of delivery of BEST in CLASS practices associated with positive child outcomes. The flexibility of the practices embedded within BEST in CLASS allows teachers to use them throughout the school day during regularly scheduled classroom activities with focal children, increasing the number of opportunities to increase positive interactions between teachers and children. To illustrate, as opposed to a more targeted Tier 2 or Tier 3 program that is delivered in a small group or one-to-one by another professional

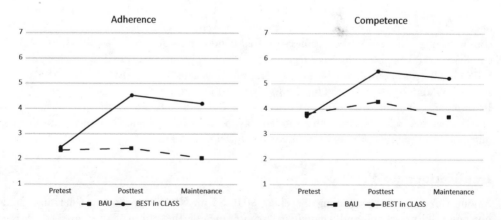

Figure 15.2 Adherence to and competence of delivery

or is delivered in a pull-out session, teachers are trained and coached to deliver BEST in CLASS practices at any time during the school day when problem behavior might occur. Therefore, teachers can prevent problem behavior from occurring by reminding a child of the rules at the beginning of language arts, precorrect a child behavior prior to transition to lunch, or provide increased opportunities to respond if the child begins to be off task during math. The flexibility and usability of BEST in CLASS across different contexts may therefore lead to a higher dose of program exposure, strengthening the overall impact of the intervention. As a result, interventions that target improvements of teacher–child interactions across a variety of activities throughout the school day may hold particular promise for improving child outcomes.

That said, for children to fully benefit from high-fidelity implementation of BEST in CLASS practices throughout the school day teachers must become proficient in delivering the practices with competence. This requires teachers to be responsive to the needs of the focal children, time delivery of the practice for maximum effectiveness, and use developmentally appropriate language, among other indicators of quality implementation (Sutherland, McLeod, Conroy, & Cox, 2013). For teachers to achieve this level of proficiency requires intensive professional development support beyond typical one-time trainings. As highlighted in Sutherland et al. (2015), teachers in the BEST in CLASS – PK study did not begin to significantly increase their adherence or competence of delivery until the practice-based coaching began. Therefore, efforts to increase teacher delivery of evidence-based practices, particularly with adherence and competence towards children with and at risk for EBD during ongoing classroom and school activities, would appear to require a systematic approach to coaching that supports teachers' development of proficiency.

Conclusion

Research consistently indicates that many children enter school demonstrating chronic problem behaviors that result in negative interaction patterns with their teachers who often are poorly prepared to teach children with behavioral problems. The relationships children with chronic problem behavior have with their teachers, and, more proximally, the ongoing interactions they have with their teachers, impacts their educational outcomes. Therefore, interactions with teachers can be viewed as either risk or protective factors. When teachers and children have strong, positive relationships characterized by positive interactions, these relationships can serve as a protective barrier, minimizing the risks and potential development of behavioral difficulties and school failure. However, when these interactions are coercive and or highly conflictual, the relationship may become a risk factor that contributes to the development or persistence of children's learning and behavior problems. Thus, the early school years appear to be a key time for interventions targeting high quality teacher–child interactions in school to maximize school success for children with chronic problem behaviors. Furthermore, interventions such as BEST in CLASS that target value-added evidence-based practices that can be delivered throughout the school day by teachers have particular promise at improving the social, behavioral, and academic outcomes of children with and at risk for EBD.

Author Note

This research was supported by grants from the U.S. Department of Education, Institute for Education Sciences (R305A150246; R324A160158). The opinions expressed by the authors are not necessarily reflective of the position of or endorsed by the U.S. Department of Education.

224 *Kevin S. Sutherland et al.*

References

Achenbach, T. M., & Rescorla, L. A. (2000). *CBCL/1, 5-5 & C-TRF/1, 5-5 profiles.* Burlington, VT: Research Center for Children, Youth, and Families. doi: 10.3109/08039480903456595

Brauner, C. B., & Stephens, C. B. (2006). Estimating the prevalence of early childhood serious emotional/behavioral disorders: Challenges and recommendations. *Public Health Reports, 121*(3), 303–310. doi:10.1177/003335490612100314

Bronfenbrenner, U. (1979). *The ecology of human development: Experiments by nature and design.* Cambridge, MA: Harvard University Press.

Bronfenbrenner, U. (2005). *Making human beings human: Bioecological perspectives on human development.* Thousand Oaks, CA: Sage Publications.

Brouwers, A., & Tomic, W. (2000). A longitudinal study of teacher burnout and perceived self-efficacy in classroom management. *Teaching and Teacher Education, 16*(2), 239–253. doi:10.1016/S0742-051X(99)00057-8

Conroy, M. A., Alter, P., Boyd, B., & Bettini, E. (2014). Teacher preparation for students who demonstrate challenging behaviors. In P. T. Sindelar, E. D. McCray, M. T. Brownell, & B. Lingnugaris/Kraft (Eds.), *Handbook of research on special education teacher preparation* (pp. 320–333). New York: Routledge, Taylor, & Francis.

Conroy, M. A., Sutherland, K. S., Algina, J., Ladwig, C., Werch, B., Martinez, J., ... Gyure, M. (2019). Outcomes of the BEST in CLASS intervention on teachers' use of effective practices, self-efficacy, and classroom quality. *School Psychology Review, 48,* 31–45. doi:10.17105/SPR-2018-0003.V48-1

Conroy, M. A., Sutherland, K. S., Algina, J., Werch, B., & Ladwig, C. (2018). Prevention and treatment of externalizing problem behaviors in young children: Clinical implications from a randomized controlled trial of BEST in CLASS. *AERA Open, 4*(1), 1–16. doi:10.1177/2332858417750376

Conroy, M. A., Sutherland, K. S., Wilson, R. E., Martinez, J., Whalon, K. J., & Algina, J. (2015). Measuring teacher implementation of the BEST in CLASS intervention program and corollary child outcomes. *Journal of Emotional and Behavioral Disorders, 23,* 144–155. doi:10.1177/1063426614532949

Cook, B. G., & Odom, S. L. (2013). Evidence based practices and implementation science in special education. *Exceptional Children, 79,* 135–144. doi:10.1177/001440291307900201

Danielson, L., & Rosenquist, C. (2014). Introduction to the TEC special issue on data-based individualization. *TEACHING Exceptional Children, 46*(4), 6–12. doi:10.1177/0040059914522965

Dellinger, A. B., Bobbett, J. J., Olivier, D. F., & Ellett, C. D. (2008). Measuring teachers' self-efficacy beliefs: Development and use of the TEBS-self. *Teaching and Teacher Education, 24*(3), 751–766. doi:10.1016/j.tate.2007.02.010

Domitrovich, C. E., Bradshaw, C. P., Poduska, J. M., Hoagwood, K., Buckley, J. A., Olin, S., ... Ialongo, N. S. (2008). Maximizing the implementation quality of evidence-based preventive interventions in schools: A conceptual framework. *Advances in School Mental Health Promotion, 1*(3), 6–28. doi:10.1080/1754730X.2008.9715730

Domitrovich, C. E., Gest, S. D., Jones, D., Gill, S., & DeRousie, R. M. S. (2010). Implementation quality: Lessons learned in the context of the head start REDI trial. *Early Childhood Research Quarterly, 25*(3), 284–298. doi:10.1016/j.ecresq.2010.04.001

Durlak, J. A. (2010). The importance of doing well in whatever you do: A commentary on the special section, "Implementation research in early childhood education". *Early Childhood Research Quarterly, 25*(3), 348–357. doi:10.1016/j.ecresq.2010.03.003

Durlak, J. A. (2016). Programme implementation in social and emotional learning: Basic issues and research findings. *Cambridge Journal of Education, 46*(3), 333–345. doi:10.1080/0305764X.2016.1142504

Durlak, J. A., Weissberg, R. P., Dymnicki, A. B., Taylor, R. D., & Schellinger, K. B. (2011). The impact of enhancing students' social and emotional learning: A meta-analysis of school-based universal interventions. *Child Development, 82,* 405–432. doi:10.1111/j.1467-8624.2010.01564.x

Early, D. M., Bryant, D. M., Pianta, R. C., Clifford, R. M., Burchinal, M. R., Ritchie, S., ... Barbarin, O. (2006). Are teachers' education, major, and credentials related to classroom quality and children's academic gains in pre-kindergarten? *Early Childhood Research Quarterly, 21*(2), 174–195. doi:10.1016/j.ecresq.2006.04.004

Garcia-Ros, R., Fuentes, M. C., & Fernandez, B. (2015). Teachers' interpersonal self-efficacy: Evaluation and predictive capacity of teacher burnout. *Electronic Journal of Research in Educational Psychology*, *13*(3), 483–502. doi:10.14204/ejrep.37.14105

Gresham, F. M., & Elliott, S. N. (2008). *Social skills improvement system-rating scales*. Minneapolis, MN: Pearson Assessments.

Grimes, D. (2018). Measuring student SEL can help you target intervention for young learners. *Principal*, *97*(3), 19–21.

Gunter, P., & Coutinho, M. (1997). Negative reinforcement in classrooms: What we're beginning to learn. *Teacher Education and Special Education*, *20*(3), 249–264. doi:10.1177/088840649702000306

Hendrickx, M. M., Mainhard, M. T., Boor-Klip, H. J., Cillessen, A. H., & Brekelmans, M. (2016). Social dynamics in the classroom: Teacher support and conflict and the peer ecology. *Teaching and Teacher Education*, *53*, 30–40. doi:10.1016/j.tate.2015.10.004

Henricsson, L., & Rydell, A. (2004). Elementary school children with behavior problems: Teacher-child relations and self-perception. A prospective study. *Merrill-Palmer Quarterly-Journal of Developmental Psychology*, *50*(2), 111–138.

Horner, R. H., Sugai, G., & Anderson, C. M. (2010). Examining the evidence base for school-wide positive behavior support. *Focus on Exceptional Children*, *42*(8), 1–14.

Howes, C., Burchinal, M., Pianta, R., Bryant, D., Early, D., Clifford, R., & Barbarin, O. (2008). Ready to learn? Children's pre-academic achievement in pre-kindergarten programs. *Early Childhood Research Quarterly*, *23*, 27–50. doi:10.1016/j.ecresq.2007.05.002

Hughes, J. N., Im, M. H., & Wehrly, S. E. (2014). Effect of peer nominations of teacher-student support at individual and classroom levels on social and academic outcomes. *Journal of School Psychology*, *52*, 309–322. doi:10.1016/j.jsp.2013.12.004

Kellam, S. G., Ling, X. G., Merisca, R., Brown, C. H., & Ialongo, N. (1998). The effect of the level of aggression in the first grade classroom on the course and malleability of aggressive behavior into middle school. *Development and Psychopathology*, *10*, 165–185. doi:10.1017/S0954579498001564

Kokkinos, C. M. (2007). Job stressors, personality and burnout in primary school teachers. *British Journal of Educational Psychology*, *77*, 229–243. doi:10.1348/000709905X90344

McLeod, B. D., Sutherland, K. S., Martinez, R. G., Conroy, M. A., Snyder, P. A., & Southam-Gerow, M. A. (2017). Identifying common practice elements to improve social, emotional, and behavioral outcomes of young children in early childhood classrooms. *Prevention Science*, *18*, 204–213. doi:10.1007/s11121-016-0703-y

Myers, S. M., & Pianta, R. C. (2008). Developmental commentary: Individual and contextual influences on student-teacher relationships and children's early problem behaviors. *Journal of Clinical Child and Adolescent Psychology*, *37*(3), 600–608. doi:10.1080/15374410802148160

O'Connor, E. (2010). Teacher–child relationships as dynamic systems. *Journal of School Psychology*, *48*(3), 187–218. doi:10.1016/j.jsp.2010.01.001

O'Connor, E. E., Dearing, E., & Collins, B. A. (2011). Teacher-child relationship and behavior problem trajectories in elementary school. *American Educational Research Journal*, *48*(1), 120–162. doi:10.3102/0002831210365008

Pianta, R. C., & Hamre, B. (2001). *Students, teachers, and relationship support (STRS)*. Lutz, FL: Psychological Assessment Resources.

Pianta, R. C., La Paro, K. M., & Hamre, B. K. (2008). *Classroom assessment scoring system (CLASS) manual, pre-K*. Baltimore, MD: Paul H. Brookes Publishing Company.

Reinke, W. M., Herman, K. C., & Stormont, M. (2013). Classroom-level positive behavior supports in schools implementing PBIS: Identifying areas for enhancement. *Journal of Positive Behavior Interventions*, *15*, 39–50. doi:10.1177/1098300712459079

Reinke, W., Stormont, M., Herman, K., Puri, R., Goel, N., & Kamphaus, R. W. (2011). Supporting children's mental health in schools: Teacher perceptions of needs, roles, and barriers. *School Psychology Quarterly*, *26*(1), 1–13. doi: 10.1037/a0022714

Ringeisen, H., Stambaugh, L., Bose, J., Casanueva, C., Hedden, S., Avenevoli, S., ... West, J. (2017). Measurement of childhood serious emotional disturbance: State of the science and issues for consideration. *Journal of Emotional and Behavioral Disorders, 25*, 195–210. doi:10.1177/1063426616675165

Sameroff, A. J. (1983). Developmental systems: Contexts and evolution. In P. Mussen (Ed.), *Handbook of child psychology* (Vol. 1, pp. 237–294). New York, NY: Wiley.

Sameroff, A. J. (1995). General systems theories and developmental psychopathology. In D. Cicchetti & D. J. Cohen (Eds.), *Wiley series on personality processes. Developmental psychopathology, vol. 1. Theory and methods* (pp. 659–695). Oxford, England: John Wiley & Sons.

Skinner, B. F. (1954). The science of learning and the art of teaching. *Harvard Educational Review, 24*, 86–97.

Snyder, P. A., Hemmeter, M. L., & Fox, L. (2015). Supporting implementation of evidence-based practices through practice-based coaching. *Topics in Early Childhood Special Education, 35*, 133–143. doi:10.1177/0271121415594925

Spilt, J. L., Koomen, H. M., Thijs, J. T., & van der Leij, A. (2012). Supporting teachers' relationships with disruptive children: The potential of relationship-focused reflection. *Attachment & Human Development, 14* (3), 305–318. doi:10.1080/14616734.2012.672286

Spybrook, J., & Raudenbush, S. W. (2009). An examination of the precision and technical accuracy of the first wave of group-randomized trials funded by the Institute of Education Sciences. *Educational Evaluation and Policy Analysis, 31*(3), 298–318. doi:10.3102/0162373709339524

Sutherland, K. S., Conroy, M. A., Algina, J., Ladwig, C., Jessee, G., & Gyure, M. (2018). Reducing child problem behaviors and improving teacher-child interactions and relationships: A randomized controlled trial of BEST in CLASS. *Early Childhood Research Quarterly, 42*, 31–43. doi:10.1016/j.ecresq.2017.08.001

Sutherland, K. S., Conroy, M. A., Abrams, L., Vo, A., & Ogston, P. (2013). An initial evaluation of the Teacher-Child Interaction Direct Observation System: Measuring teacher-child interaction behaviors in classroom settings. *Assessment for Effective Intervention, 39*, 12–23. doi: 10.1177/1534508412463814

Sutherland, K. S., Conroy, M. A., McLeod, B. D., Granger, K., Nemer, S. L., Kunemund, R. L., ... Miles, C. (2019). Adapting an evidence-based early childhood tier 2 program for early elementary school. *Elementary School Journal.* doi:10.1086/703103

Sutherland, K. S., Conroy, M. A., McLeod, B. D., Kunemund, R., & McKnight, K. (2019). Common practice elements for improving social, emotional and behavioral outcomes of young elementary school students. *Journal of Emotional and Behavioral Disorders,* doi:10.1177/1063426618784009

Sutherland, K. S., Conroy, M. A., Vo, A., & Ladwig, C. (2015). Implementation integrity of practice-based coaching: Preliminary results from the BEST in CLASS efficacy trial. *School Mental Health, 7*, 21–33. doi:10.1007/s12310-014-9134-8

Sutherland, K. S., McLeod, B. D., Conroy, M. A., & Cox, J. R. (2013). Measuring treatment integrity in the implementation of evidence-based programs in early childhood settings: Conceptual issues and recommendations. *Journal of Early Intervention, 35*, 129–149. doi:10.1177/1053815113515025

Sutherland, K., & Oswald, D. (2005). The relationship between teacher and student behavior in classrooms for students with emotional and behavioral disorders: Transactional processes. *Journal of Child and Family Studies, 14*(1), 1–14. doi:10.1007/s10826-005-1106-z

Sutherland, K. S., Wehby, J. H., & Yoder, P. J. (2002). Examination of the relation between teacher praise and opportunities for students with EBD to respond to academic requests. *Journal of Emotional and Behavioral Disorders, 10*, 5–13.

Tschannen-Moran, M., & Hoy, A. W. (2001). Teacher efficacy: Capturing an elusive construct. *Teaching and Teacher Education, 17*, 783–805. doi:10.1016/S0742-051X(01)00036-1

Van Acker, R., Grant, S. H., & Henry, D. (1996). Teacher and student behavior as a function of risk for aggression. *Education and Treatment of Children, 19*, 316–334.

Wehby, J. H., Symons, F. J., & Shores, R. E. (1995). A descriptive analysis of aggressive behavior in classrooms for children with emotional and behavioral disorders. *Behavioral Disorders, 20*, 87–105. doi:10.1177/019874299502000207

16 An Adaptive, Correlated Constraints Model of Classroom Management

The Behavioral, Academic, and Social Engagement (BASE) Program

Thomas W. Farmer, Jill Hamm, David Lee, Brittany Sterrett, Karen Rizzo, and Kate Norwalk

Classroom management is fundamental for supporting students with or at risk of emotional and behavioral disorders (EBD: Oliver, Lambert, & Mason, 2017; Owens et al., 2018). Researchers have focused on identifying evidence-based practices (EBPs), promoting their implementation with fidelity in classrooms, and presenting EBPs to practitioners in a scripted manner (Cook et al., 2015). Yet, multiple factors tend to contribute to students' problem behavior (Maggin, Wehby, Farmer, & Brooks, 2016; Wehby, Symons, & Shores, 1995). To promote students' adjustment, it is often necessary to use a combination of strategies, intervene with the student and the context, and adapt EBPs to specific situations and students (Lee, 2018; McDaniel, Bruhn, & Mitchell, 2017). Although there is a tendency to describe EBPs as stand-alone strategies used independent of other interventions, this is often not the case in "real world" practice. Teachers may need to use and adapt multiple strategies to address interconnected domains of student functioning without a guiding framework for such efforts (Ludlow, 2014).

Grounded in a systems perspective of EBD (Cairns & Cairns, 1994; Farmer & Farmer, 2001; Sameroff, 2000), the BASE model was created to address the dynamic, multi-determined aspects of adjustment difficulties by providing a conceptual and practice framework to guide teachers as they manage the behavior of students within the classroom context. We provide an overview of the foundations and development of BASE, summarize intervention components, describe the use and adaptation of BASE to manage classrooms and support students with or at risk of EBD, review empirical support for the BASE model, and consider future directions.

Conceptual Foundations and Development of the BASE Model

The BASE model of classroom management is grounded in three complementary concepts that reflect a dynamic systems perspective of development and adaptation. First, multiple factors and domains of functioning operate as a system of correlated constraints. The term correlated constraints posits that factors within the individual (e.g., self-regulatory capacity, temperament, social-cognitive skills), the social ecology (e.g., family, peer group, classroom, school, neighborhood), and the functioning of the individual tend to become synchronized in ways that support and sustain each other (Farmer & Farmer, 2001; Magnusson & Cairns, 1996). As depicted in Figure 16.1, there are three primary domains of school functioning (i.e., academic, behavioral, and social). As the bidirectional arrows indicate, each domain influences the others. Second, to understand the development and adaptation of behavior, it is

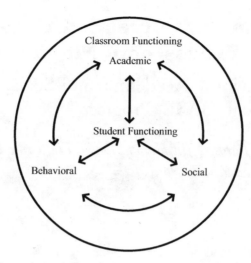

Figure 16.1 Developmental systems/correlated constraints model of classroom/student functioning

important to situate the person-in-context (Bronfenbrenner, 1996). This means it is necessary to consider the relevant characteristics of the student (e.g., academic functioning, social functioning, self-regulation, social history, strengths, and difficulties) and how these factors align and become synchronized with the context. In some cases, the context may evoke and reinforce maladaptive behaviors. Third, when intervening to support new behaviors or adaptation in a specific domain or context, it is important to consider how other relevant domains or contexts may constrain the child's functioning and support the undesired behavior and prevent the consolidation of a newly acquired behavior or skill. Therefore, it is often necessary to go beyond intervening with the antecedents and consequences of the behavior and to also address relevant developmental factors and processes that would otherwise constrain adaptation (Farmer, Gatzke-Kopp, Lee, Dawes, & Talbott, 2016).

The BASE model was developed while working with elementary and middle schools in high poverty rural and urban areas across the United States that included high concentrations of students with aggressive and disruptive behavior, academic difficulties, and social problems. It was developed primarily as a universal intervention but is designed to be adapted to the specific needs of students, contexts, and resources and capacities available to teachers in a process known as directed consultation (Farmer et al., 2018; Motoca et al., 2014). The BASE model is particularly well suited for a Tiered System of Adaptive Support (TSAS) that centers on: (a) identifying the various developmental factors and processes that are operating for a child as a system of correlated constraints, and (b) adapting evidence-based strategies accordingly, both within and across tiers (Farmer, Farmer, Estell, & Hutchins, 2007; Farmer, Gatzke-Kopp, & Latendresse, 2020; Sutherland, Farmer, Kunemund, & Sterrett, 2018).

BASE Intervention Components

Reflecting correlated constraints and person-in-context perspectives (Figure 16.1), the BASE model involves integrating academic, behavioral, and social support strategies to manage the classroom context (Dawes et al., 2019; Farmer, Hamm, Dawes, Barko-Alva, & Cross, 2020; Farmer et al., 2013). It is comprised of three components: Academic Engagement Enhancement (AEE), Competence Enhancement Behavior Management (CEBM), and Social Dynamics Management (SDM).

Academic Engagement Enhancement

The *AEE* component is aimed at creating a context where learning is valued, students support each other, instructional time is protected, and instruction is carefully paced for students who struggle and may become off-task or disruptive without adaptive supports (Gut et al., 2004; Lee, 2006). As academic instruction is the central focus of school classrooms, the AEE component is the foundation of the BASE model and its overarching goal is to create a classroom culture that values learning and reinforces the academic engagement of all students. To accomplish this, the AEE component is organized into three distinct but complementary categories of instructional management strategies (see Table 16.1): academic context management, pacing activities for success, and reinforcing desired behaviors.

Competence Enhancement Behavior Management

The *CEBM* component centers on creating a classroom ecology that reinforces desired behaviors while using problems as opportunities to teach new behaviors (Farmer et al., 2006). This involves managing the classroom, the behavior of students, and the interplay between students and contexts. This requires using evidence-based and data driven practices, but it also involves adapting strategies to balance the needs of specific students and the general classroom ecology (Sutherland et al., 2018; Wehby & Kern, 2014). In addition, it is helpful for teachers to approach behavior management with a positive mindset, to have high expectations for students, to use problems as opportunities to teach desired behaviors, and to communicate to students they are worth taking the time to ensure they learn the skills and behaviors necessary to be successful in the classroom (Farmer et al., 2006; Milner, 2018). It is also important to structure the classroom so there are natural rewards and consequences that promote a sense of community and a mindset that we are all in this together and need to support each other (Farmer et al., 2020). Accordingly, the overarching goal of CEBM is to foster a general classroom climate of productive and supportive behavior and the sustained engagement of students with behavioral difficulties in positive behavior patterns. To accomplish this, the CEBM component is organized into three categories (see Table 16.1): behavioral context management; eliciting and reinforcing desired behavior; and positive behavioral redirection.

Social Dynamics Management

The *SDM* component involves shaping natural social processes to create peer cultures that foster students' academic effort and engagement while promoting positive social roles and relationships for struggling students (Farmer et al., 2018). The SDM component of the BASE model centers on using knowledge of the classroom social system to harness the power of the peer group in the management of the instructional and behavioral context while fostering students' positive social roles and relationships. Classroom social dynamics refers to how classrooms are socially structured and how this structure influences and is influenced by student interactions (Farmer et al., 2018). Students coordinate their behaviors with each

Table 16.1 The BASE Classroom Management Model for Adapting Supports for Students with EBD

Intervention Components	Goal	Aims	Strategies
Academic Engagement™ Enhancement	Promote the productive academic engagement of all students (including students with EBD) by establishing a general classroom climate that values instructional engagement, academic effort, and academic success	• Create a positive and engaged classroom climate • Support a positive peer culture for academic engagement/school valuing • Data driven adaptation of strategies to address individual student academic engagement	*Academic Context Management* • Review instructional rules & expectations • Class routines and rituals • Verbal/visual cues of the value of academic effort/achievement *Pacing Activities for Success* • Routines/cues to start & transition to new activities • Alternative activities • Behavior momentum sequences • Premack schedule *Reinforcing Desired Behaviors* • Opportunities to respond • Academic behavior feedback • Using preferred peers to model & reinforce academic effort • End activity/class with success

| *Competence Enhancement Behavior Management* | Promote positive behavior patterns of all students (including students with EBD) by establishing a general classroom climate of productive and supportive behavior and fostering positive engagement and success of students who have difficulty regulating and coordinating their behavior with others | • Promote productive classroom behavior
• Use EBPs with appropriate frequency and quality
• Data driven adaptation to address individual student behavior needs
• Teachers approach BM to communicate that the student is important | *Behavioral Context Management*

• Review behavioral rules and specific task expectations
• Routines for class activities
• Classroom rituals/goals
• Monitoring/modeling behavior

Elicit/reinforce Desired Behavior

• Goals/prompts/reminders
• Behavior-specific direction/praise
• Use of natural consequences
• Contingencies & rewards

Behavioral Redirection

• Verbal group redirection
• Nonverbal individual redirection
• Proximity management
• Antiseptic bouncing
• Premack schedule
• Positive practice
• Teaching desired behaviors |

(Continued)

Table 16.1 (Cont.)

Intervention Components	Goal	Aims	Strategies
Social Dynamics Management	Promote a classroom climate of peer support for academic engagement and productive behavior and foster a positive peer social system that enhances the social roles and successful relationships of all students including those with EBD	• Reduce social hierarchies and coercive peer groups • Promote positive social roles and relationships for students with EBD • Support culture of peer support and protection against bullying	*Social Context Management* • Attunement to students' social roles, reputations, & peer groups • Rules and expectations for social behaviors and relationships • Model desired social interactions • Monitor/manage social hierarchy *Peer Affiliation and Group Supports* • Seating/proximity arrangements • Grouping strategies • Monitor/support positive intra-group relationships • Monitor support positive inter-group relationships *Managing Students' Roles/Relations* • Monitor social synchrony • Realign negative patterns • Strengthen positive patterns • Promote positive social opportunities and roles for students with EBD • Reframe negative identities

other, sort themselves into peer groups, create social hierarchies, and develop social roles (Adler & Adler, 1998; Ahn & Rodkin, 2014; Trach, Lee, & Hymel, 2018). Although social dynamics are peer driven, teachers can facilitate students' social experiences, opportunities, and roles (Gest, Madill, Zadzora, Miller, & Rodkin, 2014; van den Berg & Stoltz, 2018). The goal of the SDM component is to create a classroom climate of peer support for academic engagement and productive behavior by fostering a positive social system to promote supportive social relationships for all students. The SDM component involves three categories (see Table 16.1): general social context management; monitoring and managing students' peer affiliations and peer group supports; and managing students' social roles and relationships.

The Use and Adaptation of BASE to Manage Classrooms and Support Students

The three components (i.e., AEE, CEBM, SDM) and corresponding goals, aims, and strategies of the BASE model are summarized in Table 16.1. The full BASE model can serve as the foundation for managing classrooms in general (see also Farmer et al., 2020) but the focus of this model as outlined in Table 16.1 is to create a classroom context for students with EBD that provides a base for adapting and intensifying interventions to the specific needs and circumstances of students who struggle behaviorally, emotionally, and socially.

It is beyond the scope and purpose of this chapter to go through each component and describe the implementation of each strategy. Rather, our goal is to discuss the general delivery and application of the AEE, CEBM, and SDM components as an integrated model that synergistically leverages the interplay between a system of correlated constraints. Unlike many evidence-based models that are scripted and designed to follow a specific scope and sequence of implementation, BASE is a dynamic model that centers on managing the moment-to-moment aspects of the daily functioning of students and classrooms to foster positive alignment among key developmental factors and the long-term adaptation and adjustment of youth with or at risk of EBD. Next, we describe: (a) teachers' general management of the classroom context and the adaptation of EBPs to students' needs; (b) directed consultation as a framework that intervention specialists (i.e., special educators, school social workers, behavior analysts, counselors, school psychologists, mental health professionals) can use to support teachers as they adapt and intensify strategies across TSAS to promote the adaptation of students with or at risk of EBD; and (c) the scouting report as a data collection process to guide the adaptation of strategies to the circumstances and needs of specific students and classrooms.

Managing Classroom Contexts and Adapting Strategies to Students' Needs

Reflective of dynamic systems and person-in-context perspectives, the BASE model recognizes that classroom management is not a "one size fits all" proposition. Strategies must be adapted to the characteristics of individual students, the classroom composition and culture, the characteristics and strengths of the teacher, the resources and supports available in the school, and the values and expectations of the broader community (Farmer et al., 2013). The BASE model can serve as a TSAS that involves: (a) clarifying the developmental factors and processes that operate as a correlated system at both the individual student and classroom levels; and (b) adapting EBPs to foster the adjustment and productive growth of all students

234   *Thomas W. Farmer et al.*

including those who are at risk for developing EBD and those who have manifested EBD (Farmer et al., 2020; Sutherland et al., 2018). The universal aspects (Tier 1) of BASE involve creating contexts that support the social, emotional, and behavioral growth and adjustment of all students in the moment-to-moment functioning of daily activities; the selected aspects (Tier 2) of BASE involve screening to identify youth who are at risk for the negative reorganization of their developmental systems and adapting and individualizing EBPs to prevent the emergence of a system of negative correlated constraints; and the targeted aspects (Tier 3) of BASE involve screening to identify youth who manifest a system of correlated risks/difficulties across multiple developmental domains and establishing a coordinated system of services aimed at carefully reorganizing the child's developmental system and promoting a trajectory of positive adaptation across various domains (Farmer et al., 2007, 2018, 2020).

As indicated in Table 16.1, the three BASE intervention components (i.e., AEE, CEBM, SDM) have a core focus on managing the context to support students' positive engagement and success. Consistent with a correlated constraints perspective, efforts to manage the context in one domain should not be done in isolation. The use of strategies in each domain should be done with a careful eye toward how they may impact and be impacted by strategies in the other two domains. As teachers review rules, create routines, and develop and implement instructional activities, they should consider how particular instructional efforts impact and are impacted by their strategies to manage the behavioral and social context and how the behavioral and social context may contribute to how students respond to particular instructional approaches. For example, a well-intentioned small group academic activity may have poor results if the teacher does not go beyond explicit academic instruction and include pre-teaching, reviewing necessary behavioral rules, activating relevant routines, taking into consideration group composition, and providing guidance about the roles and interactional dynamics for each person in the group.

BASE Universal (Tier 1) Approaches

At the universal (Tier 1) level, the BASE intervention centers on having routines and supports for all students to help them be successful academically, behaviorally, and socially (see also Emmer & Stough, 2001; Leinhardt, Weidmand, & Hammond, 1987). The goal is to have clear expectations, guidance, and structure for the common activities in the daily schedule while adapting specific strategies for particular students and adjusting strategies depending on changes in moment-to-moment circumstances or events (Long, Morse, Fecser, & Newman, 2007). For example, it is important to have a common routine for starting class. Yet, students with attention or behavior regulation difficulties many need more structure, guidance, and explicit instruction than the class in general. Therefore, the teacher can use a general routine for starting class that everyone knows and understands while creating more individualized routines for struggling students that will help them to start class successfully. This may include having an alternative activity that serves as pre-teaching or review that the struggling student can independently complete with success while the teacher is getting class started (Farmer et al., 2006).

Once class starts, the teacher can go to struggling students and give them individual explicit instruction on the day's activities to ensure their success. For both the general class and for struggling students, it is important to pace and sequence instruction in a manner that keeps students engaged and reinforced for their effort. Strategies such as carefully using opportunities to respond (Haydon et al., 2010; Sutherland, Alder, & Gunter, 2003; Sutherland & Wehby, 2001), behavior momentum (Belfiore, Lee, Scheeler, & Klein, 2002; Knowles, Meng,

& Machalicek, 2015; Lee, 2006), and premack schedules (Billingsley, 2016; Hosie, Gentile, & Carroll, 1974; Long et al., 2007; Premack, 1959) can all be important for fostering a context that positively guides students through instructional activities and helps them to feel as though instructional engagement is not only important, it is something they can do with success.

It is important to help students develop positive mindsets about their ability to complete academic tasks. Self-efficacy for academic success is influenced by whether students view intelligence as a fixed quantity that they either do or do not possess (i.e., a fixed mindset) or a malleable quantity that reflects a growth mindset in which they believe intelligence can be increased or improved with effort and learning (Dweck & Leggett, 1988). Students with fixed mindsets tend to focus on proving their intelligence and when they experience wrong answers may view themselves as "dumb" and give up trying; whereas students with a growth mindset view incorrect responses as opportunities to learn and are resilient when they face academic challenges. Students with fixed mindsets tend to develop performance goals (i.e., prove I'm smart) while those with growth mindsets are likely to have learning goals that involve improving one's ability (Pintrich, 2000). Because students' mindsets and goals impact effort and persistence on instructional tasks, it is important for teachers to foster and reinforce growth mindsets and learning goals as they manage the classroom context (Dweck, Walton, & Cohen, 2014).

Reinforcement of desired behavior is critical for promoting a positive classroom context, but it is a concept that is often misunderstood and applied ineffectively (Shores & Wehby, 1999). Teachers frequently interpret reinforcement to mean giving a student something that is pleasant; something they like or want to have. Reinforcement is a process by which behavior is increased and is "defined objectively by two facts: a contingency between a behavior and its consequences, and a strengthening of the behavior" (Cullinan, Epstein, & Lloyd, 1983, p. 77). Desired behaviors can be reinforced (strengthened or increased) in a variety of ways. The BASE model focuses on increasing desired behaviors by: (a) pacing instruction to promote engagement and success with a variety of strategies (e.g., opportunities to respond, behavior momentum, premack schedules) that guide students to a reinforcing outcome (Billingsley, 2016; Lee, 2006; Sutherland et al., 2003); (b) providing supportive and engaging academic feedback that does not involve telling students whether they have the correct answer but that teaches and motivates students in how to work to get the correct answer (Dweck et al., 2014; Pintrich, 2000); (c) promoting a positive peer culture using preferred peers to model and reinforce effort and achievement and by creating a collective peer group mindset and norms that view learning as valuable and achievable (De-Lade O'Connor, Alvarez, Murray, & Milner, 2017; Hamm, Hoffman, & Farmer, 2012; Wentzel, Muenks, McNeish, & Russell, 2017); and (d) ending specific activities and the class with success (Farmer et al., 2006; Hobbs, 1982; Milner & Tenore, 2010).

BASE Selected (Tier 2) Approaches

At the selected (Tier 2) level, BASE focuses on students who experience problems in a specific domain (i.e., academic, behavioral, social) and who are at risk for developing difficulties in other domains (Farmer et al., 2007). For example, some academically struggling students may engage in problem behavior to avoid public display of their academic difficulties and they may become increasingly noncompliant until teachers negatively reinforce their behavior by not asking them to do work they are unable or unwilling to do (Gunter, Denny, Jack, Shores, & Nelson, 1993). Relatedly, students who classmates perceive as having academic or behavior problems and who are also perceived to be disliked by teachers are more likely to have difficulty developing positive relations with engaged classmates and may develop peer affiliations and social positions that consolidate defiant, disruptive behavior that supports a difficult to manage classroom (Adler & Adler, 1998; Hendrickx, Mainhard, Boor-Klip, Cillessen, & Brekelmans, 2016; Hughes, Im, & Wehrly, 2014; Shores & Wehby, 1999). In short, problems in one domain have the potential to contribute to problems in other domains when teachers are not able to effectively support a student and when they become engaged in patterns of coercive interactions with the student that contribute to the student developing social roles and relationships that maintain difficulties in the academic and behavioral domains (Lee, 2018; Shores, Gunter, & Jack, 1993; Van Acker, Grant, & Henry, 1996; Wehby et al., 1995).

Within a TSAS, the goal of selected (Tier 2) BASE intervention centers on preventing developmental cascades (Masten & Cicchetti, 2010) by stopping problems in one domain from spreading to other domains. Thus, while it is necessary to screen for problems early on, the emphasis is not only on identifying a problem but also on determining whether other domains are involved or are at risk of becoming involved in the problem. To screen for difficulties, teachers can complete brief rating scales on students' academic and interpersonal adaptation and these ratings can be used to identify students who experience distinct profiles or configurations of school functioning that are differentially associated with school adjustment. For example, a recent study using person-oriented analysis of students' adjustment during the middle school transition year (i.e., sixth grade) identified five distinct interpersonal competence patterns (ICPs) that included no-risk, single risk, and multiple risk configurations (Chen et al., 2019). Students in no-risk ICPs tended to report good adjustment during the middle school transition and perceived the school context favorably, students in single risk ICPs reported less favorable adjustment that tended to be associated with their domain of difficulty but many had favorable adjustment and positive perceptions of the school context in other domains, and students in multi-risk ICPs tended to report problems across multiple domains and had unfavorable views of the school context across the academic, behavioral, and social domains. Consistent with these findings and the concept of correlated constraints, person-oriented longitudinal studies have found that no-risk, single-risk, and multi-risk ICPs in childhood and early adolescence are differentially related to students long-term outcomes with multi-risk ICPs being linked to academic failure, suspension and expulsion, school dropout, adolescent criminality, substance use, and teen parenthood (Bergman & Magnusson, 1997; Cairns & Cairns, 1994; Farmer et al., 2004; Janosz, Le Blanc, Boulerice, & Tremblay, 2000; Roeser & Peck, 2003; Xie, Cairns, & Cairns, 2001).

Therefore, selected (Tier 2) BASE interventions are aimed at preventing students who experience difficulties/risk in a single domain from developing a correlated system of difficulties across multiple domains (Farmer et al., 2007). Building upon ICP data, it is helpful to observe the student's functioning in the classroom and the broader school context to determine whether the domain of difficulty is promoting risk in other domains and whether there are strengths and competencies that reduce the student's vulnerability for developing disorder. Ameliorating problems, supporting strengths, and building new competencies and positive social relationships and social roles are all part of the BASE Tier 2 framework. This is a data driven individualized approach that involves identifying developmental process leverage points (i.e., potentially malleable factors that may support positive adaptation in other factors), linking these leverage points to corresponding practice elements of EBPs, adapting and coordinating multiple strategies to address and support multiple factors, collecting ongoing progress monitoring data, and making adaptations to strategies based on data (2020; Farmer et al., 2018). Such a process is likely to require the support of an intervention specialist to help teachers collect data and modify strategies to the needs and circumstances of individual students and the classroom (Farmer et al., 2016; Sutherland et al., 2018). As described below, directed consultation and the scouting report process have been developed to provide intervention specialists with a framework for supporting teachers in the adaptation of BASE across Tiers 1, 2, and 3.

BASE Targeted (Tier 3) Approaches

At the targeted (Tier 3) level, BASE strategies center on promoting the reorganization of a correlated system of developmental risks for youth who have manifested problems that span multiple domains of school functioning (i.e., academic, behavioral, social). The goal is to develop coordinated, intensive, multi-factored interventions that address a system of developmental leverage points, ameliorate the student's functioning and circumstances in correlated problem domains and contexts, build upon strengths to support and sustain new competencies and desired behaviors, and establish both informal (e.g., friendships, peer group, community activities) and formal (e.g., community mental health, social services, health, therapeutic recreation) supports that can bolster and strengthen the child's adaptation (Farmer & Farmer, 2001; Farmer et al., 2007; Farmer, Gatzke-Kopp, Latendresse, 2020).

Tier 3 and Tier 2 are similar, with three critical differences. First, Tier 3 focuses on promoting the positive reorganization of the developmental system of youth who manifest disorder while Tier 2 focuses on preventing the negative reorganization of the developmental system of youth with difficulties in a single domain. Therefore, for Tier 3 intervention, the focus is not on fixing a single problem but rather on promoting positive and coordinated change in multiple domains in ways that will sustain adaptation in each other. Second, youth who have difficulties in multiple domains are likely to have problems that extend beyond school and are manifested in multiple ecologies including the family, neighborhood, and broader community. Difficulties in various ecologies are likely to require supports and interventions that focus on the ecology itself and not just the functioning of the child. Third, because youth who manifest EBD have complex problems that extend across multiple ecologies, they are likely to be involved with or need supports of multiple service sectors including education, special education, mental health, social services, juvenile justice, and community recreation. Therefore, Tier 3 BASE interventions should involve a system of care and the establishment of a coordinated system of informal and agency supports that requires significant progress monitoring and communication aimed at clarifying how strategies in different domains and ecologies may contribute to each other and the overall adaptation of the child (Farmer & Farmer, 2001; Talbott, De Arment, Sterrett, & Chen, 2020).

Directed Consultation

Classroom management is a complex and often difficult process for teachers. The complexity and difficulty are magnified when classrooms have multiple students with or at risk of EBD. It is not feasible to expect general education teachers to effectively manage classrooms with students with or at risk of EBD without support and guidance for adapting and intensifying intervention (Maggin et al., 2016). There is a need for well-trained intervention specialists to provide such support and guidance to general education teachers and there is a corresponding need for a framework to help guide the efforts of intervention specialists in such efforts (Farmer et al., 2016; Talbott et al., 2020).

Directed consultation (DC) is a professional development and coaching model that was created to address this need. Often, there is a concern that schools do not implement EBPs with fidelity. Efforts to address this issue tend to center on getting teachers to adhere to a structured protocol in a lock-step fashion. However, classroom management is a moment-to-moment process and teachers have considerable discretion to address issues in ways that cannot easily be programmed into a structured model. Also, schools often have many ongoing programs and typically teachers do some things well while needing support in other areas. Further, different classrooms and teachers tend to have different competencies, needs, and difficulties.

Within BASE, intervention specialists use DC to train and support teachers in the use and adaptation of the practice elements of EBPs that align with the developmental process needs of their classrooms and students (Farmer et al., 2018). Specifically, DC involves: (a) pre-intervention assessments of the school ecology, individual classroom functioning, and students' needs with a focus on identifying what seems to be working, what is not working, and what is needed to promote success in the classroom; (b) Tier 1 universal professional development in EBP strategies that are aligned and adapted to the schools' characteristics and ongoing programs as well as approaches for adapting intervention to specific students and classrooms; (c) ongoing training, implementation assessment, and clarification of the day-to-day use of specific strategies across Tiers 1, 2, and 3; and (d) consultation and coaching to foster the adaptation of strategies to the needs of specific classrooms and schools guided by ongoing progress monitoring data (Farmer & Hamm, 2016; Farmer et al., 2018; Motoca et al., 2014).

The Scouting Report Process

As noted above, screening that involves brief teacher ratings of students' academic and inter-personal functioning along with person-oriented analytic techniques can be used to identify students who have difficulties in a single domain (i.e., need Tier 2 supports) and students who experience a system of multiple risks (i.e., correlated constraints) that require Tier 3 supports. But this is only part of the equation. Teachers need information and guidance about the general functioning of the classroom and the support needs of specific students. The scouting report is an ecological assessment framework intervention specialists can use to gather information about the resources and culture of the school, the current practices of the teacher, the functioning of the classroom, the needs and circumstances of students, and the ongoing use and adaptation of specific intervention strategies (Farmer et al., 2016; Farmer & Hamm, 2016).

To do this, the scouting report process begins with interviews with key stakeholders and may include central office and building level administrators, student support personnel (e.g., school psychologists, counselors, behavior analysts, school resource officers, librarians), teachers, parents, community members, and students (Farmer et al., 2018). The goal is to not only collect information about what seems to be working and what is needed but to also determine whether consistency or differences in stakeholders' perspectives need to be addressed in the intervention process. Once this information is gathered, the intervention specialist conducts observations in the school and classroom to determine whether the various perspectives are accurate as well as to identify factors that should be addressed in the intervention process, to clarify what practices should be continued and/or modified, to determine what practices should be terminated or replaced, and to identify potential key leverage points that should be a priority in the intervention process. After observations are complete, the intervention specialist checks back in with relevant stakeholders to clarify any information that may be important for the intervention process. The intervention specialist then uses the totality of this information to develop a comprehensive classroom management program of the practice elements of EBPs that align with the circumstances of the classroom and the needs of students (Farmer et al., 2016; Farmer & Hamm, 2016). From this foundation, professional development, ongoing training, and consultation activities are conducted across the school year while collecting ongoing progress monitoring data to guide adaptations and modifications in the intervention process (Farmer et al., 2013, 2020; Motoca et al., 2014).

Empirical Support for the BASE Model

The BASE model has been used in several randomized control trials that have included small pilot studies with pairs of schools and two cluster randomized trials (one in metropolitan and one in rural settings) with over 30 schools. This work has demonstrated that teachers trained in this model tend to create a classroom context that promotes academic engagement and achievement while reducing social risks and peer support for problem behavior (Farmer et al., 2013). Teachers who have been trained in the BASE model tend to have more effective use of key management strategies including classroom structure, communication with students, motivation strategies, and management of groups and classroom social dynamics and they tend to use more positive feedback and less negative feedback and redirection (Motoca et al., 2014). In addition, BASE teachers have a greater sense of efficacy for supporting students (Farmer et al., 2010) and are better attuned to (i.e., aware of) classroom peer groups and students' social roles and relationships (Hamm, Farmer, Dadisman, Gravelle, & Murray, 2011).

In classrooms where teachers use BASE strategies, students tend to be more positively engaged (Dawes et al. 2019; Farmer et al., 2013). Academically and behaviorally struggling students are more likely to view the peer culture as supportive of positive academic effort and achievement (Hamm, Farmer, Lambert, & Gravelle, 2014), they are more likely to feel like they belong and that the ecology supports them (Hamm, Schmid, Farmer, & Locke, 2011), and they may have greater behavioral engagement in academic activities and improvement in academic grades and test scores (Hamm et al., 2010). Students with behavioral risks in BASE classrooms are more likely to affiliate with and develop positive relations with prosocial peers (Farmer et al., 2010) and students with disabilities tend to perceive less peer support for bullying directed against them (Chen, Hamm, Farmer, Lambert, Mehtaji, & 2015).

Future Directions and Considerations

Research on the BASE model has centered on the impact of universal (Tier 1) strategies on the classroom context, particularly in the middle school years. Additional work is needed that uses this model in elementary and high school settings. Further, there is a significant need for research that focuses on melding general context (Tier 1) centered interventions with selected (Tier 2) strategies to prevent the negative reorganization of the developmental systems of youth who are at risk for developing disorder and targeted (Tier 3) strategies to promote the positive reorganization and developmental adaptation of youth who manifest disorder (Farmer et al., 2007; Maggin et al., 2016; Sutherland et al., 2018). Prior work with universal strategies suggests that the BASE model does promote classroom contexts that are supportive of students with or at risk of EBD. But research on more intensive interventions at the Tier 2 and Tier 3 level is needed to clarify the processes, strategies, and supports necessary to enhance the adaptation of students with or at risk of EBD.

240 *Thomas W. Farmer et al.*

To move the field forward on this front, new research designs and approaches are needed that can examine changes in dynamic and developing contexts and equally dynamic and adapting developmental systems of youth in relation to multi-factored interventions that are purposefully dynamic and designed to be responsive to changing phenomena (Bronfenbrenner, 1996; Farmer et al., 2016; Maggin et al., 2016). This is a very different approach to research than the cluster randomized trials that involve the structured implementation of rigorous standardized interventions that are assessed in an equally rigorous manner. However, if our aim is to foster the adaptation and adjustment of youth with or at risk of significant EBD, the focus needs to be on the dynamic processes of development and not exclusively on the effectiveness of a specific intervention strategy in isolation. Research designs that utilize local analytics along with person-oriented analysis to examine patterns and trajectories of adaptation of subtypes of youth should be a productive approach for enhancing and evaluating dynamic, multi-factored interventions that are tailored to align the changing needs of youth and the ecologies in which they live and develop (Bergman & Magnusson, 1997; Cairns & Cairns, 1994; Maggin et al., 2016). This does not mean abandoning experimental designs, but it does mean complementing them with much more complex and individualized approaches that recognize that the most effective intervention will be responsive to the dynamic and unique needs of the child and the ecologies in which they live, grow, and adapt.

Authors' Note

This work was supported by grants from the Institute of Education Sciences (R305A040056; R305A160398). The views expressed in this paper are those of the authors and do not reflect the views of the granting agency.

References

Adler, P. A., & Adler, P. (1998). *Peer power: Preadolescent culture and identity*. New Brunswick, NJ: Rutgers University Press.

Ahn, H.-J., & Rodkin, P. C. (2014). Classroom-level predictors of the social status of aggression: Friendship centralization, friendship density, teacher–student attunement, and gender. *Journal of Educational Psychology, 106*, 1144–1155. doi:10.1037/a0036091

Belfiore, P. J., Lee, D. L., Scheeler, C., & Klein, D. (2002). Implications of behavioral momentum and academic achievement for students with behavior disorders: Theory, application, and practice. *Psychology in the Schools, 39*, 171–179. doi:10.1002/pits.10028

Bergman, L. R., & Magnusson, D. (1997). A person-oriented approach in research on developmental psychopathology. *Developmental Psychopathology, 9*, 291–319.

Billingsley, G. M. (2016). Combating work refusal using research-based practices. *Intervention in School and Clinic, 52*, 12–16. doi:10.1177/1053451216630289

Bronfenbrenner, U. (1996). Foreword. In R. B. Cairns, G. H. Elder, Jr., & E. J. Costello (Eds.), *Developmental science* (pp. iv–xvii). New York, NY: Cambridge University Press.

Cairns, R. B., & Cairns, B. D. (1994). *Lifelines and risks: Pathways of youth in our time*. New York, NY: Harvester Wheatsheaf.

Chen, C. C., Farmer, T. W., Hamm, J. V., Lee, D. L., Dawes, M., & Brooks, D. S. (2019). Adjustment difficulties of students with disabilities during the transition to middle school: Configurations and perceptions. *Journal of Emotional and Behavioral Disorders*, doi:10.1177/1063426619866829

Chen, C.-C., Hamm, J. V., Farmer, T. W., Lambert, K., & Mehtaji, M. (2015). Exceptionality and peer victimization involvement in late childhood: Subtypes, stability, and social marginalization. *Remedial and Special Education, 36*, 312–324.

Cook, B. G., Buysse, V., Klinger, J., Landrum, T. J., McWilliam, R. A., Tankersley, M., & Test, D. W. (2015). CEC's standards for classifying the evidence base of practices in special education. *Remedial and Special Education, 36*, 220–234.

Cullinan, D., Epstein, M. H., & Lloyd, J. W. (1983). *Behavior disorders of children and adolescents*. Englewood Cliffs, NJ: Prentice-Hall, Inc.

Dawes, M., Farmer, T. W., Hamm, J. V., Lee, D., Norwalk, K., Sterrett, B., & Lambert, K. (2019: online first). Creating supportive contexts during the first year of middle school: Impact of a developmentally responsive multi-component intervention. *Journal of Youth and Adolescence*.doi: 10.1007/s10964-019-01156-2.

De-Lade O'Connor, L. A., Alvarez, A. J., Murray, I. E., & Milner, H. R. (2017). Self-efficacy beliefs, classroom management, and the cradle-to-prison pipeline. *Theory into Practice, 56*, 178–186.

Dweck, C. S., & Leggett, E. L. (1988). A social-cognitive approach to motivation and personality. *Psychological Review, 95*, 256–273. doi:10.1037/0033-295X.95.2.256

Dweck, C. S., Walton, G. M., & Cohen, G. L. (2014). *Academic tenacity: Mindsets and skills that promote long-term learning*. Seattle, WA: Bill & Melinda Gates Foundation.

Emmer, E. T., & Stough, L. (2001). Classroom management: A critical part of educational psychology, with implications for teacher education. *Educational Psychologist, 36*, 103–112. doi:10.1207/S15326985EP3602_5

Farmer, T. W., Chen, -C.-C., Hamm, J. V., Moates, M. M., Mehtaji, M., Lee, D., & Huneke, M. R. (2016). Supporting teachers' management of middle school social dynamics: The scouting report process. *Intervention in School and Clinic, 52*, 67–76.

Farmer, T. W., Dawes, M., Hamm, J. V., Lee, D., Mehtaji, M., Hoffman, A. S., & Brooks, D. S. (2018). Classroom social dynamics management: Why the invisible hand of the teacher matters for special education. *Remedial & Special Education, 39*, 177–192.

Farmer, T. W., & Farmer, E. M. Z. (2001). Developmental science, systems of care, and prevention of emotional and behavioral problems in youth. *American Journal of Orthopsychiatry, 71*, 171–181.

Farmer, T. W., Farmer, E. M. Z., Estell, D., & Hutchins, B. C. (2007). The developmental dynamics of aggression and the prevention of school violence. *Journal of Emotional and Behavioral Disorders, 15*, 197–208.

Farmer, T. W., Gatzke-Kopp, L., & Latendresse, S. (2020, this volume). The development, prevention, and treatment of emotional and behavioral disorders: An interdisciplinary developmental systems perspective. In T. W. Farmer, M. Conroy, E. M. Z. Farmer, & K. S. Sutherland (Eds.), *Handbook of research on emotional & behavioral disorders: Interdisciplinary developmental perspectives on children and youth*. New York and London: Routledge.

Farmer, T. W., Gatzke-Kopp, L. M., Lee, D. L., Dawes, M., & Talbott, E. (2016). Research and policy on disability: Linking special education to developmental science. *Policy Insights from the Behavioral and Brain Sciences, 3*, 138–145.

Farmer, T. W., Goforth, J. B., Hives, J., Aaron, A., Hunter, F., & Sgmatto, A. (2006). Competence enhancement behavior management. *Preventing School Failure, 50*, 39–44.

Farmer, T. W., Hamm, J. L., Petrin, R. A., Robertson, D. L., Murray, R. A., Meece, J. L., & Brooks, D. S. (2010). Creating supportive classroom contexts for academically and behaviorally at-risk youth during the transition to middle school: A strength-based perspective. *Exceptionality, 18*, 94–106.

Farmer, T. W., & Hamm, J. V. (2016). Promoting supportive contexts for minority youth in low-resource rural communities: The SEALS model, directed consultation, and the scouting report approach. In L. J. Crockett & G. Carlo (Eds.), *Rural ethnic minority youth and families in the United States* (pp. 247–265). Cham, Switzerland: Springer.

Farmer, T. W., Hamm, J. V., Dawes, M., Barko-Alva, K., & Cross, J. R. (2020). Promoting inclusive communities in diverse classrooms: Teacher attunement and social dynamics management. *Educational Psychologist*. doi:10.1080/00461520.2019.1635020

Farmer, T. W., Hamm, J. V., Lee, D., Lane, K. L., Sutherland, K. S., Hall, C. M., & Murray, R. M. (2013). Conceptual foundations and components of a contextual intervention to promote student engagement during early adolescence: The supporting early adolescent learning and social success (SEALS) model. *Journal of Educational and Psychological Consultation, 23*, 115–139. doi:10.1080/10474412.2013.785181

Farmer, T. W., Hamm, J. V., Lee, D. L., Sterrett, B. I., Rizzo, K., & Hoffman, A. S. (2018). Directed consultation and supported professionalism: Promoting adaptive evidence-based practices in rural schools. *Rural Special Education Quarterly*, *37*, 164–175.

Farmer, T. W., Price, L., O'Neal, K. K., Leung, M.-C., Goforth, J. B., Cairns, B. D., & Reese, L. E. (2004). Exploring risk in African-American youth. *American Journal of Community Psychology*, *33*, 51–59.

Farmer, T. W., Sutherland, K. S., Talbott, E., Brooks, D., Norwalk, K., & Huneke, M. (2016). Special educators as intervention specialists: Dynamic systems and the complexity of intensifying intervention for students with emotional and behavioral disorders. *Journal of Emotional and Behavioral Disorders*, *24*, 173–186.

Farmer, T. W., Talbott, B., Dawes, M., Huber, H. B., Brooks, D. S., & Powers, E. (2018). Social dynamics management: What is it and why is it important for intervention? *Journal of Emotional and Behavioral Disorders*, *26*, 1–10.

Gest, S. D., Madill, R. A., Zadzora, K. M., Miller, A. M., & Rodkin, P. C. (2014). Teacher management of elementary classroom social dynamics: Associations with changes in student adjustment. *Journal of Emotional and Behavioral Disorders*, *22*, 107–118.

Gunter, P. L., Denny, R. K., Jack, S. L., Shores, R. E., & Neslon, C. M. (1993). Aversive stimuli in academic interactions between students with serious emotional disturbance and their teachers. *Behavioral Disorders*, *18*, 265–274. doi:10.1177/019874299301800405

Gut, D. M., Farmer, T. W., Bishop, J. L., Hives, J., Aaron, A., & Jackson, F. (2004). The school engagement project: The academic engagement enhancement component. *Preventing School Failure*, *48*, 4–9.

Hamm, J. V., Farmer, T. W., Dadisman, K., Gravelle, M., & Murray, R. A. (2011). Teachers' attunement to students' peer group affiliations as a source of improved student experiences of the school social-affective context following the middle school transition. *Journal of Applied Developmental Psychology*, *32*, 267–277.

Hamm, J. V., Farmer, T. W., Lambert, K., & Gravelle, M. (2014). Enhancing peer cultures of academic effort and achievement in early adolescence: Promotive effects of the SEALS intervention. *Developmental Psychology*, *50*, 216–228. doi:10.1037/a0032979

Hamm, J. V., Farmer, T. W., Robertson, D., Dadisman, K., Murray, A. R., Meece, J., & Song, S. (2010). Effects of a developmentally-based intervention with teachers on Native American and white early adolescents' schooling adjustment in rural settings. *Journal of Experimental Education*, *78*, 343–377. doi:10.1080/00220970903548038

Hamm, J. V., Hoffman, A., & Farmer, T. W. (2012). Peer cultures of academic success in adolescence: Why they matter and what teachers can do to promote them. In A. Ryan & G. Ladd (Eds.), *Peer relationships and adjustment at school* (pp. 219–250). New York, NY: Information Age Publishing.

Hamm, J. V., Schmid, L, Farmer, T. W., & Locke, B. L. (2011). The influence of injunctive and descriptive peer group norms on the academic adjustment of rural early adolescents. *Journal of Early Adolescence*, *31*, 41–73.

Haydon, T., Conroy, M. A., Scott, T. M., Sindelar, P. T., Barber, B. R., & Orlando, A.-M. (2010). A comparison of three types of opportunities to respond on student academic and social behaviors. *Journal of Emotional and Behavioral Disorders*, *18*, 27–40.

Hendrickx, M. M., Mainhard, M. T., Boor-Klip, H. J., Cillessen, A. H., & Brekelmans, M. (2016). Social dynamics in the classroom: Teacher support and conflict and the peer ecology. *Teaching and Teacher Education*, *53*, 30–40. doi:10.1016/j.tate.2015.10.004

Hobbs, N. J. (1982). *The troubled and troubling child*. San Francisco, CA: Jossey-Bass.

Hosie, T. W., Gentile, J. R., & Carroll, J. D. (1974). Pupil preferences and the premack principle. *American Educational Research Journal*, *11*, 241–247.

Hughes, J. N., Im, M. H., & Wehrly, S. E. (2014). Effect of peer nominations of teacher-student support at individual and classroom levels on social and academic outcomes. *Journal of School Psychology*, *52*, 309–322. doi:10.1016/j.jsp.2013.12.004

Janosz, M., Le Blanc, M., Boulerice, B., & Tremblay, R. E. (2000). Predicting types of school dropouts: A typological approach with two longitudinal samples. *Journal of Educational Psychology*, *92*, 171–190.

Knowles, C., Meng, P., & Machalicek, W. (2015). Task sequencing for students with emotional and behavioral disorders: A systematic review. *Behavior Modification, 39*, 136–166.

Lee, D. (2006). Facilitating academic transitions: An application of behavioral momentum. *Remedial and Special Education, 27*, 312–317. doi:10.1177/07419325060270050601

Lee, D. L. (2018). Social dynamics management and functional behavioral assessment. *Journal of Emotional and Behavioral Disorders, 26*(62–64), 1063426617742345.

Leinhardt, G. C., Weidmand, C., & Hammond, K. M. (1987). Introduction and integration of classroom routines by expert teachers. *Curriculum Inquiry, 17*, 135–176.

Long, N. J., Morse, W. C., Fecser, F. A., & Newman, R. G. (2007). *Conflict in the classroom: Positive staff support for troubled students* (6th ed.). Austin, TX: Pro-Ed, Inc.

Ludlow, B. (2014). Intensifying intervention: Kicking it up a notch. *Teaching Exceptional Children, 46*, 4.

Maggin, D. M., Wehby, J. H., Farmer, T. W., & Brooks, D. S. (2016). Intensive interventions for students with emotional and behavioral disorders: Issues, theory, and future directions. *Journal of Emotional and Behavioral Disorders., 24*, 127–137.

Magnusson, D. M., & Cairns, R. B. (1996). Developmental science. Toward a unified framework. In R. B. Cairns, G. H. Elder, & E. J. Costello (Eds.), *Developmental science* (pp. 7–30). Cambridge: Cambridge University Press.

Masten, A. S., & Cicchetti, D. (2010). Developmental cascades. *Development and Psychopathology, 22*, 491–495.

McDaniel, S. C., Bruhn, A. L., & Mitchell, B. S. (2017). A responsive Tier 2 process for a middle school student with behavior problems. *Preventing School Failure, 61*, 280–288.

Milner, H. R. (2018). Development over punishment: An unhealthy fixation on punishment hurts underserved students. *Educational Leadership, 75*, 93–94.

Milner, H. R., & Tenore, F. B. (2010). Classroom management in diverse classrooms. *Urban Education, 45*, 560–603.

Motoca, L., Farmer, T. W., Hamm, J. V., Byun, S.-Y., Lee, D., Brooks, D. S., … Moohr, M. (2014). Directed consultation, the SEALS Model, and teachers' classroom management. *Journal of Emotional of Behavioral Disorders, 22*, 119–129.

Oliver, R. M., Lambert, M. C., & Mason, W. A. (2017). A pilot study for improving classroom systems within schoolwide positive behavior support. *Journal of Emotional and Behavioral Disorders*. doi:10.1177/1063426617733718

Owens, J. S., Holdaway, A. S., Smith, J., Evans, S. W., Himawan, L. K., Coles, E. K., … Dawson, A. E. (2018). Rates of common classroom behavior management strategies and their associations with challenging student behavior in elementary school. *Journal of Emotional and Behavioral Disorders, 26*, 156–169.

Pintrich, P. R. (2000). Multiple goals, multiple pathways: The role of goal orientation in learning and achievement. *Journal of Educational Psychology, 92*, 544–555.

Premack, D. (1959). Toward empirical behavior laws. I. Positive reinforcement. *Psychological Review, 66*, 219–233. doi:10.1037/h0040891

Roeser, R. W., & Peck, S. C. (2003). Patterns and pathways of educational achievement across adolescence: A holistic-developmental perspective. *New Directions for Child and Adolescent Development, 101*, 39–62.

Sameroff, A. J. (2000). Developmental systems and psychopathology. *Development and Psychopathology, 12*, 297–312.

Shores, R. E., Gunter, P. L., & Jack, S. L. (1993). Classroom management strategies: Are they setting events for coercion? *Behavioral Disorders, 18*, 92–102.

Shores, R. E., & Wehby, J. H. (1999). Analyzing the classroom social behavior of students with EBD. *Journal of Emotional and Behavioral Disorders, 7*, 194–199.

Sutherland, K. S., Alder, N., & Gunter, P. L. (2003). The effects of varying rates of opportunities to respond to academic requests on the classroom behavior of students with EBD. *Journal of Emotional and Behavioral Disorders, 11*, 239–248.

Sutherland, K. S., Farmer, T. W., Kunemund, R. L., & Sterrett, B. I. (2018). Learning, behavioral, and social difficulties within MTSS: A dynamic perspective of intervention intensification. In N. D. Young,

244 *Thomas W. Farmer et al.*

K. Bonanno-Sotiropoulos, & T. A. Citro (Eds.), *Paving the pathway for educational success: Effective classroom interventions for students with learning disabilities* (pp. 15–32). New York, NY: Rowman & Littlefield.

Sutherland, K. S., & Wehby, J. H. (2001). Exploring the relationship between increased opportunities to respond to academic requests and the academic and behavioral outcomes of students with EBD – A review. *Remedial and Special Education, 22*, 113–121.

Talbott, E., De Arment, S., Sterrett, B., & Chen, C.-C. (2020, this volume). Leading the team for youth with emotional and behavioral disorders: Special educators as intervention specialists. In T. W. Farmer, M. Conroy, E. M. Z. Farmer, & K. S. Sutherland (Eds.), *Handbook of research on emotional & behavioral disorders: Interdisciplinary developmental perspectives on children and youth.* Taylor & Francis.

Trach, J., Lee, M., & Hymel, S. (2018). A social-ecological approach to addressing emotional and behavioral problems in school: Focusing on group processes and social dynamics. *Journal of Emotional and Behavioral Disorders, 26*, 11–20.

Van Acker, R., Grant, S. H., & Henry, D. (1996). Teacher and student behavior as a function of risk for aggression. *Education and Treatment of Children, 19*, 316–334.

van den Berg, Y. H. M., & Stoltz, S. (2018). Enhancing social inclusion of children with externalizing problems through classroom seating arrangements: A randomized control trial. *Journal of Emotional and Behavioral Disorders, 26*, 31–41.

Wehby, J. H., & Kern, L. (2014). Intensive behavior intervention: What is it, what is its evidence base, and why do we need to implement now? *Teaching Exceptional Children, 46*, 38–44. doi:10.1177/0040059914523956

Wehby, J. H., Symons, F. J., & Shores, R. E. (1995). A descriptive analysis of aggressive behavior in classrooms for children with emotional and behavioral disorders. *Behavioral Disorders, 20*, 87–105. doi:10.1177/019874299502000207

Wentzel, K. R., Muenks, K., McNeish, D., & Russell, S. (2017). Peer and teacher supports in relation to motivation and effort: A multi-level study. *Contemporary Educational Psychology, 49*, 32–45.

Xie, H. L., Cairns, B. D., & Cairns, R. B. (2001). Predicting teen motherhood and teen fatherhood: Individual characteristics and peer affiliations. *Social Development, 10*, 488–511.

17 Multi-Tiered Social-Emotional Learning

PATHS and Friendship Group in the Fast Track Program

Karen L. Bierman, Mark T. Greenberg, and The Conduct Problems Prevention Research Group*

Deficits in social-emotional skills are common among students with (or at high-risk for) emotional and behavioral disorders (EBD) (Farmer et al., 2008; Gresham, Cook, Crews, & Kern, 2004). Social-emotional skill deficits are particularly prominent in students who display attention deficits (Mikami & Hinshaw, 2006), disruptive behaviors (Waas, 2006), and children with autism spectrum disorder (Ratcliffe, Wong, Dossetor, & Hayes, 2014), and they disrupt children's functioning at school, impairing social, behavioral, and academic performance. This chapter provides an overview of the social-emotional skill deficits that are common among students with (or at high-risk for) EBD. It describes interventions that have been effective in promoting skill development and fostering school adjustment, emphasizing the utility of a multi-tiered approach that includes tier one classroom-wide (and school-wide) programming along with tier two small group programming for children who need extra support for social-emotional skill development. This chapter features the Fast Track adaptation of the PATHS® Curriculum (Kusché & Greenberg, 2011) as an exemplary tier one program and the Fast Track Friendship Group (Bierman et al., 2017) as a coordinated and complementary tier two program. Program content and implementation are described, along with evidence from the Fast Track randomized-controlled trial and other studies demonstrating the efficacy of these programs, when integrated, to promote social competence, self-regulation skills, and adaptive learning behaviors, and to reduce aggressive-disruptive behavior in children with or at risk for EBDs.

Multi-Tiered Social-Emotional Learning Models

Social-emotional learning (SEL) involves the acquisition of knowledge, attitudes, and skills associated with understanding and managing emotions, controlling impulses and behaviors, establishing and maintaining positive interpersonal relationships, and making responsible decisions (Domitrovich, Durlak, Staley, & Weissberg, 2017). In their comprehensive model, the Collaborative for Academic, Social, and Emotional Learning (CASEL) identifies five inter-related competencies that comprise adaptive SEL – self-awareness, self-management, social awareness, relationship skills, and responsible decision-making (CASEL, 2013). Developmental delays or distortions in SEL contribute to impairments in children's emotional functioning, behavioral control, and social adjustment (Dusenbury & Weissberg, 2016).

Children with (or at risk for) EBD often have problems initiating and sustaining friendships and working cooperatively with others (Gresham, Elliott, & Kettler, 2010); many get into frequent conflicts with peers and teachers (Bierman, 2004). Many also experience significant emotional distress about their social difficulties, including social anxiety, loneliness, and depression (La Greca & Landoll, 2011).

When accompanied by poor SEL, social and behavioral difficulties often escalate over time. Children who exhibit socially unskilled behavior tend to alienate peers, who react with counter-aggression and/or avoidance and exclusion. These negative peer responses become an active force that intensifies children's behavioral and emotional difficulties, contributing to a negative cycle of social dysfunction (Mikami & Hinshaw, 2006). Negative peer experiences also amplify feelings of loneliness and social anxiety, undermining perceived efficacy, learning engagement, and academic performance (Fite, Wimsatt, Vitulano, Rathert, & Schwartz, 2012). Chronic peer difficulties are associated with a negative cascade of social problems over the course of elementary school, as peers exclude disliked children and thereby restrict opportunities to learn the more complex social skills that support social integration later in life. When children are actively disliked and rejected by peers, they are particularly likely to experience increasing social alienation, school disengagement, underachievement, risky adolescent behaviors, and early school drop-out (Bierman, 2004). Social-emotional skill deficits can also undermine student–teacher relationships. Especially when accompanied by impulsive, off-task, or aggressive behavior, unskilled children often experience decreasing support from teachers and increasing conflict (Sutherland & Oswald, 2005) which exacerbates maladjustment (Lee & Bierman, 2018).

Given the general importance of SEL and positive classroom interactions to school success, educational researchers recommend that schools provide multiple levels of systematic support to help students develop social-emotional skills (Gresham et al., 2004). These include "universal" tier one classroom-level curriculum-based efforts to promote SEL for all students, and more intensive tier two supports to remediate social-emotional skill deficits, matched to the level of student need (CASEL, 2013; Greenberg, Domitrovich, Weissberg, & Durlak, 2017).

Universal SEL Programs (Tier One)

Universal tier one SEL interventions are typically taught by classroom teachers and provide primary prevention support. They benefit all students, improving social and behavioral adjustment, enhancing emotional functioning, and fostering academic success (Durlak, Weissberg, Dymnicki, Taylor, & Schellinger, 2011; Schonert-Reichl & Weissberg, 2015). In a large meta-analysis of universal SEL programs, Durlak et al. (2011) documented an average 11% gain on measures of academic achievement, and similar significant improvements in behavior and emotional functioning. By increasing positive behavior and support in the classroom, universal SEL programs also create a context that is beneficial to students experiencing social adjustment difficulties.

Targeted SEL Programs (Tier Two)

It is generally expected that approximately 15% of students need additional social-emotional skill training in small groups to address their social-emotional skill deficits and social adjustment problems (Sugai & Horner, 2002). Targeted, small group SEL programs focus on building the social skills of students who are experiencing significant peer difficulties or demonstrating problematic behaviors that undermine their social adjustment. Gresham, Cook, Crew, and Kern (2004) reviewed six meta-analyses examining the effectiveness of targeted social skill training programs for students with or at risk for EBD. These studies demonstrated that small group social skills training is an effective intervention strategy with an overall mean effect size d of .29 (range = .19 – .40), corresponding to an improvement rate of 65% versus 35% for children in the intervention and control groups, respectively. In addition, social skill training proved effective for children who varied substantially in terms of their specific emotional and behavioral problems, including those exhibiting a wide range of externalizing and internalizing problems.

Coordinated Universal and Targeted SEL Programs

Implementing coordinated universal and targeted SEL programs has the potential to amplify positive benefits for children with (or at risk for) EBD, relative to the provision of either tier alone. Given the key role that teacher and peer responses play in either amplifying or reducing the social adjustment difficulties of peer-rejected children, interventions need to both reduce the SEL deficits of these children and also improve interpersonal responses to them (Pepler & Bierman, 2018). Universal interventions help with this second goal, creating a more positive and supportive classroom context, and improving teacher and peer attitudes and behaviors. In addition, when universal interventions focus on the same skills and use the same support strategies as small targeted social skill training groups, they facilitate the generalization of gains made from the small groups to the larger classroom and school settings in which peer interaction takes place (Greenberg et al., 2017).

Multi-Tiered SEL in the Fast Track Program

The coordinated implementation of a classroom-level tier one SEL program with a small-group tier two SEL program provided the foundation for the Fast Track Program, a multicomponent prevention program designed to promote the SEL of children at risk for conduct disorders (CPPRG, 1992). Fast Track involved a multisite research project with a set of concurrent randomized-controlled field trails undertaken in four geographically and demographically diverse areas of the United States – rural Pennsylvania; Seattle, Washington; Durham, North Carolina, and Nashville, Tennessee. At each site, matched pairs of schools were randomly assigned to intervention or "usual practice" comparison groups. Children were identified as at risk for the development of conduct disorders based on teacher and parent ratings of aggressive behavior problems in kindergarten (see Lochman & CPPRG, 1995 for details).

The multicomponent design of Fast Track recognized that many of the parents of children who have (or are at high risk for developing) EBD are multiply-stressed and uncertain about how to help their children at school. For example, compared to students without disabilities, students with EBD are more likely to live in poverty, have a single or unemployed parent, and to have another household member who has a disability (Wagner, Kutash, Duchnowski, Epstein, & Sumi, 2005). As a function of exposure to the adversity associated with these family risks, children with or at risk for EBDs often show complex social-emotional difficulties. Correspondingly, Fast Track included multiple integrated components and covered a ten-year period. In addition to SEL programming, Fast Track included components to enhance positive parenting practices (parent groups), family organization and problem solving (home visiting) and parent–child relationships (parent–child interaction time), along with academic support (reading tutoring). In the following sections, we focus on the multi-tiered SEL components that were implemented during the elementary phase of Fast Track (grades

1–5). These included a universal tier one SEL program (the PATHS Curriculum) and a targeted tier two SEL program (Fast Track Friendship Group and peer-pairing), both focused in a coordinated way on strengthening children's social-cognitive skills, self-regulation capabilities, and interpersonal competencies.

In Fast Track, children were screened for inclusion based on elevated aggressive-disruptive behavior problems; the majority also displayed deficits in prosocial and cooperative behaviors, emotional difficulties (e.g., easily aroused feelings of anxiety, anger, or ambivalence in interpersonal contexts), and social-cognitive biases (e.g., impulsive and inaccurate perceptions, negatively biased evaluations, and inadequate or aggression-prone problem-solving skills). For this reason, it was important for the SEL interventions to address the behavioral, affective-motivational, and social-cognitive features of children's adjustment difficulties. Early exposure to adversity has been linked with emotional reactivity and difficulties with self-regulation, creating a need for SEL programming to support neurocognitive functioning, including the development of executive functioning (Greenberg, 2006). In the following sections, we describe the two SEL programs that were used in Fast Track (the PATHS Curriculum and the Fast Track Friendship Group program), followed by the research findings from Fast Track and other studies supporting the efficacy of these programs.

The Universal SEL Intervention Used in Fast Track: The PATHS Curriculum

The PATHS curriculum (Greenberg & Kusché, 1998) is a comprehensive program for promoting social and emotional competencies and reducing aggression and behavior problems in elementary school-aged children, while simultaneously building a positive classroom climate characterized by harmonious and engaged students. Originally designed to support special education students, this multi-year (preschool through sixth grade) classroom SEL program was adapted to fit the needs of regular education students for the Fast Track program. The grade level PATHS Curriculum consists of separate volumes for grade levels 1–5 which include developmentally appropriate lesson plans and associated materials (e.g., pictures, handouts, posters) (www.channing-bete.com/preven tion-programs/paths/).

Across the grade levels, PATHS targets skills in five domains: positive relationships, emotional understanding, self-control, positive self-esteem, and interpersonal problem-solving skills. Each lesson includes specific objectives and illustrative scripts; teachers are encouraged to use these guides flexibly to maximize the engagement of the students in their classrooms. Skill concepts are presented via instruction, discussion, and modeling stories, and discussion and role-playing activities follow to support skill practice. Lessons are organized hierarchically to build on each other across the years. Ideally, teachers lead two to three lessons per week and include extension activities and daily supports to promote the generalized use of the targeted skills.

For example, lessons designed to increase *positive relationship skills* focus on specific activities (e.g., taking turns, helping, sharing at the younger grade levels; communicating effectively and respecting others' perspectives at the older grade levels). Daily classroom activities support these skills. During each PATHS lesson, one child (selected on a rotating basis) serves as the teacher's helper (the PATHS Kid of the Day). At the end of the lesson, these children receive compliments from classmates, the teacher, and themselves. The compliment sheets are then sent home with the request that family members add compliments to the list.

In the domain of *emotional understanding*, lessons at the younger grade levels teach children to recognize the internal and external cues of different feelings and to label them with appropriate terms. By teaching the verbal skills needed to identify, express, redirect, and reduce negative arousal, PATHS provides young children with a foundation for self-control and interpersonal problem solving. In additional lessons, children are taught to distinguish feelings from behaviors, and they learn that "feelings are OK, but behaviors can be OK or not OK." "Feeling face" cards support growth in emotional understanding. After each feeling word is introduced, children receive a card with that feeling face expression. Children can display a card to share their feelings during the day and change their card as their feelings change. Teachers have their own set of feeling faces and use them as models to help children generalize the skill. At older levels, children compile a "Feelings Dictionary" and are encouraged to recognize more complex and mixed feelings in the stories they read and write.

The lessons on social problem-solving skills also follow a development sequence. At the younger grade levels, teachers use a "control signals poster" with a traffic light illustrating a three-step model of problem solving. Children are taught that when they are in a challenging situation (such as a playground conflict or difficult work situation) they: (1) "go to the red light" to stop and think before they act; tell themselves to stop, take a long, deep breath to calm down, and explain the problem and how they feel; (2) move to the yellow light to "make a plan," considering the possible solutions and choosing the best option; and (3) try out the plan at the green light and evaluate its effects. At the older grade levels, additional features are added to the problem-solving guide, including goal-setting, anticipating consequences for various solutions, and self-reflection on the effectiveness of the chosen solution. Across grade levels, teachers are instructed in the method for holding classroom problem-solving meetings, which are designed to help children use the problem-solving steps to address the problems currently facing them in their classroom. PATHS also includes parent letters and home activity assignments to keep parents informed of the targeted skills and to encourage parent involvement and support.

In the Fast Track program, teachers were trained to deliver the PATHS Curriculum. Teachers received consultation and support from Fast Track project staff (educational consultants (ECs) in PATHS implementation. In addition, ECs met regularly with teachers to consult on the effective classroom management of disruptive behavior (e.g. establishing clear rules and directions, providing positive and corrective feedback for appropriate behavior, applying response cost procedures to reduce problematic behavior). ECs also helped teachers develop positive behavioral management plans for individual high-risk children in the classroom on an as-needed basis. At the school level, ECs also consulted with the school principal to bring the philosophy of PATHS to the entire school; various efforts resulted (on a school-by-school basis), such as placing PATHS posters in school hallways, implementing new school behavior guidelines, and painting problem-solving "stoplights" on school playgrounds.

PATHS was revised and extended for Fast Track based on previous field trials with different versions of the PATHS curriculum that focused on typically developing children as well as children who are deaf (Greenberg & Kusché, 1998) and children with special needs (Greenberg, Kusché, Cook, & Quamma, 1995; Kam, Greenberg, & Walls, 2003; Riggs, Greenberg, Kusché, & Pentz, 2006). These studies documented the efficacy of the PATHS curriculum to boost children's social understanding and socially competent behaviors, and to reduce both internalizing and externalizing behavior (Kam et al., 2003; Riggs et al., 2006).

The Targeted SEL Intervention Used in Fast Track: Friendship Group

The Fast Track Friendship Group (Bierman et al., 2017) was designed to complement the classroom PATHS Curriculum and provide more intensive remediation and support for the development of key social-emotional competencies. Parallel to the PATHS curriculum, Friendship Group addresses behavioral skills (collaborating and cooperating with others), emotional features of social behavior (emotion understanding and regulation) and the thinking skills that underlie effective interaction (negotiation, conflict management, and related social problem-solving skills). Specifically, the program includes a total of 45 lessons that address skill deficits in six domains: (1) *prosocial engagement* (social participation and cooperation); (2) *communication skills*; (3) *emotion regulation and self-control*; (4) *responsible social behavior* (fair play, respecting others, good sportsmanship); (5) *social problem-solving skills* (negotiation, conflict resolution, and collaborative planning); and (6) *managing stress* (coping effectively with bullying, teasing, and disappointment). There are two developmental levels, with lessons for younger (grades Kindergarten–grade 2) and older elementary students (grades 3–5). The program is aligned with the organization of the classroom PATHS program. For example, as feeling words or social skill concepts are introduced in PATHS, these same words and concepts are incorporated into the group program. Just as in PATHS, the control signals poster is used as the framework for teaching social problem-solving skills and for processing interpersonal conflicts.

Friendship Group uses core coaching strategies to build new skills (Gresham, Van Bao, & Cook, 2006). This includes the use of: (1) skill presentations, involving the use of instructions, modeling, and discussions to clarify skill concepts and provide exemplars of positive and negative skill performance; (2) structured and supportive opportunities to practice those skills in the context of interactive games and activities with peers; (3) performance feedback, including specific praise to reinforce skill performance and non-critical redirection or corrective input that allows the child to adjust and improve skill performance; (4) opportunities to self-monitor, using emotion coaching, induction strategies, and problem-solving dialogue to increase self- and social-awareness and promote self-regulation; and (5) generalization programming, including practice in multiple game and peer activity formats to foster use in natural settings, along with efforts to coordinate support for skill performance with teachers and parents. To provide students with remedial support in social-emotional skill training, Friendship Group incorporates extended practice in multiple play and conversation contexts that increase in complexity over the course of the year. Practice activities move from structured social opportunities that provide maximal support for skill acquisition to activities that gradually increase the level of difficulty and naturalistic challenge. Each session includes a "Friendship Tips" handout to be shared with teachers and parents to keep them informed about the focus of the group session. Periodic meetings with parents and teachers are encouraged to review each child's progress and discuss positive peer interaction opportunities that they might support outside of the group context.

The management of group processes in social skill training programs has an important impact on child skill acquisition (Lavallee, Bierman, Nix, & CPPRG, 2005). The nature of the interpersonal exchanges that occur determines the degree to which children have opportunities to practice new social strategies and the way that they are reinforced by peers within sessions (see also Bierman, 1986). Skill acquisition and generalization are enhanced in groups when children feel competent using new social-emotional skills and when they receive reinforcement from peers for these skills. Hence, it is important to use management strategies that increase feelings of efficacy and increase positive responses from all group members, as well as decreasing any deviancy training in which group members laugh, copy, or otherwise reinforce negative social behavior (Dodge, Lansford, & Dishion, 2006). With this goal in mind, a set of therapeutic strategies are used in the Friendship Group program to manage and process group interactions. They include: (1) positive support to increase children's comfort in social interaction and reduce anxiety; (2) emotion coaching to foster emotional awareness, empathy, and emotion coping; (3) induction strategies to support self-regulation; and (4) social problem-solving dialogue to enhance flexible thinking and conflict management skills. These strategies are designed to promote a positive climate within the group, increase positive responding, enhance positive control beliefs, and encourage self-regulation. Friendship Group also includes group planning and reflection discussions to help children consider the behaviors that helped them have fun together (and those that interfered with group success).

In Fast Track, Friendship Group was delivered as an extracurricular program. Target children who exhibited elevated aggressive-disruptive behaviors were invited to attend two-hour extracurricular sessions with their families, held after-school, in the evening, or on the weekend. Groups of six children met for 60–90 minutes in Friendship Group while their parents attended Parent Groups. These sessions were followed by a 30-minute period of guided parent–child sharing activities. Fast Track ECs led the Friendship Group with a paraprofessional assistant leader. The timing of Friendship Group sessions was coordinated with the PATHS Curriculum, so that the classroom program provided an introduction to the skills and the Friendship Group providing at risk target children with additional coaching and practice to remediate skill deficits.

Implementing Friendship Group outside of the school setting provided the opportunity to interface sessions with parents, which was an important design feature of Fast Track. At the same time, these groups included only children who exhibited high rates of aggressive-disruptive behavior. As a result, they limited children's exposure to normative peer interactions and provided no direct opportunity to practice skills with classmates, reducing opportunities to promote the generalization of the targeted skills to the school setting. Hence, Fast Track also included weekly half-hour peer-pairing sessions (Asher & Oden, 1977) in the early elementary years during the school day. These were 30-minute supervised indoor play sessions that included a target child and a classmate partner who rotated over the course of the year. These sessions provide additional skill practice and were designed to foster positive relationships with classmates. In general, including peer partners in social skill training sessions and using naturalistic peer activities for skill practice both strengthen the impact of social skill training programs, relative to individual training or a reliance on role-play skill practice alone (Bierman, 2004; Bierman & Furman, 1984; Pelham & Fabiano, 2008; Troop & Asher, 1999).

Although Fast Track implemented Friendship Group in an extracurricular setting, it is worth noting that several subsequent disseminations have conducted Friendship Group as a school-based program. For example, in the PATHS to Success program (Greenberg, 2012) described later in this chapter, 45-minute Friendship Group sessions were held during school and included classmates as rotating partners in groups for targeted aggressive children (Greenberg, 2012). Running Friendship Group in this way has several advantages. First, managing groups that contain only aggressive children can be difficult and can increase the risk of negative peer dynamics undermining effective sessions (Lavallee et al., 2005). Including classmates as partners in the group provides more exposure to normative peer models and also increases the ease with which groups can be managed. In addition, meta-analyses suggest that social skill training interventions may have more benefits for aggressive children when they use heterogeneous grouping, rather than grouping aggressive children together (Ang & Hughes, 2001). Finally, smaller groups run in school settings require only one facilitator, which may be a school counselor, special education teacher, or other well-trained school personnel.

The specific sessions and activities used in Friendship Group were developed for the Fast Track program based on a strong set of studies demonstrating the efficacy of the approach. Lessons in the Fast Track Friendship Group manual draw from manuals evaluated in randomized trials that pre-dated Fast Track and focused on disliked, withdrawn 5th–6th graders (Bierman, 1986; Bierman & Furman, 1984), and rejected-aggressive 2nd–3rd graders (Bierman et al., 1987). In each of these studies, randomized trials documented significant effects on improved social skills and social behaviors, and also on the peer nominations provided by the peer partners.

Efficacy of the Fast Track Multi-Tiered SEL Programming

As noted above, based on prior evidence of the efficacy of the approaches in building social-emotional competencies and reducing aggressive-disruptive behaviors, Fast Track developed, adapted, and implemented its universal and targeted SEL programs. The research study evaluating Fast Track compared the progress of targeted high-risk children assigned randomly to the intervention or control groups, based on the school in which they matriculated in first grade. Overall, 891 children participated in the Fast Track study, with 445 receiving the Fast Track intervention and 446 in the control group. Two-thirds of the participating children were boys; 51% were African American, 47% were European American, and 2% were from other ethnic/racial groups. Annual assessments were conducted to track child progress, including annual ratings completed by teachers and direct assessments of child competencies. In addition, in the early years of the program, peer ratings and observations were collected.

In this chapter, we focus on intervention benefits that emerged in areas of social-emotional competencies and school behavioral adjustment. These benefits were likely driven primarily by the SEL programming used in Fast Track. However, given that Fast Track also included parent groups, home visits, and academic tutoring, the findings may also reflect benefits associated with those components in combination with the SEL programming.

Elementary School Findings for High-Risk Children

After one year of Fast Track intervention, high-risk children in the intervention group, relative to the control group, showed improved emotion recognition, emotion coping, and social problem-solving skills in direct assessments, reflecting the focus of the Friendship Group and PATHS Curriculum (CPPRG, 1999a, 2002a). In addition, children in the intervention group increased their rates of positive peer interaction at school and were nominated more often as "most liked" and less often as "least liked" by their classmates in sociometric interviews, demonstrating the effectiveness of the multi-tiered SEL programming in improving peer relations. Parents and teachers reported reductions in child aggression. By the end of third grade, 37% of the children in the Fast Track intervention group showed no signs of elevated risk – they were not diagnosed with an oppositional defiant disorder or conduct disorder in structured interviews with parents, did not have an individualized education plan (IEP) reflecting a need for special education, and were not rated by teachers or parents as having significant aggressive-disruptive behavior problems. In contrast, only 27% of the children in the control group had reduced risk status, demonstrating that the intervention produced a powerful one-third increase in the rate of low risk status by the end of third-grade among children who entered school at high risk (CPPRG, 2002a).

Fast Track continued intervention beyond the elementary school years through the tenth grade, including additional components in adolescence focused on helping reduce the risks target youth faced for involvement in antisocial activity and substance use. Following the end of intervention, target youth were followed through age 25 (to date). Overall, Fast Track was successful in its primary goal of reducing youth risk for antisocial outcomes, as intervention youth were less likely than those in the control group to be arrested as juveniles, and they were 24% less likely to commit serious juvenile crimes (CPPRG, 2010a). At age 25, youth in the Fast Track intervention group also demonstrated significantly lower levels of internalizing and externalizing behavior problems and lower rates of substance abuse.

These later Fast Track outcomes no doubt reflect the impact of multiple Fast Track intervention components and not only the multi-tiered SEL programming. Yet interestingly, mediation analyses suggest that the early gains children made in the area of social-emotional skill development played a key role in promoting these later-emerging reductions in adolescent and young adult criminal activity and problem behaviors. Sorensen, Dodge, and CPPRG (2016) conducted longitudinal analyses to test the links between children's improvement in three different domains (academic, self-regulation, and interpersonal skills) measured during the elementary school years (ages 6–11 years old) and their later criminal activity (based on arrest records and self-reported delinquency through age 20 years old). Mediation analyses indicated that improvements in children's self-regulation and social functioning during elementary school significantly predicted reduced risk for delinquency and crime outcomes in adolescence, mediating the intervention impact on these outcomes. Intervention-produced improvements in proximal academic outcomes during the elementary years also played a role, mediating intervention effects on adolescents' reduced use of mental health services. These analyses demonstrate the long-term value of multi-tiered SEL programming in the elementary years for realigning the developmental trajectories of children with or at risk for EBDs and reducing their risks for later negative adjustment outcomes.

Elementary Findings for Classmates

In addition to examining the benefits for the high-risk target children, the Fast Track research study also assessed effects on the non-targeted classmates who received PATHS through grades 1–3 (CPPRG, 1999b, 2010b). The high-risk target children were removed from these analyses that compared classmates attending schools assigned to the intervention versus control conditions. At the end of first grade, PATHS produced reduced aggression and improved peer relations in participating classrooms (CPPRG, 1999b). Teacher ratings and peer nominations of aggressive-disruptive behaviors were lower in intervention versus control classrooms (effect sizes $d = -.22$ for each). Observers documented higher levels of rule following, on-task behavior, and positive climate in intervention classrooms.

Additional analyses examined the longitudinal effects of PATHS on classmates. Relative to children who stayed in control schools for three years, those who received PATHS for three years ($N = 2,937$; CPPRG, 2010b) were rated as less aggressive-disruptive and more socially competent and engaged in learning engagement (effect sizes ranging from $d = .10$ to .40). In addition, intervention boys were significantly less likely to be nominated by peers as aggressive or hyperactive-disruptive. These findings are consistent with other research on the positive effects of universal SEL programming (Durlak et al., 2011; Greenberg & Abenavoli,

254 Karen L. Bierman, Mark T. Greenberg et al.

2017). Given that Fast Track included the Friendship Group program and other components to support high-risk children along with the universal PATHS program, these findings support the hypothesis that an integrated approach that combines universal and selected intervention can have powerful effects at the universal level of analysis.

PATHS to Success Program Findings

The findings from one additional randomized trial also warrant mention here. In 2009, the Fast Track Friendship Group and the PATHS Curriculum were used together in the PATHS to Success project, designed to promote the social-emotional and self-regulatory skills of kindergarten and first-grade children screened for elevated aggressive behavior at school entry (Greenberg, 2012). In this study, all children (universal-only and multi-tiered intervention groups) received the PATHS Curriculum in their classrooms. Within class-room, some aggressive children were randomly assigned to receive Friendship Group and additional parent training whereas the comparison group received only PATHS. Thus, this study addressed the specific question of whether children at high behavioral risk benefit when a coordinated tier-two SEL program (Friendship Group) is added to a universal tier-one SEL program (the PATHS Curriculum). In this study, children in the universal-only group (those identified as high in aggression but who were not assigned to Friendship Group) participated in the PATHS program as part of their normal classroom curriculum. Children assigned to the multi-tiered intervention group partici-pated in PATHS as well as weekly friendship groups that reinforced the skills of the PATHS program and provided the opportunity for structured practice of new skills. Children were screened for participation in the fall of the kindergarten year based on elevated aggressive behavior. Intervention occurred during the spring of the kindergarten year and fall of first grade. Post-intervention assessments occurred in the spring of first grade.

The models evaluating the effects of this study included a set of covariates to account for pre-existing differences between children in the universal-only and multi-tiered SEL conditions and used multiple imputation to address missing data (details in Greenberg, 2012). Specifically, propensity scores were estimated based on a broad range of child and family characteristics and used as pretreatment covariate, along with the pre-intervention baseline assessments of child outcomes (Stuart, 2010). Examination of the means showed that identified children in both the universal-only and multi-tiered intervention groups decreased in teacher-rated aggression and improved in teacher-rated social competence and peer-nominated social preference. The mean differences all favored the multi-tiered intervention group, but analyses revealed no significant difference. In other words, children who received multi-tiered SEL programming and those who received universal SEL programming only showed equivalent improvements. However, several other measures revealed group differences. On direct assessments of emotion recognition skills, children who had received the multi-tiered PATHS plus Friendship Group made significantly more gains than children who received universal PATHS alone ($d = .25$). In addition, significant incremental benefits associated with multi-tiered SEL emerged on teacher-rated measures of school readiness ($d = .19$). School readiness includes adaptive approaches to learning and the skills necessary to succeed in school, such as the ability and willingness to follow classroom routines and complete tasks. In addition, children in the multi-tiered SEL intervention condition exhibited fewer symptoms of inattention as rated by teachers, and this difference was highly statistically significant ($d = -.31$). At the follow-up assessments conducted one year later, multi-tiered intervention continued to have a significant impact on teacher ratings of child school readiness and adaptive learning engagement relative to universal intervention only, and in addition, children who received the multi-tiered SEL programming expressed significantly more empathy and kindness when presented with vignettes regarding the distress of others ($d = .24$). In addition, although non-significant, children in the multi-tiered intervention group showed lower average scores on self-report of depressed feelings, and higher averages scores on perceived social competence and friendship quality than those in the universal-only group.

In addition, we conducted a Latent Profile Analysis (LPA) to see which children were most likely to improve during the course of the intervention. The LPA analysis identified groups of children who improved, stayed the same, or declined in adjustment between the kindergarten pre-test and first-grade post-test. Overall, more children in the multi-tiered intervention group than in the universal-only group showed notable social and academic improvement (46% vs. 34%). In contrast, about half as many of the children in the multi-tiered intervention group (14%) vs. universal alone (24%) were in the group that got worse by the end of first grade. When the degree of initial risk was also examined, it was clear that the children who were at the highest risk were most likely to improve from the multi-tiered intervention. Among the children in the most aggressive group, 58% who received the multi-tiered intervention showed improvement, whereas only 40% who received the universal intervention alone showed improvement. This indicates that there was almost a 50% increase in the number of highly aggressive children who improved with multi-tiered SEL intervention as compared to the universal intervention alone.

Summary

Together, these studies demonstrate that multi-tiered SEL programming can be very effective. In Fast Track, positive benefits emerged for the classmates who received only the universal PATHS program as well as for the high-risk target children who received the combination of PATHS and tier-two Friendship Group (along with other Fast Track components). The results of the PATHS to Success study reflect the specific ways in which the addition of Friendship Group benefitted high-risk aggressive children in ways that extended beyond the effect of the universal program alone. The findings from that study on children's attention skills and learning engagement are important, given the contributions these skills make to future school success, along with social-emotional competencies (Blair & Raver, 2012).

It has been well-recognized that there is a need for supportive infrastructure or training and coaching at the school and the district levels to support effective SEL implementation by classroom teachers. However, there is also a need for infrastructure to support vertical integration of SEL programming across tiers based on level of need. Observers have noted a lack of coordination and fragmentation among school-based mental health services (Dwyer & Osher, 2000). It is rare to see school providers (e.g., classroom teachers, counselors, special-needs teachers, psychologists) coordinate their services, and it's even rarer to see coordination with community mental health service providers. As a result, schools rarely have aligned strategies and practices that support children across the classroom, pull-out services, and family support.

Moreover, the work of professionals such as school counselors, social workers, psychologists should be coordinated with universal efforts in the classroom and the school so that children interact with adults who use the same language and promote the same skills. For students who need a higher level of support, such student-support professionals supplement classroom-based instruction, often through small group work such as Friendship Groups. But rarely are classroom teachers taught the skills to reinforce and support the competencies children learn during these groups. Reciprocally, there is a need for training for local providers of evidenced-based mental health services (such as community mental health programs) to connect them to universal programs that are being conducted in classrooms (Weist, 2014). If these professionals know the social-emotional content and instructional practices that teachers are using in classrooms, they can integrate them into their own work with students (Domitrovich et al., 2017). A key challenge will be to synthesize research from different disciplines so that we recognize the essential elements of diverse programs and policies that support coordination between universal modes and tiered services – and to put these elements in place to sustain comprehensive school- and district-wide SEL programming.

Summary and Conclusions

Extensive research has demonstrated the efficacy of universal SEL programs in boosting the positive social-emotional skills of elementary school children, promoting increases in positive behavior and decreases in aggressive and disruptive behaviors in the classroom (Durlak et al., 2011; Dusenbury & Weissberg, 2016; Schonert-Reichl & Weissberg, 2015). The skills promoted by these programs, including emotional understanding, interpersonal relationship skills, self-control, and social problem-solving skills foster success at school and beyond. Indeed, Jones, Greenberg, and Crowley (2015) found that these social-emotional skills measured in kindergarten by teacher ratings predicted a wide range of early adult outcomes, including high school graduation, employment, mental health, and reduced criminal arrests. The PATHS curriculum is one example of an evidence-based universal SEL program that effectively promotes these skills, and a number of others are available for schools to choose from. For example, in the 2013 review by CASEL, eight universal SEL programs were supported by replicated randomized trials with significant positive effects evident at least two years after program implementation: Caring School Community, PATHS, Positive Action, Resolving Conflicts Creatively Program, Responsive Classroom, Second Step, Social Decision Making/Problem Solving Program, and Steps to Respect (Schonert-Reichl & Weissberg, 2015).

At the same time, universal SEL programs alone are unlikely to meet the needs of the 10% to 15% of children who have or are at risk for EBDs as a function of delays or deficits in their social-emotional and self-regulatory skill development. These children benefit from tier two SEL programming in the form of small groups that use evidence-based social-emotional skill training programs to remediate and strengthen skill knowledge and skill performance. An extensive research base documents the efficacy of social-emotional skill training programs to promote the social-emotional skills and social behavior of children with or at risk for EBDs, including children exhibiting a diverse set of social difficulties ranging from aggressive social behavior to social awkwardness and withdrawal (Ang & Hughes, 2001; Gresham et al., 2004). In addition to the Fast Track Friendship Group program, a number of other tier two social skill training programs have proven successful at improving the ability of aggressive children to manage strong feelings and control impulses, with the goal of reducing disruptive and aggressive behaviors that undermine peer relationships. Like Fast Track, many of these programs include parents to extend support for self-control skills to the home. Two examples are the Coping Power program (Lochman & Wells, 2004) that promoted improved school behavior and reduced aggression in a randomized-controlled trial, and the Stop Now and Plan (SNAP) program (Burke & Loeber, 2015) that similarly reduced aggression, conduct problems, and externalizing behavior problems among children who screened in on the basis of elevated aggression. In addition, the S.S.Grin program (DeRosier, 2004) warrants mention, given its positive effects in a randomized trial on peer liking, feelings of self-efficacy, and reductions in social anxiety and antisocial affiliates among elementary school children with poor peer relations.

This chapter has highlighted the value of coordinating universal and tier two programming, providing evidence from the Fast Track Program and the PATHS to Success program that coordinated programming can be implemented with high quality and promote concurrent improvements in the social-emotional skills and behaviors of both targeted high-risk students as well as their classmates. These findings highlight the potential benefit to all students, particularly those with or at risk for EBD that will occur if schools commit to the high-quality and sustained implementation of coordinated, evidence-based tier one and tier two SEL programming in the elementary school years. Keys to success include the selection of SEL programs with strong empirical evidence of effectiveness, and the commitment to professional development support necessary to help school personnel implement programs with high fidelity.

Acknowledgments

* Members of the Conduct Problems Prevention Research Group (CPPRG) in alphabetical order are Karen L. Bierman, John D. Coie, Kenneth A. Dodge, Mark T. Greenberg, John E. Lochman, Robert J. McMahon, and Ellen E. Pinderhughes.

The development of the original Fast Track Friendship Group program was supported by National Institute of Mental Health (NIMH) Grants R18MH48043, R18MH50951, R18MH50952, R18MH50953, K05MH00797, and K05MH01027; National Institute on Drug Abuse (NIDA) Grants DA016903, K05DA15226, RC1DA028248, and P30DA023026; and Department of Education Grant S184U30002. The Center for Substance Abuse Prevention also provided support through a memorandum of agreement with the NIMH. In addition, the Friendship Group program was further developed and refined in the context of projects funded by the NIMH R34MH085889, the Pennsylvania Department of Health, and R305A150488 funded by the Institute of Educational Sciences. The opinions expressed are those of the authors and are not necessarily endorsed by the funding agencies.

In developing this program, we are grateful for the close collaboration of the Altoona Area School District, Bellefonte Area School District, Durham Public Schools, Harrisburg School District, Highline Public Schools, Juniata County School District, Middletown Area School District, Mifflin County School District, Metropolitan Nashville Public Schools, State College Area School District, Seattle Public Schools, Steelton-Highspire School District, Tyrone Area School District, York City School District, Barnardos Children's Charity of Ireland, and Barnardos Children's Charity of the United Kingdom. We greatly appreciate the hard work and dedication of the many staff members who implemented the project, provided feedback and suggestions, collected the evaluation data, and assisted with data management and analyses.

References

Ang, R., & Hughes, J. (2001). Differential benefits of skills training with antisocial youth based on group composition: A meta-analytic investigation. *School Psychology Review, 31*, 164–185.

Asher, S. R., & Oden, S. (1977). Coaching children in social skills for friendship making. *Child Development, 48*, 495–506.

Bierman, K. L. (1986). Process of change during social skills training with preadolescents and its relation to treatment outcome. *Child Development, 57*, 230–240.

Bierman, K. L. (2004). *Peer rejection: Developmental processes and intervention strategies.* New York: Guilford Press.

Bierman, K. L., & Furman, W. (1984). The effects of social skills training and peer involvement on the social adjustment of preadolescents. *Child Development, 55*, 151–162.

Bierman, K. L., Greenberg, M. T., Coie, J. D., Dodge, K. A., Lochman, J. E., & McMahon, R. J. (2017). *Social and emotional skills training for children: The Fast Track Friendship Group Manual.* New York: Guilford Press.

Bierman, L. L., Miller, C. L., & Stabb, S. D. (1987). Improving the social behavior and peer acceptance of rejected boys: Effects of social skill training with instructions and prohibitions. *Journal of Consulting and Clinical Psychology, 55*, 194–200.

Blair, C., & Raver, C. C. (2012). Individual development and evolution: Experiential canalization of self-regulation development. *Developmental Psychology, 48*, 647–657.

Burke, J. D., & Loeber, R. (2015). The effectiveness of the Stop Now and Plan (SNAP) Program for boys at risk for violence and delinquency. *Prevention Science, 16*, 242–253.

Collaborative for Academic, Social and Emotional Learning. (2013). *The 2013 CASEL Guide: Effective social and emotional learning programs – Preschool and elementary school edition.* Chicago, IL: Author.

Conduct Problems Prevention Research Group (CPPRG). (1992). A developmental and clinical model for the prevention of conduct disorders: The Fast Track Program. *Development and Psychopathology, 4*, 509–528.

Conduct Problems Prevention Research Group (CPPRG). (1999a). Initial impact of the fast track prevention trial for conduct problems: I. The high-risk sample. *Journal of Consulting and Clinical Psychology, 67*, 631–647.

Conduct Problems Prevention Research Group (CPPRG). (1999b). Initial impact of the Fast Track prevention trial for conduct problems: II. Classroom effects. *Journal of Consulting and Clinical Psychology, 67*, 648–657.

Conduct Problems Prevention Research Group (CPPRG). (2002a). Evaluation of the first 3 years of the Fast Track prevention trial with children at high risk for adolescent conduct problems. *Journal of Abnormal Child Psychology, 30*, 19–35.

Conduct Problems Prevention Research Group (CPPRG). (2010a). Fast Track intervention effects on youth arrests and delinquency. *Journal of Experimental Criminology, 6*, 131–157. doi:10.1007/s11292-010-9091-7

Conduct Problems Prevention Research Group (CPPRG). (2010b). The effects of a multiyear social-emotional learning program: The role of student and school characteristics. *Journal of Consulting and Clinical Psychology, 78*, 156–168.

DeRosier, M. E. (2004). Building relationships and combating bullying: Effectiveness of a school-based social skill group intervention. *Journal of Clinical Child and Adolescent Psychology, 33*, 196–201.

Dodge, K., Lansford, J. E., & Dishion, T. J. (2006). The problem of deviant peer influences in intervention programs. In K. A. Dodge, T. J. Dishion, & J. E. Lansford (Eds.), *Deviant peer influences in programs for youth* (pp. 3–13). New York: Guilford Press.

Domitrovich, C. E., Durlak, J. A., Staley, K. C., & Weissberg, R. P. (2017). Social-emotional competence: An essential factor for promoting positive adjustment and reducing risk in schoolchildren. *Child Development, 88*, 408–416.

Durlak, J. A., Weissberg, R. P., Dymnicki, A. B., Taylor, R. D., & Schellinger, K. B. (2011). The impact of enhancing students' social and emotional learning: A meta-analysis of school-based universal interventions. *Child Development, 82*, 405–432.

Dusenbury, L., & Weissberg, R. P. (2016). *Social and emotional learning for elementary-school children: Finding from research and implications for policy.* Chicago, IL: Collaborative for Academic, Social, and Emotional Learning.

Dwyer, K. P., & Osher, D. (2000). *Safeguarding our children: An action guide.* Washington, DC: US Departments of Education and Justice, American Institutes for Research.

Farmer, T. W., Estell, D. B., Hall, C. M., Pearl, R., Rodkin, P., & Van Acker, R. M. (2008). Interpersonal competence configurations, behavior problems, and social adjustment in preadolescence. *Journal of Emotional and Behavior Disorders, 16*, 195–212.

Fite, P. J., Wimsatt, A. R., Vitulano, M. L., Rathert, J. L., & Schwartz, S. (2012). Examination of peer rejection and depressive symptoms as mediators of the link between rule-breaking behavior and poor academic performance. *Journal of Psychopathology and Behavioral Assessment, 34*, 164–171.

Greenberg, M. (2012). *PATHS to success – Final project report.* Pennsylvania Department of Health, Health Research Grants Unpublished report.

Greenberg, M. T. (2006). Promoting resilience in children and youth: Preventive interventions and their interface with neuroscience. *Annals of the New York Academy of Sciences, 1094*, 139–150.

Greenberg, M. T., & Abenavoli, R. (2017). Universal interventions: Fully exploring their impacts and potential to produce population-level impacts. *Journal of Research on Educational Effectiveness, 10*, 40–67.

Greenberg, M. T., Domitrovich, C. E., Weissberg, R. P., & Durlak, J. A. (2017). Social and emotional learning as a public health approach to education. *Future of Children, 27*(1), 13–32.

Greenberg, M. T., & Kusché, C. A. (1998). Preventive intervention for school-age deaf children: The PATHS curriculum. *Journal of Deaf Studies and Deaf Education, 3*(1), 49–63.

Greenberg, M. T., Kusché, C. A., Cook, E. T., & Quamma, J. P. (1995). Promoting emotional competence in school-aged children: The effects of the PATHS curriculum. *Development and Psychopathology, 7*, 117–136.

Gresham, F. M., Cook, C., Crews, S., & Kern, L. (2004). Social skills training for children and youth with emotional and behavioral disorders: Validity considerations and future directions. *Behavioral Disorders, 30*, 32–46.

Gresham, F. M., Elliott, S. N., & Kettler, R. J. (2010). Base rates of social skills acquisition/performance deficits, strengths, and problem behaviors: An analysis of the Social Skills Improvement System – Rating scales. *Journal of Psychological Assessment, 22*(4), 809–815.

Gresham, F. M., Van Bao, M., & Cook, C. R. (2006). Social skills training for teaching replacement behaviors: Remediating acquisition deficits in at-risk students. *Behavioral Disorders, 31*(4), 363–377.

Jones, D. E., Greenberg, M., & Crowley, M. (2015). Early social-emotional functioning and public health: The relationship between kindergarten social competence and future wellness. *American Journal of Public Health, 105*(11), 2283–2290.

Kam, C. M., Greenberg, M. T., & Walls, C. T. (2003). Examining the role of implementation quality in school-based prevention using the PATHS curriculum. *Prevention Science, 4*, 55–63.

Kusché, C. A., & Greenberg, M. T., & CPPRG. (2011). *Grade level PATHS (Grades 1–2).* South Deerfield: Channing-Bete Co.

La Greca, A. M., & Landoll, R. R. (2011). Peer influences. In W. K. Silverman & A. Field (Eds.), *Anxiety disorders in children and adolescents: Research, assessment, and intervention* (2nd ed.) (pp. 323–346). London: Cambridge University Press.

Lavallee, K. L., Bierman, K. L., Nix, R. L., & CPPRG. (2005). The impact of first-grade "friendship group" experiences on child social outcomes in the Fast Track Program. *Journal of Abnormal Child Psychology, 33*, 307–324.

Lee, P., & Bierman, K. L. (2018). Year-to-year variations in student-teacher relationship quality: Associations with aggressive-disruptive behavior problems. *Journal of School Psychology, 70*, 1–15.

Lochman, J. E., & CPPRG. (1995). Screening of child behavior problems for prevention programs at school entry. *Journal of Consulting and Clinical Psychology, 63*, 549–559.

Lochman, J. E., & Wells, K. C. (2004). The coping power program for preadolescent aggressive boys and their parents: Outcome effects at the 1-year follow-up. *Journal of Consulting and Clinical Psychology, 72*(4), 571.

Mikami, A. Y., & Hinshaw, S. P. (2006). Resilient adolescent adjustment among girls: Buffers of childhood peer rejection and attention-deficit/hyperactivity disorder. *Journal of Abnormal Child Psychology, 34*, 825–839.

Pelham, W. E., & Fabiano, G. A. (2008). Evidence-based psychosocial treatment for attention deficit/hyperactivity disorder: An update. *Journal of Clinical Child and Adolescent Psychology, 37*, 185–214.

Pepler, D. J., & Bierman, K. L. (2018). With a little help from my friends: The importance of peer relationships for social-emotional development, Edna Bennett Pierce Prevention Research Center,

Pennsylvania State University. Retrieved from http://prevention.psu.edu/uploads/files/rwjf450248-PeerRelationships.pdf accessed January 21, 2020.

Ratcliffe, B., Wong, M., Dossetor, D., & Hayes, S. (2014). Teaching social-emotional skills to school-age children with autism spectrum disorder: A treatment versus control trial in 41 mainstream schools. *Research in Autism Spectrum Disorders, 8*, 1722–1733.

Riggs, N. R., Greenberg, M. T., Kusché, C. A., & Pentz, M. A. (2006). The mediational role of neurocognition in the behavioral outcomes of a social-emotional prevention program in elementary school: Effects of the PATHS curriculum. *Prevention Science, 7*, 91–102.

Schonert-Reichl, K. A., & Weissberg, R. P. (2015). Social and emotional learning: Children. In T. P. Gullotta & M. Bloom (Eds.), *Encyclopedia of primary prevention and health promotion Part II* (2nd ed., pp. 936–949). New York: Springer.

Sorensen, L. C., & Dodge, K. A., and the Conduct Problems Prevention Research Group (2016). How does the fast track intervention prevent adverse outcomes in young adulthood? *Child Development, 87*(2), 429–445.

Stuart, E. A. (2010). Matching methods for causal inference: A review and a look forward. *Statistical science: A review journal of the Institute of Mathematical Statistics, 25*(1), 1–21.

Sugai, G., & Horner, R. (2002). The evolution of discipline practices: School-wide positive behavior supports. *Child and Family Behavior Therapy, 24*, 23–50.

Sutherland, K. S., & Oswald, D. P. (2005). The relationship between teacher and student behavior in classrooms for students with emotional and behavioral disorders: Transactional processes. *Journal of Child and Family Studies, 14*, 1–14.

Troop, W. P., & Asher, S. R. (1999). Teaching peer relationship competence in schools. In R. J. Stevens (Ed.), *Teaching in American schools* (pp. 141–171). Columbus, OH: Merrill.

Waas, G. A. (2006). Peer relationships. In G. A. Waas (Ed.), *Children's needs III: Development, prevention, and intervention* (pp. 325–340). Washington, DC: National Association of School Psychologists.

Wagner, M., Kutash, K., Duchnowski, A. J., Epstein, M. H., & Sumi, W. C. (2005). The children and youth we serve: A national picture of the characteristics of students with emotional disturbances receiving special education. *Journal of Emotional and Behavioral Disorders, 13*(2), 79–96.

Weist, M. D. (2014). Challenges and ideas from a research program on high quality, evidence-based practice in school mental health. *Journal of Clinical Child and Adolescent Psychology, 43*, 244–255.

18 Checking the Connections between Effective Interventions for Students with Emotional/Behavioral Disorders

Allison Bruhn, Sara McDaniel, and Kay Augustine

Over the last 30 years, the percentage of students receiving special education services under the "emotional disturbance" label has remained stable at less than 1% of the school-age population (U.S. Department of Education, 2015). Unfortunately, the experiences and outcomes for this small group of students also remain relatively unchanged. Compared to students with other disabilities, students with emotional/behavioral disorders (EBD) are more likely to be living in poverty, in a single-parent household, and with a parent who does not have a formal post-high school education (Lipscomb, Lacoe, Liu, & Haimson, 2018). Further, they are more likely to attend multiple schools and low performing schools, which may be a result of a required reassignment or suspension/expulsion (Lipscomb et al., 2018). These factors alone present elevated risk for poor academic and social outcomes, while also highlighting potential leverage points for intervention. For instance, being deliberate and purposeful in communicating with parents, as well as providing positive mentoring may be critical in addressing these risk factors. Socially, students with EBD are significantly more likely to have been bullied and to have engaged in bullying behavior than their peers with other disabilities (Lipscomb et al., 2018), thus underscoring the need for safe and supportive schools that help students develop positive relationships. Given their social struggles in school, it is not surprising that students with EBD report significantly fewer positive views about school, such as being happy at school and feeling like part of the school, compared to their peers with other disabilities (Lipscomb et al., 2018).

The abysmal outcomes, and the risk factors that contribute to them, signify an urgent need to identify and support students with or at risk for EBD as well as those students who exhibit persistent emotional and behavioral problems that may lead to negative outcomes. In schools, supporting these students requires consistent and high quality implementation of evidence-based practices. Though evidence-based practices generally refer to a collection of scientifically tested practices resulting in consistently positive outcomes for a specific population, researchers have distilled these practices into individual components or elements (Sutherland, Conroy, McLeod, Kunemund, & McKnight, 2019). The logic is that an evidence-based practice is often a combination of multiple, effective, individual practices (i.e., components, elements; Sutherland et al., 2019). Ideally, implementation involves matching practice elements to students' individual needs (McDaniel, Bruhn, & Mitchell, 2015).

In this chapter, we examine three individual practices with evidence of improving students' social, emotional, behavioral, and academic well-being: adult–student mentoring, home–school collaboration, and data-based decision-making. We focus on these practices due to their strong theoretical and empirical evidence of effectiveness in addressing the critical risk factors associated with youth who have or are at risk for EBD. Ecological systems theory (Bronfenbrenner, 1992), for example, highlights the importance of the interaction between

262 *Allison Bruhn et al.*

a child's development and their environment, including home, school, and community "units." Each of these "units" contributes to the child's social system, and in turn, directly impacts how the child develops. As such, adult–student mentoring and home–school collaboration align with theoretical underpinnings for improving youth development as each has the potential to affect the child's social system. Further, research has shown data-based decision-making within and across tiers of intervention is integral to improving student outcomes (Bruhn, Rila, Mahatmya, Estrapala, & Hendrix, 2018; Fuchs et al., 2014). In this chapter we describe each of these practices and how they relate to the risk factors and outcomes for students with or at risk for EBD. Then, we review three common school-based, multi-component, research-based interventions that incorporate these practice elements: Check-In/Check-Out (CICO); Check & Connect (C&C); and Check, Connect, and Expect (CCE).

Mentoring

As previously described, students with EBD may experience risk factors from home and community stressors (e.g., poverty, single parent home; Lipscomb et al., 2018). Familial factors such as mobility, household dysfunction, abuse, and neglect can further impact outcomes for this high-risk population (Lloyd, Bruhn, Sutherland, & Bradshaw, 2019; National Institute of Mental Health, 2018). Thus, the need for children and youth to develop positive relationships with adults is critical, as this can serve as a protective factor against the deleterious outcomes that might otherwise result from a difficult home life.

Although positive relationships may evolve organically through informal conversation, more deliberate relationship-building may come through formal mentoring. The goal of mentoring is to facilitate healthy relationships between an adult and child, and in turn, improve social, academic, and behavioral outcomes (Caldarella, Adams, Valentine, & Young, 2009). Though all adult/student relationships are important, in mentoring, the focus is on a singular adult being a critical contact for an individual student, shifting from a typical informal adult–student relationship in a school to a formal mentoring relationship. In schools, an adult mentor's responsibilities may include, but are not limited to, providing unconditional positive regard, care, and concern; giving pre-corrections; listening; encouraging; establishing trust; and providing performance feedback in the form of specific praise and error correction (Cook et al., 2015).

Some evaluation of mentoring programs indicates enduring mentoring relationships that last a year or longer are the most effective, while early termination of mentoring relationships can be detrimental to students' emotional well-being (Grossman & Rhodes, 2002). If students have a history of neglectful, abusive, or combative relationships with adults, they may be particularly vulnerable when a mentoring relationship does not progress as intended or is prematurely ended (Grossman & Rhodes, 2002). These findings align with ecological systems theory (Bronfenbrenner, 1992) in that how a student experiences relationships at home or in the community may impact how they experience or progress in a mentoring relationship at school.

Research on the effects of matching adult mentors to students based on age, gender, and ethnicity appears to be mixed, with a recent study on Check & Connect indicating these variables were not significant predictors of the quality of the mentor–mentee relationship (Kern, Harrison, Custer, & Mehta, 2018). Generally, adult mentors are selected based on interest, availability, and capacity to establish a positive relationship with the student (Hawken, 2006). Research has shown school-based mentoring programs can improve outcomes of students with externalizing or internalizing problems, though most research has focused on reducing externalizing issues (Cook et al., 2015). Recently, Cook and colleagues (2015) demonstrated a functional relation between students' reduced internalizing behaviors and a school-based structured mentoring program. The finding that students with internalizing problems can benefit from mentoring is particularly encouraging, given the limited research on and supports for this subgroup of students with or at risk for EBD (Cook et al., 2015).

Home–School Communication

A second practice element essential to improving student outcomes is communication between home and school (Sutherland et al., 2019), with literature suggesting social interaction between caregiver systems (e.g., home and school) can serve as a conduit for child development (Neal & Neal, 2013). As it relates to students with EBD who may be receiving special education services under IDEA (2004), caregivers have specific and guaranteed rights related to securing appropriate educational services for their children. Simultaneously, educators are mandated to involve parents (or caregivers) in their child's education (Turnbull, 2005). Meta-analyses indicate parental involvement has a positive impact on student achievement that is consistent across ages and race (Jeynes, 2007, 2012). To this end, one way to facilitate parental or caregiver involvement is for school personnel to initiate communication with families.

Home–school communication has been defined as "a regular system for communicating with the focal student's parents or guardians about the student's social, behavioral, or academically related skills and/or difficulties" (Sutherland et al., 2019, p. 81). Traditionally, schools have engaged in one-way communication through handbooks, newsletters, or reports cards (Muscott et al., 2008) with the purpose of informing caregivers about things going on at school. Although informing caregivers about events, activities, or student progress is important, effective home–school communication also must include a two-way, reciprocal exchange of information (Muscott et al., 2008). This involves teachers delivering information about student progress, asking families for feedback, and similarly, families providing information and feedback to the teacher. For caregivers who speak limited or no English, translated materials are critical for understanding and relationship building. Further, one key to implementing effective home–school communication procedures is for teachers to be aware of student culture, interests, and home situations that may impede caregivers from communicating (e.g., time, work, disability, lack of technology access, language) or that result in students being severely punished at home (Hawken, 2006).

Data-Based Decision-Making

A third practice element is data-based decision-making, which should be used to identify students with or at risk for EBD who need intervention and to monitor student progress once in intervention. A school site team identifies students for intervention using multiple data sources such as office discipline referrals (ODRs), systematic behavior screeners, teacher nomination, attendance, and academic data such as grades or work completion (Mitchell, Bruhn, & Lewis, 2016). In positive behavioral intervention and support frameworks (PBIS), the general rule is that once students accrue 2 to 5 ODRs then they are eligible for targeted interventions such as Check-in/Check-out (Mitchell et al., 2016). Validated screening tools such as the Strengths and Difficulties Questionnaire (SDQ; Goodman, 1997), the Behavioral and Emotional Screening System (BASC-2 BESS; Kamphaus & Reynolds, 2007), and the Systematic Screening for Behavior Disorders (SSBD; Walker & Severson, 1992) may be completed universally (i.e., all students in the building are rated) to identify students for targeted or intensive supports (e.g., Tiers 2 or 3), or they may be completed after a student has been identified for a Tier 2 intervention with data from the assessment used to match students to an appropriate intervention (McDaniel et al., 2015).

Once the student is in intervention, data-based decision-making involves collecting student-level data on an on-going basis, evaluating the data to determine how the student is responding to intervention, and making programmatic changes as needed (Jung, McMaster, Kunkel, Shin, & Stecker, 2018). Although data-based decision-making traditionally has been used for assessing academic progress and modifying academic instruction, researchers agree this is also a necessary practice for behavior (Wehby & Kern, 2014). Schools may use ODRs, behavioral rating scales, or systematic direct observation to measure behavior at baseline (prior to intervention) and during intervention. Other important data may include course failures, grade point average, and attendance. While there is no set of standard decision rules for judging behavioral progress, student support teams charged with tracking data may set a priori decision rules related to establishing mastery criteria, demonstrating adequate progress, and fading or intensifying intervention.

When data indicate a student is not responding to a single intervention, additional or different interventions may be necessary. For example, researchers have demonstrated that integrating check-in/check-out with pull-out cognitive-behavioral instruction may accelerate improvements in behavior (McDaniel & Bruhn, 2019). Similarly, Bruhn and colleagues (2018) found significant improvements in students' positive behavior when teachers implemented a technology-based self-monitoring intervention, monitored data on an on-going basis, and implemented adaptations to intervention based on student response.

Check-In/Check-Out

Check-In/Check-Out (CICO); Check & Connect (C&C); and Check, Connect, and Expect (CCE) are three research-based, multi-component interventions that incorporate the theoretically and empirically supported practice elements of adult–student mentoring, home–school communication, and data-based decision-making. CICO is considered the least intensive of the three interventions, and it is also the most widely used Tier 2 intervention in schools implementing PBIS (Conley, Kittleman, Massar, & McIntosh, 2018). CICO, also known as the Behavior Education Program (BEP), was designed to align with critical features of Tier 2 supports. Specifically, Tier 2 interventions should be readily available, require minimal time and effort from teachers, be easy to implement consistently regardless of skill and training, and align with Tier 1 systems and practices (Mitchell et al., 2016).

Students are assigned an adult mentor with whom the students meet to start and end the day. During "check in," the adult mentor engages students in a brief conversation to see how they are feeling (e.g., did they eat breakfast), check if they have all class materials, and review their daily progress report (DPR). The purpose of the check-in is for the mentor to gauge the student's readiness for the day, while also providing positive attention and encouragement to meet the DPR goal. The DPR is a form that lists the positive behaviors the student is expected to display (e.g., Be Respectful). Students take the DPR to each class throughout the day. At the end of each class, teachers rate the student on how well they displayed the listed behaviors. After DPR completion, the teacher reviews the scores with the student while also providing specific praise or corrective feedback. Ideally, this interaction is

Checking the Connections 265

positive, as the goal is to provide multiple opportunities for the student to receive positive attention.

At the end of the day, the student and mentor complete the "check-out." If the DPR goal is met, the mentor provides specific praise, and possibly, additional reinforcement (e.g., PBIS ticket). If the goal is not met, the mentor may ask the student about any issues or problems occurring that day, and then follow with corrective and encouraging feedback. Finally, the mentor checks to make sure the student has all materials necessary to take home (e.g., homework) and sends a copy of the DPR with the student to bring home to his/her caregiver. The DPR may include a note to the caregiver further describing how the student's day went. The caregiver views and signs the DPR, with the student returning the signed DPR to the mentor at the next morning's check-in. The purpose of this component is to enhance home–school communication.

This process continues daily with the mentor and/or school-site team regularly reviewing DPR data to determine whether the student is responding to intervention. Based on DPR data indicating a student is or is not responding, the team can make data-driven decisions to continue, adapt, or discontinue CICO. For students who are initially non-responsive, a midday check-in with the mentor may be added (Swoszowski, McDaniel, Jolivette, & Melius, 2013), the DPR goal may be lowered (Crone, Hawken, & Horner, 2010), or reinforcement beyond praise may be added (Bruhn, McDaniel, Rila, & Estrapala, 2018). Conversely, for students who are responsive, a variety of fading strategies such as gradually increasing goals and decreasing rates of reinforcement may be employed so that the student maintains positive behavior changes and successfully transitions back to Tier 1 supports only (Lane, Capizzi, Fisher, & Ennis, 2012; McDaniel & Bruhn, 2016; Miller, Durfene, Sterling, Olmi & Bachmayer, 2014).

CICO Research

As the most widely implemented Tier 2 intervention, CICO is also the most researched Tier 2 intervention with at least four published systematic reviews on CICO (Hawken, Bundock, Kladis, O'Keeffe, Barrett, 2014; Maggin, Zurheide, Pickett, & Baillie, 2015; Mitchell, Adamson, & McKenna, 2017; Wolfe et al., 2016). Across reviews, studies have included single-subject and group designs with elementary, middle, and high school students with or at risk for EBD. Though, most studies have occurred at the elementary and middle school level (Hawken et al., 2014). Although these four reviews indicated positive changes in academic engagement, off-task behavior, disruptive behavior, DPR scores, and ODR, some reviews reported mixed findings as well as potential moderators of response to CICO.

For instance, in the first review of CICO which included 28 studies, Hawken and colleagues (2014) reported the eight group design studies demonstrated small median effect sizes (e.g., $d = .37$ [n = 6]; $R^2 = .23$ [n = 2]) and single-subject studies approached criteria for effectiveness (i.e., >70% PND; Scruggs & Mastropieri, 1998). Three reviews of CICO included quality appraisals for methodological rigor using specific standards (Maggin et al., 2015; Mitchell et al., 2017; Wolfe et al., 2016). Of 22 studies reviewed, Maggin and colleagues (2015) found only nine single-case studies (with 35 participant cases) met the What Works Clearinghouse (WWC) standards. Of these, 28 cases met design standards and provided evidence of effectiveness, thus indicating the practice is evidence-based per WWC standards. Of the five group studies, only one study met WWC design standards. Findings from group studies produced no discernable positive effects, thus differing from single-case findings. Although this is concerning, plausible explanations related to moderating variables such as behavioral function and disability were not evaluated.

Similarly, Wolfe and colleagues (2016) appraised the quality of the research base using standards from Horner et al. (2005); Gersten et al. (2005); and Lane, Kalberg, & Shepcaro (2009). Authors noted the most robust effects of CICO were limited to students with attention-maintained behavior, and thus deemed it an evidence-based practice for this subgroup of students. This is not surprising, given the heavy role adults play in building a relationship and providing feedback to students in CICO. Although CICO can be modified to address other behavioral functions, this review indicated there were not enough studies to determine whether CICO is an evidence-based practice for students with problem behavior maintained by something other than adult attention.

Another review of CICO applied quality indicators from the Council for Exceptional Children Standards for Evidence-Based Practices in Special Education (2014; Mitchell et al., 2017). Of the 29 studies reviewed, only five met the CEC standards for quality research, with all five showing reductions in problem behavior. Authors acknowledged CICO as an evidence-based practice, but with serious caution due to the lack of clarity about under what conditions and for whom CICO is effective (Mitchell et al., 2017).

These reviews indicate the quality of some research on CICO is not meeting various scientific standards. However, there is still a breadth of high-quality evidence to suggest CICO is effective for students exhibiting signs of risk for an EBD. For students with a confirmed EBD diagnosis, most studies have taken place at residential educational facilities (Ennis, Jolivette, Swoszowski, & Johnson, 2012; Swoszowski, Jolivette, Fredrick, & Heflin, 2012; Swoszowski, McDaniel, Jolivette, & Melius, 2013). In two of these studies, researchers conducted functional behavior assessments (FBA) to determine whether CICO was effective for attention- and escape-maintained behavior (Ennis et al., 2012; Swoszowski et al., 2012). Results were inconsistent, with one study demonstrating better effects for students with attention-maintained behavior than with escape-motivated behavior (Ennis et al., 2012) and the other study demonstrating students did not respond differentially based on function (Swoszowski et al., 2012). In a third study at a residential facility with students who had varying DSM-IV diagnoses (e.g., disruptive behavior disorder, encopresis, post-traumatic stress disorder, attention deficit disorder, reactive attachment disorder), three of four students were responsive to CICO as evidenced by decreases in off-task behavior. For one student who was nonresponsive, adding an extra check-in with the mentor at midday to increase feedback proved an effective way to intensify CICO, and in turn, reduce problem behavior (Swoszowski et al., 2013). Interestingly, all four participants had attention-maintained behavior.

Evidence suggests CICO is effective for students who are motivated by attention, yet the role of function in moderating the effects of CICO continues to perplex researchers (Wolfe et al., 2016). Given CICO is predicated on providing frequent, positive attention from adults through check-ins with a mentor and teacher interactions about the DPR, it makes sense students who thrive on adult attention would be successful in this intervention. For students with escape-maintained behavior, it is possible basic CICO could be effective, but adapting CICO to meet students' avoidance motivation is warranted. For instance, this may include providing students with escape-based reinforcement for meeting a daily DPR goal (e.g., timed break during class, homework pass; Ennis et al., 2012).

Similarly, researchers have begun to examine how to adapt CICO for students with internalizing behaviors, as most research on CICO has been conducted with students demonstrating disruptive, non-compliant behavior (e.g., Hunter, Chenier, & Gresham, 2014). Adaptations must begin with the identification process. If schools rely solely on

Checking the Connections 267

ODRs or other measures of externalizing behaviors, students with internalizing issues are not likely to be referred for CICO. Thus, validated screening tools that capture internalizing behaviors may be necessary (Hunter et al., 2014). Potential adaptations for internalizing behavior include (a) aligning DPR expectations and goals with positive replacement behaviors (Hunter et al., 2014); and (b) peer-mediated CICO in which peers serve as mentors with some adult supervision (Dart et al., 2015).

Check & Connect

Check & Connect (C&C; Christenson, Stout, & Pohl, 2012) is an intervention designed to support the school engagement of elementary and secondary students. In some states (e.g., Iowa), C&C has been identified as a more intense Tier 2 intervention; that is, it requires more time and resources than basic CICO or other Tier 2 supports. Others consider it a Tier 3, intensive intervention. Regardless, C&C is used with students who need a longer-term, more intensive intervention rather than a "quick fix," as the recommended duration is two years (Christenson et al., 2012).

To be successfully implemented, schools must commit to intervention training, monitoring the process and outcomes; and providing on-going recruitment, training, and support for mentors. Because of the nature and intensity of C&C, it is systematized through specific implementation steps: preparation, implementation, evaluation, and maintenance (Christenson et al., 2012, p. 21). The implementation process involves oversight from a building coordinator who assists with referrals, training and support of mentors, coordinating data, connecting mentors with resources in the school and community, and monitoring fidelity of implementation (Christenson et al., 2012, p. 78). Initially, implementing sites use building or district data to determine the specific criteria for referring students to C&C. These criteria are selected from observable indicators of disengagement such as time on task, grades, course credits, attendance, ODRs, and suspensions (www.checkandconnect.umn.edu). More specifically, early warning signs of risk include absence of 10% or more of school days, more than two ODRs, inability to read by the end of third grade, a course failure in math or English in sixth to ninth grades, a GPA of less than 2.0, and two or more failures in ninth grade (Balfanz, Bridgeland, Bruce, & Fox, 2012).

Once students have been identified for C&C, a mentor uses observable indicators (i.e., academic and behavioral data) in conjunction with internal indicators such as cognitive and affective engagement to identify areas of student risk and as a guide to determine potential interventions (Christenson et al., 2012, p. 105). Cognitive internal indicators include students' perceived relevance of schoolwork and self-regulation skills (e.g., persistence toward goals), whereas affective internal indicators include students' sense of belonging to school and connectedness to peers and teachers. The logic is that once these indicators have been identified, the mentor can work with the student on areas targeted for support. Many mentoring programs rely upon building relationships through participation in recreational activities in informal settings. Instrumental mentoring is different because through a relationship with an adult, students are expected to learn specific skills and achieve goals. For example, targeting academic skills may involve getting students additional tutoring or homework support. Behavioral supports may include behavior contracts and small group instruction in problem-solving and anger management. Cognitive supports may focus on developing self-determination skills, whereas affective supports focus on building relationships and school involvement. The mentor helps facilitate these supports, as the relationship between the mentor and student is considered the primary mechanism for changes in students' connection to, and engagement with, school.

268   *Allison Bruhn et al.*

As the name implies, there are two main components to C&C. The "Check" component involves systematic monitoring of students' levels of engagement and educational progress using school data (Christenson et al., 2012). The "Connect" component involves personalized intervention facilitated and monitored by the mentor, as well as engagement with families (Christenson et al., 2012). The formal weekly meeting of the mentor and student is usually between 10 and 30 minutes depending on the identified needs and goals of the student and the level of intervention needed (Christenson et al., 2012). The mentor is not to serve as a disciplinarian, therapist, or social worker, but rather as a positive connection to school that can help the student stay on track, communicate with families, and connect the student to available and useful resources (Adamson & Grupe, 2015).

C&C has two levels of intensity based on student need and response to intervention. At the basic level, students meet with their mentor once per week to review the students' data, discuss current issues, set goals, and conduct problem-solving. Problem-solving involves identifying the problem and potential solutions, and then evaluating the consequences. At the intensive level, which is reserved for students who are more at risk and need more focused attention to one or more specific areas of need, the components of the basic intervention are used along with more individualized supports tailored to students' needs. This may require schools to leverage local community resources. The intent is to foster a change in the environment by including the school, teachers, and family to identify and refine any policies, practices, or procedures that may be limiting students' engagement with school. Including multiple stakeholders from a students' life is consistent with the theory that interactions between a student and their environment (e.g., home, school, community) have a direct impact on their well-being and development (Bronfenbrenner, 1992).

The primary role of the mentor is to build relationships with students and help students to make changes that positively impact their engagement in school, and in turn, learning. In addition to learning about the student's beliefs about education, motivations, sense of belonging, areas of interest or hobbies, future goals, influences from their families and/or culture, and other circumstances that may be causing barriers to their successful engagement in school, mentors monitor students' data. They help students reflect on their own data and use those data to identify short- and long-term goals, monitor progress towards these goals, problem-solve as needed, and celebrate as they achieve them. Additionally, mentors work with the student to determine interventions, resources, and strategies available to support goal achievement (e.g., tutoring, counseling). Finally, mentors connect with caregivers in the students' life on a regular basis to build a relationship where they can collaborate on strategies and resources needed to assist the student and help navigate the educational system.

Check & Connect Research

C&C is marketed as a dropout prevention program for K-12 students who show early warning signs of disengagement, and thus, risk for dropping out (www.checkandconnect. umn.edu). As such, the What Works Clearinghouse (WWC) reviewed group design studies on C&C for the Dropout Prevention topic area of the WWC Intervention Reports (U.S. Department of Education, 2015). Though 13 studies on C&C were identified as of March 2014, only two studies met WWC criteria for both the Dropout Prevention topic and group design standards. Across 238 student participants in the two studies, which included students receiving special education services for learning, emotional, or behavioral disabilities, the WWC report indicated C&C resulted in "positive effects on staying in school, potentially positive effects on progressing in school, and no discernible effects on completing school for high school students with learning, behavioral, or emotional disabilities" (p. 1).

In the initial study on C&C, which was included in the WWC report, 94 students with learning or emotional/behavioral disabilities received C&C during seventh and eighth grades (Sinclair, Christenson, Evelo, & Hurley, 1998). Then, after eighth grade, students were randomly assigned to continue in C&C through ninth grade to support their transition from middle to high school. The study showed students participating in C&C were significantly "more likely to be engaged in school and on track to graduate" than the control group as evidenced by enrollment, credits toward graduation, and assignment completion (Sinclair et al., 1998, p. 17).

Multiple studies on C&C have since followed, representing a range of settings and students (Sinclair, Christenson, Lehr, & Anderson, 2003). In a longitudinal randomized study on student engagement of urban high school students with EBD, 144 ninth graders were randomly assigned to C&C or a control group (Sinclair, Christenson, & Thurlow, 2005). Students in C&C group demonstrated significantly better outcomes related to student engagement on a number of measures. For instance, C&C students had lower dropout rates, which were comparable to all students in the district and better than the national average, whereas non-C&C students had dropout rates substantially worse than the national average. C&C students also demonstrated much better attendance patterns as well as greater participation in IEP meetings and planning.

The findings of C&C studies corroborate previous research demonstrating that interventions which include effective practice elements such as mentoring, home–school communication, and data-based decision-making can improve engagement and connection to school, while also making school completion more likely for youth with or at risk for EBD. This is particularly important given the dropout rates of students with EBD are the highest of all subgroups of students with disabilities.

Check, Connect, & Expect

A third intervention that builds on the primary features of C&C and CICO, is Check, Connect, & Expect (CCE; Cheney, Flower, & Templeton, 2008). These features include

> (a) students checking in and out daily with adult mentors, (b) students receiving DPRs from mentors, (c) teachers providing behavioral feedback to students throughout the day on DPRs, (d) mentors holding problem-solving sessions with students when they did not meet daily goals, (e) students receiving feedback from mentors at check-out about whether daily behavioral goals were met, (f) mentors charting and reviewing DPR data weekly, and (g) mentors using charted data to reinforce students when met daily and weekly goals.
>
> (Cheney et al., 2009, p. 228)

Like CICO, DPRs are sent home to caregivers and returned each day. This represents the "Basic" level of CCE. Like C&C, CCE provides varying levels of support based on need, almost making it a tiered system of support within itself. Additional levels include Basic Plus, Intensive, Self-Monitoring, and Graduation. Implementation, communication, and decision-making hinges on the role of the mentor, who in CCE is called a coach. Generally, coaches work with 20–25 students at a time and are employed full-time (Cheney et al., 2010).

Students who are successful at the Basic level go on to the Self-Monitoring level in which they begin rating their own behavior on the DPR. Student ratings are compared to teacher ratings for about two weeks until a predetermined degree of matching occurs, at which point the student then rates independently for another two weeks. If students are successful with Self-Monitoring for four weeks, they graduate from the program. Graduates of CCE are celebrated and may serve as mentors for students entering CCE.

Students who are not successful at the Basic level after eight weeks as measured by DPR (i.e., percentages consistently below 75%) move into Basic Plus. Here, daily DPR goals are adjusted to make it more likely the student will be successful and additional sources of reinforcement are included to incentivize goal attainment. In addition, students are provided with academic or social skill instruction depending on their DPR data, which may suggest specific problem areas. In previous studies of CCE, the *Stop and Think* curriculum (Knoff, 2001) was used to teach explicit social skills (Cheney et al., 2009).

If students are successful in Basic Plus after eight weeks (i.e., meeting goals 80% of the time), they may return to the Basic level and follow the same sequence depending on response (i.e., responders move to Self-Monitoring). Students who do not meet criteria after eight weeks go on to receive the Intensive level of CCE. This level requires school personnel (e.g., teacher, school psychologist) to conduct a functional behavior assessment (FBA) consisting of an interview with the assigned teacher, an interview with the target student, and direct observations. Depending on the results of the FBA, one of three interventions is selected (1) differential reinforcement, (2) the *Good Behavior Game* (Barrish, Saunders, & Wolf, 1969), or (3) a multi-component intervention.

Check, Connect, & Expect Research

In a 2-year longitudinal study, researchers examined the effects of CCE on elementary-age students at risk for developing EBD (Cheney et al., 2008). Students at risk for EBD (n = 127) participated in CCE for a minimum of 80 days. These students were compared to 127 students who did not receive CCE. Students attended demographically matched elementary schools in regard to race, size, the number of students with IEPs, and the number of students receiving free and reduced lunch. Results suggested 67% of participants responded positively to intervention, 50% showed improved behavior as perceived by teachers, and only 9% went on to be referred for special education services.

In a follow-up 2-year longitudinal study of CCE, 121 elementary-age students at risk for EBD received CCE and 86 at risk students were in a matched comparison group (Cheney et al., 2009). Results indicated that 60% of participating students graduated from the CCE program and significantly improved their problem behavior as measured by teacher ratings, though teachers' ratings of students' social skills and academic measures did not significantly change over time.

More recently, McDaniel, Houchins, and Robinson (2016) examined the effects of CCE in an alternative education school setting. Twenty-two elementary students in second to -fourth grade (19 males, 14 African-American) with EBD participated in this quasi-experimental within-subjects design. Students receiving CCE demonstrated significant improvements in DPR scores and on-task behavior from baseline to intervention. Additionally, reading and math fluency improved, though not significantly.

In short, studies of CCE have demonstrated positive effects on behavior for students identified as at risk for EBD, as well as those with EBD who are receiving special education services. Taken together, one might presume CCE can be used both as a preventive intervention for students showing elevated risk for an EBD, as well as a responsive intervention for students already identified with an emotional or behavioral disability.

Moving Forward

Providing timely and effective interventions to students with or at risk for EBD is critical to mitigating the negative academic, social, and behavioral outcomes prevalent in this population. We have highlighted three interventions (CICO, C&C, CCE) that each have their own unique components but share common high-leverage practice elements of mentoring, home–school communication, and data-based decision-making. These interventions, which draw upon theoretical and empirical evidence of effective practices, have been implemented and evaluated as targeted and intensive interventions across a range of students. As implementation of these interventions continues to expand across the country, several areas for further research are necessary for fully understanding the capacity of CICO, C&C, and CCE to meet the varied needs of students with or at risk for EBD.

First, the number of students with internalizing difficulties such as anxiety and depression continue to rise, thus creating an increased need for effective interventions to address these mental health issues. This is particularly important given the equally (as compared to students with externalizing behaviors) poor outcomes for students with internalizing problems (Merikangas et al., 2010). And, yet, the number of interventions and supports for mental health issues lags behind those available for students with externalizing behavior problems (Lloyd et al., 2019). Researchers have begun to examine how to modify CICO for internalizing behaviors, but further work is needed not just with CICO (Hunter et al., 2014), but also with C&C and CCE. Similarly, questions remain about how to best support students whose behavior is escape, rather than attention, motivated. Because these interventions rely heavily on positive contact with adults, it may be worth considering how to adapt mentoring interventions for students who might otherwise want to avoid adults. This may include assigning a peer, rather than adult, mentor, or allowing the student to choose the adult mentor.

A second area warranting further exploration is how to enhance and sustain home–school communication. Lloyd and colleagues (2019) note the importance of "identifying effective ways to meaningfully involve families" (p. 91) in the process of coordinating home–school collaborations. Increasing home–school communication for students with mental health issues and challenging behavior improves consistency in expectations, language, and consequences across the two settings (Lochman et al., 2019). With coordinated efforts between caregivers and educators, intervention effects can be maximized in a more efficient, timely manner. This type of planning, which parallels systems-of-care models in mental health, has been recommended as a comprehensive approach to improving outcomes for students with or at risk for EBD (Lloyd et al., 2019). However, home–school communication and collaboration requires additional time, buy-in, and flexibility. In studies of CICO, fidelity problems often are related to sending the DPR home with students and getting it signed and returned the next day. Given varying schedules of caregivers and students, it is possible that a daily signature is not practical or feasible, and thus, a weekly signature may work better although without daily feedback and progress updates, home–school collaboration effects may be limited. Utilizing technology such as mobile apps and email may offer a viable alternative. Beyond a simple signature, however, engaging caregivers in a meaningful way that facilitates two-way communication and, in turn, helps caregivers to become more invested and connected to the school is imperative.

Third, although research has demonstrated strong, positive effects for students with EBD, much of the research has taken place in alternative education settings (e.g., residential facilities, self-contained schools). Questions remain about how effectively these interventions

272 *Allison Bruhn et al.*

can meet the needs of students with EBD in less restrictive, general education settings. In less restrictive, general education settings the student–teacher ratios are higher and navigating the social and academic expectations is more complex, with students interacting with more adults across varied settings each day. These variables add a potential layer of difficulty to completing DPR ratings, making team-based decisions, and mentoring in a meaningful and effective way. By understanding the conditions under which these interventions are most effective, researchers and practitioners can explore potential adaptations to malleable intervention components that will increase the likelihood of success. Similarly, understanding how to support students transitioning from alternative settings back to traditional school settings warrants further investigation. This may be particularly important for students who have established strong mentoring relationships in the alternative setting, as that relationship may end once the student changes placements. One suggestion is to transition students to their home school with the same intervention in place, but with a new mentor. Another model for transition is to gradually introduce the transitioning students to the home school by having them check-in with the mentor and attend the home school for only part of the day while concurrently working to establish a new mentoring relationship. Once that relationship has been firmly established, students may complete the transition to attending full time. Additionally, involving multiple stakeholders in the planning process (similar to *wraparound* services) is likely to be beneficial (Lloyd et al., 2019).

Finally, over 15 years of research has yielded positive results for students with or at risk for EBD receiving CICO, C&C, and CCE. These interventions share several core components: mentoring, data-based decision-making, and home–school communication. It is important to understand the similar and different components of each intervention and individual student characteristics (e.g., function of behavior, age, dual language learners, severity of disability) in order to match the most effective intervention to the needs of students. This underscores the need to explore how student characteristics moderate response to intervention. Future researchers should continue to work towards validating these interventions for students with or at risk for EBD while testing the effectiveness of adaptations across settings and students with varying diagnoses (e.g., depression, conduct disorder, post-traumatic stress disorder) and characteristics. Further, though evidence suggests these interventions can result in immediate improvements in behavior, a next step is examining the degree to which these changes in behavior maintain over time and across different environments. While positive changes in behavior are certainly desirable and important, perhaps more important is understanding how these effective interventions mitigate the myriad risk factors for students with or at risk for EBD, and in turn, result in better life outcomes (e.g., graduating from high school, attending college or maintaining a job, avoiding criminal activity, living with adequate means). Research on maintenance and generalization in short-term studies, as well as longitudinal research, are needed to address these questions.

References

Adamson, R., & Grupe, M. (2015) Check & connect. A presentation at the PBIS Forum. Chicago, IL.

Balfanz, R., Bridgeland, J. M., Bruce, M., & Fox, J. H. (2012). *Building a grad nation: Progress and challenge in ending the high school dropout epidemic*. Washington, DC: Civic Enterprises.

Barrish, H. H., Saunders, M., & Wolf, M. M. (1969). Good behavior game: Effects of individual contingencies for group consequences on disruptive behavior in a classroom 1. *Journal of applied behavior analysis, 2*(2), 119–124.

Bronfenbrenner, U. (1992). Ecological systems theory. In R. Vasta (Ed.), *Annals of child development. Six theories of child development: Revised formulations and current issues* (pp. 187–249). London: Jessica Kingsley.

Bruhn, A. L., McDaniel, S., Rila, A., & Estrapala, S. (2018). A step-by-step guide to tier 2 behavioral progress monitoring. *Beyond Behavior*. Advance Online Publication. doi:10.1177/1074295618756984

Bruhn, A. L., Rila, A., Mahatmya, D., Estrapala, S., & Hendrix, N. (2018). Analyzing the effects of data-based, individualized interventions using multilevel modeling and visual analysis. *Journal of Emotional and Behavioral Disorders*. Advance online publication. doi:10.1177/1063426618806279

Caldarella, P., Adams, M. B., Valentine, S. B., & Young, K. R. (2009). Evaluation of a mentoring program for elementary school students at risk for emotional and behavioral disorders. *New Horizons in Education, 57*(1), 1–15.

Cheney, D., Flower, A., & Templeton, T. (2008). Applying response to intervention metrics in the social domain for students at risk of developing emotional or behavioral disorders. *Journal of Special Education, 42*, 108–126.

Cheney, D., Lynass, L., Flower, A., Waugh, M., Iwaszuk, W., Mielenz, C., & Hawken, L. (2010). The check, connect, and expect program: A targeted, tier 2 intervention in the schoolwide positive behavior support model. *Preventing School Failure, 54*, 152–158.

Cheney, D., Stage, S., Hawken, L., Lynass, L., Mielenz, C., & Waugh, M. (2009). A two-year outcome study of the check, connect, and expect intervention for students at-risk of severe behavior problems. *Journal of Emotional and Behavioral Disorders, 17*, 226–243.

Christenson, S., Stout, K., & Pohl, A. (2012). *Check & connect: A comprehensive student engagement intervention: Implementing with fidelity*. Minneapolis, MN: University of Minnesota, Institute on Community Integration.

Conley, K., Kittleman, A., Massar, M., & McIntosh, K. (2018). *What are patterns and predictors of CICO participation in U.S. schools?* Retrieved from: https://www.pbis.org/resource/what-are-patterns-and-predictors-of-cico-participation-in-u-s-schools

Cook, C. R., Xie, S. R., Earl, R. K., Lyon, A. R., Dart, E., & Zhang, Y. (2015). Evaluation of the courage and confidence mentor program as a Tier 2 intervention for middle school students with identified internalizing problems. *School Mental Health, 7*(2), 132–146.

Crone, D., Hawken, L., & Horner, R. (2010). *The Guilford Practical Intervention in the Schools Series. Responding to problem behavior in schools, second edition: The behavior education program*. New York, NY: Guilford Press.

Dart, E. H., Furlow, C. M., Collins, T. A., Brewer, E., Gresham, F. M., & Chenier, K. H. (2015). Peer-mediated check-in/check-out for students at-risk for internalizing disorders. *School Psychology Quarterly, 30*(2), 229–243.

Ennis, R. P., Jolivette, K., Swoszowski, N. C., & Johnson, M. L. (2012). Secondary prevention efforts at a residential facility for students with emotional and behavioral disorders: Function-based check-in, check-out. *Residential treatment for children & youth, 29*(2), 79–102.

Fuchs, D., Fuchs, L. S., & Vaughn, S. (2014). What is intensive instruction and why is it important? *TEACHING Exceptional Children, 46*(4), 13–18. doi: 10.1177/0040059914522966.

Gersten, R., Fuchs, L. S., Compton, D., Coyne, M., Greenwood, C., & Innocenti, M. S. (2005). Quality indicators for group experimental and quasi-experimental research in special education. *Exceptional children, 71*(2), 149–164.

Goodman, R. (1997). The Strengths and Difficulties Questionnaire: A research note. *Journal of Child Psychology and Psychiatry and Allied Disciplines, 38*, 581–586.

Grossman, J. B., & Rhodes, J. E. (2002). The test of time: Predictors and effects of duration in youth mentoring relationships. *American Journal of Community Psychology, 30*, 199–219.

Hawken. (2006). School psychologists as leaders in the implementation of a targeted intervention: The behavior education program. *School Psychology Quarterly, 21*, 91–111.

Hawken, L. S., Bundock, K., Kladis, K., O'Keeffe, B., & Barrett, C. A. (2014). Systematic review of the check-in, check-out intervention for students at risk for emotional and behavioral disorders. *Education and Treatment of Children, 37*(4), 635–658.

Horner, R. H., Carr, E. G., Halle, J., McGee, G., Odom, S., & Wolery, M. (2005). The use of single-subject research to identify evidence-based practice in special education. *Exceptional children, 71*(2), 165–179.

Hunter, K. K., Chenier, J. S., & Gresham, F. M. (2014). Evaluation of check in/check out for students with internalizing behavior problems. *Journal of Emotional and Behavioral Disorders, 22*(3), 135–148. doi:10.1177/1063426613476091

Individuals with Disabilities Education Improvement Act of 2004, 20 U.S.C., 1415 *et seq.* (2004)

Jeynes, W. (2012). A meta-analysis of the efficacy of different types of parental involvement programs for urban students. *Urban Education, 47,* 706–742.

Jeynes, W. H. (2007). The relationship between parental involvement and urban academic achievement: A meta-analysis. *Urban Education, 42,* 82–110.

Jung, P. G., McMaster, K. L., Kunkel, A. K., Shin, J., & Stecker, P. M. (2018). Effects of data-based individualization for students with intensive learning needs: A meta-analysis. *Learning Disabilities Research & Practice, 33*(3), 144–155.

Kamphaus, R. W., & Reynolds, C. R. (2007). *BASC 2, Behavioral and Emotional Screening System.* San Antonio, TX: Pearson.

Kern, L., Harrison, J. R., Custer, B. E., & Mehta, P. D. (2018). Factors that enhance the quality of relationships between mentors and mentees during check & connect. *Behavioral Disorders.* doi:10.1177/0198742918779791

Knoff, H. M. (2001). *The stop & think social skills program.* Longmont, CO: Sopris West.

Lane, K. L., Capizzi, A. M., Fisher, M. H., & Ennis, R. P. (2012). Secondary prevention efforts at the middle school level: An application of the behavior education program. *Education and Treatment of Children, 35,* 51–90.

Lane, K. L., Kalberg, J. R., & Shepcaro, J. C. (2009). An examination of the evidence base for function-based interventions for students with emotional and/or behavioral disorders attending middle and high schools. *Exceptional Children, 75*(3), 321–340.

Lipscomb, S., Lacoe, J., Liu, A. Y., & Haimson, J. (2018). *Preparing for life after high school: The characteristics and experiences of youth in special education. A summary of key findings from the national longitudinal transition study 2012.* NCEE Evaluation Brief. National Center for Education Evaluation and Regional Assistance.

Lloyd, B. P., Bruhn, A. L., Sutherland, K. S., & Bradshaw, C. P. (2019). Progress and priorities in research to improve outcomes for students with or at risk for emotional and behavioral disorders. *Behavioral Disorders, 44,* 85–96. doi:10.1177/0198742918808485

Lochman, J. E., Boxmeyer, C. L., Ialongo, N. S., McDaniel, S. C., Pas, E. T., & Powell, N. P. (2019). Tier II family-school partnership programs. In A. Garbacz (Ed.), *Implementing family-school partnerships: Student success in school psychology research and practice* (pp. 88–110). New York, NY: Routledge.

Maggin, D. M., Zurheide, J., Pickett, K. C., & Baillie, S. J. (2015). A systematic evidence review of the check-in/check-out program for reducing student challenging behaviors. *Journal of Positive Behavior Interventions, 17*(4), 197–208.

McDaniel, S., & Bruhn, A. L. (2016). Using a changing-criterion design to evaluate the effects of individualized goals within check-in/check-out. *Journal of Positive Behavior Interventions, 18,* 197–208. doi:10.1177/1098300715588263

McDaniel, S., Bruhn, A. L., & Mitchell, B. (2015). Tier 2: A framework for identification and intervention. *Beyond Behavior, 24*(1), 10–17.

McDaniel, S. C., Houchins, D. E., & Robinson, C. (2016). The effects of check, connect, and expect on behavioral and academic growth. *Journal of Emotional and Behavioral Disorders, 24*(1), 42–53.

McDaniel, S. M., & Bruhn, A. L. (2019). Examining the additive effects of check-in/check-out to coping power. *Elementary School Journal.* Advance online publication. doi: 10.1086/703125.

Merikangas, K. R., He, J. H., Burstein, M., Swanson, S. A., Avenevoli, S., Cui, L., … Swendsen, J. (2010). Lifetime prevalence of mental disorders in U.S. adolescents: Results from the national comorbidity survey replication–adolescent supplement (NCS-A). *Journal of the American Academy of Child & Adolescent Psychiatry, 50,* 32–45.

Miller, L. M., Dufrene, B. A., Sterling, H. E., Olmi, D. J., & Bachmayer, E. (2014). The effects of check-in/check-out on problem behavior and academic engagement in elementary school students. *Journal of Positive Behavior Interventions.* Advance online publication. doi: 1098300713517141

Mitchell, B. S., Adamson, R., & McKenna, J. W. (2017). Curbing our enthusiasm: An analysis of the check-in/check-out literature using the council for exceptional children's evidence-based practice standards. *Behavior modification, 41*(3), 343–367.

Mitchell, B. S., Bruhn, A. L., & Lewis, T. J. (2016). Essential features of tier 2 & 3 school-wide positive behavioral supports. In S. R. Jimerson, M. K. Burns, & A. M. VanDerHeyden (Eds.), *Handbook of response to intervention: The science and practice of assessment and intervention* (2nd ed., pp. 539–562). New York, NY: Springer.

Muscott, H. S., Szczesiul, S., Berk, B., Staub, K., Hoover, J., & Perry-Chisholm, P. (2008). Creating home–school partnerships by engaging families in schoolwide positive behavior supports. *Teaching Exceptional Children, 40*(6), 7–14.

National Institute of Mental Health. (2018). *Child traumatic stress research program*. Retrieved from www.nimh.nih.gov

Neal, J. W., & Neal, Z. P. (2013). Nested or networked? Future directions for ecological systems theory. *Social Development, 22*(4), 722–737.

Scruggs, T. E., & Mastropieri, M. A. (1998). Summarizing single-subject research: Issues and applications. *Behavior Modification, 22*, 221–242.

Sinclair, M. F., Christenson, S. L., Evelo, D. L., & Hurley, C. M. (1998). Dropout prevention for high-risk youth with disabilities: Efficacy of a sustained school engagement procedure. *Exceptional Children, 65*, 7–21.

Sinclair, M. F., Christenson, S. L., Lehr, C. A., & Anderson, A. R. (2003). Facilitating student engagement: Lessons learned from check & connect longitudinal studies. *The California School Psychologist, 8*(1), 29–41.

Sinclair, M. F., Christenson, S. L., & Thurlow, M. L. (2005). Promoting school completion of urban secondary youth with emotional or behavioral disabilities. *Exceptional Children, 71*(4), 465–482.

Sutherland, K. S., Conroy, M. A., McLeod, B. D., Kunemund, R., & McKnight, K. (2019). Common practice elements for improving social, emotional and behavioral outcomes of young elementary school students. *Journal of Emotional and Behavioral Disorders, 27*, 76–85. doi:10.1177/1063426618784009

Swoszowski, N. C., Jolivette, K., Fredrick, L. D., & Heflin, L. J. (2012). Check in/check out: Effects on students with emotional and behavioral disorders with attention-or escape-maintained behavior in a residential facility. *Exceptionality, 20*(3), 163–178.

Swoszowski, N. C., McDaniel, S. C., Jolivette, K., & Melius, P. (2013). The effects of Tier II check-in/check-out including adaptation for nonresponders on the off-task behavior of elementary students in a residential setting. *Education and Treatment of Children, 36*, 63–79.

Turnbull, H. R. (2005). Individuals with disabilities education act reauthorization: Accountability and personal responsibility. *Remedial and Special Education, 26*, 320–326.

U.S. Department of Education, Institute of Education Sciences, What Works Clearinghouse. (2015, May). Dropout prevention intervention report: Check & connect. Retrieved from https://ies.ed.gov/ncee/wwc/Docs/InterventionReports/wwc_checkconnect_050515.pdf

Walker, H. M., & Severson, H. H. (1992). *Systematic screening for behavior disorders (SSBD): User's guide and administration manual*. Longmont, CO: Sopris West.

Wehby, J. H., & Kern, L. (2014). Intensive behavior intervention: What is it, what is its evidence base, and why do we need to implement now? *TEACHING Exceptional Children, 44*, 38–44. doi:10.1177/0040059914523956

Wolfe, K., Pyle, D., Charlton, C. T., Sabey, C. V., Lund, E. M., & Ross, S. W. (2016). A systematic review of the empirical support for check-in check-out. *Journal of Positive Behavior Interventions, 18*(2), 74–88.

19 Multisystemic Therapy for High-Risk Youth

Emotional/Behavioral Disorders

Michael R. McCart, Ashli J. Sheidow, and Phillippe B. Cunningham

This chapter describes Multisystemic Therapy (MST; Henggeler, Schoenwald, Borduin, Rowland, & Cunningham, 2009), an intensive family- and community-based treatment for youth at imminent risk for out-of-home placement (e.g., detention, residential treatment) due to serious antisocial behaviors, such as delinquent offending and substance abuse. Based on findings from two decades of research, MST has been recognized by the National Institutes of Health, U.S. Surgeon General, President's New Freedom Commission on Mental Health, and other entities as a leading evidence-based treatment for antisocial youth (Henggeler et al., 2009). Indeed, MST is one of the most widely implemented treatments for youth antisocial behavior; as of 2019, MST programs have been transported to more than 34 states and 15 nations, treating tens of thousands of antisocial youth and their families annually (see mstservices.com). This chapter outlines the theoretical bases of MST and provides an overview of the treatment model. A case example is used to illustrate the clinical aspects of the MST approach. The remainder of the chapter summarizes research on MST for antisocial youth and describes efforts to adapt the model for other high-risk groups.

Theoretical and Empirical Bases of MST

Bronfenbrenner's (1979) social ecological theory serves as the conceptual model for MST. According to this theory, human behavior is influenced by the multiple systems in which individuals are embedded (e.g., family, peer, school, community) as well as the reciprocal interplay between those systems. Consistent with this view, decades of research have shown that risk factors for antisocial behavior are present at both individual and environmental levels (Deater-Deckard, Dodge, Bates, & Pettit, 1998; Elliott, 1994; Loeber, Farrington, Stouthamer-Loeber, & Van Kammen, 1998; Thornberry & Krohn, 2003). At the level of the individual, for example, antisocial behavior is associated with social skill deficits and cognitive biases. Among families, specific characteristics of parents (e.g., high stress, mental health problems) and ineffective parenting practices (e.g., low monitoring, inconsistent discipline, poor affective relations) are well-established predictors of youth antisocial behavior. Regarding peers, research shows youth are more likely to participate in antisocial behavior if they associate with peers who are frequently in trouble. School-level influences include low academic achievement, low commitment to education, and an overly authoritarian teaching style. Further, communities characterized by high poverty, high residential mobility, and drug availability predict elevated rates of antisocial behavior in youth.

Social ecological theory, and evidence regarding the multi-determined nature of antisocial behavior in youth, support the notion that for interventions to be maximally effective, they must target risk factors across multiple ecological systems. Consistent with that view, MST is designed to address determinants of antisocial behavior within each aspect of a youth's social ecology and also between two or more ecological systems (e.g., parents' interactions with their youth's school). To further enhance the treatment's ecological validity, MST employs a home- and community-based model of service delivery so antisocial behaviors can be targeted in their natural settings.

Of note, one key assumption of MST is that parents are critical to achieving lasting youth behavior change. Thus, early in treatment, MST therapists devote considerable time teaching parents how to manage their youths' needs more effectively, with the goal of building sustainable skills that will be effective immediately, but also throughout the remainder of the youth's adolescence. As parents develop competencies, MST therapists guide parents to also address contributors to their youth's antisocial behavior from other ecological systems, such as the youth's peer network, school, and community.

Characteristics of MST Treatment

MST is delivered by a team that includes 2–4 full-time Master's level therapists and a Master's level or doctoral level supervisor who devotes at least 50% of his or her time to supervising the team. Members of an MST team typically work for private service provider organizations contracted by public juvenile justice, child welfare, and/or mental health authorities. MST therapists carry a caseload of 4–6 families each. Treatment is intensive, with therapists having an average of 60 direct contact hours with each family over a typical treatment duration of 3–5 months. Therapeutic contacts tend to be more frequent early in treatment. For example, a therapist might meet with a family as many as 3–4 times per week during the first few months, as behavior change efforts are being developed, implemented, and refined. Later in treatment, after therapeutic progress has been made, contacts become less frequent and focus on enhancing sustainability of positive behavior changes. Further, therapists are available to families 24 hours per-day, seven days a week so sessions can be scheduled at times convenient to the family and so therapists can respond to clinical crises whenever they occur.

The interventions employed by MST therapists are empirically supported and drawn from theoretical perspectives that complement social ecological theory. These include cognitive behavioral theory (e.g., problem-solving skills), behavioral theory (e.g., behavior plans), social learning theory (e.g., modeling and reinforcement), structural formulations (e.g., understanding family members' roles and patterns of interactions that regulate each individual's behaviors), and strategic formulations (e.g., emphasizing present-focused, brief interventions within the family to change problematic recursive sequences).

MST Treatment Principles and Process

As opposed to following a manualized protocol, MST individualizes treatment to each youth and family through adherence to nine principles and a detailed analytical process that guides problem conceptualization and treatment planning. Individualized MST treatment plans incorporate a tailored set of interventions targeted to each family's unique strengths and struggles. This tailoring makes MST more efficient (i.e., limits interventions to those that are necessary), increases the likelihood of achieving the family's alignment with treatment, and ensures sustainability of skill development. The nine MST principles and analytic process are described next, accompanied by their application to an example case.

MST Principles

Principle 1. Finding the Fit – The primary purpose of assessment is to understand the "fit" between the identified problems and their broader systemic context.

Within MST, assessment is focused and aims to identify how antisocial behaviors are sustained by factors in the youth's ecology. Therapists use a "fit analysis" to map out this ecological conceptualization, in which relevant factors are listed as "drivers" of a given behavior. These drivers become the "fit factors" for the fit analysis. A thorough fit analysis may include factors at the level of the youth (e.g., cognitions, biological processes, low academic functioning), family (e.g., ineffective parenting practices, low warmth and high conflict, parent psychopathology, or substance use), community (e.g., poor housing quality, high crime, limited resources), and peers (e.g., access to drugs, modeling of criminal behavior, beliefs, and norms). The therapist's role is to identify factors that might be relevant for a given family; this provides the individualized conceptualization for a case. Further, this conceptualization is updated in response to newly identified or appropriately resolved fit factors.

Consider the case of a 16-year-old boy, referred by juvenile probation for running away, theft, and drug abuse. The boy spends most of his time at friends' homes where they play video games, smoke marijuana, and experiment with other drugs. The boy used to be involved in positive school activities, but dropped out when he became more interested in hanging out with friends. The boy's parents are unaware of the extent of his drug use. They give him an allowance each week, but are unaware how he uses the money; in reality, he uses the money to purchase drugs. When his parents become strict, he sneaks out of his bedroom window and stays at friends' homes for the night. A few times, when he and his friends were bored, they stole items out of cars, pawning the items to make money to purchase drugs, and have been arrested twice when caught. Primary fit factors for this case are boredom and negative peer associations (and corresponding lack of activities with prosocial peers), low monitoring and parental supervision, easy access to money, and lack of meaningful consequences.

Principle 2. Positive and Strength Focused – Therapist contacts should emphasize the positive and use systemic strengths as levers for change.

Focusing on strengths can decrease negative affect, build hopefulness, create an environment of mutual problem solving (improving chances for generalization; see Principle 9), and enhance parent confidence. This approach is emphasized throughout treatment. Therapists actively investigate youth factors (e.g., competencies, altruism), family factors (e.g., resources, affective bonds), community factors (e.g., business involvement, neighbor concern), and peer factors (e.g., competencies, prosocial activities), drawing upon strengths to develop interventions. An example of this principle is that therapists, with assistance from their team and supervisor, try to highlight any movement toward desired behaviors. Specifically, the therapist might attempt to understand the "fit" of a reduced problem behavior, even if elimination of the behavior is the ultimate goal. By identifying factors driving the reduction, the therapist is providing positive feedback to the family, but also identifying fit factors that might be further targeted to eliminate the behavior. Suppose, for example, that the 16-year-old boy described previously had two instant drug screens conducted over the past week by a parent; the first was negative (indicating no use), but the second was positive (indicating use). Although the youth has recently used drugs, the therapist conducts a "positive fit analysis" to determine what factors drove abstinence earlier in the week versus drug use later in the week; perhaps the parent did not provide money to the youth earlier in the week, coincidentally eliminating the youth's ability to purchase drugs. This type of factor could be replicated in the future.

Another example of this principle is that MST therapists and supervisors strive to avoid language that blames families. This is sometimes a struggle in the difficult cases seen by an MST therapist, such as when a family is not following through with plans developed in session. Instead of blaming, the MST team attempts to see things from the family's perspective, identifying barriers the family members may be experiencing that prevent them from following through with plans. Using the example case, a positive fit analysis indicates that limiting access to money might drive reduced drug use, so the therapist suggests the parents not give money to the youth each week. The youth later has a positive drug screen and admits to drug use; after a fit analysis on the recent use, the therapist finds that the youth still has access to money. The therapist tries to identify barriers that prevented the parents from withholding the money and finds that they work long hours and are concerned the youth does not have food for lunch and snacks after school. Although the parents initially agreed to the plan of withholding money, they were unable to follow through due to practical barriers. Rather than expressing frustration or "giving up," the therapist appreciates the parents' perspective and engages them in problem-solving to overcome these practical barriers (e.g., reducing the amount of money and requiring receipts from food purchases before providing additional money to the youth).

Principle 3. Increasing Responsibility – Interventions should be designed to promote responsible behavior and decrease irresponsible behavior among family members.

As noted previously, a fundamental goal of MST is to empower parents to effectively address problem behaviors presented by their youth both now and throughout the youth's adolescence (see Principle 9: Generalization). MST views parents as the key to positive youth outcomes, and therefore as the strongest lever for change (i.e., the "change agent"). With this in mind, parents participate in every step of assessment and intervention, engaging other indigenous supports as needed. Therefore, rather than relying on individual therapy for the youth or doing the interventions *for* the family, therapists align with parents on treatment goals and provide them with the instruction and support needed to have parents be in the driver's seat of implementing interventions.

As an example, consider the case of the 16-year-old boy. The parents and therapist completed a fit assessment (Principle 1) and are in agreement that some primary "drivers" are negative peer involvement and lack of prosocial peer involvement. Through the assessment, the therapist learns that the youth used to be involved in baseball but stopped, in part, because he felt disconnected from the coach and team. The parents and therapist align on a treatment goal to re-engage the youth in this afterschool activity. It would be easy for the therapist to contact the coach directly about these concerns; however, the therapist would be taking the responsibility away from the parents and would lose a valuable opportunity to improve the parents' skills in accessing ecological supports. Instead, the therapist supports the parents in arranging their own meeting with the coach, including creating an agenda for the meeting, role-playing the meeting, and planning for "what ifs."

Principle 4. Present-focused, Action-oriented, and Well-defined – Interventions should be present-focused and action-oriented, targeting specific and well-defined problems.

Clear treatment goals form the basis for MST interventions and are behaviorally defined so it is obvious what is being targeted. A parent with a nonspecific goal such

280 *Michael R. McCart et al.*

as "be more responsible" would be guided to identify what this might look like for the youth (e.g., follow rules at home and school) and a behaviorally defined goal would be developed (e.g., youth will demonstrate responsibility as evidenced by following household and school rules). This wording allows the treatment team and family to be action-oriented in developing plans to achieve goals, closely tracking progress, and identifying criteria for treatment termination. MST is an intensive treatment, so therapists develop weekly "sub-goals" that target prioritized fit factors (Principle 1). Given this action-oriented approach, rapid and measurable treatment change is expected. Further, emphasis is placed on present-focused fit factors (i.e., those presently sustaining the behaviors, as opposed to historical factors responsible for initial development of the behaviors).

Imagine that the parents of the 16-year-old boy believed their son's antisocial behavior was being driven by a decline in the parent–child relationship when the mother lost her job two years ago, and the related economic stressors when the youth was starting high school. At that time, the youth struggled to adjust to this change and the parents became more lenient in their supervision to try to accommodate his emotional difficulty. Such a change in the family's financial circumstances and the youth's adjustment may have been the initial drivers of his antisocial behavior, but other drivers have since become more primary (e.g., poor supervision) and present-focused and therefore are prioritized for intervention.

Principle 5. Targeting Sequences – Interventions should target sequences of behavior within or between multiple systems that maintain identified problems.

In MST, problem behaviors are viewed as having a multisystemic set of causal and sustaining factors. Interventions are thus focused on changing family members' interactions with one another, as well as their interactions with the ecology. As such, MST therapists often will have the family detail a given instance of a behavior, as well as its antecedents and consequences, as a method to identify the sequence. This sequence of events is used to identify the fit factors (Principle 1) from across the ecology (e.g., family members, peers) that are driving that particular youth's behavior. MST interventions are then designed to eliminate these drivers and thus alter future sequences.

Take the example case. The therapist guided the parents through detailing the sequence of events involving the youth sneaking out of the house the prior weekend. While there were drivers identified within this sequence such as negative peer pressure to sneak out and lack of effective consequences, the most easily addressable drivers to disrupt the sequence were access to sneaking out of his window and lack of parents' monitoring at night. To target these fit factors, the family and therapist developed an initial plan that included the youth having to sleep on a cot in the parent's room until the parents could install a lock on the youth's window. The youth greatly disliked having to go to bed at the same time as his parents, so was motivated to earn back their trust. The parents allowed the youth to move back to his room after they installed the window lock, but removed the door from its hinges to ensure they could hear attempts to remove the window lock and also let the youth know they would be conducting random room checks throughout the night. Following a few weeks of this, improvements in the youth's involvement in prosocial activities, and a number of consecutive negative drug screens (i.e., indicating no drug use), the parents placed the door back on the hinges, but continued using the window lock and conducting random room checks at night.

Principle 6. Developmentally Appropriate – Interventions should be developmentally appropriate and fit the developmental needs of the youth.

MST therapists ensure interventions are well-matched to the youth's and family's developmental needs. Thus, the competencies youth typically develop during adolescence are emphasized (e.g., peer relations, academic planning). To illustrate, the parents of our example case could have packed a lunch and snack for the youth to take to school instead of providing money for him to purchase food (which he then was using to purchase drugs). Instead, when choosing intervention strategies, the family and therapist decided to use a more developmentally appropriate plan for a 16-year-old in which they held him accountable for the use of the money rather than removing the money altogether.

Principle 7. Continuous Effort – Interventions should be designed to require daily or weekly effort by family members.

Changing behavior requires practice. Thus, an MST therapist works with parents and families to practice the new behaviors on a daily or weekly basis. This, in turn, provides more opportunities for identifying barriers to intervention effectiveness, and more opportunities for families to feel empowered as they come to learn they are the "change agents" (Principle 3) for altering the youth's behavior. For example, the therapist for the 16-year-old boy checked in briefly by phone each evening to ensure parents were prepared to do the nighttime room checks and then in the morning to see how the room checks went. The therapist used these brief calls to predict and plan for potential barriers, coach parents through the new plan, and praise parents for their consistent efforts. After a week of check ins, the parents felt confident to continue the plans on their own without the calls. The intensity of MST, compounded with therapists' low caseloads, result in frequent in-person and phone contact. Further, therapists employ homework assignments to also ensure daily or weekly effort by family members.

Principle 8. Evaluation and Accountability – Intervention effectiveness is evaluated continuously from multiple perspectives with providers assuming accountability for overcoming barriers to successful outcomes.

Because goals are well defined (Principle 4) and interventions are devised to require continuous effort from the family (Principle 7), measurable outcomes can be monitored and evaluated frequently. This ensures adherence to the MST assessment and treatment planning process, which is ongoing and iterative (see MST Analytical Process). The MST therapist gathers data from multiple sources (e.g., key participants, school or probation records) to ensure accurate evaluation. Importantly, the MST therapist is responsible for monitoring outcomes on at least a weekly basis (i.e., continuously), as well as being responsible (i.e., assuming accountability) for rapidly identifying and problem-solving barriers to treatment progress. As with all aspects of MST, the therapist avoids blaming or negatively labeling individuals as "resistant" (Principle 2); instead, the therapist focuses on generating creative ways to overcome impediments to success and ensuring a "can-do" attitude (see the examples for Principle 2). Evaluating treatment progress continuously from multiple perspectives as applied to the example case includes youth self-reports and parent-reports about behaviors, as well as probation reports, school reports, and urine drug screens.

Principle 9. Generalization – Interventions should be designed to promote treatment generalization and long-term maintenance of therapeutic change by empowering caregivers to address family members' needs across multiple systemic contexts.

From an MST perspective, long-term therapeutic change is achieved by empowering parents to address the family and youth's needs across the multiple systems in which they participate. By

282   *Michael R. McCart et al.*

leveraging strengths (Principle 2), increasing responsibility (Principle 3), and requiring present-focused (Principle 4) and continuous (Principle 7) effort, parents can develop the skills necessary for achieving and continuing the progress made during treatment. Whenever possible, the MST therapist guides the family to rely more on themselves and indigenous supports (e.g., extended family, friends) to sustain favorable outcomes rather than relying on the therapist. Further, as treatment progresses, the MST therapist changes from a teacher/clinician to an advisor/consultant to ensure changes are sustained after termination.

Consider the 16-year-old example case. Rather than dictating to the parents the interventions to prevent the youth from sneaking out at night, the therapist and parents brainstormed a list of possible interventions. The therapist then guided the parents to consider the pros and cons of each, so the parents made the determination on which interventions to try. As part of brainstorming, the parents initially identified using formal systems (e.g., asking the probation officer (PO) to punish the youth for sneaking out), but the therapist highlighted the cons of that approach, such as the PO's consequences to date not being effective and the short-term nature of the PO's involvement with the youth. Instead, and as described previously, the parents decided to target their son's sneaking out behavior directly, which better positions them to target new problematic behaviors that might emerge as their youth ages.

MST Analytical Process

The MST Analytical Process (see Figure 19.1) provides the framework for identifying youth and family problems, prioritizing drivers for change, designing interventions for implementation, and measuring successes and barriers to goal attainment. The MST team uses this framework to guide treatment, but does so while adhering to the nine MST principles. Of note, this process can only be successful when the therapist has created an environment of engagement and alignment (the largest box in the Figure). Thus, throughout treatment, the MST team uses varied strategies to engage families, such as delivering treatment in the home and community at times convenient to families, understanding family members' perspectives, being on-call in times of crisis, assisting families with practical needs, and maintaining a strength-focused perspective.

At the start of treatment (top of the Figure), the therapist must identify the referral behaviors and elicit the desired outcomes for treatment from key participants (e.g., immediate family, formal and informal supports). This information is then translated into well-defined overarching treatment goals, providing direction for the duration of treatment. The therapist guides the family through fit analyses of the behaviors identified in the overarching goals (top of the circle in the Figure), engaging key participants to identify multisystemic factors driving each behavior. These factors are prioritized based either on their potential for triggering antisocial behavior or on those that must be targeted prior to targeting the primary factors (i.e., prerequisite factors). The prioritized fit factors help the MST team generate working hypotheses that are used to tailor interventions to the family. From this, the therapist and family determine the best-suited interventions, attempt the interventions (bottom of the circle in the Figure), and evaluate the effectiveness of the interventions. Based on the evaluation, the conceptualization (i.e., fit factors, hypotheses; back to the top of the circle in the Figure) may be revised and new or redesigned interventions are implemented. This iterative process repeats (the circle of the Figure) until the behaviors are targeted successfully, at which point the factors driving the sustained improvements are identified (understanding the fit) and concrete plans are developed for the family to sustain those factors into the future.

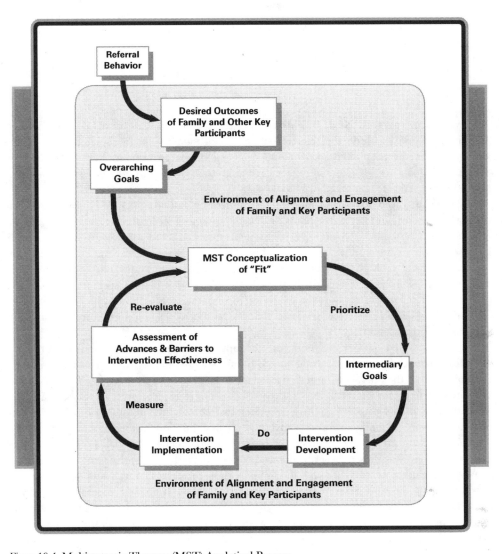

Figure 19.1 Multisystemic Therapy (MST) Analytical Process

Henggeler, S. W., & Schoenwald, S. K. (1998). *The MST supervisory manual: Promoting quality assurance at the clinical level.* Charleston, SC: MST Institute.

To illustrate, consider the case of the 16-year-old male referred for running away, theft, and drug abuse. The MST therapist begins by building clear baseline definitions of the problem behaviors, including their intensity and frequency, and how long the youth has exhibited these behaviors. The assessment indicates that the youth began seriously acting out at the end of his freshman year of high school. He started running away overnight and had at least three instances where he disappeared for several days. Two of these extended instances were in the past three months when he was arrested after stealing items from parked cars, such as change, phone cords, and sunglasses. He was placed on probation for these incidents. At the time of intake into MST, the youth's parents and PO report that he leaves the house at night a few times per week and, although the youth denies using drugs, the PO reports the youth has had positive drug screens for marijuana, synthetic marijuana, and alcohol.

The MST therapist works with the parents to identify their desired outcomes, including elimination of the referral behaviors and improved completion of schoolwork. The PO, school guidance counselor, and former baseball coach are identified as key participants in treatment and engaged by the MST therapist; these individuals report the same desired outcomes as the parents. Next, overarching goals for treatment are developed. MST overarching goals must include the referral behaviors and achieve the desired outcomes. They also guide the direction of treatment and establish discharge criteria. For this youth, the overarching goals are: (1) eliminate theft; (2) eliminate drug use; (3) obtain permission before leaving home; and (4) complete all schoolwork.

The MST therapist now begins the "fit" assessment by gathering detailed information from the youth, parents, and key participants on recent sequences of theft, drug use, running away, and not completing schoolwork. These sequences help the therapist and family identify factors that drive the youth's behaviors. The MST therapist ensures that fit factors from each layer of the ecology (individual, family, peer, school, community) are considered. The therapist and family then prioritize the fit factors. For instance, specific to drug use, prioritized fit factors are: boredom, access to money to purchase drugs, no negative consequences for drug use, few rewards for drug abstinence, low parental monitoring, and negative peer association.

The fit assessment guides the therapist and family to develop interventions targeting the prioritized fit factors, while ensuring interventions adhere to the MST principles. For the example youth, the therapist targets drivers of drug use by educating the parents about principles of behavior modification, and they collaboratively develop a behavior plan. The plan includes monitoring the youth's whereabouts, conducting instant urine drug screens purchased from an online source, delivering meaningful and immediate negative consequences for drug use (as documented by positive drug screens), and delivering appropriate and immediate rewards for drug abstinence (as documented by negative drug screens). This plan also includes parents limiting the money they provide to the youth and requiring documentation on how it is used (e.g., provide receipts from purchases) before giving additional money, as well as placing locks on the youth's bedroom window and conducting random nighttime checks. Before initiating the behavior plan, the therapist and parents consider possible barriers to its implementation. For instance, the PO reports that the youth once tried to "cheat" his urine drug screen by diluting the sample with toilet water. Therefore, the therapist teaches the parents how to prevent this in the home by placing food coloring in the toilet before conducting the screen.

Simultaneously, the therapist helps the family intervene on boredom and negative peer association. Although the youth is not truthful with his parents about his peers (nor the drug use and other illegal behaviors when with these peers), the parents can attempt to leverage the PO, school counselor, and coach to gather such information. The parents and ecology work together to place restrictions on the time the youth spends with these negative peers. In setting restrictions, the parents identify their long work hours and the youth's lack of prosocial activities as barriers to reducing time spent with negative peers. Therefore, the therapist guides the family to invite the boy's former baseball coach into treatment for support. The coach agrees to work with the youth to prepare for the next baseball season, providing monitored workouts with other prosocial youth in the afternoon. Further, to improve grades so that the youth is academically eligible for baseball, the guidance counselor is engaged to (a) re-assign the youth to a study period at the end of each school day that supports students in completing schoolwork and (b) assist parents to communicate weekly with teachers for monitoring schoolwork completion. The family and therapist also generate a list of the youth's strengths and talents to identify other prosocial activities. Using this list, they contact people in the community who provide low-cost opportunities for outdoor recreation such as rock climbing, kayaking, and fishing, which used to interest the youth when he was younger. The youth and his parents arrange weekend outings once a month to try these outdoor activities together. The PO is so pleased with the family's efforts that he allows the monthly outings to take the place of one-third of the youth's required community service hours.

The family and therapist, with input from other key participants, assess the youth's progress each week, problem-solving barriers as they proceed. MST is concluded following sustained reduction in the target behaviors and development of a long-term sustainability plan that the family can continue implementing on their own.

MST Quality Assurance

A comprehensive quality assurance (QA) system is used to train therapists in MST and ensure their adherence to the model. Therapists first participate in a 5-day orientation training, during which they learn the theoretical foundations of MST and participate in role-plays to develop specific skills. Following training, therapists deliver MST to families under the guidance of a Master's or doctoral level MST-trained clinical supervisor. Supervisors meet weekly with therapists to review cases, help problem-solve barriers to family engagement, and ensure interventions follow the nine MST principles. In addition, each team is assigned an expert MST consultant who helps facilitate adherence through quarterly booster trainings and weekly review of cases. Important components of the QA system also include validated surveys that measure implementation adherence by therapists and supervisors, and a web-based tracking system that provides teams with ongoing feedback about adherence. Considerable resources are devoted to the MST QA system because research has identified a strong association between therapist adherence to MST and positive youth and family outcomes (Henggeler, Melton, Brondino, Scherer, & Hanley, 1997; Henggeler, Pickrel, & Brondino, 1999; Schoenwald, Carter, Chapman, & Sheidow, 2008).

Of note, aside from providing weekly consultation to the team, MST consultants also provide support to agencies who are interested in developing new MST programs. Key components of this assistance include community assessments to ensure that an MST program would effectively address stakeholder needs, determination of whether sufficient financial and other resources are in place to support an MST team, and cultivation of stakeholder buy-in and commitment to the success of the program. After an MST program has been implemented in a community, consultants provide ongoing organizational support in the form of semi-annual program reviews and assistance in problem-solving barriers to implementation.

Empirical Support for MST

Several researchers (e.g., Eyberg, Nelson, & Boggs, 2008; Hoge, Guerra, & Boxer, 2008; McCart & Sheidow, 2016; Waldron & Turner, 2008) and entities charged with evaluating research (e.g., Elliott, 1998; Margo, 2008; National Alliance on Mental Illness, 2008; National Institute on Drug Abuse, 1999) have concluded that MST is effective for reducing antisocial behavior in youth. To date, MST has been evaluated in 25 published randomized controlled trials, most of which examined outcomes with adolescents presenting serious conduct problems. Across published studies, MST reduced re-arrest rates by a median of 42% and out-of-home placements by a median of 54%, in addition to improvements in family functioning, substance use, cost savings, and other key variables. A range of variables were examined within each published study, but the following provides a brief overview of MST outcome studies. This research is detailed more extensively in Henggeler and colleagues (2009) and MST Services (2019), which include citations for the dozens of original MST empirical publications.

Efficacy Trials

In the initial MST efficacy trials, graduate student therapists delivered MST under close supervision of the model developers (Scott Henggeler and Charles Borduin). The studies were conducted through university-based clinics, although MST's home-based model of service delivery was used. The first efficacy trial, published in 1986, evaluated MST with juvenile offenders in an inner city. Later efficacy trials were conducted with maltreating families, juvenile sexual offenders, and chronic juvenile offenders. Across all studies, findings supported the efficacy of the MST model. Specifically, relative to youth in control conditions, youth receiving MST evidenced decreased antisocial behavior, re-arrests, and incarceration. Further, MST was associated with improved family relations and youths' decreased association with antisocial peers. Importantly, long-term follow-up studies indicate that many of these positive outcomes have been sustained for up to 22 years post-treatment, including 36% fewer felony arrests, 75% fewer violent felony arrests, and 33% fewer days incarcerated for MST relative to control group participants. These long-term results have critical implications for the cost effectiveness of MST (i.e., savings earned through reduced justice involvement and out-of-home placements; cost–benefit studies found savings ranging from $35,582 to $199,374 per juvenile offender).

Effectiveness Trials

Effectiveness studies of MST were conducted in collaboration with community mental health centers, using clinic-based therapists as treatment providers. Such studies aimed to evaluate whether the favorable findings from MST efficacy trials could be replicated in real-world clinical practice settings. In one of these studies, MST developer Henggeler served as the off-site MST expert, providing weekly consultation to the community clinic therapists and their local supervisor. Participants were juvenile offenders at imminent risk of incarceration. Results demonstrated that, relative to the comparison condition, MST was more effective at improving family functioning and decreasing youth antisocial behavior and out-of-home placements (e.g., 53% lower placement rate at 20-month follow up).

Results of subsequent effectiveness studies provided further support for the capacity of MST to improve family relations and decrease re-arrest and incarceration rates among juvenile offenders. Importantly, this work also highlighted the vital role that MST treatment adherence plays in achieving favorable outcomes. Specifically, secondary analyses have shown that when therapists adhere to the nine MST treatment principles, rates of re-arrest are significantly lower than when treatment adherence is poor. These findings support the MST QA system and demonstrate the importance of treatment adherence in achieving desired clinical outcomes.

Of note, due to some favorable reductions in substance use observed in the early MST efficacy studies, two effectiveness trials were conducted with juvenile offenders meeting diagnostic criteria for a substance use disorder. The first study demonstrated favorable MST effects in several areas, including the reduction of substance use. The second study showed that MST enhanced the favorable effects of juvenile drug court, a program providing specialized services for drug-involved youth and their families, in reducing substance use and criminal behavior. Together, this body of effectiveness research demonstrates the capacity of MST to be implemented effectively in community-based settings.

Independent Transportability Trials

In addition to efficacy and effectiveness trials, a number of MST evaluations have been conducted by independent investigators who have no affiliation with the treatment developers. These studies provide a strong test of the transportability of MST. For such independent trials, QA was overseen by an MST purveyor organization (MST Services, Inc.), and treatment was provided by community-based practitioners. For example, Ogden conducted a multi-site, randomized trial of MST in Norway. Results replicated the favorable outcomes found in earlier studies. Specifically, relative to the comparison condition, MST was more effective at reducing youth antisocial behavior, mental health symptoms, and out-of-home placements (e.g., 78% lower placement rate at 6-month and 56% lower placement rate at 24-month follow ups). However, consistent with other research on MST, treatment adherence impacted trial results. That is, one of the four sites in the Norway study demonstrated poor adherence to MST, and that site did not evidence positive clinical outcomes. Consistent with that finding, a multi-site trial conducted in neighboring Sweden failed to replicate favorable MST treatment effects. In attempting to understand this failure to replicate, investigators noted that treatment adherence was very low across all sites.

Timmons-Mitchell and her colleagues conducted the first independent trial of MST in the U.S. Participants included juvenile felons at risk of out-of-home placement. When compared to usual treatment services, MST was more effective at decreasing youth substance use problems and re-arrests (e.g., 23% lower arrest rate at 18-month follow up). Subsequently, another independent trial was conducted by Stambaugh and colleagues with youth presenting serious emotional disturbance. MST was compared with Wraparound, a widely used intensive intervention in system-of-care sites in the U.S. MST was more effective than Wraparound at decreasing youth symptoms, improving youth functioning, and reducing out-of-home placements (e.g., 54% lower placement rate at 18-month follow up).

In summary, the effectiveness of MST has been replicated by independent investigators in community-based settings with an MST purveyor organization providing ongoing QA – such as currently being provided for MST programs worldwide. A critical caveat, however, pertains to the importance of treatment adherence in achieving favorable outcomes from MST, which also applies to most other evidence-based treatments transported to real-world contexts (McCart & Sheidow, 2016).

Adaptations to the MST Model

Several investigators have adapted the basic MST model to target high-risk populations other than youth with antisocial behavior. Such adaptations leverage the key features of

288   *Michael R. McCart et al.*

MST, including its (a) focus on serious clinical problems with multi-determined causation, (b) home-based model of service delivery, (c) strong QA system, and (d) integration of evidence-based treatment techniques. As an example, MST has been adapted for youth with Problem Sexual Behavior (MST-PSB), and several randomized trials have documented effectiveness of the model. MST-PSB targets aspects of the youth's ecology that are functionally related to the youth's sexual delinquency. Specific adaptations include creating a safety plan to minimize the youth's access to potential victims, addressing youth and caregiver denial about the severity of the offense, and improving youth's peer relations so that more age-appropriate and normative sexual experiences can occur with peers (for more information about MST-PSB, see www.mstpsb.com). Other clinical problems for which MST has been adapted and demonstrated to be effective include youth with serious emotional disturbance/psychiatric crises, chronic pediatric health care conditions (e.g., diabetes, HIV-positive youth), and child maltreatment.

More recently, Sheidow and McCart developed an adaptation of MST for emerging adults (aged 17–26) at the highest risk for negative outcomes – those with serious behavioral health conditions (i.e., mental illness and/or substance abuse) and extensive systems involvement. The behavioral health conditions treated in MST for emerging adults (MST-EA) are typically more severe than those targeted by standard MST. In addition, while the MST-EA model follows the standard MST principles and analytic process, minor revisions are made to make them more developmentally appropriate and applicable to the ecology of the EA client. Specifically, because MST-EA targets an older age population (standard MST is not for youth over age 17), focus is shifted away from parents as the central change agent and placed on the EA (the identified client). That is, the EA is the primary contact for the therapist and is empowered by the therapist throughout treatment to implement therapeutic changes. Further, because MST-EA clients might be living in varied settings (e.g., on their own, with family or friends, or in group or foster homes), parent involvement is not required as it is for standard MST. However, involvement of family or other natural supports is recommended and all efforts are made to identify such supports and include them in treatment. Two multi-site randomized controlled trials evaluating the effectiveness of MST-EA are currently under way.

Conclusions

MST is a family- and community-based intervention with demonstrated empirical support for reducing antisocial behavior in youth. A key feature of MST is its emphasis on addressing known risk factors for antisocial behavior comprehensively, with parents viewed as critical to achieving sustainable positive outcomes. Further, services incorporate pragmatic, behaviorally oriented intervention techniques guided by nine core principles and a detailed analytic process. Promising results from initial MST efficacy studies were replicated by later effectiveness trials, and these have been supported by independent evaluations conducted in distal sites. This research, however, also has demonstrated the critical importance of treatment adherence in the success of MST. Hence, all MST programs worldwide currently participate in an intensive QA system to sustain program adherence and to facilitate positive youth and family outcomes. Building off the strong evidence base for MST, several research groups have developed and validated adaptations of MST for treating other types of complex and serious clinical problems. Such adaptations are made possible by the defining features of MST, which are not necessarily specific to youth antisocial behavior.

References

Bronfenbrenner, U. (1979). *The ecology of human development: Experiments by design and nature.* Cambridge, MA: Harvard University Press.

Deater-Deckard, K., Dodge, K. A., Bates, J. E., & Pettit, G. S. (1998). Multiple risk factors in the development of externalizing behavior problems: Group and individual differences. *Development and Psychopathology, 10,* 469–493.

Elliott, D. S. (1994). Serious violent offenders: Onset, developmental course, and termination. The American Society of Criminology 1993 presidential address. *Criminology, 32,* 1–21.

Elliott, D. S. (1998). *Blueprints for violence prevention* (Series ed.). University of Colorado, Center for the Study and Prevention of Violence. Boulder, CO: Blueprints Publications.

Eyberg, S. M., Nelson, M. M., & Boggs, S. R. (2008). Evidence-based psychosocial treatments for children and adolescents with disruptive behavior. *Journal of Clinical Child and Adolescent Psychology, 37,* 215–237.

Henggeler, S. W., Melton, G. B., Brondino, M. J., Scherer, D. G., & Hanley, J. H. (1997). Multisystemic therapy with violent and chronic juvenile offenders and their families: The role of treatment fidelity in successful dissemination. *Journal of Consulting and Clinical Psychology, 65,* 821–833.

Henggeler, S. W., Pickrel, S. G., & Brondino, M. J. (1999). Multisystemic treatment of substance abusing and dependent delinquents: Outcomes, treatment fidelity, and transportability. *Mental Health Services Research, 1,* 171–184.

Henggeler, S. W., Schoenwald, S. K., Borduin, C. M., Rowland, M. D., & Cunningham, P. B. (2009). *Multisystemic therapy for antisocial behavior in children and adolescents* (2nd ed.). New York, NY: Guilford Press.

Hoge, R. D., Guerra, N. G., & Boxer, P. (Eds.). (2008). *Treating the juvenile offender.* New York, NY: Guilford Press.

Loeber, R., Farrington, D. P., Stouthamer-Loeber, M., & Van Kammen, W. B. (1998). *Antisocial behavior and mental health problems: Explanatory factors in childhood and adolescence.* Mahwah, NJ: Lawrence Erlbaum Associates.

Margo, J. (2008). *Make me a criminal: Preventing youth crime.* London: Institute for Public Policy Research.

McCart, M. R., & Sheidow, A. J. (2016). Evidence-based psychosocial treatments for adolescents with disruptive behavior. *Journal of Clinical Child and Adolescent Psychology, 45,* 529–563.

MST Services. (2019). *Multisystemic therapy research at a glance: Published MST outcome, implementation and benchmarking studies.* Retrieved from www.mstservices.com/mst-whitepapers

National Alliance on Mental Illness. (2008, Winter). Medicaid coverage of multisystemic therapy. *NAMI Beginnings, (10),* 5–8.

National Institute on Drug Abuse. (1999). *Principles of drug addiction treatment: A research-based guide* (NIH Publication No. 99-4180). Rockville, MD: U.S. Department of Health and Human Services, National Institutes of Health.

Schoenwald, S. K., Carter, R. E., Chapman, J. E., & Sheidow, A. J. (2008). Therapist adherence and organizational effects on change in youth behavior problems one year after multisystemic therapy. *Administration and Policy in Mental Health and Mental Health Services Research, 35,* 379–394.

Thornberry, T. P., & Krohn, M. D. (Eds.). (2003). *Taking stock of delinquency: An overview of findings from contemporary longitudinal studies.* New York, NY: Kluwer/Plenum.

Waldron, H. B., & Turner, C. W. (2008). Evidence-based psychosocial treatments for adolescent substance abuse. *Journal of Clinical Child and Adolescent Psychology, 37,* 238–261.

20 Treatment Foster Care

Providing Out-of-Home Treatment in Community- and Family-Based Environments

Elizabeth M.Z. Farmer, Maureen E. Murray, Barbara J. Burns, and Allison D. Little

Introduction

Treatment Foster Care (TFC) is a widely used approach that provides family-based and community-based treatment for youth in out-of-home placements. It is often viewed as a critical service in a system and continuum of care. Trained treatment foster parents within a TFC program provide more intensive intervention than traditional or kinship foster care for youth with serious emotional and/or behavioral problems, all within the context of a treatment foster family's own home. Therefore, it serves a critical role in the continuum of care by providing an out-of-home option for youth who are too challenging for foster care without evoking concerns that are often raised about institutional or congregate residential treatment (see Lee, this volume, for a description of these concerns). TFC's potential to play a critical role in systems and trajectories of care has also been bolstered in recent years by its inclusion in lists of evidence-based treatments. Given its implementation in private homes of trained treatment foster parents, TFC also is significantly less expensive than other more restrictive residential treatment options. Therefore, from a paradigmatic, empirical, and fiscal lens, TFC is a valued intervention approach and treatment setting for youth with emotional and/or behavioral problems.

It is critical to remember that TFC refers to both a treatment approach and a specific organizational setting within which treatment is provided. Rigorous empirical studies of several models of TFC have shown positive results (e.g., Chamberlain & Mihalic, 1998; Farmer, Burns, Wagner, Murray, & Southerland, 2010; Farmer, Dorsey, & Mustillo, 2004; Fisher & Gilliam, 2012). Additional research is currently under way to examine additional models and increase understanding of effective implementation and dissemination (e.g., Bishop-Fitzpatrick, Jung, Nam, Trunzo, & Rauktis, 2015; Murray, Khoury, Farmer, & Burns, 2018; Price, Chamberlain, Landsverk, & Reid, 2009). It is sometimes assumed that these "branded" or "named" models (e.g., Treatment Foster Care Oregon (TFCO), formerly known as Mulitdimensional Treatment Foster Care (MTFC); Together Facing the Challenge (TFTC)) are what is typically delivered when an organization says that it provides TFC. This is far from true. The vast majority of TFC programs do not implement one of the currently recognized evidence-based models of TFC (recent estimates, based on discussions among knowledgeable experts in the field, suggest that fewer than 20% of TFC programs across the nation implement a recognized evidence-based TFC model) (Boyd & Devlin, 2018, personal communication). Rather, most TFC programs incorporate some elements of practice aligned with the FFTA Program Standards for Treatment Foster Care (1995, 2013); locally derived models built from practice-based evidence and (in some cases) familiarity with the evidence-based models; and/or intervention components borrowed from other non-residential EBPs (e.g., Motivational Interviewing, Cognitive

Behavioral Therapy) that are utilized within the TFC context (Farmer, Marshall, Palazzolo, 2018). Therefore, it is important to understand what is known about current evidence-based models of TFC and to understand the tremendous variation that occurs in implementation among and across TFC programs. As would be expected, little empirical evidence about effectiveness is available on this more eclectic range of TFC programs that exist in most service systems across the nation.

As with several other intervention approaches or modalities discussed in this volume, TFC is also a somewhat amorphous and confusing treatment to clearly define and bound. It is known by a range of names across different states and localities (e.g., therapeutic foster care; specialized foster care; professional parenting; treatment family care). For the sake of this chapter, we are using the generic term Treatment Foster Care (TFC) to talk about a type of service with a recognition that this service may be known by different names in different systems and locations.

History and Key Components of TFC

TFC occupies an interesting position in a continuum of care for youth in out-of-home placements: it is more treatment-focused and intensive than foster care and less restrictive than congregate residential treatment. Therefore, it fits well within the model laid out under early CASSP principles (Stroul & Friedman, 1986) and the subsequent wide-scale adoption of systems of care paradigms and approaches (Pumariega & Winters, 2003) that focus on least-restrictive, appropriate, child- and family-centered, individualized, culturally competent services (Stroul, 2003). TFC is viewed as a family-based treatment approach that can adequately and appropriately serve youth with serious emotional/behavioral disorders in a less restrictive setting than other residential, institutional, or congregate options (Chamberlain, 2002). At its heart, TFC is defined as a model where youth are placed in the homes of specially trained treatment foster parents (Kutash & Rivera, 1996). This relatively simple sentence underlines two critical dimensions of TFC – its core involves specially trained treatment foster parents (1) who serve as both front-line mental health providers and substitute caregivers (Farmer & Lippold, 2016); (2) who have the youth living with them in their own personal home.

The Family Focused Treatment Association (FFTA – formerly known as the Foster Family-based Treatment Association) developed Program Standards that provide detailed definitions and guidance around (1) key elements of TFC programs; (2) requirements for treatment parents; and (3) rights, priorities, and supports for children and their families (FFTA, 2013). These standards highlight several key dimensions that should exist in all TFC programs. These include: individualized treatment (designed, coordinated, and implemented to meet the unique needs and strengths of the child and family) that is family-based (provided in the homes of treatment foster parents), culturally competent (training and implementation to respect and support each child and family's identities and cultures), and addresses varying levels of care (so that treatment can be modified to meet emerging and changing needs and opportunities). FFTA's standards include a focus on coordination and collaboration with and among professionals on a treatment team who should be working with the youth and treatment foster parents to develop and implement an individualized treatment plan. There is also attention to the inclusion and valuing of youth's families in this process and the importance of focusing on long-term permanence and stability for the youth (FFTA, 2013). Many of these foci are hallmarks of high quality treatment for youth, regardless of setting or modality. What sets TFC apart is the primary centrality of trained treatment foster parents, working in their own homes, to work with youth as both front-line interventionists and temporary primary caregivers.

TFC can trace its roots from three prongs: foster care; residential treatment in mental health; and the search for alternatives to incarceration in juvenile justice (Dore & Mullin, 2006). TFC's underpinnings can be traced most directly to efforts that began in the 1970s as family alternatives to institutional placements (McGuinness & Dyer, 2007). Knitzer's pivotal work around Unclaimed Children (1982) and subsequent federal efforts to develop the Child and Adolescent Service Systems Program (CASSP) (Stroul & Friedman, 1986) shone national attention on the challenges of effectively addressing youth's challenging emotional and behavioral disorders while providing them with opportunities for growth, socialization, and relationships in community-based and normative environments.

TFC's combination of programming that allowed for intensive individualized intervention within the privately owned homes of trained treatment parents seemed a potentially optimal means to bridge these underlying priorities and needs. A string of key publications in the early 1990s (e.g., Bryant & Snodgrass, 1990; Chamberlain, 1994; Chamberlain, Moreland, & Reid, 1992; Gross & Campbell, 1990; Hawkins, Almeida, Fabry, & Reitz, 1992; Meadowcroft, Thomlison, & Chamberlain, 1994) described both the need for this type of intervention and early blueprints for how it could be done. Also critical in this period were new understandings about the development of antisocial behavior, particularly in the context of family dynamics and relationships (e.g., Forgatch & Patterson, 1989; Patterson, 1975; Patterson & Forgatch, 1987; Patterson & Gullion, 1968; Reid & Eddy, 1997). By building upon this underlying conceptual model of antisocial behavior, Chamberlain's (1994) *Family Connections: A Treatment Foster Care Manual* was particularly clear and compelling in its portrayal of TFC as a promising model to effectively serve some of the nation's most difficult to treat youth in a conceptually appealing, effective, and financially viable way (Fisher & Chamberlain, 2000). This model – known then as Multidimensional Treatment Foster Care (MTFC) and more recently as Treatment Foster Care Oregon (TFCO) – includes five key foci: consistent and reinforcing environment; daily structure with clear expectations and consequences; consistent supervision; minimizing interactions with deviant peers and supporting affiliations with prosocial peers; supporting school attendance and homework (Chamberlain, 2002; www.tfcoregon.com).

During the 1990s, there was a strong shift in the children's mental health field towards evidence-based treatments (Pumariega & Winters, 2003). There were very few community-based interventions that had substantial rigorous research to support them, particularly residential options for children and youth with serious emotional and/or behavioral problems. Chamberlain's continuing development of the MTFC model (now known as TFCO) and randomized trials on this model meant that TFC was well-positioned to be seen as one of the leading evidence-based interventions as the field was clamoring for such programs. Recognition of the intervention by the U.S. Department of Justice in its Blueprints for Preventing Violence series (Chamberlain & Mihalic, 1998), mention in the U.S. Surgeon General's Report (U.S. Department of Health and Human Services, 1999), and inclusion on SAMHSA's National Registry of Evidence-based Practices and Programs (NREPP) as well as Chamberlain's team's multi-pronged and sustained program of research, solidified TFC as a leading contender and evidence-based option for out-of-home treatment.

Near the turn of the 21st century, TFCO was often regarded (along with Multisystemic Therapy (MST: see McCart, Shidow, & Cunningham, this volume)) as "the" effective approach to community-based treatment for children and adolescents with serious mental health problems. However, within the field, there was growing concern that TFCO was too expensive, resource intensive, and demanding for widespread dissemination and implementation. Chamberlain and colleagues continued to study, improve, and disseminate TFCO (Chamberlain, Saldana, Brown, & Leve, 2010; Hansson & Olsson, 2012). They also recognized the potential and need for a less intensive version to be utilized with a wider range of youth and developed KEEP (Keeping Foster Parents Trained and Supported) to infuse TFC principles and practices into traditional foster care (Chamberlain et al., 2010; Price et al., 2008; Price, Roesch, Walsh, & Landsverk, 2015).

While TFCO was viewed as evidence based, most agencies that were implementing TFC in the early 2000s were not implementing Chamberlain's model (Farmer, Burns, Dubs, & Thompson, 2002). Many agencies were developing their own "home grown" models based on combinations of their own experience, resources, and needs in their organizations and communities, and knowledge of the growing range of evidence-based interventions in the field (including TFCO). Many of these are now well-defined approaches, but none (at the time of this writing) have been officially recognized as evidence based by the major repositories that catalogue such interventions.

Farmer and colleagues took a somewhat different approach. Rather than developing a new model of TFC, they sought to develop an approach to training and consultation that could combine elements from evidence-based TFC, increase implementation of "what worked" in existing usual-care TFC programs, and fill perceived gaps in both the evidence-based and usual-care TFC. A large-scale statewide study of existing TFC agencies clarified challenges and discrepancies between many existing TFC agencies' orientation, size, and system-level supports and assumptions of TFCO (Farmer et al., 2002). Hence, they conducted a program of federally funded research that resulted in *Together Facing the Challenge* (TFTC) (Farmer et al., 2010; Murray, Dorsey, Farmer, Burns, & Ballentine, 2015).

TFTC is built around a resource toolkit and training/consultation approach designed to increase effective practices among TFC agencies in a way that is viable within available resources, capacities, and costs of a wide range of currently operating TFC agencies. The TFTC team developed a "hybrid" model – one that included evidence-based elements around training for treatment foster parents while recognizing constraints and opportunities posed by existing programs and practice-based evidence (Farmer et al., 2010; Murray, Culver, Farmer, Jackson, & Rixon, 2014). Core components that are highlighted in training with administrators, supervisors, and treatment parents include: (1) building relationships and teaching cooperation; (2) setting expectations; (3) use of effective parenting tools; (4) implementing effective consequences; (5) cultural sensitivity; (6) preparing youth to transition to adulthood; and (7) effective communication and taking care of self (Murray et al., 2015).

Treatment Foster Care Oregon (TFCO) and Together Facing the Challenge (TFTC) are, as of this writing, the only two TFC approaches recognized as evidence-based on a national list of such interventions (California Clearinghouse of Evidence-based Practices in Child Welfare, www. cebc4cw.org). They may be viewed as complementary, rather than competing, models that fit different types of agencies with different missions, resources, and contexts. TFCO is a relatively resource intense and highly prescribed model for delivering relatively short-term (6–9 months) TFC. TFTC is designed to provide relatively low-cost training (with an explicit train-the-trainer approach), coaching, and consultation to allow TFC agencies to more flexibly augment their practice by incorporating systematic and structured evidence-based elements and approaches.

It is important to recognize that TFC is built on a core set of processes and approaches, regardless of whether a specific TFC program is implementing one of the two evidence-based models. These include (1) treatment foster parents as key agents of change; (2) team approach to treatment (that includes treatment foster parents as key members); (3) service coordination; and (4) focus on the child's ecology beyond the treatment foster family (e.g., work with the child's family, focus on peer affiliations). As would be expected in "real world" practice, how well each of these is implemented in any particular TFC program varies (see Farmer et al., 2002). The two evidence-

294 *Elizabeth M.Z. Farmer et al.*

based approaches both focus on the importance of core skills that treatment foster parents must have to effectively intervene with youth. Each addresses the need for systematic, high-quality, focused supervision and support for treatment foster parents by their agency supervisor. TFCO has a very specific approach to these that includes a strong behavioral focus (including points/ levels) and specific roles for treatment foster parents, auxiliary professionals and paraprofessionals, and their supervisors (Chamberlain, 2002). TFTC, given its focus on training/consultation to improve practice in existing TFC programs, provides training and extended coaching and consultation on each of these to develop knowledge and skills and create a system that supports effective practice (Murray et al., 2014, 2015).

Changes in the broader context of children's mental health services also brought changes to TFC models. By the time that TFTC was being developed in the early 2000s, the field was grappling with new information about the centrality of trauma and adverse childhood experiences (e.g., Deblinger & Heflin, 1996; Deblinger, Stauffer, & Steer, 2001) and the particularly problematic longitudinal outcomes for youth with emotional/behavioral problems (e.g., Farmer, 1993, 1995; Kutash & Rivera, 1996). Therefore, TFTC explicitly incorporated these foci into the core training and consultation/coaching model.

At present, TFC is a widely practiced approach to out-of-home treatment for youth. It is difficult to get a full count of the number of programs or of youth served in TFC. There are currently approximately 350 member agencies of FFTA, but comparison of this list with known TFC agencies in selected states suggest that this represents a fraction of existing agencies and programs. However, this database provides a rough description of the range of TFC programs. They exist across nearly every state in the U.S. (and are common throughout North America and internationally). Programs vary tremendously in size – based on annual budgets, they range from "mom and pop" programs with small annual budgets to large programs with budgets over $250M. The majority of TFC agencies are organizationally designated as non-profits, but TFC is also run via public agencies, and some operate as for-profits. Nearly all TFC programs are operated within broader organizations that provide child/family-focused services (e.g., outpatient, case management, group residential, intensive in-home, independent living). While most youth in TFC are school aged and meet criteria for at least one psychiatric diagnosis, its individualized and community-based focus makes it adaptable and useful with a wide range of ages, issues, and disorders (e.g., medically fragile youth, pregnant/teen mothers, young children). In most communities where it is practiced, TFC is a scarce resource. Its widespread applicability, relatively low costs (for residential treatment), concordance with contemporary priorities around community- and family-based treatment, and recognition as an evidence-based treatment (even though most implementation does not utilize one of the recognized evidence-based models) all work together to make it a positively valued approach where demand frequently outpaces availability. Hence, one of the challenges (to be discussed later in this chapter) revolves around dissemination and implementation approaches to increase availability of high-quality TFC that can serve a wide range of youth, with assurances for safe, appropriate, and effective treatment, within the resource constraints of financial and personnel resources.

Current State of Knowledge for TFC

TFC Practice and Role in a System/Continuum of Care

TFC's rise to prominence coincided with paradigmatic shifts in the broader children's mental health system and child welfare systems towards a focus on systems of care, coordinated and collaborative care, and a strong focus on least-restrictive placements (Stroul, 2003). As such, there was a good deal of attention to the role that TFC could play in more fully operationalizing this set of principles. TFC was often portrayed as a "step down" placement; a way to transition youth from more restrictive placements back into community-based settings. Data suggest that for some youth, TFC appeared to function in this way (i.e., youth were in more restrictive placements before their focal placement in TFC) (Baker & Curtis, 2006; Bishop-Fitzpatrick et al., 2015; Farmer, Wagner, Burns, & Richards, 2003). However, for a significant portion of youth who reside in TFC (35–75% across various studies), such placement was either a move to a more restrictive placement (e.g., from home, foster care) or a lateral move (i.e., movement among TFC homes). Findings across studies have fairly consistently found that youth are likely to be discharged to less restrictive settings (e.g., home, foster care) (Bishop-Fitzpatrick et al., 2015; Chamberlain, 1994; Farmer et al., 2003). How stable and sustainable these less restrictive placements are varies (Farmer et al., 2003) and studies have found such instability to be a risk factor, in itself, for continued problems in the post-discharge period (Hussey & Guo, 2005).

Implementation of TFC across programs varies widely. Farmer and colleagues (Farmer et al., 2002) used the FFTA Program Standards (FFTA, 1995, 2013) to develop an interview for TFC program directors. The 52 resulting items covered the FFTA criteria related to program, treatment parents, and child/youth/families. Scoring of the full measure had a potential range from 0–104; actual range of the 42 included agencies was 53–93 (M=69.9). Seventeen percent of agencies were below average on all three included domains (program; treatment parents; children/youth/families), and 21% were above average on all three domains. More recent data collection among FFTA member agencies (i.e., organizations that are connected to a national infrastructure and are aware of national standards of practice) suggest that many TFC programs incorporate elements of evidence-based practices into their programs, but few implement a full-standing evidence-based model of TFC (Farmer et al., 2018). These data suggest that programs most consistently implemented planning and child-centered work (e.g., timing of plan development, effectively address child's behavior) and were substantially less consistent on implementing outreach and adequate coverage of child/family needs (e.g., coordinate with other agencies, keep caseloads small, provide follow-up supports).

A final question about TFC's role in a system or continuum of care focuses on the severity of youth being served in TFC and whether there is effective triaging between TFC and more restrictive levels of placement (usually group homes or other congregate placement options). It appears that group homes tend to serve youth with somewhat more severe disorders, but the differences between youth in the two settings are not large (and often not statistically significant) (Curtis, Alexander, & Lunghofer, 2001). In a large multi-agency, multi-state study, Baker and colleagues (Baker, Kurland, Curtis, Alexander, & Papa-Lentini, 2007) found that 52% of youth in TFC vs. 55% of youth in residential treatment were in the clinical range on Total Problems for the Child Behavior Check List (CBCL) (not statistically different). Breland-Noble and colleagues also found no significant differences in clinical severity between youth in TFC and those in group homes (Breland-Noble, Farmer, Dubs, Potter, & Burns, 2005). However, they did find significant differences in other service use while in placement (more clinical and intensive services associated with group homes; more community-based and proactive services in TFC; higher rates of medication and polypharmacy in group homes) (Breland-Noble et al., 2004, 2005; Brenner, Southerland, Burns, Wagner, & Farmer, 2014).

296   *Elizabeth M.Z. Farmer et al.*

Effectiveness of TFC

Treatment Foster Care Oregon (TFCO)

The core research on TFC revolves around a series of randomized trials and is largely based on research conducted by Chamberlain and colleagues on TFCO (e.g., Chamberlain, 1994, 1996, 1999; Chamberlain & Mihalic, 1998; Chamberlain et al., 2010). Initial randomized trials showed that TFCO was related to decreased detention, delinquency, offenses, and arrests when compared to a group of similar youth who were randomly assigned to group homes in the same geographic region (Chamberlain & Reid, 1998; Leve, Chamberlain, & Reid, 2005). Extended follow-up of these study participants showed sustained improvements in behavior and arrests in the years following discharge (Eddy, Whaley, & Chamberlain, 2004). Additional work examined broader dimensions of impact and found that TFC was also associated with improved educational attainment (Chamberlain, Leve, & DeGarmo, 2007; Leve & Chamberlain, 2007) and clinical symptoms (e.g., Harold, Kerr, Ryzin, DeGarmo, Rhoades, & Leve, 2013). Analyses also examined potential cost effectiveness of TFCO by examining initial lower costs of treatment than group home placements as well as reduced days incarcerated, increased days in public school, and increased residence with family (e.g., Chamberlain et al., 2007).

This set of randomized trials has also made it possible to analyze key hypothesized mediational factors that may improve outcomes in TFCO compared to other (particularly congregate) residential placements. A variety of these have been shown to be more prominent in TFCO than in group residential settings and, when present, to influence outcomes. These include close and consistent adult supervision, effective discipline, adult mentoring, and decreased association with deviant peers (Eddy & Chamberlain, 2000; Leve, Chamberlain & Reid, 2005).

More recent work has focused on dissemination and implementation of TFCO (Chamberlain, Sladana, Brown, & Leve, 2010). This has included a randomized trial in California to identify system-level factors that influence implementation and dissemination and evaluation internationally (e.g., Bergström & Höjman, 2016; Hansson & Olsson, 2012). At present, TFCO is being implemented in sites in North America, Europe, Australia, and New Zealand.

Variations Derived from TFCO

TFCO was designed originally for adolescents, particularly adolescents with extensive histories of antisocial behavior and involvement with the juvenile justice system. Positive findings suggested the potential utility of this framework for addressing a broader population of youth and recognized the possibilities of intervening earlier in youth's development and system involvement.

Fisher and colleagues adapted MTFC to intervene with young children who were in the foster care system (Fisher, Burraston, & Pears, 2005; Fisher, Gunnar, Chamberlain, & Reid, 2000). Initially known as Early Intervention Foster Care (EIFC) and later as the Multidimensional Treatment Foster Care Program for Preschoolers (MTFC-P) (and, then, TFCO-P), this adaptation uses the same key ingredients of the adolescent version of MTFC (e.g., training and consultation for foster parents, therapy for children, work with children's families, focus on appropriately and effectively addressing problematic behaviors, consistent limit setting, and close supervision). It includes developmentally focused approaches to assure a nurturing environment for young children, consistent structure and routines, and understanding of young children's developmental needs (Fisher et al., 2005). Randomized trial results showed that children in the TFCO-P condition were more likely to achieve and maintain permanency (Fisher et al., 2005) and showed more positive attachment-related behaviors (Fisher & Kim, 2007) than youth in traditional foster care.

Another variation on TFCO took the general principles of TFCO and distilled them to core elements that could be more easily utilized in regular foster care. There has been increasing concern for quite a while about high rates of problem behaviors among youth in foster care (Landsverk & Garland, 1999). TFCO was found to be effective in reducing such problems among youth with very serious emotional, behavioral, and conduct problems, but it was too intensive and expensive to disseminate broadly in regular foster care settings. A team of collaborators identified potentially key factors for this type of broader dissemination and application. Project KEEP focused primarily on teaching foster parents more effective approaches to managing behavior, with specific focus on positive reinforcement (Chamberlain, Price, & Leve, 2008). Initial randomized trial results showed that foster parents could be engaged in this effort, could improve their use of positive reinforcement, and that such increases were associated with improved behavior for children and increased the likelihood of a positive exit from foster care (e.g., reunification with parent(s), adoption) (Chamberlain, Price, Leve et al., 2008; Price et al., 2008). Interest in the potential for widespread dissemination of this approach led to testing of a "cascading dissemination" model to systematically engage local paraprofessionals as trainers. Results showed that paraprofessionals could implement the training and effectively teach new paraprofessionals to do so (Chamberlain, Price, Reid, & Landsverk, 2008).

Together Facing the Challenge (TFTC)

As described above, TFTC was developed from a different angle to address the need to make high-quality TFC available to a broad range of agencies. Work with TFC agencies across North Carolina in the mid-1990s suggested that program directors wanted to improve quality of care, but did not have the financial resources/infrastructure to implement the then-current version of MTFC. They also had philosophical concerns about the strong behavioral underpinnings of MTFC, particularly the use of points and levels in a non-congregate care setting. Therefore, Farmer and colleagues conducted a study of what "usual care" TFC involved, modeled effects of key factors on youth outcomes, and then brought this information together with the existing FFTA Practice Standards and available information from MTFC to create a "hybrid" approach to improve practice within the confines of ongoing TFC programs' fiscal, infrastructure, and philosophical realities (Farmer, Burns, & Murray, 2009).

Results from the initial observational study of usual practice TFC showed that TFC, as broadly practiced, varied considerably and did not fully adhere to either the FFTA Standards or MTFC core elements (Farmer et al., 2002). However, variations in certain practices were found to be associated with improved outcomes for youth. These included improved use of proactive behavior management strategies and increased training and supervision of treatment foster parents (Farmer et al., 2009, 2010). TFTC was designed to be accessible to a broad range of TFC programs and to be sustainable. Hence, it was developed as a training and consultation model – designed as a train-the-trainer model to work with treatment foster parents and their supervisors and provide extended consultation and coaching to supervisors as they implemented the approaches in TFTC with their treatment parents. Training includes a multi-day training with supervisors and administrators (so that they can be champions of the new approaches and assist in training their treatment parents) and

298 *Elizabeth M.Z. Farmer et al.*

a curriculum for training treatment parents (Murray et al., 2015; Murray, Farmer, Souther-land, & Ballentine, 2010). After the initial training, TFC supervisors engage in a minimum of 12 months of regular consultation and coaching with the TFTC trainers to provide support, additional training, and guidance as they work within their agency to improve practice (Murray et al., 2010, 2014).

An initial randomized trial showed that TFTC resulted in reduced symptoms and improved functioning for youth compared to youth receiving usual-practice TFC from other agencies in the geographic region (Farmer et al., 2010). Positive results were seen for symptoms, behaviors, and strengths at six months and changes in youths' behavior remained significantly better for TFTC youth than comparison youth at the 12-month follow-up (Farmer et al., 2010). Post-hoc analyses of differences in process showed that improved behavior management, stronger relationships between treatment foster parents and youth, and additional training and supervision were all associated with improved outcomes for youth. It should be noted that TFTC was compared to and found to be more effective than usual-care TFC. Nearly all other work on assessing effectiveness of TFC has compared it to an adjacent level of care (usually group homes).

Recent work on TFTC has built upon the initial positive findings to help fill a gap in available and feasible evidence-based options for improving TFC. This has included improvements to address concerns about decreased significance of effects by 12 months. This led to a focus on increasing intensity of the consultation and coaching after initial training. A randomized trial showed that an enhanced dose and more focused strategies for follow-up consultation/coaching resulted in better implementation of the model (Murray et al., 2018). At present, TFTC is being implemented by more than 100 agencies in over 25 states. Ongoing work focuses on efforts to streamline and improve training approaches to assure access and quality across the full organizational and geographic range of TFC providers (Ballentine, Morris, & Farmer, 2012; Murray et al., 2010, 2014; Southerland, Farmer, Murray, Stambaugh, & Rosenberg, 2018).

Other Evidence and Relevant Findings

The evidence base for TFC has centered largely on TFCO and TFTC. Studies of other models of TFC have shown mixed effects. For example, Bishop-Fitzpatrick and colleagues (2015) showed positive pre-post outcomes for Pressley Ridge-TFC (PR-TFC) and showed potential moderators and mediators of change. In contrast, Lee and Thompson's (2008) study of Boys Town's TFC vs. the same organization's group home model suggested more positive outcomes for group care than for TFC.

Since 2000, there have been several reviews of literature on TFC to examine overall state of the field and knowledge. Curtis et al. (2001) reviewed available literature to examine what was known about the characteristics of youth served and outcomes between TFC and group homes. They concluded that youth in group homes were slightly more likely to be older, male, and in contact with the justice system, but overall youth in the two settings were quite similar and outcomes were also mostly comparable. More recent reviews (Hahn et al., 2005; Lee, Bright, Svoboda, Fakunmoju, & Barth, 2011; Osei, Gorey, & Hernandez Jozefowicz, 2016; Turner & Macdonald, 2011) supported the relative effectiveness of TFC over group homes on outcomes including delinquency and criminal behavior and less restrictive community-based placements. Also, when examined, TFC was consistently less expensive than other interventions (Turner & Macdonald, 2011). All reviews point to the overall positive and promising nature of the accumulated results and also to the relative dearth of studies.

Current Directions and Dilemmas for TFC

Strengths and Appeal of TFC

TFC occupies an interesting position in the world of services for youth with emotional and behavioral disorders and in the realm of evidence-based treatments. It spans two child-serving sectors – child welfare and children's mental health. As such, it clearly recognizes the intersection of these two sectors and the fact that youth with EBD often require services from both. TFC plays a mid-level and boundary spanning role in its provision of intensive individualized treatments within the private homes of treatment foster families.

TFC also fits well into discussions of evidence-based treatments. It has at least two models or approaches that have been identified as evidence-based practices, based on positive findings from randomized trials. However, most TFC programs do not implement either of these models, and usual-care practice appears to be a muted version of both established practice standards and evidence-based models. Many locally developed models share core components and key features, and many include elements of a wide range of evidence-based practices from the broader children's mental health field.

Available evidence (from randomized trials, systematic reviews, and a range of other research designs) suggests that TFC is associated with significant improvements in youth's behavior, symptoms, and functioning. These gains are observed across time in nearly all studies and appear to be stronger in programs implementing more structured and/or evidence-based models than those with more eclectic intervention approaches. Data on mediators of outcomes suggest that stronger relationships between treatment foster parents and youth, proactive positively focused discipline practices, consistent monitoring and supervision, and improved training and supervision of treatment foster parents are associated with improved outcomes.

Challenges and Future Directions

One of the major challenges for TFC is the need to increase the evidence-base about what works in the wide range of models that are currently implemented in TFC and to increase access to empirically supported models of treatment across the full range of TFC agencies. At present, relatively few programs implement one of the two recognized evidence-based models. However, many programs incorporate evidence-based elements or components derived from other settings into their TFC programming, and many locally developed programs are built around practice-based evidence and common elements that are also prominent in evidence-based TFC. Most of these programs have not conducted rigorous research or evaluations to examine effectiveness of these approaches and programs. There is a need to develop an efficient approach to assessing effectiveness of this range of locally developed and delivered TFC programming. This requires specification of core essential elements, a way to systematically measure implementation of these elements in usual practice, and low-burden approaches to evaluating outcomes for youth and families. There is also a need for broader dissemination and implementation research on the existing evidence-based models (and any others that attain this designation as the field moves forward). It is important to know what works, assess the degree to which these known programs and/or components are being implemented, and determine both the short-term and sustained effects of intervention for youth and their families. It is likely that this will require coordinated research/evaluation across a wide range of TFC agencies to provide data that can be used to guide practice and policy.

There are a variety of reasons why TFC agencies have not widely and rapidly implemented evidence-based models (e.g., costs for training and implementation, fit of models to existing system/context, correspondence between EBPs and agency conceptual or theoretical underpinnings, availability of local personnel and resources). Beyond these concrete explanations or reasons, though, remains an underlying reality – change is difficult. Work in California (Chamberlain et al., 2010; Price et al., 2009) and North Carolina (Murray et al., 2010, 2014) to implement TFCO, KEEP, and TFTC show the extensive and intensive collaborative relationships, partnering, buy-in, sustained engagement, substantial consultation/coaching, requirements for agency leadership, and collective will that is necessary to change knowledge, attitudes, and behavior to implement new practices. There is a growing knowledge base on the implementation and dissemination process across evidence-based practices. This is useful. Examples from previous work in TFC are also useful guides. However, the challenges in widespread implementation of improved TFC are daunting. In addition to the challenges in disseminating and implementing any EBP, TFC has core features that may make such work even more difficult. These include, among many others: high turnover in supervisory/administrative positions within many TFC agencies; implementation of an intervention that is, by design, individualized; geographic dispersion of families and supervisors that may make it difficult to have providers interact with colleagues in a way that facilitates shared learning, culture, supervision, and change; and a fundamental requirement of TFC to provide treatment within the context and flow of families' lives and communities. Given these complexities, widespread implementation of improved TFC is likely to require resources, use of technology, expanded training, consultation, and supervision, and overarching infrastructure that significantly exceeds that which is currently widely available across agencies and localities.

TFC also faces challenges in having an adequate supply of personnel. This is particularly acute for treatment foster parents, but is also challenging for supervisory positions. Being a treatment foster parent is an extremely challenging role (Farmer & Lippold, 2016; Wells, Farmer, Richards, & Burns, 2004). The role requires individuals to simultaneously serve as front-line treatment providers who work closely with a team to develop and implement an intensive treatment plan and to function as the youth's primary caregiver to meet the emotional, developmental, and social needs of the whole child. Treatment foster parents vary in their interpretation and enactment of the role (Farmer & Lippold, 2016; Wells et al., 2004). Finding individuals, couples, and families who are willing to take on this complex set of demands while also meeting all of the economic, community, social, recreational, spiritual, medical, etc. needs of the entire family unit is challenging. Finding people who have the aptitude, skills, personality, and stability to do this well and over an extended period of time is even more challenging. Conversations with TFC program directors across the country suggest that recruitment and retention of treatment parents and other staff is a central challenge and unending effort (Farmer et al., 2018).

Another challenge for TFC (and nearly all out-of-home treatment approaches (see Lee, this volume)) is sustaining positive changes after youth are discharged. In most situations, TFC agencies' ability to bill for or be paid for services in the post-discharge period is quite limited. Duration varies by funding source and across states, but most programs have 0–60 days within which they can receive remuneration for supporting youth and families after discharge from TFC. Anecdotal data from discussions with TFC providers across the nation suggest that much of the post-discharge support is unfunded and provided by treatment foster parents and other staff who continue informally supporting youth after discharge. While such long-term connections and devotion are admirable, relying on volunteer labor to support youth and families with long-standing and complex challenges and needs is not a sustainable or sufficient approach to systematically assuring continuity of intervention and supports or sustainability of in-treatment gains.

Another ongoing challenge for TFC is its role in a system of care and shifting parameters of that system. TFC is usually classified according to Medicaid eligibility criteria to serve youth who have demonstrated need (via diagnoses, symptoms, impairment) but whose level of need does not require round-the-clock monitoring/supervision. In recent years, there have been concerns about the level of difficulty of youth being served in TFC. As systems, payers, policy makers, and advocates have raised questions about group homes and other forms of more restrictive residential treatment, many states have dramatically reduced the number of youth served in such settings. As facilities are closed, youth who historically would have been served in these settings must be served elsewhere. In many communities, TFC is the next-available level of treatment. There are currently not systematic data about whether or to what extent this is causing problems in TFC. Discussions among TFC providers across the country suggest that it is seen as a significant problem that strains the ability of TFC agencies to adequately serve referred youth and to assure adequate combinations of treatment and safety for youth, families, and communities (Farmer et al., 2018).

Conclusions

There are clearly many challenges and a great deal of work to be done. However, TFC is currently a highly regarded and widely utilized approach to meet the complex needs of youth with serious emotional and behavioral disorders who require out-of-home treatment and care. Unlike its adjacent level of care – group homes – TFC aligns well with contemporary principles of community-based, family-based, least-restrictive treatment. It is also substantially less expensive than group homes or other forms of out-of-home treatment. In addition, it has a relatively well-developed evidence base compared to other community-based and/or out-of-home treatments. There are available evidence-based models that have established training, dissemination, and implementation approaches and are currently being used in communities and agencies across the U.S. and internationally. TFC is based on core principles of structure, treatment, and process that allow for tremendous individualization, intensity of intervention in community- and family-based settings, and work with a team of professionals to ecologically support youth with very diverse characteristics, strengths, and needs. Hence, it is an established and promising intervention for treating youth with complex and extended individual and family issues.

While all of this makes TFC conceptually and practically appealing, there is still a great deal of work to ensure that high-quality TFC becomes typical. At present, many TFC programs incorporate evidence-based elements/approaches, but relatively few implement one of the existing evidence-based TFC models. This may or may not be a problem – at present there is insufficient data on the wide range of TFC approaches, models, and programs currently being delivered to assess their effectiveness. This challenge of knowing "what works" and, once this is identified, how to efficiently and effectively move the field towards more effective processes, approaches, and practices is a major challenge. TFC also struggles with a bit of an identity crisis – spanning children's mental health and child welfare, TFC is a conceptually appealing and widely applicable intervention. However, its role and utility may not be fully realized because of this lack of clear "fit" within a single existing system or domain. This creates challenges for the professionalism of the approach, clear

302 *Elizabeth M.Z. Farmer et al.*

understanding of relevant comparison or alternative interventions, and eligibility for potentially relevant funding sources.

As the field moves forward, TFC's positioning and flexibility is likely to be a strong asset to serve youth with complex and multifaceted needs and issues. TFC is a very promising model that has tremendous potential. It is important to advance knowledge and practice to assure that every youth who is served in TFC receives high-quality treatment that effectively supports the youth, their treatment foster parents, and their families. It is also important to create systematic and sustainable infrastructure and supports to ensure that TFC programs and youth served by them are able to develop, flourish, and grow across time.

References

Baker, A. J., & Curtis, P. (2006). Prior placements of youth admitted to therapeutic foster care and residential treatment centers: The Odyssey Project population. *Child and Adolescent Social Work Journal, 23* (1), 38–60.

Baker, A. J., Kurland, D., Curtis, P., Alexander, G., & Papa-Lentini, C. (2007). Mental health and behavioral problems of youth in the child welfare system: Residential treatment centers compared to therapeutic foster care in the Odyssey Project population. *Child Welfare, 86*(3), 97.

Ballentine, K. L., Morris, A. N., & Farmer, E. M. Z. (2012). Following youth after out-of-home placement: Navigating a data collection obstacle course. *Residential Treatment for Children & Youth, 29*(1), 32–47.

Bergström, M., & Höjman, L. (2016). Is multidimensional treatment foster (MTFC) more effective than treatment as usual in a three-year follow-up? Results from MTFC in a Swedish setting. *European Journal of Social Work, 19*(2), 219–235.

Bishop-Fitzpatrick, L., Jung, N., Nam, I., Trunzo, A. C., & Rauktis, M. E. (2015). Outcomes of an agency-developed treatment foster care model for adolescents. *Journal of Emotional and Behavioral Disorders, 23*(3), 156–166.

Breland-Noble, A. M., Elbogen, E. B., Farmer, E. M. Z., Dubs, M. S., Wagner, H. R., & Burns, B. J. (2004). Use of psychotropic medications by youths in therapeutic foster care and group homes. *Psychiatric Services, 55*(6), 706–708.

Breland-Noble, A. M., Farmer, E. M. Z., Dubs, M. S., Potter, E., & Burns, B. J. (2005). Mental health and other service use by youth in therapeutic foster care and group homes. *Journal of Child and Family Studies, 14*(2), 167–180.

Brenner, S. L., Southerland, D. G., Burns, B. J., Wagner, H. R., & Farmer, E. M. Z. (2014). Use of psychotropic medications among youth in treatment foster care. *Journal of Child and Family Studies, 23*(4), 666–674.

Bryant, B., & Snodgrass, R. (1990). Therapeutic foster care: Past and present. In P. Meadowcroft & B. A. Trout (Eds.), *Troubled youth in treatment homes: A handbook of therapeutic foster care* (pp. 1–20). Washington, DC: Child Welfare League of America.

Chamberlain, P. (1994). *Family connections: A treatment foster care model for adolescents with delinquency.* Eugene, OR: Castalia Publishing Company.

Chamberlain, P. (1996). Community-based residential treatment for adolescents with conduct disorder. In T. H. Ollendick & R. J. Prinz (Eds.) *Advances in clinical child psychology* (pp. 63–90). Boston, MA: Springer.

Chamberlain, P. (1999). Residential care for children and adolescents with oppositional defiant disorder and conduct disorder. In H. C. Quay & A. E. Hogan (Eds.), *Handbook of disruptive behavior disorders* (pp. 495–506). Boston, MA: Springer.

Chamberlain, P. (2002). Treatment foster care. In B. J. Burns & K. Hoagwood (Eds.), *Community treatment for youth: Evidence-based interventions for severe emotional and behavioral disorders* (pp. 117–138). Oxford, UK: Oxford University Press.

Chamberlain, P., Leve, L. D., & DeGarmo, D. S. (2007). Multidimensional Treatment Foster Care for girls in the juvenile justice system: 2-year follow-up of a randomized clinical trial. *Journal of Consulting and Clinical Psychology, 75*(1), 187–193.

Chamberlain, P., & Mihalic, S. (1998). *Blueprints for violence prevention, book eight: Multidimensional Treatment Foster Care*. Boulder, CO: Center for the Study and Prevention of Violence.

Chamberlain, P., Moreland, S., & Reid, K. (1992). Enhanced services and stipends for foster parents: Effects on retention rates and outcomes for children. *Child Welfare, 71*(5), 387–401.

Chamberlain, P., Price, J., Leve, L. D., Laurent, H., Landsverk, J. A., & Reid, J. B. (2008). Prevention of behavior problems for children in foster care: Outcomes and mediation effects. *Prevention Science, 9*(1), 17–27.

Chamberlain, P., Price, J., Reid, J., & Landsverk, J. (2008). Cascading implementation of a foster and kinship parent intervention. *Child Welfare, 87*(5), 27–48.

Chamberlain, P., & Reid, J. B. (1998). Comparison of two community alternatives to incarceration for chronic juvenile offenders. *Journal of Consulting and Clinical Psychology, 66*(4), 624–633.

Chamberlain, P., Saldana, L., Brown, C. H., & Leve, L. D. (2010). Implementation of Multidimensional Treatment Foster care in California: A randomized trial of an evidence-based practice. In M. Roberts-DeGennaro & S. Fogel (Eds.), *Empirically supported interventions for community and organizational change* (pp. 218–234). Chicago, IL: Lyceum.

Curtis, P. A., Alexander, G., & Lunghofer, L. A. (2001). A literature review comparing the outcomes of residential group care and therapeutic foster care. *Child and Adolescent Social Work Journal, 18*(5), 377–392.

Deblinger, E., & Heflin, A. H. (1996). *Interpersonal violence: The practice series, Vol. 16. Treating sexually abused children and their nonoffending parents: A cognitive behavioral approach.* Thousand Oaks, CA: Sage Publications, Inc.

Deblinger, E., Stauffer, L. B., & Steer, R. A. (2001). Comparative efficacies of supportive and cognitive behavioral group therapies for young children who have been sexually abused and their nonoffending mothers. *Child Maltreatment, 6*(4), 332–343.

Dore, M. M., & Mullin, D. (2006). Treatment family foster care: Its history and current role in the foster care continuum. *Families in Society, 87*(4), 475–482.

Eddy, J. M., & Chamberlain, P. (2000). Family management and deviant peer association as mediators of the impact of treatment condition on youth antisocial behavior. *Journal of Consulting and Clinical Psychology, 68*(5), 857–863.

Eddy, J. M., Whaley, R. B., & Chamberlain, P. (2004). The prevention of violent behavior by chronic and serious male juvenile offenders: A 2-year follow-up of a randomized clinical trial. *Journal of Emotional and Behavioral Disorders, 12*(1), 2–8.

Farmer, E. M. Z. (1993). Externalizing behavior in the life course: The transition from school to work. *Journal of Emotional and Behavioral Disorders, 1*(3), 179–188.

Farmer, E. M. Z. (1995). Extremity of externalizing behavior and young adult outcomes. *Journal of Child Psychology and Psychiatry, 36*(4), 617–632.

Farmer, E. M. Z., Burns, B., & Murray, M. (2009). Enhancing treatment foster care: An approach to improving usual care practice. *Report on Emotional and Behavioral Disorders in Youth, 9*, 79–84.

Farmer, E. M. Z., Burns, B. J., Dubs, M. S., & Thompson, S. (2002). Assessing conformity to standards for treatment foster care. *Journal of Emotional and Behavioral Disorders, 10*(4), 213–222.

Farmer, E. M. Z., Burns, B. J., Wagner, H. R., Murray, M., & Southerland, D. G. (2010). Enhancing "usual practice" treatment foster care: Findings from a randomized trial on improving youths' outcomes. *Psychiatric Services, 61*(6), 555–561.

Farmer, E. M. Z., Dorsey, S., & Mustillo, S. A. (2004). Intensive home and community interventions. *Child and Adolescent Psychiatric Clinics, 13*(4), 857–884.

Farmer, E. M. Z., & Lippold, M. A. (2016). The need to do it all: Exploring the ways in which treatment foster parents enact their complex role. *Children and Youth Services Review, 64*, 91–99.

Farmer, E. M. Z., Marshall, L. M., & Palazzolo, S. L. (2018). *Supporting successful reunification of children and youth served in treatment foster care.* Hackensack, NJ: Family Focused Treatment Association.

Farmer, E. M. Z., Wagner, H. R., Burns, B. J., & Richards, J. T. (2003). Treatment foster care in a system of care: Sequences and correlates of residential placements. *Journal of Child and Family Studies, 12*(1), 11–25.

304 *Elizabeth M.Z. Farmer et al.*

Fisher, P. A., Burraston, B., & Pears, K. (2005). The early intervention foster care program: Permanent placement outcomes from a randomized trial. *Child Maltreatment, 10*(1), 61–71.

Fisher, P. A., & Chamberlain, P. (2000). Multidimensional Treatment Foster Care: A program for intensive parenting, family support, and skill building. *Journal of Emotional and Behavioral Disorders, 8*(3), 155–164.

Fisher, P. A., & Gilliam, K. S. (2012). Multidimensional Treatment Foster Care: An alternative to residential treatment for high risk children and adolescents. *Intervencion Psicosocial, 21*(2), 195–203.

Fisher, P. A., Gunnar, M. R., Chamberlain, P., & Reid, J. B. (2000). Preventive intervention for maltreated preschool children: Impact on children's behavior, neuroendocrine activity, and foster parent functioning. *Journal of the American Academy of Child & Adolescent Psychiatry, 39*(11), 1356–1364.

Fisher, P. A., & Kim, H. K. (2007). Intervention effects on foster preschoolers' attachment-related behaviors from a randomized trial. *Prevention Science, 8*(2), 161–170.

Forgatch, M., & Patterson, G. (1989). *Parents and adolescents living together, Pt. 2: Family problem solving.* Eugene, OR: Castalia.

Foster Family-Based Treatment Association. (1995). *Program standards for treatment foster care.* Hackensack, NJ: Author.

Foster Family-Based Treatment Association. (2013). *Program standards for treatment foster care (revised).* New York: Author.

Gross, N., & Campbell, P. (1990). Recruiting and selecting treatment parents. In P. Meadowcroft & B. A. Trout (Eds.), *Troubled youth in treatment homes: A handbook of therapeutic foster care* (pp. 33–50). Washington, DC: Child Welfare League of America.

Hahn, R. A., Bilukha, O., Lowy, J., Crosby, A., Fullilove, M. T., Liberman, F., … Corso, P. (2005). The effectiveness of therapeutic foster care for the prevention of violence: A systematic review. *American Journal of Preventive Medicine, 28*(2), 72–90.

Hansson, K., & Olsson, M. (2012). Effects of Multidimensional Treatment Foster Care (MTFC): Results from a RCT study in Sweden. *Children and Youth Services Review, 34*(9), 1929–1936.

Harold, G. T., Kerr, D. S. R., Van Ryzin, M., DeGarmo, D. S., Rhoades, K. A., & Leve, L. D. (2013). Depressive symptom trajectories among girls in the juvenile justice system: 24-month outcomes of an RCT on Multidimensional Treatment Foster Care. *Prevention Science, 14*(5), 437–446.

Hawkins, R. P., Almeida, M. C., Fabry, B., & Reitz, A. L. (1992). A scale to measure restrictiveness of living environments for troubled children and youths. *Psychiatric Services, 43*(1), 54–58.

Hussey, D. L., & Guo, S. (2005). Characteristics and trajectories of treatment foster care youth. *Child Welfare, 84*(4), 485–506.

Knitzer, J., & Olson, L. (1982). *Unclaimed children: The failure of public responsibility to children and adolescents in need of mental health services.* Washington, DC: Children's Defense Fund.

Kutash, K., & Rivera, V. R. (1996). *What works in children's mental health services?: Uncovering answers to critical questions* (Vol. 3). Baltimore, MD: Paul H Brookes Publishing Company.

Landsverk, J., & Garland, A. F. (1999). Foster care and pathways to mental health services. In P. A. Curtis, G. Dale, & J. C. Kendall (Eds.), *The foster care crisis: Translating research into policy and practice* (pp. 193–210). Lincoln: University of Nebraska Press.

Lee, B. R., Bright, C. L., Svoboda, D., Fakunmoju, S., & Barth, R. P. (2011). Outcomes of group care for youth: A review of comparative studies. *Research on Social Work Practice, 21*(2), 177–189.

Lee, B. R., & Thompson, R. (2008). Comparing outcomes for youth in treatment foster care and family-style group care. *Children and Youth Services Review, 30*(7), 746–757.

Leve, L. D., & Chamberlain, P. (2007). A randomized evaluation of multidimensional treatment foster care: Effects on school attendance and homework completion in juvenile justice girls. *Research on Social Work Practice, 17*(6), 657–663.

Leve, L. D., Chamberlain, P., & Reid, J. B. (2005). Intervention outcomes for girls referred from juvenile justice: Effects on delinquency. *Journal of Consulting and Clinical Psychology, 73*(6), 1181–1184.

McGuinness, T. M., & Dyer, J. G. (2007). Catchers in the rye: Treatment foster parents as a system of care. *Journal of Child and Adolescent Psychiatric Nursing, 20*(3), 140–147.

Meadowcroft, P., Thomlison, B., & Chamberlain, P. (1994). Treatment foster care services: A research agenda for child welfare. *Child Welfare, 73*(5), 565–581.

Murray, M., Culver, T., Farmer, E., Jackson, L. A., & Rixon, B. (2014). From theory to practice: One agency's experience with implementing an evidence-based model. *Journal of Child and Family Studies, 23* (5), 844–853.

Murray, M., Dorsey, S., Farmer, E. M. Z., Burns, B. J., & Ballentine, K. (2015). *Together facing the challenge: A therapeutic foster care resource toolkit* (2nd ed.). Retrieved from https://sites.duke.edu/tftc/files/2015/09/TTT_Intro-Session-1-Sample1.pdf

Murray, M., Farmer, E. M. Z., Southerland, D. G., & Ballentine, K. (2010). Enhancing and adapting treatment foster care: Lessons learned in trying to change practice. *Journal of Child and Family Studies, 19* (4), 393–403.

Murray, M., Khoury, D. Y., Farmer, E. M. Z., & Burns, B. J. (2018). Is more better? Examining whether enhanced consultation/coaching improves implementation. *American Journal of Orthopsychiatry, 88*(3), 376–385.

Osei, G. K., Gorey, K. M., & Hernandez Jozefowicz, D. M. (2016). Delinquency and crime prevention: Overview of research comparing treatment foster care and group care. *Children and Youth Care Forum, 45* (1), 33–46.

Patterson, G. R. (1975). *Families: Applications of social learning to family life.* Champaign, IL: Research Press.

Patterson, G. R., & Forgatch, M. (1987). *Parents and adolescents living together: Part 1: The basics.* Eugene, OR: Castalia.

Patterson, G. R., & Gullion, M. E. (1968). *Living with children: New methods for parents and teachers.* Champaign, IL: Research Press.

Price, J. M., Chamberlain, P., Landsverk, J., & Reid, J. (2009). KEEP foster-parent training intervention: Model description and effectiveness. *Child & Family Social Work, 14*(2), 233–242.

Price, J. M., Chamberlain, P., Landsverk, J., Reid, J. B., Leve, L. D., & Laurent, H. (2008). Effects of a foster parent training intervention on placement changes of children in foster care. *Child Maltreatment, 13*(1), 64–75.

Price, J. M., Roesch, S., Walsh, N. E., & Landsverk, J. (2015). Effects of the KEEP foster parent intervention on child and sibling behavior problems and parental stress during a randomized implementation trial. *Prevention Science, 16*(5), 685–695.

Pumariega, A. J., & Winters, N. C. (2003). *The handbook of child and adolescent systems of care: The new community psychiatry.* San Francisco, CA: Jossey-Bass.

Reid, J. B., & Eddy, J. M. (1997). The prevention of antisocial behavior: Some considerations in the search for effective interventions. In D. M. Stoff, J. Breiling, & J. D. Maser (Eds.), *Handbook of antisocial behavior* (pp. 343–356). Hoboken, NJ: John Wiley & Sons.

Southerland, D. G., Farmer, E. M. Z., Murray, M. E., Stambaugh, L. F., & Rosenberg, R. D. (2018). Measuring fidelity of empirically-supported treatment foster care: Preliminary psychometrics of the Together Facing the Challenge – Fidelity of Implementation Test (TFTC-FIT). *Child & Family Social Work, 23*(2), 273–280.

Stroul, B. A. (2003). Systems of care. In *The handbook of child and adolescent systems of care, the new community psychiatry* (pp. 17–34). San Francisco, CA: Jossey-Bass.

Stroul, B. A., & Friedman, R. M. (1986). *A system of care for severely emotionally disturbed children & youth.* Washington, DC: Georgetown University CASSP Technical Assistance Center.

Turner, W., & Macdonald, G. (2011). Treatment foster care for improving outcomes in children and youth people: A systematic review. *Research on Social Work Practice, 21*(5), 501–527.

U.S. Department of Health and Human Services. (2001). *Youth violence: A report of the Surgeon General.* Retrieved from https://stacks.cdc.gov/view/cdc/51661/cdc_51661_DS1.pdf

Wells, K., Farmer, E. M. Z., Richards, J. T., & Burns, B. J. (2004). The experience of being a treatment foster mother. *Qualitative Social Work, 3*(2), 117–138.

21 Residential Programs

Opportunities and Challenges in the 21st-Century Treatment Environment

Bethany R. Lee

Some critics may be surprised to find a chapter on residential treatment in a section entitled "effective programs and practices." The role of residential treatment for youth with emotional and behavioral disorders has evolved over time, from a treatment of choice to a "treatment of last resort" (Frensch & Cameron, 2002; Holmes, Connolly, Mortimer, & Hevesi, 2018). Initiatives to promote family-based care and least restrictive environments (Blau et al., 2010) as well as concerns about residential program quality and safety (GAO, 2007) have contributed to the changing role of residential programs. However, residential treatment remains an environment that has the potential to facilitate transformational change for youth and families (Lyons, 2015).

This chapter provides an overview of the current challenges and opportunities within the residential treatment environment. It begins with an overview of the evidence base for residential programs, reviewing what is known about how residential programs compare with other services and what questions remain. Next, program characteristics associated with positive outcomes from residential treatment are explored, including program model, family involvement, staff structure and training, and engagement with evidence-based practices. Finally, the chapter closes by describing three types of residential programs that merit further attention in research and practice: (a) short-term residential settings that deliver seamlessly integrated evidence-based interventions using the immersive environment to support clinical progress; (b) hybrid residential/home-based services where residential staff support parents during home visits, provide extended aftercare, and offer flexible respite; and (c) residential education programs that provide youth with EBD a specialized academic experience.

Defining Residential Treatment

One of the obstacles within the field of residential programs is a lack of clarity in terminology (GAO, 2007; Lee & Barth, 2011). Residential programs are labeled as residential treatment, congregate care, therapeutic residential care, group care, or even residential institutions, and these labels are often used interchangeably. Within this chapter, the terms residential care and residential programs will be favored as they are more broadly encompassing.

Regardless of what a residential program is called, these environments have several common characteristics. To promote a shared understanding, an international work group on Therapeutic Residential Care (TRC) developed a consensus statement that defines TRC as the planful use of a purposefully constructed, multi-dimensional living environment designed to enhance or provide treatment, education, socialization, support, and protection to children and youth with identified mental health or behavioral needs in partnership with their families and in collaboration with a full spectrum of community based formal and informal helping resources.

(Whittaker et al., 2016, p. 94)

This definition outlines the key elements of residential programs; however, the variation of how these elements are expressed or emphasized within a residential program can influence the aggregate effects of this intervention. To ensure that these programmatic differences are disclosed, group care reporting standards that specify what characteristics of residential programs should be described in research studies were proposed (Lee & Barth, 2011) and adopted by at least one journal (Weems, 2011).

Prevalence of Residential Programs

Determining the number of residential programs or youth served in those programs is anything but straightforward (Friedman et al., 2006). Because residential programs vary in their funding and regulatory structure, there is not a single entity that catalogues their prevalence and use. Public child-serving systems offer some estimates. For youth in the care of public child welfare, about 50,000 youth were served in group homes and institutions on September 30, 2016 (Child Welfare Information Gateway, 2017). Juvenile justice programs also place youth in residential programs. According to data from the 2015 Census of Juveniles in Residential Placement, about 48,000 youth offenders were placed in just under 2,000 residential programs (US DOJ, 2018). Youth can also be placed in residential treatment for behavioral health needs via Medicaid or private insurance. The National Survey on Drug Use and Health estimated that 271,000 youth age 12 to 17 received mental health services through a residential treatment center (RTC) in 2015 (SAMHSA, 2015). Unfortunately, it is not possible to know whether the counts of youth from child welfare, juvenile justice, and mental health are distinct or overlapping, making the full measure of prevalence difficult to capture.

Although the point-in-time prevalence of programs and their capacity is unknown, trends in the use of residential care consistently reflect a decline in recent years. Within child welfare, about 18% of youth in child welfare placements were in residential programs in 2004 compared to 14% in 2013 (USDHHS, 2015) and 12% in 2016 (Child Welfare Information Gateway, 2017). Within juvenile justice placements, this decrease is more dramatic, with a 50% drop in the number of youth in residential settings in 2015 compared to 1997 (US DOJ, 2018). These estimates suggest that fewer youth are receiving residential services. However, therapeutic residential care remains an essential setting within the child-serving continuum. From the above counts (that likely under-represent private placements), anywhere from one-quarter to one-half of a million youth are receiving residential services in the United States at any given time. Regardless of size, this population is important because they are commonly understood to be the most challenging youth who have not been well served by community-based services and their families are no longer able to support them safely at home. Residential placement can be a family's last hope.

Residential Treatment's Changing Role

Residential programs have experienced a significant shift in acceptance over time, as reflected by the changing rates of use. Although the future role of residential programs is somewhat uncertain, recent legislation suggests that residential settings will continue to play a role in behavioral health treatment for youth. The 2018 Family First Prevention Services Act (FFPSA) allows for the use of federal funds for residential programs that are licensed and accredited as Qualified Residential Treatment Programs (QRTP). To qualify as a QRTP, programs must have a trauma-informed treatment model, engage families, and offer aftercare supports following discharge.

Further, FFPSA ushers in an explicit emphasis on the importance of research evidence, albeit only for placement prevention services. Under FFPSA, a state's federal reimbursement rates will be tied to the level of evidence supporting each community-based prevention service. Although some implementation details for FFPSA are still being finalized, implications from this policy are likely to drive changes to residential programs' prevalence, functioning, and potentially even their evidence base.

Evidence of Residential Programs' Effectiveness

Despite the long history of residential programs, the evidence base remains underdeveloped. Randomizing assignment into residential treatment can be problematic and is rarely attempted. As a result, it is difficult to assess the relative benefits of residential placement compared to other treatments. Most of the empirical evidence comes from quasi-experimental or single-group designs, which limits causal attribution. A systematic review of two-group studies that compared outcomes for group care interventions with an alternative treatment was conducted in 2011 (Lee, Bright, Svoboda, Fakunmoju, & Barth, 2011). Results from the 19 identified and relevant studies suggested that significant effects varied depending on the residential program's characteristics and to what it was being compared. Studies that compared outcomes for family foster care with those of residential programs found better outcomes for foster care, but pre-treatment differences were not considered. For treatment foster care studies, Multidimensional Treatment Foster Care showed better outcomes than group care, but other TFC studies found effects that favored group care. This review study illustrated the complexity of the empirical evidence for and against residential programs.

A more recent multi-level meta-analysis compared behavioral and delinquency outcomes of two-group controlled studies that compared youth outcomes from residential care to non-group-based settings (Strijbosch et al., 2015). Overall outcomes favored family-based care settings with a small to medium effect size. However, when the residential program was evidence-based, there were no outcome differences between residential and family care settings, suggesting the quality of the program influences its effectiveness.

In a multi-national study of almost 3,000 orphaned or abandoned children age 6–12 in low and middle income countries, developmental and well-being outcomes for youth living in group-based care were compared to youth in family care. Findings at baseline suggested youth in group-based settings were doing at least as well as youth in family care (Whetten et al., 2009). At 3-year follow-up, youth in group care settings had better height for age development and fewer caregiver health issues (Whetten et al., 2014) as well as lower annual incidence of physical or sexual abuse (Gray et al., 2015). Similar to the empirical evidence from studies in the United States, these findings suggest that group care settings are not inherently worse and high quality group care may produce equivalent or better outcomes than family care.

Taken as a whole, assessing the evidence for residential care's effectiveness is difficult. The literature is constrained by research design and often study samples are limited to a single program or non-representative populations. However, findings also point to the importance of within program characteristics, including using an evidence-supported treatment model, which may be as important as the treatment setting. The next section considers the two-part question that guides research on residential programs: "what works?" and "for whom?"

What Works? In Pursuit of Quality Residential Care

A consistent theme within the empirical evidence reviewed in the prior section is the high level of variation in program characteristics and quality, which may determine youth outcomes. Several approaches have been proposed to minimize variation in quality and improve residential practice as usual. The American Association for Children's Residential Centers (now known as ACRC) asserted that, at a minimum, residential programs should be licensed, accredited, and have internal continuous quality improvement and monitoring activities (AACRC, 2009b). They point out that these elements within themselves are not indicators of quality, but that these components are important for creating a foundation for accountability and transformation.

Licensing and accreditation standards may be necessary but, as satirized by McMillen (2007), are not sufficient indicators of quality. Researchers who conducted on-site quality reviews of 26 residential treatment programs in a Midwestern county found no measurable or observable differences in quality between accredited and non-accredited programs (Pavkov, Negash, Lourie, & Hug, 2010). Some of the programs they visited were high quality, but most ranged from fair to poor, with quality concerns related to treatment planning, medication management, and disciplinary practices. Rather than rely on coarse indicators of quality such as accreditation, Pavkov, Lourie, Hug, and Negash (2010) suggested an external consultative review process to provide quality assurance to residential programs. On-site visits included interviews with administrators, staff, and youth as well as case record reviews. Exit interviews were strengths based but also identified areas for improvement. This level of periodic monitoring and feedback to residential programs was associated with sizable improvements in treatment planning, psychiatric care, educational services, and aftercare planning, suggesting the value of continuous quality improvement efforts to create progress.

Quality standards have been proposed as another path forward to promoting quality. Child Welfare League of America developed both Standards of Excellence for Residential Services (2004) and Quality Indicators for Residential Treatment (Carman & Farragher, 1994). A review of these standards along with the Performance Standards for Residential Care published by Boys Town (Daly & Peter, 1996) identified both unique and common domains of importance, but lacked direction on how to measure quality (Lee & McMillen, 2008). A more recent review of seven published quality standards for youth residential programs (Huefner, 2018) showed that although the number of organizations creating quality standards may be increasing, reaching a consensus in how to measure and create accountability around quality remains stagnant.

In an effort to develop an empirically based framework for quality, Farmer, Murray, Ballentine, Rauktis, and Burns (2017) tested theoretically derived group home quality dimensions and indicators to assess their association with youth outcomes. This research team had access to a variety of data sources, including observational measures in the home,

310   *Bethany R. Lee*

as well as interviews with youth, staff, and agency directors. They found the following treatment model, staff, and setting characteristics associated with improved youth outcomes at or after discharge:

- motivational systems that were positively focused,
- staff whose interactions with youth incorporated appropriate humor,
- youth who reported their staff as fair and caring,
- more pre-service training requirements,
- more age/interest-appropriate items in the home, and
- a prohibition on restraints.

Although limited to group homes in a single state, this study makes a unique contribution to identifying the quality elements within a residential setting that may be essential for improved youth outcomes.

... *For Whom? Level of Care Decision-Making*

Empirical evidence supporting residential interventions is based on the average treatment effect across all participants; individual youth may be differentially impacted for better or worse. A study of latent class modeling found that some youth benefit from residential placement more than others (Lee & Thompson, 2009). Unfortunately, knowing in advance who those youth are remains a mystery. Generally, youth who enter residential programs have previously failed in less restrictive placements (Barth et al., 2007; James et al., 2006). Hence, they have experienced multiple placements by the time they are included in evaluations of residential programs. These additional placement changes can contribute to or escalate behavioral health issues (James, Landsverk, Slymen, & Leslie, 2004). If it could be determined prior to placement what level of care a youth optimally needs, it may be possible to reduce placement failures and changes.

Several states have sought to minimize placement disruption by improving placement-matching, often through structured decision-making or standardized assessments (Blakey et al., 2012). In one study, multi-level analysis found that assessment scores at intake from the Child and Adolescent Needs and Strengths (CANS) were strongly associated with youth's level of care, but since the assessment was completed after the placement had begun, the finding may be confounded by confirmation bias (Lardner, 2015). In Illinois, placement decisions made by multidisciplinary teams were compared to those made by a decision support algorithm that also relied on CANS assessments (Chor, McClelland, Weiner, Jordan, & Lyons, 2012, 2015). The placement options considered residential treatment centers (RTC) the most restrictive, group homes as slightly less restrictive, followed by specialized foster care and regular foster home settings. A few key findings were noted from this innovative study. First, for placements in RTC, the algorithm and treatment team agreed on placement more than half the time. In contracts, for group home placement, agreement was only 13% (Chor et al., 2015). Second, youth who were placed in less restrictive settings than recommended by the algorithm showed slower rates of improvement over time compared to other youth in that setting (Chor et al., 2015). Third, youth placed in residential treatment centers (regardless of decision-making tool) showed improved functioning and fewer risk behaviors during treatment (Chor et al., 2012). Conclusions from this study underscore the importance of youth receiving the level of care that corresponds to their reported needs. In addition, combining machine-learning and predictive analytics with multidisciplinary team decisions may offer promise for proactively identifying what works best for whom.

Creating Positive Residential Program Outcomes

Although there are limited studies with rigorous designs comparing outcomes between residential programs and other settings, there is a larger field of literature examining within-program factors associated with positive youth outcomes. In this section, several key components of effective residential programs will be summarized with supporting literature. Specifically, these components are use of evidence-based practices, program model, staffing issues, and family involvement.

Evidence-Based Practices

An increased interest in evidence-based practice is evident in all areas of practice with youth who have emotional and behavioral disorders. In residential settings, the integration of evidence-based interventions can take different forms, including using an evidence-based program model, delivering manualized clinical treatments within the residential settings, or developing a practice-based model that becomes established as evidence-based (for more discussion, see Lee & McMillen, 2017). Integrating a manualized evidence-supported treatment into a residential setting requires significant investment, including an assessment of the organization's treatment model, preparation of staff, assessment of readiness for implementing these structured interventions and having an infrastructure to support evaluation (James, 2017). A recent review found only ten empirical studies of manualized treatments that included youth in residential settings (James, Alemi, & Zepeda, 2013). Nevertheless, the utilization of evidence-based practices in residential programs is presumed to be much higher. In a survey of the use of manualized evidence-based practices in residential settings, almost 90% of responding residential programs reported using at least one practice they consider to be evidence-based (James et al., 2015). Despite their prevalence, contextual factors within a residential environment may hamper implementation and fidelity to structured evidence-based interventions in these settings (James, Thompson, & Ringle, 2017).

Program Models

A residential program's model of care directs the therapeutic approach and the functioning of the milieu (i.e., the physical, social, and emotional environment of the residential program). As James (2011) identified, five residential treatment models have been reviewed by the California Evidence-based Clearinghouse for Child Welfare. Four of these models (Positive Peer Culture, Teaching Family Model, Sanctuary Model, and Stop-Gap) are considered supported or promising based on their evidence base. A recent multi-site study assessed the role of the program model by comparing youth symptom outcomes for Teaching Family group care programs with programs that did not follow a specified model. Farmer, Seifert, Wagner, Burns, and Murray (2017) found that Teaching Family homes had significantly greater improvement in symptoms by eight months post-discharge compared to youth served by less well-defined program models. However, youth across both types of environments demonstrated improvements, with average change from a clinical score to a score within the normal range. Beyond just the type of program model, implementing the model with fidelity is also relevant. In a study of a Teaching Family program, fidelity to the program model was significantly associated with improved youth behavioral functioning (Duppong Hurley, Lambert, Gross, Thompson, & Farmer,

312   *Bethany R. Lee*

2017). These findings suggest that program model does matter and adherence to a program model may create a consistency in treatment that promotes improved youth outcomes. Notably, both of these studies are focused on the Teaching Family model, which is the most well studied. More studies are needed to understand other program models and their relative benefits on outcomes.

Staffing Issues

Although direct care staff roles are often entry-level positions with minimal education requirements, these individuals are tasked with critical and challenging work: creating a therapeutic residential environment for youth. The importance of building a trusting relationship with youth has long been established as a key ingredient in promoting clinical progress in residential settings (Manso & Rauktis, 2011). Therapeutic alliance between youth and their residential care staff has been shown to predict subsequent treatment motivation (Roest, Van der Helm, & Stams, 2016) as well as behavior problems even following placement (Ayotte, Lanctot, & Tourigny, 2016). Beyond just the interpersonal factors, the structure of the staffing model in residential settings is associated with youth perceptions of care and satisfaction. In a follow-up study of youth who had experienced either the live-in houseparent model or a shift care model, youth reported higher satisfaction ratings with houseparents (Jones, 2018). Youth perceived houseparents as providing a stronger family atmosphere, greater consistency, and higher rates of retention. These perceptions of increased continuity of care and decreased experience of turnover for houseparents were empirically supported (Jones, Landsverk, & Roberts, 2007).

Family Involvement

Even when not residing with their family, maintaining connections and positive relationship during residential care is important to youth success. Family involvement can take many forms, including visitation on and off-site, family therapy, family workshops, and parent mentors (Affronti & Levison-Johnson, 2009). Engaging families in treatment for their child's behavioral health needs is a challenge in any setting (Ingoldsby, 2010), but growing evidence supports practices such as motivational interviewing, family check-up, and the parent engagement model (Herman et al., 2011). More studies are needed to test these interventions in residential programs.

Residential programs vary in their level of family involvement. In a study of almost 300 residential programs, almost 90% of programs report including family members on the treatment team, but only 12% reported that family members have a primary decision-making role in developing a treatment plan and 17% reported family members have a limited role (Brown et al., 2010). Providing opportunities for family members to be meaningfully engaged with their youth during a residential stay has been consistently associated with improved outcomes, like greater likelihood of returning to a family-like setting (Nickerson, Salamone, Brooks, & Colby, 2008) and improved youth functioning with fewer problem behaviors (Robst et al., 2013).

The Future of Residential Care: Three Models to Consider

Thus far, the chapter has described the current state of research and practice in residential programs. Residential settings continue to evolve in accordance with changes to policy and society values. This section will describe three models for residential programs that should be further developed and studied: short-term residential treatment centered on evidence-based practices, hybrid models that blur the lines between residential and family-based services, and residential education programs.

Short-Term Residential Treatment as Intensive EBP Lab

Several recent papers have explored how evidence-based practices can be better integrated into residential settings (Boel-Studt & Tobia, 2016; James, 2017; Lee & McMillen, 2017). James and colleagues (2015) found that residential programs are committed to delivering evidence-based interventions and have some capacity to do so within their programs. Designing residential treatment settings as laboratories for the efficient delivery of EBPs can be an effective way of improving treatment quality and youth outcomes.

Youth with emotional and behavioral disorders can benefit from receiving evidence-based interventions that target their specific needs. However, connecting youth to EBPs that are delivered with fidelity requires engagement with the entire mental health systems ecology (Southam-Gerow, Rodriguez, Chorpita, & Daleiden, 2012), including the youth and family, therapist, agency, and larger systems. Barriers to engaging and retaining youth in community-based EBPs have been well-documented (Ingoldsby, 2010) and can include logistical barriers such as scheduling, attendance challenges, and finding EBP-trained clinicians. Residential treatment settings, by design, can remove many of these barriers and facilitate coordination across the mental health system, which can improve access to and completion of manualized treatments. Unlike in community settings where youth may have a weekly appointment with a clinician, a clinician in a residential program could complete several sessions each week, expediting progress in completing multi-session interventions. Further, the frontline staff members at the residential program can reinforce the clinical intervention with "homework" or other therapeutic activities in the residential unit. By leveraging the milieu as an asset to promote clinical change, a youth can have a transformative experience that is grounded in a manualized intervention shown to be effective.

This idea of creating an EBP-rich residential environment can be seen in Norway's implementation of Multifunctional Treatment in Residential and Community Settings (MultifunC). MultifunC is a youth program built on research evidence of what works for youth with serious behavior problems (Andreassen, 2015). Structurally, youth complete about six months of residential placement and about four months in an intensive aftercare program with their family. The residential program is based on a collection of EBPs: motivational interviewing (MI) to promote commitment to change, cognitive behavioral therapy (CBT), social skills training, and aggression replacement training (ART). Parents are engaged in Parent Management Therapy and Multisystemic Therapy (MST). Although the design and structure holds promise, evaluation findings are not yet available and the implementation of MultifunC is thus far limited to juvenile justice populations in Norway, Sweden, and Denmark. However, the success of the implementation offers proof of concept that residential programs can serve as lab settings for the delivery of EBPs.

A few questions must be resolved before we can "redefine residential care as evidence-based care" (James, 2017, p. 158). Historically, the goals of short-term programs have been focused on assessment or diagnosis as well as crisis resolution, which do not align well with many EBPs or the lasting impact expected for an intensive treatment like residential

314 *Bethany R. Lee*

placement. Clinical goals must be meaningful but also reasonable within the limited time-frame. A second structural issue is the readiness of direct care staff to be engaged agents of change with youth in care. The low pay and limited training often provided to direct care staff may be limiting factors in the quality of the milieu. Creating a well-trained and appropriately compensated youth care staff may necessitate a professionalization of the role that can be seen in places such as Canada and Scotland, where child and youth care or even residential caring is an academic major or certificate program in university settings. Despite these system-level implications, the example of MultifunC demonstrates that a model of short-term residential treatment as an intensive EBP environment is feasible and could be a promising direction for the U.S.

Hybridization of Residential and Family-Based Care

In any institutional setting, the challenge of connecting with the larger community and generalizing clinical progress to a different environment is present. An early residential model, Project Re-Ed (Hobbs, 1982) recognized the importance of maintaining connections between the residential program and the youth's family life. In standard implementation of the Re-Ed model, youth spend the weekdays in the residential setting with their educators and complete home visits each weekend to practice behavior changes in the family setting. Findings from Re-Ed studies showed decreases in youth problem behaviors during treatment and sustained from at least six months post-discharge (Fields, Farmer, Apperson, Mustillo, & Simmers, 2006) to some growth evident even two years later (Hooper, Murphy, Devaney, & Hultman, 2000). These single-group pre/post study designs lack rigor, but provide evidence for the feasibility and potential promise of a hybridized residential program.

These five-day models with weekly home visits are of renewed interest as the importance of family engagement (AACRC, 2009a), generalizing clinical gains beyond the residential setting, and appreciating the need for aftercare (Tyler, Thompson, Trout, Lambert, & Synhorst, 2016) has taken a stronger hold. In current iterations, this model even considers cross-training direct care staff to not just complete shifts on the residential unit but to also accompany youth on home visits where their role becomes a coach for parents to support boundary-setting, relationship-building, and other practical parenting skills. By maintaining consistency in the involvement of supportive adults, youth can begin to generalize skills across settings and build new patterns of healthy family interactions.

The dilemma of how to better bridge the residential program with family and community-based services was one impetus for the development of California's Residentially-Based Services (RBS) reform project. Through a partnership with Casey Family Programs and California Department of Social Services, this effort sought to transform residential programs from a placement setting to a service, where families were involved early and often to promote permanency and shorter residential stays, and residential interventions transitioned seamlessly into post-placement supports in the community. Several agencies participated in the pilot efforts and initial evaluation reports are available (Chance, Dickson, Bennett, & Stone, 2010; Hay & Franz, 2013; Knecht & Hargrave, 2002). Despite the anticipated difficulties in carrying out organizational changes that include re-training staff and finding creative solutions to funding constraints, results suggest that engaging family as true partners and equipping them with skills to recover their parenting role has promise.

Residential Education

Boarding schools have educated upper class youth for generations and remain a popular option for elite families in many countries around the world. Youth of lesser means should have similar educational opportunities. In the United States, there are a few well-known residential education programs for youth. These include the Milton Hershey School, a free residential school for more than 2,000 youth from pre-kindergarten through high school graduation; and the SEED Foundation Schools, public charter schools located in three cities, provide five-day boarding during the academic year for students beginning in sixth grade. Specific to youth in the foster care system, San Pasqual Academy in California provides a boarding school environment for youth who are not able to reunify with family. These limited examples underscore the potential of this model.

Due to limited research, there are many gaps in knowledge about the value of residential education for youth with behavioral and emotional disorders (Lee & Barth, 2009). Available research from San Pasqual academy, where all residents have had histories of trauma, suggests that most youth experienced a positive outcome (school retention/graduation or exit to permanency; Jones, 2012), and had lower rates of criminal justice involvement and homelessness compared to other foster care alumni (Jones, 2008). Importantly, the school completion and college attendance rates of San Pasqual students were higher than other foster care alumni (Jones & Landsverk, 2006). These educational gains are especially important for youth in child welfare placements as changes to placement can often short-change their academic progress and opportunities (Pecora, 2012).

Similar to the questions raised above for residential programs in general, what works for whom in residential education remains unknown. More studies are needed about recruitment, admissions decision-making, and retention for youth with special emotional and behavioral needs. Balancing the academic orientation of a rigorous educational program with the therapeutic needs of youth may be challenging. There is an inherent tension between removing youth whose behaviors may create a distraction versus creating an environment that accommodates all youth needs at the cost of becoming a treatment program rather than a school. Further, although the rates of initial college acceptance are impressive, four-year graduation records are significantly lower. Helping prepare youth for college may include providing supports (academic, psychosocial, and financial) beyond high school graduation.

Residential education programs are expensive and require long-term investments before producing results. Although public funds can be used to support the basic academic costs, public–private partnerships or other fiscal resources are needed to cover the necessary residential and supplemental resources. Residential school programs should consider emulating the funding structure of Promise Neighborhood grants provided by the U.S Department of Education, which require match funds from private and public sources. If residential education programs can produce evidence to demonstrate their ability to close the achievement gap and overcome patterns of intergenerational poverty, their value to society could justify the significant investments needed.

At this time, residential education as an option for any youth with emotional and behavioral disorders is more of an idea than reality. However, the potential for boarding schools to provide a high-quality educational experience for privileged youth is well established. More attention towards developing similar opportunities for all youth is needed.

Conclusion

This chapter has considered the role of residential programs in a continuum of care, including its promise and challenges. Although policy and practice initiatives have decreased the number of youth served in residential programs, there will likely always need to be a placement option for youth who cannot be maintained in a family setting (Ainsworth & Hansen, 2005). Research reviewed in this chapter has demonstrated that high quality residential programs have the potential to be transformational.

Through empirical inquiry, we are building an understanding of program components associated with improved outcomes for youth. These include integrating evidence-based interventions within the therapeutic services, following an organizing framework within the residential milieu, supporting front-line staff to be key agents of change, and involving the youth's family in every possible way. High quality residential programs can create positive peer pressures, model healthy relationships, and build bridges between the residential home and family home, so that gains made during placement are sustained beyond placement. Organizations such as Building Bridges (Blau et al., 2010; www.BuildingBridges4Youth.org), and Casey Family Programs (Pecora, English, & Casey Family Programs, 2016) have also brought attention to effective practice in residential programs and partner with agencies to promote high quality care.

In addition to programming around program and practice elements that can promote effectiveness, the future of therapeutic residential care should consider expansion of innovative models that focus on EBPs, hybrid placement, or are academically centered. As the world changes, cutting-edge solutions are needed to address new challenges and residential settings can respond. Recently, therapeutic residential care programs have been developed to support immigrant and refugee unaccompanied minors (Estoura & Roberto, 2019; Munoz & Venta, 2019), the opioid epidemic (Bosk, Paris, Hanson, Ruisard, & Suchman, 2019), and human trafficking (Reichert & Sylwestrzak, 2013). Residential programs offer a unique treatment environment and should continue to evolve to serve youth with the greatest emotional and behavioral health needs.

References

Affronti, M. L., & Levison-Johnson, J. (2009). The future of family engagement in residential care settings. *Residential Treatment for Children & Youth, 26*, 257–304.

Ainsworth, F., & Hansen, P. (2005). A dream come true- no more residential care: A corrective note. *International Journal of Social Welfare, 14*, 195–199.

American Association of Children's Residential Centers (AACRC). (2009a). Redefining residential: Becoming family-driven. *Residential Treatment for Children & Youth, 26*, 230–236.

American Association of Children's Residential Centers (AACRC). (2009b). Redefining residential: Ensuring the pre-conditions for transformation through licensing, regulation, accreditation and standards. *Residential Treatment for Children & Youth, 26*, 237–240.

Andreassen, T. (2015). MultifunC: Multifunctional treatment in residential and community settings. In J. Whittaker, J. Del Valle, & L. Holmes (Eds.), *Therapeutic residential care for children and youth* (pp. 100–110). London, UK: Jessica Kingsley Publishers.

Ayotte, M., Lanctot, N., & Tourigny, M. (2016). How the working alliance with adolescent girls in residential care predicts the trajectories of their behavior problems. *Residential Treatment for Children & Youth, 33*, 135–154.

Barth, R. P., Lloyd, E. C., Green, R. L., James, S., Leslie, L. K., & Landsverk, J. (2007). Predictors of placement moves among children with and without emotional and behavioral disorders. *Journal of Emotional and Behavioral Disorders, 15*, 46–55.

Blakey, J. M., Leathers, S. J., Lawler, M., Washington, T., Natschke, C., Strand, T., & Walton, Q. (2012). A review of how states are addressing placement stability. *Children and Youth Services Review*, *34*, 369–378.

Blau, G., Caldwell, B., Fisher, S. K., Kuppinger, A., Levinson-Johnson, J., & Lieberman, B. (2010). The building bridges initiative: Residential and community-based providers, families and youth coming together to improve outcomes. *Child Welfare*, *89*(2), 21–38.

Boel-Studt, S. M., & Tobia, L. (2016). A review of trends, research, and recommendations for strengthening the evidence-base and quality of residential group care. *Residential Treatment for Children & Youth*, *33*, 13–35.

Bosk, E. A., Paris, R., Hanson, K. E., Ruisard, D., & Suchman, N. E. (2019). Innovations in child welfare interventions for caregivers with substance use disorders and their children. *Children & Youth Services Review*, *101*, 99–112.

Brown, J. D., Barrett, K., Ireys, H. T., Allen, K., Pires, S. A., & Blau, G. (2010). Family-driven youth-guided practices in residential treatment: Findings from a national survey of residential treatment facilities. *Residential Treatment for Children & Youth*, *27*, 149–159.

Carman, G. O., & Farragher, B. J. (1994). *Quality indicators for residential treatment programs: A survey instrument*. Washington, DC: Child Welfare League of America.

Chance, S., Dickson, D., Bennett, P. M., & Stone, S. (2010). Unlocking the doors: How fundamental changes in residential care can improve the ways we help children. *Residential Treatment for Children & Youth*, *27*, 127–148.

Child Welfare Information Gateway. (2017). *Foster care statistics 2016*. Washington, DC: US Department of Health and Human Services, Children's Bureau.

Child Welfare League of America. (2004). *CWLA standards of excellence for residential services* (Rev. ed.). Washington, DC: Author.

Chor, K. H. B., McClelland, G. M., Weiner, D. A., Jordan, N., & Lyons, J. S. (2012). Predicting outcomes of children in residential treatment: A comparison of a decision support algorithm and a multidisciplinary team decision model. *Children and Youth Services Review*, *34*, 2345–2352.

Chor, K. H. B., McClelland, G. M., Weiner, D. A., Jordan, N., & Lyons, J. S. (2015). Out-of-home placement decision-making and outcomes in child welfare: A longitudinal study. *Administration in Policy and Mental Health Services Research*, *42*, 70–86.

Daly, D. L., & Peter, V. J. (1996). *National performance standards for residential care: A policy initiative from Father Flanagan's Boys' Home*. Boys Town, NE: Boys Town Press.

Duppong Hurley, K., Lambert, M. C., Gross, T. J., Thompson, R. W., & Farmer, E. M. Z. (2017). The role of therapeutic alliance and fidelity in predicting youth outcomes during therapeutic residential care. *Journal of Emotional and Behavioral Disorders*, *25*, 37–45.

Estoura, D., & Roberto, S. (2019). The RAISE model: Psychosocial intervention in residential care for unaccompanied minors. *Residential Treatment for Children & Youth*, *36*, 102–117.

Farmer, E. M. Z., Murray, M. L., Ballentine, K., Rauktis, M. E., & Burns, B. J. (2017). Would we know it if we saw it? Assessing quality of care in group homes for youth. *Journal of Emotional and Behavioral Disorders*, *25*, 28–36.

Farmer, E. M. Z., Seifert, H., Wagner, H. R., Burns, B. J., & Murray, M. (2017). Does model matter? Examining change across time for youth in group homes. *Journal of Emotional and Behavioral Disorders*, *25*(2), 119–128.

Fields, E., Farmer, E. M. Z., Apperson, J., Mustillo, S., & Simmers, D. (2006). Treatment and posttreatment effects of residential treatment using a re-education model. *Behavioral Disorders*, *31*, 312–322.

Frensch, K. M., & Cameron, G. (2002). Treatment of choice or a last resort? A review of residential mental health placements for children and youth. *Child & Youth Care Forum*, *31*, 307–339.

Friedman, R. M., Pinto, A., Behar, L., Bush, N., Chirolla, A., Epstein, M., & Young, C. K. (2006). Unlicensed residential programs: The next challenge in protecting youth. *American Journal of Orthopsychiatry*, *76*, 295–303.

General Accountability Office (GAO). (2007). *Residential treatment programs: Concerns regarding abuse and death in certain programs for troubled youth*. GAO-08-146T. Retrieved from www.gao.gov/new.items/d08146t.pdf

Gray, C. L., Pence, B. W., Ostermann, J., Whetten, R. A., O'Donnell, K., Thielman, N. M., & Whetten, K. (2015). Experiences among orphans in institutional and family-based settings in 5 low and middle-income countries: A longitudinal study. *Global Health: Science and Practice, 3*, 395–404.

Hay, L. A., & Franz, J. (2013). *Permanency, partnership and perseverance: Lessons from the California residentially based services reform project.* Casey Family Programs. Retrieved from www.rbsreform.org/materials/RBS%20Lessons%20Learned%20Report%202013%20(2).pdf

Herman, K. C., Borden, L. A., Hsu, C., Schultz, T., Carney, M., Brooks, C. M., & Reinke, W. M. (2011). Enhancing family engagement in interventions for mental health problems in youth. *Residential Treatment for Children & Youth, 28*, 102–119.

Hobbs, N. (1982). *The troubled and troubling child: Reeducation in mental health, education, and human services programs for children and youth.* San Francisco, CA: Jossey-Bass Inc.

Holmes, L., Connolly, C., Mortimer, E., & Hevesi, R. (2018). Residential group care as a last resort: Challenging the rhetoric. *Residential Treatment for Children & Youth, 35*, 209–224.

Hooper, S. R., Murphy, J., Devaney, A., & Hultman, T. (2000). Ecological outcomes of adolescents in a psychoeducational residential treatment facility. *American Journal of Orthopsychiatry, 70*(4), 491–500.

Huefner, J. C. (2018). Crosswalk of published quality standards for residential care for children and adolescents. *Children & Youth Services Review, 88*, 267–273.

Ingoldsby, E. M. (2010). Review of interventions to improve family engagement and retention in parent and child mental health programs. *Journal of Child and Family Studies, 19*, 629–645.

James, S. (2011). What works in group care? A structured review of treatment models for group homes and residential care. *Children & Youth Services Review, 33*, 308–321.

James, S. (2017). Implementing evidence-based practice in residential care: How far have we come? *Residential Treatment for Children & Youth, 34*, 155–175.

James, S., Alemi, Q., & Zepeda, V. (2013). Effectiveness and implementation of evidence-based practices in residential care settings. *Children and Youth Services Review, 35*, 642–656.

James, S., Landsverk, J., Slymen, D. J., & Leslie, L. K. (2004). Predictors of outpatient mental health service use- role of foster care placement change. *Mental Health Services Research, 6*, 127–141.

James, S., Leslie, L. K., Hurlbert, M. S., Slymen, D. J., Landsverk, J., Davis, I., … Zhang, J. (2006). Children in out-of-home care: Entry into intensive or restrictive mental health and residential care placements. *Journal of Emotional and Behavioral Disorders, 14*, 196–208.

James, S., Thompson, R., Sternberg, N., Schnur, E., Ross, J., Butler, L., & Muirhead, J. (2015). Attitudes, perceptions, and utilization of evidence-based practices in residential care. *Residential Treatment for Children & Youth, 32*, 144–166.

James, S., Thompson, R. W., & Ringle, J. L. (2017). The implementation of evidence-based practices in residential care. *Journal of Emotional & Behavioral Disorders, 25*, 4–18.

Jones, L. (2008). Adaptation to early adulthood by a sample of youth discharged from a residential education placement. *Child & Youth Care Forum, 37*, 241–263.

Jones, L. (2018). The perceptions and satisfactions of youth in residential care with two caregiving models. *Families in Society*, doi:10.1606/1044-3894.3893

Jones, L., & Landsverk, J. (2006). Residential education: Examining a new approach for improving outcomes for foster youth. *Children and Youth Services Review, 28*, 1152–1168.

Jones, L., Landsverk, J., & Roberts, A. (2007). A comparison of two caregiving models in providing continuity of care for youth in residential care. *Child & Youth Care Forum, 36*, 99–109.

Jones, L. P. (2012). Predictors of success in a residential education placement for foster youths. *Children & Schools, 34*, 103–113.

Knecht, R., & Hargrave, M. C. (2002). Familyworks: Integrating family in residential treatment. *Residential Treatment for Children & Youth, 19*, 25–35.

Lardner, M. (2015). Are restrictiveness of care decisions based on youth level of need? A multilevel model of analysis of placement levels using the child and adolescent needs and strengths assessment. *Residential Treatment for Children & Youth, 32*, 195–207.

Lee, B. R., & Barth, R. P. (2009). Residential education: An emerging resource for improving educational outcomes for youth in foster care? *Children & Youth Services Review, 31*, 155–160.

Lee, B. R., & Barth, R. P. (2011). Defining group care programs: An index of reporting standards. *Child and Youth Care Forum, 40*(4), 253–266.

Lee, B. R., Bright, C. L., Svoboda, D., Fakunmoju, S., & Barth, R. P. (2011). Outcomes of group care for youth: A review of comparative studies. *Research on Social Work Practice, 21*, 177–189.

Lee, B. R., & McMillen, J. C. (2008). Measuring quality in residential treatment for children and youth. *Residential Treatment for Children and Youth, 24*(1/2), 1–18.

Lee, B. R., & McMillen, J. C. (2017). Pathways forward for embracing evidence based practice in group care settings. *Journal of Emotional & Behavioral Disorders, 25*, 19–27.

Lee, B. R., & Thompson, R. (2009). Examining externalizing behavior trajectories of youth in group homes: Is there evidence for peer contagion? *Journal of Abnormal Child psychology, 37*(1), 31–44.

Lyons, J. S. (2015). The myths of outcomes management: Implications for residential treatment. *Residential Treatment for Children & Youth, 32*, 184–194.

Manso, A., & Rauktis, M. E. (2011). What is the therapeutic alliance and why does it matter? *Reclaiming Children & Youth, 19*, 45–50.

McMillen, J. C. (2007). The business of accreditation. *Families in Society, 88*, 1–4.

Munoz, C., & Venta, A. (2019). Referring unaccompanied minors to psychiatric residential treatment: When is it worth the disruption to adaptation and shelter integration? *Residential Treatment for Children & Youth, 36*, 137–156.

Nickerson, A. B., Salamone, F. J., Brooks, J. L., & Colby, S. A. (2008). Promising approaches to engaging families and building strengths in residential treatment. *Residential Treatment for Children & Youth, 22*(1), 1–18.

Pavkov, T. W., Lourie, I. S., Hug, R. W., & Negash, S. (2010). Improving the quality of services in residential treatment facilities: A strength-based consultative review process. *Residential Treatment for Children & Youth, 27*, 23–40.

Pavkov, T. W., Negash, S., Lourie, I. S., & Hug, R. W. (2010). Critical failures in a regional network of residential treatment facilities. *American Journal of Orthopsychiatry, 80*, 151–159.

Pecora, P. J. (2012). Maximizing educational achievement of youth in foster care and alumni: Factors associated with success. *Children and Youth Services Review, 34*, 1121–1129.

Pecora, P. J., & English, D. & Casey Family Programs (2016, March). *Elements of effective practice for children and youth served by therapeutic residential care: Research brief.* Casey Family Programs. Retrieved from https:// caseyfamilypro-wpengine.netdna-ssl.com/media/Group-Care-complete.pdf

Reichert, J., & Sylwestrzak, A. (2013). *National survey of residential programs for victims of sex trafficking.* Chicago, IL: The Illinois Criminal Justice Information Authority.

Robst, J., Rohrer, L., Armstrong, M., Dollard, N., Sharrock, P., Batsche, C., & Reader, S. (2013). Family involvement and changes in child behavior during residential mental health treatment. *Child & Youth Care Forum, 42*, 225–238.

Roest, J. J., Van der Helm, G. H. P., & Stams, G. J. J. M. (2016). The relation between therapeutic alliance and treatment motivation in residential youth care: A cross-lagged panel analysis. *Child and Adolescent Social Work, 33*, 455–468.

Southam-Gerow, M. A., Rodriguez, A., Chorpita, B. F., & Daleiden, E. L. (2012). Dissemination and implementation of evidence based treatments for youth: Challenges and recommendations. *Professional Psychology: Research and Practice, 43*, 527–534.

Strijbosch, E. L. L., Huijs, J. A. M., Stams, G. J. J. M., Wissink, I. B., van der Helm, G. H. P., de Swart, J. J. W., & van der Veen, Z. (2015). The outcome of institutional youth care compared to non-institutional youth care for children of primary school age and early adolescence: A multi-level meta-analysis. *Children & Youth Services Review, 58*, 208–218.

Substance Abuse and Mental Health Services Administration, US Department of Health and Human Services. (2015). *Results from the 2015 national survey on drug use and health detailed tables.* Retrieved from www. samhsa.gov/data/report/results-2015-national-survey-drug-use-and-health-detailed-tables

Tyler, P. M., Thompson, R. W., Trout, A. L., Lambert, M. C., & Synhorst, L. L. (2016). Availability of aftercare for youth departing group homes. *Residential Treatment for Children & Youth, 33*, 270–285.

United States Department of Health and Human Services (USDHHS). Administration for Children and Families, Children's Bureau. (2015, May). *A national look at the use of congregate care in child welfare.* Retrieved from www.acf.hhs.gov/sites/default/files/cb/cbcongregatecare_brief.pdf

United States Department of Justice, Office of Justice Programs, Office of Juvenile Justice and Delinquency Prevention. (2018). *Juveniles in residential placement, 2015.* Juvenile Justice Statistics, National Report Series Bulletin. Retrieved from www.ojjdp.gov/pubs/250951.pdf

Weems, C. F. (2011). Guidelines for empirical papers on group care programs. *Child & Youth Care Forum, 40,* 251–252.

Whetten, K., Ostermann, J., Pence, B. W., Whetten, R. A., Messer, L. C., Ariely, S., … Thielman, N. M., & the Positive Outcomes for Orphans (POFO) Research Team. (2014). Three-year change in the wellbeing of orphaned and separated children in institutional and family-based care settings in five low- and middle-income countries. *PLoS One, 9,* e104872–e104880. doi:10.1371/journal.pone.0104872

Whetten, K., Ostermann, J., Whetten, R. A., Pence, B. W., O'Donnell, K., Messer, L. C., … The Positive Outcomes for Orphans (POFO) Research Team. (2009). A comparison of the wellbeing of orphans and abandoned children ages 6–12 in institutional and community-based care settings in 5 less wealthy nations. *PLoS ONE, 4,* e8169–e8181. doi:10.1371/journal.pone.0008169

Whittaker, J. K., Holmes, L., delValle, J. F., Ainsworth, F., Andreassen, T., Anglin, J., & Zeira, A. (2016). Therapeutic residential care for children and youth: A consensus statement of the international work group on therapeutic residential care. *Residential Treatment for Children & Youth, 33,* 89–106. doi:10.1080/0886571X.2016.1215755

22 Managing and Adapting Practice (MAP)

Michael A. Southam-Gerow, Julia R. Cox, and Abigail Kinnebrew

The Managing and Adapting Practice (MAP) system is an approach designed to provide clinicians and systems with a method to leverage available evidence to make clinical decisions, particularly in the context of planning and delivering mental health services. We trace some of the history of MAP, provide a description of the system, and then review available data on MAP.

Context of Children's Mental Health Services

Clinical scientists have focused considerable efforts on the development and testing of mental health treatments. In fewer than 40 years, more than 1000 randomized controlled trial (RCT) papers have been published testing more than 2500 different psychosocial treatment programs designed to ameliorate a wide variety of childhood problems (e.g., Chorpita & Daleiden, 2009; Weisz et al., 2017). Although the development of a multitude of what have been called evidence-based treatments (EBTs) represents a critical step for the field, several identified limitations create challenges and opportunities for continued advancement of the field (e.g., Beidas & Kendall, 2010; Chorpita et al., 2011; Southam-Gerow, Rodríguez, Chorpita, & Daleiden, 2012). These limitations include, among many other things the following: (a) most EBTs are designed for a single or small set of child problems (e.g., single diagnosis), (b) they involve lengthy and invariant session sequences, (c) they seldom address comorbidity, and (d) they rarely include guidance on how the program should be adapted for diversity. Scientists and policy makers have come to recognize that a dissemination and implementation (D&I) science focus that identifies multilevel and ecological approaches to improving mental health care is needed to address the limitations of treatment research (Greenhalgh, Robert, MacFarlane, Bate, & Kyriakidou, 2004).

D&I science has helped the field identify strategies for implementing interventions across diverse contexts, develop measurement tools to gauge success of implementation efforts, and encourage a focus on organizational and policy-level efforts needed to promote uptake of scientific evidence (e.g., Cox & Southam-Gerow, in press). Another direction has been identifying innovative ways to adapt and/or develop interventions. Nearly all interventions developed for children's mental health have focused on discrete problem types, such as anxiety or disruptive behavior, and generally for a specific age group. There have been benefits to this approach, mainly that the field has identified numerous interventions that produce reliable positive effects for a variety of problem types. However, as a method for improving mental health care at scale, the approach has notable shortcomings. Most relevant to the focus of the current chapter, the approach offers limited guidance for how to plan and deliver services for individuals with multiple problems and/or problems for which there is not

322   *Michael A. Southam-Gerow et al.*

already an identified program. Nor does the approach guide providers in how to change clinical focus, address diversity (e.g., of child/family, setting), or how to solve the myriad emergent life events that so often intervene in clinical care (e.g., Guan, Park, & Chorpita, 2019). These are some (though not all) of the problems that led to the development of an approach now called Managing and Adapting Practice (MAP).

Brief History of MAP

The history of MAP is well documented across several papers over the past decade (see e.g., Chorpita & Daleiden, 2010; Chorpita et al., 2002; Higa-McMillan et al., in press; Nakamura et al., 2011). Thus, this historical overview will be brief and is not meant to be comprehensive. MAP was born in Hawai'i in part as a response to the Felix consent decree (Chorpita & Donkervoet, 2005), as a result of a lawsuit brought by parents of students in the public schools of Hawai'i who claimed the state was in violation of the Individuals with Disabilities Education Act. The court sided with the plaintiffs; as a result, the state was required to provide a system of care to support students in schools. In short, the state suddenly had to significantly expand mental health services for students in their public school system.

Thus, there was a need to scale up services in an unprecedented way. The first efforts focused on identifying evidence-based treatment programs (EBTs) that would address the needs of Hawai'i's families. Rapidly, there was a realization that many factors, including funding, precluded adequate coverage of those in need of services by relying on EBTs alone. As a result, the Child and Adolescent Mental Health Division (CAMHD) of the Hawai'i Department of Health established the Hawai'i Empirical Basis to Services Task Force in 1999. One of the task forces' many jobs was to identify the optimal way to serve children whose needs, conditions, or circumstances were not covered by one of the state-adopted EBTs. Through a series of quality improvement efforts, the approach started as a set of ad hoc resources and became the formal system of MAP (For more on these early days of MAP, see Chorpita et al. (2002) and Nakamura et al. (2011).

Another strong spur to the growth and development of MAP was a meeting at a national mental health services conference between the developers of MAP and state mental health officials in Minnesota. Like most states in the late 1990s, Minnesota was struggling to find ways to reduce costs. Drs. Glenace Edwall and Pat Nygaard saw the Hawai'i approach, MAP, as a part of the solution and were some of the earliest adopters of the system (Chorpita, 2004). This led to a long-term relationship between the MAP team and the state. For more on the Minnesota chapter of the MAP story, see Higa-McMillan et al. (in press).

The last stop on this brief history of MAP is California. As in Hawai'i, there is important local context to consider. In 2004, the voters of California passed the Mental Health Services Act (MHSA). As a result, a new and dedicated funding source was created solely for new and transformed mental health services in the State of California by taxing 1% of each dollar of income earned over $1 million. By early 2011, the MHSA had generated more than $6.5 billion in additional revenue, with annual revenues over $750 million per year anticipated moving forward (Southam-Gerow et al., 2014). Each county in the state was tasked with developing a plan to transform their system to access these funds. For Los Angeles county, the most populous county in the state (and second most populous in the nation), this meant challenges and opportunities.

In 2007, the Los Angeles County (LAC) Department of Mental Health started planning for their MHSA related plan. In the end, the plan included the implementation of more than 50 evidence-based treatments (EBTs), promising practices, and community-defined-evidence practices in eight different geographic regions within LAC. While generating the list of programs, the policy makers encountered the same challenge that was faced in Hawai'i: each program covered a small subset of youth. There was a desire for a single approach that could cover a wider group of children, especially children not covered by the programs identified to date. To make a long story short, then MAP entered the picture. Practitioner and service organizations were vocal and persuasive in their demands to bring MAP to LAC (Southam-Gerow et al., 2014). As MAP was implemented across LAC, the system helped the county better meet youth's needs. (In a later section, we review the results of the implementation of MAP in Los Angeles County.)

Description of MAP System

MAP is a *system* or infrastructure for supporting evidence-based practice and empirically informed health and human services. The MAP approach to providing direct services for mental health is *not* a manualized approach and is in fact not a treatment program. Rather, MAP is a set of decision-guidance frameworks and tools to help therapists, supervisors, and systems manage the implementation and adaptation of evidence-informed care across a diverse service array and multiple treatment targets (see also Chorpita & Daleiden, 2010, 2018). In providing services with a family, a MAP therapist uses evidence from a variety of sources to make choices about what treatments to try, how to know if they are working, and when to change directions; MAP therapists have at their disposal a set of tools and models that they use to take these steps (see Chorpita, Bernstein, & Daleiden, 2008; Chorpita & Daleiden, 2010, 2014, 2018). The MAP coordination models, described in more detail shortly, provide structure to the choices that therapists make. The MAP tools, described shortly, provide easy access to data needed to make those choices.

The MAP Coordination Models

Because MAP is not a program, there is no manual and no predetermined plan for how to deliver mental health services. Instead, the system provides several fundamental coordination models, abstracted from hundreds of EBTs, that act as decision-making guides for the variety of decisions made in mental health service provision.

Evidence-based Services System Model

The first of these is the evidence-based services system model or EBS system model. Although none of the coordination models is considered foundational, the EBS system model is a key to understanding how MAP defines the word *evidence* in evidence-informed, and thus is an important conceptual skill for MAP therapists to develop. The EBS system model is depicted in Figure 22.1.

The EBS system model moves from left to right, from evidence to choices. The left side of the figure represents the four evidence bases that inform all of the choices in the rest of the diagram. These are the sources of information potentially available to a therapist any time they are deciding how to work with a particular youth. The evidence bases are divided into two categories: *general knowledge* and *local knowledge*. *Clinical theory* is the first in the general knowledge category, representing empirical and theoretical papers that provide evidence on the causes of mental health problems. These can be broad psychodynamic or cognitive-behavioral theories, or they can be specific findings from developmental psychopathology research, such as the finding that caregiver stress reduces the effectiveness of giving instructions to a youth.

324 *Michael A. Southam-Gerow et al.*

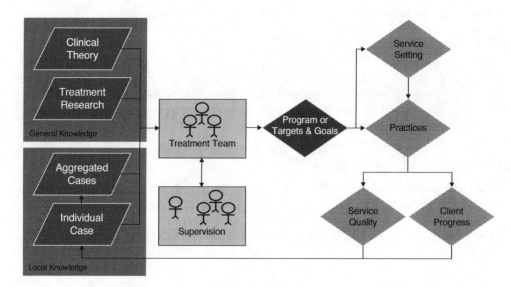

Figure 22.1 The evidence-based services system model

The second general knowledge evidence base is *treatment research*, encompassing the whole of the literature on which treatments work and for whom and under what conditions. Included in this box are randomized controlled trials as well as other clinical studies.

The *local knowledge* category includes two sub-categories: *data on an individual person* or *the historical record of all previous cases* (i.e., *aggregated cases*). The second category refers to evidence drawn from the history of all cases in a particular context. That can mean a few different things, ranging from the history of an individual therapist to the history of treatment team or supervision group all the way to the history of an entire agency or a system. The aggregated case category represents the historical record of the person or agency – a record that can be used as data to inform choices. As an example, an agency might have operated in a particular neighborhood for many years and have data that suggests a particular intervention works well with folks there. As one might imagine, the quality of the aggregated case data varies. Some individuals and agencies collect data systematically, whereas the data can also be collected (and used) less intentionally. As an example, in Hawai'i, effort was made to collect state-wide data on clinical care ranging from practices used, problems treated, and outcomes achieved. The efforts in Hawai'i represent one of the most systematic ways of using local aggregate data (see Daleiden, Chorpita, Donkervoet, Arensdorf, & Brogan, 2006). Aggregated case data is likely never as rigorous or controlled as the data from either of the general knowledge evidence bases. However, the aggregated cases data has advantages to either of the other sources. As one example, to the extent that context matters in delivering treatment, local data may be more relevant than general data to guide future decisions and approaches.

The other local evidence base is the individual case data. These data include information collected on a specific youth (at intake as well as all data collected throughout treatment). These data, then, represent the single case design for each child. Least systematic, these data are likely the most important to privilege. At the end of the day, what matters most to the child and their family is their own personal outcome.

The two general knowledge categories are probably familiar to most readers. At one time, evidence-based practice meant a focus on the *treatment research* section of the model in Figure 22.1. And a more case conceptualization driven model often focused on the *clinical theory* box. The local knowledge boxes in the EBS system model are not new. They draw on the traditions of single-case design and practice-based evidence. What is novel here is that all four evidence bases are given similar status in the model. A MAP therapist is trained to consider all four when making choices, with none being privileged.

Moving to the right across the figure, the next two boxes represent the treatment team. Here are represented the therapist (or therapists) and the supervision team. These are usually locally determined in their details, though ideally their composition would be based on the four evidence bases.

Next on the figure is the *program* or *targets/goals* diamond. Here, there are two main choices: one can select a treatment program (e.g., EBT) or one can instead choose a set of targets or goals for the child. If a program is selected, the four choices on the far right (e.g., setting, practices) are determined by that program. In MAP, one can choose an EBT and still be using MAP. As noted, though, given program costs and child heterogeneity, a system or agency is unlikely to be able to have a program for every child. That is where the targets/goals option becomes operative. In MAP, one selects a target (e.g., anxiety, trauma) or a goal (e.g., reduce disruptive behavior, reduce substance use) and then uses the four evidence bases to make the selections on the far right.

On the far right side of the figure are the decisions or choices that one must make when planning and delivering services. These include the setting, or where to provide the service, the program or practices to be provided, how one will gauge the quality of that service, and how one will gauge whether or not progress is being made. With many EBTs, these choices are predetermined. MAP also permits a more open set of choices, each made by leveraging the four evidence bases. In particular, as discussed later, MAP provides a wealth of resources for the practice box. Daleiden and Chorpita (2005) have written in more detail on the evidence-based services system model.

Session and Treatment Planners

The next two MAP coordination models are treatment planning tools at the event/session and episode levels. At the event-level, the model is called the *Session Planner*, a tool designed to provide a structure for each individual session or meeting with the child. The heart of the model is the three-part structure for the session that includes *opening*, *working*, and *closing* phases. In the *opening* phase, meant to be brief, the therapist checks in with the child, reviews homework if assigned, collects ongoing outcome data, and sets an agenda for the session. The *working* phase, meant to be the longest, focuses on a small number of ideas or skills from the treatment plan, with an emphasis on connecting whatever the content is to the child's life and helping them practice. As an example, if relaxation was the focus of the working phase, the therapist may engage in a conversation with the child designed to uncover a rationale for why relaxation may be helpful and then proceed to practicing using different relaxation techniques. The closing phase of the session is designed to summarize and wrap up the session, confirm any homework, lock down the next appointment, and for some children, engage in a fun activity, like a game, as a reward for the hard work in the session. The session planner also has extensive guidance for actions to consider before and after sessions to help prepare for each session.

326   *Michael A. Southam-Gerow et al.*

MAP also has an episode level model called the *Treatment Planner*, designed to help a therapist develop a treatment plan. The Treatment Planner contains two major concepts: the focus-interference framework and a phase model. The focus-interference framework structures therapists through the differentiation of a focal or target problem from other, so-called, interference problems. These latter problems are labeled as interference because the challenges raised by them could make work on the focus problem challenging. MAP therapists are trained to view interference problems as future/potential focus problems. The focus and interference problems can be, and often are, diagnostic or problem area categories, though they need not be. Problems like "housing disrupted" or "job loss" can be considered as interference when using the treatment planner.

The focus-interference framework is designed to provide a therapist with a method for sorting through the multiple problems facing each child and selecting one of them on which to focus – the choice ending up in the targets/goals diamond in the EBS system model. The framework also is an acknowledgement that although one may choose a singular focus, that choice is often made with incomplete data. As new data emerge, a different focus may be more sensible. As a result, the focus-interference choice is meant to be malleable; therapists are encouraged to revisit the choice regularly, using evidence to determine whether to stay the course or revise the plan.

Once a focus is selected, the treatment planner also provides guidance for sequencing the practices to be used for the focus problem. The sequence is a set of phases summarized by three Cs: Connect-Cultivate-Consolidate. In the Connect phase, the therapist selects practices that create a connection between the child(ren) and the therapist. In MAP, there are no required practices – the therapist is free to choose those that they believe will accomplish the goal. Common examples are rapport building, engagement, and psychoeducation. The Cultivate phase emphasizes skill development, insight building, and other kinds of more challenging clinical work. Again, there are no required practices; instead, the therapist determines which fit the child best. Finally, in the Consolidation phase, the therapist chooses practices to wrap up the episode of therapy and prepare the child for future challenges. Though there are no required practices, maintenance is a common one selected here.

The treatment planner is used at the start of treatment and is open to revision throughout. Therapists are trained to make the plan using the EBS system model, as well as using tools and other models, that we describe shortly.

CARE Process

Because MAP is not designed for a specific diagnosis or child, there are models that guide adaptation of a treatment plan once developed. The first of these, the CARE process, is the basic adaptation model. The CARE process was originally operationalized as a decision-making cycle initiated with a question in the *Consider* phase, gathering and reflecting on the data to *Answer* that question, choosing a strategy to *Respond* to the answer, and then *Evaluating* the effect of the response. The last phase leads right back to the first one – a circular process. Figures 22.2 and 22.3 provide two examples of the CARE process.

The MAP

The CARE process is a generic adaptation model, meant to accommodate almost any question a therapist might have. The process emphasizes the use of evidence, in the evaluate phase, as a key component. The two examples provided in the figures are common ones in

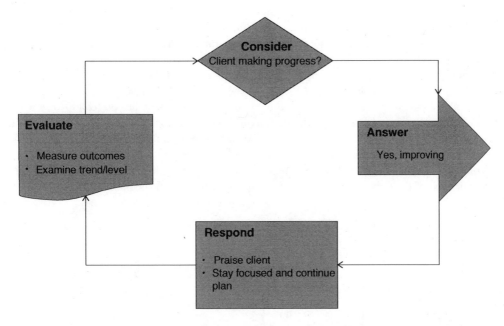

Figure 22.2 CARE process example: Clinical progress

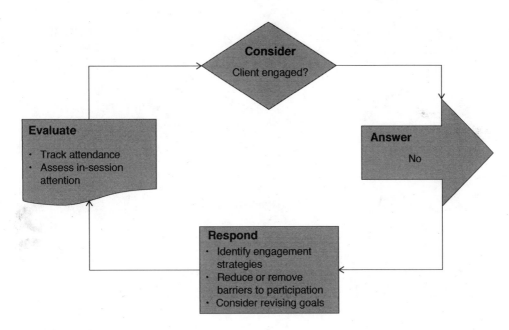

Figure 22.3 CARE process example: Client engagement

328 *Michael A. Southam-Gerow et al.*

clinical treatment; the CARE process can be used for any question. MAP also includes a standardized set of CARE processes, called the MAP, that address six perennial questions. Shown in Figure 22.4, these questions are elaborated horizontally as individual CARE processes and vertically in the typical order one might pose them.

As an example, take the fifth Consider question, *Poor treatment fit?* Here the E step of the CARE process relies on two tools from MAP, the dashboard and PWEBS (both described later), as potential resources to consult to determine whether the treatment fits the child. One would examine the practices delivered on the dashboard and determine whether they match up with the evidence for the child (i.e., results from a PWEBS search). If the plan fits, the answer is no, not a poor treatment fit and the therapist moves to the next question down, *Treatment integrity?*. However, if the answer is yes (bad treatment fit), a therapist considers the responses on the right: identification of barriers to a fitting treatment plan and revision of the plan.

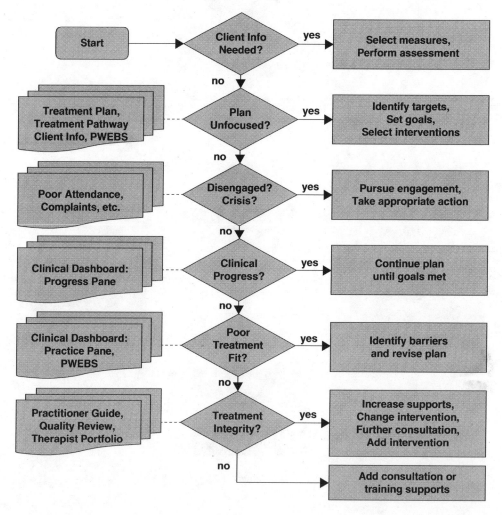

Figure 22.4 The Map

Embracing Diversity

Finally, MAP provides an adaptation guide emphasizing how treatment can be adapted for diverse children: Embracing Diversity. The model is another special case of the CARE process in which the Consider question is, *Are adaptations needed to address child diversity?* The model provides guidance on how one might adapt for diversity, emphasizing two broad categories of adaptation: process and content. In brief, process adaptations involve changes to the way that an intervention or practice is delivered. As examples, one might involve specific individuals or change agents in session, such as grandparents or siblings, or adopt a different style, such as using play or storytelling, to be more congruent with the child and their family. One may also change the content that is delivered, such as varying the metaphor used to explain a particular concept or presenting the main message in a way that fits the child's culture best.

The *embracing diversity* model is a good example of a common feature of MAP. The system provides general models that are used to guide choices. However, the models themselves rarely provide specific instructions to the therapist. Instead, the therapist is trained to lean on the four evidence bases from the EBS system model to identify specific ideas to use. In the case of embracing diversity, a therapist would be encouraged to consult both the general and local knowledge evidence bases to source ways to adapt treatment in their work with diverse children.

The MAP Tools

The coordination models represent the conceptual heart of MAP, providing evidence-informed guardrails for MAP therapists. MAP also provides three tools to guide some of the most critical therapist actions. These tools are the PracticeWise Evidence-Based youth mental health Services literature database (PWEBS), the Practitioner Guides, and the Clinical Dashboard.

PWEBS

PWEBS is an online search engine that includes (nearly) all available randomized controlled trials conducted with children/adolescents. As such, PWEBS represents a resource related to the *treatment research* evidence base from the EBS system model described earlier. To use PWEBS, a therapist enters specific parameters of an individual child, including problem, age, gender/sex, ethnicity, and setting, along with the desired evidence level. Evidence levels range from 1 to 5, largely following the approach used by APA's Divisions 12 and 53 (APA Presidential Task Force on Evidence-Based Practice, 2006; Southam-Gerow & Prinstein, 2014), with 1 representing "best support," 2 representing "good support," 3 representing "moderate support," 4 representing "minimal support," and 5 representing "no support." In MAP, a level 2 search is considered the default level.

A PWEBS search result includes all available treatment families and practices with evidence supporting them for the parameters entered. By treatment family, PracticeWise is referring to a broad categorization of a multiple treatment program that represents the basic treatment approach (e.g., theory underlying the approach, target of treatment) rather than a specific named treatment program. In other words, the treatment family results include options such as individual CBT or interpersonal therapy rather than Coping Cat (Kendall & Hedtke, 2006) or Mufson's interpersonal therapy for adolescents (e.g., Mufson et al., 2004). PWEBS results show the proportion of each treatment family meeting the level of evidence criteria and the parameter(s) provided. As an example, Tables 22.1 and 22.2 demonstrate two different searches at level 2 – the first for depression and the second for depression for an African-American child. For example, in Table 22.1 we see that 50% of successful treatments were individual CBT whereas 6% were CBT with parents included.

330 *Michael A. Southam-Gerow et al.*

Table 22.1 PWEBS search for depression, level 2, treatment families

Family	Percent of groups
Cognitive Behavior Therapy	50
Interpersonal Therapy	10
Cognitive Behavior Therapy and Medication	8
Client Centered Therapy	6
Cognitive Behavior Therapy with Parents	6
Expression	4
Family Therapy	4
Physical Exercise	4
Problem Solving	4
Relaxation	4
Attention Training	2
Cognitive Behavioral Psychoeducation	2
Motivational Interviewing/Engagement and Cognitive Behavior Therapy	2
n=43 papers	

PWEBS results also include treatment practices or practice elements. Practice element is defined (see Chorpita & Daleiden, 2009) as a discrete clinical technique or strategy (e.g., "time out," "relaxation") used as part of a larger intervention plan (e.g., a manualized treatment program for youth depression). For a more detailed definition, see Chorpita and Daleiden (2009). Tables 22.3 and 22.4 provide examples of the previous searches, this time at the practice element level. As earlier, "percent of groups" refers to the percent of times that the practice was included in successful treatment groups. For example, in Table 22.3, we see that 68% of successful treatments for depression included cognitive interventions as one of their practice elements.

In addition to these results, a PWEBS search provides a wealth of other information on the literature for a given set of parameters, including the number of papers leading to the result, links to summaries of the results of each paper, and more. In short, the PWEBS search provides a lightning-fast way to identify which treatments and practice elements to consider when planning a treatment for a particular child.

Table 22.2 PWEBS search for depression, level 2, African-American only, treatment families

Family	Percent of groups
Cognitive Behavior Therapy	42
Client Centered Therapy	12
Cognitive Behavior Therapy and Medication	12
Expression	12
Family Therapy	6
Interpersonal Therapy	6
Motivational Interviewing/Engagement and Cognitive Behavior Therapy	6
Physical Exercise	6
n=12 papers	

Managing and Adapting Practice (MAP)

Table 22.3 PWEBS search for depression, level 2, treatment practices (partial)

Practice	Percent of groups
Cognitive	68
Psychoeducation – Child	64
Activity Selection	57
Maintenance/Relapse Prevention	51
Problem Solving	51
Goal Setting	42
Social Skills Training	39
Self-Monitoring	35
Communication Skills	33
Psychoeducation – Caregiver	33
Relaxation	28
Self-Reward/Self-Praise	24
Relationship/Rapport Building	22
Behavioral Contracting	20
and more than 25 more.	<20
n=43 papers	

Table 22.4 PWEBS search for depression, level 2, African-American only, treatment practices (partial)

Practice	Percent of groups
Cognitive	59
Psychoeducation – Child	59
Activity Selection	48
Relationship/Rapport Building	42
Communication Skills	36
Maintenance/Relapse Prevention	30
Problem Solving	30
Psychoeducation – Caregiver	30
Goal Setting	24
Motivational Enhancement	24
Self-Monitoring	24
Social Skills Training	24
and more than 15 more.	<20
n=17 papers	

Practitioner Guides

Another MAP tool is called the Practitioner Guides. These are an online and searchable large set of practice and process guides that provide one-page (front and back) descriptions of key

332   *Michael A. Southam-Gerow et al.*

treatment practices and coordination models. Currently numbering 58, these guides represent descriptions of commonly used treatment practices derived from treatment programs with strong evidence bases. PracticeWise develops new practice guides as new information is available and several new ones are added each quarter. The information in each guide represents a generic version of the particular practice element, gleaned from reviewing all available treatment manuals describing the practice and distilling them into a single, summary description.

Each of the guides has two main sections: objectives and steps. In the objectives section, the main goals of the practice are enumerated in a brief manner. For example, the relaxation guide lists four objectives:

- To present the idea that staying calm and relaxing is a good way to affect the way we feel.
- To demonstrate what relaxation feels like to children who have difficulty relaxing.
- To increase a child's awareness about his or her own tension so that relaxation skills can be applied at the proper time.
- To teach the child to relax on demand in certain situations (e.g., bedtime, before a test).

The steps section of the guide contains a checklist of the steps involved in the practice, listed in the order one might present them in a session. The steps are presented in a simple format on the left side and with more details on the right. The more detailed version would be useful for therapists relatively new to the practice whereas those with more experience may prefer just the brief version of the steps. Figure 22.5 provides a partial set of the steps from the relaxation guide.

Steps

☐ **Introduce benefits of relaxation**	Present the idea that staying calm and relaxing is a good way to affect the way we feel – especially when we are stressed out and tense.
☐ **Relay the idea that being tense can make us feel bad**	Discuss with the child times when he/she has felt up-right, tense, or stressed, particularly focusing on the somatic or physical responses he/she experiences at such times. If the child has difficulty recalling somatic or physical feelings associated with stressful experiences, imaginal techniques might be used to help the child identify the physical experssions of his/her feelings.
☐ **Discuss how bad feelings can make the body tense**	Introduce the idea that many of the physical sensations associated with feelings of worry, sadness, or stress involve muscle tension. Suggest that when a person becomes upset, some parts of the body become tense,and that these somatic or physical responses are the result of that tension.
☐ **Introduce idea that learning to relax can help combat bad feelings**	1. Ask the child to think of a time or situation in which he/she is really calm and happy. 2. Ask him/her to imagine him- or herself in that scence and to then focus on how his/her body feels. 3. Discuss with the child the difference between how his/her body feels when it is tense and when it is relaxed. ○ Reinforce this idea by asking the child to make a tight first by clenching his/her hand while you count to five and to focus on how it feels. ○ Then tell the child to relax his fist to the count of five and to focus on the warm, relaxed feeling.
☐ **Initial training in deep-muscle relaxation**	Tell the child that if he/she can relax tense parts, he/she will be taking the first step in coping with these feelings. Scripts are available for these exercises, but yo will want to adapt your training to the child's age level and other characteristics (e.g., emotional maturity). Steps (10-20 minutes): 1. Ask child to get into a comfortable position, with closed eyes 2. Practice deep breathing 3. Prompt child to progressively tense and relax various muscles groups until the child feels relaxed

Figure 22.5 Partial example of steps from the relaxation practice guide

In addition to practice guides, the practitioner guides also include a set of process guides. These cover the main coordination models described in the previous section, such as the EBS system model, the MAP, and embracing diversity. The process guides include both a description of the model and how it is used as well as a worksheet for use with children.

Clinical Dashboard

Yet another MAP tool is the clinical dashboard, a practice and progress monitoring tool. The dashboard is a spreadsheet that allows the input of data on the child (e.g., age, gender, ethnicity, target problem), progress (i.e., measures used to gauge child outcome), and practices (i.e., treatment practices planned for the case). As data are entered into the spreadsheet, they are depicted on a chart that displays progress and practice delivery over time. Therapists are trained in the selection of appropriate standardized and idiographic instruments to use to measure treatment progress. They are also trained to interpret the data trends in the dashboard over time. The tool turns each case into a single case experimental study, where therapists can test the effectiveness of their treatment plans and see the results in real time. Figure 22.6 provides an example of a dashboard for a 16-year-old child with depression.

Days in treatment is depicted on the x-axis in both panels. In the top or progress panel, the two y-axes represent scores on the measures, with two different scales (set by the therapist). In the bottom or practice panel, the diamonds indicate that a practice was delivered. The therapist can include practices as well as other notable events, such as missed appointments, medication changes, or family transitions (e.g., move, divorce). The dashboard in Figure 22.6 suggests a lack of engagement at the outset, including several missed sessions. The therapist instituted a change in therapeutic tactics (including more involvement of the caregiver and different practices), changes that appear to have led to gradual improvements.

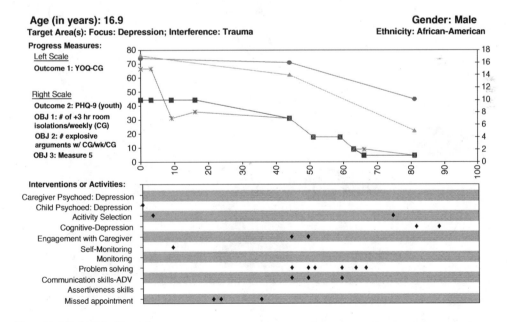

Figure 22.6 Partial dashboard

The dashboard represents a key MAP tool, providing data for many of the questions from the MAP and CARE process questions that arise in treatment. Further, the dashboard represents the individual case evidence base in the EBS system model. In MAP, a spreadsheet is one way to implement progress and practice monitoring. However, such a technological version is not required in MAP. One could graph progress using pencil and paper, as was typical in the early days of MAP in Hawai'i.

In total, then, these several coordination models and tools comprise a curriculum covering the conceptual and procedural aspects of MAP. The core concepts have been consistent since the late 2000s and represent the MAP system as it is practiced across the country and world. In the late 2000s, a formal professional development program was designed; we turn to a description of that program next.

The MAP Professional Development Program

The professional development program (PDP) created a formal set of role descriptions to help systems and agencies determine the best method for implementing MAP. Roles defined in the PDP include resource use, direct service provision, and supervisory and training (a.k.a., train-the-trainer) classes. Figure 22.7 depicts a portion of the PDP.

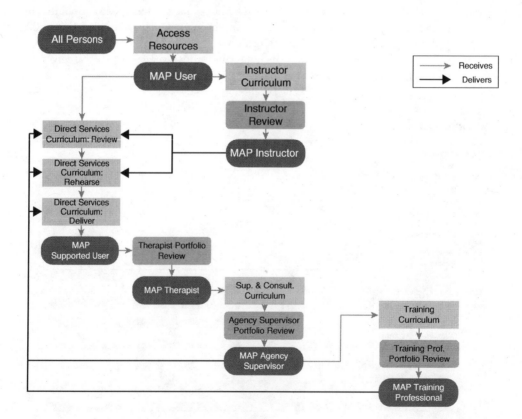

Figure 22.7 MAP professional development program

In the figure, specific roles are in dark grey and experiences needed to achieve those roles are noted in light grey. As the figure depicts, MAP Therapist status is achieved by engaging in the direct services curriculum in didactic (review), active, and service delivery capacities. These experiences can be trained and/or overseen by a variety of individuals trained in MAP, including MAP instructors, agency supervisors, or national trainers. The reason for the variety of roles was the desire to permit maximum local capacity to train rather than relying on national trainers. Regardless of the training path, the required professional development experiences should include at least 52 hours of training and supervision over at least a six (6) month period, provision of services to at least two (2) children, and successful completion of a promotion review. The first step in becoming a MAP Therapist is getting access to the core information resources upon which the direct service system relies. Doing so gives the practitioner the title, MAP User.

As shown in Figure 22.7, there are several paths to becoming credentialed as a MAP Therapist. One proceeds along the right side of the figure through what is called the Direct Services Curriculum. On this path, a practitioner participates in a Direct Services training provided by national trainers. These trainings vary but usually consist of five days (40 hours) training and six months of bi-weekly phone consultation (i.e., 12 calls), meeting the 52-hour requirement. After the 52 hours, the practitioner submits materials in a MAP Therapist Portfolio for review.

As is apparent in Figure 22.7, though, there are many other ways to achieve the 52 required hours, including training from an Agency Supervisor (AS) or a MAP Instructor. As depicted in Figure 22.7, an AS has already achieved MAP Therapist status and completed an additional supervisor training and portfolio review process, including coverage of the Supervision and Consultation Curriculum (16 hours of training plus six hours of monthly consultation calls). Once credentialed, an AS can train and supervise anyone at their agency in MAP without involvement of the national training team.

A MAP Instructor is an individual who completes the instructor curriculum and review process via the national team. These individuals are generally faculty members at higher education institutions. A MAP Instructor can provide training opportunities up to 40 hours for an aspiring MAP Therapist. However, the instructor cannot provide the 12 hours of supervision/consultation. Those can be obtained from the national training team or from an AS.

Figure 22.7 makes clear that an aspiring MAP has several ways to obtain the required experiences for promotion to MAP Therapist. PracticeWise has also made available online resources that make access to the training even easier. Through online learning, an aspiring MAP Therapist can learn many of the key concepts of MAP and then spend time with an instructor, AS, or national trainer focused on rehearsing those skills.

Empirical Studies of MAP

Because MAP is not a treatment program and is not designed for a discrete patient population, amassing evidence for its efficacy via the traditional route of randomized controlled trials is challenging. That said, there have been a number of empirical studies of MAP.

Hawai'i *quality improvement studies*. As noted in the section on the history of MAP, MAP and its early beta-versions were implemented in the state of Hawai'i in response to the Felix consent decree. Because the state was intentional in its efforts, the influence of MAP on practice and outcomes was measured carefully. In two papers, Daleiden and Chorpita (2005)

336   *Michael A. Southam-Gerow et al.*

and Daleiden et al. (2006) describe the timeline for implementation of early versions of MAP. As reported, MAP led to a notable average functional improvement for children: specifically, a twofold increase in change rate of functioning over a three-year MAP implementation period. These early data were a driver to the popularity of MAP for other systems (e.g., Higa-McMillan et al., in press).

MAP Implementation in LA County

When MAP was added as one of the options in the LA County transformation, an opportunity was presented to gauge several important indicators of the success of the system because the entire transformation was being evaluated by an independent organization, the California Institute for Mental Health (CiMH). The LAC implementation had mandated that a set of standardized child outcome measures be collected on a systematic basis as part of the way to receive payment. Hence, all youth and caregivers completed the Youth Outcome Questionnaire. Different instruments were used for each target problem area (i.e., anxiety, depression, disruptive behavior, trauma). For example, the Patient Health Questionnaire-9 (PHQ-9; Kroenke, Spitzer, & Williams, 2001) was used to gauge depression outcomes. Southam-Gerow et al. (2014) reported results of the early implementation of MAP. Effect sizes for the four problem areas billable with MAP (anxiety, depression, disruptive behavior, and trauma) were as follows: YOQ Anxiety=0.70 (n=303); YOQ-SR Anxiety=0.94 (n=104); YOQ Depression=0.80 (n=437); YOQ-SR Depression=0.97 (n=249); YOQ Disruptive=0.79 (n=569); YOQ-SR Disruptive=0.54 (n=198); YOQ Trauma=0.59 (n=42); YOQ-SR Trauma=0.79 (n=23). From a benchmarking perspective (e.g., Hunsley & Lee, 2007), these effect sizes are better than those reported in the Weisz et al. (2017) meta-analysis of the child/adolescent treatment literature, where the average post-treatment ES was 0.61 for anxiety, 0.46 for disruptive, and 0.29 for depression.

Southam-Gerow et al. (2014) also evaluated other important implementation outcomes. For example, in the fiscal year 2012 (the first full year MAP was included in the transformation), 11,929 children and youth received MAP services. In that period, MAP accounted for 28% of children and youth receiving services and 22% of claims and expenditures, making MAP one of the most widely used of the programs in the transformation. These data suggested that MAP rapidly became a popular choice for providers across the county.

Southam-Gerow et al. (2014) reported data on whether the different training pathways (i.e., trained by a national trainer or by a local agency supervisor) led to different training outcomes. These comparisons represented a key implementation outcome, as the local agency supervisor option has considerable cost benefits to agencies. Structured, external ratings of the case materials submitted by practitioners for their therapist portfolio reviews were used to test for differences between the therapists trained by National Trainer (NT) or Agency Supervisor (AS). The average ratings for both the NT ($M = 2.15$, SD = 0.27, $n = 874$ cases) and AS ($M = 2.02$, SD = 0.25, $n = 554$ cases) pathways were in the proficient range (i.e., 1 = needs work, 2 = proficient, 3 = advanced). While both the NT and AS training resulted in proficiency, comparisons between the two approaches showed that local supervisors were able to train therapists to proficiency, though not quite as successfully as the national trainers t (1,416) = 8.87, p = .000, ES = .485.

In a more recent set of studies evaluating the LAC transformation writ large (i.e., across all EBTs), Brookman-Frazee, Lau, and colleagues reported a few findings relevant to MAP. Quantitative analysis of electronic health records indicated that clinicians recorded using MAP most frequently over time (i.e., used in the highest average proportion of clinical encounters, used by the highest proportion of therapists, used with the highest proportion of children and agencies; Brookman-Frazee et al., 2016, 2018) compared to the array of EBTs included in the transformation. Survey data focused on attitudes and perceptions from agency clinicians and leaders are somewhat mixed; one study indicated that MAP was perceived more favorably by agency leadership than frontline clinicians (Stadnick et al., 2018). The authors highlight a number of MAP-specific design features that may appeal to agency leadership (e.g., the breadth of clinical problems covered by MAP, greater level of clinical oversight with the Clinical Dashboard; Stadnick et al., 2018). Whereas the breadth of coverage may also appeal to frontline clinicians, MAP is likely to require more preparation time (e.g., completing PWEBS searches, using Clinical Dashboard) than a standard, structured program, posing a possible challenge (Brookman-Frazee, Drahota, Stadnick, & Palinkas, 2012; Drahota, Stadnick, & Brookman-Frazee, 2014).

Social Work Training Study

MAP has been integrated into clinical education programs for pre-service professionals (e.g., master's in social work (MSW) programs, clinical psychology doctoral programs, child psychiatry fellowships). To our knowledge, several such programs have adopted MAP into their curriculum to date for at least one training cycle (e.g., the MSW program at the University of Southern California; the clinical psychology program at Virginia Commonwealth University; the child psychiatry fellowship program at the University of California Los Angeles).

One project to date (Cox & Southam-Gerow, 2019) has evaluated training outcomes in an MSW program for a semester-long adaptation of the MAP training curriculum relative to curriculum-as-usual (CAU) of 39 participants (17 in the MAP condition, 22 in the CAU). The majority of participants were women (92.3%) and identified as white (59.0%); participants' average age was 27.0 (SD = 5.84; range 22–52) and had 0.89 years of direct clinical experience (SD = 0.48; range 0–2.25 years) at the beginning of their semester of participation. Outcomes of interest were twofold: (1) cognitive indicators of skill gain as measured through a written task designed to measure MAP-relevant skills (e.g., in response to a clinical vignette, designing an initial treatment plan and plan to monitor progress); (2) behavioral indicators of skill gain as measured through a brief standardized patient interaction that was recorded and subsequently coded using the Therapy Process Observational Coding System for Child Psychotherapy, Revised Strategies scale (TPOCS-RS; McLeod, Smith, Southam-Gerow, Weisz, & Kendall, 2015); attitudinal indicators, including attitudes toward evidence-based practice broadly (e.g., Aarons, 2004) and, for those in the MAP condition, perceived acceptability, feasibility, understanding, and presence of system-level support to use the MAP system.

Initial findings are encouraging. On the written MAP skill task, students in the MAP condition indicated that they would use idiographic instruments for treatment progress monitoring post-semester with greater frequency than their CAU peers. In the standardized patient interaction, students in the MAP condition demonstrated significantly greater use of cognitive (e.g., cognitive restructuring) and behavioral (e.g., relaxation training) therapeutic strategies relative to their CAU peers post-semester. Finally, students in the MAP course agreed that MAP itself was largely acceptable, feasible, and understandable. Taken together, these findings highlight the feasibility of integrating MAP into masters-level training programs as a means to bolster the clinical skill set of the next generation of mental health clinicians.

Conclusion

In this chapter, we provided an overview of the Managing and Adapting Practice (MAP) system. MAP represents a unique approach to evidence-based practice, providing a set of coordination models and tools designed to help therapists plan and deliver highly personalized treatment to children and adolescents. Evidence suggests MAP has great promise for mental health systems. To date, MAP has not only been shown to reduce symptoms for children and adolescents – MAP can be implemented at scale and maintained over time. Ongoing studies in Los Angeles County and South Carolina as well as implementation in several other states will provide more data on MAP in the near future.

Author Note

The opinions expressed by the authors are not necessarily reflective of the position of or endorsed by the PracticeWise, LLC, the developers of MAP.

References

Aarons, G. A. (2004). Mental health provider attitudes toward adoption of evidence-based practice: The Evidence-Based Practice Attitude Scale (EBPAS). *Mental Health Services Research, 6*, 61–74.

APA Presidential Task Force on Evidence-Based Practice. (2006). Evidence-based practice in psychology. *American Psychologist, 61*, 271–285.

Beidas, R. S., & Kendall, P. C. (2010). Training therapists in evidence-based practice: A critical review of studies from a system-contextual perspective. *Clinical Psychology, 17*, 1–30.

Brookman-Frazee, L., Drahota, A., Stadnick, N., & Palinkas, L. A. (2012). Therapist perspectives on community mental health services for children with autism spectrum disorders. *Administration and Policy in Mental Health and Mental Health Services Research, 39*, 365–373. doi:10.1007/s10488-011-0355-y

Brookman-Frazee, L., Stadnick, N., Roesch, S., Regan, J., Barnett, M., Innes-Gomberg, D., … Lau, A. (2016). Measuring sustainment of multiple practices fiscally mandated in children's mental health services. *Administration and Policy in Mental Health and Mental Health Services Research, 43*, 1009–1022. doi:10.1007/s10488-016-0731-8

Brookman-Frazee, L., Zhan, C., Stadnick, N., Sommerfeld, D., Roesch, S., Aarons, G. A., … Lau, A. S. (2018). Using survival analysis to understand patterns of sustainment within a systems-driven implementation of multiple evidence-based practices for children's mental health services. *Frontiers in Public Health, 6*, 1–12. doi:10.3389/fpubh.2018.00054

Chorpita, B. F. (2004, January). *Strategies for implementing evidence based services in a system of care.* Workshop presented for the 2004 System of Care Community Meeting, San Antonio, TX.

Chorpita, B. F., Bernstein, A., & Daleiden, E. L. (2008). Driving with roadmaps and dashboards: Using information resources to structure the decision models in service organizations. *Administration and Policy in Mental Health and Mental Health Services Research, 35*(1–2), 114–123.

Chorpita, B. F., & Daleiden, E. L. (2009). Mapping evidence-based treatments for children and adolescents: Application of the distillation and matching model to 615 treatments from 322 randomized trials. *Journal of Consulting and Clinical Psychology, 77*, 566–579.

Chorpita, B. F., & Daleiden, E. L. (2010). Building evidence-based systems in children's mental health. In J. R. Weisz & A. E. Kazdin (Eds.), *Evidence-based psychotherapies for children and adolescents* (pp. 482–499). New York, NY: The Guilford Press.

Chorpita, B. F., & Daleiden, E. L. (2014). Structuring the collaboration of science and service in pursuit of a shared vision. *Journal of Clinical Child and Adolescent Psychology, 43*, 323–338.

Chorpita, B. F., & Daleiden, E. L. (2018). Coordinated strategic action: Aspiring to wisdom in mental health service systems. *Clinical Psychology: Science & Practice, 25*. doi:10.1111/cpsp.12264

Chorpita, B. F., & Donkervoet, C. (2005). Implementation of the felix consent decree in Hawaii: The impact of policy and practice development efforts on service delivery. In R. G. Steele & M. C. Roberts (Eds.), *Issues in clinical child psychology. Handbook of mental health services for children, adolescents, and families* (pp. 317–332). New York, NY: Kluwer Academic/Plenum Publishers.

Chorpita, B. F., Rotheram-Borus, M. J., Daleiden, E. L., Bernstein, A., Cromley, T., Swenderman, D., & Regan, J. (2011). The old solutions are the new problem: How do we better use what we already know about reducing the burden of mental illness?. *Perspectives on Psychological Science, 6*, 493–497.

Chorpita, B. F., Yim, L. M., Donkervoet, J. C., Arensdorf, A., Amundsen, M. J., McGee, C., & Morelli, P. (2002). Toward large-scale implementation of empirically supported treatments for children: A review and observations by the Hawai'i Empirical Basis to Services Task Force. *Clinical Psychology: Science and Practice, 9*, 165–190.

Cox, J. R., & Southam-Gerow, M. A. (2019). Dissemination and implementation of evidence-based treatments for children and adolescents. In R. G. Steele & M. Roberts (Eds.), *Handbook of evidence-based therapies for children and adolescents: Bridging science and practice.* New York: Springer Publishing.

Daleiden, E., & Chorpita, B. F. (2005). From data to wisdom: Quality improvement strategies supporting large-scale implementation of evidence based services. *Child and Adolescent Psychiatric Clinics of North America, 14*, 329–349.

Daleiden, E. L., Chorpita, B. F., Donkervoet, C. M., Arensdorf, A. A., & Brogan, M. (2006). Getting better at getting them better: Health outcomes and evidence-based practice within a system of care. *Journal of the American Academy of Child and Adolescent Psychiatry, 45*, 749–756.

Drahota, A., Stadnick, N., & Brookman-Frazee, L. (2014). Therapist perspectives on training in a package of evidence-based practice strategies for children with autism spectrum disorders served in community mental health clinics. *Administration and Policy in Mental Health and Mental Health Services Research, 41*, 114–125. doi:10.1007/s10488-012-0441-9

Greenhalgh, T., Robert, G., MacFarlane, F., Bate, P., & Kyriakidou, O. (2004). Diffusion of innovations in service organizations: Systematic review and recommendations. *The Milbank Quarterly, 82*, 581–629.

Guan, K., Park, A. L., & Chorpita, B. F. (2019). Emergent life events during youth evidence-based treatment: Impact on future provider adherence and clinical progress. *Journal of Clinical Child & Adolescent Psychology, 48*, S202–S214.

Higa-McMillan, C. K., Nakamura, B. J., Daleiden, E. L., Edwall, G. E., Nygaard, P., & Chorpita, B. F. (in press). Fifteen years of MAP implementation in Minnesota: Tailoring training to evolving provider experience and expertise. *Journal of Family Social Work.*

Hunsley, J., & Lee, C. M. (2007). Research-informed benchmarks for psychological treatments: Efficacy studies, effectiveness studies, and beyond. *Professional Psychology: Research and Practice, 38*, 21–33. doi:10.1037/0735-7028.38.1.21

Kendall, P. C., & Hedtke, K. (2006). *The coping cat workbook* (2nd ed.). Ardmore, PA: Workbook Publishing.

Kroenke, K., Spitzer, R. L., & Williams, J. B. W. (2001). The PHQ-9: Validity of a brief depression severity measure. *Journal of General Internal Medicine, 16*, 606–613. doi:10.1046/j.1525-1497.2001.016009606.x

McLeod, B. D., Smith, M. M., Southam-Gerow, M. A., Weisz, J. R., & Kendall, P. C. (2015). Measuring treatment differentiation for implementation research: The therapy process observational coding system for child psychotherapy revised strategies scale. *Psychological Assessment, 27*, 314–325. doi:10.1037/pas0000037

Mufson, L. H., Dorta, K. P., Wickramaratne, P., Nomura, Y., Olfson, M., & Weissman, M. M. (2004). A randomized effectiveness trial of interpersonal psychotherapy for depressed adolescents. *Archives of General Psychiatry, 61*, 577–584.

Nakamura, B. J., Chorpita, B. F., Hirsch, M., Daleiden, E., Slavin, L., Amundson, M. J., … Vorsino, W. M. (2011). Large-scale implementation of evidence-based treatments for children 10 years later: Hawai'i's evidence-based services initiative in children's mental health. *Clinical Psychology: Science and Practice, 18*, 24–35.

Southam-Gerow, M. A., Daleiden, E. L., Chorpita, B. F., Bae, C., Mitchell, C., Faye, M., & Alba, M. (2014). MAPping Los Angeles County: Taking an evidence-informed model of mental health care to scale. *Journal of Clinical Child and Adolescent Psychology, 43*, 190–200.

Southam-Gerow, M. A., & Prinstein, M. J. (2014). Evidence-based treatment updates: The evolution of the evaluation of psychological treatments for children & adolescents. *Journal of Clinical Child & Adolescent Psychology, 43*, 1–6.

Southam-Gerow, M. A., Rodríguez, A., Chorpita, B. F., & Daleiden, E. L. (2012). Dissemination and implementation of evidence-based treatments for youth: Challenges and recommendations. *Professional Psychology: Research and Practice, 43*, 527–534.

Stadnick, N. A., Lau, A. S., Barnett, M., Regan, J., Aarons, G. A., & Brookman-Frazee, L. (2018). Comparing agency leader and therapist perspectives on evidence-based practices: Associations with individual and organizational factors in a mental health system-driven implementation effort. *Administration and Policy in Mental Health and Mental Health Services Research, 45*, 447–461. doi:10.1007/s10488-017-0835-9

Weisz, J. R., Kuppens, S., Ng, M. Y., Eckshtain, D., Ugueto, A. M., Vaughn-Coaxum, R., … Fordwood, S. R. (2017). What five decades of research tells us about the effects of youth psychological therapy: A multilevel meta-analysis and implications for science and practice. *American Psychologist, 72*, 79–117.

23 Best Practices for Prescribing and Deprescribing Psychotropic Medications for Children and Youth

Christopher Bellonci and Jonathan C. Huefner

Psychotropic medications are medications used to treat emotional or behavioral conditions. These medications can be a critical component of the service and supports provided to a youth diagnosed with a behavioral health disorder. While there have been significant gains in the evidence base for the use of psychotropic medications for children, these medications are often used for conditions or in age groups where the efficacy (i.e. does the medication work?) and safety (i.e. there are minimal harmful side-effects when using this medication with a youth of this age with this specific condition) have yet to be established. This is especially true when medications are combined (i.e. polypharmacy) or used for long periods of time (i.e. more than 60 days, see Chen, Patel, Sherer, & Aparasu (2011); most medication research trials are 6–8 weeks in duration). In the first half of this chapter we will outline best practices in the use of psychotropic medications for youth. We will then focus the second half of this chapter on a relatively new concept in medicine, "Deprescribing," the process of reassessing the need for medication after a period of stability has been achieved or when the risks or side-effects of the medication outweigh the benefits. In many cases deprescribing is needed to bring psychotropic medication regimens in line with best practice principles.

Throughout this discussion we will emphasize that medications in children's behavioral health are not curative. At best, psychotropic medications can alleviate symptoms and create conditions that help a youth engage in treatment. Unlike medications such as antibiotics that cure infections and then can be discontinued, psychotropic medications have to continue to be taken in order to maintain symptom reduction. This is the rationale for medications not being used in isolation from evidence-based psychotherapies that actively teach skills for managing and coping with the symptoms of behavioral health conditions. *Medications do not teach skills*. Combination treatment with medication *and* psychotherapy are typically the approach called for in most clinical practice guidelines for more severe children's behavioral health disorders. Mild or moderate conditions would typically first be treated with an evidence-based therapy prior to the initiation of psychotropic medications.

Rates of Psychotropic Medication Use by Children in the U.S.

An increasing percentage of youth in the U.S. are being prescribed psychotropic medications with this trend accelerating during the last two decades. Data from the National Center for Health Statistics (Howie, Pastor, & Lukacs, 2014) found that 7.5% of U.S. children aged 6–17 used a psychotropic medication in the past six months (see Figure 23.1). Males (9.7%) used psychotropic medications more than females (5.2%). This may be because males are more likely to display their emotions through externalizing behaviors such as aggression that can drive medication use. Females more commonly display internalizing symptoms (e.g. anxiety

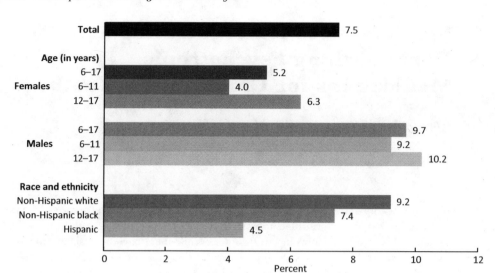

Figure 23.1 Percentage of children aged 6–17 years prescribed medication during the past six months for emotional or behavioral difficulties, by sex and age group, and race and Hispanic origin: United States, 2011–2012

Note: Parents were asked, "During the past 6 months, was the [same child] prescribed medication or taking prescription medication for difficulties with emotions, concentration, behavior or being able to get along with others?" See NCHS report for more detailed information on how these groups differed (Howie et al., 2014). Source: CDC/NCHS, National Health Interview Survey.

and depression) that may be less obvious to parents or caregivers. Non-Hispanic white (9.2%) children had the highest psychotropic medication use reported followed by non-Hispanic black (7.4%) children and Hispanic (4.5%) children.

Additionally, a higher percentage of children insured by Medicaid or the Children's Health Insurance Program (9.9%) used prescribed medication for emotional or behavioral difficulties compared with Tricare/other (military, MEDICARE, other government insurance; 7.9%), private health insurance (6.7%) or no insurance (2.7%). The NCHS report also showed that a higher percentage of children in families having income below 100% of the poverty level (9.2%) used prescribed medication for emotional or behavioral difficulties compared with children in families having income at 100–200% of the poverty level (6.6%); 200–400% (7.3%) or greater than 400% (7.2%).

Data from the National Health and Nutrition Examination Survey (Jonas, Gu, & Albertorio, 2013) indicated that for adolescents aged 12–19 antidepressants and medications to treat attention deficit hyperactivity disorder (ADHD) were the most commonly used psychotropic medications in the past month. A concerning finding from this survey was that only approximately one-half of adolescents reporting any psychotropic medication use in the last month had seen a mental health professional in the past year. To meet best practice standards, children taking psychotropic medications should be seen on a monthly basis and minimally every three months.

The rates of psychotropic medication use by children in the U.S. are typically higher than rates in other developed nations (Bachmann et al., 2016; Raman et al., 2018; Zito et al., 2008). The U.S. is only exceeded recently by the Netherlands for stimulant and antipsychotic use (Bachmann et al., 2017; Kalverdijk et al., 2017).

Psychotropic medication rates for youth in foster care are 58% to 330% higher than for Medicaid enrolled youth in general (all youth in foster care are eligible for Medicaid; Matone et al., 2015; Raghavan et al., 2014). Research examining youth in intensive residential programs that serve youth with more serious emotional and behavioral problems has found that between 78% and 88% of youth were on a psychotropic medication at admission, with 57–67% being on two or more psychotropic medications (Huefner, Griffith, Smith, Vollmer, & Leslie, 2014; Lyons et al., 2004).

For youth on at least one psychotropic medication, there is an increasing psychotropic polypharmacy trend from 21.2% in 1999–2001 to 27.7% in 2008–2010 (Hincapie-Castillo, Liu, Bussing, & Winterstein, 2017; Saucedo et al., 2018). An examination of Medicaid claims found a 6.2-fold increase in polypharmacy from 6.7% to 41.6% for depressed adolescents between 1996 and 2005 (McIntyre & Jerrell, 2009). Similarly, between 1996 and 2007, the polypharmacy rate increased from 14% to 20% for youth prescribed psychotropic medication by an office-based physician (Comer, Olfson, & Mojtabai, 2010), and has been reported to be as high as 60% for youth seeing an office-based psychiatrist (Mojtabai & Olfson, 2010). Polypharmacy rates can be even higher for specific medications, where 85% of Medicaid enrolled children using second generation antipsychotic medications (SGAs) were also concurrently prescribed one or more other psychotropic medications (Kreider et al., 2014). This is an area of particular concern as much polypharmacy seen in practice is untested or not supported by clinical trials. The growing trend for youth to be on two or more medications far outpaces our capacity to evaluate and assess efficacy and safety of these medication combinations (Saldaña et al., 2014; Tishler & Reiss, 2012; Vitiello, 2007).

What Is Known and Unknown about the Use of Psychiatric Medications for Children and Adolescents?

Off-label prescribing is the use of medications lacking Food and Drug Administration (FDA) approval for the specific age of the child or for the condition being treated by the medication (Sharma et al., 2016). Off-label includes prescribing specific medications that have not been tested with pediatric populations; and also includes most polypharmacy, doses exceeding maximum recommendations, and the use of psychotropic medications with very young children (Barnett et al., 2016). Current estimates are that 32–75% of all pediatric prescribing is "off label" (Ansermot, Jordanov, Smogur, Holzer, & Eap, 2018; Braüner, Johansen, Roesbjerg, & Pagsberg, 2016; Roberts, Rodriguez, Murphy, & Crescenzi, 2003). In spite of researchers questioning and challenging this practice, the use of off-label psychotropic medication continues to rise (Harrison, Cluxton-Keller, & Gross, 2012; Olfson, Crystal, Huang, & Gerhard, 2010). Because many psychotropic medications have not been developed for and tested in pediatric populations, the data relating to long-term safety and effectiveness for many medications used in pediatric pharmacotherapy is extremely limited (Braüner et al., 2016; Sharma et al., 2016).

It has been long argued that, given the unknowns about pediatric pharmacotherapy, non-pharmacological treatments should be prioritized (Foxx, 1998; McKay, 2007; Rhoades, 1982). There is a particular concern in relation to the adverse effects of psychotropic medications to the developing brain and body of children and adolescents (Correll & Carlson, 2006; Singh & Chang, 2012). The implications of adding a psychoactive medication to the brain of a developing child, particularly very young children, is largely unknown. The neurotransmitters that these medications target are not in just one part of the brain, and the medications cannot be directed just to the regions of the brain that are theorized to be related to the behavioral health condition under treatment. When these medications interact with neurotransmitters that may be unrelated to the etiology of the behavioral health condition being treated, side-effects can develop. There are examples of medications that were safe for adults but caused untoward side-effects for children (e.g. Reye's syndrome secondary to taking aspirin; Hurwitz, 1989). This would include second-generation anti-psychotic medications that have been associated with significant amounts of weight gain, increased risk of diabetes and metabolic syndrome far in excess of what was seen in adult studies of these medications.

In spite of these concerns, psychotropic medications for youth can play a critical role in managing a child or adolescent's psychiatric symptoms. For some conditions like Psychotic or Bipolar disorders that have no evidence-based psychosocial therapies, medication may be the primary treatment. For other conditions, such as mild or moderate depressive and anxiety disorders, an evidence-based therapy, such as cognitive behavioral therapy, would be the recommended first line of treatment. Generally, conservative medication practice reserves the use of medication for more severe conditions such as those resulting in hospitalization, if the young person was suicidal or experiencing significant functional impairment, or if after a sufficient period in therapy symptoms persisted or worsened. Many studies have shown combination treatments (medication plus therapy) can have the best response (Bennett et al., 2016; Catalá-López et al., 2017; Malik & Azeem, 2017), especially when the symptoms prevent the young person from being able to engage in treatment (Walkup, 2009). Ideally, once the child learns the skills to manage symptoms the medication can be discontinued.

Recommended Practices for the Use of Psychotropic Medications in Children

The American Academy of Child and Adolescent Psychiatry's (AACAP) Practice Parameter (PP; 2009) on the use of psychotropic medications clearly outlines best-practice guidelines for the use of these medications in children and adolescents. The following section uses the 13 Principles outlined in the practice parameter as the framework for discussing recommended practices for the use of psychotropic medications for youth with emotional and behavioral disorders.

Principle 1: Before Initiating Pharmacotherapy, a Psychiatric Evaluation Is Completed

All effective treatment starts with a working clinical hypothesis of what may be driving the emotional or behavioral issues for which the child is being referred. In child mental health, a focus on the history of the presenting concern would include details on the duration, setting, context, and severity of the symptom(s). Screening tools and rating scales can be very helpful in obtaining this information either by having the youth, parent, and potentially the youth's teacher complete the screening tool or rating scale directly or solicited during an initial intake assessment. Developmental, family, educational, and past treatment histories must be collected and integrated into a narrative that helps to explain the child's behavior. This becomes the basis of the biopsychosocial formulation. Medication decisions should be informed by the clinical needs of the child via an evidence-based indication or clinical guidelines for psychotropic use, as well as by response to treatment using objective data.

Psychotropic Medications Best Practices   345

Principle 2: Before Initiating/Adding Pharmacotherapy, a Medical History Is Obtained, and a Medical Evaluation Is Considered When Appropriate

There are a number of physical conditions that can cause psychiatric symptoms (such as hypothyroidism resulting in depression). In order to rule out a physical cause for psychiatric symptoms it is important to gather information about the child's physical health status and whether the symptoms can be accounted for by a physical health disorder. If so, appropriate testing and assessment should be conducted. Many psychotropic medications can cause physical side-effects (e.g. changes in weight, blood pressure, prolactin and other hormone levels). By conducting a careful baseline medical history, physical exam, and laboratory testing prior to the initiation of a medication trial, the prescriber will know whether the abnormal health or laboratory measures were present before the medication trial or the result of a medication trial. This information can then inform treatment decisions about whether the benefits of the medication trial are outweighed by the emergent adverse effects of the medication.

Principle 3: The Prescriber Is Advised to Communicate with Other Professionals Involved with the Child to Obtain Collateral History and Set the Stage for Monitoring Outcome and Side-Effects during the Medication Trial

Children have many adults involved in their lives. They have their parents or caregivers, their pediatrician, their teacher or school personnel, and if they are involved in the child welfare, mental health, or juvenile justice system they are likely to have case managers and others involved in their care. In order to get the best data to inform the treatment of a child, as many sources of information as possible about the course and nature of the child's emotional and behavioral difficulties should be accessed. Good history taking is the basis of good treatment. Similarly, if a decision is made to medicate a child, the adults involved in that child's life need to understand what to look for in terms of benefits from the medication trial as well as any treatment-emergent side-effects. There should be a discussion of what might be considered emergent or urgent to be reported to the prescriber as well as less urgent, but still significant side-effects.

Principle 4: The Prescriber Develops a Psychosocial and Psychopharmacological Treatment Plan Based on the Best Available Evidence

Together the youth, the family, their advocates and treatment team write a treatment plan based on the biopsychosocial formulation, with clear measures that can be tracked in order to monitor the youth's response to treatment. This includes treatment goals for any and all medications and how response to any medication changes will be measured. It would be a rare circumstance where a child would be prescribed a medication and not also benefit from therapy, so as the medication plan is being considered, a plan to engage in therapy to learn skills to manage the symptoms should also be developed.

Principle 5: The Prescriber Develops a Plan to Monitor the Patient, Short and Long Term

In order to assess whether the psychotropic treatment is resulting in more benefits than side-effects, the child should be closely monitored. At the initiation of a medication trial the child may need to be monitored as frequently as weekly (e.g. to monitor for antidepressant-induced suicidal ideation, antipsychotic weight gain). The monitoring does not have to be conducted by the treating prescriber and may be assigned to the therapist working with the child provided it has been clearly communicated to the therapist what to look for and there is a reliable means for the therapist to reach the prescriber with their observations and concerns. If the prescriber, in consultation with the parents/caregiver and youth, determines a prolonged course of treatment with medication is warranted, there should continue to be regular monitoring of risks and benefits. As developmental skills become available to the growing youth or the child learns skills in therapy there may be opportunities to reconsider the medication trial. Some medication-related adverse events only appear after the child has been on the medication for a prolonged period of time, further warranting continued engagement with the prescriber even when symptoms have been resolved.

Principle 6: Prescribers Should Be Cautious when Implementing a Treatment Plan that Cannot Be Appropriately Monitored

If the child is not able to have on-going follow-up with the prescriber who initiated the medication trial, consideration of whether to start the medication may be needed. One alternative would be to have someone with medical training monitor the medication trial, such as the child's pediatrician. If this course of treatment is undertaken it is critically important that the prescriber and pediatrician discuss the rationale for the medication trial, how long the trial is being undertaken, and what to look for in terms of benefits and potential side-effects. Ultimately, it remains the responsibility of the prescribing clinician to ensure their patient does not come to harm as a result of their treatment recommendations.

Principle 7: The Prescriber Provides Feedback about the Diagnosis and Educates the Patient and Family Regarding the Child's Disorder and the Treatment and Monitoring Plan

Child behavioral health providers should be consultants in the care of the youth and family. It is critical that the parents and youth retain the "locus of control" and not be led to believe that the psychotropic medication will fix everything or that they are passive participants in their own or their child's treatment. Youth and family attitudes towards and beliefs about medication should be carefully adhered to and open dialog encouraged. Resulting treatment outcomes can be optimized by thus incorporating youth and family perspectives, including cultural factors influencing beliefs about medication treatment. Therapeutic alliance, patient autonomy and understanding the meaning of the treatment intervention have positive, powerful, and measurable impacts on the effectiveness of psychotropic medication treatment (Mintz & Flynn, 2012).

Principle 8: Complete and Document the Assent of the Child and Consent of the Parents before Initiating Medication Treatment and at Important Points during Treatment

Documentation of the rationale for a medication recommendation is critical in order for others working with the child or future treaters of the child to understand why the medication was initiated and the outcome of the trial. If a child is in the care of a child welfare system, it is the prescriber's responsibility to know who is empowered to give informed consent for the medication and what process is needed to obtain that consent. Laws vary widely with some states requiring that all psychotropic medications be preapproved by a judge (e.g., California) to others who have developed centralized, web-based consent processes (e.g., Connecticut). In addition to whatever written documentation the child welfare system may require, the prescriber should also document the consent in the child's record.

Principle 9: The Assent and Consent Discussion Focuses on the Risks and Benefits of the Proposed and Alternative Treatments

Informed consent requires a discussion of what is known and unknown about each specific psychotropic medication for the specific condition for which it is being prescribed and for the specific age group of the child or youth. The goals of both medication and psychosocial interventions need to be clearly communicated to the children and youth in a developmentally appropriate way and their assent sought. Similarly, parents and guardians should understand the rationale for the treatment recommendations, both pharmacologic and non-pharmacologic and how a positive or negative response will be measured. Frequent communication about the response to the intervention should occur in order to determine whether benefits of the intervention outweigh any side-effects that may develop. There should be clear communication about how long the medication will take to work, alternatives to the proposed treatment, and the best prediction of what might occur if the proposed treatment was not initiated.

Principle 10: Implement Medication Trials Using an Adequate Dose and for an Adequate Duration of Treatment

Dosage guidelines for many psychotropic medications do not exist for youth. The clinical pearl, "start low and go slow" meaning start at a low dose and increase the dose slowly, as regards any new medication trial dosing is critical when working with youth, given the medication unknowns and youth sensitivities to these medications. Using data, as referenced above, to measure and monitor responses to medication and psychosocial interventions can result in rational psychopharmacological trials (including medication tapering or "washes"). Since objective determination of response to medication and psychosocial interventions can take weeks or even months, it is critical to plan for proper supports and oversight during the medication trial in order to ensure adequate exposure to the regimen and determination of the intervention's efficacy.

Typical human development is a continual process of youth acquiring new skills and normative behavior changes over time. Psychopharmacological practice should take this into account and periodically reassess the continuing need for a medication. As the youth develops coping skills to manage what the medication is meant to treat (e.g., anxiety or affect management) the medication may no longer be needed. In fact, psychosocial interventions should specifically promote the acquisition of these skills. The only way to know whether a medication continues to be warranted is to stop the medication and assess the response after a period of stable functioning.

Principle 11: The Prescriber Reassesses the Patient if the Child Does Not Respond to the Initial Medication Trial as Expected

Reassessment of the original biopsychosocial formulation developed at admission should occur during every meeting of the treatment team and include the youth, family, and advocates. This reassessment should be informed by routine clinical data that is being used to measure the youth's on-going emotional and behavioral progress in relation to the treatment plan goals. This data-driven decision making will allow a medication management process that uses the lowest effective dose of a medication and the fewest number of medications needed to ensure the youth's continued progress. Rather than simply changing from one medication to another, there should be a continual reassessment of the original hypothesis of the problem and updates to the biopsychosocial formulation as new information becomes available which may impact medication and other treatment recommendations.

Principle 12: The Prescriber Needs a Clear Rationale for Using Medication Combinations

Combinations of more than one psychotropic medication concurrently is becoming more common in child psychiatry resulting in practices that some have characterized as irrational. Specifically, some researchers have postulated that high pediatric polypharmacy rates result from reasons such as insufficient trials of monopharmacy (e.g., inadequate dose, sufficient time frame, etc.), symptom-based prescribing, clinical encounter time constraints, managed care restrictions, and insufficient attention to psychosocial issues (Kingsbury, Yi, & Simpson, 2001; Rosenheck, 2005).

There are some studies showing improved outcomes by combining a stimulant and an alpha-agonist to treat ADHD in circumstances where one medication was ineffective. There have also been studies looking at combinations of a mood-stabilizer with a second-generation antipsychotic to treat Bipolar disorder. However, in general, there is very little research supporting the use of more than one medication concurrently and virtually no studies looking at combinations of more than two medications. Despite the dearth of research supporting this practice, it has become increasingly common that these combinations are used in clinical practice, especially for youth living in foster or residential care. The prescriber of such a regimen should have a well-articulated rationale for any polypharmacy and should be able to explain that rationale during the informed consent process. It should be specifically articulated that the polypharmacy regimen has not been studied in clinical trials so the parent or guardian providing the consent can truly make an informed decision.

Principle 13: Discontinuing Medication in Children Requires a Specific Plan

For many youth on psychotropic medications, adherence to psychotropic medication regimens receives considerable attention, but far less focus is placed on intentional, proactive deprescribing of psychotropic medications that are no longer justified (i.e., ineffective, unsafe, or unwanted). In fact, most of AACAP's practice parameters are silent about if, when, or how to thoughtfully and safely discontinue medications (i.e. deprescribe). Deprescribing is not about denying effective psychotropic treatment for children and adolescents. It is the process of discontinuing or decreasing psychotropic medications when existing or potential harms outweigh existing or potential benefits. It also takes the youth and caregiver perspectives into account. Deprescribing is part of the good prescribing continuum that ensures that the current psychotropic medication regimen is consistent with the principles described above. We discuss discontinuation in more detail in the next section, and highlight how discontinuation is consistent with several of the principles we just discussed.

Psychotropic Medication Discontinuation in Pediatric Populations

Scott et al. (2015) define deprescribing as "the systematic process of identifying and discontinuing drugs in instances in which existing or potential harms outweigh existing benefits within the context of an individual patient's care goals, current level of functioning, life expectancy, values and preferences" (p. 827). Deprescribing is the obvious, and often unrecognized, solution to ensure that at any point in time in the course of a child or adolescent's treatment for a behavioral health condition the medication they are taking remains warranted.

Deprescribing, like prescribing, starts with a comprehensive psychiatric assessment (Principle 1; see American Academy of Child and Adolescent Psychiatry's Practice Parameters on the Assessment of Children and Adolescents; e.g., Geller, March, & Workgroup on Quality Issues, 2012; Pliszka & Workgroup on Quality Issues, 2007). This is especially important when a youth is entering the clinician's care already on medications. The clinician should make every attempt to review the records of past psychiatric treatment and any past testing to understand the rationale for the current medication regimen and in their absence exercise sound professional judgment (Principle 2). Developing an independent biopsychosocial formulation is critical to guide any consideration of deprescribing. Consideration of whether the current medication regimen may actually be contributing to side-effects or symptoms that might be mistaken as remaining targets for medication intervention should prompt thoughtful consideration of deprescribing rather than treating with additional medications (Principle 3). Periodic reassessment of the diagnosis and formulation is indicated, especially as additional historical information is obtained and the clinician is able to observe the response to treatment interventions including deprescribing.

The diagnosis and knowledge of the course of the disorder should inform the decision of whether and when to taper or discontinue a medication (Principles 4 and 5). For example, there is more clinical support for longer maintenance treatment in ADHD or well-documented psychotic disorders than in PTSD-related symptoms or for single episode depression and anxiety disorders where treatment protocols typically call for medication discontinuation after 6–12 months (see AACAP Practice Parameters on Depression and Anxiety disorders: Birmaher, Brent, & AACAP Work Group on Quality Issues, 2007; Connolly & Bernstein, & Workgroup on Quality Issues, 2007).

Any recommendation to taper or discontinue a psychotropic medication should be done while engaging in developmentally appropriate shared decision making with the youth and caregiver (Principle 7). Assent from the youth and consent from the caregiver should be obtained after the appropriate risks, benefits, and alternatives are discussed (Principles 8 and 9). If the youth is in foster care, consent needs to be obtained from the person who is authorized in that state or county to provide consent for psychotropic medication decisions. This is often the biological parent and ideally the parent will be a part of the youth's behavioral health treatment and will have had an opportunity to understand the diagnosis, treatment formulation, and rationale for medication prior to the medication being initiated or continued. If a transitioning-age youth (typically 18 years old) is planning on discontinuing their medication when they reach the age of consent, it may be clinically advisable to taper medications in advance in order to prevent the side-effects of sudden cessation and/or to demonstrate to the young person the effects of stopping the medication while they are still in care.

Stability is defined as showing significant symptom reduction (i.e. no longer scoring in the clinical range on a standardized rating scale); no hospitalizations or other signs of regression in academics, relationships, or behavior, and no recent placement disruptions. For youth on monotherapy, deprescribing would typically consist of reducing the dose and observing for a return of the target symptoms for which the medication was originally prescribed (Principles 10 and 11). When a child or adolescent is on multiple medications and the plan is to deprescribe more than one, it is best to deprescribe one at a time so it is clear which taper is responsible for any adverse responses. If the youth is prescribed more than one medication concurrently, consider the following:

- Start tapering medication that has the least evidence of efficacy and/or greatest evidence of side-effects or risk of side-effects (e.g. SGAs);
- Start tapering medication that is prescribed at a supra-therapeutic dose without obvious justification;
- Start tapering medication that is prescribed at doses that are sub-therapeutic or has limited or no evidence of effectiveness for the condition it is prescribed (e.g. SGAs for sleep).

- When deprescribing medications, the half-life of the medication can affect the speed at which it can safely be deprescribed.
- When anticonvulsants (including Benzodiazepines) are used for psychiatric reasons, it is important to remember that rapid tapering can precipitate seizures even if patients have not previously had seizures.

Combined psychotropic and psychosocial interventions are typically more effective than either treatment alone. During a medication trial the youth should be receiving an evidence-based psychosocial therapy teaching skills to manage the target symptoms for the prescribed medication (e.g., a psychotherapy, such as Cognitive Behavioral Therapy (CBT), for anxiety for a child prescribed an anti-anxiety medication) or to implement new skills as symptoms have improved on beneficial medication. If in the course of a medication taper or discontinuation, target symptoms recur, based on the specific clinical circumstances of the youth and the youth and family's preferences, consideration should be given whether to provide more intensive therapeutic supports, refreshers of the skills that were taught or booster sessions of the therapy; restarting the medicine or increasing the dose back to the last effective dosage; or considering an alternative therapeutic, academic, or medication intervention (Principle 11).

Treating some medication responsive conditions with psychotropic medication may facilitate deprescribing other medications, especially those with less supported indications. For example, combined anti-anxiety medication and psychotherapy, such as CBT, may be more effective than either treatment alone for childhood anxiety disorders. In addition, for youth with co-occurring ADHD and disruptive behavior whose parents are participating in parent skills training, treating ADHD with medication may further reduce disruptive behavior. This may permit deprescribing of other medications that were prescribed for the disruptive behavior such as an antipsychotic that brings more risks of side-effects than stimulant medications.

In addition to knowing what prescribed medication a youth is taking for medical conditions, the clinician should ask about the use of over-the-counter medications, supplements, and vitamins. Increasingly youth are taking pills that could interact with psychotropic medications that it would behoove the clinician to be aware of. One approach is to have the parent or caretaker bring all medications they are administering to the child to the appointment so the clinician can carefully review the indication and potential interactions between prescribed and non-prescribed pills.

A return to some degree of defiance, aggression, or other problem behaviors in the context of a significant life stressor (e.g. parental rights termination), may not represent a loss of stability, but an expected variance within the case formulation. Once the youth is discontinued from those prescribed psychotropic medications that can be tapered, the clinician should remain available to the family as needed for support, should resumption or intensification of symptoms occur. It is best for the child to also continue in therapy for a period of time to ensure there is no relapse. If discontinuation of a medication is being prompted by abnormal lab values or concerning side-effects, the youth should be observed to see whether the side-effects have remitted following medication discontinuation, and/or follow-up laboratory studies should be completed to document normalization of any abnormal laboratory values. If normalization does not occur or there is active symptomatology the youth should be referred to the appropriate health care professional for treatment. In sum, deprescribing follows the best practice elements outlined by AACAP.

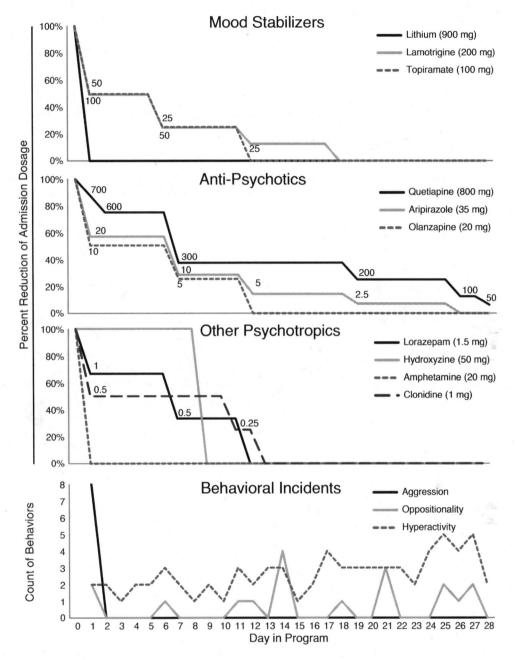

Figure 23.2 Psychotropic medication discontinuation and disruptive behavior for case example (with starting dosages and dosage reductions over time)

352   *Christopher Bellonci and Jonathan C. Huefner*

Case Example

Alexa*, a 16-year-old female was referred to a psychiatric residential treatment facility (PRTF) by the state director of a private insurance company. She was from a rural town where she was receiving care from a psychiatric advanced practice nurse (under the direction of a psychiatrist). During her admission interview she spent much of the time sleeping and noticeably drooled, and was concurrently on ten psychotropic medications and 12 additional medical medications. Prior to admission to the PRTF, her life-time psychotropic bill was approximately $275,000.

She was removed from her mother at eight months of age secondary to her mother's struggles with substance abuse resulting in severe neglect. After some back and forth between her biological mother and a foster family, Alexa was adopted. When Alexa was ten years old her family changed residences, moving from an urban to a rural setting, and Alexa began demonstrating significant problem behaviors. This included aggression toward her parents, combative interactions with classmates at school, threatening to kill her adoptive mother, stealing, running away, self-harm behavior (cutting her arms and clawing her face), running into traffic, and frequent police contact. By the time she was admitted to the PRTF she had been on psychotropic medications for five years, and her adoptive parents reported that it was "difficult to tell what medications were helping."

Alexa was diagnosed with an intermittent explosive disorder and oppositional defiant disorder by the PRTF's staff psychiatrist. She was only in the program for 28 days during which time she was taken off all but one of her ten psychotropic medications (see Figure 23.2), at which point her parents felt she was doing well and brought her home. Her attending psychiatrist observed that the increase in hyperactive behavior was probably a case of her gaining energy after coming off so many sedating medications. If she had remained in care a bit longer the plan was to discontinue the remaining medication. Six months after departure she was still being seen by one of the PRTF's psychiatrists, was doing well in school and at home, and was taking only one medication having successfully come off nine others.

Unfortunately, there are several barriers to deprescribing including inertia, family and managed care expectations, and knowledge gaps. Inertia includes discomfort with changing the status quo, fear of making problems worse, and not understanding when to consider deprescribing. Family and managed care frequently request adding medications as a perceived quick solution to emotional and behavioral problems.

Finally, the lack of deprescribing guidelines and protocols, combined with seeing psychotropic medications as a cure to emotional and behavioral problems, result in misunderstandings about the role of psychotropic medications in the treatment of troubled youth. Good medication practice is multifaceted and includes deprescribing.

Conclusion

The use of psychotropic medications for youth with emotional and behavioral disorders has increased exponentially over the last two decades. Research to support these practice trends remains sparse. While medications can be a great aid in the management of the symptoms of behavioral health disorders, they are not curative and can carry significant side-effects. Rarely should a medication be used for a child or adolescent without an accompanying therapy designed to teach the youth and their parents or caregivers new skills for managing the child or adolescent's condition. By learning new skills, the youth develops a sense of mastery that they can call upon should symptoms reemerge as they move through life. When medications are used, they should be thought of as an adjunct to effective treatment and rarely would they be the sole treatment or even the primary treatment intervention. Once the child and parent/caregiver learn the skills to manage their symptoms, deprescribing should be considered.

References

American Academy of Child & Adolescent Psychiatry. (2009). Practice parameter on the use of psychotropic medication in children and adolescents. *Journal of the American Academy of Child & Adolescent Psychiatry, 48*(9), 961–973. doi:10.1097/CHI.0b013e3181ae0a08

Ansermot, N., Jordanov, V., Smogur, M., Holzer, L., & Eap, C. B. (2018). Psychotropic drug prescription in adolescents: A retrospective study in a Swiss psychiatric university hospital. *Journal of Child and Adolescent Psychopharmacology, 28*(3), 192–204. doi:10.1089/cap.2017.0054

Bachmann, C. J., Aagaard, L., Burcu, M., Glaeske, G., Kalverdijk, L. J., Petersen, I., ... Hoffmann, F. (2016). Trends and patterns of antidepressant use in children and adolescents from five western countries, 2005–2012. *European Neuropsychopharmacology, 26*(3), 411–419. doi:10.1016/j.euroneuro.2016.02.001

Bachmann, C. J., Wijlaars, L. P., Kalverdijk, L. J., Burcu, M., Glaeske, G., Schuiling-Veniga, C. C. M., ... Zito, J. M. (2017). Trends in ADHD medication use in children and adolescents in five western countries, 2005–2012. *European Neuropsychopharmacology, 27*(5), 484–493. doi:10.1016/j.euroneuro.2017.03.002

Barnett, E. R., Butcher, R. L., Neubacher, K., Jankowski, M. K., Daviss, W. B., Carluzzo, K. L., ... Yackley, C. R. (2016). Psychotropic medications in child welfare: From federal mandate to direct care. *Children and Youth Services Review, 66*, 9–17. doi:10.1016/j.childyouth.2016.04.015

Bennett, K., Manassis, K., Duda, S., Bagnell, A., Bernstein, G. A., Garland, E. J., ... Wilansky, P. (2016). Treating child and adolescent anxiety effectively: Overview of systematic reviews. *Clinical Psychology Review, 50*, 80–94. doi:10.1016/j.cpr.2016.09.006

Birmaher, B., Brent, D., & AACAP Work Group on Quality Issues. (2007). Practice parameter for the assessment and treatment of children and adolescents with depressive disorders. *Journal of the American Academy of Child & Adolescent Psychiatry, 46*(11), 1503–1526. doi:10.1097/chi.0b013e318145ae1c

Bräuner, J. V., Johansen, L. M., Roesbjerg, T., & Pagsberg, A. K. (2016). Off-label prescription of psychopharmacological drugs in child and adolescent psychiatry. *Journal of Clinical Psychopharmacology, 36* (5), 500–507. doi:10.1097/JCP.0000000000000559

Catalá-López, F., Hutton, B., Núñez-Beltrán, A., Page, M. J., Ridao, M., Saint-Gerons, D. M., ... Moher, D. (2017). The pharmacological and non-pharmacological treatment of attention deficit hyperactivity disorder in children and adolescents: A systematic review with network meta-analyses of randomised trials. *PLoS ONE, 12*(7), e0180355. doi:10.1371/journal.pone.0180355

Chen, H., Patel, A., Sherer, J. T., & Aparasu, R. (2011). The definition and prevalence of pediatric psychotropic polypharmacy. *Psychiatric Services, 62*(12), 1450–1455. doi:10.1176/appi.ps.000642011

Comer, J. S., Olfson, M., & Mojtabai, R. (2010). National trends in child and adolescent psychotropic polypharmacy in office-based practice, 1996–2007. *Journal of the American Academy of Child & Adolescent Psychiatry, 49*(10), 1001–1010. doi:10.1016/j.jaac.2010.07.007

Connolly, S. D., Bernstein, G. A., & Workgroup on Quality Issues. (2007). Practice parameter for the assessment and treatment of children and adolescents with anxiety disorders. *Journal of the American Academy of Child & Adolescent Psychiatry, 46*(2), 267–283. doi:10.1097/01.chi.0000246070.23695.06

Correll, C. U., & Carlson, H. E. (2006). Endocrine and metabolic adverse effects of psychotropic medications in children and adolescents. *Journal of the American Academy of Child & Adolescent Psychiatry, 45*(7), 771–791. doi:10.1097/01.chi.0000220851.94392.30

Foxx, R. M. (1998). A comprehensive treatment program for inpatient adolescents. *Behavioral Interventions, 13*(1), 67–77.

Geller, D. A., March, J., & Workgroup on Quality Issues. (2012). Practice parameter for the assessment and treatment of children and adolescents with obsessive-compulsive disorder. *Journal of the American Academy of Child & Adolescent Psychiatry, 51*(1), 98–113. doi:10.1016/j.jaac.2011.09.019

Harrison, J. N., Cluxton-Keller, F., & Gross, D. (2012). Antipsychotic medication prescribing trends in children and adolescents. *Journal of Pediatric Health Care*, *26*(2), 139–145. doi:10.1016/j.pedhc.2011.10.009

Hincapie-Castillo, J. M., Liu, X., Bussing, R., & Winterstein, A. G. (2017). Prevalence of psychotherapy surrounding initiation of psychotropic polypharmacy in the medicaid-insured population, 1999–2010. *Psychiatric Services*, *68*(11), 1120–1126. doi:10.1176/appi.ps.201600511

Howie, L. D., Pastor, P. N., & Lukacs, S. L. (2014). *Use of medication prescribed for emotional or behavioral difficulties among children aged 6–17 years in the united states, 2011–2012*. (Vol. NCHS Data Brief, no. 148). Hyattsville, MD: National Center for Health Statistics.

Huefner, J. C., Griffith, A. K., Smith, G. L., Vollmer, D. G., & Leslie, L. K. (2014). Reducing psychotropic medications in an intensive residential treatment center. *Journal of Child and Family Studies*, *23*(4), 675–685. doi:10.1007/s10826-012-9628-7

Hurwitz, E. S. (1989). Reye's syndrome. *Epidemiologic Reviews*, *11*(1), 249–253. doi:10.1093/oxfordjournals.epirev.a036043

Jonas, B. S., Gu, Q., & Albertorio, D. J. R. (2013). *Psychotropic medication use among adolescents: United States, 2005–2010*. NCHS data brief, no. 135. Hyattsville, MD: National Center for Health Statistics.

Kalverdijk, L. J., Bachmann, C. J., Aagaard, L., Burcu, M., Glaeske, G., Hoffmann, F., … Zito, J. M. (2017). A multi-national comparison of antipsychotic drug use in children and adolescents, 2005–2012. *Child and Adolescent Psychiatry and Mental Health*, *11*(1), 55. doi:10.1186/s13034-017-0192-1

Kingsbury, S. J., Yi, D., & Simpson, G. M. (2001). Rational and irrational polypharmacy. *Psychiatric Services*, *52*(8), 1033–1035. doi:10.1176/appi.ps.52.8.1033

Kreider, A. R., Matone, M., Bellonci, C., dosReis, S., Feudtner, C., Huang, Y. S., … Rubin, D. M. (2014). Growth in the concurrent use of antipsychotics with other psychotropic medications in Medicaid-enrolled children. *Journal of the American Academy of Child & Adolescent Psychiatry*, *53*(9), 960–970. doi:10.1016/j.jaac.2014.05.010

Lyons, J. S., MacIntyre, J. C., Lee, M. E., Carpinello, S., Zuber, M. P., & Fazio, M. L. (2004). Psychotropic medications prescribing patterns for children and adolescents in New York's public mental health system. *Community Mental Health Journal*, *40*(2), 101–118. doi:10.1023/B:COMH.0000022731.65054.3e

Malik, S., & Azeem, M. W. (2017). Pediatric depression: The latest in diagnosis and treatment. *Psychiatric Annals*, *47*(10), 502–506. doi:10.3928/00485713-20170911-01

Matone, M., Zlotnik, S., Miller, D., Krelder, A., Rubin, D., & Noonan, K. (2015). *Psychotropic medication use by Pennsylvania children in foster care and enrolled in Medicaid: An analysis of children ages 3-18 years*. Philadelphia, PA: PolicyLab at The Children's Hospital of Philadelphia.

McIntyre, R. S., & Jerrell, J. M. (2009). Polypharmacy in children and adolescents treated for major depressive disorder: A claims database study. *Journal of Clinical Psychiatry*, *70*(2), 240–246. doi:10.4088/JCP.08m04212

McKay, M. (2007). Forced drugging of children in foster care: Turning child abuse victims into involuntary psychiatric patients. *Journal of Orthomolecular Medicine*, *22*(2), 63–74.

Mintz, D. L., & Flynn, D. F. (2012). How (not what) to prescribe: Nonpharmacologic aspects of psychopharmacology. *Psychiatric Clinics of North America*, *35*(1), 143–163. doi:10.1016/j.psc.2011.11.009

Mojtabai, R., & Olfson, M. (2010). National trends in psychotropic medication polypharmacy in office-based psychiatry. *Archives of General Psychiatry*, *67*(1), 26–36. doi:10.1001/archgenpsychiatry.2009.175

Olfson, M., Crystal, S., Huang, C., & Gerhard, T. (2010). Trends in antipsychotic drug use by very young, privately insured children. *Journal of the American Academy of Child & Adolescent Psychiatry*, *49*(1), 13–23. doi:10.1097/00004583-201001000-00005

Pliszka, S. & Workgroup on Quality Issues. (2007). Practice parameter for the assessment and treatment of children and adolescents with attention-deficit/hyperactivity disorder. *Journal of the American Academy of Child & Adolescent Psychiatry*, *46*(7), 894–921. doi:10.1097/chi.0b013e318054e724

Raghavan, R., Brown, D. S., Allaire, B. T., Garfield, L. D., Ross, R. E., & Snowden, L. R. (2014). Racial/ethnic differences in Medicaid expenditures on psychotropic medications among maltreated children. *Child Abuse & Neglect*, *38*, 1002–1010. doi:10.1016/j.chiabu.2014.02.013

Raman, S., Man, K. K. C., Bahmanyar, S., Berard, A., Bilder, S., Boukhris, T., ... Wong, I. C. K. (2018). Trends in attention-deficit hyperactivity disorder medication use: A retrospective observational study using population-based databases. *Lancet Psychiatry*, *5*(10), P824–835. doi:10.1016/S2215-0366(18)30293-1

Rhoades, L. J. (1982). Psychosocial intervention: A way out for chronic patients. *Hospital & Community Psychiatry*, *33*(9), 709–710.

Roberts, R., Rodriguez, R., Murphy, D., & Crescenzi, T. (2003). Pediatric drug labeling: Improving the safety and efficacy of pediatric therapies. *JAMA*, *290*(7), 905–911.

Rosenheck, R. (2005). The growth of psychopharmacology in the 1990s: Evidence-based practice or irrational exuberance. *International Journal of Law and Psychiatry*, *28*(5), 467–483.

Saldaña, S. N., Keeshin, B. R., Wehry, A. M., Blom, T. J., Sorter, M. T., DelBello, M. P., & Strawn, J. R. (2014). Antipsychotic polypharmacy in children and adolescents at discharge from psychiatric hospitalization. *Pharmacotherapy*, *34*(8), 836–844. doi:10.1002/phar.1453

Saucedo, R. S., Liu, X., Hincapie-Castillo, J. M., Zambrano, D., Bussing, R., & Winterstein, A. G. (2018). Prevalence, time trends, and utilization patterns of psychotropic polypharmacy among pediatric medicaid beneficiaries, 1999–2010. *Psychiatric Services*, *69*(8), 919–926. doi:10.1176/appi.ps.201700260

Scott, I. A., Hilmer, S., Reeve, E., Potter, K., Le Couteur, D., Rigby, D., ... Martin, J. H. (2015). Reducing inappropriate polypharmacy: The process of deprescribing. *JAMA Internal Medicine*, *175*(5), 827–834. doi:10.1001/jamainternmed.2015.0324

Sharma, A. N., Arango, C., Coghill, D., Gringras, P., Nutt, D. J., Pratt, P., ... Hollis, C. (2016). BAP position statement: Off-label prescribing of psychotropic medication to children and adolescents. *Journal of Psychopharmacology*, *30*(5), 416–421. doi:10.1177/0269881116636107

Singh, M. K., & Chang, K. D. (2012). The neural effects of psychotropic medications in children and adolescents. *Child and Adolescent Psychiatric Clinics of North America*, *21*(4), 753–771. doi:10.1016/j.chc.2012.07.010

Tishler, C. L., & Reiss, N. S. (2012). Psychotropic drugs and paediatrics: A critical need for more clinical trials. *Journal of Medical Ethics*, *38*(4), 250–252.

Vitiello, B. (2007). Research in child and adolescent psychopharmacology: Recent accomplishments and new challenges. *Psychopharmacology*, *191*(1), 5–13. doi:10.1007/s00213-006-0414-3

Walkup, J. (2009). Practice parameter on the use of psychotropic medication in children and adolescents. *Journal of the American Academy of Child & Adolescent Psychiatry*, *48*(9), 961–973. doi:10.1097/CHI.0b013e3181ae0a08

Zito, J. M., Safer, D. J., van den Berg, L. T. W. d., Janhsen, K., Fegert, J. M., Gardner, J. F., ... Valluri, S. C. (2008). A three-country comparison of psychotropic medication prevalence in youth. *Child and Adolescent Psychiatry and Mental Health*, *2*(26). doi:10.1186/1753-2000-2-26

24 The Homework, Organization, and Planning Skills (HOPS) Intervention

Joshua M. Langberg, Rosanna Breaux, Melissa R. Dvorsky, Stephen J. Molitor, Zoe R. Smith, and Elizaveta Bourchtein

Homework, Organization, Time-Management, and Planning (OTMP) Deficits and ADHD

Attention-deficit/hyperactivity disorder (ADHD) is one of the most prevalent neurodevelopmental disorders of childhood, and symptoms and impairment frequently persist into adolescence (Biederman, Petty, Evans, Small, & Faraone, 2010; Visser et al., 2014). The core symptoms of ADHD include developmentally inappropriate levels of inattention, hyperactivity, and impulsivity. In addition, the disorder is often associated with deficits in organization, time management, and planning (OTMP) skills (American Psychiatric Association, 2013). OTMP skills are considered part of a broader set of cognitive abilities known as executive functions (EF; Pennington & Ozonoff, 1996). Many of the leading theoretical models link the core symptoms of ADHD with EF deficits, which may explain the high frequency of OTMP difficulties for youth with the disorder (Barkley, 1997; Sonuga-Barke, 2005). EF abilities develop continuously throughout childhood and are not considered fully mature until young adulthood (Anderson, 2002; Blakemore & Choudhury, 2006). Further, OTMP skills are developed after some of the more basic aspects of EF (e.g., working memory), with typically developing youth making significant strides in OTMP abilities during adolescence (Anderson, 2002; Luciana, Collins, Olson, & Schissel, 2009). Notably, EF and OTMP deficits are not universal for individuals with ADHD, and OTMP deficits are not solely indicative of an ADHD diagnosis (Molitor, Oddo, Eadeh, & Langberg, 2018; Willcutt, Doyle, Nigg, Faraone, & Pennington, 2005). However, difficulties with organization and planning are one of the more persistent aspects of the disorder and individuals who continue to exhibit symptoms of ADHD into adulthood also endorse significant difficulties with OTMP skills (Erhardt, Epstein, Conners, Parker, & Sitarenios, 1999). Therefore, it is important to understand how OTMP deficits relate to the long-term functional outcomes of youth with ADHD.

For students with ADHD, OTMP deficits frequently lead to impairment in academic functioning. Perhaps one of the most salient OTMP skills deficits is the management of personal belongings. Youth with ADHD often lose school materials such as writing utensils, home–school notes, and homework assignments (Power et al., 2006). They are also likely to forget to bring necessary materials to class or to their homes or after-school programs to complete assignments. Additionally, they frequently have trouble keeping track of their assigned work, including daily assignments and upcoming exams or project deadlines (Langberg, Epstein, Becker, Girio-Herrera, & Vaughn, 2012). Other aspects of OTMP deficits are more difficult to observe, but are impairing nonetheless. For example, youth with ADHD often have trouble estimating the amount of time needed to complete an assignment, usually underestimating the amount of time actually needed (Barkley, Murphy, & Bush, 2001). This can be especially problematic for the completion of long-term, multi-step assignments or projects. Finally, youth with ADHD frequently have difficulty developing an efficient plan to complete assignments. For daily assignment completion, planning deficits may result in students using out-of-school time inefficiently, leading to late nights and reduced sleep duration in order to complete homework or to a failure to complete work (Niermann & Scheres, 2014). In summary, OTMP deficits interfere with the completion of school assignments, which in turn is likely to lead to penalties for late assignment completion, failure to complete some assignments altogether, and ultimately lower grades in school (Langberg et al., 2016; Langberg, Dvorsky, & Evans, 2013).

The impact of OTMP deficits is perhaps most notable as students transition from elementary school into middle school (Jacobson, Williford, & Pianta, 2011). During this transition, several changes occur that place increased demands on OTMP skills. For example, individual subjects are typically taught by different instructors rather than a single core teacher. Homework expectations and deadlines may vary between instructors and more complex, multi-step assignments (e.g., studying for exams, completing long-term projects) become more common. At the same time, students are required to keep track of school materials across multiple locations (e.g., classrooms, locker or backpack, home and school). These increased demands on OTMP skills occur around the same time that youth typically experience marked growth in their EF abilities (Anderson, Anderson, Northam, Jacobs, & Catroppa, 2001). However, youth with ADHD often experience delayed development of these abilities, and many do not fully catch up to their typically developing peers (Halperin, Trampush, Miller, Marks, & Newcorn, 2008; Shaw et al., 2007).

Given these strong theoretical connections, it is not surprising that a growing body of evidence now highlights the detrimental effects OTMP deficits can have on the academic functioning of students with ADHD, especially during adolescence. In a recent longitudinal study, middle school students (grades 6–8) with ADHD were found to turn in an average of 12% fewer assignments than the overall classroom average, and baseline levels of homework completion predicted student grades 18 months later even after accounting for students' general intelligence and academic achievement abilities (Langberg et al., 2016). Further, parent ratings of their child's OTMP skills were predictive of homework completion 18 months later. Similar associations between homework completion and student grades have been observed throughout high school and college (Kent et al., 2011; Weyandt et al., 2013). Together, these findings demonstrate clear links between OTMP skills and academic functioning, as well as the need for additional support in developing these skills among students with ADHD.

Development of the HOPS Intervention

Given the importance of OTMP skills for the academic performance of youth with ADHD, the Homework, Organization, and Planning Skills (HOPS) intervention was developed. HOPS was initially developed and evaluated for delivery through an eight-week after-school program (16 meetings total; Langberg, Epstein, Urbanowicz, Simon, & Graham, 2008) with two, one-hour parent meetings. However, feedback from school providers and school administration suggested that from a cost and feasibility perspective, HOPS needed to be delivered during the school day to increase the potential for widespread dissemination and implementation.

Based upon this stakeholder feedback (Langberg, 2011), HOPS was reduced to consist of bi-weekly, 20-minute meetings delivered by school mental health providers (SMHP) during the school day over eight weeks (16 meetings total). To increase the potential for students to fully learn to self-manage their new OTMP systems, the intervention was spread out across

358   Joshua M. Langberg et al.

11 weeks. Initially, meetings are twice per week and then at week 11, meeting frequency changes to once per week to place more self-management responsibility with the student. In addition, to further bolster the dissemination/implementation potential, the manual for SMHP included checklists, example scripts, and brief but specific session-by-session instructions. The goal was for SMHP to be able to implement HOPS with minimal or no training and with no on-going supervision or consultation.

The HOPS treatment manual outlines multiple service delivery models, including individual, small group, and class-wide. Struggles with OTMP skills and balancing responsibilities in middle and high school is not unique to students with ADHD. In fact, to some extent, it is normative for students to struggle with staying organized with their materials, managing their time, writing down assignments, and studying effectively following the transition to middle school (Jacobson, Williford, & Pianta, 2011). As such, many schools are interested in providing structure and support surrounding OTMP skills more broadly. Teaching OTMP skills to all students fits well within a tiered Response to Intervention (RTI) service delivery model. Such a model would begin with setting clear school-wide expectations for OTMP skills and would include a system for monitoring skills use. This would be followed by small group (e.g., $n = 8$) and individualized (1:1) intervention models for students who need additional support. These models are briefly discussed below.

Tier 1 – School-Wide HOPS

The HOPS program is based upon the core principles of behavioral intervention. As with all behavioral interventions, the first step is specifically defining target behavior(s) and setting clear expectations. This step is the foundation for monitoring and tracking student progress and setting realistic goals. Tier 1 HOPS uses the same types of organization and time-management checklists also used in the individual model in order to provide operationalized definitions of OTMP behaviors that can be readily tracked by teachers in a "yes/no" fashion. For feasibility reasons, there are fewer OTMP criteria on the Tier 1 checklists than with small group or individual. The foundation of Tier 1 HOPS is having a specific system for materials organization, homework recording, and planning that is recommended to students. Specifically, all students are expected to bring their school binders to class each day. In addition, all students are given a homework folder and instructed that homework to be completed always goes on the left side and homework to be turned in to the teacher goes on the right side. Only homework materials go in that folder and all other papers get filed in the class sections of the binder (e.g., math section). Teachers also need to be clear about what homework and assignment/exam planning tasks should be recorded and why, and then gradually remove this support to allow students to take more responsibility.

One important benefit of a HOPS Tier 1 model is that students regularly hear discussions about how their peers are recording homework and planning to study for upcoming tests. Twice per week, a four-item checklist is completed to monitor student use of OTMP skills. For feasibility reasons, a peer model is used, and students' pair up and evaluate each other's systems while the teacher observes. Classroom average OTMP checklist scores are calculated weekly and prizes are given to the class with the highest average. Some schools complete the checklists and track points during homeroom period, others use study halls, and others have outside staff such as counselors facilitate checklist completion in core classes. One of the main benefits of a Tier 1 approach is that a consistent system of OTMP measurement is in place. If a student is not meeting expectations (e.g., >90% mastery of organization skills on the checklist and turning in >90% of homework assignments), a referral can be made for Tier 2 HOPS.

Tier 2 – Small Group HOPS

The small group model is very similar to the individual model that is described in detail in the next section with three exceptions. First, the curriculum is delivered with groups of eight to ten students rather than individually. Second, there are no parent meetings. Third, meetings with students are scheduled for 30 minutes instead of 20 minutes to allow sufficient time to complete the checklists of all group members and acknowledging that behavioral management challenges may slow the pace of instruction. Although seemingly minor, these are important differences from a cost effectiveness and feasibility of implementation perspective. As with the individual model, initially meetings are twice per week and halfway through the intervention move to once per week. As such, the entire intervention is completed in 11 weeks. The HOPS organization and time-management checklists are completed at every meeting. Group contingencies are attached to the scores on the checklists. For example, if everyone in the group scores 90% or higher on the organizational skills checklists, then a reward may be provided (e.g., food during the meeting). However, unlike Tier 3, these rewards are all at the group level rather than individualized. The groups can be run by a single SMHP but ideally, a teacher or student (e.g., a student who does well with OTMP skills in a higher grade) assists. Typically, HOPS small groups are run within grade level (e.g., all sixth graders) as expectations and abilities regarding OTMP may vary substantially across middle school grades.

Tier 3 – Individual Implementation of HOPS

The individual model of HOPS is designed for students who have a history of significant homework problems due to OTMP deficits. Research on this model has focused on middle school students with ADHD and significant homework problems. In this model, adolescents are pulled from their regularly scheduled classes to complete the intervention; traditionally students have been pulled from electives. A summary of session content is provided Table 24.1; here we provide a general description of session content and order. The goal of the HOPS intervention is to develop or further enhance three skills: (1) organization and management of school materials, (2) accurate recording of assignments and projects, and (3) development of daily and long-term plans to complete assignments and projects and study for tests (Langberg et al., 2018). These skills are introduced sequentially, beginning with materials organization and ending with planning skills, with skills introduction complete by the tenth session.

When learning materials organization skills, students are introduced to a specific organizational system for their backpack, binder, and locker. Students also learn a system for transitioning all necessary school materials to and from school and develop a strategy for consistently monitoring their adherence to the organizational system. When learning assignment recording skills, students are introduced to the use of a daily planner for tracking all relevant schoolwork (e.g., assignment due dates, upcoming exams). When planning skills are introduced, students learn how to break larger tasks, such as long-term projects or studying for an exam, into a series of smaller steps that can then be incorporated into their assignment recording system. They also learn how to develop a schedule for the completion of assignments in the context of their other after-school activities (e.g., extracurricular activities, family events). After all skills are introduced, the remainder of the intervention focuses on helping students troubleshoot difficulties with their organization and planning systems and on developing a self-management system to maintain skills use after the intervention concludes.

Table 24.1 HOPS Session Components

Session Number	Session Components
1	• Introduce the purpose of the HOPS intervention • Assess current material organization system • Collaborate with student to develop rewards menu
2	• Introduce binder/bookbag organization system • Facilitate transfer of materials to new organization system • Assess current homework recording strategies and accuracy
3	• Continue setting-up binder/bookbag organization systems • Introduce new strategies for accurate homework recording • Introduce HOPS reward system, including point tracking sheet
4–6	• Finish setting-up binder/bookbag organization systems • Continue teaching strategies for accurate homework recording • Troubleshoot and problem solve difficulties with implementation • Adjust goals and rewards menu as needed • Prepare for parent meeting [Session 5 only]
Parent 1	• Brief overview of HOPS • Provide summary of skills taught to date and student progress • Introduce abbreviated checklists for parent to complete • Establish feasible monitoring schedule
7	• Continue using checklists to monitor organization and homework recording • Track points earned and provide rewards based upon menu • Introduce time management skills; preparing for tests and quizzes • Practice test/quiz recording/planning
8	• Continue using checklists to monitor organization and homework recording • Track points earned and provide rewards based upon menu • Review tests and quizzes time-management strategies • Introduce planning for long-term projects
9	• Continue using checklists to monitor organization, homework, and time-management skills • Track points earned and provide rewards based upon menu • Introduce using an evening schedule to accurately estimate time and balance school and extracurricular responsibilities
10	• Continue using checklists to monitor organization, homework, and time-management skills • Track points earned and provide rewards based upon menu • Review utility and accuracy of initial evening schedule and complete new evening schedule
11	• Continue using checklists to monitor organization, homework, and time-management skills • Track points earned and provide rewards based upon menu • Revisit organization and accurate homework recording systems and make adjustments as necessary
12	• Continue using checklists to monitor organization, homework, and time-management skills • Track points earned and provide rewards based upon menu • Introduce self-management checklist and develop self-monitoring plan
13	• Continue using checklists to monitor organization, homework, and time-management skills • Track points earned and provide rewards based upon menu

(*Continued*)

Table 24.1 (Cont.)

Session Number	Session Components
	• Review effectiveness of the self-monitoring plan and make adjustments
	• Prepare for parent meeting
Parent 2	• Review student progress
	• Review progress with parent monitoring of organization and accurate homework recording and make adjustments
	• Establish home-based rewards menu
14	• Continue using checklists to monitor organization, homework, and time-management skills
	• Track points earned and provide rewards based upon menu
	• Review effectiveness of the self-monitoring plan and make adjustments
	• Review parent meeting and implementation of home-based rewards
15	• Continue using checklists to monitor organization, homework, and time-management skills
	• Track points earned and provide rewards based upon menu
	• Review effectiveness of the self-monitoring plan and make adjustments
	• Review implementation of home-based rewards system
16	• Celebrate progress, including completion of fun activity (e.g., game)

The individual model of HOPS includes a behavioral reward system to reinforce students' use of the newly learned organizational skills. Each session, SMH providers monitor students' use of skills using a set of intervention checklists. Students earn a point for each criterion where they earn a "yes", such as keeping all homework assignments in a designated homework folder or for accurately recording their assignments from each class during the previous day. During the two parent meetings, parents learn how to use abbreviated checklists and to take over the points and rewards system.

The first parent meeting focuses on introducing OTMP skills monitoring to parents in order to increase generalization to the home setting. Parents are encouraged to bring their adolescents to the meetings in order for the SMHP to facilitate a family conversation regarding organization and homework. When adolescents are able to attend the parent meetings, they are prompted to teach the skills they are learning to their parents. Parents also learn how OTMP skills are being monitored by the SMHP using checklists and develop strategies to monitor their adolescent's skill use at home. The first parent meeting happens early in the intervention around session 5 or 6. The second parent meeting focuses on troubleshooting the behavior monitoring system parents developed during the first meeting and on implementing a home-based reward system.

Evidence Supporting the Efficacy of the HOPS Intervention

The seven published empirical studies focusing on the HOPS intervention are summarized in Table 24.2. All of the studies used multi-informant (parent, teacher) report and objective (assignment completion, GPA) outcome measures to evaluate efficacy of the HOPS program. Together, these studies support that the HOPS intervention significantly improves parent- and teacher-reported organization and homework management skills (Homework Performance Questionnaire, Homework Problems Checklist, Academic Performance Rating Scale,

Table 24.2 Efficacy Studies of the HOPS Intervention

Reference	Study Type	Implementation Model	Sample (% male, % White, grades)	Follow-up	Primary Findings
Langberg et al. (2008)	Pilot RCT	Small group HOPS implemented as an afterschool program	$N = 37$ $N = 24$ HOPS $N = 13$ WLC (84% male; 70% White), grades 4–7	Immediate, post, and 8-week follow-up	• Significant improvements in organization and homework management skills • Moderate improvements in parent-reported homework problems ($d = .71$) • Small decrease in teacher-reported academic impairment ($d = .28$) and small/negligible improvements in GPA ($d = .18$) • Gains maintained at 8-week follow-up
Langberg et al. (2012)	Open trial (no control group)	1:1 model, implemented by SMHPs, during school	$N = 11$ (90% male; 60% White); grades 6–8	Immediate and post	• Large improvements in parent-rated organization skills ($d = 1.8$) and homework problems ($d = 1.6$) • No improvements on teacher ratings • SMHP implemented HOPS with fidelity (90%) despite no formal ongoing consultation • Qualitative results from focus groups across 3 districts and 10 SMHPs used to refine HOPS intervention
Langberg et al. (2012)	RCT of HOPS	1:1 model, implemented by SMHPs, during school	$N = 47$ $N = 23$ HOPS $N = 24$ WLC (76% male; 72% White), grades 6–8	Immediate, post, and 3-month follow-up	• Large improvements in parent-rated organized action ($d = .88$), planning ($d = 1.05$), and homework completion behaviors ($d = .85$). • No improvements on teacher ratings

					• Moderate to large improvement in GPA (ds from .69 to .82)
					• SMHP implemented HOPS with fidelity (91%) despite no formal ongoing consultation provided
Langberg, Becker, Epstein, Vaughn, & Girio-Herrera (2013)	Predictors of treatment response	1:1 model, implemented by SMHPs during school day	$N = 23$[a] (74% male; 78% White), grades 6–8	Immediate and post	• Students who obtained teacher initials in planner demonstrated large improvements in organization skills (β = .36–.54, ps < .05)
					• Student implementation of the HOPS binder materials organizational system and student-rated therapeutic alliance predicted gains in homework behaviors and organization
					• Adoption of the HOPS binder system predict parent-rated academic improvements above and beyond the therapeutic alliance (β = .42–.60, ps < .05)
Langberg et al. (2018)	RCT with active comparison and WLC groups	1:1 model, implemented by SMHPs during school day	$N = 280$ $N = 111$ HOPS $N = 115$ CHIEF $N = 52$ WLC (72% male, 54% White), grades 6–8)	Immediate, post, and 6-month follow-up	• Large improvements in parent-rated homework completion behaviors (ds = .87–1.29)
					• Large gains in parent- rated organization (ds =. 79–1.14) and moderate gains in teacher-rated organization (ds = .53–.55)
					• For students who received HOPS, GPA improved slightly (2.15 to 2.33)
					• Homework and organization improvements were sustained at follow-up
					• Students with higher behavior severity that received HOPS had significantly fewer homework and organization problems at post-intervention

(*Continued*)

Table 24.2 (Cont.)

Reference	Study Type	Implementation Model	Sample (% male, % White, grades)	Follow-up	Primary Findings
Breaux et al. (2018)	Mechanisms of treatment response	1:1 model, implemented by SMHPs during school day	$N = 222$[b] $N = 111$ HOPS $N = 111$ CHIEF (72% male; 54% White), grades 6–8)	Immediate and post	• SMHP implemented HOPS with fidelity (85%) despite no formal ongoing consultation • SMHP-rated working alliance and adolescent involvement were the strongest predictors of treatment gains in teacher-rated homework and grades • Parent attendance, parent involvement, and parent commitment to homework plan were *ns* after controlling for the effects of other therapeutic processes
Breaux et al. (2018)	Predictors of treatment response and trajectories of organization skills	1:1 model, implemented by SMHPs during school day	$N = 111$[b] (72% male; 54% White), grades 6–8	Immediate, post, and trajectories of skill acquisition	• Accurate homework recording and time management skills were unique predictors of parent-reported homework and organizational skills outcomes • Parent-reported use of monitoring and contingencies to support adolescent skills implementation was not associated with outcomes. • All participants showed rapid improvement in organizational skills across the first two weeks of intervention • The majority (75%) of participants increased on homework recording; however, the remainder showed decreases in homework recording

					• 68% of participants displayed high acquisition of both organizational and homework recording skills
Breaux et al. (2018)	Predictors of treatment response trajectories	1:1 model, implemented by SMHPs during school day	$N = 111$[b] (72% male; 54% White), grades 6–8	Immediate, post, and trajectories of skill acquisition	• The majority (68–81% across outcomes) of participants displayed a significant and positive response according to both parent and teacher ratings of academic functioning as well as percentage of assignments turned-in
					• Students with ADHD and severe academic impairment (i.e., GPA lower than 2.0 at baseline) are less likely to respond to brief homework interventions, and may require more intensive interventions to address homework problems and academic impairment

Note. WLC = Waitlist control group. 1:1 = one-on-one or individual implementation. SMHP = school mental health providers. HI = hyperactivity/impulsivity symptoms. ODD = Oppositional defiant disorder symptoms. ns = non significant. [a] This is a follow-up study to the (Langberg et al., 2012) RCT that examined predictors of response within the subsample that received the HOPS intervention. [b] These are follow-up studies to the (Langberg et al., 2018) RCT, which examined predictors of response within the subsample that received HOPS.

366   *Joshua M. Langberg et al.*

Children's Organizational Skills Scale) and student grades post-intervention, and that gains are maintained at short-term (8 weeks) and moderate-term (3 and 6 months) follow-up. Results also suggest that the majority of students who complete HOPS improve on intervention-specific skills and on global measures of homework performance.

To date, there have been seven empirical studies published on the HOPS intervention, reporting results from four distinct intervention trials. The 1:1 implementation model of the HOPS intervention has been evaluated in one open trial (no control group; Langberg, 2011) and two randomized controlled trials (RCTs; Langberg et al., 2012, 2018). Small group HOPS has been evaluated in one small RCT (Langberg et al., 2008), with the groups implemented in an after-school program. In addition, there have been five studies evaluating predictors of response to the HOPS intervention (Breaux, Langberg, Bourchtein, et al., 2018; Breaux, Langberg, McLeod, et al., 2018; Breaux, Langberg, Molitor, et al., 2018; Langberg, Becker et al., 2013; Langberg et al., 2018).

Implementation

In the majority of studies with HOPS, the intervention implementation conditions were realistic, with SMHPs implementing the interventions during the school day. Studies suggest that HOPS can be implemented with high fidelity: approximately 85% overall adherence to the student meetings, and 93% overall adherence across parent meetings. Additionally, studies have found high attendance rates for adolescents (92% of participants attending all 16 sessions) and parents (87% of parents attending both parent meetings). Follow-up data also show that a majority of parents monitor adolescent skill use and provide contingencies at home on a regular and consistent basis.

Main Outcomes

Across all of the studies completed to date, students have uniformly made large gains in binder, bookbag, and locker organization according to the checklists and have recorded more homework assignments accurately and in sufficient detail. In addition, across all studies, parent ratings of homework, organization, and planning skills have shown large and significant improvements (average Cohen's *d* effect size approximately .8 to 1.3). Importantly, improvements on the checklists and parent ratings have been sustained at follow-up assessments (Langberg et al., 2018). Further, multiple studies have demonstrated improvement or significant group differences in GPA, with small to moderate effect sizes (Langberg et al., 2008, 2012, 2018). Consistent with other studies focused on adolescents with ADHD, participant improvement as evaluated by teachers was not as large as improvement rated by parents (e.g., Evans et al., 2016; Sibley et al., 2016).

Trajectory analyses suggest that the majority of students (68–81%) displayed a significant positive treatment response across outcomes (parent- and teacher-reported homework performance, parent-reported homework problems, and assignment completion). Promisingly, these positive response trajectories are similar to those found in more intensive, long-term interventions (e.g., Evans et al., 2005; Swanson et al., 2007). However, for each outcome, groups of students were identified who did not respond (19–32%) or who had a poor response (12–18%).

Predictors of Treatment Response

Recent studies of the HOPS intervention have focused on more closely evaluating treatment response, including the evaluation of who responds well and what factors predict response.

These studies have examined therapeutic processes (i.e., working alliance, parent engagement, and youth involvement; Breaux et al., 2018) and skill acquisition (i.e., adolescent performance on checklists targeting materials organization, homework recording, and time management skills; parent monitoring and reinforcement of adolescent key skill behaviors; Breaux et al., 2018) in understanding response to the HOPS intervention.

Examination of the trajectories of skill acquisition suggest that all HOPS participants make rapid gains in organizational skills across the first two weeks of the intervention, with trajectories being differentiated by level of skill acquisition: "high acquisition" group (76.4% of participants), "moderate acquisition" group (16.5% of participants), and "low acquisition" group (18.1% of participants). Individuals in the high acquisition group had significantly fewer homework and organization, planning, and time management problems and a higher GPA post-intervention. In contrast, while the majority of students steadily improved on their homework recording accuracy throughout the course of the intervention ("adopters"; 71.3% of participants), a group of "non-responders" was identified who decreased in homework recording throughout the course of the intervention (28.7% of participants). Not surprisingly, adopters had significantly better homework performance; significantly less organization, planning, and time management problems; and significantly higher GPA post-intervention. Findings suggest that the skills that are most important for treatment outcomes depend upon the perspective of the rater and the outcome of interest. As such, a modular approach might be valuable for implementing the HOPS intervention. Specifically, rather than implementing HOPS as a package, SMHP could use assessment using the Homework Completion Cycle (Langberg et al., 2018) to determine which OTMP skills are most problematic and where to focus intervention efforts.

GPA and academic achievement proved to be the strongest predictors of treatment response across outcomes (i.e., differentiating responders from non-responders or poor responders; Breaux et al., 2018). Findings suggest that schools could realistically use data from students' academic records to determine whether brief school-based interventions for homework problems like HOPS are likely to succeed or whether a more intensive intervention is warranted. Specifically, results suggested that students with ADHD who display severe academic impairment (i.e., GPA lower than 2.0 at baseline) may benefit from a more long-term, intensive intervention. Identification of potential responders prior to beginning an intervention may help streamline use of limited time and resources.

Implications for Schools

The basic premise behind the HOPS intervention is that students are most likely to be successful when schools clearly define what it means to record homework accurately, plan for tests and projects, and keep materials organized, and consistently monitor student progress. The most important component of the HOPS intervention is the checklists, which clearly define homework, organization, and time-management for students, parents, and teachers. Using these checklists, the HOPS intervention can be delivered using a variety of models (e.g., school-wide, small group, individual) and by a variety of providers (e.g., teachers, counselors, psychologists), as long as skills implementation is monitored consistently.

Another important aspect of the HOPS intervention is the use of a reward system to help motivate students to implement the skills and strategies. It is important to note that not all students will need a rewards system. Schools may find it helpful to clearly define and monitor homework, organization, and time-management skills for all students, similar to how they develop benchmarks and monitor progress with math and reading. For many students, simply defining what it means to be organized and monitoring progress will be sufficient to motivate them to consistently utilize the skills and strategies. However, for other groups of students, such as students with ADHD, linking the checklists to points and rewards menus will be important. This is because for some students, homework completion is a negative process, which is associated with a history of perceived failures. Unfortunately, because of this history, some students are not motivated to try to learn new skills and strategies, as they believe they will just fail. In these cases, setting realistic and achievable goals and linking the HOPS checklists to a rewards menu is important to help motivate students.

Conclusions

The HOPS program is a brief intervention that targets homework, organization, and planning skills. The intervention can be implemented by SMH providers as a Tier 1, 2, or 3 intervention. The majority of empirical evidence supporting the HOPS intervention is for the individual Tier 3 model as implemented with students with ADHD. Importantly, in this model fidelity for administration of the HOPS intervention is high, even with limited training and no ongoing supervision. The HOPS intervention significantly improves parent- and teacher-reported organization and homework management skills and gains are maintained at short-term (8 week) and moderate-term (3 and 6 month) follow-up. Additionally, response trajectories are favorable for the majority of participants (68–81% depending on outcome), with trajectories being consistent with more long-term, intensive OTMP interventions.

Author Note

This research was supported by grants from the U.S. Department of Education, Institute for Education Sciences (R305A130011; R305A100996). The opinions expressed by the authors are not necessarily reflective of the position of or endorsed by the U.S. Department of Education.

References

American Psychiatric Association. (2013). *Diagnostic and statistical manual of mental disorders* (5th ed.). Retrieved from https://doi.org/10.1176/appi.books.9780890425596

Anderson, P. (2002). Assessment and development of executive function (EF) during childhood. *Child Neuropsychology, 8*(2), 71–82.

Anderson, V. A., Anderson, P., Northam, E., Jacobs, R., & Catroppa, C. (2001). Development of executive functions through late childhood and adolescence in an Australian sample. *Developmental Neuropsychology, 20*(1), 385–406.

Barkley, R. A. (1997). Behavioral inhibition, sustained attention, and executive functions: Constructing a unifying theory of ADHD. *Psychological Bulletin, 121*(1), 65.

Barkley, R. A., Murphy, K. R., & Bush, T. (2001). Time perception and reproduction in young adults with attention deficit hyperactivity disorder. *Neuropsychology, 15*(3), 351.

Biederman, J., Petty, C. R., Evans, M., Small, J., & Faraone, S. V. (2010). How persistent is ADHD? A controlled 10-year follow-up study of boys with ADHD. *Psychiatry Research, 177*(3), 299–304.

Blakemore, S. J., & Choudhury, S. (2006). Development of the adolescent brain: Implications for executive function and social cognition. *Journal of Child Psychology and Psychiatry, 47*(3–4), 296–312.

Breaux, R. P., Langberg, J. M., Bourchtein, E., Eadeh, H. M., Molitor, S. J., & Smith, Z. R. (2018). Brief homework interventions for adolescents with ADHD: Trajectories and predictors of response. *School Psychology Quarterly, 34*(2), 201–211. doi:10.1037/spq0000287

Breaux, R. P., Langberg, J. M., McLeod, B., Molitor, S. J., Smith, Z. R., Bourchtein, E., & Green, C. D. (2018). The importance of therapeutic processes in school-based psychosocial treatment of homework problems in adolescents with ADHD. *Journal of Consulting and Clinical Psychology, 86*, 427–438. doi:10.1037/ccp0000300

Breaux, R. P., Langberg, J. M., Molitor, S. J., Dvorsky, M. R., Bourchtein, E., Smith, Z. R., & Green, C. D. (2018). Predictors and trajectories of response to the Homework, Organization, and Planning Skills (HOPS) intervention for adolescents with ADHD. *Behavior Therapy, 50*(1), 140–154. doi:10.1016/j.beth.2018.04.001

Erhardt, D., Epstein, J. N., Conners, C. K., Parker, J. D. A., & Sitarenios, G. (1999). Self-ratings of ADHD symptomas in auts II: Reliability, validity, and diagnostic sensitivity. *Journal of Attention Disorders, 3*(3), 153–158.

Evans, S. W., Langberg, J., Raggi, V., Allen, J., & Buvinger, E. C. (2005). Development of a school-based treatment program for middle school youth with ADHD. *Journal of Attention Disorders, 9*, 343–353. doi:10.1177/108705470527930

Evans, S. W., Langberg, J. M., Schultz, B. K., Vaughn, A., Altaye, M., Marshall, S. A. & Zoromski, A. K. (2016). Evaluation of a school-based treatment program for young adolescents with ADHD. *Journal of Consulting and Clinical Psychology, 84*(1), 15–30. doi:10.1037/ccp0000057

Halperin, J. M., Trampush, J. W., Miller, C. J., Marks, D. J., & Newcorn, J. H. (2008). Neuropsychological outcome in adolescents/young adults with childhood ADHD: Profiles of persisters, remitters and controls. *Journal of Child Psychology and Psychiatry, 49*(9), 958–966.

Jacobson, L. A., Williford, A. P., & Pianta, R. C. (2011). The role of executive function in children's competent adjustment to middle school. *Child Neuropsychology, 17*(3), 255–280.

Kent, K. M., Pelham, W. E., Molina, B. S., Sibley, M. H., Waschbusch, D. A., Yu, J., … Karch, K. M. (2011). The academic experience of male high school students with ADHD. *Journal of Abnormal Child Psychology, 39*(3), 451–462.

Langberg, J. M. (2011). *Homework, Organization, and Planning Skills (HOPS) interventions: A treatment manual.* Bethesda, MD: National Association of School Psychologists.

Langberg, J. M., Becker, S. P., Epstein, J. N., Vaughn, A. J., & Girio-Herrera, E. (2013). Predictors of response and mechanisms of change in an organizational skills intervention for students with ADHD. *Journal of Child and Family Studies, 22*(7), 1000–1012.

Langberg, J. M., Dvorsky, M. R., & Evans, S. W. (2013). What specific facets of executive function are associated with academic functioning in youth with attention-deficit/hyperactivity disorder?. *Journal of Abnormal Child Psychology, 41*(7), 1145–1159.

Langberg, J. M., Dvorsky, M. R., Molitor, S. J., Bourchtein, E., Eddy, L. D., Smith, Z., … Evans, S. W. (2016). Longitudinal evaluation of the importance of homework assignment completion for the academic performance of middle school students with ADHD. *Journal of School Psychology, 55*, 27–38.

Langberg, J. M., Dvorsky, M. R., Molitor, S. J., Bourchtein, E., Eddy, L. D., Smith, Z. R., … Eadeh, H. M. (2018). Overcoming the research-to-practice gap: A randomized trial with two brief homework and organization interventions for students with ADHD as implemented by school mental health providers. *Journal of Consulting and Clinical Psychology, 86*(1), 39–55. doi:10.1037/ccp0000265

Langberg, J. M., Epstein, J. N., Becker, S. P., Girio-Herrera, E., & Vaughn, A. J. (2012). Evaluation of the Homework, Organization, and Planning Skills (HOPS) intervention for middle school students with ADHD as implemented by school mental health providers. *School Psychology Review, 41*(3), 342–364.

Langberg, J. M., Epstein, J. N., Urbanowicz, C. M., Simon, J. O., & Graham, A. J. (2008). Efficacy of an organization skills intervention to improve the academic functioning of students with attention-deficit/hyperactivity disorder. *School Psychology Quarterly, 23*(3), 407–417. doi:10.1037/1045-3830.23.3.407

Luciana, M., Collins, P. F., Olson, E. A., & Schissel, A. M. (2009). Tower of London performance in healthy adolescents: The development of planning skills and associations with self-reported inattention and impulsivity. *Developmental Neuropsychology, 34*(4), 461–475.

Molitor, S. J., Oddo, L. E., Eadeh, H. M., & Langberg, J. M. (2018). EF deficits in youth with ADHD: Untangling possible sources of heterogeneity. *Journal of Emotional and Behavioral Disorders*. doi:10.1177/1063426618763125

Niermann, H. C., & Scheres, A. (2014). The relation between procrastination and symptoms of attention-deficit hyperactivity disorder (ADHD) in undergraduate students. *International Journal of Methods in Psychiatric Research*, *23*(4), 411–421.

Pennington, B. F., & Ozonoff, S. (1996). Executive functions and developmental psychopathology. *Journal of Child Psychology and Psychiatry*, *37*(1), 51–87.

Power, T. J., Werba, B. E., Watkins, M. W., Angelucci, J. G., & Eiraldi, R. B. (2006). Patterns of parent-reported homework problems among ADHD-referred and non-referred children. *School Psychology Quarterly*, *21*(1), 13.

Shaw, P., Eckstrand, K., Sharp, W., Blumenthal, J., Lerch, J. P., Greenstein, D. E. E. A., … Rapoport, J. L. (2007). Attention-deficit/hyperactivity disorder is characterized by a delay in cortical maturation. *Proceedings of the National Academy of Sciences*, *104*(49), 19649–19654.

Sibley, M. H., Graziano, P. A., Kuriyan, A. B., Coxe, S., Pelham, W. E., Rodriguez, L., … & Ward, A. (2016). Parent–teen behavior therapy+ motivational interviewing for adolescents with ADHD. *Journal of Consulting and Clinical Psychology*, *84*(8), 699.

Sonuga-Barke, E. J. (2005). Causal models of attention-deficit/hyperactivity disorder: From common simple deficits to multiple developmental pathways. *Biological Psychiatry*, *57*(11), 1231–1238.

Swanson, J. M., Hinshaw, S. P., Arnold, L. E., Gibbons, R. D., Marcus, S. U. E., Hur, K., … Hechtman, L. (2007). Secondary evaluations of MTA 36-month outcomes: Propensity score and growth mixture model analyses. *Journal of the American Academy of Child & Adolescent Psychiatry*, *46*, 1003–1014. doi:10.1097/CHI.0b013e3180686d63

Visser, S. N., Danielson, M. L., Bitsko, R. H., Holbrook, J. R., Kogan, M. D., Ghandour, R. M., … Blumberg, S. J. (2014). Trends in the parent-report of health care provider-diagnosed and medicated attention-deficit/hyperactivity disorder: United States, 2003–2011. *Journal of the American Academy of Child & Adolescent Psychiatry*, *53*(1), 34–46.

Weyandt, L., DuPaul, G. J., Verdi, G., Rossi, J. S., Swentosky, A. J., Vilardo, B. S., … Carson, K. S. (2013). The performance of college students with and without ADHD: Neuropsychological, academic, and psychosocial functioning. *Journal of Psychopathology and Behavioral Assessment*, *35*(4), 421–435.

Willcutt, E. G., Doyle, A. E., Nigg, J. T., Faraone, S. V., & Pennington, B. F. (2005). Validity of the executive function theory of attention-deficit/hyperactivity disorder: A meta-analytic review. *Biological Psychiatry*, *57*(11), 1336–1346.

25 The Daily Report Card Intervention
Summary of the Science and Factors Affecting Implementation

Julie Sarno Owens, Chelsea L. Hustus, and Steven W. Evans

Broadly speaking the daily report card intervention (DRC[1]) is a behavioral contract designed to modify clearly-defined target behaviors (e.g., interruptions, work completion) and enhance student academic and/or behavioral functioning. When designed and implemented by a multi-disciplinary team and in partnership with parents, this contract can be (a) adapted to a variety of contexts (e.g., general and special education classrooms, cafeteria, and home setting) to address the student's evolving needs and competencies, (b) integrated with other support services provided to the student, (c) used as an effective communication tool between home and school, and (d) leveraged as a progress monitoring tool by school professionals. In this chapter, we describe the DRC intervention and the evidence supporting why it should be prioritized as an intervention for students with emotional and behavioral disorders (EBD), highlight strategies for maximizing the effectiveness of this intervention in schools, and make recommendations for future research and practice.

The Daily Report Card: Description and Theoretical Underpinnings

There are several strategies, grounded in behavioral theory, that are effective in preventing and reducing disruptive behavior and promoting positive behavior in children and adolescents. These strategies include the use of contingent and specific praise, differential reinforcement of desirable and undesirable behaviors, use of clear instructions and explicit expectations, and strategic responses to noncompliance and violations of expectations (Epstein, Atkins, Culinan, Kutash, & Weaver, 2008; McLeod et al., 2017; Simonsen, Fairbanks, Briesch, Myers, & Sugai, 2008). When used as intended, these strategies shape and modify behavior through the behavioral processes of antecedent control, extinction, and contingent reinforcements and consequences. These strategies are most effective when they are tailored to the child's developmental level and when applied in the context of a positive adult–child relationship. To address the unique needs of students with EBD, these strategies can be applied in an individualized and targeted manner in the context of a DRC intervention, which can be used at home, school, or any treatment setting, and as part of a multi-component intervention plan. In this chapter, we will focus on the DRC in the school setting.

The DRC is a behavioral contract designed to modify clearly-defined target behaviors (e.g., aggression, work accuracy) and enhance student academic and/or behavioral functioning. The DRC directly builds upon the behavioral strategies described above, but tailors them to each student's unique needs. When using a school-based DRC, teachers first identify and define two to four target behaviors that create impairment for the student and track those behaviors for one week. The resulting data provide the teacher with the information needed to establish the initial, achievable goals for each behavior (e.g., completes 50% of daily math assignments, respects others with seven or fewer violations). The teacher is encouraged to review the goals with the student at the start of the day, give feedback to the student at the point of performance throughout the day, and review success at the end of the day. Following shaping procedures, the goals for each behavior are modified until the student's behavior falls in the normative range. New goals can be added as previous goals are mastered.

Although the DRC is grounded in behavioral theory, it also aligns well with social interaction and ecological frameworks (Bronfenbrenner, 1979; Farmer, Reinke, & Brooks, 2014). Both of these theoretical frameworks posit that students develop within multiple contexts (e.g., peer group, classroom, family) and that these contexts *and* their interactions (e.g., home–school communication) shape and impact student functioning. Within these frameworks, disruptive behavior is viewed as a function of the interaction between student characteristics (e.g., skills and abilities) and the context (classroom structure, teacher instructional and classroom strategies, peer group) rather than as a function of the student. Thus, when attempting to change student behavior via the DRC intervention, school teams should consider targeting behaviors within specific contexts (e.g., respect within peer interactions, compliance within student–teacher interactions, work completion within classroom expectations and instructions). Subsequently, teachers must consider (a) how he/she can structure these contexts to maximize success for the student and (b) how she and others in the classroom may contribute to the maintenance or desistance of problematic behavior through antecedent conditions, social modeling, and reinforcement (intentional or unintentional).

The DRC intervention can also facilitate positive interactions across contexts outside of the classroom (communication between home and school; communication between general and special education teachers). For example, the DRC is designed to serve as a mechanism for collaborative problem solving and daily communication between home and school. When the DRC is developed in the context of a meeting attended by the parents, teacher, student, and school-based consultant (e.g., school psychologist; behavioral consultant) (Sheridan, Kratochwill, & Bergan, 2013), this can facilitate a common understanding of the contributors to the student's behavior, shared goals, and consistency in intervention implementation across contexts, all of which can maximize positive intervention outcomes.

The DRC is an effective targeted intervention that can be used when universal classroom management and social emotional learning strategies are insufficient to meet the needs of a student. When implemented with high quality in the general education environment, it can reduce the behaviors that often lead teachers to refer a student for a special education evaluation, and therefore may be able to reduce unnecessary referrals to more intensive services (although this has not been explicitly empirically tested). In addition, among students identified with EBD, the DRC can be used in both general education and special education classrooms and, in many cases, can provide the external supports needed to compensate for student deficits in self-regulation. If a student has an individual education program (IEP), it is recommended that the school-based team create alignment between the DRC and the IEP. For example, the DRC can be used to address impairments in academic enabling behaviors (pays attention, participates) and in behavioral functioning (following classroom rules). Additionally, DRC target behaviors can be aligned with IEP goals and modified over time to facilitate achievement of IEP goals. Lastly, the DRC can be used in combination with other approaches. For example, a student can bring the DRC to small group academic interventions or therapeutic inventions for consistency across environments. Thus, the DRC is a flexible tool that can be tailored and adapted to address complex needs of the student.

Empirical Evidence Supporting Prioritization of the DRC

There have been several reviews of studies evaluating the effectiveness of the DRC (Barth, 1979; Chafouleas, Riley-Tillman, & McDougal, 2002; Riden, Taylor, Lee, & Scheeler, 2018), two meta-analyses of single case design studies (Pyle & Fabiano, 2017; Vannest, Davis, Davis, Mason, & Burke, 2010), and one meta-analysis of group design studies (Iznardo, Rogers, Volpe, Labelle, & Robaey, 2017). The extant body of literature documents that the DRC is effective in reducing a wide variety of problematic behaviors (e.g., Owens et al., 2012; Vannest et al., 2010), is acceptable to teachers (Girio & Owens, 2009), and can be used for several months (i.e., is feasible; Fabiano et al., 2010; Owens et al., 2012). Most studies have been conducted with elementary school students, with evidence of developmental adaptation across grades K – 5 (e.g., pictorial representation of target behaviors with younger students; student participation in the development and evaluation process with older elementary students). The DRC also has promise with middle school students (Vannest et al., 2010).

Effectiveness

The three meta-analyses provide a comprehensive evaluation of the effectiveness of the DRC. The two meta-analyses examining the use of the DRC in single case studies provide evidence of the promise of the DRC for children in both elementary and middle school, demonstrating a variety of inattentive and disruptive behaviors (Pyle & Fabiano, 2017;Vannest et al., 2010). In both analyses, the average effect sizes (ES) of included studies was moderate to large depending on the specific indicator (0.59–0.94). The meta-analyses also indicate that DRC produces better outcomes when implemented for more than one hour of the day (average ES = .87), rather than for just one class (average ES = .51;Vannest et al., 2010) and may demonstrate greater effects when home–school collaboration is high (Williams, Noell, Jones, & Gansle, 2012). No moderating effects of grade level/age, gender, or target type (disruptive behaviors versus on-task behaviors) were found in these analyses, highlighting the broad applicability of the DRC (Vannest et al., 2010).

Iznardo and colleagues (2017) conducted a meta-analysis on group design studies (N = 7) that examined the DRC for children with attention-deficit/hyperactivity disorder (ADHD). In contrast to the previous meta-analyses where the outcome of interest was change in behavior targeted on the DRC, the outcome of interest in these studies was ADHD symptoms as measured by a rating scale or direct observation of the behaviors targeted by the DRCs. Across studies, the average Hedge's g ES was 0.59. Outcomes were significantly stronger when obtained via direct observation (ES=1.05) than via parent and teacher ratings (ES = 0.36) as expected, given the specificity of the observations and breadth of the rating scales. These meta-analyses demonstrate that, under many conditions, the DRC is an effective tool for modifying disruptive behaviors, time on/off task, and classroom rule violations (as evidenced by moderate to large ESs).

Acceptability

Several studies have examined the acceptability of the DRC intervention as rated by classroom teachers (e.g., Chafouleas, Riley-Tillman, & Sassu, 2006; Girio & Owens, 2009; Power, Hess, & Bennett, 1995). For example, using vignette methodology, Girio and Owens (2009) evaluated elementary school teachers' (N = 156) perceptions of acceptability of the DRC, time-out, peer tutoring, self-reinforcement, and social skills training. The DRC received the highest overall acceptability score and was statistically more acceptable than all other interventions except self-reinforcement (Girio & Owens, 2009). Other studies have examined parent and teacher acceptability and satisfaction with the intervention following multiple months of use (e.g., Murray, Rabiner, Schulte, & Newitt, 2008; Owens, Murphy, Richerson, Girio, & Himawan, 2008) and have found high ratings from both informants. Taken together, these studies demonstrate that those most likely to implement a DRC support its use in the classroom and in many cases, view it as more favorable than other possible strategies.

Feasibility

Given the many competing demands faced by teachers, school-based intervention teams must prioritize interventions that are feasible, meaning they are low cost and can be seamlessly integrated into the classroom context. Several studies offer indicators of the feasibility of the DRC. For example, multiple studies show that, with implementation support, teachers can implement the DRC for multiple months, and in some cases, across the entire school year (Fabiano et al., 2010; Holdaway et al., 2018; Murray et al., 2008; Owens et al., 2012). This is important because changing student behavior can take several months, and because most students may have multiple behaviors that would benefit from intervention. In addition, these studies document that implementation adherence is relatively strong. For example, both Fabiano et al. (2010) and Owens et al. (2008) found that teachers implemented the DRC on at least 75% of school days, suggesting that teachers found a way to integrate the intervention into typical daily procedures.

Because the above findings occurred in the context of high implementation supports (i.e., ongoing support from a behavioral consultant), which may not be available in many schools, recently investigators have examined the extent to which technology can be leveraged to support teacher's use of the DRC (Mixon, Owens, Hustus, Serrano, & Holdaway, 2018; Owens et al., 2019). Two pilot studies suggest that with access to an interactive web-based system that provides professional development and implementation supports related to the DRC (see www.oucirs.org/daily-report-card-preview/), a meaningful subset of teachers (20% to 50%) can implement the DRC with acceptable adherence procedures for up to eight weeks, and can achieve positive change in student behavior (moderate to large effects) with limited supports from consultants (e.g., less than 30 minutes of face-to-face consultation for the duration of implementation). These results offer promise for the widespread use of this effective intervention.

Maximizing DRC Effectiveness in Schools

Although many teachers can implement the DRC with high quality, a substantial portion of teachers may experience barriers to implementation, leading to underutilization of the intervention and/or low quality implementation (Hart et al., 2017; Martinussen, Tannock, & Chaban, 2011). Barriers to teacher use of high quality classroom interventions include inadequate access to training (Parsad, Lewis, & Farris, 2001; Reinke, Stormont, Herman, Puri, & Goel, 2011), forgetting to implement the interventions (Collier-Meek, Sanetti, & Boyle, 2019), limited skills in problem solving and data-driven decision making (Farley-Ripple & Buttram, 2015), and limited implementation supports and accountability (Long et al., 2016). Because these are likely barriers to the implementation of many interventions for students with EBD (e.g., social skills programs, check-in/check-out programs), interdisciplinary school-based teams need to carefully consider these barriers and develop plans for overcoming them. An effective solution is for an experienced member of the team to provide consultation and support to the teacher attempting implementation. Because schools differ in how they approach building-level teams and implementation supports, the individual who provides this support may be a special education teacher, a peer teacher who leads positive behavior support efforts, a behavioral consultant, school psychologist, or assistant principal. Below, we describe consultation strategies that take a problem-solving approach to this process.

Problem-Solving Consultation to Support Implementation

Problem-solving consultation is an effective strategy for identifying and overcoming barriers to the success of a classroom intervention (Frank & Kratochwill, 2014). Effective problem solving in the context of intervention implementation typically follows a five-step cyclical approach that includes the following elements: (1) consultant–teacher relationship development, (2) problem identification, (3) problem analysis, (4) intervention implementation, and (5) evaluation. Once the intervention is launched, on-going consultation can include encouraging the teachers' continued use of the intervention, periodic review of data for accountability purposes and to inform intervention modification, and helping the teacher generate and evaluate ideas for overcoming barriers. The first step to providing this support is relationship development with the teacher.

Relationship Development

Without teacher engagement, there will be no classroom intervention. Thus, teacher engagement and the development of a positive consultation relationship is critical. We encourage consultants to (a) express enthusiasm for working together (*I'm excited to work together to address this student's needs*), (b) show empathy for the teacher's challenging experiences with the student (*That sounds very stressful/challenging. It will be important that we find a way to address this behavior*), (c) inquire about and actively listen to the teacher's current approach to the student, classroom management, and goals for his/her class, and (d) explain or clarify your role as a consultant (e.g., *My goal is to support you and help you focus on strategies that may produce success for you and the student; My goal is to work with you to identify effective strategies that also align with the goals you have for your classroom*). When parents are involved in the DRC development phase, the consultant and/or teacher should consider adopting a similar approach to relationship development with parents.

Problem Identification: Target Behavior Interview

A Target Behavior Interview (see example at http://oucirs.org/daily-report-card/ and in Volpe & Fabiano, 2013) is designed to help teachers identify problematic behaviors, prioritize those that are most important for enhancing academic or behavioral functioning, and develop operational definitions for each behavior. This can occur in a dyadic conversation between a consultant and teacher (with or without parents present) or in the context of an intervention team meeting. Initially, the consultant can help the teacher create a list of all problematic student behaviors. Then, for practicality purposes, the consultant can help the teacher prioritize the two to four behaviors that, if changed, would maximize success for the student. When prioritizing, teachers should prioritize behaviors that (a) address a safety concern (e.g., aggression), (b) are of high frequency (e.g., interruptions), as these behaviors are often most disruptive to the class, stressful for the teacher, and most amenable to change, (c) relate to academic productivity (e.g., percent complete), as this behavior is incompatible with disruptive behaviors (e.g., out of seat), and (d) are antecedents to other behaviors, as targeting these behaviors can address additional cascading behaviors (e.g., disrespect to peers may only occur when the student is out of seat; thus by focusing on remaining seated, the teacher can address disrespect as well). Consultants should help the teacher develop specific definitions for the negative behaviors and ask the teacher to track these behaviors for five school days.

Problem Analysis: Baseline Data

Although collecting baseline data may seem onerous to some, these data serve multiple functions and are critically important to the initial success. First, if the teacher struggles to collect these data, it may be an important foreshadowing of implementation challenges. With this knowledge, teachers and consultants can brainstorm strategies to overcome tracking and implementation barriers before launching the intervention. Second, the baseline data may reveal important relationships that inform decisions about target behaviors. For example, if the data reveal that work productivity is highest on days when out of seat is lowest and vice-versa, then targeting work productivity may serve to improve both behaviors (and the teacher would not need to target *out of seat* separately). Alternatively, it is common that after tracking a given behavior (verbal disrespect), a teacher may realize that the behavior is not as frequent as suspected, is better accounted for by an alternative behavior (e.g., noncompliance), or only occurs in situations when the student is overwhelmed by an academic challenge (math word problems). In these situations, it may be most effective to target the alternative behavior and/or provide an academic support strategy (e.g., have a math facts chart available when completing word problems). Thus, when reviewing the baseline data with teachers, consultants can listen for clues that might point to antecedent behaviors, behaviors that occur in a chain, and contextual information that may provide clues to the function of the behavior.

Again, the review of baseline data can occur in a dyadic conversation between a consultant and teacher (with or without parents present) or in the context of an intervention team meeting. Once the teacher has decided upon the behaviors to target on the DRC, the DRC can be created with consideration of two elements. First, during the baseline period, the teacher tracked the negative behaviors (e.g., out of seat; interruptions); however, on the DRC that the student and parents see, the behaviors should be phrased in the positive (*remains in seat with X or fewer violations; raises hand to speak with X or fewer interruptions*). Common DRC targets can be found at http://oucirs.org/daily-report-card/ and in Volpe and Fabiano (2013). Second, the baseline data can be used as a guide to setting the initial goal criterion. Namely, teachers are encouraged to set the initial goal criterion (e.g., five or fewer interruptions) at a level that the student could have achieved at least 3 out of 5 days during baseline. Setting the goal well within the student's current repertoire of behaviors will increase the likelihood that the student experiences success during the first week. This success (particularly when paired with praise from parents and teacher, and/or a privilege system) often motivates the student to put forth additional effort toward goal attainment and behavior change. Ideas for home and school-based privilege systems can be found at http://oucirs.org/daily-report-card/ and in Volpe and Fabiano (2013).

Intervention Implementation

There are many nuances to implementation and a consultant can assist teachers in attending to these. First, the DRC can be tailored to the child's developmental level. For example, for young children, clip art can be used to depict target behaviors and or checkboxes can be used to make goal criteria more concrete (see Figure 25.1). For older students, the teacher may initially do all the tracking, but as the student becomes familiar with the process, the teacher may ask the student to self-track the behaviors and then reinforce accuracy (in addition to staying below the goal criterion). Second, the DRC is likely to be most effective when it is framed as a positive behavioral support to the student and peers (*some children need glasses to read, others needs programs to help them stay on task or follow classroom rules*) and with encouragement rather than reprimand. Thus, teachers are encouraged to greet the student each morning, briefly review the behaviors and goals with the student and ask the student what privilege they are working toward. It may be helpful for the consultant to periodically participate in this review to legitimize the process for the student and observe the teacher. The consultant can support the teacher by highlighting the teacher's strengths and/or offering additional ideas for maximizing the success of this interaction. Third, one of the mechanisms of behavior change is feedback at the point of performance. We encourage teachers to *label* the behavior (*That's an interruption*), *connect* the behavior to the DRC (*Let's put a mark on your card*), and *track* the infraction (actually making the mark), and refers to this with a memorable acronym of TLC. Indeed, there is recent evidence that documents the important relationship between teachers' effective response to rule violations and disruptive behavior (Owens, Allan, Hustus, & Erchul, 2018). Fourth, teachers will maximize skill development if they pair behavioral infractions with opportunities for skills practice (e.g., allowing students to raise their hand and wait to be called upon, followed by praise for the improved behavior). Just as teachers shape phonemic awareness into reading, they can shape behavioral skills practice in appropriate self-regulation. Again, if teachers are comfortable with periodic observations by the

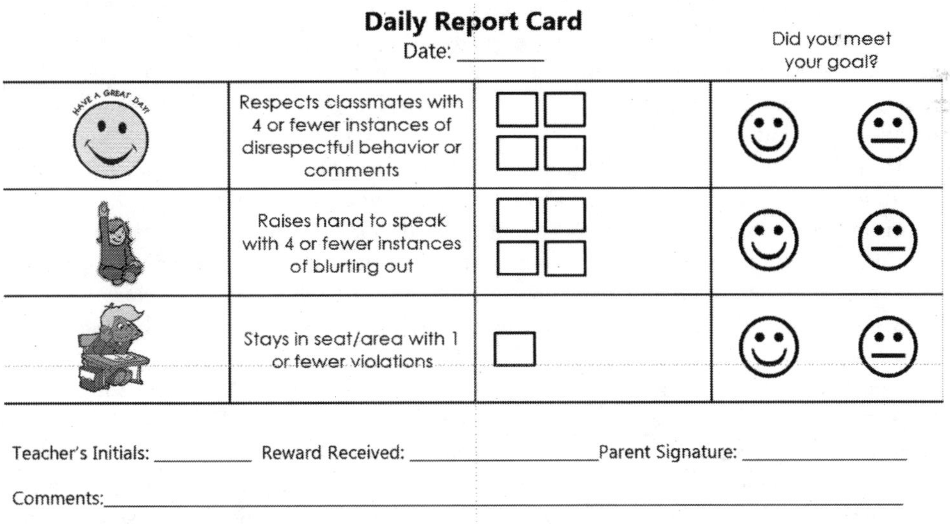

Daily Report Card

Date: ________

			Did you meet your goal?
HAVE A GREAT DAY!	Respects classmates with 4 or fewer instances of disrespectful behavior or comments		
	Raises hand to speak with 4 or fewer instances of blurting out		
	Stays in seat/area with 1 or fewer violations		

Teacher's Initials: ________ Reward Received: ________ Parent Signature: ________

Comments: ________

Figure 25.1 Sample Daily Report Card

378   *Julie Sarno Owens et al.*

consultant, it provides an opportunity for the consultant to praise the teacher and brainstorm ways to maximize success. Lastly, at the end of the day, the teacher and student can review the student's progress on each goal, praise the student for success, and offer relevant privileges. The student is encouraged to take the DRC home for parental review and signature (and potentially home-based privileges).

Evaluation: Progress Monitoring with Consideration to Benchmarks

In the context of school-based multi-tiered systems of supports (MTSS;Benner, Kutash, Nelson, & Fisher, 2013), the level of intervention intensity should be matched to the student need, and intensified or reduced based on the student's response to a given level of intervention. This goal can only be achieved if school personnel monitor the student's response to intervention and have benchmarks to determine whether the response is satisfactory or not.

With regard to monitoring student progress with a DRC, it is recommended that the student's progress be reviewed every two weeks. If the student has met the goal for a given target behavior for 8 of 10 school days, then the team can consider shaping the goal toward more normative levels. When teachers modify a goal, it is recommended that the same principle used during initial goal setting be applied. Namely, modify the goal to a new level, but one that the student can still succeed more days than not. These modification decisions can be made efficiently if student DRC data are graphed. Given that most teachers report not graphing DRC data (Chafouleas et al., 2002), consultants may maximize effective decision making if they can offer support in this domain of implementation.

With regard to benchmarking, there are two studies that offer benchmark data for consideration (Holdaway et al., 2018;Owens et al., 2012) with elementary school students. Benchmarks reveal how much change in student behavior can be expected over a given time period when using a specific intervention.Owens et al. (2012) examined the trajectories of change in behavioral DRC targets (e.g., interrupting, aggression, out of seat) incrementally over each month of intervention, and cumulatively over four months of intervention. They documented the change in behavior using a standard mean difference within-subjects effect size. The results revealed that, overall, students can be expected to experience a large magnitude of change in behavior by the end of the first month of intervention (ES = .78) with additional small benefits (ES = .3 per month) in each subsequent month of intervention. This study provides preliminary benchmarks for intervention decision making. For example, if a student is making less than moderate progress after the first month (i.e., small and inconsistent changes), school personnel should consider implementation integrity, the saliency of rewards, and intervention trouble shooting. If improvement is not observed following these checks and revisions, then the team can assume that the likelihood of achieving a large change in behavior may be unlikely and should consider supplemental or alternative interventions.

Holdaway et al. (2019) attempted to replicate these effects with a separate sample of elementary school students ($N = 37$), and expand the study of benchmarks (a) using both standard mean difference and a Tau-based effect size to account for possible baseline trends, (b) examining change in both academic and behavioral DRC target behavior, and (c) examining teacher behaviors associated with positive outcomes. This study offers replication that a large magnitude of change in behavior can be expected following the first month of intervention for both behavioral (ES = .94) and academic targets (ES = 1.04). This pattern

The Daily Report Card Intervention   379

was replicated when using a more stringent Tau effect size as well, although the magnitude of effects was more modest (ES = .4). This study also replicated that small incremental effects are observed in subsequent months. Lastly, this study revealed that higher rates of teacher feedback at the point of performance was associated with better outcomes for behavioral targets, but not academic targets. This suggests that behavioral and academic targets may warrant separate consideration in future studies.

Leveraging Technology

We recognize that the individual consultation process described above requires face-to-face supports and this resource may be unavailable in some schools. If individual consultation is not available, support and guidance can be provided to teachers in the context of school-based positive behavior support or intervention teams. Arguably, there is a sizable portion of teachers who can implement the DRC with sufficient quality with minimal consultation and support. Thus, advances in technology provide a viable alternative to face-to-face consultation to improve the accessibility and feasibility of support for teachers. In some cases, these alternatives show comparable effects to face-to-face consultation (Mixon et al., 2018; Owens et al., 2019).

One example of a technological alternative to face-to-face consultation is the Daily Report Card Online (DRC.O), an interactive web-based system that provides professional development and implementation supports related to the DRC (see www.oucirs.org/daily-report-card-preview/; Mixon et al., 2018; Owens et al., 2019). The DRC.O offers the information and materials needed to understand and implement the DRC intervention, as well as video demonstrations of implementation. Teachers can access this content in their own time and at a pace that suits their needs. The DRC.O system includes novel interactive features designed to mirror the problem-solving approach recommended above. The system guides teachers through a process of selecting and prioritizing target behaviors, collecting baseline data about those behaviors, and using the baseline data to set individualized student goals. The system also graphs student progress and has algorithms that offer data-driven decision supports, making recommendations about when goals should be changed (i.e., to gradually shape student behavior into the normative range) and by how much (so that the student continues to experience success).

The initial evaluation of the DRC.O was conducted with 33 elementary teachers in the U.S. who were provided access to the DRC.O program and asked to implement a DRC with one elementary school student for eight weeks using supports from the DRC.O website and brief, in-person consultation, as needed (Mixon et al., 2018). In total, 54.54% ($n = 18$) of teachers implemented the intervention for at least one month and 51.51% ($n = 17$) implemented it for at least two months. These teachers ($n = 17$) demonstrated acceptable levels of observed implementation integrity (i.e., comparable to that observed in some consultation studies; Owens, Evans et al., in press), and their students demonstrated improvements in total ($d = .53$) and hyperactive and inattentive ($d = .83$) problems on the *Strengths and Difficulties Questionnaire* (Goodman, 2001). Importantly, teachers achieved these outcomes using an average of 32 minutes of face-to-face consultation. This is a substantial reduction in time compared to studies on DRC effectiveness with traditional consultation, in which teachers participated in 6 to 10, 30-minute meetings (Fabiano et al., 2010; Owens et al., 2012). These results suggest that, for some teachers, online supports offer a feasible means of supporting DRC implementation.

Following the first pilot, teachers provided feedback about the website that informed subsequent website modifications. The authors conducted a second evaluation of the DRC.O with 54 teachers in Calgary, Canada, using the same methods as the first pilot (Owens et al., 2019). However, in this study, there was no face-to-face consultation provided by the research team and the school had not engaged in prior research with the university partners. In total, 39% ($n = 21$) implemented for at least one month, and 20% ($n = 11$) implemented for at least two months. These lower rates, relative to the first pilot may represent the importance of some face-to-face support being available, and/or the impact of a long-term university–community partnership on teacher behavior. On average, teachers (who implemented for a least one month) input daily data on 74.93% of days (SD = 22.91). Notably, this level of implementation and data entry matches that observed in studies with extensive face-to-face supports (Fabiano et al., 2010; Owens et al., 2008). For students, total scores on the Strengths and Difficulties Questionnaire (SDQ) (Goodman, 2001), moved, on average, from the clinically significant range at baseline ($M = 19.5$) to the near normative range at post-assessment ($M = 13.2$), a within-subjects effect size of $d = 1.01$.

Website analytics revealed that, on average, long-term adopters completed all steps of DRC development in less than one hour and spent only three minutes per day engaged in data entry for progress monitoring. These data demonstrate how technology may be able to enhance efficiencies in this process relative to face-to-face. Collectively, these data suggest that the DRC.O is a promising tool for overcoming barriers to adoption and implementation of effective practices; high quality randomized control trials, and evaluations by other author teams are warranted to confirm this conclusion.

An Ecology of Support for Teachers: A Continuum of Professional Development

Whether using intervention support teams, consultants, or technology, the above described processes will likely be most effective when administrators and school mental health professionals create a school culture that values innovation, implementation of positive behavioral support, and peer-to-peer collaboration (Forman, Olin, Hoagwood, Crowe, & Saka, 2009; Hustus & Owens, 2018). In addition, studies are starting to show that professional development is most effective when tailored to the teacher's individual needs (Coles, Owens, Serrano, Slavec, & Evans, 2015; Owens et al., 2017; Sanetti, Collier-Meek, Long, Kim, & Kratochwill, 2014). Some teachers need intensive face-to-face consultation; however, a substantial portion do not. Ideally, school administrators could reserve intensive face-to-face consultation for teachers who have significant difficulty implementing interventions and/or whose students demonstrate the greatest need, whereas less intensive supports could be offered (e.g., via technology) to the majority of teachers (i.e., those with less intensive needs). In order to differentiate resources in this way, research that examines predictors of teachers' intervention adoption and implementation patterns is needed. The above-described DRC.O studies, as well as studies examining predictors of teachers' implementation of other interventions offer preliminary insights into possible innovations in professional development for teachers.

In the Mixon et al. (2018) study, the authors categorized teachers into short-term adopters (implemented the DRC for 1 to 8 weeks; $n = 6$); and long-term adopters (implemented the DRC for 8 weeks or longer; $n = 17$), and examined characteristics of these two groups. Long-term adopters were more likely than short-term and non-adopters to have a Master's degree, and to have previously used a DRC intervention. Other demographic characteristics (e.g., age, years in the profession) were not significantly associated with this group status. This suggests that the DRC.O technology may offer efficiencies for those with previous DRC experience and can serve to facilitate sustainment of the use of this effective practice. In addition, short-term adopters took twice as long to set up the DRC (i.e., number of weeks between receiving the website link and launching the DRC) than long-term adopters. This suggests that, if progress is stalled during the development phase, these teachers may benefit from face-to-face support to problem solve and overcome barriers to intervention implementation.

In the second pilot study, the authors monitored implementation via the number days that the teacher entered daily DRC data into the system. Two baseline factors predicted higher data entry: (1) higher scores on a knowledge test of behavioral theory and (2) lower scores on a measure assessing teacher stress related to student discipline (Owens et al., 2019). This is consistent with a study that found that higher teacher stress was related to less implementation of a universal classroom intervention focused on preventing and reducing disruptive behavior (Domitrovich et al., 2015). Further, another recent study found that higher levels of work-related stress was associated with lower receptivity to consultation provided by a consultant with relevant expertise and information about intervention (Owens et al., 2018). Taken together, this suggests that teacher stress could be assessed and used to match teacher needs to specific types of professional development and implementation supports. Studies that directly assess this match are needed.

Lastly, additional work is underway to examine the potential interaction between teacher perceptions of intervention acceptability (prior to and during implementation), implementation behaviors (e.g., feedback to students, daily DRC data entry), and student response to the intervention. One study (Girio-Herrera et al., 2019) found that higher acceptability ratings *prior to implementation* were related to higher levels of teacher knowledge about ADHD, but were not related to acceptability ratings *during implementation*, implementation behaviors, or student outcomes. In contrast, the student's initial response to the intervention (i.e., the magnitude of improvement in DRC target behaviors) predicted higher acceptability ratings during implementation and greater implementation behaviors. Further, higher acceptability ratings during implementation predicted that the teacher implemented the DRC for more school days. Thus, knowledge of ADHD (Girio-Herrera et al., 2019) and of behavioral theory (Owens et al., 2019) may be related to a teacher's capacity and/or willingness to adopt the DRC; however, supportive monitoring by a school-based consultant may facilitate ongoing implementation via problem solving if the teacher has difficulty launching the DRC (Owens et al., 2019) and/or if the student's initial response is less than desirable (Girio-Herrera et al., 2019).

Recommendations for Future Research and Practice

Expanded Evaluation of the DRC

We hope that the above review convincingly documents the empirical evidence supporting the DRC. However, additional practice-based research is needed in several areas. First, the magnitude of change in behavioral outcomes produced by the DRC is large. However, the data are mixed for academic outcomes. Thus, research is needed to learn what components of the DRC could be enhanced, or what supplemental supports could be added, to better address change in academic outcomes. Second, to date, the DRC has largely been used to address inattention and disruptive behavior. Because students with EBD present with a host of presenting problems, including anxiety, fearfulness, and emotion dysregulation, it is worth examining the extent to which DRCs could be helpful for internalizing problems. Third, there are few high quality studies assessing the impact of the DRC with middle school students. Although this intervention may have promise with adolescents, additional developmental modifications are likely needed. Systematic study of these nuances may offer middle school teachers additional tools for managing challenging behavior. Lastly, it is critically important to examine the extent to which these findings replicate under more natural conditions, such as when the consultants to the teacher are school employees rather than project-based research staff.

Evaluation of Technology

In many fields, technological advances are being leveraged to enhance access to services, and enhance the efficiency and quality of services. In this chapter, we highlight one example of the application of technology to enhance teachers' use of DRC. However, only pilot demonstrations have been conducted; thus, examination in the context of rigorous design standards is needed. In addition, it is important to study the extent to which technology can be leveraged to enhance other aspects of targeted interventions, such as enhancing remote consultation to teachers (e.g., Fischer, Erchul, & Schultz, 2018) and for enhancing work directly with students (Schultz & Evans, 2018).

Evaluation of Individually Tailored Professional Development

There is emerging evidence that professional development that is individually tailored to the teacher's needs may produce better outcomes than a one size fits all approach (e.g., Owens et al., 2017). However, in order to adopt this approach, teachers must be able to self-assess and/or administrators must be able to efficiently assess teacher characteristics that best match various professional development approaches. Emerging evidence suggests that knowledge, attitudes, stress, and previous experience with an intervention may be characteristics that offer guideposts for professional development decision making. Additional work that adaptively assesses the utility of implementation supports at various time points (e.g., if progress is stalled during DRC development) and/or that assesses various combinations between teacher profiles and types of implementation supports (e.g., technology-driven or face to face) could be critically informative.

Obtain Data that Facilitates Intervention Benchmarking

Lastly, most elementary schools operate within a multi-tiered framework of supports. Thus, school teams need benchmarks for determining whether an intervention, such as the DRC, is likely to produce success for a given student. Thus, as additional studies are conducted on the DRC, investigators are encouraged to report outcomes at key time points (e.g., weekly or monthly) so that collectively, we can begin to benchmark the proximal outcomes that produce desired distal outcomes.

Conclusion

The DRC is the most widely studied targeted intervention for elementary school students demonstrating inattentive and disruptive behaviors in the classroom environment. When high quality implementation occurs, the DRC is effective in reducing a wide variety of problematic behaviors, is acceptable to teachers, and can feasibly be used for several months. Further, the DRC can be designed and implemented within the context of a multi-disciplinary team and in partnership with parents, allowing for the intervention to be adapted to a variety of contexts and integrated with other support services provided to the student. Implementation integrity can be maximized through a variety of supports including problem-solving consultation and interactive web technologies such as the DRC.O. For best outcomes for the teacher and the student, school teams should consider what implementation supports are most feasible and appropriate within the context of their extant approach to the treatment of EBD. Although there is already a breadth of research supporting the use of the DRC in the classroom environment, future research in this area should focus on expanding the study of the DRC with new populations and problem behaviors, the development of implementation supports, and better understanding benchmarking data related to the DRC intervention.

Note

1 The DRC intervention has also been referred to as a school–home note (Kelley, 1990) and daily behavior report card (DBRC; Chafouleas, Riley-Tillman, & McDougal, 2002).

References

Barth, R. (1979). Home-based reinforcement of school behavior: A review and analysis. *Review of Educational Research, 49*(3), 436–458.

Benner, G. J., Kutash, K., Nelson, J. R., & Fisher, M. B. (2013). Closing the achievement gap of youth with emotional and behavioral disorders through multi-tiered systems of support. *Education and Treatment of Children, 36*(3), 15–29.

Bronfenbrenner, U. (1979). *The ecology of human development: Experiments by nature and design.* Cambridge, MA: Harvard University Press.

Chafouleas, S. M., Riley-Tillman, T. C., & McDougal, J. L. (2002). Good, bad, or in-between: How does the daily behavior report card rate? *Psychology in the Schools, 39*(2), 157–169.

Chafouleas, S. M., Riley-Tillman, T. C., & Sassu, K. A. (2006). Acceptability and reported use of daily behavior report cards among teachers. *Journal of Positive Behavior Interventions, 8*(3), 174–182.

Coles, E. K., Owens, J. S., Serrano, V., Slavec, J., & Evans, S. W. (2015). From consultation to student outcomes: The role of teacher knowledge, skills, and beliefs in increasing integrity in classroom behavior management. *School Mental Health, 7*, 34–48.

Collier-Meek, M. A., Sanetti, L. M., & Boyle, A. M. (2019). Barriers to implementing classroom management and behavior support plans: An exploratory investigation. *Psychology in the Schools, 56*(1), 5–17.

Domitrovich, C. E., Pas, E. T., Bradshaw, C. P., Becker, K. D., Keperling, J. P., Embry, D. D., & Ialongo, N. (2015). Individual and school organizational factors that influence implementation of the PAX good behavior game intervention. *Prevention Science, 16*(8), 1064–1074.

Epstein, M., Atkins, M., Culinan, D., Kutash, K., & Weaver, R. (2008). *Reducing behavior problems in the elementary school classroom.* IES Practice Guide. (NCEE 2008-012). U.S. Department of Education, National Center for Education Statistics. Washington, DC: U.S. Government Printing Office.

Fabiano, G. A., Vujnovic, R. K., Pelham, W. E., Waschbusch, D. A., Massetti, G. M., Pariseau, M. E., … Greiner, A. R. (2010). Enhancing the effectiveness of special education programming for children with attention deficit hyperactivity disorder using a daily report card. *School Psychology Review, 39*, 219.

Farley-Ripple, E., & Buttram, J. (2015). The development of capacity for data use: The role of teacher networks in an elementary school. *Teachers College Record, 117*(4), 1–34.

Farmer, T. W., Reinke, W. M., & Brooks, D. S. (2014). Managing classrooms and challenging behavior: Theoretical considerations and critical issues.

Fischer, A. J., Erchul, W. P., & Schultz, B. K. (2018). Teleconsultation as the new frontier of educational and psychological consultation: Introduction to the special issue. *Journal of Educational and Psychological Consultation, 28*(3), 1–6.

Forman, S. G., Olin, S. S., Hoagwood, K. E., Crowe, M., & Saka, N. (2009). Evidence-based interventions in schools: Developers' views of implementation barriers and facilitators. *School Mental Health, 1*, 26–36.

Girio, E. L., & Owens, J. S. (2009). Teacher acceptability of evidence-based and promising treatments for children with attention-deficit/hyperactivity disorder. *School Mental Health, 1*, 16–25.

Girio-Herrera, E. L., Egan, T. E., Owens, J. S., Evans, S. W., Coles, E. K., Holdaway, A. S., … Kassab, H. (2019). *Teacher ratings of acceptability for a daily report card intervention prior to and during implementation: Relations to implementation integrity and student outcomes.* Manuscript under review.

Goodman, R. (2001). Psychometric properties of the strengths and difficulties questionnaire. *Journal of the American Academy of Child & Adolescent Psychiatry, 40*(11), 1337–1345.

Hart, K. C., Fabiano, G. A., Evans, S. W., Manos, M. J., Hannah, J. N., & Vujnovic, R. K. (2017). Elementary and middle school teachers' self-reported use of positive behavioral supports for children with ADHD: A national survey. *Journal of Emotional and Behavioral Disorders, 25*(4), 246–256.

Holdaway, A. S., Owens, J. S., Evans, S. W., Coles, E. K., Egan, T., & Himawan, L. K. (2018, October). *Incremental benefits of a daily report card over time for youth with disruptive behavior: Replication and extension.* Poster presented at the Annual Conference on Advancing School Mental Health, Las Vegas, NV (under review).

Holdaway, A. S., Owens, J. S., Evans, S. W., Coles, E. K., Egan, T. E., & Himawan, L. K. (2019, October). *Incremental benefits of a daily report card over time for youth with or at-risk for ADHD: Replication and extension.* Poster presented at the annual conference on Advancing School Mental Health, Las Vegas, NV.

Hustus, C., & Owens, J. S. (2018). Assessing readiness for change among school professionals and its relationship with adoption and reported implementation of mental health initiatives. *Child and Youth Care Forum, 47*, 829–844.

Iznardo, M., Rogers, M. A., Volpe, R. J., Labelle, P. R., & Robaey, P. (2017). The effectiveness of daily behavior report cards for children with ADHD: A meta-analysis. *Journal of Attention Disorders.* doi:10.1177/1087054717734646.

Kelley, M. L. (1990). *School-home notes: Promoting children's classroom success.* New York: Guilford Press.

Frank, J. L., & Kratochwill, T. R. (2014). School-based problem-solving consultation. In W. P. Erchul & S. M. Sheridan (Eds.) *Handbook of research in school consultation* (2nd ed., pp. 18–39). New York, NY: Routledge..

Long, A. C., Sanetti, L. M. H., Collier-Meek, M. A., Gallucci, J., Altschaefl, M., & Kratochwill, T. R. (2016). An exploratory investigation of teachers' intervention planning and perceived implementation barriers. *Journal of School Psychology, 55*, 1–26.

Martinussen, R., Tannock, R., & Chaban, P. (2011). Teachers' reported use of instructional and behavior management practices for students with behavior problems: Relationship to role and level of training in ADHD. *Child & Youth Care Forum, 40*(3), 193–210.

McLeod, B. D., Sutherland, K. S., Martinez, R. G., Conroy, M. A., Snyder, P. A., & Southam-Gerow, M. A. (2017). Identifying common practice elements to improve social, emotional, and behavioral outcomes of young children in early childhood classrooms. *Prevention Science, 18*(2), 204–213.

Mixon, C. S., Owens, J. S., Hustus, C., Serrano, V. J., & Holdaway, A. S. (2018). Evaluating the impact of online professional development on teachers' use of a targeted behavioral classroom intervention. *School Mental Health.* doi:10.1007/s12310-018-9284-1

Murray, D. W., Rabiner, D., Schulte, A., & Newitt, K. (2008). Feasibility and integrity of a parent–Teacher consultation intervention for ADHD students. *Child & Youth Care Forum, 37*, 111–126.

Owens, J. S., Allan, D. M., Hustus, C., & Erchul, W. P. (2018). Examining correlates of teacher receptivity to social influence strategies within a school consultation relationship. *Psychology in the Schools, 55*, 1041–1055.

Owens, J. S., Coles, E. K., Evans, S. W., Himawan, L. K., Girio-Herrera, E., Holdaway, A. S., … Schulte, A. (2017). Using multi-component consultation to increase the integrity with which teachers implement behavioral classroom interventions: A pilot study. *School Mental Health, 9*, 218–234.

Owens, J. S., Evans, S. W., Coles, E. K., Himawan, L. K., Holdaway, A. S., Mixon, C., & Egan, T. (in press). Consultation for classroom management and targeted interventions: Examining benchmarks for teacher practices that produce desired change in student Behavior. *Journal of Emotional and Behavioral Disorders*. doi:10.1177/106342661879544

Owens, J. S., Holdaway, A. S., Zoromski, A. K., Evans, S. W., Himawan, L. K., Girio-Herrera, E., & Murphy, C. E. (2012). Incremental benefits of a daily report card intervention over time for youth with disruptive behavior. *Behavior Therapy, 43*, 848–861.

Owens, J. S., McLennan, J. D., Hustus, C. L., Haines-Saah, R., Mitchell, S., Mixon, C. S., & Troutman, A. (2019). Leveraging technology to facilitate teachers' use of a targeted classroom intervention: Evaluation of the daily report card. Online (DRC. O) System. *School Mental Health, 11*(4), 665–677.

Owens, J. S., Murphy, C. E., Richerson, L., Girio, E. L., & Himawan, L. K. (2008). Science to practice in underserved communities: The effectiveness of school mental health programming. *Journal of Clinical Child & Adolescent Psychology, 37*(2), 434–447.

Parsad, B., Lewis, L., & Farris, E. (2001). *Teacher preparation and professional development: 2000*. (NCES 2001-088). U.S. Department of Education, National Center for Education Statistics. Washington, DC: U.S. Government Printing Office.

Power, T. J., Hess, L. E., & Bennett, D. S. (1995). The acceptability of interventions for attention-deficit hyperactivity disorder among elementary and middle school teachers. *Journal of Developmental and Behavioral Pediatrics, 16*(4), 238–243.

Pyle, K., & Fabiano, G. A. (2017). Daily report card intervention and attention deficit hyperactivity disorder: A meta-analysis of single-case studies. *Exceptional Children, 83*(4), 378–395.

Reinke, W. M., Stormont, M., Herman, K. C., Puri, R., & Goel, N. (2011). Supporting children's mental health in schools: Teacher perceptions of needs, roles, and barriers. *School Psychology Quarterly, 26*(1), 1.

Riden, B. S., Taylor, J. C., Lee, D. L., & Scheeler, M. C. (2018). A synthesis of the daily behavior report card literature from 2007 to 2017. *The Journal of Special Education Apprenticeship, 7*(1), 3–27.

Sanetti, L. M. H., Collier-Meek, M. A., Long, A. C., Kim, J., & Kratochwill, T. R. (2014). Using implementation planning to increase teachers' adherence and quality to behavior support plans. *Psychology in the Schools, 51*(8), 879–895.

Schultz, B. K., & Evans, S. W. (2018). *Development of a game-supported intervention to improve learning and study strategies among at-risk students*. Grant proposal funded by Institute of Education Sciences (unpublished).

Sheridan, S. M., Kratochwill, T. R., & Bergan, J. R. (2013). *Conjoint behavioral consultation: A procedural manual*. New York, NY: Springer Science & Business Media.

Simonsen, B., Fairbanks, S., Briesch, A., Myers, D., & Sugai, G. (2008). Evidence-based practices in classroom management: Considerations for research to practice. *Education and Treatment of Children, 31*(3), 351–380.

Vannest, K. J., Davis, J. L., Davis, C. R., Mason, B. A., & Burke, M. D. (2010). Effective intervention for behavior with a daily behavior report card: A meta-analysis. *School Psychology Review, 39*(4), 654–672.

Volpe, R. J., & Fabiano, G. A. (2013). *Daily behavior report cards: An evidence-based system of assessment and intervention*. New York, NY: Guilford Press.

Williams, K. L., Noell, G. H., Jones, B. A., & Gansle, K. A. (2012). Modifying students' classroom behaviors using an electronic daily behavior report card. *Child & Family Behavior Therapy, 34*(4), 269–289.

26 Cognitive-Behavioral Prevention and Intervention Approaches to Student Emotional and Behavioral Functioning

Stephen W. Smith, Joni W. Splett, Daniel V. Poling, and Joseph W. Graham

Current estimates suggest that up to 20% of children and youth exhibit some type of emotional and behavioral difficulties that impedes school success (Perou et al., 2013); however, school professionals identify less than 1% of students for the provision of special education services for emotional and behavioral disorders (Snyder, de Brey, & Dillow, 2018). A lack of necessary programming is particularly consequential for students with the most significant behavioral and mental health needs identified with emotional and behavioral disorders (EBD). For students with externalizing behaviors (e.g., hyperactivity, chronic disruption and noncompliance, aggression, general conduct problems), failure to provide effective prevention and intervention can result in persistent maladaptive and aggressive school behavior patterns that result in escalating conflict with adults, peers, and family members and lead to poor social trajectories into adulthood (Bradley, Doolittle, & Bartolotta, 2008; Sanford et al., 2011). Untreated internalizing difficulties such as anxiety, depression, fear, and post-traumatic stress can interfere with inter- and intrapersonal functioning, academic progress, and can result in self-harm or even suicide (Centers for Disease Control and Prevention, 2015; Merry et al., 2012). Given that these students spend a large part of their day in schools, this provides a natural entry point for (a) early identification of students at risk for EBD and implementation of early prevention to counter the onset of significant behaviors, and (b) delivery of intensive interventions for students who, despite preventative efforts, display chronic problematic behavioral difficulties.

The continuum of prevention and intervention delivered in schools consists of tiered models of support (see Kern, McIntosh, Commisso, & Austin, this edition), which includes universal prevention programs for typically developing children regardless of need or risk, whereas intervention programs target a select group of students based on identified risk (e.g., history of disruptive behavior, poor academic performance, identified disability, attention difficulties). Within this tiered approach for support for students with EBD, school professionals typically provide an array of reinforcement and punishment strategies (e.g., token economies, time out) to shape behavior and function-informed behavior improvement plans. While contingent reinforcement for appropriate behavior, behavior reduction procedures, and behavioral programming informed by functional assessment are indeed strategic supports, they do not foster the self-regulatory processes to override the maladaptive and habitual and response sequences that prohibit independent and sustained positive interpersonal functioning (Smith, Poling, & Worth, 2018). The complex and challenging social-emotional and behavioral needs of students with EBD necessitates that they receive the most intensive evidenced-based interventions available (Mattison & Schneider, 2009; Nelson et al., 2009), however, these practices are rarely implemented for students with EBD, especially at levels necessary to maximize positive outcomes (Bradley et al., 2008; Smith et al., 2018).

There is a pressing need for intensive, evidenced-based programming for students with significant behavior problems that includes instructional skill components such as goal setting, perspective taking, social awareness, social problem solving, along with coping strategies and emotion control (Smith et al., 2018). Such targeted skill instruction can be accomplished through the use of cognitive-behavioral interventions (CBIs) that focus on deficits in the integration of cognition and emotion and the processing of emotional and social information. Importantly, provision of effective school-based prevention and intervention requires the coordination of specially trained educators and mental health practitioners (e.g., school counselors, school social workers, school psychologists) along with access to evidence-based CBIs with associated training and professional development.

In this chapter we (a) describe the use of CBIs in school settings, (b) review prevailing guiding theories and empirical evidence for CBIs, (c) preview several prevention and intervention programs that use a cognitive-behavioral approach to prevent or reduce externalizing and internalizing behavior problems experienced by students, and (d) discuss briefly teacher training issues, collaboration among professionals, intensity issues, and benefits of delivering CBIs in school settings.

Cognitive-Behavioral Interventions

The ultimate goal of any effort to moderate the deleterious effects of maladaptive behavior is for students to regulate their own behavior by skillfully using positive behaviors that can replace their more problematic ones. When students who exhibit behavioral problems learn to manage their own behavior, they reduce their dependence on external sources of control (e.g., school-wide token economies, frequent and specific praise, punishment strategies), thereby increasing their freedom of choice and self-determination (Polsgrove & Smith, 2004). Having proficient command of their self-regulatory processes, students can interpret, manage, and monitor effectively their behavior along with their emotions, and set, monitor, and achieve personal goals.

As students enter upper elementary grades and matriculate into middle school, self-regulatory processes become increasingly critical, as they are subject to intensifying pressure from peers and begin to rely less on adult supervision and support (Lerner & Steinberg, 2004). Many of the behavior problems exhibited by students with significant behavior problems are the result of deficits in self-regulating processes (i.e., goal-directed effortful control of thought, action, emotion) manifesting in negative externalizing behaviors such as physical and verbal aggression and internalizing problems, including anxiety, depression, and somatic complaints (Polsgrove & Smith, 2004; Smith & Daunic, 2010). For school professionals, however, working with students who exhibit EBD and have difficulty with regulating effectively their own behavior, is not without its complex and demanding challenges. Thus, access to highly efficient and effective cognitive-based interventions which are rigorous and comprehensive enough in scope to temper the effects of significant behavior problems, are clearly needed. Fortunately, CBIs provide a well-researched teaching technology to facilitate the necessary development by students of their use of prosocial behaviors (Smith & Daunic, 2004).

Multiple literature reviews and meta-analyses (e.g., Barnes, Smith, & Miller, 2014; Merrill, Smith, Cumming, & Daunic, 2017; Robinson, Smith, Miller, & Brownell, 1999) have confirmed the efficiency and effectiveness of CBIs for the prevention and remediation of behavioral problems while assisting students to learn more appropriate behavior for school success. Specifically, teaching cognitive strategies to school-aged children and youth has been found to decrease hyperactivity/impulsivity and disruption/aggression, strengthen pro-social behavior, increase social cognition, and improve peer relations. A research-based approach to teaching students positive coping strategies, CBIs incorporate behavior therapy techniques such as modeling, feedback, and reinforcement, and cognitive mediation techniques such as instructional think-alouds and teaching students to use positive self-talk (Smith, Taylor, Barnes, & Daunic, 2012). The use of CBIs operates under three primary assumptions: (1) a person's active cognitive interpretation of events affects behavior, (2) a person's cognition can be monitored and altered, and (3) through cognitive change, a person's behavior can change (Smith, Graber, & Daunic, 2009). Inherent in CBIs is the fundamental idea that behavior is mediated through self-talk (Mahoney, 1974; Meichenbaum, 1977; Smith et al., 2012). Thus, the use of language in altering cognitions is often a common component of the approach, and most CBI programs promote the active engagement of participants in the process of understanding and modifying their thought processes, feelings, and behaviors. Employable in a school setting, CBI instruction focuses on altering students' thought processes that frequently provoke behavioral problems along with the use of reinforcement contingencies (Riggs, Greenberg, Kusché, & Pentz, 2006; Smith & Daunic, 2010).

The strength of the CBI approach is that it provides skill development necessary for generalization to a variety of problem situations as opposed to focusing on behavior change by teaching how to respond in specific situations. Teaching strategies imbedded in CBIs can include whole class and small group instruction, guided discussions, demonstration/cognitive modeling, self-study, rehearsal and performance-related activities such as role-play with feedback, student homework, attending to and challenging automatic thoughts through the use of self-talk (Smith & Daunic, 2010).

For example, teachers might use modeling to demonstrate their own self-talk (cognitive modeling), and students would then be encouraged to work through simulated situations using overt self-talk while they receive coaching and feedback. The long-term goal is for students to use self-talk covertly and automatically over time in in-vivo situations. Kaplan and Carter (1995) delineate five characteristics that set CBIs apart from other approaches designed to manage student behavior:

(1) the student, rather than the teacher is the agent of change,
(2) verbalization is the primary component for learning,
(3) the student is often taught steps for identifying and solving social conflict,
(4) instruction involves the use of modeling, and
(5) gaining self-regulation is the ultimate goal.

The CBI programs we include in this chapter are reflective of a cognitive instructional approach including elements such as social competence, emotional literacy, problem solving, stress reduction, anger management, goal setting, and coping skills for trauma induced fear and anxiety. Since evidence-based school-wide, selected, and indicated behavioral programming is a fundamental aspect of tiered models of support, the overall aim is to reduce the need to identify students with EBD. As such, we chose to describe several universal programs to highlight the essential prevention approach to promote well-being, deter problems, and encourage appropriate behaviors and one intervention designed for small group instruction for those students displaying at risk behaviors. Given the severity of the behavioral needs of students served as EBD, our fourth program is an example of an intensive, multi-component

Cognitive-Behavioral Approaches 389

CBI for students who have experienced post-traumatic stress and anxiety. From our perspective, these four curricula/programs are representative of the diverse types of CBIs available and demonstrate the applicability of the approach across grade levels, especially during the elementary years. Moreover, these programs draw upon developmental models of externalizing and internalizing behavior and target multiple risk factors that include individual child and context (e.g. peer and parent) components.

Select CBIs in Schools

There is a sundry of empirically based CBIs intended to prevent or reduce emotional and behavioral problems of school-aged children and youth. As an effort to examine the universe of appropriate programs, we consulted key resource guides (e.g., Weissberg, Goren, Domitrovich, & Dusenbury, 2013; Wrabel, Hamilton, Whitake, & Grant, 2018), literature reviews (e.g., Merrill et al., 2017), and meta-analyses (e.g., Durlak, Weissberg, Dymnicki, Taylor, & Schellinger, 2011) related to effective prevention and intervention programs that fit Kaplan and Carter's (1995) description of CBIs. We scanned for programs that met the our inclusionary criteria: (a) must demonstrate empirically positive effects on students' externalizing and/or internalizing behavior problems, (b) feasible delivery by typical school personnel such as general and special education teachers, school counselors, school social workers, and/or school psychologists during a typical school day, (c) instruction includes sequenced explicit skill instruction and modeling in identifying and modifying one's thoughts, feelings, and behavior, and (d) programs not described elsewhere in this handbook. Our intention was not to provide a capacious account of available programs, rather, we wanted to provide examples of several CBIs to highlight the use of explicit skill instruction to prevent behavior problems from occurring and when behaviors start to escalate and negatively affect a student's school success. We delineate several CBI programs that are intended for universal classroom application to prevent emotional and behavioral problems (i.e., *Tools for Getting Along* [Daunic, Smith, Brank, & Penfield, 2006; Daunic et al., 2012; Smith et al., 2014] and *Second Step* [Low, Cook, Smolkowski, & Buntain-Ricklefs, 2015]). We also describe two small group interventions for students with escalating behavior problems including *Coping Power* (Lochman, Coie, Underwood, & Terry, 1993), designed to decrease anger and aggression, and *Bounce Back* (Langley, Gonzalez, Sugar, Solis, & Jaycox, 2015), intended to reduce post-traumatic stress symptoms and other internalizing behavior problems. Inclusion of many of the notable empirically-based CBIs such as *Promoting Alternative Thinking Strategies* (*PATHS*, Conduct Problems Prevention Research Group, 2010), *Incredible Years* (Webster-Stratton, Reid, & Stoolmiller, 2008), *I Can Problem Solve* (Shure & Spivack, 1979*), Making Choices* (Fraser, Thompson, Day, & Macy, 2014), and the *RULER* approach (Rivers, Brackett, Reyes, Elbertson, & Salovey, 2013) would be beyond the scope of this chapter.

Tools for Getting Along

Originating from the Cognitive-Behavioral Research Group at the University of Florida, Tools for Getting Along (TFGA) is a preventative CBI that introduces social emotional curriculum to upper elementary students. The primary objectives of TFGA include helping students understand anger and how it can cause or compound social problems, learn how to recognize and manage anger, and use problem-solving steps requisite to generate, apply, and evaluate positive solutions to social situations. In line with the characteristics of CBIs, the TFGA curriculum is manualized and sequenced, containing specific step-by-step objectives, a collection of learned skills, and scaffolded individual and group activities for fourth and fifth grade students (Smith et al., 2009). There are 20 core lessons followed by six booster lessons provided one to three times weekly for approximately 25–35 minutes per lesson. During lessons, TFGA incorporates CBI strategies such as modeling, reinforcement, role-playing real-life scenarios, and feedback to promote generalizability (Smith et al., 2014).

The sequenced lessons include both cognitive instructional and behavioral reinforcement techniques in 15 lessons that cover the curriculum's six problem-solving steps and five other role-play lessons strategically interspersed between problem-solving lessons to help students practice and apply the steps they are learning. Following an introductory lesson, students learn to recognize there is in fact a problem, and these problems can create or aggravate negative situations. Self-regulation coping strategies (e.g., calm down and think) are introduced in step two. Step three teaches students how to identify and define problems by identifying barriers and setting goals. Step four involves brainstorming for solutions and finally, steps five and six teach students the processes to select, enact, and evaluate a choice. TFGA incorporates six booster sessions to increase students' opportunities to practice the skills learned during instructions. Booster sessions resemble the same format as previous lessons but are delivered less frequently (e.g., once every two weeks) and include behavioral reinforcement techniques to generalize skills learned from the curriculum. Here, students have the opportunity to problem solve real-life scenarios through student constructed role-play (Smith et al., 2014).

Overall, outcomes of TFGA are positive for students' social problem-solving skills, aggressive behavior, teacher-reported executive function, and/or student-reported anger and anger management immediately following intervention (Daunic et al., 2006, 2012) and at one (Smith et al., 2014) and two-year follow ups (Daunic, Smith, Aydin, & Barber, 2019). These main effects for all students were also attenuated for students with higher risk of teacher-rated aggression, behavioral adjustment, and self-control at baseline. Similarly, in a replication study, Smith and colleagues (2016) found positive treatment effects consistent with those detected in prior efficacy trials (Daunic et al., 2006, 2012), such that main effects were detected for all students and baseline by treatment effects detected for those students at highest risk at baseline.

Second Step

Second Step is a classroom curriculum aimed to promote social-emotional development and reduce aggression by promoting empathy, impulse control, anger management, and problem-solving skills in children and adolescents (Frey, Hirschstein, & Guzzo, 2000). It is designed for children ages 4 to 14 and delivered in three groupings, including pre-K to third grade, fourth to fifth grade, and middle school. Each grouping includes curriculum with engaging lessons for students, staff training materials, family materials such as take-home activities and letters home, resources for school administrators to share with faculty and in assemblies, implementation ideas, and summative knowledge assessments.

The curriculum for each grouping includes 15 to 25 lessons intended to last about 35 minutes each and be delivered sequentially in one to two school years. Each lesson includes age-appropriate games, role-plays, media (e.g., video clips, PowerPoint slides), and homework, and can be delivered by typical school personnel, such as classroom teachers and school counselors. The Second Step curriculum teaches a five-step problem-solving model aligned with the CBI approach, including (a) identify the problem; (b) brainstorm solutions; (c) evaluate solutions by asking "Is it safe? Is it fair? How might people feel? Will it work?"; (d) select, plan, and try the

Cognitive-Behavioral Approaches 391

solution; and (e) evaluate if the solution worked and what to do next. Lessons also include stories that provide children with opportunities to identify problems, evaluate contexts, and brainstorm potential solutions to the problems. This format provides opportunities for direct instruction, a cognitive technique, and practice with feedback, a behavioral reinforcement strategy, as well as concrete examples for discussion to improve students' understanding and problem solving of complex social situations.

Several researchers have examined the effects of Second Step during the last 20 years from its first edition (Grossman et al., 1997) to most recent updates (Low et al., 2015; Upshur, Heyman, & Wenz-Gross, 2017). Findings demonstrate consistent treatment effects of prior program editions on decreased problem behavior, such as aggression and peer conflict, and increased prosocial behaviors at immediate posttests and three to 12-month follow-ups (Edwards, Hunt, Meyers, Grogg, & Jarrett, 2005; Frey, Nolen, Edstrom, & Hirschstein, 2005; Grossman et al., 1997).

In the primary grades, Low and colleagues (2015) and Upshur and colleagues (2017) examined treatment effects of the most recent edition of Second Step on students in grades K to 2 and preschools, respectively. Low et al. (2015) tested Second Step in 61 schools across six school districts including 7,300 students and 321 teachers. Results of the one-year randomized controlled trial indicated limited main effects, but differential treatment effects on teacher-reported social-emotional competencies and behavioral difficulties. That is, Low et al. found treatment effects for those students who started the school year with teacher-rated problem behaviors and/or social-emotional skill deficits in the areas of teacher-rated conduct problems, hyperactivity, peer problems, prosocial behaviors, social-emotional competency, learning skills, emotional management, and problem solving. These findings suggest Second Step, like TFGA, is most impactful for students with the lowest baseline competencies and highest problem behaviors. Upshur and colleagues (2017) conducted an efficacy trial of Second Step with 492 preschool-age students randomized to a treatment or control group. At posttest following one year of intervention, students in the treatment group exhibited significantly greater executive functioning and social-emotional skills than the students in the control group.

At the middle school level, a new edition was released in 2017, but only the prior edition has been tested empirically (Espelage, Low, Polanin, & Brown, 2013; Espelage, Rose, & Polanin, 2015). Espelage and colleagues (2013, 2015) conducted a randomized controlled trial with matched pairs of 36 middle schools and 3,616 sixth graders. After one year of implementing 15 weekly Second Step lessons from the 2008 edition, Espelage et al. (2013) found main treatment effects for reductions in physical aggression but no significant effects for other forms of aggression and victimization (e.g., verbal, relational, homophobic, and sexual). Subsequent analyses also revealed intervention effects for students with disabilities with a significant decrease in bullying perpetration across the three-year study compared to those in the control group (Espelage et al., 2015).

Coping Power

The Coping Power Program (CPP) is an intervention for students aged eight to 14 with heightened levels of disruptive and aggressive behavior. CPP was derived from an earlier iteration of the Anger Coping Program (Lochman, Nelson, & Sims, 1981) which was refined and tested as a multi-component CBI for both children and parents (Lochman & Wells, 2002). CPP is designed to increase social competence, self-regulation, and positive parental involvement via school-based group sessions for targeted students and parent training sessions for their caregivers delivered over the course of 15 to 18 months by a master's level clinician, such as typical school mental health staff (e.g., school counselor, social worker, school psychologist). The child component includes 33 group sessions lasting approximately 40–60 minutes delivered over the course of two intervention years with four to six children in each group. The group sessions include skill instruction and modeling in the areas of personal goal setting, awareness of feelings, coping self-statements, distraction techniques, relaxation methods, organizational and study skills, perspective taking, and social skills (Lochman & Wells, 2002). Students learn these skills via cognitive mediation instruction and behavioral therapy techniques by engaging in interactive methods through puppetry, videos, and demonstrations by the group leader and their peers. In addition to group sessions, the group leader engages each student in an individual 30-minute session every two months. The parent component of CPP also occurs at school led by the child component group leader and includes 16 90-minute sessions. Participating parents receive training in areas about the identification of prosocial and disruptive behaviors, rewarding appropriate child behaviors, giving effective instructions, establishing age-appropriate rules and expectations, developing effective consequences, and creating open communication.

Several research trials show positive effects of CPP, including both child and parent components, as well as variations to the original model (i.e., abbreviated child component, Lochman et al., 2014; class-wide applications, Muratori et al., 2015; individual delivery Lochman et al., 2015; internet enhancement for parent and child components, Lochman et al., 2017). Positive treatment effects of CPP have been detected immediately after intervention period and in one, three, and six-year follow-ups on substance use, delinquent behavior, teacher-rated behavioral problems, and/or academic performance (Lochman, 1992; Lochman, Lampron, Gemmer, Harris, & Wyckoff, 1989; Lochman & Wells, 2004; Muratori et al., 2019). Although effect sizes of CPP in one to three-year follow-ups are in the small to medium range, treatment effects have been found for preventing a decline in language arts grades two years following intervention (Lochman et al., 2012) and teacher-rated externalizing behavior (Lochman, Wells, Qu, & Chen, 2013). Researchers have also demonstrated these intervention effects are mediated by changes in children's social cognitions and parents' use of consistent discipline, in part validating the cognitive-behavioral component of the intervention's skill instruction (Lochman & Wells, 2002). Researchers have compared treatment effects of CPP to a common behavioral intervention strategy, Check-In/Check-Out (Maggin, Zurheide, Pickett, & Baillie, 2015) which relies on positive reinforcement strategies to shape behavior but does not include the cognitive or instructional components foundational to CBIs such as CPP (McDaniel et al., 2018). Although both the behavioral intervention strategy and CPP reduced externalizing behavior relative to the no treatment control condition, only CPP produced statistically and clinically significant within-group pre-post changes on measures of teacher-rated externalizing behavioral and total emotional and behavioral risk indices (McDaniel et al., 2018). Specifically, more students proportionally in the CPP group moved from heightened risk levels at pretest to below risk cutoffs at posttest than in the Check-In/Check-Out group and the intervention x time effect was only significant for the CPP group on a measure of both emotional and behavioral difficulties.

Bounce Back

Bounce Back is a multifaceted intervention for elementary school students who have experienced trauma that integrates school-based trauma interventions with evidence-based CBI strategies. Originally, Bounce Back was developed as an adaptation to lengthier, individually focused trauma interventions (i.e., Cognitive Behavioral Intervention for

Trauma in Schools [Kataoka et al., 2003; Stein et al., 2003] and Trauma-Focused Cognitive Behavioral Therapy [Cohen, Deblinger, Mannarino, & Steer, 2004]) to provide diverse communities with more feasible and acceptable school-based interventions (Langley et al., 2015). Bounce Back includes lessons for groups of four to six elementary students (ages 5–11) who are experiencing clinically significant levels of traumatic stress following a traumatic event (e.g., natural disasters; experienced or witnessed family, community, or school violence; traumatic separation due to the death, incarceration, deportation of a loved one).

Bounce Back includes ten manualized group lessons, two to three individual sessions, and up to three parent sessions designed specifically to normalize reactions to traumatic experiences, provide psychoeducation, and teach coping strategies. Each school-based group lesson lasts approximately 60 minutes, with the individual and parent sessions lasting 30 minutes. Each group session includes an agenda, reviewing assignments, introducing new concepts, and assigning activities for the next group. Lesson plans rely heavily upon CBI strategies that provide psychoeducation on learning the cognitive-behavioral relationships associated with feelings, relaxation training, cognitive restructuring, social problem solving, behavioral activation, and trauma-focused interventions, including gradual exposure to anxiety-provoking situations and trauma narrative. To provide developmentally appropriate experiential learning and make concepts taught in the group lessons concrete, trauma narratives are first portrayed through picture stories developed by students. Each story is individualized to reflect personal student experiences. Then, in individual and parent sessions students share and retell their trauma narrative relying on skills taught in group sessions to reduce anxious and fear responses to the event.

Results from Bounce Back demonstrate a multi-component intervention program can significantly improve post-traumatic stress and anxiety symptoms within a diverse population of elementary-aged students. Specifically, Langley et al. (2015) demonstrated that students who participated in the Bounce Back Program immediately reported substantial improvements in anxiety and post-traumatic stress symptoms when compared to a randomized 3-month waitlist group. These researchers also documented a high parent participation rate with 97% of participants having at least one session with a parent during the intervention group (Langley et al., 2015). At a 3-month follow-up assessment, students exposed to Bounce Back continued to show decreased internalizing symptoms. Moreover, following receipt of intervention from the delayed group, parent- and student-reported levels of post-traumatic stress, depression, and anxiety symptoms showed significant improvements (Langley et al., 2015). A subsequent replication study by Santiago and colleagues (2018) provided further support of Langley et al.'s initial efficacy study. Participants were mostly male, Latino elementary school students randomly assigned to immediate treatment or waitlist control. Researchers detected main treatment effects for greater reductions in post-traumatic stress symptoms and improved coping in the immediate treatment group compared to the delayed group. At 3-month follow up, the immediate treatment group also demonstrated reduced post-traumatic stress and depression symptoms and improved coping (Santiago et al., 2018). Additional research has documented the social validity and acceptability of Bounce Back in school-based programming (Distel et al., 2019).

Conclusion

An increasing number of researchers, teachers, and other school professionals recognize that providing explicit skill instruction through the use of CBIs can provide students with the skills to control their behaviors and emotions that are fundamental to healthy interpersonal functioning, mental health, and academic success (Durlak, Weissberg, Dymnicki, Taylor, &

Schellinger, 2011). A contributing factor for increasing this type of skill instruction in schools can be attributed to the Every Student Succeeds Act, the federal legislation that offers the provision of social-emotional learning (SEL) curricula and programs through a variety of funding streams to support districts and schools in their SEL implementation (Grant et al., 2017). These funding opportunities can provide a catalyst for key stakeholders to infuse CBIs within their school culture; however, there are personnel-level and programmatic challenges that exist such as (a) school professional training, support, and pedagogical fit, and (b) intervention intensity for students with EBD.

Teachers who work with students with behavioral problems are more likely to adopt an intervention when it aligns with their views on behavior change and when they are fluent with the teaching strategies required by the program (Han & Weiss, 2005). As such, preparation programs should orient teachers to cognitive behavioral theory as an approach for remediating significant behavior problems including pedagogical techniques of teaching positive self-talk, cognitive modeling, performance feedback, and the use of role-play inherent in CBIs (Smith & Daunic, 2006; Smith, Lochman, & Daunic, 2005). Han and Weiss (2005) explain that in-service teachers must receive intensive training followed by performance feedback with enough intensity and duration to internalize the principles of a program. Relatedly, research on working conditions of teachers of students with EBD suggest that learning opportunities and collegial support are fundamental for the implementation of evidence-based practices (Bettini, Cumming, Merrill, Brunsting, & Liaupsin, 2017). With adequate awareness and training of skills to implement CBIs, coordination among special educators and other school professionals (e.g., school psychologists, mental health staff, school counselors) to deliver CBIs enhances the opportunity for professional collaboration and provision of planned feedback, both of which may increase the likelihood of sustained CBI use. Moreover, coordination among a variety of school professionals can facilitate the generalization of learned skills across numerous settings, especially for secondary settings where students typically have daily contact with numerous teachers.

Implementing measures to mollify the effects of externalizing behaviors should align with the knowledge and skillset of certified special education teachers; however, it is unlikely these teachers possess the requisite psychoeducational training necessary to deliver therapeutic, multi-component interventions such as Bounce Back that address depression, anxiety, or trauma-induced stress. Thus, state and local education agencies may have to provide schools with more skilled mental health professionals and build substantive partnerships with community agencies (Splett et al., 2017) to assist with implementing CBIs.

To alter the significant and sometimes extreme maladaptive behavioral patterns of students with EBD, cognitive-behavioral type interventions must be of sufficient intensity as universal and targeted level supports may not be potent enough to affect change. No doubt, school-based CBIs may not be intensive enough for significant change, so incorporating the student's natural support systems such as family, community members, and agency professionals in therapeutic wrap-around services can help overcome mental health or behavioral issues (Suter & Bruns, 2009).

A salient factor in the use of CBIs is the collateral benefit to teachers and other school professionals responsible for their delivery. For example, Domitrovich et al. (2016) examined the impact of a CBI on teacher-reported indices of burnout, self-efficacy, and SEL competency when implemented in primary grades. Their results indicated that teachers who implemented the program reported higher levels of personal accomplishment and self-efficacy for behavior management and social-emotional interactions with students. The promise of CBIs to positively impact teachers and other school professionals who work with students with EBD is particularly relevant considering special education teacher shortages and the high level of teacher stress, burnout, and low job satisfaction (e.g., Brunsting, Sreckovic, & Lane, 2014).

References

Barnes, T. N., Smith, S. W., & Miller, M. D. (2014). Cognitive-behavioral interventions in the treatment of aggression in schools in the United States: A meta-analysis. *Aggression and Violent Behavior, 19*, 311–321. doi:org/10.1016/j.avb.2014.04.013

Bettini, E. A., Cumming, M. M., Merrill, K. L., Brunsting, N. C., & Liaupsin, C. J. (2017). Working conditions in self-contained settings for students with emotional disturbance. *The Journal of Special Education, 51*(2), 83–94. doi:org/10.1177/0022466916674195

Bradley, R., Doolittle, J., & Bartolotta, R. (2008). Building on the data and adding to the discussion: The experiences and outcomes of students with emotional disturbance. *Journal of Behavioral Education, 17*, 4–23. doi:10.1007/s10864-007-9058-6

Brunsting, N. C., Sreckovic, M. A., & Lane, K. L. (2014). Special education teacher burnout: A synthesis of research from 1979 to 2013. *Education and Treatment of Children, 37*, 681–711. doi:10.1353/etc.2014.0032

Centers for Disease Control and Prevention. (2015). *National Suicide Statistics.* Retrieved from www.cdc.gov/violenceprevention/suicide/statistics/

Cohen, J. A., Deblinger, E., Mannarino, A. P., & Steer, R. A. (2004). A multisite, randomized controlled trial for children with sexual abuse-related PTSD symptoms. *Journal of the American Academy of Child & Adolescent Psychiatry, 43*, 393–402. doi:org/10.1097/00004583-200404000-00005

Conduct Problems Prevention Research Group. (2010). The effects of a multiyear universal social-emotional learning program: The role of student and school characteristics. *Journal of Consulting and Clinical Psychology, 78*, 156–168. doi:org/10.1037/a0018607

Daunic, A. P., Smith, S. W., Aydin, B., & Barber, B. R. (2019). Lowering risk for significant behavior problems through cognitive-behavioral intervention: Effects of the Tools for Getting Along curriculum two years following implementation. *Journal of Primary Prevention, 40*, 463–482. doi: 10.1007/s10935-019-00554-3.

Daunic, A. P., Smith, S. W., Brank, E. M., & Penfield, R. D. (2006). Classroom-based cognitive–Behavioral intervention to prevent aggression: Efficacy and social validity. *Journal of School Psychology, 44*, 123–139. doi:org/10.1016/j.jsp.2006.01.005

Daunic, A. P., Smith, S. W., Garvan, C. W., Barber, B. R., Becker, M. K., Peters, C. D., … Naranjo, A. H. (2012). Reducing developmental risk for emotional/behavioral problems: A randomized controlled trial examining the *Tools for Getting Along* curriculum. *Journal of School Psychology, 50*, 149–166. doi:org/10.1016/j.jsp.2011.09.003

Distel, L. M., Torres, S. A., Ros, A. M., Brewer, S. K., Raviv, T., Coyne, C., … Santiago, C. D. (2019). Evaluating the implementation of Bounce Back: Clinicians' perspectives on a school-based trauma intervention. *Evidence-Based Practice in Child and Adolescent Mental Health, 4*(1), 1–17. doi:org/10.1080/23794925.2019.1565501

Domitrovich, C. E., Bradshaw, C. P., Berg, J. K., Pas, E. T., Becker, K. D., Musci, R., … Ialongo, N. (2016). How do school-based prevention programs impact teachers? Findings from a randomized trial of an integrated classroom management and social-emotional program. *Prevention Science, 17*, 325–337. doi:org/10.1007/s11121015-0618-z

Durlak, J. A., Weissberg, R. P., Dymnicki, A. B., Taylor, R. D., & Schellinger, K. B. (2011). The impact of enhancing students' social and emotional learning: A meta-analysis of school-based universal interventions. *Child Development, 82*, 405–432. doi:org/10.1111/j.1467-8624.2010.01564.x

Edwards, D., Hunt, M. H., Meyers, J., Grogg, K. R., & Jarrett, O. (2005). Acceptability and student outcomes of a violence prevention curriculum. *The Journal of Primary Prevention, 26*, 401–418. doi:10.1007/s10935-005-0002-z

Espelage, D. L., Low, S., Polanin, J. R., & Brown, E. C. (2013). The impact of a middle school program to reduce aggression, victimization, and sexual violence. *Journal of Adolescent Health, 53*, 180–186. doi:org/10.1016/j.jadohealth.2013.02.021

Espelage, D. L., Rose, C. A., & Polanin, J. R. (2015). Social-emotional learning program to reduce bullying, fighting, and victimization among middle school students with disabilities. *Remedial and Special Education, 36*, 299–311. doi:org/10.1177/0741932514564564

Every Student Succeeds Act (ESSA) of 2015, Pub.L. 114-95. (2015).

Fraser, M. W., Thompson, A. M., Day, S. H., & Macy, R. J. (2014). The Making Choices program: Impact of social-emotional skills training on the risk status of third graders. *Elementary School Journal, 114*, 354–379. doi:10.1086/674055

Frey, K. S., Hirschstein, M. K., & Guzzo, B. A. (2000). Second Step: Preventing aggression by promoting social competence. *Journal of Emotional and Behavioral Disorders, 8*, 102–112. doi:10.1177/106342660000800206

Frey, K. S., Nolen, S. B., Edstrom, L. V., & Hirschstein, M. K. (2005). Effects of a school-based social-emotional competence program: Linking children's goals, attributions, and behavior. *Journal of Applied Developmental Psychology, 26*, 171–200. doi:org/10.1016/j.appdev.2004.12.002

Grant, S., Hamilton, L. S., Wrabel, S. L., Gomez, C. J., Whitaker, A., & Ramos, A. (2017). *How the Every Student Succeeds Act can support social and emotional learning.* Santa Monica, CA: RAND Corporation.

Grossman, D. C., Neckerman, H. J., Koepsell, T. D., Liu, P. Y., Asher, K. N., Beland, K., … Rivara, F. P. (1997). Effectiveness of a violence prevention curriculum among children in elementary school: A randomized controlled trial. *Journal of American Medical Association, 277*, 1605–1611. doi:org/10.1001/jama.277.20.1605

Han, S. S., & Weiss, B. (2005). Sustainability of teacher implementation of school-based mental health programs. *Journal of Abnormal Child Psychology, 33*, 665–679. doi:org/10.1007/s10802-005-7646-2

Kaplan, J. S., & Carter, J. F. (1995). *Beyond behavior modification: A cognitive-behavioral approach to behavior management in the school.* Austin, TX: Pro Ed.

Kataoka, S. H., Stein, B. D., Jaycox, L. H., Wong, M., Escudero, P., Tu, W., … Fink, A. (2003). A school-based mental health program for traumatized Latino immigrant children. *Journal of the American Academy of Child & Adolescent Psychiatry, 42*, 311–318. doi:org/10.1097/00004583-200303000-00011

Langley, A. K., Gonzalez, A., Sugar, C. A., Solis, D., & Jaycox, L. (2015). Bounce Back: Effectiveness of an elementary school-based intervention for multicultural children exposed to traumatic events. *Journal of Consulting and Clinical Psychology, 83*, 853–865. doi:10.1037/ccp0000051

Lerner, R., & Steinberg, L. (2004). *Handbook of adolescent psychology* (2nd ed.). Hoboken, NJ: John Wiley & Sons.

Lochman, J. E. (1992). Cognitive-behavioral intervention with aggressive boys: Three-year follow-up and preventive effects. *Journal of Consulting and Clinical Psychology, 60*, 426–432. doi:org/10.1037/0022-006X.60.3.426

Lochman, J. E., Baden, R. E., Boxmeyer, C. L., Powell, N. P., Qu, L., Salekin, K. L., & Windle, M. (2014). Does a booster intervention augment the preventive effects of an abbreviated version of the Coping Power Program for aggressive children? *Journal of Abnormal Child Psychology, 42*, 367–381. doi:org/10.1007/s10802-013-9727-y

Lochman, J. E., Boxmeyer, C. L., Jones, S., Qu, L., Ewoldsen, D., & Nelson, W. M., III. (2017). Testing the feasibility of a briefer school-based preventive intervention with aggressive children: A hybrid intervention with face-to-face and internet components. *Journal of School Psychology, 62*, 33–50. doi:org/10.1016/j.jsp.2017.03.010

Lochman, J. E., Boxmeyer, C. L., Powell, N. P., Qu, L., Wells, K., & Windle, M. (2012). Coping Power dissemination study: Intervention and special education effects on academic outcomes. *Behavioral Disorders, 37*, 192–205. doi:org/10.1177/019874291203700306

Lochman, J. E., Coie, J. D., Underwood, M. K., & Terry, R. (1993). Effectiveness of a social relations intervention program for aggressive and nonaggressive, rejected children. *Journal of Consulting and Clinical Psychology, 61*, 1053–1058. https://doi.org/10.1037/0022-006X.61.6.1053

Lochman, J. E., Dishion, T. J., Powell, N. P., Boxmeyer, C. L., Qu, L., & Sallee, M. (2015). Evidence-based preventive intervention for preadolescent aggressive children: One-year outcomes following randomization to group versus individual delivery. *Journal of Consulting and Clinical Psychology, 83*, 728–735. doi:org/10.1037/ccp0000030

Lochman, J. E., Lampron, L. B., Gemmer, T. C., Harris, S. R., & Wyckoff, G. M. (1989). Teacher consultation and cognitive-behavioral interventions with aggressive boys. *Psychology in the Schools, 26*, 179–188. doi:org/10.1002/1520-6807(198904)26:2<179::AID-PITS2310260209>3.0.CO;2-Z

Lochman, J. E., Nelson, W. M., & Sims, J. P. (1981). A cognitive behavioral program for use with aggressive children. *Journal of Clinical Child Psychology, 10*, 146–148. doi:org/10.1080/15374418109533036

Lochman, J. E., & Wells, K. C. (2002). Contextual social-cognitive mediators and child outcome: A test of the theoretical model in the Coping Power program. *Development and Psychopathology, 14*, 945–967. doi:org/10.1017/S0954579402004157

Lochman, J. E., & Wells, K. C. (2004). The Coping Power program for preadolescent aggressive boys and their parents: Outcome effects at the 1-year follow-up. *Journal of Consulting and Clinical Psychology, 72*, 571. doi:org/10.1037/0022-006X.72.4.571

Lochman, J. E., Wells, K. C., Qu, L., & Chen, L. (2013). Three year follow-up of Coping Power intervention effects: Evidence of neighborhood moderation? *Prevention Science, 14*, 364–376. doi:org/10.1007/s11121-012-0295-0

Low, S., Cook, C. R., Smolkowski, K., & Buntain-Ricklefs, J. (2015). Promoting social–Emotional competence: An evaluation of the elementary version of Second Step®. *Journal of School Psychology, 53*, 463–477. doi:org/10.1016/j.jsp.2015.09.002

Maggin, D. M., Zurheide, J., Pickett, K. C., & Baillie, S. J. (2015). A systematic evidence review of the Check-In/Check-out program for reducing student challenging behaviors. *Journal of Positive Behavior Interventions, 17*, 197–208. doi:http://dx.doi.org/10.1177/1098300715573630

Mahoney, M. J. (1974). *Cognition and behavior modification*. Cambridge: Ballinger.

Mattison, R. E., & Schneider, J. (2009). First-year effectiveness on school functioning of a self-contained ED middle school. *Behavioral Disorders, 34*, 60–71. doi:org/10.1177/019874290903400201

McDaniel, S. C., Lochman, J. E., Tomek, S., Powell, N., Irwin, A., & Kerr, S. (2018). Reducing risk for emotional and behavioral disorders in late elementary school: A comparison of two targeted interventions. *Behavioral Disorders, 43*, 370–382. doi:http://dx.doi.org/10.1177/0198742917747595

Meichenbaum, D. H. (1977). *Cognitive-behavior modification: An integrative approach*. New York, NY: Plenum Press.

Merrill, K. L., Smith, S. W., Cumming, M. M., & Daunic, A. P. (2017). A review of social problem-solving interventions: Past findings, current status, and future directions. *Review of Educational Research, 87*, 71–102. doi:org/10.3102/0034654316652943

Merry, S. N., Hetrick, S. E., Cox, G. R., Brudevold-Iversen, T., Bir, J. J., & McDowell, H. (2012). Cochrane review: Psychological and educational interventions for preventing depression in children and adolescents. *Evidence-Based Child Health: A Cochrane Review Journal, 7*, 1409–1685. doi:10.1002/ebch.1867

Muratori, P., Bertacchi, I., Giuli, C., Lombardi, L., Bonetti, S., Nocentini, A., … Lochman, J. E. (2015). First adaptation of Coping Power program as a classroom-based prevention intervention on aggressive behaviors among elementary school children. *Prevention Science, 16*, 432–439. doi:org/10.1007/s11121-014-0501-3

Muratori, P., Milone, A., Levantini, V., Ruglioni, L., Lambruschi, F., Pisano, S., … Lochman, J. E. (2019). Six-year outcome for children with ODD or CD treated with the Coping Power program. *Psychiatry Research, 271*, 454–458. doi:org/10.1016/j.psychres.2018.12.018

Nelson, J. R., Hurley, K. D., Synhorst, L., Epstein, M. H., Stage, S., & Buckley, J. (2009). The child outcomes of a behavioral model. *Exceptional Children, 76*, 7–30. doi:org/10.1177/001440290907600101

Perou, R., Bitsko, R. H., Blumberg, S. J., Pastor, P., Ghandour, R. M., Gfroerer, J. C., … Huang, L. N. (2013). Mental health surveillance among children–United States, 2005–2011. *Morbidity and Mortality Weekly Report, 62*(Suppl. 2), 1–35.

Polsgrove, L., & Smith, S. W. (2004). Informed practice in teaching self-control to children with emotional and behavioral disorders. In R. B. Rutherford, M. M. Quinn, & S. R. Mathur (Eds.), *Handbook of research in emotional and behavioral disorders* (pp. 399–425). New York, NY: Guilford.

Riggs, N. R., Greenberg, M. T., Kusché, C. A., & Pentz, M. A. (2006). The mediational role of neurocognition in the behavioral outcomes of a social-emotional prevention program in elementary school students: Effects of the PATHS curriculum. *Prevention Science, 7*, 91–102. doi:org/10.1007/s11121-005-0022-1

Rivers, S. E., Brackett, M. A., Reyes, M. R., Elbertson, N. A., & Salovey, P. (2013). Improving the social and emotional climate of classrooms: A clustered randomized controlled trial testing the RULER approach. *Prevention Science, 14*, 77–87. doi:org/10.1007/s11121-012-0305-2

Robinson, T. R., Smith, S. W., Miller, M. D., & Brownell, M. T. (1999). Cognitive behavior modification of hyperactivity-impulsivity and aggression: A meta-analysis of school-based studies. *Journal of Educational Psychology, 91*, 195–203. doi:org/10.1037/0022-0663.91.2.195

Sanford, C., Newman, L., Wagner, M., Cameto, R., Knokey, A. M., & Shaver, D. (2011). *The post-high school outcomes of young adults with disabilities up to 6 years after high school: Key findings from the National Longitudinal Transition Study-2 (NLTS2). NCSER 2011-3004.* Washington, DC: National Center for Special Education Research, Institute of Education Sciences. Retrieved from http://files.eric.ed.gov/fulltext/ED524044.pdf

Santiago, C. D., Raviv, T., Ros, A. M., Brewer, S. K., Distel, L. M. L., Torres, S. A., ... Langley, A. K. (2018). Implementing the Bounce Back trauma intervention in urban elementary schools: A real-world replication trial. *School Psychology Quarterly, 33*, 1–9. doi:10.1037/spq0000229

Shure, M. B., & Spivack, G. (1979). Interpersonal cognitive problem solving and primary prevention: Programming for preschool and kindergarten children. *Journal of Clinical Child Psychology, 2*, 89–94. doi:org/10.1080/15374417909532894

Smith, S. W., & Daunic, A. P. (2004). Research on preventing behavior problems using a cognitive-behavioral intervention: Preliminary findings, challenges, and future directions. *Behavioral Disorders, 30*, 72–76. doi:org/10.1177/019874290403000105

Smith, S. W., & Daunic, A. P. (2006). *Managing difficult behavior through problem solving instruction: Strategies for the elementary classroom.* Boston, MA: Allyn & Bacon.

Smith, S. W., & Daunic, A. P. (2010). Cognitive-behavioral interventions in school settings. In R. Algozzine, A. P. Daunic, & S. W. Smith (Eds.), *Preventing problem behaviors: A handbook of successful prevention strategies* (2nd ed., pp. 53–70). Thousand Oaks, CA: Corwin Press.

Smith, S. W., Daunic, A. P., Aydin, B., Van Loan, C. L., Barber, B. R., & Taylor, G. G. (2016). Effect of Tools for Getting Along on student risk for emotional and behavioral problems in upper elementary classrooms: A replication study. *School Psychology Review, 45*(1), 73–92. doi:org/10.17105/SPR45-1.73-92

Smith, S. W., Daunic, A. P., Barber, B. R., Aydin, B., Van Loan, C. L., & Taylor, G. G. (2014). Preventing risk for significant behavior problems through a cognitive-behavioral intervention: Effects of the *Tools for Getting Along* curriculum at one-year follow-up. *Journal of Primary Prevention, 35*, 371–387. doi:org/10.1007/s10935-014-0357-0

Smith, S. W., Graber, J., & Daunic, A. P. (2009). Cognitive-behavioral interventions for anger/aggression: Review of research and research-to-practice issues. In M. Mayer, R. Van Acker, J. Lochman, & F. Gresham (Eds.), *Cognitive-behavioral interventions for emotional and behavioral disorders: School-based practice* (pp. 111–142). New York, NY: Guilford.

Smith, S. W., Lochman, J. E., & Daunic, A. P. (2005). Managing aggression using cognitive- behavioral interventions: State of the practice and future directions. *Behavioral Disorders, 30*, 227–240. doi:10.1177/019874290503000307

Smith, S. W., Poling, D. V., & Worth, M. R. (2018). Intensive intervention for students with emotional and behavioral disorders. *Learning Disabilities Research and Practice, 33*, 168–175. doi:org/10.1111/ldrp.12174

Smith, S. W., Taylor, G. G., Barnes, T. N., & Daunic, A. P. (2012). Cognitive-behavioral interventions to prevent aggression of students with emotional and behavioral disorders. In B. G. Cook, M. Tankersley, & T. J. Landrum (Eds.), *Advances in learning and behavioral disabilities, Volume 25* (pp. 47–70). Bingley, UK: Emerald Publishing.

Snyder, T. D., de Brey, C., & Dillow, S. A. (2018). *Digest of Education Statistics 2016 (NCES 2017-094)*. Washington, DC: National Center for Education Statistics, Institute of Education Sciences, U.S. Department of Education.

Splett, J. W., Perales, K., Halliday-Boykins, C. A., Gilchrest, C., Gibson, N., & Weist, M. D. (2017). Best practices for teaming and collaboration in the Interconnected Systems Framework. *Journal of Applied School Psychology, 33*(347-368). doi:http://dx.doi.org/10.1080/15377903.2017.1328625

Stein, B. D., Jaycox, L. H., Kataoka, S. H., Wong, M., Tu, W., Elliott, M. N., & Fink, A. (2003). A mental health intervention for school children exposed to violence: A randomized controlled trial. *Journal of the American Medical Association, 290*, 603–611. doi:org/10.1001/jama.290.5.603

Suter, J. C., & Bruns, E. J. (2009). Effectiveness of the wraparound process for children with emotional and behavioral disorders: A meta-analysis. *Clinical Child and Family Psychology Review, 12*, 336–351. doi:10.1007/s10567-009-0059-y

Upshur, C. C., Heyman, M., & Wenz-Gross, M. (2017). Efficacy trial of the Second Step Early Learning (SSEL) curriculum: Preliminary outcomes. *Journal of Applied Developmental Psychology, 50*, 15–25. doi:org/10.1016/j.appdev.2017.03.004

Webster-Stratton, C., Reid, M. J., & Stoolmiller, M. (2008). Preventing conduct problems and improving school readiness: Evaluation of the incredible years teacher and child training programs in high-risk schools. *Journal of Child Psychology and Psychiatry, 49*, 471–488.

Weissberg, R. P., Goren, P., Domitrovich, C., & Dusenbury, L. (2013). *CASEL guide effective social and emotional learning programs: Preschool and elementary school edition.* Chicago, IL: CASEL.

Wrabel, S. L., Hamilton, L. S., Whitaker, A. A., & Grant, S. (2018). *Investing in evidence-based social and emotional learning: Companion guide to social and emotional learning interventions under the Every Student Succeeds Act: Evidence review.* Santa Monica, CA: RAND Corporation.

27 School-based Mental Health

Steven W. Evans, R. Elizabeth Capps, and Julie Sarno Owens

Approximately 12% of young people experience any mental health disorder in a given year based on parent report and evidence suggests that only 36% of youth who experience a mental health disorder receive treatment (Leaf et al., 1996). Even among those who do receive care, they attend so few sessions (Merikangas et al., 2011) that the value of the treatment provided is questionable. Given the large numbers of youth who do not receive care or receive less than optimal services it is not surprising that the long-term outcomes of youth with emotional and behavioral disorders (EBD) are quite poor (Bradley, Henderson, & Monfore, 2004). For example, evidence from the National Longitudinal Transition Study-2 (NLTS-2) indicated that 56% of high school-aged youth with EBD finished high school and this rate is among the lowest high school completion rate of all disability categories (Wagner, Newman, Cameto, & Levine, 2005). Further, among all disability categories in the 2015–2016 school year, youth with EBD evidenced the highest rates of school suspensions, expulsions, and removal to alternative school placements due to drugs, weapons, or serious injury (U.S. Department of Education, 2018). School mental health professionals (SMHPs; intervention specialists, school psychologists, school counselors, school social workers) are uniquely trained and ecologically well situated to address the problems faced by these students. The purpose of the chapter is to describe advantages of school-based delivery, types of school mental health (SMH) services and frameworks for how these services can be systematically applied in schools. We also review cultural and developmental considerations and the critical importance of moving strategies developed in the scientific arena to practice to improve the outcomes of students with EBD.

Advantages of School-Based Service Delivery

Although clinics have historically been the location for the provision of services to youth with EBD, the emergence of SMH over the last half century has contributed to the importance of schools in this role (Burns et al., 1995). Despite the benefits that clinic-based care can offer to a subset of youth, SMH has many advantages over clinic-based care. First and foremost, SMH delivery models enhance access to care by removing logistic barriers (travel time, transportation). Second, SMH models facilitate ecologically based assessment. For example, when completing evaluations of a referred student, SMHPs have unique opportunities to observe students and easy access to teachers and other staff who interact with them. For youth with EBD the school setting often presents social, academic, and behavioral challenges. SMHPs have the opportunity to witness the students' impairment and the context in which the impairment manifests. The observations can improve professionals' understanding of the problems and enhance conceptualization of the student's strengths and weaknesses. In contrast, clinic-based clinicians have little access to information from schools and typically rely on parent or child report and possibly teacher-completed rating scales. Rating scales can provide insight into a referred child's strengths and weaknesses in relation to normative data about the child's functioning in school, but they provide little in relation to the context and function of behaviors. Further, these ratings are particularly valuable for elementary school-aged students, but have serious limitations for middle and high school students, as their reliability and validity are questionable (Evans, Allen, Moore, & Strauss, 2005; Molina, Pelham, Blumenthal, & Galiszewski, 1998). Clinicians in any setting can use these ratings to gather information about a student; however, the unique opportunities that SMHPs have to talk to a student's teachers, review records, and complete observations in multiple contexts (e.g., structured, unstructured, academic, social) makes these ratings only a portion of the data about school functioning instead of the entirety of the data as is often true in a clinic.

Third, SMH models also have advantages over clinic-based models when it comes to ecologically grounded interventions. Remarkably, clinic-based care has adhered to weekly 50-minute sessions as the standard for care for many decades even though many of our most effective treatments are difficult to implement well in that format. For example, exposure and habituation sessions when treating youth with anxiety can be brief or quite long depending on the response of the child. This can make the fit within a 50-minute session difficult. Although individual and group therapy interventions have been developed for delivery in schools and transported from clinics to schools (e.g., Ginsburg, Becker, Kingery, & Nichols, 2008), there is often a need to modify the interventions to the context of the school. For example, modifications to cognitive-behavioral treatment for elementary school-aged children with anxiety (e.g., Coping Cat) included increasing frequency of sessions while reducing session length, increasing use of visual aids and activity-based learning, revising the nature of parent involvement, and maintaining flexibility in student availability so exposure sessions can last as long as is needed for the student to habituate (Mychailyszyn et al., 2011). Furthermore, exposure sessions are optimally effective when they are repeated frequently and in the context in which anxiety occurs, as can be done in schools. Assigning exposure practice as "home-work" is a common practice in clinics to achieve these repetitions, yet these assignments are often inconsistently completed (Park et al., 2014). This advantage for SMH is not limited to exposure sessions. Organization and interpersonal training interventions for adolescents with ADHD are demonstrating meaningful and lasting effects and frequent practice and coaching are one key to their success (Evans, Owens, & Power, 2019). Similarly, daily report card (DRC) interventions leverage daily relational support and feedback to shape student behavior over time. SMHPs are in a unique position to provide ecologically grounded, high-frequency interventions and this can improve the quality of services provided.

Fourth, unlike clinic providers, SMHPs have the opportunity to observe the implementation of interventions and facilitate efficient modifications (e.g., timing, intensity, location). For example, behavioral approaches for children with disruptive behavior often involve a student's teacher implementing targeted behavioral practices (e.g., Owens, Hustus & Evans, Chapter 25 in this book). A SMHP has the opportunity to help the teacher implement the practice, observe attempts to use it, and provide constructive feedback. For many teachers, this level of support is necessary for effective implementation (Owens et al., 2017). Furthermore, the SMHP can observe a student's attempts to use strategies learned in sessions (e.g., problem solving, organization) and identify reasons why the strategy may or may not be working. This can lead to timely modifications to enhance effectiveness.

Lastly, SMH services also provide the unique opportunity to integrate academic, family, and mental health interventions (Atkins, Hoagwood, Kutash, & Seidman, 2010). For example, students with test anxiety and math related learning problems may benefit from an intervention plan that includes math remediation, exposure for anxiety, and parent training pertaining to supportive procedures related to math homework and coping. The level of the math tasks used in the exposure could be informed by the progress of the math remediation in a manner that substantially enhances student outcomes. This type of integrated intervention implemented by a multidisciplinary team can provide students with exemplary and unique intervention opportunities that can address both their emotional and learning needs.

In spite of these potential advantages of SMH services over clinic-based care, many of these advantages are not realized in daily practice. In fact, reviews of IEPs and 504 plans for students with EBD indicate that evidence-based practices are rarely implemented and some of the most frequently provided services have little to no evidence that they work (Kern, Hetrick, Custer, & Commisso, 2018; Spiel, Evans, & Langberg, 2014). Reasons for this state of affairs include a lack of time and priority for SMHPs to attend to the needs of students with emotional and behavioral problems (Kelly et al., 2010), an inadequate number of SMHPs in many districts, a lack of training in evidence-based practices in many of the graduate programs training SMHPs (Shernoff, Kratochwill, & Stoiber, 2003), and lack of attention to the diverse array of the types of services that can be provided under the umbrella of comprehensive SMH programming. Effectively addressing these barriers could unleash the full potential of SMH services and substantially improve the outcomes of youth with emotional and behavioral problems.

Types of Services

Comprehensive SMH programming includes services across a continuum of care including universal mental health promotion, universal skill development and/or risk prevention, screening, assessment, early targeted intervention, intensive indicated intervention, and inter-systems coordinated care. These services can be provided school-wide (e.g., halls, cafeteria, library), in general education classrooms, alternative classrooms, or as individual, group, or family-based counseling services.

School-wide services typically take an education approach to benefit students about risky behaviors (e.g., drug and alcohol use) or practices that may improve health or mental health (e.g., sleep hygiene, social or emotion regulation skills). Approaches may include a public-health campaign approach including having common expectations across contexts, posters with educational messages, articles in newsletters, and integration into themes for school projects. School-wide programs such as bullying prevention involve interdisciplinary collaboration in delivery as diverse school personnel (including teachers, principals, and SMHPs) and students apply strategies to improve students' functioning and school outcomes (Leff, Waanders, Waasdorp, & Paskewich, 2014). School-wide approaches require a great deal of sustained commitment and buy-in among school personnel and the effects may not be immediately evident (Leff et al., 2014). School-wide interventions may help establish the foundation for mental health in the student body, but targeted interventions are required to address the needs of many individual students.

Some targeted interventions are provided in the context of general education classrooms. Evidence-based use of effective classroom management strategies provides an important foundation for engaging students in academic content, maximizing instruction time, and addressing disruptive behavior (Emmer & Sabornie, 2015). Teachers' effective use of classroom management is positively associated with students' achievement (Reddy, Fabiano, Dudek, & Hsu, 2013), social development (Mikami, Owens, Hudec, Kassab, & Evans,

2019), and behavioral outcomes (Owens, Evans et al., 2019). However, many students with EBD require individualized supports, such as a daily report card. Importantly, interventions delivered in the context of the general education classroom have the potential to address behavioral, academic, and social concerns experienced by students with EBD that occur in the context where impairments in functioning are likely to present. Although teacher-delivered interventions for students with EBD may raise concerns about additional demands on teachers, classroom-based interventions have the potential to complement class-wide behavior management and reduce the need for intensive interventions.

In addition to interventions provided in the context of the general education classroom, interventions for youth with EBD may be administered in alternative classroom formats. Alternative classrooms are most frequently resource rooms or small group study halls. Multiple students typically are in the rooms at the same time, but there are usually few of them and staffing often includes a special education teacher and aide. This setting allows for more intensive interventions than can be provided in general education classrooms. They provide an ideal setting for remedial instruction, group interventions, academic skills training, and behavioral interventions too intensive for the general education classroom. For example, middle or high school students with ADHD or learning disabilities could learn note taking skills or self-management in such a setting (e.g., Evans et al., 2016). Some students in special education may receive much of their instruction each day in an alternative classroom with an intensive behavioral program in place to keep them engaged and effectively manage behavior. Some secondary students are assigned to small group study halls and these settings often include students with and without service plans, thus providing a setting for a wide range of students to receive special services. Alternative classrooms provide a valuable setting for the provision of SMH services to students with EBD.

Services provided by SMHPs such as counseling may be those that are most traditionally considered SMH services and may be most likely to be considered individualized and intensive. Services provided by SMHPs are often similar to the type of assessment and intervention that is provided in clinics. In fact, there are two common models for providing these services. The first is often referred to as a co-location model and the other is a school staff model. The co-location model usually involves clinicians from local hospitals or clinics conducting part of their work in a school. They are often paid by direct billing to families or insurers for their time with each student, or on a contracted basis with the school, or a combination of these two. One advantage of this approach is that children who need additional services that may not be available from the co-located clinician (e.g., medication, family therapy) may be able to receive coordinated care by the clinician at school and others at the clinician's "home" clinic. A disadvantage of that approach is that the co-located clinicians may be unfamiliar with the culture of a school and this may impede collaboration. In addition, for some co-located clinicians, the need to generate billable hours in the school may limit the amount of time the clinician spends with teachers, observing student behavior, and participating in team meetings. It may also limit the students who can be served (only those with Medicaid or a specific type of insurance).

Advantages of school staff providing interventions include the opportunity to collaborate with other school professionals, conduct observations, participate in team meetings, and serve all students regardless of insurance status. As their time is not influenced by the need for billable hours, it can be allocated based solely on what is best for the student. Some SMHPs are hesitant to provide "therapy" services to students citing an abundance of administrative work, unfamiliarity with effective interventions, or a discomfort with that role. Unfortunately, SMHPs are often burdened with tasks that could be completed by someone without

404   *Steven W. Evans et al.*

a professional degree (e.g., scheduling, administrative paperwork, proctoring tests, and monitoring study halls). Burdening SMHPs with these administrative tasks is an obstacle to students receiving effective care. In fact, these tasks have been identified as barriers to meeting the needs of students even when training and ongoing support for SMHPs is freely available (Kern et al., 2019).

Models for SMH Services

Given the array of services within comprehensive SMH programming, frameworks for organizing these services have emerged. Three common models for scaffolding school-based intervention decisions and implementation include schoolwide positive behavioral interventions and supports (SWPBIS; Sugai & Horner, 2006), multi-tiered system of support (MTSS; Benner, Kutash, Nelson, & Fisher, 2013), and the Life Course Model (LCM; Evans, Owens, Mautone, DuPaul, & Power, 2014). SWPBIS and MTSS are two frameworks for guiding decisions about the selection, integration, and implementation of evidence-based practices to improve students' academic and behavioral functioning. Both frameworks are designed to function similarly in schools; however, they originally differed in the area of student functioning with which they are concerned (i.e., behavioral functioning was the foci for SWPBIS; academic functioning was the foci for MTSS) (see Kern, McIntosh, Commisso, & Austin, Chapter 14, this volume). One limitation of these two models is that they do not guide the decisions of SMHPs about *how* to select a service for a student within a given level of impairment or within a given tier of service. In contrast, the LCM does provide guidance about how to sequence and prioritize services for students with EBD.

The LCM is grounded on the premise that providers should prioritize interventions that have the best chance to increase the functioning of students so they can independently meet age-appropriate expectations. Based on this premise, a model for sequencing types of services was developed (Evans et al., 2014). The first priority for services involves evaluating and intervening to improve the context in which the problems occur. The rationale is that if the classroom or home situation is chaotic or otherwise problematic, intervening with the student may have little benefit until the context changes. The second priority is psychosocial interventions designed to build skills or competencies (e.g., behavioral regulation, organization, coping). When psychosocial interventions are effective, the student should be able to independently meet age-appropriate expectations for behavior and academic performance after the intervention ends. According to the LCM, medications are the third priority. Parents can be encouraged to give psychosocial interventions time to work before initiating a medication trial for many children. Although medications can help children meet age-appropriate expectations, there is little reason to believe that their benefits will extend beyond their use. Although SMHPs may prefer to refrain from recommending medications, it is well within their purview to help parents become educated consumers about this decision (e.g., review advantages and disadvantages, help parents develop questions to ask the pediatrician or psychiatrist). In the LCM, accommodations are a last resort. In schools, strategies commonly categorized as accommodations are those that reduce expectations as a means of reducing impairment (e.g., shortening or removing homework assignments, offering extended time for tests or assignments, providing class notes). The primary reason that accommodations are last is because although these approaches can reduce parent, teacher, and student stress, and/or improve grades, they do not help students develop skills to be an independent learner or for success after high school. According to the LCM, if the only services provided to a student are accommodations, then parents and professionals are essentially giving up on

School-based Mental Health   405

the student being able to function similar to peers. However, a combined approach may benefit some students. In accordance with the LCM, students may be given copies of a teacher's notes (accommodation) while being taught how to take accurate notes (intervention).

Research on the benefits of a combined approach to prioritizing services is limited, but some evidence exists. For example, in a study evaluating the sequencing of medication and psychosocial interventions for children with ADHD, Pelham and colleagues (2016) reported benefits for providing psychosocial interventions prior to medication. In another study with middle school students with ADHD that addressed the benefits of interventions in relation to accommodations, gains after services ended were apparent for students who received interventions but not for students who received accommodations (Harrison et al., 2019). In addition, Harrison and colleagues' study highlights the possible undesirable side-effects associated with accommodations. Namely, some participants who received accommodations during the school day resisted learning how to effectively take notes or keep their materials organized because these behaviors were no longer expected of them by their teachers (teachers provided notes or managed materials for them). As a result, this subset of students refused to engage in the training interventions offered. These findings suggest that providing adolescents with accommodations instead of interventions may further impair students by diminishing their developmentally appropriate progress towards autonomy. Both of these studies support the sequence for prioritizing services in the LCM and can provide critical guidance for SMHPs when determining and recommending services. Additional studies on the sequencing of services for students with EBD is warranted (August, Piehler, & Miller, 2018), and it is important to acknowledge that the optimal sequence may vary by student.

Implications of Culture, Race, SES, and Community in SMH

SMH services are delivered to students in a wide variety of school settings and to a diverse body of students. Thus, effective SMH services must take into consideration the cultural, racial, and socioeconomic diversity of the schools in which they are integrated. Although some evidence suggests students of racial and ethnic minorities are more likely to be referred for special education services (Skiba, Middelberg, & McClain, 2014), other evidence indicates that students of racial and ethnic minorities are less likely to be identified as having an EBD and referred for special education services when controlling for student sex, socioeconomic status, academic achievement, and externalizing behaviors (Morgan et al., 2015). Whether minorities are over or under represented among students with EBD, there is little to no evidence to indicate that any interventions are differentially effective based on race or culture. Nevertheless, there may be differences in methods for engaging children and families based on differences in race and culture. There is evidence that parent education levels are positively associated with children's responses to psychosocial interventions (Rieppi et al., 2002) and unfortunately, children of higher educated parents are often overrepresented in the samples of intervention studies (Evans, Owens, Wymbs, & Ray, 2018). As a result, some studies may exaggerate the benefits of treatments in relation to children from the full spectrum of parent education levels.

Students with EBD are more likely than their peers to exhibit disruptive behavior at school and student race and ethnicity may be related to the perception of that behavior by school staff (Stevens, 1980). Evidence has consistently suggested that there are racial disparities in school discipline across primary and secondary schools and across severity levels of discipline (Skiba et al., 2014), whereby African American students have consistently been

406 *Steven W. Evans et al.*

overrepresented in teachers' disciplinary referrals (Bradshaw, Mitchell, O'Brennan, & Leaf, 2010; Rocque, 2010; Skiba, Michael, Nardo, & Peterson, 2002). However, the evidence of disproportionality in disciplinary events is less conclusive among other racial and ethnic groups (Skiba et al., 2014). This evidence suggests teachers may be more likely to interpret African American students' behavior as more disruptive and therefore over-discipline such behaviors. Such over-discipline of African American students is particularly problematic when it results in missing class time in the case of out-of-school suspensions or when it occurs instead of SMH services. Thus, when making interpretations about students' behavior in class, teachers should be mindful of evidence that suggests an over-identification of behavioral problems in minority students, particularly among African American students. Biases may also affect assessments of emotional and behavioral problems as evidence exists that teachers may be biased in their ratings of some youth based on race and SES variables (Stevens, 1980); however, more recent research has raised questions about those findings (Hosterman, DuPaul, & Jitendra, 2008).

In addition to race and ethnicity, community is also an important factor in the prioritization of SMH services in rural compared to urban areas. For example, researchers have observed trends of greater rates of death by suicide in rural compared to urban youth (Fontanella et al., 2015), accounted for, at least in part, by access to firearms (Hirsch & Cukrowicz, 2014). In response to such trends, Capps, Michael, and Jameson (2019) increased the scope of an existing high school-based suicide risk assessment and response protocol to assess for rural students' access to firearms in the context of a suicidal crisis. During a year of implementation the protocol was used for 78 events in one high school resulting in referrals for SMH and community-based services as well as the psychiatric hospitalization of three students due to imminent danger of self-harm (Capps et al., 2019). By identifying the aspect of rural homes that contributed to the increased rates of suicide, these investigators adapted services to specifically target a mitigating factor in rural communities.

Developmental Considerations

Effective SMH services are tailored to the developmental and contextual changes that exist across the pre-K to grade 12 continuum. In addition to the differences related to services across the grades, there are also important changes in assessment and progress monitoring due to maturation and a changing environment. For example, teachers play an important role in screening the student population for students showing signs of emotional or behavioral problems. There may be no better context for screening students than the formal (e.g., instruction, work completion) and informal (e.g., recess, interpersonal conversations) settings associated with a classroom. Benefiting from years of experience, teachers become experts at recognizing normal and abnormal behavior for youth within a restricted age range. Because elementary teachers spend most of the day with the same students, they play a particularly important role in screening, early detection of risk, and in shaping the development of student social and emotional skills. Further, early identification and subsequent intervention with these students is often less intensive and cheaper than interventions for older students (Kern, Hilt-Panahon, & Sokol, 2009). In secondary schools, teachers do not gain the same depth of expertise with each student as they typically spend time with over 100 students per day seeing each one for an hour or less. Nevertheless, secondary teachers have been found to be a valuable resource for screening, although they tend to be better at identifying disruptive behavior problems than emotional problems (Margherio, Evans, & Owens, 2019).

As keen observers in this challenging context for students, elementary school teachers have a critical role in progress monitoring. Research has identified that elementary school teacher ratings correspond with classroom observations and are sensitive to change (Hustus, Owens, Volpe, Briesch, & Daniels, 2019); however, this was not true for high school teachers (Miller, Crovello, & Chafouleas, 2017). Nevertheless, indices of academic and social functioning from school are critically important for measuring the effects of interventions and investigators continue to develop and evaluate measures to use in this context (Brady, Evans, Berlin, Bunford, & Kern, 2012; DuPaul et al., 2019).

Developmental considerations are also important when applying behaviorally oriented strategies tailored to students' developmental level. For example, in the early elementary school years students may need visual displays of steps in a routine and may be easily reinforced via sticker charts. In the intermediate elementary school years, students may provide input about how the teacher provides feedback (subtle hand signals) and what rewards are motivating, and may play an increasing role in monitoring their own behavior (e.g., matching self-tracking with teacher tracking). In middle school and high school, tangible rewards are less acceptable and naturalistic reinforcements (e.g., pride in work, positive regard from teachers), combined with high repetitions of strategies for skills may take precedence in shaping student behavior.

Some challenges associated with providing SMH therapy services in an elementary school are even greater in secondary schools. For example, scheduling time to meet with students can be difficult in secondary schools as each student has multiple teachers instead of just one in elementary school. Nevertheless, we have conducted multiple clinical trials in middle and high schools and finding time to meet with students is usually possible (e.g., Evans et al., 2016). Meeting at the very beginning of the day, while eating lunch, during non-academic courses, and during homeroom are common options. Shortening sessions and meeting more often than weekly is also a good approach in secondary schools as student availability can fluctuate. Scheduling with students to conduct group interventions in high schools can be challenging; however, depending on the flexibility of the staff and the students' schedules group sessions can happen consistently (e.g., Kern et al., 2019). Finally, the independence afforded adolescents in school can be both helpful and difficult. Some students come to their scheduled sessions without prompts; however, others frequently "forget" and miss meetings. In these situations, we have asked teachers to provide subtle reminders, met students at their classroom door, and had announcements directed to their classroom asking the student to come to the office. These techniques have helped students get into a routine. Collaboratively working with educators at each academic level can help to identify methods for integrating SMH interventions into the school day.

Dissemination and Implementation

Although many school-based interventions for children and adolescents are now considered evidence-based (Fabiano & Evans, 2019), facilitating the dissemination of evidence-based practices to schools can be challenging for many contextual reasons including local control, lack of clear methods for sustaining best practices, variability in the training of SMHPs, and resources (see review by Owens et al., 2014). In addition, our nation's schools have witnessed the spread of MTSS and the SWPBIS framework (as they are promoted by many state departments of education; e.g., Barrett, Bradshaw, & Lewis-Palmer, 2008). However, the extent to which these frameworks are applied as intended, with high quality and/or sustained is limited (McIntosh et al., 2013).

408 *Steven W. Evans et al.*

The issue of local control is a longstanding value of local public schools and allows communities to shape their local public school system. Although federal regulations related to schools have accumulated over the years (e.g., special education), the crux of most decision-making is the locally elected board of education. Local control has many strengths, but it also limits dissemination of evidence-based SMH practices in the United States. For example, the Mindmatters Program was disseminated nationally throughout Australia (Wyn, Cahill, Holdsworth, Rowling, & Carson, 2000) and the Achievement for All program was broadly disseminated and evaluated throughout schools in England (Humphrey, Lendrum, Barlow, Wigelsworth, & Squires, 2013). Although the broad distribution of programs and large evaluations that can be accomplished when decisions are more centralized than they are in the United States has some appeal, there are limitations with regard to the degree with which these mandates adequately consider the resources and needs of local communities and this can lead to considerable variability in fidelity (Humphrey et al., 2013).

Unfortunately, there is little known about how to sustain effective SMH practices in schools. Identifying school leaders such as principals to support new practices is an important strategy (Owens et al., 2014), but leaders can also include teachers who have formal or informal leadership roles in the school (i.e., key opinion leaders, Atkins et al., 2008). Although these individuals can be important for the initiation of new practices, their role in sustaining those practices over time has not been adequately evaluated. One possible reason for this limitation is that principals and teachers frequently move to other schools, especially in large districts, or leave the profession. This instability in leadership can dramatically end the practice of an effective program as others come to replace these leaders who have other priorities. A potentially more stable alternative that may facilitate sustaining effective practices is professional learning communities (Akiba & Liang, 2016). These involve a collection of school staff interested in professional development related to best practices within a specific domain. They meet regularly, read the literature, and discuss the potential application of best practices to their work. Although their operation in schools has been associated with small gains in student math achievement (Akiba & Liang, 2016), professional learning communities have not been evaluated in relation to school mental health outcomes. Overall, these approaches are viable candidates for achieving implementation of SMH best practices over time; however, research is needed to determine whether this potential can be achieved.

Finally, dissemination is also limited by the lack of SMH expertise in many schools. Educators and SMHPs report feeling unprepared to meet the needs of their students and especially those with emotional and behavioral problems (Parsad, Lewis, & Farris, 2001). This is partly due to limitations in our graduate training programs as described previously, but it is also a problem when school districts do not employ enough SMHPs to meaningfully address the need in their student populations. When SMH staffing is inadequate, then the SMHPs in the district are often in a position to simply try to "put out fires." Their days can be consumed by attending to student crises and attending to overdue paperwork. This approach does little to improve the well-being of the students over time and makes discussion of evidence-based practices seem irrelevant.

In spite of these obstacles, there are advancements in the dissemination of evidence-based practices. At the global level there are service delivery models that focus on organizing services across the spectrum from prevention to intervention and integrating school-based services with community providers (e.g., Link to Learning; Atkins, Cappella, Shernoff, Mehta, & Gustafson, 2017). They promote advocating for a shared objective of child and adolescent well-being to bring community resources into the school community. Link to Learning is a model that was designed for and evaluated in high-poverty communities and prioritized universal and classroom-based targeted interventions (e.g., daily report card) for school staff and school-based mental health services provided by community-based providers. Financial support for the community-based providers was provided by Medicaid billing. Billing models for SMH are sometimes more feasible in high-poverty communities due to common Medicaid coverage throughout the student population as opposed to communities with diverse economic conditions and a variety of potential payors with some being very restrictive. Nevertheless, models of SMH care such as Link to Learning are a powerful example of how bringing together the resources inherent in a community can dramatically change the types of school-based services available to students.

Other advances involve specific techniques for facilitating dissemination and sustained use of evidence-based practices with school staff. For example, Owens and colleagues (2017) evaluated a set of consultation and individually tailored training procedures to help elementary classroom teachers implement effective classroom management techniques and a daily report card. Their consultation techniques were designed to address the unique needs of teachers with a specific profile of knowledge and beliefs about effective classroom management. Although this approach takes more resources than standard performance feedback procedures (Noell & Gansle, 2014), it also targeted teachers for whom standard performance feedback procedures were inadequate. Furthermore, they have since identified a group of teachers who initiate use of similar practices with much less support than provided through standard performance feedback. In fact, approximately 30% of teachers needed little more than access to a web-based system of professional development to consistently implement a daily report card (Owens, McLennan et al., 2019). This line of research is making clear that consultation and training can be enhanced when individualized to the specific strengths and weaknesses of teachers, and that technology can be leveraged as an implementation and dissemination tool.

There continues to be a need to develop and evaluate additional tools to achieve dissemination and sustained use of evidence-based practices. The education system includes many barriers as described above and there is little accountability in the system to provide best practices. The research and development work continues to be driven by the magnitude of benefit for youth when meaningful gains are made (see Lyon & Bruns, 2019 for additional future directions).

Conclusions

As described in this chapter, there is tremendous potential for SMH services to dramatically improve children's access to services and the effectiveness of those services. In order for this to happen, use of evidence-based practices will have to increase, additional research is needed to develop effective interventions and methods of dissemination, and the organization and coordination of these services need to improve. More research is needed to ensure SMH services may effectively address EBD for students of diverse backgrounds, developmental levels, and communities. These efforts may not necessitate completely unique or different services. Rather, systematic studies of how SMH services benefit diverse students in various communities may increase the evidence base for school-based practices. Leadership in schools is needed that makes these services a priority. SMHPs should have their time protected to provide these services and strategies for coordinating their time within schools established. Furthermore, tracking service provision, types of services, and outcomes can help school professionals enhance these strategies over time and inform choices of professional development activities. These services are prioritized at some schools to the benefit of their students;

410 *Steven W. Evans et al.*

however, it has been our experience that in far more schools, addressing the needs of students with EBD is a low priority as evidenced by uncoordinated systems of referral, assessment and interventions, poor record keeping, and SMHPs whose time is diverted to administrative tasks. Overall, the SMH field is advancing and our ability to help students is improving. Our biggest challenge is to advance the integration of science and practice of SMH so research is focused on the most important topics and generates feasible tools and practitioners incorporate scientific advances into their practice. The ultimate beneficiaries of this work will be the students and families.

References

Akiba, M., & Liang, G. (2016). Effects of teacher professional learning activities on student achievement growth. *The Journal of Educational Research, 21*, 1–12.

Atkins, M. S., Cappella, E., Shernoff, E., Mehta, T., & Gustafson, E. (2017). Schooling and children's mental health: Realigning resources to reduce disparities and advance public health. *Annual Review of Clinical Psychology, 13*, 123–147.

Atkins, M. S., Frazier, S., Leathers, S., Graczyk, P., Talbott, E., Jakobsons, L., … Bell, C. (2008). Teacher key opinion leaders and mental health consultation in low-income urban schools. *Journal of Consulting and Clinical Psychology, 76*, 905–908.

Atkins, M. S., Hoagwood, K., Kutash, K., & Seidman, E. (2010). Toward the Integration of Education and Mental Health in Schools. *Administration and Policy in Mental Health and Mental Health Services Research, 37*, 40–47.

August, G., Piehler, T., & Miller, F. (2018). Getting "SMART" about implementing multi-tiered systems of support to promote school mental health. *Journal of School Psychology, 66*, 85–96.

Barrett, S., Bradshaw, C. P., & Lewis-Palmer, T. (2008). Maryland statewide PBIS initiative: Systems, evaluation, and next steps. *Journal of Positive Behavior Interventions, 10*, 105–114.

Benner, G., Kutash, K., Nelson, J., & Fisher, M. (2013). Closing the achievement gap of youth with emotional and behavioral disorders through multi-tiered systems of support. *Education and Treatment of Children, 36*, 15–29.

Bradley, R., Henderson, K., & Monfore, D. (2004). A national perspective on children with emotional disorders. *Behavioral Disorders, 29*, 211–223.

Bradshaw, C. P., Mitchell, M., O'Brennan, L., & Leaf, P. (2010). Multilevel exploration of factors contributing to the overrepresentation of black students in office disciplinary referrals. *Journal of Educational Psychology, 10*, 508–520.

Brady, C., Evans, S. W., Berlin, K., Bunford, N., & Kern, L. (2012). Evaluating school impairment with adolescents using the Classroom Performance Survey. *School Psychology Review, 41*, 429–446.

Burns, B., Costello, E., Angold, A., Tweed, D., Stangle, D., Farmer, E., & Erkanli, A. (1995). Children's mental health service use across service sectors. *Health Affairs, 14*, 147–159.

Capps, R. E., Michael, K., & Jameson, J. (2019). Lethal means and adolescent suicidal risk: An expansion of the PEACE protocol. *Journal of Rural Mental Health, 43*, 3–16.

DuPaul, G. J., Evans, S. W., Allan, D., Puzino, K., Xiang, J., Cooper, J., & Owens, J. S. (2019). High school teacher ratings of academic, social, and behavioral difficulties: Factor structure and normative data for the School Functioning Scale. *School Psychology, 34*, 479–491.

Emmer, E., & Sabornie, E. (2015). *Handbook of classroom management.* New York, NY: Routledge Publishing.

Evans, S. W., Allen, J., Moore, S., & Strauss, V. (2005). Measuring symptoms and functioning of youth with ADHD in middle schools. *Journal of Abnormal Child Psychology, 33*, 695–706.

Evans, S. W., Langberg, J., Schultz, B., Vaughn, A., Altaye, M., Marshall, S., & Zoromski, A. (2016). Evaluation of a school-based treatment program for young adolescents with ADHD. *Journal of Consulting and Clinical Psychology, 84*, 15–30.

Evans, S. W., Owens, J. S., Mautone, J., DuPaul, G., & Power, T. (2014). Toward a comprehensive life-course model of care for youth with attention-deficit/hyperactivity disorder. In M. Weist, N. Lever,

C. Bradshaw, & J. S. Owens (Eds.), *Handbook of school mental health: Research, training, practice, and policy* (pp. 413–426). Boston, MA: Springer.

Evans, S. W., Owens, J. S., & Power, T. (2019). Attention-deficit/hyperactivity disorder. In M. Prinstein, E. Youngstrom, E. Mash, & R. Barkley (Eds.), *Treatment of childhood disorders, fourth edition* (pp. 47–101). New York, NY: Guilford Press.

Evans, S. W., Owens, J. S., Wymbs, B., & Ray, A. (2018). Evidence-based psychosocial treatments for children and adolescents with attention deficit/hyperactivity disorder. *Journal of Clinical Child & Adolescent Psychology, 47*, 157–198.

Fabiano, G., & Evans, S. W. (2019). Introduction to the special issue of School Mental Health on best practices in effective multi-tiered intervention frameworks. *School Mental Health, 11*, 1–3.

Fontanella, C., Hiance-Steelesmith, D., Phillips, G., Bridge, J., Lester, N., Sweeney, H., & Campo, J. (2015). Widening rural-urban disparities in youth suicides, United States, 1996–2010. *Journal of the American Medical Association Pediatrics, 169*, 466–473.

Ginsburg, G., Becker, K., Kingery, J., & Nichols, T. (2008). Transporting CBT for childhood anxiety disorders into inner-city school-based mental health clinics. *Cognitive and Behavioral Practice, 15*, 148–158.

Harrison, J., Evans, S. W., Baran, A., Khondker, F., Press, K., Wassserman, S., ... Belmonte, C. (2019). *Comparison of teacher-mediated and self-mediated classroom-based strategies for youth with ADHD: A randomized controlled trial.* Manuscript under review.

Hirsch, J., & Cukrowicz, K. (2014). Suicide in rural areas: An updated review of the literature. *Journal of Rural Mental Health, 38*, 65–78.

Hosterman, S., DuPaul, G., & Jitendra, A. (2008). Teacher ratings of ADHD symptoms in ethnic minority students: Bias or behavioral difference? *School Psychology Quarterly, 23*, 418–435.

Humphrey, N., Lendrum, A., Barlow, A., Wigelsworth, M., & Squires, G. (2013). Achievement for All: Improving psychosocial outcomes for students with special educational needs and disabilities. *Research in Developmental Disabilities, 34*, 1210–1225.

Hustus, C., Owens, J. S., Volpe, R., Briesch, A., & Daniels, B. (2019). Treatment sensitivy of direct behavior rating-multi-item scales in the context of a daily report card intervention. *Journal of Emotional and Behavioral Disorders.* Retrieved from https://journals.sagepub.com/doi/full/10.1177/1063426618806281

Kelly, M., Berzin, S., Frey, A., Alvarez, M., Shaffer, G., & O'Brien, K. (2010). The state of school social work: Findings from the national school social work survey. *School Mental Health, 2*, 132–141.

Kern, L., Evans, S. W., Lewis, T., State, T., Mehta, P., Weist, M., ... Gage, N. (2019). *Evaluation of a comprehensive assessment-based intervention for secondary students with social, emotional, and behavioral problems.* Manuscript under review.

Kern, L., Hetrick, A., Custer, B., & Commisso, C. (2018). An evaluation of IEP accommodations for secondary students with emotional and behavioral problems. *Journal of Emotional and Behavioral Disorders, 27*(3), 178–192.

Kern, L., Hilt-Panahon, A., & Sokol, N. (2009). Further examining the triangle tip: Improving support for students with emotional and behavioral needs. *Psychology in the Schools, 46*, 18–32.

Leaf, P., Alegria, M., Cohen, P., Goodman, S. H., Horwitz, S. M., Hoven, C., ... Regier, D. (1996). Mental health service use in the community and schools: Results from the four-community MECA study. *Journal of the American Academy of Child & Adolescent Psychiatry, 35*, 889–897.

Leff, S., Waanders, C., Waasdorp, T., & Paskewich, B. (2014). Bullying and aggression in school settings. In H. Walker & F. Gresham (Eds.), *Handbook of evidence-based practices for emotional and behavioral disorders: Applications in schools* (pp. 277–291). New York, NY: The Guilford Press.

Lyon, A., & Bruns, E. (2019). From evidence to impact: Joining our best school mental health practices with our best implementation strategies. *School Mental Health, 11*, 106–114.

Margherio, S., Evans, S. W., & Owens, J. S. (2019). Universal screening in middle and high schools: Who falls through the cracks? *School Psychology, 34*, 591–602.

McIntosh, K., Mercer, S., Hume, A., Frank, J., Turri, M., & Mathews, S. (2013). Factors related to sustained implementation of schoolwide positive behavior support. *Exceptional Children, 79*, 293–311.

Merikangas, K., He, J., Burstein, M., Swendsen, J., Avenevoli, S., Case, B., … Olfson, M. (2011). Service utilization for lifetime mental disorder in U.S. adolescents: Results of the National Comorbidity Survey-Adolescent Supplement (NCS-A). *Journal of the American Academy of Child & Adolescent Psychiatry, 50*, 32–45.

Mikami, A., Owens, J. S., Hudec, K., Kassab, H., & Evans, S. W. (2019). Classroom strategies designed to reduce child problem behavior and increase peer inclusiveness: Does teacher use predict students' sociometric ratings? *School Mental Health*. Retrieved from https://link.springer.com/article/10.1007/s12310-019-09352-y

Miller, F., Crovello, N., & Chafouleas, S. (2017). Progress monitoring the effects of daily report cards across elementary and secondary settings using Direct Behavior Rating: Single Item Scales. *Assessment for Effective Intervention, 43*, 34–47.

Molina, B., Pelham, W., Blumenthal, J., & Galiszewski, E. (1998). Agreement among teachers' behavior ratings of adolescents with a childhood history of attention deficit hyperactivity disorder. *Journal of Clinical Child Psychology, 27*, 330–339.

Morgan, P., Farkas, G., Hillemeier, M., Mattison, R., Maczuga, S., Li, H., & Cook, M. (2015). Minorities are disproportionately underrepresented in special education: Longitudinal evidence across five disability conditions. *Educational Researcher, 44*, 278–292.

Mychailyszyn, M., Beidas, R., Benjamin, C., Edmunds, J., Podell, J., Cohen, J., & Kendall, P. (2011). Assessing and treating child anxiety in schools. *Psychology in the Schools, 48*, 223–232.

Noell, G., & Gansle, K. (2014). Research examining the relationships between consultation procedures, treatment integrity, and outcomes. In W. Erchul & S. Sheridan (Eds.), *Handbook of research in school consultation, second edition* (pp. 386–408). New York, NY: Routledge.

Owens, J. S., Coles, E., Evans, S. W., Himawan, L., Girio-Herrera, E., Holdaway, A., … Schulte, A. (2017). Using multi-component consultation to increase the integrity with which teachers implement behavioral classroom interventions: A pilot study. *School Mental Health, 9*, 218–234.

Owens, J. S., Evans, S. W., Coles, E., Holdaway, A., Himawam, L., Mixon, C., & Egan, T. (2019). Consultation for classroom management and targeted interventions: Examining benchmarks for teacher practices that produce desired change in student behavior. *Journal of Emotional and Behavioral Disorders*. Retrieved from https://journals.sagepub.com/doi/full/10.1177/1063426618795440

Owens, J. S., Hustus, C., & Evans, S. W. (2020). The daily report card intervention: Summary of the science and factors affecting implementation. In T. Farmer, M. Conroy, B. Farmer, & K. Sutherland (Eds.), *Handbook of research on emotional & behavioral disabilities: Interdisciplinary developmental perspectives on children and youth.*

Owens, J. S., Lyon, A., Brandt, N., Warner, C., Nadeem, E., Spiel, C., & Wagner, M. (2014). Implementation science in school mental health: Key constructs in a developing research agenda. *School Mental Health, 6*, 99–111.

Owens, J. S., McLennan, J., Hustus, C., Haines-Saah, R., Mitchell, S., Mixon, C., & Troutman, A. (2019). Leveraging technology to facilitate teachers' use of a targeted classroom intervention: Evaluation of the daily report card.online (DRC.O) system. *School Mental Health, 11*, 665–677.

Park, J., Small, B., Geller, D., Murphy, T., Lewin, A., & Storch, E. (2014). Does d-Cycloserine augmentation of CBT improve therapeutic homework compliance for pediatric OCD? *Journal of Child and Family Studies, 23*, 863–871.

Parsad, B., Lewis, L., & Farris, E. (2001). *Teacher preparation and professional development: 2000 (NCES 2001–088)*. U.S. Department of Education, National Center for Education Statistics. Washington, DC: U.S. Government Printing Office.

Pelham, W., Fabiano, G., Waxmonsky, J., Greiner, A., Gnagy, E., Pelham, W., … Murphy, S. (2016). Treatment sequencing for childhood ADHD: A multiple-randomization study of adaptive medication and behavioral interventions. *Journal of Clinical Child and Adolescent Psychology, 45*, 396–415.

Reddy, L., Fabiano, G., Dudek, C., & Hsu, L. (2013). Predictive validity of the Classroom Strategies Scale— Observer Form on statewide testing scores: An initial investigation. *School Psychology Quarterly, 28*, 301–316.

Rieppi, R., Greenhill, L., Ford, R., Chuang, S., Wu, M., Davies, M., ... Wigal, T. (2002). Socioeconomic status as a moderator of ADHD treatment outcomes. *Journal of the American Academy of Child and Adolescent Psychiatry, 41*, 269–277.

Rocque, M. (2010). Office discipline and student behavior: Does race matter? *American Journal of Education, 116*, 557–581.

Shernoff, E., Kratochwill, T., & Stoiber, K. (2003). Training in evidence-based interventions (EBIs): What are school psychology programs teaching? *Journal of School Psychology, 41*, 467–483.

Skiba, R., Michael, R., Nardo, A., & Peterson, R. (2002). The color of discipline: Sources of racial and gender disproportionality in school punishment. *Urban Review, 34*, 317–342.

Skiba, R., Middelberg, L., & McClain, M. (2014). Multicultural issues for schools and students with emotional and behavioral disorders. In H. Walker & F. Gresham (Eds.), *Handbook of evidence-based practices for emotional and behavioral disorders: Applications in schools* (pp. 54–70). New York, NY: The Guilford Press.

Spiel, C., Evans, S. W., & Langberg, J. (2014). Evaluating the content of individualized education programs and 504 plans of young adolescents with attention deficit/hyperactivity disorder. *School Psychology Quarterly, 29*, 452–468.

Stevens, G. (1980). Bias in attributions of positive and negative behavior in children by school psychologists, parent, and teachers. *Perceptual and Motor Skills, 50*, 1283–1290.

Sugai, G., & Horner, R. (2006). A promising approach for expanding and sustaining school-wide positive behavior support. *School Psychology Review, 35*, 245–259.

U.S. Department of Education. (2018). *40th annual report to Congress on the implementation of the Individuals with Disabilities Education Act, 2018*. Washington, DC: U.S. Department of Education.

Wagner, M., Newman, L., Cameto, R., & Levine, P. (2005). *Changes over time in the early post school outcomes of youth with disabilities: A report of findings from the National Longitudinal Transition Study (NLTS) and the National Longitudinal Transition Study-2 (NLTS-2)*. Menlo Park, CA: SRI International.

Wyn, J., Cahill, H., Holdsworth, R., Rowling, L., & Carson, S. (2000). MindMatters, a whole-school approach promoting mental health and wellbeing. *Australian and New Zealand Journal of Psychiatry, 34*, 594–601.

Part 4

Preparing and Supporting the EBD Workforce

28 Leveraging Implementation Science and Practice to Support the Delivery of Evidence-Based Practices in Services for Youth with Emotional and Behavioral Disorders

Bryce D. McLeod, Rachel Kunemund, Shannon L. Nemer, and Aaron R. Lyon

As many as 12% of youth display social, emotional, and behavioral problems (Forness, Freeman, Paparella, Kauffman, & Walker, 2012). When social, emotional, and behavioral problems become chronic they can lead to the development of emotional and behavioral disorders (EBDs). These EBDs are known to be related to difficulties with academic performance (Spilt, Koomen, Thijs, & van der Leij, 2012), particularly in comparison with their same-age peers without EBDs (Bradley, Doolittle, & Bartolotta, 2008; Lane, Barton-Arwood, Nelson, & Wehby, 2008). In addition to academic difficulties, these youth are at risk to experience negative consequences (e.g., high school dropout, unemployment) throughout school and into adulthood (Wagner & Newman, 2012).

To address the social, emotional, and behavioral problems of youth, research in psychology has focused on the development and evaluation of interventions and practices (see Weisz et al., 2017; What Works Clearinghouse, 2017). Collectively, these efforts have produced a number of evidence-based programs (e.g., see PK PATHS, Domitrovich, Cortes, & Greenberg, 2007; Incredible Years, Webster-Stratton, Reid, & Hammond, 2004) and practices (e.g., opportunities to respond; Sutherland, Alder, & Gunter, 2003) designed to be delivered by professionals (e.g., mental health clinicians). Many of these programs and practices have demonstrated positive effects (hereafter called evidence-based practices, or EBPs) and shown promise for reducing the social, emotional, and behavioral problems of youth with EBDs.

Stakeholders sometimes turn to EBPs in an effort to improve youth outcomes. Yet these stakeholders have struggled to deliver EBPs brought into community settings with integrity or to the degree of efficacy seen in published studies (Damschroder et al., 2009; Gottfredson & Gottfredson, 2002). This gap between the science and practice of EBPs in services for youth with EBDs represents a critical public health issue. Implementation science is designed to help meet this challenge. Emerging over the past decade, implementation science is defined as "the scientific study of methods to promote the systematic uptake of research findings and other EBPs into routine practices" (Eccles & Mittman, 2006, p. 1). As research in implementation science expands, it will continue to inform implementation practice.

Within services for youth with EBDs, implementation science focuses on the strategies needed to help transfer EBPs into community settings and maximize the likelihood of

418   *Bryce D. McLeod et al.*

sustainable success. Research to date suggests that the successful implementation of EBPs in community settings is challenging. In instances when a new EBP is adopted in a community setting, such as a school or community mental health center, it is rarely implemented with sufficient integrity required to bring about expected effects (Gottfredson & Gottfredson, 2002). And, ultimately, only one in three EBPs are successfully installed and sustained in community settings (Damschroder et al., 2009).

As we will describe, formidable challenges are posed by conducting implementation science in the settings that service youth with EBDs. One obstacle is that the application of implementation science to settings that serve youth with EBDs is relatively new, so there are few comprehensive discussions of the conceptual and methodological issues involved in conducting implementation science in these settings. This chapter seeks to redress this problem. We start by defining key terms, including description of two example conceptual frameworks intended to help guide research. In the second section of the chapter, we review factors that might influence the implementation of EBPs services for youth with EBDs. We finish the chapter with directions for future research.

What Is Implementation Science?

In 2000, Balas and Boren concluded that in medicine under normal circumstances it takes 17 years for 14% of original work on EBPs to find their way from research to community settings. This report helped give rise to the field of implementation science designed to span the research to practice gap. To achieve this goal, a key focus of implementation science is to identify the strategies and methods needed to hasten the transition of research to practice.

Since the mid-2000s, the National Institutes of Health (NIH) has funded implementation science. Strategic plans released by specific NIH institutes (e.g., National Institute of Mental Health, National Cancer Institute) have articulated a vision for implementation science that have shaped the field and encouraged innovative research in medicine and behavioral health. During this time, NIH created a special panel to review grants focused on dissemination and implementation science submitted across participating NIH institutes (i.e., Dissemination and Implementation Research in Health). These activities were followed by the formation of an annual NIH Dissemination and Implementation conference and the creation of the field's first journal in 2006, *Implementation Science*. Together, these efforts helped to launch the field and shape the direction of research over the past decade.

NIH situates implementation science at the end of the translational research pipeline. The pipeline describes how innovations, such as EBPs, move from basic scientific discovery, to intervention, and to large scale, sustained delivery in routine community practice (Khoury et al., 2007). By placing implementation science along this continuum, NIH articulated the need for a specific scientific discipline to promote the effective delivery and sustainment of EBPs in community settings. This move acknowledged that simply demonstrating an EBP is effective is not enough to guarantee uptake in community contexts – specific strategies are needed to support adoption, effective delivery, and sustainment.

As implementation science in medicine and behavioral health has progressed, new measurement and research designs have emerged to support the evaluation and improvement of medical and behavioral health systems (Brown et al., 2016; Glasgow, 2013; Landsverk, Brown, Reutz, Palinkas, & Horwitz, 2010). A characteristic of these new measurement and research designs is an emphasis on practical considerations. These new "pragmatic" research and measurement approaches are designed to remain rigorous while incorporating the local context and stakeholder perspectives with the goal of accelerating and broadening the impact of implementation science on policy and practice (Glasgow, 2013; Stanick et al., 2018).

As research studying the implementation of EBPs in medicine and behavioral health has progressed, notable advances have been made. For example, implementation science has helped to improve patient outcomes in oncology care (see Mitchell & Chambers, 2017) and mental health care (Lewis et al., 2016). However, research has also served to illustrate how difficult it is to implement and sustain new innovations in community contexts as efforts to implement EBPs do not always achieve expected results (Damschroder et al., 2009). Moreover, implementation science has not been applied equally across all service contexts with certain sectors receiving less empirical attention, such as school settings (Lyon & Bruns, in press). As implementation science is increasingly applied to the settings that serve youth with EBDs, researchers can learn from advances in other fields, though it is likely these advancements will require modification and replication in these new settings (Aarons, Sklar, Mustanski, Benbow, & Brown, 2017).

Implementation Science and Practice: Definition and Objectives

Implementation science and practice is a relative newcomer to research focused on youth with EBD. As with many emerging areas of inquiry, numerous terms are used to refer to the goals and objectives of implementation science and practice (Rabin & Brownson, 2012). The inconsistent use of terms can slow the progress of science, so we will provide definitions of implementation science and practice and define the objectives of this field of inquiry.

We define "implementation science" as "the scientific study of methods to promote the systematic uptake of research findings and other EBPs into routine practices" (Eccles & Mittman, 2006, p. 1). We define "implementation practice" as specific efforts to apply knowledge gained through implementation science to deliver EBPs in community settings (Lyon, 2017). Importantly, implementation science is distinct from efficacy (does it work) and effectiveness research (does it work in community settings). Effectiveness of an EBP can be established without the necessary supports required to promote the uptake and sustained delivery of that EBP in community settings. Implementation science thus focuses on gathering scientific knowledge about the specific activities and strategies required to integrate an EBP into a specific context through implementation practice.

Implementation science and practice is multilevel, focusing on individuals, groups, organizations, and systems to change behavior and promote quality improvement (Bauer, Damschroder, Hagedorn, Smith, & Kilbourne, 2015). Frequently, the objectives of implementation science include the identification of multilevel determinants that serve as facilitators or barriers to the uptake of EBPs as well as specific strategies for improving EBP adoption and sustainment (Powell et al., 2015; Proctor et al., 2011). Figure 28.1 outlines a model that articulates the space within the field focused on providing services for youth with EBDs in which implementation science and practice operates. This figure depicts the relation among interventions, implementation strategies, implementation determinants, implementation mechanisms, implementation outcomes, and youth outcomes. As these terms have sometimes been used interchangeably in the implementation literature, we provide definitions of each in the following sections.

Interventions

In Figure 28.1, the intervention represents the EBP that is being implemented. Research efforts have mostly focused on evaluating the efficacy (i.e., does an intervention produce optimal outcomes in a tightly controlled research settings) or effectiveness (i.e., does an

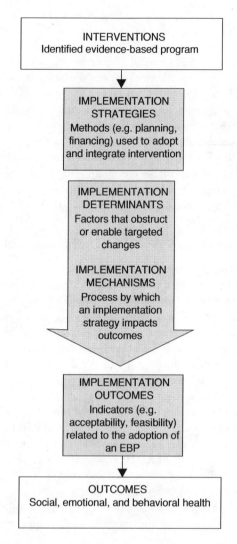

Figure 28.1 Conceptual model of implementation science

intervention produce optimal youth outcomes in a specific community setting) of interventions, but have not asked questions related to implementation. Demonstrating that an EBP is effective in a specific setting is typically an important precondition to engaging in implementation science and practice in support of that EBP. However, Curran, Bauer, Mittman, Pyne, and Stetler (2012) have articulated how intervention and implementation research can progress simultaneously by employing hybrid effectiveness-implementation designs. Combining elements of effectiveness (does it work in a particular setting) and implementation (factors that influence adoption of an EBP) trials can speed up the translation of research knowledge into community contexts.

Implementation Strategies

Implementation strategies are "systematic intervention process[es] to adopt and integrate evidence-based health innovations into usual care" (Powell et al., 2012, p. 124). To date, over 70 implementation strategies have been identified in the literature (Cook, Lyon, Locke, Waltz, & Powell, 2019; Lyon et al., 2019). Powell et al. (2012) reviewed existing strategies and placed them into six broad categories: planning, educating, financing, restructuring, quality management, and attending to policy contexts (see Table 28.1 for definitions). Despite their relevance to services for youth with EBDs, many strategies are skipped or overlooked when implementing EBPs in these settings, especially school settings. Specifically, there is a tendency to focus on education and to use one-time, "train and hope" professional development sessions, which are unlikely to produce change in professional behavior (Lyon, Stirman, Kerns, & Burns, 2011). Instead, multiple strategies may be needed to help ensure uptake and sustainment. For example, adapting an EBP for a specific context as well as providing dynamic and ongoing training and real-time feedback could be provided to help support the effective implementation of EBPs (Lyon et al., 2018). Broadly, however, the selection of strategies should be guided by implementation frameworks (e.g., Aarons, Hurlburt, & Horwitz, 2011;

Table 28.1 Descriptions of implementation strategies and outcomes

	Description
Implementation Strategies	
Plan	Help stakeholders gather data, select strategies, build buy-in, initiate leadership, and develop relationships
Educate	Inform stakeholders about the intervention and its implementation
Finance	Incentivize the use of the intervention and provide resources for professional development
Restructuring	Facilitate implementation by changing staffing, roles, physical structures, and equipment
Quality Management	Develop and apply data systems and support networks to continually evaluate and enhance the delivery of the intervention with fidelity
Attending to Policy Context	Encourage the promotion of interventions through accreditation, licensing, and legal systems
Implementation Outcomes	
Acceptability	The perception among stakeholders that the intervention is agreeable, feasible, or satisfactory
Adoption	The intention, initial decision, or effort put toward using an evidence-based program
Appropriateness	The perception of fit, relevance, or compatibility of the intervention for the specific setting or problem
Cost	The cost of an implementation effort, which can vary based on complexity and setting
Feasibility	The extent to which an intervention can be successfully carried out in the setting
Fidelity	The degree to which the intervention was implemented as intended by the program developers
Penetration	The integration of an intervention within a context
Sustainment	The extent to which the new intervention is maintained or institutionalized

Note. Adapted from Powell et al. (2012) and Proctor et al. (2011).

422   *Bryce D. McLeod et al.*

Damschroder et al., 2009) to help ensure that the implementation of an EBP in community settings is effective and likely to be sustained.

Implementation Determinants

Implementation determinants are defined as factors that help or hinder an implementation strategy from producing an optimal effect (Lewis et al., 2018). Commonly called barriers and facilitators, a key goal of implementation science is to identify determinants at different levels (e.g., school, administrator, teacher, mental health professional) that influence the effect of an implementation strategy. Determinants are naturally occurring within a specific context and can take on different roles in influencing the success of implementation strategies (Lewis et al., 2018). To maximize the impact of implementation strategies it is important for researchers to identify determinants and specify the role they play in implementation (e.g., act as a moderator or precondition; see Lewis et al., 2018 for a discussion).

Implementation Mechanisms

Implementation mechanisms are defined as "process[es] or event[s] through which an implementation strategy operates to affect desired implementation outcomes" (Lewis et al., 2018). Recently there have been calls for researchers to move beyond implementation frameworks to specify and test theoretical models of how implementation strategies influence desired implementation outcomes (Lewis et al., 2018; Williams, 2016). Though very few studies have attempted to specify, measure, or test mechanisms, this represents an important direction for future research. Through the articulation of theoretical models that identify how mechanisms operate, specific hypotheses can be tested that can lead to the accumulation of knowledge about how implementation influences implementation outcomes. Understanding how implementation strategies work will ultimately improve the uptake and sustainment of EBPs in community settings.

Implementation Outcomes

Implementation outcomes are defined as key indicators related to the uptake and sustainment of an EBP (Proctor et al., 2011). Proctor et al. (2011) proposed a framework of implementation outcomes that focused on eight dimensions: Acceptability, Adoption, Appropriateness, Feasibility, Fidelity, Cost, Penetration, and Sustainment (see Table 28.1 for definitions). This framework was intended to provide the field with a consistent set of indicators that are important at different phases of the implementation process. For example, when initially introduced, EBPs may be met with either resistance or with positive perceptions by personnel, so it is important to assess acceptability. As another example, sustainment is an implementation outcome that is assessed in later phases of implementation. The framework provided by Proctor et al. (2011) can be used to guide the selection of implementation outcomes that fit the implementation phase and research questions.

Youth Outcomes

Youth outcomes represent the social, emotional, behavioral, and educational outcomes of youth with EBDs, which stem from the outcomes of the EBPs. Throughout the implementation process, it is important to document youth progress as one of several indicators. Next, we provide more detail about implementation strategies and outcomes.

Implementation Frameworks

Frameworks are needed to guide implementation science and practice. However, selecting implementation frameworks can be a daunting task. A recent count indicated that there are over 60 implementation frameworks (Tabak, Khoong, Chambers, & Brownson, 2012). Even though tools to help researchers select frameworks are beginning to emerge (e.g., Birken et al., 2018), the number of frameworks can present a challenge when researchers wish to select a framework for a given study. The early work of federally funded centers (e.g., National Implementation Research Network; https://nirn.fpg.unc.edu/) and literature reviews (see e.g., Fixsen, Naoom, Blasé, Friedman, & Wallace, 2005) have exerted an important influence on the development of existing implementation frameworks. Here our goal is to highlight frameworks with various aims and applications (Nilsen, 2015), so we propose use of (a) a determinant framework called the Consolidated Framework for Implementation Research (CFIR; Damschroder et al., 2009) and (b) a process framework called the Exploration, Preparation, Implementation, and Sustainment (EPIS; Aarons et al., 2011) framework. These frameworks overlap in content, but approach implementation through different lenses (e.g., conceptual vs. practical). The combination of these frameworks can help researchers understand the factors that might directly influence the implementation of EBPs for youth with EBDs as well as what factors may need to be considered during different phases of implementation.

Consolidated Framework for Implementation Research (CFIR)

To maximize the likelihood that EBPs are appropriate and can be translated into a service sector serving youth with EBD, it is essential to understand how the context can influence implementation. The CFIR (Damschroder et al., 2009) is designed to help researchers understand how factors in a specific context can influence the implementation of an EBP. The five major domains that comprise the CFIR include: (a) Intervention characteristics (i.e., features and design of the intervention); (b) Outer setting (i.e., economic, political, and social context within which a setting exists); (c) Inner setting (i.e., characteristics of the service setting); (d) Characteristics of individuals involved in delivering the intervention (e.g., attitudes towards the intervention, self-efficacy); and (e) The implementation process (i.e., steps associated with implementing an intervention). A core tenet of the CFIR is an EBP must be adapted to fit the specific needs of a context. How an EBP is adapted depends on the interaction between the EBP characteristics and those of the inner setting, outer setting, and individuals working within the setting. By defining the factors that may influence implementation the CFIR has helped expand the implementation knowledge base by facilitating the use of a common set of terms and concepts across implementation science in the health, business, and medical fields. As the CFIR was intended to promote theory development and theory verification it is ideal for research focused on EBPs for youth with EBD as implementation science in the service settings where these youth receive care is still in an early phase.

Exploration, Preparation, Implementation, and Sustainment (EPIS) Framework

Despite the comprehensive nature of the CFIR, the framework does not suggest relationships among the implementation phases, which is a key factor in the implementation of EBPs. The EPIS Framework (Aaron et al., 2011) is designed to provide a multilevel framework for the implementation process in community-based mental health centers. The EPIS divides the

424 *Bryce D. McLeod et al.*

implementation process into four phases: exploration, adoption/preparation, implementation, and sustainment. The exploration phase involves the identification of a problem (e.g. consistent disruptive behavior from a youth with problem behavior) or the knowledge that there are EBPs (e.g. behavioral intervention, Incredible Years; Webster-Stratton et al., 2004) for addressing an identified problem (Aarons et al., 2011). Once a problem is identified, the next phase is adoption decision and preparation. This phase includes identifying and selecting an EBP and then making the decision to adopt that EBP for a specific context. One component of this phase is the identification of the specific EBP that will be used. The third phase is active implementation. Once an EBP has been identified by stakeholders, the next step is to use and apply it in the specific setting via specific active implementation strategies. The final phase is sustainment, which represents the ongoing use of the EBP by individuals within the organization (e.g. teachers in a school; clinicians in a mental health setting) following the removal of formal supports. Importantly, the EPIS underscores the fact that different implementation strategies, determinants, and outcomes are relevant at different phases. An important starting point for researchers is thus to locate their research questions within the four phases of the EPIS framework, and then determine what strategies, determinants, and outcomes are important to consider for that phase.

Implementation Science and Practice for Youth with Emotional and Behavioral Disorders

As illustrated by the frameworks, implementation science largely agrees that determinants operate across multiple levels. Implementation strategies thus need to target multiple levels. The CFIR and EPIS models provide guidelines for identifying the levels that frequently need to be considered and targeted. We now consider each of the levels that operate in the settings in which youth with EBD receive services (e.g., schools, community mental health centers) and what implementation strategies may be considered to enhance outcomes.

Phases

What implementation phase a service system is in will determine which implementation strategies, determinants, and outcomes are relevant. Helping researchers conceptualize implementation science as involving multiple phases is important. We can learn valuable lessons from implementation science conducted in medical and behavioral health that indicate different strategies and outcomes are relevant at each phase. For example, planning strategies focused on gathering information through needs assessments may be critical for the exploration phase, while strategies for quality management take focus during the implementation phase (Powell et al., 2012). As another example, outcomes such as appropriateness for the service setting are important in the adoption phase, whereas cost and indicators of treatment integrity are important in the implementation phase. Though the EPIS framework and existing research from other fields can help researchers identify factors to consider at each phase, the relevancy of these and other factors for settings in which youth with EBD receive services are yet to be determined.

Intervention Characteristics

How EBPs are designed can influence whether stakeholders adopt and utilize the EBPs in community settings (Damschroder et al., 2007; Lyon & Bruns, 2019). EBPs that are overly complex or poorly fitted to a specific context can make it less likely that stakeholders will use these EBPs (Grol, Bosch, Hulscher, Eccles, & Wensing, 2007; Kochevar & Yano, 2006). Successful implementation of EBPs thus requires attention to issues of fit and relevance to specific settings (Stahmer, Suhrheinrich, Reed, & Schreibman, 2012). Models of community-partnered participatory research have been proposed for the redesign of EBPs in schools (e.g., Döll & Romero-Lankao, 2017; Parsons et al., 2013), and for mental health more generally (e.g., Lyon & Koerner, 2016). Common among these models are collaborative efforts between EBP designers and key stakeholders (e.g., clinicians, teachers, families), who iteratively review goals and possible EBP methods to find a good fit for the setting (e.g., schools in a particular district), emphasizing (a) designers and stakeholders form a partnership to ensure that EBP methods are feasible and acceptable, and fit the context in a culturally relevant manner; (b) that a sufficient brainstorming and pilot testing stage ensues to determine whether the proposed methods are useful in practice, whether they meet stakeholder goals, and whether redesign is needed to improve the EBP package; and (c) that effectiveness is assessed when the EBP is acceptable to stakeholders, and that implementation outcomes such as feasibility and integrity continue to be assessed in the initial testing (e.g., Parsons et al., 2013). As implementation science in settings serving youth with EBD progresses, an important objective will be to determine what intervention characteristics are most important to consider for specific contexts (e.g., community mental health center, school).

Outer Setting

Macro factors outside of a service setting (e.g., policy), either in isolation or in combination, influence the implementation or outcomes of EBPs. Federal, state, and district-level legislative action (e.g., No Child Left Behind (2002), Every Student Succeeds Act (2015–2016)), can have both a positive and negative impact, primarily through fiscal, regulatory, and administrative channels (Domitrovich et al., 2008). For example, many developers of behavior-focused EBPs for school settings identified the high-stakes testing atmosphere brought on by No Child Left Behind as a barrier to implementation (Forman, Olin, Hoagwood, Crowe, & Saka, 2009), due to the intense focus on core academic subjects such as reading and math. At the same time, however, the federal government was also identified as an implementation facilitator, particularly through the provision of funding and technical assistance. Unfortunately, in some districts, it can be difficult to mix this funding with money available at the local level, as it is often earmarked for specific purposes (Domitrovich et al., 2008). Thus, as this example from education illustrates, attending to the policy context is a critical strategy in implementation, as it can determine the necessary financial strategies and greatly impact the appropriateness of an intervention for a given setting.

While legislative policies tend to have the greatest external influence on implementation, other outer-setting factors should also be considered. In particular, the community surrounding a service setting can work to either help or hinder the implementation of EBPs (Forman et al., 2009). Domitrovich et al. (2008) highlight important community-level factors, including the availability of qualified professionals in a region and the strength of community–university partnerships. Gathering information on the community context and availability of human resources is key in planning, as successful implementation may require the development of additional relationships.

Inner Setting

The importance of organizational factors as inputs and moderators of implementation outcomes cannot be overstated. Both culture, which includes the norms and expectations of personnel within a service setting, and climate can influence the acceptability of interventions and may be more critical to the implementation of EBPs than individual characteristics (Aarons et al., 2011; Durlak, 2010). For example, Baker, Kupersmidt, Voegler-Lee, Arnold, and Willoughby (2010) highlighted the influence of organizational factors, including administrative leadership and collaboration in the work environment, when examining variance in teacher participation at multiple levels (e.g. individual, school; Durlak, 2010). This affirms the qualitative findings of Forman et al. (2009), in which 79% of intervention developers noted the importance of school leadership in facilitating intervention. Thus, building the buy-in of individuals within the setting, through system-level incentives or identified champions, is a critical strategy (Lyon et al., 2018). Given the consistent findings linking organizational factors to implementation outcomes, researchers should attend to organizational culture and climate when seeking to understand the impact of strategies on implementation outcomes.

Individuals

Critical to the long-term goal of implementing EBPs in service settings for youth with EBDs is developing a competent workforce (Fairburn & Patel, 2014; Kazdin & Rabbitt, 2013). Professionals that can deliver EBPs with integrity can foster settings that provide a foundation for the long-term academic and social-emotional success of youth with EBDs. However, many stakeholders do not have access to opportunities for professional development that could provide instruction in EBPs. To help stakeholders learn how to deliver effective EBPs, teachers and clinicians need access to effective professional development opportunities. Still, uptake of EBPs by stakeholders can be limited even when expert training is given (Gottfredson & Gottfredson, 2002), as long-term sustainment frequently relies on resource-heavy ongoing consultation and technical assistance (Durlak, 2010).

Future Directions

We believe that the services for youth with EBD can learn valuable lessons from implementation science in healthcare and behavioral health; however, research is needed to determine the extent to which these lessons will apply to contexts that most commonly provide services to youth with EBDs. Towards this goal, we now discuss a few specific research questions that may be addressed by the field to help accelerate efforts to implement EBPs in settings serving youth with EBDs.

First, it is important to understand how the unique structure of settings (e.g., schools, juvenile justice, community mental health centers) influence implementation at each phase (Lyon et al., 2018). Leadership, organizational climate, and organizational culture play critical roles in the implementation of EBPs in other service sectors (Aarons et al., 2011). Leadership can include a wide range of individuals within a system. For example, leadership in schools can include grade leads, principals, administrators, or those even further removed from the classroom such as superintendents or state-level officials. School administrators can thus play an important role in the exploration phase as they are often involved in the decision-making process and also play a key role in adoption because if a principal is not supportive of a particular EBP then this may influence buy-in and adoption at the teacher-level (Brackett,

Rivers, Reyes, & Salovey, 2012; McIntosh, Mercer, Nese, Strickland-Cohen, & Hoselton, 2016). Understanding how leadership, culture, and climate influence implementation in the various settings that influence youth with EBD is thus an important future research direction.

Second, critical to the goal of implementing EBPs in service settings for youth with EBD is the development of feasible, efficient, and effective training and coaching strategies. Most efforts to implement EBPs have relied on the "gold-standard" training and consultation procedures used in efficacy trials (i.e., protocol, training workshop, and ongoing practice-based coaching) to establish and maintain treatment integrity (Sutherland, McLeod, Conroy, & Cox, 2013). Professional development models use similar procedures to engage professionals in didactic and consultation activities. Some evidence suggests that these models impact professionals' implementation of EBPs (Joyce & Showers, 2002; Trivette, Dunst, Hamby, & O'Herin, 2009). However, these models are not scalable, and relatively little is known about their feasibility and effectiveness. Thus, a challenge for the field is to develop feasible, efficient, and effective training and consultation procedures that produce sustainable changes in behavior related to delivering EBPs for youth with EBD (Becker & Stirman, 2011; Chambers, Glasgow, & Stange, 2013). Research that helps identify effective teaching and consultation strategies is needed, so that we can respond to this challenge by producing professional development strategies that are feasible, efficient, and can be taken to scale.

Third, EBPs need to be adapted for the unique needs of the specific contexts that serve youth with EBDs. EBPs that have been redesigned to fit a specific context have proven to produce superior outcomes to EBPs that were not redesigned (e.g., Rahman, Malik, Sikander, Roberts, & Creed, 2008; Weisz et al., 2012). User-Centered Design frameworks offer guidance on methods to maximize the fit of EBPs for specific service settings (e.g., Lyon & Koerner, 2016). User-Centered Design is an approach for product development that emphasizes the consumers' or stakeholders' needs and preferences from the inception of the design process. As noted by Lyon and Koerner (2016), good design entails simplicity, efficiency, ease of use, and attunement to "fit" with the needs of the end user (e.g., teacher, clinician). From this perspective, the difficulty, complexity, and specificity of many EBPs for youth may negate their usability and potency under realistic conditions in settings serving youth, such as schools or community mental health centers. User-Centered Design emphasizes principles such as learnability, low cognitive load, and fit with natural constraints. More research is needed to determine how EBPs can be designed to better fit specific contexts so that they can produce maximum benefit.

Fourth, youth characteristics are particularly critical to consider when implementing innovative services for youth with EBDs. Although aspects of individual service providers are most commonly considered among individual-level determinants of implementation (Damschroder et al., 2009), service recipient demographics, presenting problems, and values also represent key aspects of intervention-setting fit (Lyon et al., 2014; Tornatzky & Klein, 1982). Furthermore, youth with EBDs are frequently connected to services across multiple domains (e.g., mental health, academic), thus increasing the complexity of care and need for inter-organizational communications. At the individual level growing emphasis across sectors and problem domains is being placed on personalized and precision services that attend explicitly to the specific needs of individual service recipients. Mental health (Bickman, Lyon, & Wolpert, 2016) and education (Cook, Kilgus, & Burns, 2018) have seen similar calls with direct relevance to youth. Future research in contexts serving youth with EBDs would be well advised to follow these trends through the explicit incorporation of data elements that both drive tailoring of care and facilitate implementation (Bickman et al., 2016) as well as patient choice models that empower service recipients though shared decision making (Edwards & Elwyn, 2009).

428 *Bryce D. McLeod et al.*

Finally, methods and models from implementation science are uniquely positioned to support efforts to adapt EBPs to better account for developmental factors and the diverse contexts in which youth with EBD receive services. An overarching theme of this book is the idea that adapting EBPs to attend to diverse developmental backgrounds, ecologies, and service resources of youth with EBDs may help maximize effectiveness. As noted by Farmer, Gatzke-Kopp, and Latendresse (2020), youth with EBD come from a wide variety of ecological contexts and are served by a complicated set of youth-serving sectors and services. A key goal and strength of implementation science is the identification and development of strategies needed to màximize the fit of an EBP to a given setting and population. Conceptual models and methods, reviewed in this chapter, for adapting innovations can aid in these efforts as we seek to maximize the effectiveness of EBPs with youth with EBDs across developmental periods and in diverse service contexts. Merging implementation models and methods with a developmental viewpoint that can help ensure we engage in interdisciplinary efforts that leverage our knowledge of the development of EBD to adapt EBPs will potentially help maximize the effectiveness of EBPs for this population.

Conclusions

This chapter highlighted several points about the implementation of EBPs for youth with EBD in community settings. Whereas promising EBPs for youth with EBD have been developed, the research on how best to implement EBPs is relatively sparse. Implementation science that has been conducted has served to illustrate the challenges inherent in delivering EBPs with adherence. Going forward, the field stands to benefit from lessons and exemplars pulled from other fields in which EBPs have been implemented with success to inform increasingly systematic selection of implementation strategies. Beyond learning from these lessons, it will be important for funding agencies to consider ways to provide guidance and financial support for implementation research. In the next phase of implementation science and practice, exploring key questions related to the influence of leadership, adapting EBPs for specific contexts, youth characteristics, and developing competency in the workforce may be a fruitful path forward towards better EBP options that are more widely available to youth with EBD in variety of service settings.

References

Aarons, G. A., Hurlburt, M., & Horwitz, S. M. (2011). Advancing a conceptual model of evidence-based practice implementation in public service sectors. *Administration and Policy in Mental Health and Mental Health Services Research, 38*(1), 4–23.

Aarons, G. A., Sklar, M., Mustanski, B., Benbow, N., & Brown, C. H. (2017). "Scaling-out" evidence-based interventions to new populations or new health care delivery systems. *Implementation Science, 12*, 111.

Baker, C. N., Kupersmidt, J. B., Voegler-Lee, M. E., Arnold, D., & Willoughby, M. T. (2010). Predicting teacher participation in a classroom-based, integrated preventive intervention for preschoolers. *Early Childhood Research Quarterly, 25*, 270–283.

Balas, E. A., & Boren, S. A. (2000). Managing clinical knowledge for health care improvement. In *Yearbook of medical informatics: Patient-centered systems.* Retrieved from https://augusta.openrepository.com/augusta/handle/10675.2/617990

Bauer, M. S., Damschroder, L., Hagedorn, H., Smith, J., & Kilbourne, A. M. (2015). An introduction to implementation science for the non-specialist. *BMC Psychology, 3*(1), 1–12.

Becker, K. D., & Stirman, S. W. (2011). The science of training in evidence-based treatments in the context of implementation programs: Current status and prospects for the future. *Administration and Policy in Mental Health and Mental Health Services Research, 38*(4), 217–222.

Bickman, L., Lyon, A. R., & Wolpert, M. (2016). Achieving precision mental health through effective assessment, monitoring, and feedback processes. *Administration and Policy in Mental Health and Mental Health Services Research, 43*(3), 271–276.

Birken, S. A., Rohweder, C. L., Powell, B. J., Shea, C. M., Scott, J., Leeman, J., ... Haines, E. R. (2018). T-CaST: An implementation theory comparison and selection tool. *Implementation Science, 13*(1), 143.

Brackett, M. A., Rivers, S. E., Reyes, M. R., & Salovey, P. (2012). Enhancing academic performance and social and emotional competence with the RULER feeling words curriculum. *Learning and Individual Differences, 22*(2), 218–224.

Bradley, R., Doolittle, J., & Bartolotta, R. (2008). Building on the data and adding to the discussion: The experiences and outcomes of students with emotional disturbance. *Journal of Behavioral Education, 17* (1), 4–23.

Brown, C. H., Curran, G., Palinkas, L. A., Aarons, G. A., Wells, K. B., Jones, L., ... Tabak, R. G. (2017). An overview of research and evaluation designs for dissemination and implementation. *Annual Review of Public Health, 38*, 1–22.

Chambers, D. A., Glasgow, R. E., & Stange, K. C. (2013). The dynamic sustainability framework: Addressing the paradox of sustainment amid ongoing change. *Implementation Science, 8*, 117.

Cook, C. R., Kilgus, S. P., & Burns, M. K. (2018). Advancing the science and practice of precision education to enhance student outcomes. *Journal of School Psychology, 66*, 4–10.

Cook, C. R., Lyon, A. R., Locke, J., Waltz, T., & Powell, B. (2019). Adapting a compilation of implementation strategies to advance school-based implementation science and practice. *Prevention Science*, 914–935.

Curran, G. M., Bauer, M., Mittman, B., Pyne, J. M., & Stetler, C. (2012). Effectiveness-implementation hybrid designs: Combining elements of clinical effectiveness and implementation science to enhance public health impact. *Medical Care, 50*(3), 217.

Damschroder, L. J., Aron, D. C., Keith, R. E., Kirsh, S. R., Alexander, J. A., & Lowery, J. C. (2009). Fostering implementation of health services research findings into practice: A consolidated framework for advancing implementation science. *Implementation Science, 4*(1), 50.

Damschroder, L. J., Pritts, J. L., Neblo, M. A., Kalarickal, R. J., Creswell, J. W., & Hayward, R. A. (2007). Patients, privacy and trust: Patients' willingness to allow researchers to access their medical records. *Social Science & Medicine, 64*(1), 223–235.

Döll, P., & Romero-Lankao, P. (2017). How to embrace uncertainty in participatory climate change risk management – A roadmap. *Earth's Future, 5*(1), 18–36.

Domitrovich, C. E., Bradshaw, C. P., Poduska, J. M., Hoagwood, K., Buckley, J. A., Olin, S., ... Ialongo, N. S. (2008). Maximizing the implementation quality of evidence-based preventive interventions in schools: A conceptual framework. *Advances in School Mental Health Promotion, 1*(3), 6–28.

Domitrovich, C. E., Cortes, R. C., & Greenberg, M. T. (2007). Improving young children's social and emotional competence: A randomized trial of the preschool "PATHS" curriculum. *The Journal of Primary Prevention, 28*, 67–91.

Durlak, J. A. (2010). The importance of doing well in whatever you do: A commentary on the special section, "Implementation science in early childhood education". *Early Childhood Research Quarterly, 25*, 348–357.

Eccles, M. P., & Mittman, B. S. (2006). Welcome to implementation science. *Implementation Science, 1*, 1.

Edwards, A., & Elwyn, G. (Eds.). (2009). *Shared decision-making in health care: Achieving evidence-based patient choice.* Oxford: Oxford University Press. Retrieved from www.oxfordscholarship.com/view/10.1093/acprof:oso/9780198723448.001.0001/acprof-9780198723448.

Every Student Success Act of 2015, Pub. L. No. 114-95 § 114 Stat. 1177 (2015–2016).

Fairburn, C. G., & Patel, V. (2014). The global dissemination of psychological treatments: A road map for research and practice. *American Journal of Psychiatry, 171*(5), 495–498.

Farmer, T. W., Gatzke-Kopp, L., & Latendresse, S. (2020). The development, prevention, and treatment of emotional and behavioral disabilities: An interdisciplinary developmental systems perspective. In T. W. Farmer, M. A. Conroy, E. M. Z. Farmer, & K. S. Sutherland (Eds.), *Handbook of research on emotional and behavioral disorders: Interdisciplinary developmental perspectives on children and youth*. New York: Routledge/Taylor & Francis.

Fixsen, D. L., Naoom, S. F., Blasé, K. A., Friedman, R. M., & Wallace, F. (2005). *Implementation science: A synthesis of the literature*. Tampa, FL: University of South Florida, Louis de la Parte Florida Mental Health Institute, The National Implementation Science Network (FMHI Publication #231).

Forman, S. G., Olin, S. S., Hoagwood, K. E., Crowe, M., & Saka, N. (2009). Evidence-based intervention in schools: Developers' views of implementation barriers and facilitators. *School Mental Health: A Multidisciplinary Research and Practice Journal, 1*(1), 26–36.

Forness, S. R., Freeman, S. F., Paparella, T., Kauffman, J. M., & Walker, H. M. (2012). Special education implications of point and cumulative prevalence for children with emotional or behavioral disorders. *Journal of Emotional and Behavioral Disorders, 20*(1), 4–18.

Glasgow, R. E. (2013). What does it mean to be pragmatic? Pragmatic methods, measures, and models to facilitate research translation. *Health Education and Behavior, 40*(3), 257–265.

Gottfredson, D. C., & Gottfredson, G. D. (2002). Quality of school-based prevention programs: Results from a national survey. *Journal of Research in Crime and Delinquency, 39*(1), 3–35.

Grol, R. P., Bosch, M. C., Hulscher, M. E., Eccles, M. P., & Wensing, M. (2007). Planning and studying improvement in patient care: The use of theoretical perspectives. *Milbank Quarterly, 85*(1), 93–138.

Joyce, B., & Showers, B. (2002). *Student achievement through staff development* (3rd ed.). Alexandria, VA: Association for Supervision and Curriculum Development.

Kazdin, A. E., & Rabbitt, S. M. (2013). Novel models for delivering mental health services and reducing the burdens of mental illness. *Clinical Psychological Science, 1*(2), 170–191.

Khoury, M. J., Gwinn, M., Yoon, P. W., Dowling, N., Moore, C. A., & Bradley, L. (2007). The continuum of translation research in genomic medicine: How can we accelerate the appropriate integration of human genome discoveries into health care and disease prevention? *Genetics in Medicine, 9*(10), 665–674.

Kochevar, L. K., & Yano, E. M. (2006). Understanding health care organization needs and context. *Journal of General Internal Medicine, 21*(2), 25–29.

Landsverk, J., Brown, C. H., Reutz, J. R., Palinkas, L., & Horwitz, S. M. (2010). Design elements in implementation science: A structured review of child welfare and child mental health studies. *Administration and Policy in Mental Health and Mental Health Services Research, 38*(1), 54–63.

Lane, K. L., Barton-Arwood, S. M., Nelson, J. R., & Wehby, J. (2008). Academic performance of students with emotional and behavioral disorders served in a self-contained setting. *Journal of Behavioral Education, 17*(1), 43–62.

Lewis, C., Darnell, D., Kerns, S., Monroe-DeVita, M., Landes, S. J., Lyon, A. R., … Puspitasari, A. (2016, June). Proceedings of the 3rd Biennial Conference of the Society for Implementation science Collaboration (SIRC) 2015: Advancing efficient methodologies through community partnerships and team science. *Implementation Science, 11*(1), 85). BioMed Central.

Lewis, C. C., Klasnja, P., Powell, B., Tuzzio, L., Jones, S., Walsh-Bailey, C., & Weiner, B. (2018). From classification to causality: Advancing understanding of mechanisms of change in implementation science. *Frontiers in Public Health, 6*, 136.

Lyon, A. R. (2017). Implementation science and practice in the education sector. Brief prepared for Project AWARE grant recipients. Substance Abuse and Mental Health Services Administration.

Lyon, A. R., & Bruns, E. J. (2019). User-centered redesign of evidence-based psychosocial interventions to enhance implementation – Hospitable soil or better seeds? *JAMA Psychiatry, 76*(1), 3–4.

Lyon, A. R., & Bruns, E. J. (2019). From evidence to impact: Joining our best school mental health practices with our best implementation strategies. *School Mental Health, 11*, 1–3.

Lyon, A. R., Cook, C. R., Locke, J., Davis, C., Powell, B. J., & Waltz, T. J. (2019). Importance and feasibility of an adapted set of strategies for implementing evidence-based mental health practices in schools. *Journal of School Psychology, 76*, 66–77.

Lyon, A. R., & Koerner, K. (2016). User-centered design for psychosocial intervention development and implementation. *Clinical Psychology: Science and Practice, 23*(2), 180–200.

Lyon, A. R., Ludwig, K., Romano, E., Koltracht, J., Vander Stoep, A., & McCauley, E. (2014). Using modular psychotherapy in school mental health: Provider perspectives on intervention-setting fit. *Journal of Clinical Child & Adolescent Psychology, 43*, 890–901.

Lyon, A. R., Stirman, S. W., Kerns, S. E., & Bruns, E. J. (2011). Developing the mental health workforce: Review and application of training approaches from multiple disciplines. *Administration and Policy in Mental Health and Mental Health Services Research, 38*(4), 238–253.

Lyon, A. R., Whitaker, K., Locke, J., Cook, C. R., King, K. M., Duong, M., … Aarons, G. A. (2018). The impact of inter-organizational alignment (IOA) on implementation outcomes: Evaluating unique and shared organizational influences in education sector mental health. *Implementation Science, 13*. Retreieved from https://implementationscience.biomedcentral.com/articles/10.1186/s13012-018-0721-1.

McIntosh, K., Mercer, S. H., Nese, R. N. T., Strickland-Cohen, M. K., & Hoselton, R. (2016). Predictors of sustained implementation of school-wide positive behavioral interventions and supports. *Journal of Positive Behavior Interventions, 18*(4), 209–218.

Mitchell, S. A., & Chambers, D. A. (2017). Leveraging implementation science to improve cancer care delivery and patient outcomes. *Journal of Oncology Practice, 13*(8), 523–529.

Nilsen, P. (2015). Making sense of implementation theories, models, and frameworks. *Implementation Science, 10*(53). Retrieved from https://implementationscience.biomedcentral.com/articles/10.1186/s13012-015-0242-0.

No Child Left Behind Act of 2001, P.L. 107–110, 20 U.S.C. § 6319 (2002).

Parsons, S., Charman, T., Faulkner, R., Ragan, J., Wallace, S., & Wittemeyer, K. (2013). Commentary–bridging the research and practice gap in autism: The importance of creating research partnerships with schools. *Autism, 17*(3), 268–280.

Powell, B. J., McMillen, J. C., Proctor, E. K., Carpenter, C. R., Griffey, R. T., Bunger, A. C., … York, J. L. (2012). A compilation of strategies for implementing clinical innovations in health and mental health. *Medical Care Research and Review, 69*(2), 123–157.

Powell, B. J., Waltz, T. J., Chinman, M. J., Damschroder, L. J., Smith, J. L., Matthieu, M. M., … Kirchner, J. E. (2015). A refined compilation of implementation strategies: Results from the Expert Recommendations for Implementing Change (ERIC) project. *Implementation Science, 10*(1), 1.

Proctor, E., Silmere, H., Raghavan, R., Hovmand, P., Aarons, G., Bunger, A., … Hensley, M. (2011). Outcomes for implementation science: Conceptual distinctions, measurement challenges, and research agenda. *Administration and Policy in Mental Health and Mental Health Services Research, 38*(2), 65–76.

Rabin, B. A., & Brownson, R. C. (2012). Developing the terminology for dissemination and implementation science. In R. C. Brownson, G. C. Colditz, & E. K. Proctor, *Dissemination and implementation science in health: Translating science to practice* (pp. 23–51). New York: Oxford University Press.

Rahman, A., Malik, A., Sikander, S., Roberts, C., & Creed, F. (2008). Cognitive behaviour therapy-based intervention by community health workers for mothers with depression and their infants in rural Pakistan: A cluster-randomised controlled trial. *The Lancet, 372*(9642), 902–909.

Spilt, J. L., Koomen, H. M., Thijs, J. T., & van der Leij, A. (2012). Supporting teachers' relationships with disruptive children: The potential of relationship-focused reflection. *Attachment & Human Development, 14*(3), 305–318.

Stahmer, A. C., Suhrheinrich, J., Reed, S., & Schreibman, L. (2012). What works for you? Using teacher feedback to inform adaptations of pivotal response training for classroom use. *Autism Research and Treatment, 2012*, 1–11.

Stanick, C. F., Halko, H. M., Dorsey, C. N., Weiner, B. J., Powell, B. J., Palinkas, L. A., & Lewis, C. C. (2018). Operationalizing the 'pragmatic measures construct using a stakeholder feedback and a multi-method approach. *BMC Health Services Research, 18*(1), 882.

Sutherland, K. S., Alder, N., & Gunter, P. L. (2003). The effect of varying rates of opportunities to respond to academic requests on the classroom behavior of students with EBD. *Journal of Emotional and Behavioral Disorders, 11*(4), 239–248.

Sutherland, K. S., McLeod, B. D., Conroy, M. A., & Cox, J. R. (2013). Measuring implementation of evidence-based programs targeting young children at risk for emotional/behavioral disorders conceptual issues and recommendations. *Journal of Early Intervention, 35*, 129–149.

Tabak, R. G., Khoong, E. C., Chambers, D. A., & Brownson, R. C. (2012). Bridging research and practice: Models for dissemination and implementation science. *American Journal of Preventive Medicine, 43* (3), 337–350.

Tornatzky, L. G., & Klein, K. J. (1982). Innovation characteristics and innovation adoption-implementation: A meta-analysis of findings. *IEEE Transactions on Engineering Management, 1*, 28–45.

Trivette, C. M., Dunst, C. J., Hamby, D. W., & O'Herin, C. E. (2009). Characteristics and consequences of adult learning methods and strategies. *Research Brief, 3*(1), 1–16.

Wagner, M., & Newman, L. (2012). Longitudinal transition outcomes of youth with emotional disturbances. *Psychiatric Rehabilitation Journal, 35*(3), 199.

Webster-Stratton, C., Reid, M. J., & Hammond, M. (2004). Treating children with early-conduct problems: Intervention outcomes for parent, child, and teacher training. *Journal of Clinical Child and Adolescent Psychology, 33*, 105–124.

Weisz, J. R., Chorpita, B. F., Palinkas, L. A., Schoenwald, S. K., Miranda, J., Bearman, S. K., … Gray, J. (2012). Testing standard and modular designs for psychotherapy treating depression, anxiety, and conduct problems in youth: A randomized effectiveness trial. *Archives of General Psychiatry, 69*(3), 274–282.

Weisz, J. R., Kuppens, S., Ng, M. Y., Eckshtain, D., Ugueto, A., & Fordwood, S. R. (2017). What five decades of research tells us about the effects of youth psychological therapy: A multilevel meta-analysis and implications for science and practice. *American Psychologist, 72*(2), 79–117.

What Works Clearinghouse. (2017). *Procedures and standards handbook (Version 4.0)*. Retrieved from https://ies.ed.gov/ncee/wwc/Docs/ReferenceResources/wwc_standards_handbook_v4_draft.pdf

Williams, N. J. (2016). Multilevel mechanisms of implementation strategies in mental health: Integrating theory, research, and practice. *Administration and Policy in Mental Health & Mental Health Services Research, 43* (5), 783–798.

29 Recruiting, Preparing, and Retaining a Diverse Emotional and Behavioral Disorders Educator Workforce

LaRon Scott, Cassandra Willis, Lauren Bruno, Katherine Brendli, Colleen A. Thoma, and Robin Walsh

The need to diversify the teaching workforce has been recognized for a number of years (e.g. Billingsley, Bettini, & Williams, 2019; Gershenson, Lindsay, Holt, & Papageorge, 2017; Goldhaber, Theobald, & Tien, 2019; Scott, Thoma, Puglia, Temple, & D'Aguilar, 2017), and this need is arguably more pronounced related to the education of students identified with emotional/behavioral disorders (EBD) who are more likely to be Black male students (Harry & Klingner, 2014). Scholars conducting research on the academic, social/emotional, and behavioral needs of students with EBD have proposed that EBD is not solely a characteristic of the student or the environment, but is a reflection of the fit (or lack thereof) between the two (Farmer, Farmer, & Brooks, 2010; Hobbs, 1982; Milner & Tenore, 2010). Currently, students of color are disproportionately represented in EBD programs, are disproportionately referred for discipline problems and receive harsher and more exclusionary consequences for behavioral infractions, and tend to have among the poorest long-term outcomes of all students with disabilities (e.g., U.S. Department of Education; Mitchell, Kern, & Conroy, 2019).

If we consider that this indicates a lack of fit between the student and his/her environment, then it's critically important that teachers and other professionals understand how to minimize that discrepancy by making simultaneous changes to the environment and supporting the student. It is argued that a first step would be in the preparation of professionals in the field of EBD who can help adapt evidence-based practices to the characteristics, needs, and ecologies of diverse learners and this should include professionals who reflect the characteristics, culture, and background of the students they serve (Farmer et al., 2016). Therefore, examining key issues related to developing and supporting a diverse workforce who can contribute to positive academic and functional outcomes among students with EBD is critical, and the purpose of this chapter. In the sections that follow, we (a) describe the literature that undergirds the need to recruit and retain a diverse EBD educator workforce, (b) present emerging strategies and techniques for bridging racial disparities in the EBD workforce, and (c) review factors associated with diversifying the specialized instructional personnel (e.g., school counselors, psychologists) that support students with EBD. Throughout this chapter, we discuss how a lack of access to diverse and culturally competent teachers and support personnel of color threatens equitable educational opportunities, and contributes to disproportionate outcomes (e.g., overrepresentation in special education, exclusionary discipline) for students with EBD. We also describe the extent to which culturally accessible teaching frameworks such as Universal Design for Learning and Universal Design for Transition strengthens the opportunity to prepare a culturally responsive EBD workforce. Lastly, we hope that the findings of this chapter will culminate in discussion about achieving a diverse educator workforce to improve the educational and post school outcomes for students of color with EBD.

434 *LaRon Scott et al.*

EBD Workforce Professionals

This section will lay the foundation for recruiting and retaining a diverse EBD educator workforce, including a review of related services professionals whose purpose is to support more comprehensive supports (e.g., social, emotional, behavioral needs) for students. Even though there are many professionals that need to be equipped with the knowledge and expertise to meet the complex needs of students with EBD, we first begin with a literature overview of special education teachers (SETs) because of the unique preparation this group of professionals requires in order to provide intensive interventions to support students with EBD.

SETs require specialized training to support the complex needs of students with EBD, but an overwhelming shortage of teachers has created a workforce crisis limiting the pool of these professionals. Researchers have reported that one-third of new SETs leave the field in the first three to five years (Cancio, Albrecht, & Johns, 2014; Podolsky, Kini, Bishop, & Darling-Hammond, 2016), and in general, SETs are more likely to transfer to other teaching assignments based on student and school challenges (e.g., fewer academic and behavior challenges; Hanushek, Kain, & Rivkin, 2004). Across the United States, officials in 49 states reported critical shortages of SETs (Cross, 2017). As the population of students with disabilities continues to increase, with 6.7 million children covered under the Individuals with Disabilities in Education Act (IDEA) in the 2015–2016 school year (Cross, 2017), the demand for SETs is expected to increase. State officials are responding to the shortages by creating alternative pathways to licensure programs, Grow Your Own programs, and in dire circumstances, placement of unqualified personnel in vacancies, many of whom are in placements requiring intensive knowledge and training needed to work with students with EBD. Further compounding the critical shortage in special education is the abundance of evidential literature documenting the need to increase the number of racially and ethnically diverse teachers (Gershenson et al., 2017; Goldhaber et al., 2019), including closing the gap between the number of SETs of color and students with disabilities of color (Billingsley et al., 2019; Scott & Alexander, 2019).

Diversifying Special Education Teachers

The need to diversify the special education teacher workforce is critical. Although students of color comprise approximately 45% of students served under IDEA, the teacher workforce remains predominantly White and female (U.S. Department of Education, 2019). Similarly, overall enrollment in teacher education colleges has decreased, and the enrollment for racial minority candidates has decreased even more (Hrabowski & Sanders, 2015). Over the span of approximately seven years, education degrees awarded to students of color decreased by 50% based in part on increased opportunities in other fields (Hrabowski & Sanders, 2015).

The lack of teachers of color in special education has significant ramifications for equitable educational opportunities for students, specifically for students with EBD. This is particularly true as evidence suggests that teacher race matters with regards to the initial referral of students to special education, and in placement decisions for students of color (Blanchett, 2006; Coutinho, Oswald, & Best, 2002). Concerning diversifying teachers of color in special education, perhaps the best illustration of this argument can be seen in more inclusive classrooms where tiered-instruction (e.g., response to intervention) and co-teaching between general and education teachers is more common (Hoover & Patton, 2008). In this sense, the special education teacher's role has evolved into having more early communication and involvement with intervening during the initial referral and identification process (Hoover & Patton, 2008).

Relatedly, evidence suggests that same-race teacher–child matching is associated with improved academic outcomes, higher rates of engagement, increased motivation in learning, improved social skills, and fewer absences from school (Rasheed, Brown, Doyle, & Jennings, 2019). While these findings are not to suggest only Black special education teachers should teach Black students with disabilities, this realization that race matters does draw concerns as other research regarding the demographic mismatch in classrooms indicated that racial bias and lack of cultural awareness to social and emotional development (e.g., behavior; Ward, 2010) significantly influences the disproportionate referral and diagnosis of Black students in special education (Coutinho et al., 2002; Douglas, Lewis, Douglas, Scott & Garrison-Wade, 2008; Ward, 2010), and overall progress for students of color (Gershenson, Holt, & Papageorge, 2016; Rubie-Davies, 2010). For example, researchers have found that between 73% and 90% of students referred by classroom teachers for special education evaluations were eligible for special education services, and the referrals disproportionately affected students of color (Harry & Klingner, 2014). Researchers have also demonstrated that a child's race and ethnicity are significantly related to the probability that the child will be identified as having a disability (Ahram, Fergus, & Noguera, 2011; Harry & Klingner, 2014). Data from the Office of Civil Rights (2016) supports this finding, because nearly 5% of U.S. school districts had risk ratios of more than 3 in the category of EBD, which means that Black students in those districts were three times more likely to be found eligible for services under EBD than their non-Black peers. Unfortunately, students often have little exposure to SETs who matched their racial identity (Scott & Alexander, 2019). While there is a need for teachers of students with EBD to be reflective of the student population, all teachers regardless of racial and ethnic background, at a minimum, should be culturally proficient (Chakraborti-Ghosh, Mofield, & Orellana, 2010).

Culturally Competent Educators

Teachers who are unaware of how students' cultures and social backgrounds influence learning can have a negative impact on student educational outcomes (Gay, 2002). Landa (2011) referred to cultural competency as the ability of teachers to be able to empathize and educate students of all backgrounds, particularly those from marginalized groups. Without cultural competency, biases that are formed are left unchecked and can lead to deleterious outcomes for students of color, including students with EBD. Ladson-Billings (1995) referred to this awareness as cultural responsiveness, representing the dynamic and complex relationship between a student's culture and background, and the culture of the school. Cultural competence has been a policy recommendation for decades to combat the over-identification of students of color represented in special education (Cross, Bazron, Dennis, & Isaacs, 1989).

Teachers of students with EBD need to be culturally competent to work with this group of students. This type of knowledge is used to ensure that teachers are operating in the best interest of children, reducing the influence of the biases and stereotypes that often plague children of color who have behavioral and emotional needs (Gay, 2002). Grissom, Kern, and Rodriguez (2015) asserted that minority students are less likely to be found eligible for special education services when a larger number of minority teachers exist. The lack of cultural competency in the special education workforce perpetuates the systems that cause disproportionality, or in this case, the overrepresentation of minority students with EBD (Harry & Klingner, 2014). Furthermore, the lack of empathy and understanding of the unique social, emotional, and behavioral needs of students with EBD disavows the intersectionality of disability, race, and other cultural factors (Blanchett, Klingner, & Harry, 2009). Culturally competent teachers of students with EBD use best practices to understand the influence of culture on students and use this knowledge to create opportunities for students to excel (Landa, 2011). Without diversification and cultural competency, referrals for EBD may continue to be subjective and could be based on race, poverty, or implicit prejudice (Grissom et al., 2015) instead of student's true needs.

Recruiting and Retaining a Diverse EBD Educator Workforce

Above we provided information that highlights the need for closing the teacher shortage and demographic gaps to improve opportunities and outcomes for students with EBD. However, the capacity to actively close these gaps has been less than optimal, and a discussion about individual strengths and weaknesses across strategies for recruiting and retaining a more diverse EBD workforce is necessary to meet these goals. For that reason, strategies for closing the demographic (e.g., racial, ethnic, language, gender) gaps within the educator workforce have gained significant attention, often as a result of professional organizations, academic researchers, and academic leaders calling for more national and local policies addressing the consistent finding that the teacher–student cultural gaps have not improved over time (U.S. Department of Education, Office of Planning, Evaluation and Policy Development, Policy and Program Studies Services (USDOE), 2016). The latter statement can also be said of teachers of students with EBD, who have cited: (a) school administrator poor attitudes toward the inclusion of students with EBD; (b) not enough access to effective resources to support students with EBD; (c) inappropriate disciplinary actions taken against students with EBD; (d) school-based opposition of stakeholder acceptance of mental health disorders; and (e) lack of understanding program needs of students with EBD, as factors why they leave the profession (Cancio, Albrecht, & Johns, 2014). It is also important to note that while 45.1% of students with EBD spend 80% or more of their time in inclusive general education classrooms (U.S. Department of Education, National Center for Education Statistics (NCES), 2019), they account for about half of behavior-related incidents in those settings (Eber, Sugai, Smith, & Scott, 2002). Thus, this brings into question the placement of unqualified personnel as educators in those settings, who may often lack significant preparation to deal with the demands of teaching students with EBD.

Strategies for retaining teachers of students with EBD include: (a) providing support with paperwork and administration tasks related to supporting students with EBD (e.g., paperwork related to Individualized Education Programs (IEPs)); (b) providing sound administrator support (e.g., collaborative relationship with teacher/administrator); (c) providing professional development training on topics for staff to understand the needs of students with EBD; (d) collaboration and support from general education colleagues, paraprofessionals, and other related services personnel; (e) providing comprehensive and relevant induction and mentoring; and (f) providing access to curricular and other resources for teaching academics and solutions-focused interventions to combat behavior problems (CCBD, 2007; Cancio et al., 2014). Many of the strategies are consistent with other research and recommendations for recruiting and retaining educators from diverse backgrounds (e.g., Carver-Thomas, 2018; Scott & Alexander, 2019). Therefore, knowing about the factors that contribute to educators of color and EBD teachers' retention will allow a better understanding of how to respond to attempts at reducing their attrition rates.

While several literature reviews and reports explicitly addressed recruiting and retaining teachers of color (Achinstein, Ogawa, Sexton, & Freitas, 2010; Carver-Thomas, 2018; Ingersoll, May, & Collins, 2017; Scott & Alexander, 2019; Villegas & Irvine, 2010), it is clear that the wide variety of strategies for recruiting and retaining teachers of color are yet to make a significant impact on the overall diversity of the teacher workforce. Researchers and policymakers have examined and discussed strategies by surveying and interviewing teachers from diverse backgrounds; however, it is clear that these research efforts will require further investigation before these strategies receive empirical validation particularly for culturally diverse teachers (e.g., race, ethnicity, language, gender), culturally diverse SETs, and SETs of students with EBD. Table 29.1 provides a summary of literature that has examined recruitment and retention strategies for diversifying the teacher education workforce.

As shown in Table 29.1, Scott and Alexander (2019) conducted a grounded theory study with 18 Black male SETs, including teachers of students with EBD. These researchers examined how the teachers were recruited into their teacher preparation programs and

Table 29.1 Description of Information

Literature	Design	Summary of Recruitment and Retention Strategies
Scott and Alexander (2019)	Grounded theory study of 18 in-service Black male SETs in urban/suburban school districts	Based on interviews, researchers developed a theoretical model for recruiting Black male special educators. The model included providing same-race mentoring, curriculum that offered more diversity, recruiting from local communities, offering competitive salaries.
Rice and Goesling (2005)	Theoretical paper pertaining to recruitment of male SETs	Theoretical study indicated recruitment and retention strategies based on literature. Strategies included increasing salaries, use of male academic advisors, and gender-specific social gatherings as examples.
Talbert-Johnson (2001)	Theoretical paper pertaining to retaining Black teachers in special education	Potential strategies included recruitment from diverse paraprofessional pool, loan forgiveness, bonuses, and professional development to promote diversity, as some recommended examples.
Carver-Thomas (2018)	Research report	Report indicated practices for recruiting and retaining teachers of color including, providing loan forgiveness and scholarships, funding for teacher residency programs and community-based teacher pipeline programs, ongoing mentorship, adjusting teacher licensure requirements, improving teaching conditions (e.g., administration support), and creating preemptive hiring and induction strategies (e.g., include other teachers of color in the hiring process).
Ingersoll et al. (2017)	Descriptive research study	Study indicated school organization conditions (e.g., faculty decision-making, classroom autonomy), management, and school leadership matters when attempting to retain minority teachers.

special education teaching positions, and addressed motivations, attractions, and strategies for recruiting and retaining Black male SETs. Participants noted several strategies that motivated them to work with students with disabilities, and a theoretical model was developed that has implications for recruiting and retaining racially and gender diverse SETs, including settings where students with EBD are taught (Scott & Alexander, 2019). Carver-Thomas (2018) and Ingersoll et al. (2017) detailed barriers to recruiting and retaining teachers of color, and described promising strategies consistent with SETs of color retention needs. Rice and Goesling (2005) and Talbert-Johnson (2001) provided early discussion about valuing recruitment and retention strategies aimed specifically at diversifying (e.g., gender, race) the SET workforce. However, a larger body of empirical research specifically addressing recruiting and retaining strategies for diverse educators in the special education workforce, particularly for students with EBD, is required before understanding the impact of those strategies on the teacher workforce.

Research on Related Services Providers for the EBD Workforce

As previously noted, it is important to acknowledge that students with EBD require a diverse and wide variety of professionals to support their academic, developmental, and support needs. For that reason, it is important that discussion on workforce development to support students with EBD expand beyond SETs. For example, students with EBD are at a higher risk for school-related delinquency (Swearer, Wang, Maag, Siebecker, & Frerichs, 2012; Zhang, Hsu, Katsiyannis, Barrett, & Ju, 2011), higher rates of depression (Maag & Reid, 2006), and aggression (Rose & Espelage, 2012), which is likely to interrupt their learning and educational environments. As a result, school-based support professionals are often recruited to collaborate with special educators to meet the social/emotional needs of students with EBD. The Every Student Succeeds Act (ESSA) of 2015 defines these professionals as specialized instructional support personnel (SISP) who are involved in providing assessment, diagnosis, counseling, and educational, therapeutic, and other necessary services as part of a comprehensive program to meet students' needs (ESSA, 2015). Strategies for developing and collaborating with SISP (e.g., school counselors, school social workers, school nurses, therapists, psychologists, speech-language pathologists) are considered important for meeting the needs of students with EBD (Eber et al., 2002).

Support Personnel Responsibilities

A major responsibility of SISP includes providing direct services to all students, regardless of student backgrounds, beliefs, or disability. In addition, these professionals are tasked with maintaining ethical responsibilities and confidentialities of student behaviors and records, which are pertinent for students with EBD. But more recently, there has been increased concern for students around safety and mental health (Evans & Payne, 2008), specifically for students with social/emotional and behavior challenges (Taub, 2006). For example psychological and mental health counseling services are more frequently sought out than other related service types by youth with EBD (Levine, Marder, & Wagner, 2004; U.S. Department of Education, 2009), thus emphasizing the dire need to train and prepare more SISP (specifically school counselors) to meet the diverse academic, behavioral, social, and career needs of students with EBD.

Given these concerns, ESSA (2015) now emphasizes the mental and physical health of all students, further highlighting the importance of acquiring highly trained SISP who are knowledgeable in working with youth with EBD. Specifically, ESSA regulations encourage states and school districts to effectively prepare SISP, like school counselors and psychologists, with evidence-based training and practices to support students' social, emotional, and behavior needs (ESSA, 2015). Training and practices include efforts to implement multi-tiered service delivery models, including approaches to behavior interventions and trauma-informed care for students, which are known to be effective with supporting students with disabilities (Phifer & Hull, 2016).

Support Personnel Serving Students with EBD

SISP, such as school counselors and school psychologists, often support students receiving special education services, including those with EBD whose disability negatively impacts their education, through offering individual counseling, classroom lessons, small group lessons, and other services (McEachern & Kenny, 2007; Milsom, 2007). Topics may include self-awareness, communication, transition skills, coping skills, appreciating diversity, self-advocacy, bullying, and social skills development (McEachern & Kenny, 2007; Milsom, 2007; Milsom, Akos, & Thompson, 2004; Swearer et al., 2012; Taub, 2006). When working with students with disabilities, SISP should embed opportunities for choice making and self-advocacy in classrooms, lessons, and/or groups (Brotherson, Cook, Erwin, & Weigel, 2008; Thoma, Bartholomew, & Scott, 2009). Because students with EBD typically experience more symptoms related to depression than other students (Maag & Reid, 2006), SISP should identify and deliver evidence-based interventions and resources in all academic and functional skill areas to encourage greater transitional outcomes (Cho, Wehmeyer, & Kingston, 2012; Maag & Reid, 2006) and increase overall student self-determination (Taub, 2006; Thompson & Littrell, 1998). Since teachers have reported facing barriers to implementing self-determination instruction (e.g. time to teach self-determination and related skills), SISP may support and supplement their work with students in this area (Cho et al., 2012).

Universal Design for Learning and Students with EBD

One way in which SISP and teachers can work together to support their students' diverse academic, behavioral, and transition-related needs is using Universal Design for Learning (UDL). Included in the ESSA of 2015, UDL is defined as

> a scientifically valid framework for guiding educational practice that (a) provides flexibility in the ways information is presented, in the ways students respond or demonstrate knowledge and skills, and in the ways students are engaged; and (b) reduces barriers in instruction, provides appropriate accommodations, supports, and challenges, and maintains high achievement expectations for all students, including students with disabilities and students who are limited English proficient.
>
> (ESSA, 2015)

This framework, however, is not limited to students with disabilities and can assist teachers and other SISP in becoming more responsive to all linguistically and culturally diverse students, including those with EBD. For example, the UDL framework can be used to create culturally accessible classrooms and school environments for all learners, specifically engaging the whole learner, while emphasizing a strengths-based approach (Degner, 2016).

Although most studies investigating UDL in pre-K–12 settings include students with a range of different learning needs, very little research examines specific populations of students to determine the impact of using this approach on their learning and/or outcomes (Rao, Ok, & Bryant, 2014). In a few published papers (e.g., Cook, Rao, Collins, 2017; Kennedy, Thomas, Meyer, Alves, Lloyd, 2014), researchers focused on how UDL can be used to design and deliver instruction to address the targeted needs of a specific population of students, including students with EBD. Students with EBD struggle with learning academic content, possess challenging behaviors and have difficulty in establishing and maintaining interpersonal relationships with others (Kauffman & Landrum, 2013). While this typically results in less inclusive opportunities for students with EBD, students are increasingly being educated in general education classrooms (U.S. Department of Education, National Center for Education Statistics, 2019), signaling the need for frameworks like UDL to be implemented in order for educators and support personnel to meet the unique needs of all students. The UDL framework relates to researchers' arguments for more culturally responsive classroom management frameworks for teachers in order to center equity, and improve learning outcomes (e.g., student behavior, academics) for diverse learners (Milner & Tenore, 2010).

Benefits of UDL

For a UDL service delivery model to be implemented effectively in school-based settings, a concerted effort must first occur to prepare stakeholders (e.g., general education teachers, SETs, SISP) in proper UDL implementation during their preservice programs (Scott et al., 2017). UDL can also promote instructional flexibility to better meet diverse learner needs, therefore, offering a more equitable and socially just learning environment (Pliner & Johnson, 2004); this is particularly important for students with EBD from diverse backgrounds. Educators using UDL can address the culturally diverse needs of students with EBD through customizing instructional delivery (Kieran & Anderson, 2019), which can help address identified "barriers" (including behaviors) in the learning environment. Another barrier to learning for students with EBD may include lack of engagement, which often leads to disruptive behaviors (i.e., to a student being off-task) and eventually poor academic outcomes (Cook et al., 2017). Employing UDL guidelines for multiple means of engagement can help increase engagement while reducing other barriers to learning as well (Cook et al., 2017).

Implementing a UDL framework has promise for addressing many of the challenges faced by students with EBD in school, particularly students who are at risk for entering the juvenile justice system because of school misbehavior. Researchers have referred to this as the school-to-prison pipeline (Gonsoulin, Zablocki, & Leone, 2012; Hirschfield, 2008; Kim & Geronimo, 2009). While many of these researchers have pointed to harsh disciplinary methods in schools as an unintended consequence leading to the increasing numbers of youth who have entered the juvenile justice system, Gonsoulin et al. (2012) identify four factors that have contributed to the school-to-prison pipeline, two of which can be addressed by teachers and schools that implement the key components of a UDL framework. These two contributing factors include *poor conditions for learning* (CFL) and *failure to build the emotional and social capacity of students*.

Effective CFL includes providing safe learning environments, establishing connections between students and teachers, implementing activities and curricula that engage and challenge students, and facilitating positive peer support (Gonsoulin et al., 2012). A UDL framework requires that teachers start with creating that supportive learning environment and the use of multiple methods of representation provides opportunities for peer mentoring and the creation of academic instruction that holds high expectations for all students yet provides the opportunity for students to engage in the learning environment in ways that address their needs.

Strategies that build the emotional and social capacity of students can also be linked to a UDL framework, particularly the principle of multiple means of engagement. Under this principle, the "goal is to design learning environments, curricula and curricular goals, and instructional materials and methods so that all students can engage with their learning in multiple ways, becoming purposeful and motivated to learn" (Turnbull, Turnbull, Wehmeyer, & Shogren, 2020, p. 168). This principle of the UDL framework ensures that students have an opportunity to learn to self-regulate, to set their own learning goals tied to their interests. It can prevent students from becoming disengaged from the classroom environment and give them strategies they can use to set positive goals for their learning that can lead to a belief in their ability to be successful in school and life.

Supporting Empirical Research on UDL

UDL holds great promise for improving the instruction of all students, but more research on this topic is needed to support its use with students with EBD. The UDL framework has been shown to demonstrate a positive impact on the education of students with disabilities overall, including improved social skills and participation (Dymond et al., 2006); literacy (Coyne, Pisha, Zeph, Dalton & Smith, 2012); and science content learning (Rappolt-Schlictman, Daley, Lim, Lapinski, Robinson, & Johnson, 2013). However, given the complexity of the UDL framework (Edyburn, 2010), there is insufficient evidence to determine whether it improves student long-term academic outcomes, thus suggesting the need for a more transition-focused approach. As teachers and other SISP become more adept at following UDL principles in their instructional planning, delivery, and assessment practices, the hope is that more students will have access to the general education curriculum, which can provide further opportunities for them to achieve their dreams for a productive, rewarding adult life (Turnbull, Turnbull, Wehmeyer, & Shogren, 2012).

Training and Preparing Educators for EBD Students' Transition Needs

Building from UDL, Thoma et al. (2009) developed a proactive, barrier-free transition planning framework, called Universal Design for Transition (UDT), that links positive academics and transition outcomes for students with disabilities, including students with EBD. UDT is characterized by several elements that promote optimum educational opportunity and accessibility, especially emphasizing increased effective transitions for secondary students receiving special education services (Thoma et al., 2009). Specifically, UDT builds upon the UDL framework by bridging the gap between effective academic instruction and transition programming (Thoma et al., 2009). UDT extends from the major UDL principles (i.e., engagement, expression, and representation) by additionally preparing students with disabilities for the multiple life domains associated with postsecondary transition (Scott et al., 2017). Following in accordance with best practices in assessment and instruction, the UDT framework can be used to prepare students with EBD for postsecondary transitions through incorporating multiple means of assessment, multiple life domains, individual self-determination, and multiple resources/perspectives (Test et al., 2009; Thoma et al., 2009).

UDT and Preparing and Supporting Specialists from Diverse Backgrounds

In addition to preparing students for the postsecondary world, UDT also proactively accounts for individual differences, which is important when preparing specialists from diverse backgrounds. Specifically, the framework's emphasis on diversity is especially vital to prompt greater workforce diversification in American public schools. In support of greater workforce diversification throughout the field, UDT is used to address the individual student's needs by adopting a flexible curriculum that can be adapted according to diverse school personnel and their individual strengths and needs (Thoma et al., 2009). The framework emphasizes multiple means of assessment used to offer educators and SISP the creativity to gather assessment data in a multitude of ways, allowing these professionals to utilize their strengths, knowledge, and skills to foster student transition achievement. For example, the use of informal career assessments, observations, standardized academic achievement tests, and interviews can help educators better understand students' strengths and weaknesses to support them in developing and reaching individualized transition goals. Additionally, the framework is used to embrace multiple resources and perspectives to enhance collaboration amongst employers (including support personnel), community agency representatives, family members, and other stakeholders. Enhanced collaboration can allow school personnel to acquire a more holistic understanding of their students' cultures, especially when their cultures do not reflect that of the educators or support personnel (Thoma et al., 2009).

The framework's self-determination features also aid support personnel in using their unique qualities for enhanced effectiveness. Encompassing skills related to autonomy, relatedness, and competence, self-determination refers to "becoming a causal agent in one's life" (Palmer et al., 2013, p. 38), and it includes core elements such as choice-making, goal setting, and problem-solving (Palmer et al., 2013; Perry, Brenner, Collie, & Hofer, 2015). Researchers indicate that, similar to its benefits to students, self-determination has been used to support teacher retention and effectiveness (Perry et al., 2015).

Translating UDT to Meet Academic and Transition Goals

Regardless of cultural backgrounds, educators and other support personnel face the complex challenge of connecting academic content and transition goals in order to foster greater outcomes for students with disabilities (Best, Scott, & Thoma, 2015; Thoma, Cain, Wojcik, Best, & Scott, 2016). To illustrate, according to an annual report to members of Congress in 2014–2015 students with EBD were far more likely than members of any other disability category to receive out-of-school suspensions and expulsions, in-school suspensions, and removal from public school settings to more restrictive, alternative placements (U.S. Department of Education, Office of Special Education and Rehabilitative Services, 2017). Furthermore, for every academic year from 2004–2005 to 2017–2018, students with EBD had the highest dropout rates compared to any other disability category, which accounts for no less than 35% of students with EBD each year (U.S. Department of Education., 2019). In addition, students with EBD have some of the highest rates of unemployment, underemployment, and job instability (Prince, Hodge, Bridges, & Katsiyannis, 2017). These statistics indicate the need for academic solutions to support positive transition outcomes for students with EBD.

Through seeking greater connections between transition and academics, researchers of the UDT framework provided a roadmap that follows in accordance with the recent theme of U.S. education legislation at the federal level (Thoma et al., 2009). Specifically, UDT uses a framework for teachers and SISP to provide students with EBD universal learning opportunities that encourage multiple means to successfully aid students with postsecondary transitions (Thoma et al., 2009). Rather than customizing services to individual needs, UDT fosters student adaptability to assist students in identifying natural supports in multiple environments (Thoma et al., 2016). Educators can provide naturally occurring reinforcements to encourage students' pathways to accomplishing their transition goals. For example, educators can remind students that good grades will lead to their graduation from high school.

In terms of educator support, the framework requires facilitators to consider several questions during academic-focused lesson development to build relevant and appropriate connections with functional and transition skills for students with EBD (e.g., "What are the overall goals? What skills are needed for transition? What academic content will support most (or all) students' goals? How does this academic content apply to life after high school?"; (Thoma et al., 2009, p. 15). Given UDT's effectiveness in establishing academic and transition links (Scott, Saddler, Thoma, Bartholomew, Alder, & Tamura, 2011), researchers have recommended SETs, transition specialists, administrators, and other stakeholders weave UDT principles into school curricula (Scott et al., 2011, 2017; Thoma et al., 2009).

Conclusion

Even though the recruitment, preparation, and support of specialists from diverse back-grounds continue to be a challenge for the field, it has been encouraging to observe the attention the topic is receiving from researchers, policymakers, educators, and other stake-holders. Currently, no doubts exist about the contributions of educators from diverse back-grounds (e.g., race, ethnicity, language, gender) on students' with EBD academic achievement (Dee, 2004; Egalite, Kisida, & Winters, 2015), social/emotional, and behavioral well-being (Lindsay & Hart, 2017), possibly reducing racial bias when referring Black students for suspension and expulsion (Skiba, Chung, Trachok, Sheya, & Hughes, 2014), and perhaps decreasing referral and placement in special education (Neal, McCray, Webb-Johnson, & Bridgest, 2003). As further consideration is given to the role that educator preparation programs have in training and diversifying the EBD workforce, essential questions about current teachers', SISP's, and other service providers' knowledge, skills, and quality of preparation to serve in classrooms where students with EBD are served may continue to be answered by addressing retention and turnover rates. Nevertheless, the importance of holistic methods to prepare teachers, school counselors, and other service providers should continue to be supported. And as new models and methods are developed, including ways that UDL approaches can be used to help with supporting ways educators are prepared to instruct and include students in inclusive environments, more empirical evidence about these innovations is needed. Similarly, as strategies for recruiting, preparing, and retaining a diverse EBD workforce increase, the need for more empirical research validating these strategies is needed.

References

Achinstein, B., Ogawa, R., Sexton, D., & Freitas, C. (2010). Retaining teachers of color: A pressing problem and a potential strategy for "hard-to-staff" schools. *Review of Educational Research, 80*(1), 71–107. doi:10.3102/0034654309355994

Ahram, R., Fergus, E., & Noguera, P. (2011). Addressing racial/ethnic disproportionality in special education: Case studies of suburban school districts. *Teachers College Record, 113*(10), 2233–2266.

Best, K., Scott, L., & Thoma, C. A. (2015). Starting with the end in mind: Inclusive education designed to prepare students for adult life. In E. Brown, R. G. Craven, & G. McLean (Eds.), *International advances in* education: Global initiatives for equity and social justice: Vol. 9, Inclusive education for students with intellectual disabilities (pp. 45–72). Charlotte, NC: Information Age Press.

Billingsley, B., Bettini, E., & Williams, T. O. (2019). Teacher diversity in special and general education: Composition and distribution of teachers of color across schools. *Remedial and Special Education, 40*(4), 199–212.

Blanchett, W. (2006). Disproportionate representation of African American students in special education: Acknowledging the role of white privilege and racism. *Educational Researcher, 35*(6), 24–28.

Blanchett, W., Klingner, J. K., & Harry, B. (2009). The intersection of race, culture, languages, and disability: Implications for urban education. *Urban Education, 44*(4), 389–409. doi:10.1177/0042085909338686

Brotherson, M. J., Cook, C. C., Erwin, E. J., & Weigel, C. J. (2008). Understanding self-determination and families of young children with disabilities in home environments. *Journal of Early Intervention, 31*, 22–43. doi:10.1177/1053815108324445

Cancio, E. J., Albrecht, S. F., & Johns, B. H. (2014). Combating the attrition of teachers of students with EBD: What can administrators do?. *Intervention in School and Clinic, 49*(5), 306–312. doi:10.1177/1053451213513953

Carver-Thomas, D. (2018). *Diversifying the teaching profession: How to recruit and retain teachers of color*. Palo Alto, CA: Learning Policy Institute.

Chakraborti-Ghosh, S., Mofield, E., & Orellana, K. (2010). Cross-cultural comparisons and implications for students with EBD: A decade of understanding. *International Journal of Special Education, 25*(2), 162–170.

Cho, H. J., Wehmeyer, M. L., & Kingston, N. M. (2012). The effect of social and classroom ecological factors on promoting self-determination in elementary school. *Preventing School Failure, 56*, 19–28. doi:10.1080/1045988X.2010.548419

Cook, S. C., Rao, K., & Collins, L. (2017). Self-monitoring interventions for students with EBD: Applying UDL to a research-based practice. *Beyond Behavior, 26*(1), 19–27. doi:10.1177/1074295617694407

Coutinho, M. J., Oswald, D. P., & Best, A. M. (2002). The influence of sociodemographics and gender on the disproportionate identification of minority students as having learning disabilities. *Remedial and Special Education, 23*, 49–59.

Coyne, P., Pisha, B., Dalton, B., Zeph, L. A., & Smith, N. C. (2012). Literacy by design: A universal design for learning approach for students with significant intellectual disabilities. *Remedial and Special Education, 33*(3), 162–172.

Cross, F. (2017). *Teacher shortage areas nationwide listing 1990–1991 through 2017–2018*. Washington, DC: U.S. Department of Education. Office of Postsecondary Education.

Cross, T., Bazron, B. J., Dennis, K. W., & Isaacs, M. R. (1989). *Toward a culturally competent system of care*. Washington, DC: Georgetown University Child Development Center.

Dee, T. (2004). Teachers, race, and student achievement in a randomized experiment. *The Review of Economics and Statistics, 86*(1), 195–210. doi:10.1162/003465304323023750

Degner, J. (2016, November 15). How universal design for learning creates culturally accessible classrooms. *Education Week Teacher*. Retrieved from www.edweek.org/tm/articles/2016/11/14/udl-creates-culturally-competency-in-classroom.html

Douglas, B., Lewis, C. W., Douglas, A., Scott, M. E., & Garrison-Wade, D. (2008). The impact of White teachers on the academic achievement of Black students: An explanatory qualitative analysis. *Education Foundations, 22*, 47–62.

Dymond, S. K., Renzaglia, A., Rosenstein, A., Chun, E. J., Banks, R. A., Niswander, V., & Gilson, C. L. (2006). Using a participatory action research approach to create a universally designed inclusive high school science course: A case study. *Research and Practice for Persons with Severe Disabilities, 31*(4), 293–308.

Eber, L., Sugai, G., Smith, C. R., & Scott, T. M. (2002). Wraparound and positive behavioral interventions and supports in the schools. *Journal of Emotional and Behavioral Disorders, 10*(3), 171–180. doi:10.1177/10634266020100030501

Edyburn, D. L. (2010). Would you recognize universal design for learning if you saw it? Ten propositions for new directions for the second decade of UDL. *Learning Disability Quarterly, 33*(1), 33–41. doi:10.1177/073194871003300103

Egalite, A. J., Kisida, B., & Winters, M. A. (2015). Representation in the classroom: The effect of own-race teachers on student achievement. *Economics of Education Review, 45,* 44–52. doi:10.1016/j.econedurev.2015.01.007

Evans, Y. A., & Payne, M. A. (2008). Support and self-care: Professional reflections of six New Zealand high school counsellors. *British Journal of Guidance and Counselling, 36*(3), 317–330. doi:10.1080/03069880701729466

Every Student Succeeds Act (2015). Pub. Law No. 114-95 § 114 Stat. 1177.

Farmer, T. W., Farmer, E. M. Z., & Brooks, D. S. (2010). Recasting the ecological and developmental roots of intervention for students with emotional and behavioral problems: The promise of strength-based perspectives. *Exceptionality, 18,* 53–57.

Farmer, T. W., Sutherland, K. S., Talbott, E., Brooks, D., Norwalk, K., & Huneke, M. (2016). Special educators as intervention specialists: Dynamic systems and the complexity of intensifying intervention for students with emotional and behavioral disorders. *Journal of Emotional and Behavioral Disorders, 24,* 127–137.

Gay, G. (2002). Culturally responsive teaching in special education for ethnically diverse students: Setting the stage. *International Journal of Qualitative Studies in Education, 15*(6), 613–629. doi:10.1080/0951839022000014349

Gershenson, S., Holt, S. B., & Papageorge, N. W. (2016). Who believes in me? The effect of student-teacher demographic match on teacher expectations. *Economics of Education Review, 52,* 209–224. doi:10.1016/j.econedurev.2016.03.002

Gershenson, S., Lindsay, C., Holt, S. B., & Papageorge, N. W. (2017). *The long-run impact of same-race teachers.* Institute of Labor Economics. Retrieved from http://ftp.iza.org/dp10630.pdf

Goldhaber, R., Theobald, R., & Tien, C. (2019). Why we need a diverse teacher workforce. *Kappan: the Professional Journal for Educators, 100*(5). Retrieved from https://kappanonline.org/magazine-issue/

Gonsoulin, S., Zablocki, M., & Leone, P. (2012). Safe schools, staff development, and the school to prison pipeline. *Teacher Education and Special Education: the Journal of the Teacher Education Division of the Council for Exceptional Children, 35*(4), 309–319.

Grissom, J. A., Kern, E. C., & Rodriguez, L. A. (2015). The "representative bureaucracy" in education: Educator workforce diversity, policy outputs, and outcomes for disadvantaged students. *Educational Researcher, 44*(3), 185–192.

Hanushek, E. A., Kain, J. F., & Rivkin, S. G. (2004). Why public schools lose teachers. *Journal of Human Resources, 39*(2), 326–354. doi:0.2307/3559017

Harry, B., & Klingner, J. (2014). *Why are so many minority students in special education?* New York: Teachers College Press.

Hirschfield, P. J. (2008). Preparing for prison? The criminalization of school discipline in the USA. *Theoretical Criminology, 12,* 79–101.

Hobbs, N. (1982). *The troubled and troubling child: Reeducation in mental health, education, and human services programs for children and youth.* San Francisco, CA: Jossey-Bass Inc.

Hoover, J. J., & Patton, R. J. (2008). The role of special educators in a multitiered instructional system. *Intervention in School and Clinic, 43*(4), 195–202.

Hrabowski, F., & Sanders, M. (2015). Increasing racial diversity in the teacher workforce: One university's approach. *National Education Association Higher Education Journal Thoughts and Action,* Winter, 101–116.

Ingersoll, R., May, H., & Collins, G. (2017). *Minority teacher recruitment, employment, and retention: 1987 to 2013.* Palo Alto, CA: Learning Policy Institute.

Kauffman, J., & Landrum, T. (2013). *Characteristics of EBD of children and youth* (10th ed.). Upper Saddle River, NJ: Pearson.

Kennedy, M. J., Thomas, C., Meyer, P., Alves, K., & Lloyd, W. J. (2014). Using evidence-based multimedia to improve vocabulary performance of adolescents with LD: A UDL approach. *Learning Disability Quarterly, 37*(2), 71–86.

Kieran, L., & Anderson, C. (2019). Connecting universal design for learning with culturally responsive teaching. *Education and Urban Society, 51*(9), 1202–1216. doi:10.1177/0013124518785012

Kim, C. Y., & Geronimo, I. (2009). Policing in schools: Developing a governance document for school resource officers in K-12 schools (ACLU white paper). Retrieved from http://aclu.org/racial-justice/policing-schools-developing-governance-document-school-resource-officers-k-12-schools

Ladson-Billings, G. (1995). Toward a theory of culturally relevant pedagogy. *American Educational Research Journal, 32*(3), 465–491. doi:10.3102/00028312032003465

Landa, C. (2011). Cultural proficiency in education: A review of the literature focused on teachers, school leaders, and schools.

Levine, P., Marder, C., & Wagner, M. (2004). *Services and supports for secondary school students with disabilities.* Menlo Park, CA: SRI International. Retrieved from www.nlts2.org/reports/2004_05/index.html

Lindsay, C. A., & Hart, C. M. D. (2017). Exposure to same-race teachers and student disciplinary outcomes for Black students in North Carolina. *Educational Evaluation & Policy Analysis, 39*(3), 485–510. Retrieved from https://doi-org.proxy.library.vcu.edu/10.3102/0162373717693109

Maag, J. W., & Reid, R. (2006). Depression among students with learning disabilities assessing the risk. *Journal of Learning Disabilities, 39*(1), 3–10.

McEachern, A. G., & Kenny, M. C. (2007). Transition groups for high school students with disabilities. *Journal for Specialists in Group Work, 32*, 165–177. doi:10.1080/01933920701227190

Milner, H. R., & Tenore, F. B. (2010). Classroom management in diverse classrooms. *Urban Education, 45*, 560–603.

Milsom, A. (2007). Interventions to assist students with disabilities through school transitions. *Professional School Counseling, 10*(3), 273–278. doi:10.5330/prsc.10.3.c322443236564507

Milsom, A., Akos, P., & Thompson, M. (2004). A psychoeducational group approach to postsecondary transition planning for students with learning disabilities. *Journal for Specialists in Group Work, 29*(4), 395–411. doi:10.1080/01933920490516170

Mitchell, B. S., Kern, L., & Conroy, M. A. (2019). Supporting students with emotional or behavioral disorders: State of the field. *Behavioral Disorders, 44*(2), 70–84. doi:10.1177/0198742918816518

Neal, L., McCray, A. D., Webb-Johnson, G., & Bridgest, S. (2003). The effect of African American movement styles on teachers' perceptions and reactions. *The Journal of Special Education, 37*(1), 49–57.

Palmer, S. B., Summers, J. A., Brotherson, M. J., Erwin, E. J., Maude, S. P., Stroup-Rentier, V., . &., … Haines, S. J. (2013). Foundations for self-determination in early childhood: An inclusive model for children with disabilities. *Topics in Early Childhood Special Education, 33*(1), 38–47. doi:10.1177/0271121412445288

Perry, N. E., Brenner, C. A., Collie, R. J., & Hofer, G. (2015). Thriving on challenge: Examining one teacher's view on sources of support for motivation and well-being. *Exceptionality Education International, 25*(1), 6–34.

Phifer, L. W., & Hull, R. (2016). Helping students heal: Observations of trauma-informed practices in schools. *School Mental Health, 8*(1), 201–205.

Pliner, J., & Johnson, J. R. (2004). Historical, theoretical, and foundational principles of universal instructional design in higher education. *Equity & Excellence in Education, 37*, 1005–1113.

Podolsky, A., Kini, T., Bishop, J., & Darling-Hammond, L. (2016). *Solving the teacher shortage: How to attract and retain excellent educators.* Palo Alto, CA: Learning Policy Institute.

Prince, A. M. T., Hodge, J., Bridges, W., & Katsiyannis, A. (2017). Predictors of postschool education/training and employment outcomes for youth with disabilities. *Career Development and Transition for Exceptional Individuals, 41*(2), 77–87. doi:10.1177/2165143417698122

Rao, K., Ok, M. W., & Bryant, B. R. (2014). A review of research on universal design educational models. *Remedial and Special Education, 35*(3), 153–166. doi:10.1177/0741932513518980

Rappolt-Schlichtmann, G., Daley, S. G., Lim, S., Lapinski, S., Robinson, K. H., & Johnson, M. (2013). Universal design for learning and elementary school science: Exploring the efficacy, use, and perceptions of a web-based science notebook. *Journal of Educational Psychology, 105*(4), 1210.

Rasheed, D. S., Brown, J. L., Doyle, S. L., & Jennings, P. A. (2019). The effect of teacher-child race/ethnicity matching and classroom diversity on children's socioemotional and academic skills. *Child Development*, Advance online publication. doi: 10.1111/cdev.12275.

Rice, C. J., & Goesling, D. (2005). Recruiting and retaining male special education teachers. *Remedial Special Education, 26*, 347–356. doi:10.1177/07419325050260060501

Rose, C. A., & Espelage, D. L. (2012). Risk and protective factors associated with the bullying involvement of students with emotional and behavioral disorders. *Behavioral Disorders, 37*, 133–148.

Rubie-Davies, C. M. (2010). Teacher expectations and perceptions of student attributes: Is there a relationship?. *British Journal of Educational Psychology, 80*(1), 121–135. doi:10.1348/000709909X466334

Scott, L. A., Saddler, S., Thoma, C. A., Bartholomew, C., Alder, N., & Tamura, R. (2011). Universal design for transition: A multielement brief experimental single subject design study of the impact of the use of UDT on student achievement, engagement and motivation. *i-Manager's Journal on Educational Psychology, 4*(4), 21–32.

Scott, L. A., & Alexander, Q. (2019). Strategies for recruiting and retaining Black male special education teachers. *Remedial and Special Education, 40*(4), 236–247.

Scott, L. A., Thoma, C. A., Puglia, L., Temple, P., & D'Aguilar, A. (2017). Implementing a UDL framework: A study of current personnel preparation practices. *Intellectual & Developmental Disabilities, 55* (1), 25–36. doi:10.1352/1934-9556-55.1.25

Skiba, R. J., Chung, C., Trachok, T., Sheya, A., & Hughes, R. (2014). Parsing disciplinary disproportionality: Contributions of infractions, student and school characteristics to out-of-school suspension and expulsion. *American Educational Research Journal, 51*(4), 640–670.

Swearer, S. M., Wang, C., Maag, J. W., Siebecker, A. B., & Frerichs, L. J. (2012). Understanding the bullying dynamic among students in special and general education. *Journal of School Psychology, 50*(4), 503–520. doi:10.1016/j.jsp.2012.04.001

Talbert-Johnson, C. (2001). The quest for equity: Maintaining African American teachers in special education. *The Journal of Negro Education, 70*, 286–296. doi:10.2307/3211281

Taub, D. (2006). Understanding the concerns of parents of students with disabilities: Challenges and roles for school counselors. *Professional School Counseling, 10*(1), 52–57. doi:10.5330/prsc.10.1.b0mkn7k57w583266

Test, D. W., Mazzotti, V. L., Mustian, A. L., Fowler, C. H., Kortering, L., & Kohler, P. (2009). Evidence-based secondary transition predictors for improving postschool outcomes for students with disabilities. *Career Development for Exceptional Individuals, 32*(3), 160–181.

Thoma, C. A., Bartholomew, C., & Scott, L. A. (2009). *Universal design for transition: A roadmap for planning and instruction.* Baltimore, MD: Paul H. Brookes.

Thoma, C. A., Cain, I., Wojcik, A., Best, K., & Scott, L. A. (2016). Universal design for transition for students on the spectrum: Linking academic and transition education to improve postschool outcomes. In D. Zager, D. L., Cihack, & A. Stone-MacDonald (Eds.). *Autism spectrum disorders; Identification, education, and treatment* (4th ed., pp. 285–311). New York: Routledge.

Thompson, R., & Littrell, J. M. (1998). Brief counseling for students with learning disabilities. *Professional School Counseling, 2*, 60–67.

Turnull, A., Turnbull, R., Wehmeyer, M., & Shogren, K. (2012). *Exceptional lives: Special education in today's schools* (7th ed.). Upper Saddle River, NJ: Pearson.

Turnbull, A., Turnbull, R., Wehmeyer, M. L., & Shogren, K. A. (2020). *Exceptional lives: Practice, progress, & dignity in today's schools* (9th ed.). Hoboken, NJ: Pearson.

U.S. Department of Education (2009). National Longitudinal Transition Study-2 (NLTS2, 2009).

U.S. Department of Education, Office of Planning, Evaluation and Policy Development, Policy and Program Studies Service. (2016). *The state of racial diversity in the educator workforce.* Washington, DC Retrieved from https://2.ed.gov/rschstat/eval/highered/racial-diversity/state-racial-diversity-workforce.pdf

U.S. Department of Education, Office of Special Education and Rehabilitative Services, Office of Special Education Programs. (2017). *39th Annual report to congress on the implementation of the Individuals with Disabilities Education Act.* Washington, DC: U.S. Department of Education.

U.S. Department of Education. (2016). Racial and ethnic disparities in special education: A multi-year disproportionality analysis by state, analysis category, and race/ethnicity.

U.S. Department of Education. (2019). *The Condition of Education 2019*. Washington, DC: National Center for Education Statistics. Retrieved from https://nces.ed.gov/pubsearch/pubsinfo.asp?pubid=2019144

U.S. Department of Education, National Center for Education Statistics. (2019). Digest of Education Statistics, 2017 (NCES 2018-070).

Villegas, A. M., & Irvine, J. J. (2010). Diversifying the teaching force: An examination of major arguments. *The Urban Review, 42*(3), 175–192. doi:10.1007/s11256-010-0150-1

Ward, S. M. (2010). Briding the gap: Documenting Clinton school districts (CSD's) journal addressing racial/ethnic disproportion in special education. ProQuest Information & Learning. Dissertation Abstracts International Section A: Humanities and Social Sciences, 70(8) (2010–99030–015).

Zhang, D., Hsu, H. Y., Katsiyannis, A., Barrett, D. E., & Ju, S. (2011). Adolescents with disabilities in the juvenile justice system: Patterns of recidivism. *Exceptional Children, 77*, 283–298.

30 Leading the Team for Youth with Emotional and Behavioral Disorders

Special Educators as Intervention Specialists

Elizabeth Talbott, Serra De Arment, Brittany Sterrett, and Chin-Chih Chen

Students with emotional and behavioral disorders (EBD), many of whom can also experience academic difficulties, benefit from participating in individualized interventions in the context of an effective MTSS intervention framework (Darney, Reinke, Herman, Stormont, & Ialongo, 2013; Lane, Wehby, Little, & Cooley, 2005). Yet evidence-based interventions delivered with fidelity at the three tiers of intervention in MTSS have not been adequate for those youth who experience complex and severe EBD (Barrett, Eber, & Weist, 2013; Bruns et al., 2016; Kern & Wehby, 2014). Outcomes for these youth continue to be poor and include the highest rates of dropout from high school, the lowest rates of post-secondary employment or education, and the highest rates of involvement with the juvenile justice system (Aud et al., 2012; Sanford et al., 2011; Wagner, Kutash, Duchnowski, Epstein, & Sumi, 2005). Thus, we argue that interventions for youth with complex EBD delivered in the context of MTSS need to be comprehensive, individualized, interdisciplinary, and delivered across contexts (both home and school) in order to address their social, academic, and behavioral needs (Lyon et al., 2016; Talbott, 2019).

The MTSS team approach can set the stage for improved data-based decision-making and implementation of evidence-based interventions for youth with EBD at all three tiers of delivery (Bruns et al., 2016; Lyon et al., 2016). In the MTSS model, experienced special educators are well positioned to serve as leaders, adapting and intensifying interventions to meet the needs of individual students, as well as coordinating services within and outside the school system (Farmer et al., 2016; Lyon et al., 2016; Talbott & De Los Reyes, 2020). In this chapter, we describe the leadership roles, effective practices, and professional preparation of two types of special education intervention specialists: (a) those who serve as adaptive intervention specialists, working primarily within the MTSS team, and (b) those who serve as intervention specialist coordinators, leading the MTSS team and coordinating services across systems, such as school and health care systems.

School-based Collaborative Care Framework for Intervention Specialists

The school-based collaborative care model, adapted from the work of Lyon and colleagues (2016), provides a broad and useful framework to describe the leadership roles and effective team practices of special educators as intervention specialists. We view these intervention specialists as leaders of school-based MTSS intervention teams who serve youth with emotional, behavioral, and mental health disorders, particularly at Tiers 2 and 3. It is worth

450   *Elizabeth Talbott et al.*

noting that as many as 14–20% of youth can experience emotional and behavioral symptoms and disorders at any given point in their development; these include externalizing and internalizing problems, as well as problems with substance abuse (National Research Council and Institute of Medicine, 2009). Yet, fewer than 1% of youth are served in special education under the label of emotional disturbance (U.S. Department of Education, 2017). Thus, the majority of youth with EBD are likely to be served in general education under the MTSS framework. In our model, intervention specialists work within the education system as leaders and coordinators of care, collaborating with colleagues in education and pediatric health and mental health care systems.

Who Are These Intervention Specialists, and What Do They Do?

Intervention specialists in special education are well-positioned to provide individualized, flexible, data-based interventions that address students' functioning and adaptation, which includes coordination of services and collaboration with professionals who work within and outside the MTSS system (Farmer et al., 2016). These professionals can identify the people and settings that affect student behavior, and then lead the delivery of interventions across those contexts (Farmer et al., 2016). Due to the need for effective, distributed leadership in intervention and coordination of services for students with EBD (Talbott, Mayrowetz, Maggin, & Tozer, 2016), we envision these intervention specialists as leaders who work in two roles: (a) as adaptive intervention specialists who lead the work of the school MTSS team and (b) as intervention specialist coordinators who serve as leaders and case managers, coordinating and collaborating with pediatric health care team leaders and families outside the school system (Lyon, 2016; Talbott & De Los Reyes, 2020). We further illuminate the leadership roles, effective practices, and professional preparation of these individuals in the sections that follow and show how their skills and knowledge build upon those of the special education generalist.

Adaptive Intervention Specialist

Youth with EBD can struggle with successful functioning in one or more of the following areas: behavioral, social-emotional, and academics, with each type of functioning affecting the others in a correlated fashion (Farmer et al., 2016). Youth with EBD certainly benefit from participating in evidence-based Tier 1 and Tier 2 interventions delivered with fidelity, such as the Good Behavior Game (Bradshaw, Zmuda, Kellam, & Ialongo, 2009) and Check-In Check-Out (Hawken, Pettersson, Mootz, & Anderson, 2005), as well as function-based assessment and intervention delivered at Tier 3 (e.g., Kern & Wehby, 2014). However, these interventions alone are inadequate to address the multiple, complex needs of youth with EBD. Youth with EBD, particularly those served under the educational label of emotional disturbance, need more comprehensive and coordinated assessment and intervention, delivered within and beyond the school setting.

The adaptive intervention specialist, charged with leading the day-to-day work of the MTSS team, has the skills of a special education generalist, but is also a leader in the delivery of these interventions with the school (see Figure 30.1). He or she must possess the skills of an effective special education generalist, as well as have a strong conceptual understanding of the relationships among the important aspects of students' lives, such as their academic, behavioral, and social functioning, along with the relationship among evidence-based interventions employed to address their needs in these areas (Farmer et al., 2016). In the context of leading the MTSS

Special educators as generalists
☐ Positive, proactive behavior management skills
☐ Data-based decision-making skills in the areas of academic and behavioral
   intervention
☐ Skills in functional behavioral assessment (FBA) and function-based behavioral
   interventions

Adaptive intervention specialists ☐ Strong skills as generalists ☐ Skills in data monitoring and adaptive use of evidence-based interventions ☐ Leaders and champions for youth with EBD within the MTSS team and school

Intervention specialist coordinators ☐ Strong skills as generalists ☐ Leaders of work outside MTSS team ☐ Case managers who coordinate care and collaborate with professionals in health   care, mental health, and juvenile justice ☐ Help families access mental health services through private insurance and Medicaid ☐ Leaders in advocacy and public policy for youth with EBD

Figure 30.1 Knowledge and skills of special educators within the collaborative care model

team, adaptive intervention specialists are responsible for developing and monitoring ongoing data-collection systems and keeping the team focused on using evidence-based interventions (Talbott & De Los Reyes, 2020). As leaders of the MTSS teams, adaptive intervention specialists must collaborate with various school professionals, including other special and general educators, as well as parents, behavior specialists, school counselors, and psychologists to identify treatment needs and potential interventions and adaptations within various class and school settings to support student adjustment (Farmer et al., 2016; Talbott & De Los Reyes, 2020).

Given the dynamic nature of teaching in special education, it is essential that these educators maintain a flexible orientation to addressing the challenges of meeting the needs of learners in the context of MTSS; indeed, adaptive intervention specialists are leaders in this approach. Both initial and advanced preparation standards in special education (see the Council for Exceptional Children, 2015) reflect the need for an adaptive orientation within the professional practice of special education. De Arment, Reed, and Wetzel (2013) and others (e.g., Anthony, Hunter, & Hunter, 2015; Darling-Hammond & Bransford, 2005; Mason-Williams, Frederick, & Mulcahy, 2015; Soslau, 2012) argue that adaptive expertise is a critical skill in the repertoire of effective educators. Indeed, adaptive expertise is a core competency of adaptive intervention specialists.

Hatano and Inagaki (1986) have conceptualized two distinct courses of expertise in education: routine and adaptive. In demonstrating routine expertise, teachers are efficient in their application of procedural knowledge to respond to familiar or routine situations. Examples of routine knowledge in the classroom include teachers' basic pedagogical knowledge and their procedural knowledge of evidence-based practices, such as behavior management delivered across MTSS tiers (Chen et al., 2019; De Arment et al., 2013). In contrast, teachers' adaptive expertise is characterized by their use of knowledge in innovative ways to modify existing practices (De

Arment et al., 2013). Flexibility, use of metacognitive skills and data-based decision-making are key elements of an adaptive orientation to teaching (Chen et al., 2019).

Flexibility requires teachers to be open to new ideas and approaches to the application of evidence-based practices. Rather than relying solely on their existing knowledge and skills, adaptive teachers recognize the limits of what they know and seek new information and the perspectives of others for improving their teaching practice (De Arment et al., 2013). Teachers use their metacognitive skills to identify variations in settings and practices that might explain why students are non-responsive; they simultaneously use skills in data-based decision-making to identify effective practices and enhance their understanding of student responses to those practices (De Arment et al., 2013). Adaptive intervention specialists are skilled at making adaptations, but they are also skilled in the effective delivery of routine procedures. For these specialists, the two types of expertise are not mutually exclusive; rather, they are essentially problem-solving skills, applicable to all three tiers of intervention (Darling-Hammond & Bransford, 2005).

Intervention Specialist Coordinator

Intervention specialist coordinators will have mastered the skills of the generalist special educator, as well as those of the adaptive intervention specialist, as outlined in Figure 30.1. They serve as advocates and champions for individual youth with EBD and in their roles as case managers, collaborating and coordinating evidence-based assessment and intervention across education, health care, mental health, and juvenile justice systems (Lyon et al., 2016; Talbott & De Los Reyes, 2020). A major responsibility of these case managers is to protect student privacy under education and health care laws, even as they facilitate the sharing of data among professionals in the two systems. Indeed, as recent data from Michel and colleagues (2018) reveal, this is no small task. In their study of the effectiveness of an electronic communication system designed to improve the coordination of care between pediatric health care and education systems for youth with attention deficit hyperactivity disorder (the ADHD Care Assistant), Michel and colleagues (2018) reported that, through use of the ADHD Care Assistant, 64% of children's parents shared data describing their child's behavior with teachers. However, teachers and parents did not necessarily look at the data that were shared. Teachers viewed only 30% of the data that had been shared by parents and parents viewed only 16% of the data that had been shared by teachers (Michel et al., 2018).

The intervention specialist coordinator is well positioned to lead the MTSS team in viewing, evaluating, and responding to data collected across informants (i.e., parents and teachers), settings (school and home), and systems (health care, mental health, education, and juvenile justice). Having viewed and evaluated the data, intervention specialist coordinators then communicate with parents and health care providers about data-based school interventions and collaborate with them to coordinate services between the education and pediatric health care systems (Bruns et al., 2016; Lyon et al., 2016). Intervention specialist coordinators lead the team effort in identifying funding for services for youth with EBD, through students' private health insurance or Medicaid funding for interventions provided at school and in the community.

This work can occur effectively through a strategic use of school and community resources (Atkins et al., 2008; Atkins, Hoagwood, Kutash, & Seidman, 2010). For example, Atkins and colleagues identified teachers who were key opinion leaders among their peers to (a) collaborate with community mental health providers in low income neighborhoods in Chicago and (b) provide professional development with these providers in evidence-based Tier 1 and 2 interventions for youth with disruptive behavior disorders to their colleagues.

The result of this collaboration and training was increased use of mental health services by youth, as well as increases in youth academic engagement, academic competence, and the development of social skills (Atkins et al., 2015).

Preparation of Intervention Specialists

Special educators are well-positioned to serve in these teacher-leader roles, given their experience leading IEP teams and collaborating with diverse professionals (Sindelar, Washburn-Moses, Thomas, & Leko, 2014; Talbott et al., 2016). However, a shortcoming of their preparation is that they are likely to be trained as generalists, rather than specialists. Such training may be inadequate for developing their skills in managing the behavior of youth with EBD (Westling, 2010). Therefore, in order to prepare teachers with the knowledge and skills they need to address the complex needs of students with EBD, teacher educators need to prepare intervention specialists to develop skills above and beyond those of the generalist special educator. To develop these specialized skills, we first describe how teacher education programs can support candidates' development of adaptive expertise. We next address the specific needs for preparation of adaptation specialists. Finally, we argue on behalf of and describe advanced preparation for intervention specialist coordinators.

Development of Adaptive Expertise

Expert adaptive educators possess the skills and dispositions to identify problems using data, develop strategies for solving those problems, and then implement tailored interventions for students with disabilities. Such an approach is perfect for the work of the MTSS team, and requires that teachers become learners themselves, reflecting on their skills and the limitations of their practices, seeking out new knowledge and the perspectives of others, and using data in an ongoing way to drive instructional decision-making. As such, there is no pinnacle adaptive expert status; rather, as Hammerness, Darling-Hammond, and Bransford (2005) describe, there is a trajectory towards the development of adaptive expertise whereby educators continually balance the application of innovative skills (adaptive problem solving) with the application of efficient, routinized practices (routine problem solving).

Researchers who work with both novice and experienced teachers (i.e., Anthony et al., 2015; Janssen, de Hullu, & Tigelaar, 2008; Martin, Peacock, Ko, & Rudolph, 2015; Soslau, 2012) have argued that adaptive and routine expertise can develop simultaneously. Thus, the development of pedagogical knowledge and mastery of evidence-based practices can occur alongside the development of adaptive teaching skills. While developing a solid repertoire of routine practices in areas such as behavior management, novice teachers can also grapple with problems presented in case studies, problem-based scenarios, and their own clinical experiences in order to adapt and tailor interventions. By emphasizing both routine and adaptive knowledge required for effective teaching practice, professionals in teacher preparation programs can set their candidates on the trajectory toward developing adaptive expertise.

Although still an emerging body of research, development of adaptive expertise can be fostered through intentional and strategic support by faculty within an educator preparation program. First, teacher educators can establish a learner-centered environment (National Research Council, 2000) whereby teacher candidates have opportunities to take risks and experiment with approaches in a comfortable environment (Anthony et al., 2015; Crawford & Brophy, 2006; Hatano & Inagaki, 1986). Hatano and Inagaki (1986) have recommended establishing a context for learning in which understanding is stressed over performance. In

454   *Elizabeth Talbott et al.*

such an environment, teacher candidates have the opportunity to practice a given skill within standard or routine applications, as well as with variations and changing demands (Hatano & Oura, 2003). In this way, they can apply new knowledge flexibly in settings that mirror real-life complexity and variability (Bell, Horton, Blashki, & Seidel, 2012; Crawford & Brophy, 2006).

Second, reflection and deep thinking can foster the development of adaptive expertise through deliberate planning by faculty within coursework and clinical experiences. Using cycles of inquiry and knowledge-building through challenge-based or design-based instruction can prompt teachers to reflect upon connections between their teaching and student learning outcomes at Tiers 1–3 (Anthony et al., 2015; Martin et al., 2015). Using this approach, prospective teachers can repeatedly engage with their peers in teams to discuss instructional planning, data-based decision-making, and their reflections on practice. Indeed, this type of teamwork mirrors that in which teachers routinely engage. For example, the IRIS Center (https://iris.peabody.vanderbilt.edu/wp) provides modules for educators which are designed to help develop and enhance the skills of pre-service and in-service teachers in working with students with disabilities and their families; these skills can certainly be embedded within effective teamwork.

Finally, beyond the broader scope of the learning environment and course design, targeted efforts to prompt reflection within assignments, activities, and post-observation conferences can also support the development of adaptive expertise (Wetzel, De Arment, & Reed, 2015). Soslau (2012) found that using a guided and reflective approach to student teaching supervision fostered discussion of problems experienced by novices along with the critical discourse necessary to promote student teachers' articulation of their decision-making processes while teaching. By helping these teachers to self-assess and justify their instructional decisions, supervisors can prompt the development of adaptive expertise; without this specific prompting, opportunities for adaptive expertise development may be lost (Soslau, 2012). The role of the faculty member is critical here. For example, Hayden, Rundell, and Smyntek-Gworek (2013) found that a novice teacher was able to explore instructional adaptations within written reflections while working directly with a course instructor, but not during independent reflections on instruction. In recent research by Soslau, Kotch-Jester, Scantlebury, and Gleason (2018), the authors concluded that "huddles" or "brief impromptu conversations that often take place during teaching enactment" (p. 100) between student teachers and their clinical supervisors were opportunities for student teachers to seek help and implement instructional adaptations, therefore promoting the development of adaptive expertise.

The conceptual framework of adaptive expertise for special educator teacher preparation (De Arment et al., 2013) serves as a foundation for the preparation of both generalist special educators and the specialized professionals who can address the complexity of intensifying interventions for students with EBD (Farmer et al., 2016). Operationalizing the role of these professionals can provide a road map for the design of specialized preparation organized around theory, knowledge and skills, and experiential learning opportunities. Thus, we recommend core facets of preparation for adaptive intervention specialists and intervention specialist coordinators.

Preparation of Adaptive Intervention Specialists

The preparation of adaptive intervention specialists is likely to occur at the master's level, drawing candidates from a pool of individuals who have had some experience, although perhaps not formal training, in working with children and youth with EBD. Thus, the preparation of these specialists is likely to follow undergraduate level training and initial special education teacher licensure or an undergraduate degree in a related field such as social work, psychology, or human development, leading to initial teacher licensure at the master's level.

Theoretical Foundations

Prospective adaptive intervention specialists need to demonstrate knowledge of the theoretical basis for providing interventions and services to youth with EBD. A strong understanding of youth development in the context of dynamic systems theory is critical for these specialists (Farmer et al., 2016). A fundamental principle of systems theory is that change is inherent throughout child development, and that youth with EBD, through the application of comprehensive, evidence-based interventions, including behavioral interventions, delivered at key points during childhood and adolescence can experience positive, systematic change and improved outcomes (Geldhoff et al., 2013).

For example, educators recognize that early childhood is a critical developmental period for teaching prosocial skills to youth who have shown early signs of aggressive and disruptive behavior (Vo, Sutherland, & Conroy, 2012). Evidence-based interventions such as the Good Behavior Game coupled with an enhanced academic curriculum implemented during early childhood can have lasting benefits for students – benefits that persist through the high school years (Bradshaw et al., 2009). Adolescence is another critical period for the implementation of evidence-based interventions to prevent school dropout among youth with high levels of aggression and low achievement (Wagner et al., 2005), as well as prevent suicide for those who experience symptoms of anxiety and depression, which can co-occur with aggressive and disruptive behavior (Kumm, Gesel, Majeika, Talbott, & Maggin, 2019; Merikangas et al., 2010). Key skills in the repertoire of adaptive intervention specialists include developing productive relationships with family members, collaborating and coordinating care with community mental health and health care providers, and working closely with school professionals in order to assess symptoms and develop interventions for youth with EBD during these critical developmental periods (Atkins et al., 2015; Geldhoff et al., 2013; Motoca et al., 2014).

Adaptive intervention specialists recognize that changing one component of a student's environment using evidence-based assessment and intervention procedures, such as functional-behavioral assessment (FBA), may not be enough to change complex student behavior (e.g., Kern & Wehby, 2014). Thus, adaptive intervention specialists will be prepared to build upon the successes of FBA and intervention by adding and intensifying evidence-based common elements of interventions for individuals who experience complex symptoms and disorders, including anxiety and depression (Higa-McMillan, Francis, Rith-Najarian, & Chorpita, 2016; Weersing, Jeffreys, Do, Schwartz, & Bolano, 2017) and disruptive behavior disorders (Sutherland, Conroy, McLeod, Kunemund, & McKnight, 2019).

Knowledge and Skills

Knowledge and mastery of high-leverage practices in special education are perfectly appropriate to use in the preparation of special education generalists (McLeskey et al., 2017). However, high-leverage practices are likely to be inadequate for adaptive intervention specialists who teach youth who have EBD (McLeod et al., 2017). These professionals must develop and maintain a toolkit of evidence-based practices that contain common elements (Sutherland et al., 2019). Common elements are core components of effective, evidence-based interventions; they are drawn from research using rigorous experimental designs, and then endorsed by experts in the field (Higa-McMillan et al., 2016; Sutherland et al., 2019). Examples of common elements for teaching elementary students with or at risk for developing disruptive behavior disorders include: (a) developing a regular system for home–school collaboration, (b) providing instructional feedback, discussion, and error correction, (c) providing praise and reinforcement, (d) developing positive teacher–student relationships, (e) modeling appropriate academic or social skills, (f) providing opportunities to respond, and (g) establishing prescribed rules and behavioral expectations for students (Sutherland et al., 2019).

Likewise, researchers have identified common elements from cognitive behavioral therapy as most effective for helping youth manage symptoms of anxiety and depression (Higa-McMillan et al., 2016; Weersing et al., 2017). Examples include (a) exposure to anxiety-producing situations; (b) cognitive approaches to managing those situations; (c) modeling of appropriate approaches; (d) use of relaxation techniques; (e) psychoeducation; and (f) self-praise or self-administered rewards (Higa-McMillan et al., 2016). Initial data collection and ongoing progress monitoring are at the heart of the effective delivery of evidence-based common elements (Fuchs, Fuchs, & Vaughn, 2014; Kern & Wehby, 2014). As part of their training, adaptive intervention specialists will become leaders in using data to intensify and individualize interventions (Talbott et al., 2016).

Recognizing that interventions for students with the most intensive emotional and behavioral needs must be applied across contexts, adaptive intervention specialists will need the knowledge and skills to effectively collaborate with other professionals, such as we have described here in the collaborative care model (Farmer et al., 2016; Lyon et al., 2016; Talbott & De Los Reyes, 2020). As outlined in the Council for Exceptional Children's professional standards for initial preparation (CEC, 2015), collaboration in the context of special education requires understanding of strategies for effective communication and consultation as well as the development of expertise in providing individualized, intensive intervention. For intervention specialists in the two roles, preparation for collaboration must include opportunities to work with professionals across disciplines, through interdisciplinary coursework, field experiences, and internships, where prospective intervention specialists learn alongside their peers in related fields such as pediatrics, social work, counseling, and school psychology. Nurturing adaptive expertise within the preparation program further promotes the development of strong collaboration skills, solidifying a learning orientation towards collegial interactions for the purpose of supporting positive student outcomes across contexts (Bransford, Derry, Berliner, & Hammerness, 2005; Crawford & Brophy, 2006).

Experiential Learning

Field experiences are an integral part of teacher preparation whereby preservice teachers have supported experience applying theory and content and pedagogical knowledge to real-world practice (Maheady, Smith, & Jabot, 2014). Prospective adaptation specialists need opportunities to observe and participate in data-based decision-making and collaboration to see how professionals lead the implementation of effective interventions for students with EBD. Under the guidance, supervision, and coaching of experienced leaders, such as clinical supervisors and university faculty, these professionals need to experiment with adapting interventions. Furthermore, as suggested by the literature on the development of teacher adaptive expertise and as described previously, supervisors must thoughtfully prompt and probe for reflection as individuals develop, collect, and examine student data to make decisions about how to intensify and make changes (i.e., Kern & Wehby, 2014).

Service learning opportunities within community contexts can also provide rich opportunities for adaptive intervention specialists in training (Conroy, Alter, Boyd, & Bettini, 2014). Through service learning, students can obtain credit-bearing experience in meeting community-identified needs which, through critical reflection, allows for deeper understanding of the course learning objectives (Bringle & Hatcher, 1996). For prospective adaptive intervention specialists, this means gaining a hands-on understanding of the systems outside the school from which individuals and families can obtain resources and support (Bruns et al., 2016; Lyon et al., 2016).

To provide frequent opportunities for prospective adaptive intervention specialists to grapple with the challenges of real-world practice across varying contexts, preparation programs can capitalize on virtual simulations, case-based learning experiences, and role-playing in addition to fieldwork (Maheady et al., 2014). In collaboration with professionals from the community, faculty in the preparation programs can develop hypothetical scenarios based on real experience that describe, in detail, the dynamic factors and processes affecting the functioning of a given student. Then, through these approaches, trainees can "try on" and practice particular adaptation skills within the collaborative care model.

Intervention Specialist Coordinator Preparation

The preparation of intervention specialist coordinators builds directly from the theoretical foundations, knowledge and skills, and experiential learning opportunities central to the preparation of adaptation specialists. However, for this more advanced, likely post-master's degree training, there is greater emphasis on the development of leadership skills in intensifying interventions in the MTSS and coordinating the work of individuals within and across systems, including education, pediatric health, and mental health systems, as well as serving as advocates for children and the public policies that serve them.

To that end, it is critical for intervention specialist coordinators to develop leadership skills in the development of effective, evidence-based mental health interventions. Currently, the centrality of mental health services in schools, and the knowledge and awareness of school professionals about effective mental health interventions and their delivery, is highly variable (Bruns et al., 2016). Yet, this knowledge and awareness is critical. Educators who recognize and endorse the importance of student emotional and behavioral health are more likely to be receptive to professional development opportunities, as well as more successful in employing mental health care as part of their adaptive practices (Bruns et al., 2016). Thus, intervention specialist coordinators have the opportunity to lead their peers in the development and implementation of effective school mental health interventions, by acting as effective leaders who engage in effective team practices, and coordinating and collaborating across systems with leaders of education and pediatric health care and mental health care teams (Lyon et al., 2016; Talbott & De Los Reyes, 2020).

Preparation for the intervention specialist coordinator should be keenly aware of principles of adult learning to develop leadership skills. Bryan, Kreuter, and Brownson (2009) identified principles for training public health professionals that are relevant for the leadership role of the intervention specialist coordinator; among them are the principles that adult learners are motivated by the need to solve problems and seek to become actively involved in the learning process. To address these principles and the development of leadership skills, instructors can

458 *Elizabeth Talbott et al.*

select complex case studies in which prospective intervention specialist coordinators have the opportunity to use data, seek additional resources to serve students, communicate and collaborate, and build consensus with individuals from diverse professional backgrounds (i.e. social workers, pediatricians, nurses, teachers, and parents). A key outcome of their preparation is the building of these fundamental skills so that these professionals can be leaders in establishing and maintaining systems and resources for the effective delivery of adaptive, intensive intervention in the context of MTSS (Lemons, Sinclair, Gesel, Danielson, & Gandhi, 2019).

That is, intervention specialist coordinators must develop skills for designing and implementing comprehensive intervention plans across contexts and service providers as well as conceive a long-term view of each student's academic, behavioral, and social functioning. This includes leadership for collecting, managing, and using data to inform selection, adaptation, and intensification of interventions. Accordingly, intervention specialist coordinators need this specialized training, both through their advanced coursework and opportunities to observe and practice this role in action, shadowing an effective leader of MTSS intervention teams.

In this chapter, we have argued on behalf of the preparation and training of two types of intervention specialists to better serve the needs of youth with complex EBD in the context of a collaborative care model. These professionals, who serve as adaptive intervention specialists and intervention specialist coordinators, are leaders in the delivery of evidence-based assessment and intervention within and beyond the school for youth who experience complex symptoms of emotional and behavioral disorders over the course of youth development. Their work is vital to improving successful outcomes for these youth.

References

Anthony, G., Hunter, J., & Hunter, R. (2015). Prospective teachers' development of adaptive expertise. *Teaching and Teacher Education, 49*, 108–117.

Atkins, M. S., Frazier, S. L., Leathers, S. J., Graczyk, P., Talbott, E., Jakobsons, L., ... Bell, C. C. (2008). Teacher key opinion leaders and mental health consultation in low-income urban schools. *Journal of Consulting and Clinical Psychology, 76*, 905–908.

Atkins, M. S., Hoagwood, K. E., Kutash, K., & Seidman, E. (2010). Toward the integration of education and mental health in schools. *Administration and Policy in Mental Health and Mental Health Services Research, 37*, 40–47.

Atkins, M. S., Shernoff, E. S., Frazier, S. L., Schoenwald, S. K., Cappella, E., Marinez-Lora, A., ... Bhaumik, D. (2015). Redesigning community mental health services for urban children: Supporting schooling to promote mental health. *Journal of Consulting and Clinical Psychology, 83*, 839–852.

Aud, S., Hussar, W., Johnson, F., Kena, G., Roth, E., Manning, E., ... Yohn, C. (2012). *The condition of education.* Washington, DC: National Center for Education Statistics, Institute of Education Sciences, U.S. Department of Education.

Barrett, S., Eber, L., & Weist, M. D. (2013). *Advancing educational effectiveness: Interconnecting school mental health and school wide positive behavioral support.* OSEP Center on Positive Behavioral Interventions and Supports. Retrieved from www.sdcoe.net/student-services/student-support/Documents/School%20Mental%20Health%20and%20School%20Wide%20PBIS.pdf.

Bell, E., Horton, G., Blashki, G., & Seidel, B. M. (2012). Climate change: Could it help develop adaptive expertise? *Advances in Health Science Education, 17*, 211–224.

Bradshaw, C. P., Zmuda, J. H., Kellam, S. G., & Ialongo, N. S. (2009). Longitudinal impact of two universal preventive interventions in first grade on educational outcomes in high school. *Journal of Educational Psychology, 101*, 926–937.

Bransford, J., Derry, S., Berliner, D., & Hammerness, K. (2005). Theories of learning and their roles in teaching. In L. Darling-Hammond & J. Bransford (Eds.), *Preparing teachers for a changing world: What teachers should learn and be able to do* (pp. 40–87). San Francisco, CA: Jossey-Bass.

Bringle, R. G., & Hatcher, J. A. (1996). Implementing service learning in higher education. *Journal of Higher Education, 67*, 221–239.

Bruns, E. J., Duong, M. T., Lyon, A. R., Pullman, M. D., Cook, C. R., Cheney, D., & McCauley, E. (2016). Fostering SMART partnerships to develop an effective continuum of behavioral health services and supports in schools. *American Journal of Orthopsychiatry, 86*, 156–170.

Bryan, R. L., Kreuter, M. W., & Brownson, R. C. (2009). Integrating adult learning principles into training for public health practice. *Health Promotion Practice, 10*, 557–563.

Chen, C., Sterrett, B. I., Kunemund, R., Brown, C., Wilkerson, S., Maggin, D. M., ... Sutherland, K.S. (2019). *Intensifying interventions for students with emotional and behavioral difficulties: A conceptual synthesis of practice elements and adaptive expertise frameworks.* Manuscript submitted for publication.

Conroy, M. A., Alter, P. J., Boyd, B. A., & Bettini, E. (2014). Teacher preparation for students who demonstrate challenging behaviors. In P. Sindelar, E. McCray, M. Brownell, & B. Lignugaris/Kraft (Eds.), *Handbook of research on special education teacher preparation* (pp. 320–333). New York, NY: Routledge.

Council for Exceptional Children. (2015). *What every special educator must know: Ethics, standards, and guidelines.* Arlington, VA: Author.

Crawford, V. M., & Brophy, S. (2006, September). *Adaptive expertise: Theory, methods, findings, and emerging issues.* Presentation at the Adaptive Expertise Symposium, SRI International, Menlo Park, CA.

Darling-Hammond, L., & Bransford, J. (2005). *Preparing teachers for a changing world: What teachers should learn and be able to do.* San Francisco, CA: Jossey-Bass.

Darney, D., Reinke, W. M., Herman, K. C., Stormont, M., & Ialongo, N. S. (2013). Children with co-occurring academic and behavior problems in first grade: Distal outcomes in twelfth grade. *Journal of School Psychology, 51*, 117–128.

De Arment, S., Reed, E., & Wetzel, A. (2013). Promoting adaptive expertise: A conceptual framework for special educator preparation. *Teacher Education and Special Education, 36*, 217–230.

Farmer, T. W., Sutherland, K. S., Talbott, E., Brooks, D., Norwalk, K., & Huneke, M. (2016). Special educators as intervention specialists: Dynamic systems and the complexity of intensifying intervention for students with emotional and behavioral disorders. *Journal of Emotional and Behavioral Disorders, 24*, 173–186.

Fuchs, D., Fuchs, L. S., & Vaughn, S. (2014). What is intensive instruction and why is it important? *Teaching Exceptional Children, 46*, 13–18.

Geldhoff, G. J., Bowers, E. P., Johnson, S. K., Hershberg, R. M., Hilliard, L. J., Lerner, J. V., & Lerner, R. M. (2013). Relational developmental systems theories of positive youth development: Methodological issues and implications. In P. C. M. Molenaar, R. M. Lerner, & K. M. Newell (Eds.), *Handbook of developmental systems theory* (pp. 66–94). New York, NY: Guilford Press.

Hammerness, K., Darling-Hammond, L., & Bransford, J. (2005). How teachers learn and develop. In L. Darling-Hammond & J. Bransford (Eds.), *Preparing teachers for a changing world: What teachers should learn and be able to do* (pp. 358–389). San Francisco, CA: Jossey-Bass.

Hatano, G., & Inagaki, K. (1986). Two courses of expertise. In H. Stevenson, H. Azuma, & K. Hakuta (Eds.), *Child development and education in Japan* (pp. 262–272). New York, NY: Freeman.

Hatano, G., & Oura, Y. (2003). Commentary: Reconceptualizing school learning using insight from expertise research. *Educational Researcher, 32*, 26–29.

Hawken, L. S., Pettersson, H., Mootz, J., & Anderson, C. (2005). *The behavior education program: A check-in, check-out intervention for students at risk.* New York, NY: Guilford Press.

Hayden, H. E., Rundell, T. D., & Smyntek-Gworek, S. (2013). Adaptive expertise: A view from the top and the ascent. *Teaching Education, 24*, 395–414.

Higa-McMillan, C. K., Francis, S. E., Rith-Najarian, L., & Chorpita, B. F. (2016). Evidence base update: 50 years of research on treatment for child and adolescent anxiety. *Journal of Clinical Child and Adolescent Psychology, 45*, 91–113.

Janssen, F., de Hullu, E., & Tigelaar, D. (2008). Positive experiences as input for reflection by student teachers. *Teachers and Teaching: Theory and Practice, 14*, 115–127.

Kern, L., & Wehby, J. (2014). Using data to intensify behavioral interventions for individual students. *Teaching Exceptional Children, 46*, 45–53.

Kumm, S., Gesel, S., Majeika, C. E., Talbott, E., & Maggin, D. M. (2019). *Effects of school mental health interventions for youth with internalizing disorders: A meta-analysis*. Manuscript submitted for publication.

Lane, K. L., Wehby, J., Little, M. A., & Cooley, C. (2005). Academic, social, and behavioral profiles of students with emotional and behavioral disorders educated in self-contained classrooms and self-contained schools: Part I—Are they more alike than different? *Behavioral Disorders, 30*, 349–361.

Lemons, C. J., Sinclair, A. C., Gesel, S., Danielson, L., & Gandhi, A. G. (2019). Integrating intensive intervention into special education services: Guidance for special education administrators. *Journal of Special Education Leadership, 32*, 29–38.

Lyon, A. R. (2016). *Implementation science and practice in the education sector*. Washington, DC: Substance Abuse and Mental Health Services Administration. Retrieved from https://education.uw.edu/sites/default/files/Implementation%20Science%20Issue%20Brief%20072617.pdf

Lyon, A. R., Whitaker, K., French, W. P., Richardson, L. P., Wasse, J. K., & McCauley, E. (2016). Collaborative care in schools: Enhancing integration and impact in youth mental health. *Advances in School Mental Health Promotion, 9*, 148–168.

Maheady, L., Smith, C., & Jabot, M. (2014). Field experiences and instructional pedagogies in teacher education: What we know, don't know, and must learn soon. In P. Sindelar, E. McCray, M. Brownell, & B. Lignugaris/Kraft (Eds.), *Handbook of research on special education teacher preparation* (pp. 161–177). New York, NY: Routledge.

Martin, T., Peacock, S. B., Ko, P., & Rudolph, J. J. (2015). Changes in teachers' adaptive expertise in an engineering professional development course. *Journal of Pre-College Engineering Education Research, 5*, 35–48.

Mason-Williams, L., Frederick, J. R., & Mulcahy, C. A. (2015). Building adaptive expertise and practice-based evidence: Applying the implementation stages framework to special education teacher preparation. *Teacher Education and Special Education, 38*, 207–220.

McLeod, B. D., Sutherland, K. S., Martinez, R. G., Conroy, M. A., Snyder, P. A., & Southam-Gerow, M. A. (2017). Identifying common practice elements to improve social, emotional, and behavioral outcomes of young children in early childhood classrooms. *Prevention Science, 18*, 204–213.

McLeskey, J., Barringer, M.-D., Billingsley, B., Brownell, M., Jackson, D., Kennedy, M., … Ziegler, D. (2017). *High-leverage practices in special education*. Arlington, VA: Council for Exceptional Children.

Merikangas, K. R., He, J. P., Brody, D., Fisher, P. W., Bourdon, K., & Koretz, D. S. (2010). Prevalence and treatment of mental disorders among US children in the 2001–2004 NHANES. *Pediatrics, 125*, 75–81.

Michel, J. J., Fiks, A., Mayne, S., Grundmeier, R., Miller, J., Broomfield, C., & Guevara, J. (2018). A technology driven approach for sharing patient-reported outcomes in ADHD between parents, pediatricians and teachers. *Pediatrics, 142*, 618. Meeting Abstract, Council on Clinical Information Technology Program.

Motoca, L. M., Farmer, T. W., Hamm, J. V., Byun, S., Lee, D. L., Brooks, D. S., … Moohr, M. M. (2014). Directed consultation, the SEALS model, and teachers' classroom management. *Journal of Emotional & Behavioral Disorders, 22*, 119–129.

National Research Council. (2000). *How people learn: Brain, mind, experience, and school*. Washington, DC: National Academies Press.

National Research Council and Institute of Medicine. (2009). *Preventing mental, emotional, and behavioral disorders among young people: Progress and possibilities*. Washington, DC: National Academies Press.

Sanford, C., Newman, L., Wagner, M., Cameto, R., Knokey, A. M., & Shaver, D. (2011). *The post-high school outcomes of young adults with disabilities up to 6 years after high school: Key findings from the National Longitudinal Transition Study-2 (NLTS2)*. Menlo Park, CA: SRI International.

Sindelar, P. T., Wasburn-Moses, L., Thomas, R. A., & Leko, C. D. (2014). The policy and economic contexts of teacher education. In P. Sindelar, E. McCray, M. Brownell, & B. Lignugaris/Kraft (Eds.), *Handbook of research on special education teacher preparation* (pp. 3–16). New York, NY: Routledge.

Soslau, E. (2012). Opportunities to develop adaptive teaching expertise during supervisory conferences. *Teaching and Teacher Education, 28*, 768–779.

Soslau, E., Kotch-Jester, S., Scantlebury, K., & Gleason, S. (2018). Coteachers' huddles: Developing adaptive teaching expertise during student teaching. *Teaching and Teacher Education, 73*, 99–108.

Sutherland, K. S., Conroy, M. A., McLeod, B. D., Kunemund, R., & McKnight, K. (2019). Common practice elements for improving social, emotional, and behavioral outcomes of young elementary school students. *Journal of Emotional and Behavioral Disorders, 27*, 76–85.

Talbott, E. (2019, April). *Youth with mental health problems in education and health care: The collaborative care model.* Invited presentation, Evidence for Policy and Practice Information and Co-ordinating Centre (EPPI-Centre), University College London, London, UK.

Talbott, E., & De Los Reyes, A. (2020). *Effective teamwork in assessment and intervention for youth with Attention Deficit Hyperactivity Disorder (ADHD)*. Manuscript in preparation.

Talbott, E., Mayrowetz, D., Maggin, D. M., & Tozer, S. (2016). A distributed model of special education leadership for individualized education program teams. *Journal of Special Education Leadership, 29*, 23–31.

U.S. Department of Education. (2017). *39th Annual report to congress on the Implementation of the Individuals with Disabilities Education Act*. Washington, DC: Author.

Vo, A. K., Sutherland, K. S., & Conroy, M. A. (2012). Best in class: A classroom-based model for ameliorating problem behavior in early childhood settings. *Psychology in the Schools, 49*, 402–415.

Wagner, M., Kutash, K., Duchnowski, A. J., Epstein, M. H., & Sumi, W. C. (2005). The children and youth we serve: A national picture of the characteristics of students with emotional disturbances receiving special education. *Journal of Emotional and Behavioral Disorders, 13*, 79–96.

Weersing, V. R., Jeffreys, M., Do, M.-C. T., Schwartz, K. T. G., & Bolano, C. (2017). Evidence base update of psychosocial treatments for child and adolescent depression. *Journal of Clinical Child and Adolescent Psychology, 46*, 11–43.

Westling, D. L. (2010). Teachers and challenging behavior: Knowledge, views, and practices. *Remedial and Special Education, 31*, 48–63.

Wetzel, A. P., De Arment, S. T., & Reed, E. (2015). Building teacher candidates' adaptive expertise: Engaging experienced teachers in prompting reflection. *Reflective Practice: International and Multi-disciplinary Perspectives, 16*, 546–558.

31 Professional Development to Support Service Providers of Children and Adolescents with or at Risk of Emotional and Behavioral Disorders

Issues and Innovations

Cristin M. Hall, David L. Lee, Rachel Robertson, and Karen Rizzo

To promote the effective use of evidence-based practices (EBPs), service providers (e.g., general educators, special educators, behavioral and mental health professionals, counselors, school psychologists) may receive a variety of professional development (PD) opportunities related to the support needs of youth with/at risk of emotional and behavioral disorders (EBD). Research and training in PD for service providers tends to focus on two major areas: *skill-building* and *capacity-building*. *Skill-building* includes models for training, coaching, and consultation to foster the appropriate implementation of EBPs for service providers who work with students with/at risk of EBD. This includes a range of strategies such as classroom management, the development and implementation of individualized emotional and behavioral supports, and applied behavior analytic practices (Sanetti, Collier-Meek, Long, Byron, & Kratochwill, 2015; Motoca et al., 2014; Sutherland, Farmer, Kunemund, & Sterrett, 2018). *Capacity-building* includes developing infrastructure supports to foster service providers' ability to implement, refine, and modify their use of EBPs. This includes providing time for professional collaboration, training school, and agency leaders to provide feedback and guidance in intervention use, and creating communication and teaming systems to promote coordinated, consistent, and sustained use of EBPs (Brannan, Brashears, Gyamfi, & Manteuffel, 2012; Farmer et al., 2018; Horner et al., 2014; Strickland-Cohen, Kennedy, Berg, Bateman, & Horner, 2016; Stroul & Friedman, 1986).

Although PD targeting these areas has had many successes, programs have been less successful in producing sustained change in service providers' use of behavior management practices (McIntosh et al., 2014) and in obtaining broad staff acceptance of proactive behavior support strategies (Feuerborn & Tyre, 2016; Feuerborn, Wallace, & Tyre, 2016). Studies of school-based consultation indicate that after initial uptake, many service providers significantly decrease their use and fidelity of a behavioral intervention within seven to ten days of training, or after outside support has ended (Hawkins & Heflin, 2011; Johnson et al., 2014; Noell, Witt, Slider, & Connell, 2005). These studies show that even with the best PD practices available in supporting fidelity, many providers fail to implement and maintain effective support strategies.

In this chapter, we discuss how PD activities can be used to better equip service providers to address the needs of youth with/at risk of EBD. Our aim is to consider issues and innovations in PD to promote skill development and the capacity to sustain and adapt the use of EBPs to be responsive to the needs of youth and the contexts in which they are served. To this end, we discuss coaching broadly and highlight three complementary forms of PD support: Directed Consultation, the use of technology for dissemination and coaching, and "Wise" interventions. Further, we consider implications for future directions in practice and research.

The Need for Professional Development in Social, Emotional, and Behavioral Supports

Recent reports indicate that approximately 0.5–1% of the school-age population (ages 6–21) receives services for EBD under the Individuals with Disabilities Education Act (Forness, Freeman, Paparella, Kauffman, & Walker, 2012; Forness, Kim, & Walker, 2012; Office of Special Education and Rehabilitation Services, 2017). At face value, this is a relatively small number of children (approximately 4–6 students in an average school). However, this estimate fails to account for two key issues regarding services, prevalence, and the impact of students with/at risk of EBD within general education classroom contexts.

First, the number of children who receive special education services for EBD underestimates the total number of students who require social, emotional, and behavioral supports (Forness et al., 2012). Ringeisen and colleagues (2017) estimate that 9–13% of school age youth experience mental health difficulties that warrant services and treatment. Similarly, Forness, Freeman and colleagues (2012) estimate that 12% of youth experience social, emotional, and behavioral difficulties at any given time and approximately 30% of students experience difficulties at some point during their school career.

Second, the severity of social, emotional, and behavioral needs of youth with/at risk of EBD may negatively impact the engagement of all students. Nearly 50% of students with EBD spend 80% of their day in general education (OSERS, 2017), often with teachers who have little training in supporting students with social, emotional, and behavioral problems (Baker, 2006). Many youth with/at risk of EBD engage in high rates of aggression and disruptive behavior, have difficulty remaining engaged in academic tasks, and have elevated rates of non-compliance to adult instructions (Chen et al., 2019; Henricsson & Rydell, 2004). These problems contribute to negative student/teacher interactions (Gunter & Coutinho, 1997; Hendrickx, Mainhard, Boor-Klip, Cillessen, & Brekelmans, 2016), reduce instructional engagement (Sutherland & Wehby, 2001), and interfere with the instructional attention given to classmates (Barth, Dunlap, Dane, Lochman, & Wells, 2004; Shores & Wehby, 1999). This cycle of non-instruction and academic escape behavior may contribute to a "truce of non-instruction" between underprepared teachers and students with/at risk of EBD. If the teacher does not press academic demands, the student will decrease rates of problem behavior at a cost to their learning and social development.

The number of students who actually require supports (e.g., number currently served and number in need of services) and the variety of contexts create important issues for the delivery of PD. First, given that youth with/at risk for EBD are generally under-identified and subsequently under-served, there is a need to direct additional resources for PD for service providers. Second, given that students with/at risk of EBD are served in increasing numbers in general education and community settings, it is not just a matter of providing additional training to special care providers. There is a need to provide PD related to the support needs of youth with/at risk for EBD for all care providers (Farmer, Reinke, & Brooks, 2014).

Coaching to Promote Social, Emotional, and Behavioral Supports

Designing and validating effective supports for students with/at risk of EBD is important, but it is only one aspect of the equation. The appropriate use, adaptation, and sustainability of effective practices is critical to ensure that youth with/at risk of EBD receive the services and supports they need to develop the competencies and relationships necessary to promote their positive outcomes and long-term adjustment (Maggin, Wehby, Farmer, & Brooks, 2016). The

464   *Cristin M. Hall et al.*

goal of PD is to enhance the intervention repertoire of practitioners such that student outcomes are improved (Desimone, 2009; Lane et al., 2015). PD may vary in form, feature, and purpose, but a major consideration in designing learning opportunities is to address issues that impact the day-to-day management and intervention decision-making of service providers (Chorpita, 2019; DeSimone & Parmar, 2006; Farmer et al., 2018; Kazdin, 2019).

Historically, PD involves workshops, courses, and conferences. As one familiar example, an "expert" may be brought in to conduct a 3-hour presentation on a current topic selected by administrative leaders. While credit is given for attending the event, there is little evidence that such "one and done" PD activities do much to change the behavior of service providers (Wei, Darling-Hammond, & Adamson, 2010). To address these issues, reformed approaches to PD that center on coaching models have recently gained momentum (Scher & O'Reilly, 2007).

Coaching is an umbrella term that generally involves observation, feedback, and modeling or demonstration of key practices (Kraft, Blazar, & Hogan, 2018). Coaching has yielded positive learning outcomes for both novice and veteran service providers in a variety of settings using 1:1 formats as well as team and school/agency-wide PD initiatives (Desimone & Pak, 2017; Farmer et al., 2016; Lane et al., 2015). Five foundational considerations for effective coaching experiences have been identified: *content-focus, active learning, coherence, extended duration of time,* and *collective participation* (Desimone, 2009; Garet, Porter, Desimone, Birman, & Yoon, 2001).

Content and Context Focus

Coaching activities can be engineered in a manner that allows for concentration on individual service providers' needs relating to content knowledge or content pedagogy while being responsive to the contexts in which specific strategies are used (Motoca et al., 2014). The evolution and innovation of intervention practices reflect both micro (e.g., addressing needs within individual settings) and macro (e.g., new policy, legislation, etc.) processes (Farmer et al., 2014; Slavin, 2019). Coaching is an established practice for preparing providers with the adaptive skills to address the ever-changing content within the field (Chorpita, 2019; Desimone & Pak, 2017; Kahn & Lewis, 2014). To promote both the uptake and sustained use of EBPs, it is helpful to utilize coaching strategies that link critical practice elements of EBPs to the circumstances and ecological features of the settings in which they will be used (Chorpita, 2019; Farmer et al., 2018; Sutherland, Conroy, McLeod, Kunemund, & McNight, 2019).

Active Learning

Broadly defined within the context of professional development, active learning can include engagement with, inquiry, curriculum discussions, planning, or practice (Darling-Hammond, 1998; Penuel & Means, 2004). Active learning opportunities in PD are greatly enhanced by formative feedback (Scheeler, Ruhl, & McAfee, 2004). Within a coaching model, the active learning that occurs increases the intensity of the PD practice compared to more traditional approaches to PD.

Coherence

The flexibility of coaching models allows for integration and alignment of PD with school and agency initiatives. In addition, coaching can help to maintain a sustained system of support across stakeholders (Loucks-Horsley, 1996).

Duration

PD that is longer in duration tends to yield better results in providers' practice and youth adaptation than relatively shorter sessions (Wei, Darling-Hammond, Richardson, & Orphanos, 2009). Current recommendations suggest PD should be at least one year in duration. While traditional approaches are not structed in such a manner, coaching practices are typically of longer durations ranging from one semester to three years.

Collective Participation

Opportunities to collaborate with colleagues has a significant influence on providers' retention of new practices (Borko, Jacobs, Eiteljorg, & Pittman, 2008; Grossman, Wineburg, & Woolworth, 2001; Slavit & Roth McDuffie 2013). Service providers who have opportunities to collaborate with peers, colleagues, and related stakeholders are less likely to leave the profession (Slavit & Roth McDuffie, 2013). Loucks-Horsley (1996) characterize collective participation in terms of professional learning communities supported by school and agency administrations in which continued learning, risk-taking, reform, innovation, and a shared vision are a constant part of the culture.

Overall, coaching models have evolved in form to include peer, mentor, and E-coaching models. Each of these forms of coaching offers distinct benefits to support service provider development of new competencies and use of EBPs. As these coaching models have developed, so too have consultation practices emerged as a form of coaching. Consultation practices have been structured in several different ways based on contextual factors.

Directed Consultation

Directed consultation (DC) is an intervention support framework in which data are gathered and used to inform and target PD interventions tailored to contextual factors within and impacting classroom and community settings. These contextual factors include the skill set of service providers, needs of youth, school, and community initiatives, and available resources (Farmer & Hamm, 2016; Farmer et al., 2013, 2018; Motoca et al., 2014). DC is a strengths-based approach and reflects the five critical characteristics of PD identified by Desimone (2009) and Garet et al. (2001). What makes DC different from other PD approaches is the focus is on the person-in-context, clarifying leverage points in the ecology, and selecting interventions based on individual care providers' strengths and needs. Ultimately, DC promotes solutions that are responsive to immediate teacher concerns, youths' needs, and ongoing real-world issues which can improve sustainability of evidence-based practice (Odom, 2009). There are four components of DC: pre-intervention observations and interviews, a professional development workshop, on-line training modules, and on-going implementation meetings (Farmer et al., 2013, 2018).

Pre-intervention observations and interviews are conducted by intervention specialists with teachers and other service providers. An intervention specialist is an individual who demonstrates a working knowledge of developmental and ecological systems perspectives with background in evidence-based practices for students with EBD (Farmer et al., 2013, 2014). The intervention specialist develops a "scouting report" that identifies typical practices (e.g., context management, intervention approaches, teaming logistics, and data use) and the general functioning, strengths, and needs within relevant settings (Farmer et al., 2016; Farmer & Hamm, 2016). This report is used to develop plans for intervention and subsequent

PD needs by accounting for key leverage points in classrooms. Leverage points are aspects of the environment that can be used to make interventions more impactful and maintained over time. For example, identifying and recruiting a popular student to help lead discussion groups could be a leverage point to help increase participation of other youth.

The second component of DC is a *professional development workshop* that generally occurs at the beginning of the uptake of a new intervention. A major outcome associated with this component is development of shared values, purpose, and goal of on-going consultation meetings that occur across the training period (e.g., school year) between service providers/teams and intervention specialist(s). Individual service providers, content-specific teams, grade-level teams, or teams of service providers working with particular youth may collaborate with an intervention specialist. The intervention specialist's role is to serve as a guiding hand to service providers and teams. This individual serves to model a strength-based problem-solving approach, support solution-oriented discussions, and positions teachers to serve as collaborative resources for one another. A second outcome of the workshop is to initiate shared knowledge of the contextual nature of interventions.

The third and fourth components of DC provide contextually relevant intervention content knowledge through brief online *professional development modules* along with *support from intervention specialists*. In addition to the foundational professional development skills covered during the professional development workshops, the online professional development modules provide information on specific practices that can be of high leverage for student outcomes based on unique contextual factors of a given setting (Farmer et al., 2013). The modules are prescribed as part of *ongoing meetings with intervention specialists* who support the use of interventions in context. Service providers, teams, and intervention specialists meet on an on-going basis live or via videoconferencing. The purpose of on-going directed consultation meetings (DCM) is to apply the content from the workshops and modules to the immediate, real-world issues facing teachers.

In general, the process of DC begins with the collection of data to guide the PD (i.e., workshops and modules). A scouting report is generated and used to inform the initial and ongoing consultation meetings. The DCMs provide time for discussion of how to implement various features of the training within each classroom. This includes formative feedback from the intervention specialist in which "problems" are re-organized into opportunities for learning. DC meetings are uniquely positioned to offer a "just-in-time" approach to PD as youth move from less (universal) to more intensive (targeted) supports that frequently require training and adaptation (Farmer et al., 2016).

Technology Use for Teacher Professional Development Support

With the clear need for assistance and PD for service providers to successfully support youth with/at risk of EBD, the main thrust in the field has been encouraging the adoption and implementation of evidence-based, manualized programs. Despite the proliferation of programs for universal social-emotional learning and classroom management support, many of the extant PD protocols and EBPs do not necessarily provide portable and sustainable tools that educators can easily use (Hall, Breeden, & Giacobe, 2018). In light of the enormous growth of online social networks and "writable" internet options (termed Web 2.0), educators can now share tools that they have developed and reach out for solutions even if they are geographically isolated (Hunter & Hall, 2018). Given the difficulty with adoption and sustainability of EBPs (Forman et al., 2013), it is not surprising that the internet has provided user-driven resources for service providers.

The use of Web 2.0 options by teachers and related service providers has received some attention in both peer-reviewed academic outlets as well as in popular media outlets (Hall et al., 2018). Greenhow and Gleason (2014) described the engagement of teachers and educators on social media as a form of knowledge that is shared and transmitted as it is co-created by users versus receiving knowledge from a centralized authority such as national organizations or institutes of higher education. Keeping with the idea of the diffusion of innovations through existing channels (Rogers, 2004) and constructed knowledge in the field, a good example of teachers sharing knowledge with one another is TeachersPayTeachers (TpT) which was launched in 2006 (Jones, 2018). TpT is an online platform in which teachers may upload worksheets and other resources that users may download and use free or for a small fee. TpT reports that two-thirds of teachers are using their online resource cache (Teachers Pay Teachers, n.d.). Further, TpT advertises an option for schools to register for the site in order to download and use "standards aligned resources" to which they report over 8,000 schools have registered for the resource. Although TpT is one example of an online consolidation site and marketplace, it is also a critical example of how user-driven social media is filling a need for resources that are portable, accessible, and low- or no-cost. The overall expansion, beyond single websites like TpT, for PD and resource sharing is a consistent trend indicating that many educators are turning to the internet despite concerns about quality (Hughes, Ko, Lim, & Liu, 2015).

Due to reservations about quality control (i.e., use of practices with no evidence) and questions about how teachers are leveraging online sources, Hunter and Hall (2018) explored the use of online tools (i.e., Web 2.0 applications) in a survey of over 150 teachers. Respondents from the northeastern region of the United States in urban schools were the highest self-reported users of social media tools, which is consistent with previous research (Hughes et al., 2015). When asked about how often they used various applications, YouTube, online newspapers, and Pinterest were the top three sites across responders (Hunter & Hall, 2018). Teachers reported that they used social media for professional purposes most often for establishing professional relationships, connecting with colleagues, and commenting on education-related topics. Finding forms and templates, professional development activities, and getting ideas for lesson plans were the most frequently reported information-seeking activities among teachers in this sample. Although the patterns of use in the Hunter and Hall (2018) survey was consistent with popular media reports and other survey work, they extended the study to include assessing the degree to which teachers would select higher-quality resources for classroom management with a more robust evidence base when offered a menu of choices embedded in the survey. Years of experience, education level and comfort with using online resources were not significant predictors of teachers selecting higher quality classroom management strategies; however, trust in online resources was a positive predictor. More information is needed related to the selection of materials online for teachers and other service providers, yet it appears that some variables may predict more prudent use of online materials from platforms such as Pinterest and TpT.

Empirical Study of Extant Social Media Use

Although there are concerns about relative quality of online resources, little research has examined the topography of the kinds of materials shared in terms of content area, their original sources, and how they are related to components of EBPs. Using a web-scraping technique to examine over 26,000 professional practice-related pieces of content (or "pins") from Pinterest, data from a sample of followers of the National Association of School

Psychologists (NASP) were examined to provide a snapshot of the kinds of content Pinterest users shared (or "pinned") by those who had an interest in school psychology-related content (Hall et al., 2018). Results of an inductive coding process indicated that social-emotional (32%) and behavior-related (15%) content made up the majority of the sampled pins. Of the content in the social-emotional category, much of the shared content was related to coping skills, social skills, and counseling. In the behavior category, users most often shared content on class management and information related to students with externalizing disorders. The next largest percentage of shared content was related to professional issues (e.g., office organization, professional books; 17%) and academic issues (e.g., reading instruction, math instruction; 17%). Overall, it appears that content that targets social and emotional problems and behavior management is of most interest to school-psychology related professionals who use online resources to help guide their practice. Because such resources may include strategies that are not empirically supported, it is necessary for researchers and policy makers to clarify both the attraction and utility of online approaches and to use this information to develop ways to ensure that online resources are effectively leveraged to enhance the scale-up and use of EBPs in real-world settings.

In order to understand how the content shared on Pinterest may relate to EBP, Breeden and colleagues (2018) conducted a detailed component analysis of the coping skills related content from the aforementioned Pinterest sample. The research team identified common core components of extant evidence-based coping skills programs. They identified relaxation, problem-solving, goal setting, social support seeking, self-concept, emotion regulation, and cognitive reframing as core components of EPBs for coping and compared the coping-related pins ($n = 3,858$) to these common core components. Over half of the pins that were coping-related were consistent with a component of an extant EPB (59.32%), many of which were related to relaxation techniques (over 30%). In terms of evidentiary basis of those pins, only a third of the pins were consistent with evidence-based principles and about half lacked a clear evidence base. Although there is a substantial amount of content that can be linked back to EBPs, very little content was clearly related to an extant program (Breeden et al., 2018).

Leveraging Technology for Online Support

Given the dramatic increase in the use of social media to find resources for families, teachers, and other professionals there are both reasons for optimism and reasons for pause in how information is being shared and used. For those who are geographically isolated or for those who have limited training, the internet (if used wisely) can open doors for free information that was once almost unheard of outside of having access to large libraries or in-person PD. National organizations may provide leadership in the field in the way of handouts, simple intervention tools, videos, articles, and other media that can help professionals learn about low base rate phenomena or new developments in the field. Institutes of higher education, such as universities, and government entities can also leverage the reach of the internet and social media applications in similar ways. Open-access learning materials in the form of narrated PowerPoint presentations, free-access courses, and even YouTube videos can provide leading edge information and high quality training to those who may need it the most.

Although leaders in the field may leverage online platforms in the same ways that commercial entities do (e.g., mass marketing and user-friendly interfaces) little is known about the degree to which social media is being used for dissemination of evidence-based content. Many professional organizations may require membership fees in order for individuals to access materials. Large organizations may periodically redesign their interfaces and thus move materials to new locations on their website, making them difficult to access. In addition, .edu and .gov domains, while generally thought of as the highest quality, may be the least aesthetically appealing or be viewed by users such as parents or other stakeholders as difficult to understand in terms of readability (Di Pietro, Whiteley, Mizgalewicz, & Illes, 2013).

Researchers and practitioners alike are anecdotally known for having serious reservations when a teacher, family member, or other stakeholder reports that "they found something online," given the almost complete lack of vetting or quality control. Ineffective or iatrogenic practices are rampant and at best may be a waste of resources or at worst harmful to children and youth. Concerns about how to access higher quality resources may be ameliorated by a few simple practices for professionals. For those seeking intervention ideas, worksheets, curriculum, or other materials to help students with social-emotional problems, there are a few ways to ensure staying in line with best practices. First, using resources that are from higher-quality websites, such as .edu or .gov domains may be a reasonable assurance of better information and ideas. Second, when utilizing materials from personal or professional blogs or websites (such as a guidance counselor, teacher, or TpT) it is critical to examine whether or not the materials are at least consistent with theory or programming that is evidence-based, such as applied behavior analysis techniques or cognitive behavioral techniques. If a professional is not sure about the quality of the materials, consulting with a colleague who may have insight would be a simple way to assure better practice. Finally, with any technique, a data-driven approach to understand whether and how it is working for a particular student or classroom is important.

"Wise" Approaches to Teacher PD in Behavior Management

One reason traditional approaches to PD in behavior management may not result in long-term adoption of effective practices is that service providers' beliefs about a youth's behavior may contradict a proactive, evidence-based approach to behavior management in favor of a more punitive approach (Bambara, Nonnemacher, & Kern, 2009; Pinkelman, McIntosh, Rasplica, Berg, & Strickland-Cohen, 2015). For example, teachers who believe that student behavior is internally controlled (Feuerborn & Chinn, 2012; Wiley, Tankersley, & Simms, 2012) may be less likely to support proactive classroom management strategies and prefer punishment-based strategies (Andreou & Rapti, 2010; Brannan et al., 2012; Erbas, Turan, Aslan, & Dunlap, 2010; Liljequist & Renk, 2007). This belief is strongly linked to the notion that a proactive approach to behavior management rewards students for misbehavior (Brannan et al., 2012; Feuerborn & Chinn, 2012; Pinkelman et al., 2015).

PD approaches have been developed that address interfering service providers' beliefs with the goal of improving implementation of effective behavior management practices (Coles, Owens, Serrano, Slavec, & Evans, 2015; Cook, Lyon, Kubergovic, Wright, & Zhang, 2015; Okonofua, Paunesku, & Walton, 2016; Owens et al., 2017). Two non-experimental design studies found promising results. Cook et al. (2015) implemented a year-long supportive belief intervention based on the theory of planned behavior (Ajzen & Manstead, 2007) along with Tier 1 schoolwide positive behavior support training. The supportive beliefs intervention involved a variety of small group reflective exercises and testimonials from other teachers regarding the importance of proactive support for students who engaged in elevated rates of problem behaviors. After intervention, teachers with the greatest increases in supportive beliefs had the greatest increases in use of effective behavior management. Coles et al. (2015) incorporated Motivational Interviewing (Amrhein, Miller, Yahne, Palmer, & Fulcher, 2003; Reinke, Stormont, Webster-Stratton, Newcomer, & Herman, 2012) into teacher consultations to help teachers express supportive beliefs about student behavior change and implementation of effective behavior management. This intervention was associated with improvements in teacher implementation as well as improvements in student behavior.

More recently, two randomized controlled trials (RCT) experimentally tested the impact of intervening on teacher beliefs about student problem behavior. In comparison to traditional online modules of behavior intervention, one study examined online modules of reflective activities to increase teachers' empathetic perceptions of student behavior, including school-based reasons why students might engage in disruptive behavior (Okonofua et al., 2016). The treatment significantly increased empathetic mindsets in teachers and halved year-long student suspension rates; furthermore, the decrease in suspensions was greatest for students with a history of suspensions. A second study compared a best-practices consultation intervention to a best-practices plus support for teacher knowledge, skills, and beliefs regarding behavior management (Owens et al., 2017). The experimental treatment with belief change support was significantly more effective than the comparison in improving behavior management for teachers with the lowest levels of knowledge, skill, and supportive beliefs about behavior management.

Achieving PD Buy-In Using Wise Approaches

Evidence from social psychology supports the notion that people's beliefs about the behavior of others impact how they respond to that behavior. For example, growth and fixed mindset is a well-researched construct from social psychology showing that some people view behavior as unmalleable and caused by internal traits, and that people holding this mindset are more inclined to punish others for inappropriate behavior rather than educate or rehabilitate them (Dweck, 2006; Gervey, Chiu, Hong, & Dweck, 1999). Additionally, previous research indicates that these and other "mindsets" (defined as how individuals interpret and respond to external events) can be changed through an approach known as Wise Interventions (Blackwell, Trzesniewski, & Dweck, 2007; Walton, 2014; Yeager et al., 2016).

In a Wise Intervention framework, behavior is viewed as an interaction between an individual, his or her environment, and how that individual interprets the events in his or her environment (i.e., mindset; Walton, 2014; Yeager & Walton, 2011). Unlike skill- and capacity-based approaches to PD, Wise Interventions assume that many people have the ability and circumstances to succeed but do not because they possess maladaptive interpretations of their situation (Paunesku et al., 2015; Walton, 2014). Using theory developed through rigorous lab-based experiments on psychological processes, Wise Interventions consist of brief, carefully produced readings and reflective activities that lead participants to challenge and change their own previously held patterns of thinking and acting (Walton & Wilson, 2018). Researchers have demonstrated that using Wise Interventions, relatively brief interventions targeting participant beliefs can produce profound, lasting changes in behavior (Blackwell et al., 2007; Okonofua et al., 2016; Walton, 2014; Yeager et al., 2016). For example, Walton and Cohen (2011) provided letters from older college students to first-year college students conveying that it is normal to worry about whether you belong in college and that this thought passes over time. Remarkably, this intervention was related to increases in African American students' grades over the next three years. Wise Interventions are believed to produce long-term behavior changes by triggering recursive processes in which attitudinal and behavioral changes developed through the initial intervention are reinforced and strengthened during ongoing environmental interactions (Walton & Wilson, 2018). Additionally, recent research has demonstrated the effectiveness of Wise Interventions as self-administered online modules (Okonofua et al., 2016; Paunesku et al., 2015; Yeager et al., 2016), increasing the numbers of participants who can receive the intervention as well as its feasibility, replicability, and fidelity across recipients.

Wise Intervention Content and Activities

Descriptions of Wise Intervention content and activities are provided below and based on previous Wise Intervention protocols (Blackwell et al., 2007; Cook et al., 2015; Okonofua et al., 2016; Walton & Wilson, 2018; Yeager et al., 2016).

Messaging

Wise Intervention participants are often told that their participation and responses to reflective activities will be used to help develop supportive materials for others struggling with their situation. This approach is described as an *indirect appeal* made through asking participants to help others, rather than a *direct appeal* in which participants are told that PD is designed to help them. Direct appeals have been shown to trigger resistance and can further entrench participants in previously held maladaptive beliefs or mindsets (Robinson, 2010; Yeager et al., 2016) resulting in a countertherapeutic effect; alternatively, indirect appeals are associated with increasing "buy in," belief change, and behavior change (Yeager et al., 2016). In this approach, participants are treated as experts and agents of positive change for others, not as recipients of remediation (Okonofua et al., 2016).

Brief Research Articles

Participants in "Wise" interventions often read a brief research article supporting the primary message of the PD. The article is user-friendly and may assume the reader's agreement with the point of view expressed. Setting such a tone avoids the negative effects of direct appeals (Yeager & Walton, 2011) and produce the positive effects of indirect appeals (Walton, 2014; Yeager et al., 2016). The article may share insights regarding research findings directly related to the interpretation that is targeted for change. For example, Blackwell et al. (2007) shared research with students indicating that "the brain is like a muscle" in that the harder you work it the stronger it gets. This message was associated with greater student motivation during academic setbacks, as setbacks were interpreted as opportunities to grow.

Testimonials

Participants in Wise Interventions often read testimonials from others reinforcing the target interpretation. Okonofua et al. (2016) had teachers read testimonials from other teachers about the importance of empathizing with challenging students. Reading other teachers' descriptions of how behavior management practices have helped them provides new social information and suggests that using evidence-based classroom management strategies is a social norm for effective teachers (Okonofua et al., 2016). Student testimonials may also be used, in which older students describe how a teacher's use of the target practice helped them (Okonofua et al., 2016). Hearing from former students who describe the positive, long-term effects of behavior

472   *Cristin M. Hall et al.*

management strategies may increase the likelihood that teachers will use these strategies in order to be accurate and correct in their practice (Okonofua et al., 2016; Stephens, Hamedani, & Destin, 2014; Walton, 2014).

Reflective Writing Exercises

Wise Intervention participants are often asked to engage in reflective writing activities that focus their attention on the target interpretation, and told that their work will be used to help others struggling with this issue. Generating and writing an example of when the participant has successfully used the target practice or interpretation engages the participant in "prompting new meanings" (Wilson, 2011), in which the individual is led to reinterpret his or her own behavior. Often these writings are designed as persuasive writings, such as writing a letter to someone who might be struggling with this issue and relating how they have positively dealt with it. This exercise may operate through a "saying is believing" process, in which individuals who write authentic testimonials alter their future behavior to align with the behavior they described in their writings (Aronson, Fried, & Good, 2002; Walton & Cohen, 2011; Yeager & Walton, 2011). This belief change mechanism is described as preserving self-integrity, in that the individual is likely to behave in ways that are in accordance with their own words if they perceive these words as volitional and true (Walton & Wilson, 2018). Additionally, reflective writing exercises allow service providers to take ownership of the intervention message, connect it to their own practice, and advocate for it to others (Okonofua et al., 2016).

Future Directions

Completing a degree in applied behavioral analysis, behavioral health care, psychology, school psychology, social work, special education, or other related field pertaining to the social, emotional, and behavioral needs of children and adolescents is not the end of training for service providers for youth with/at risk of EBD. In reality, it is the end of the beginning of training. As society changes, so do the ecologies, circumstances, and support needs of youth with/at risk of EBD. Each passing year brings new challenges and new possibilities for professionals working with this group of children and adolescents. Learning new interventions and establishing a systematic framework to adapt them to the developmental needs and contexts of youth is an ongoing process (Chorpita, 2019; Maggin et al., 2016; Sutherland et al., 2018).

Kazdin (2019) recently observed that a critical issue in mental health services for youth is that the majority of children and adolescents with significant intervention needs do not receive adequate supports to address these needs. He suggests that traditional approaches to the delivery of services in clinical settings is necessary but inadequate and concludes there is a need for the delivery and diffusion of services through novel approaches that involve new technologies, social media, and expanding how interventions may be applied in the everyday lives of youth.

PD is important in efforts to meet the needs of children and youth with/at risk for EBD in their day-to-day activities. As others suggest (e.g., Chorpita, 2019; Farmer et al., 2018; Lloyd, Bruhn, Sutherland, & Bradshaw, 2019), effective PD involves training service providers in the implementation of EBPs with fidelity while also helping them to develop skills to use data to link and adapt practice elements of EBDs to developmental process variables that are contributing to the social, emotional, and behavioral functioning of specific youth.

Coaching is likely to be an important part of this process. But as Kazdin (2019) suggests, it is necessary to meet unmet need by exploring novel approaches. Bringing together DC, Web 2.0 resources that utilize social forms of dissemination and support, and "Wise" strategies can collectively operate to get new information to front-line service providers while giving them a platform and motivation for adapting strategies to the specific needs of youth and contexts. To do this, it is critical to have interventions specialists (see Talbott et al., Chapter 30, this volume) who serve as supports to bring together and support teams of professionals as they adapt EBPs within the theoretical and empirical parameters of effective intervention. In other words, it is necessary to recognize the dynamic developmental processes that both contribute to EBD and impact the successful use of EBPs (Chorpita, 2019; Maggin et al., 2016; Sutherland et al., 2018).

Such efforts must be guided by complementary research. Although there is a continued need for experimental-control trials that focus on what works, there is also need for a different form of research that builds on the foundations of improvement science. Improvement science centers on establishing interdisciplinary networks of researchers and practitioners who bring together different but complementary skills to address a problem of practice (Bryk, 2015). A critical aspect of this work is that it is building from the perspective and insights of front-line professionals to yield practice-based research that is likely to resonate with practitioners while being amenable to generating data-driven, adaptive approaches to intervention that can be more responsive to individual students and contexts (Farmer et al., 2018; Snow, 2015). Research that combines person-oriented approaches with local analytics can yield rigorous empirical methods that examine change in the organization of key developmental variables that are predictive of pathways to outcomes of interest (i.e., school completion, healthy adolescent/adult adjustment, successful post-secondary educational and work attainment). This involves developing tiered-systems of adaptive supports and using both local and national data to support the success of youth who are struggling (see Farmer, Gatzke-Kopp, & LaTendresse, Chapter 1, this volume).

In conclusion, professional develop cannot only focus on disseminating what works. Rather, the focus needs to be on how do we promote the adaptation of youth with/at risk of EBD with the resources and constraints of the contexts in which they are embedded. Innovations are required and current practices and new approaches to research have the field well positioned to establish frameworks of ongoing professional development that can provide supports to and learn from direct care service providers as they address the needs of youth with/at risk of EBD.

Authors' Note

This work was supported by grants from the Institute of Education Sciences (R305A040056; R305A160398; R305A120812). The views expressed in this paper are those of the authors and do not represent the views of the granting agency.

References

Ajzen, I., & Manstead, A. S. R. (2007). Changing health-related behaviors: An approach based on the theory of planned behavior. In K. van den Bos, M. Hewstone, J. de Wit, H. Schut, & M. Stroebe (Eds.), *The scope of social psychology: Theory and applications* (pp. 43–63). New York, NY: Psychology Press.

474 *Cristin M. Hall et al.*

Amrhein, P. C., Miller, W. R., Yahne, C. E., Palmer, M., & Fulcher, L. (2003). Client commitment language during motivational interviewing predicts drug use outcomes. *Journal of Consulting and Clinical Psychology, 71*, 862.

Andreou, E., & Rapti, A. (2010). Teachers' causal attributions for behaviour problems and perceived efficacy for class management in relation to selected interventions. *Behaviour Change, 27*, 53–67.

Aronson, J., Fried, C. B., & Good, C. (2002). Reducing the effects of stereotype threat on African American college students by shaping theories of intelligence. *Journal of Experimental Social Psychology, 38*, 113–125.

Atkins, M. S., Cappella, E., Shernoff, E. S., Mehta, T. G., & Gustafson, E. L. (2017). Schooling and children's mental health: Realigning resources to reduce disparities and advance public health. *Annual Review of Clinical Psychology, 13*, 123–147. doi:10.1146/annurev-clinpsy-032816-045234.

Baker, J. A. (2006). Contributions of teacher-child relationships to positive school adjustment during elementary school. *Journal of School Psychology, 44*, 211–229.

Bambara, L., Nonnemacher, S., & Kern, L. (2009). Sustaining school-based individualized positive behavior support: Perceived barriers and enablers. *Journal of Positive Behavior Interventions, 11*, 161–178.

Barth, J. M., Dunlap, S. I., Dane, H., Lochman, J. E., & Wells, K. C. (2004). Classroom environment influences on aggression, peer relations, and academic focus. *Journal of School Psychology, 42*, 115–133.

Blackwell, L. S., Trzesniewski, K. H., & Dweck, C. S. (2007). Implicit theories of intelligence predict achievement across an adolescent transition: A longitudinal study and an intervention. *Child Development, 78*, 246–263.

Borko, H., Jacobs, J., Eiteljorg, E., & Pittman, M. E. (2008). Video as a tool for fostering productive discussions in mathematics professional development. *Teaching and Teacher Education, 24*, 417–436.

Brannan, A. M., Brashears, F., Gyamfi, P., & Manteuffel, B. (2012). Implementation and development of federally-funded systems of care over time. *American Journal of Community Psychology, 49*, 476–482.

Breeden, N. C., Hall, C. M., & Giacobe, N. (2018). Component analysis and evidentiary basis of coping skills content on Pinterest. *Psychology in the Schools, 55*, 783–800.

Bryk, A. S. (2015). 2014 AERA distinguished lecture: Accelerating how we learn to improve. *Educational Researcher, 44*, 467–477.

Chen, C. C.-C., Farmer, T. W., Hamm, J. V., Lee, D. L., Dawes, M., & Brooks, D. S. (2019, online first). Emotional and behavioral risk configurations, students with disabilities, and perceptions of the middle school ecology. *Journal of Emotional and Behavioral Disorders*. Retrieved from https://journals.sagepub.com/doi/pdf/10.1177/1063426619866829

Chorpita, B. F. (2019). Commentary: Metaknowledge is power: Envisioning models to address unmet mental health needs: Reflections on Kazdin (2019). *Journal of Child Psychology and Psychiatry, 60*, 473–476.

Coles, E. K., Owens, J. S., Serrano, V. J., Slavec, J., & Evans, S. W. (2015). From consultation to student outcomes: The role of teacher knowledge, skills, and beliefs in increasing integrity in classroom management strategies. *School Mental Health, 7*, 34–48.

Cook, C. R., Lyon, A. R., Kubergovic, D., Wright, D. B., & Zhang, Y. (2015). A supportive beliefs intervention to facilitate the implementation of evidence-based practices within a multi-tiered system of supports. *School Mental Health, 7*, 49–60.

Darling-Hammond, L. (1998). Teachers and teaching: Testing policy hypotheses from a national commission report. *Educational Researcher, 27*, 5–15.

DeSimone, J. R., & Parmar, R. S. (2006). Issues and challenges for middle school mathematics teachers in inclusion classrooms. *School Science and Mathematics, 106*, 338–348.

Desimone, L. M. (2009). Improving impact studies of teachers' professional development: Toward better conceptualizations and measures. *Educational Researcher, 38*, 181–199.

Desimone, L. M., & Pak, K. (2017). Instructional coaching as high-quality professional development. *Theory Into Practice, 56*, 3–12.

Di Pietro, N. C., Whiteley, L., Mizgalewicz, A., & Illes, J. (2013). Treatments for neurodevelopmental disorders: Evidence, advocacy and the internet. *Journal of Autism and Developmental Disorders, 43*, 122–133. doi:10.1007/s10803-012-1551-7

Dweck, C. (2006). *Mindset: The new psychology of success.* New York, NY: Random House.

Erbas, D., Turan, Y., Aslan, Y. G., & Dunlap, G. (2010). Attributions for problem behaviour as described by Turkish teachers of special education. *Remedial and Special Education, 31,* 116–125.

Farmer, T. W., Chen, C., Hamm, J. V., Moates, M. M., Mehtaji, M., Lee, D., & Huneke, M. R. (2016). Supporting teachers' management of middle school social dynamics: The scouting report process. *Intervention in School and Clinic, 52,* 67–76. doi:10.1177/1053451216636073

Farmer, T. W., & Hamm, J. V. (2016). Promoting supportive contexts for minority youth in low-resource rural communities: The SEALS model, directed consultation, and the scouting report approach. In L. J. Crockett & G. Carlo (Eds.), *Rural ethnic minority youth and families in the United States: Theory, research, and applications* (pp. 247–265). New York, NY: Springer.

Farmer, T. W., Hamm, J. V., Lane, K. L., Lee, D., Sutherland, K. S., Hall, C. M., & Murray, R. (2013). Conceptual foundations and components of a contextual intervention to promote student engagement during early adolescence: The supporting early adolescent learning and social success (SEALS) model. *Journal of Educational and Psychological Consultation, 23,* 115–139. doi:10.1080/10474412.2013.785181

Farmer, T. W., Hamm, J. V., Lee, D. L., Sterrett, B. I., Rizzo, K., & Hoffman, A. S. (2018). Directed consultation and supported professionalism: Promoting adaptive evidence-based practices in rural schools. *Rural Special Education Quarterly, 37,* 164–175.

Farmer, T. W., Reinke, W. M., & Brooks, D. S. (2014). Managing classrooms and challenging behavior: Theoretical considerations and critical issues. *Journal of Emotional and Behavioral Disorders, 22,* 67–73. doi:10.1177/1063426614522693

Feuerborn, L., & Chinn, D. (2012). Teacher perceptions of student needs and implications for positive behavior supports. *Behavioral Disorders, 37,* 219–231.

Feuerborn, L. L., & Tyre, A. D. (2016). How do staff perceive schoolwide positive behavior supports? Implications for teams in planning and implementing schools. *Preventing School Failure: Alternative Education for Children and Youth, 60,* 53–59.

Feuerborn, L. L., Wallace, C., & Tyre, A. D. (2016). A qualitative analysis of middle and high school teacher perceptions of schoolwide positive behavior supports. *Journal of Positive Behavior Interventions, 18,* 219–229.

Forman, S. G., Shapiro, E. S., Codding, R. S., Gonzales, J. E., Reddy, L. A., Rosenfield, S., & Sanetti, L. M. H. (2013). Implementation science and school psychology. *School Psychology Quarterly, 28,* 77–100.

Forness, S. R., Freeman, S. F., Paparella, T., Kauffman, J. M., & Walker, H. M. (2012). Special education implications of point and cumulative prevalence for children with emotional or behavioral disorders. *Journal of Emotional and Behavioral Disorders, 20*(1), 4–18.

Forness, S. R., Kim, J., & Walker, H. M. (2012). Prevalence of students with EBD: Impact on general education. *Beyond Behavior, 21*(2), 3–10.

Garet, M., Porter, A., Desimone, L., Birman, B., & Yoon, K. (2001). What makes professional development effective? Analysis of a national sample of teachers. *American Educational Research Journal, 38,* 915–945.

Gervey, B. M., Chiu, C. Y., Hong, Y. Y., & Dweck, C. S. (1999). Differential use of person information in decisions about guilt versus innocence: The role of implicit theories. *Personality and Social Psychology Bulletin, 25,* 17–27.

Greenhow, C., & Gleason, B. (2014). Social scholarship: Reconsidering scholarly practices in the age of social media. *British Journal of Educational Technology, 45,* 392–402.

Grossman, P., Wineburg, S., & Woolworth, S. (2001). Toward a theory of teacher community. *Teachers College Record, 103*(6), 942–1012.

Gunter, P. L., & Coutinho, M. J. (1997). Negative reinforcement in classrooms: What we're beginning to learn. *Teacher Education and Special Education, 20*(3), 249–264.

Hall, C. M., Breeden, N. C., & Giacobe, N. (2018). I found it on Pinterest: An exploration of Pinterest content for followers of the National Association of School Psychologists. *Contemporary School Psychology, 22,* 413–423.

476 *Cristin M. Hall et al.*

Hawkins, S. M., & Heflin, L. J. (2011). Increasing secondary teachers' behavior-specific praise using a video self-modeling and visual performance feedback intervention. *Journal of Positive Behavior Interventions, 13*, 97–108.

Hendrickx, M. M., Mainhard, M. T., Boor-Klip, H. J., Cillessen, A. H., & Brekelmans, M. (2016). Social dynamics in the classroom: Teacher support and conflict and the peer ecology. *Teaching and Teacher Education, 53*, 30–40. doi:10.1016/j.tate.2015.10.004

Henricsson, L., & Rydell, A. M. (2004). Elementary school children with behavior problems: Teacher-child relations and self-perception. A prospective study. *Merrill-Palmer Quarterly-Journal of Developmental Psychology, 50*, 111–138.

Horner, R. H., Kincaid, D., Sugai, G., Lewis, T., Eber, L., Barrett, S., ... Algozzine, B. (2014). Scaling up school-wide positive behavioral interventions and supports: Experiences of seven states with documented success. *Journal of Positive Behavior Interventions, 16*, 197–208.

Hughes, J. E., Ko, Y., Lim, M., & Liu, S. (2015). Preservice teachers' social networking use, concerns, and educational possibilities: Trends from 2008–2012. *Journal of Technology and Teacher Education, 23*(2), 185–212.

Hunter, L. J., & Hall, C. M. (2018). A survey of K-12 teachers' utilization of social networks as a professional resource. *Education and Information Technologies, 23*, 633–658.

Johnson, L. D., Wehby, J. H., Symons, F. J., Moore, T. C., Maggin, D. M., & Sutherland, K. S. (2014). An analysis of preference relative to teacher implementation of intervention. *The Journal of Special Education, 48*, 214–224.

Jones, L. (2018). Teacher-powered: The unstoppable community behind TeachersPayTeachers. *Forbes*. Retrieved from www.forbes.com/sites/lilyjones/2018/07/19/teacher-powered-the-unstoppable-community-behind-teacherspayteachers/#196ed2bf3c8d (accessed on September 13, 2018).

Kahn, S., & Lewis, A. R. (2014). Survey on teaching science to K-12 students with disabilities: Teacher preparedness and attitudes. *Journal of Science Teacher Education, 25*(8), 885–910.

Kazdin, A. E. (2019). Annual research review: Expanding mental health services through novel models of intervention delivery. *Journal of Child Psychology and Psychiatry, 60*, 455–472. doi:10.1111/jcpp.12937

Kraft, M. A., Blazar, D., & Hogan, D. (2018). The effect of teacher coaching on instruction and achievement: A meta-analysis of the causal evidence. *Review of Educational Research, 88*, 547–588.

Lane, K. L., Oakes, W. P., Powers, L., Diebold, T., Germer, K., Common, E. A., & Brunsting, N. (2015). Improving teachers' knowledge of functional assessment-based interventions: outcomes of a professional development series. *Education and Treatment of Children, 38*(1), 93–120. doi:10.1353/etc.2015.0001.

Liljequist, L., & Renk, K. (2007). The relationships among teachers' perceptions of student behaviour, teachers' characteristics, and ratings of students' emotional and behavioural problems. *Educational Psychology, 27*, 557–571.

Lloyd, B. P., Bruhn, A. L., Sutherland, K. S., & Bradshaw, C. P. (2019). Progress and priorities in research to improve outcomes for students with or at-risk for emotional and behavioral disorders. *Behavioral Disorders, 44*, 85–96.

Loucks-Horsley, S. (1996). Principles of effective professional development for mathematics and science education: A synthesis of standards. *NISE Brief, 1*(1), 1–6.

Maggin, D. M., Wehby, J. H., Farmer, T. W., & Brooks, D. S. (2016). Intensive interventions for students with emotional and behavioral disorders: Issues, theory, and future directions. *Journal of Emotional and Behavioral Disorders, 24*, 127–137.

McIntosh, K., Predy, L. K., Upreti, G., Hume, A. E., Turri, M. G., & Matthews, S. (2014). Perceptions of contextual features related to implementation and sustainability of school-wide positive behavior support. *Journal of Positive Behavior Interventions, 16*, 29–41.

Motoca, L. M., Farmer, T. W., Hamm, J. V., Byun, S. Y., Lee, D. L., Brooks, D. S., & Moohr, M. M. (2014). Directed consultation, the SEALS model, and teachers' classroom management. *Journal of Emotional and Behavioral Disorders, 22*, 119–129.

Noell, G. H., Witt, J. C., Slider, N. J., & Connell, J. E. (2005). Treatment implementation following behavioral consultation in schools: A comparison of three follow-up strategies. *School Psychology Review, 34*, 87–106.

Odom, S. L. (2009). The tie that binds: Evidence-based practice, implementation science, and outcomes for children. *Topics in Early Childhood Special Education, 29*(1), 53–61.

Office of Special Education and Rehabilitative Services. (2017). *39th annual report to congress on the implementation of the Individuals with Disabilities Education Act.* Washington, DC: U.S. Government Printing Office.

Okonofua, J. A., Paunesku, D., & Walton, G. M. (2016). Brief intervention to encourage empathic discipline cuts suspension rates in half among adolescents. *Proceedings of the National Academy of Sciences of the United States of America, 113*, 5221–5226.

Owens, J. S., Coles, E. K., Evans, S. W., Himawan, L. K., Girio-Herrera, E., Holdaway, A. S., & Schulte, A. C. (2017). Using multi-component consultation to increase the integrity with which teachers implement behavioral classroom interventions: A pilot study. *School Mental Health, 9*, 218–234.

Paunesku, D., Walton, G. M., Romero, C., Smith, E. N., Yeager, D. S., & Dweck, C. S. (2015). Mind-set interventions are a scalable treatment for academic underachievement. *Psychological Science, 26*, 1–10.

Penuel, W. R., & Means, B. (2004). Implementation variation and fidelity in an inquiry science program: An analysis of GLOBE data reporting patterns. *Journal of Research in Science Teaching, 41*, 294–315.

Pinkelman, S. E., McIntosh, K., Rasplica, C. K., Berg, T., & Strickland-Cohen, M. K. (2015). Perceived enablers and barriers related to sustainability of school-wide positive behavioral interventions and supports. *Behavioral Disorders, 40*, 171–183.

Reinke, W. M., Stormont, M., Webster-Stratton, C., Newcomer, L. L., & Herman, K. C. (2012). The Incredible Years Teacher Classroom Management program: Using coaching to support generalization to real-world classroom settings. *Psychology in the Schools, 49*, 416–428.

Ringeisen, H., Stambaugh, L., Bose, J., Casanueva, C., Hedden, S., Avenevoli, S., … West, J. (2017). Measurement of childhood serious emotional disturbance: State of the science and issues for consideration. *Journal of Emotional and Behavioral Disorders, 25*, 195–210.

Robinson, T. N. (2010). Stealth interventions for obesity prevention and control: Motivating behavior change. In L. Dube, A. Bechara, A. Dagher, A. Drewnowski, J. Lebel, P. James, … M. Laflamme-Sanders (Eds.), *Obesity prevention: The role of society and brain on individual behavior* (pp. 319–327). New York, NY: Elsevier.

Rogers, E. M. (2004). A prospective and retrospective look at the diffusion model. *Journal of Health Communication, 9*, 13–19. doi:10.1080/10810730490271449

Sanetti, L. M. H., Collier-Meek, M. A., Long, A. C. J., Byron, J., & Kratochwill, T. R. (2015). Increasing teacher treatment integrity of behavior support plans through consultation and Implementation Planning. *Journal of School Psychology, 53*(3), 209–229. doi:10.1016/j.jsp.2015.03.002

Scheeler, M. C., Ruhl, K. L., & McAfee, J. K. (2004). Providing performance feedback to teachers: A review. *Teacher Education and Special Education, 27*, 396–407.

Scher, L., & O'Reilly, F. (2007). Professional development for K–12 math and science teachers: What do we really know? *Journal of Research on Educational Effectiveness, 2*(3), 209–249. doi:10.1080/19345740802641527

Shores, R. E., & Wehby, J. H. (1999). Analyzing the classroom social behavior of students with EBD. *Journal of Emotional and Behavioral Disorders, 7*, 194–199.

Slavin, R. E. (2019). How evidence-based reform will transform research and practice in education. *Educational Psychologist.* Retrieved from https://www-tandfonline-com.ezaccess.libraries.psu.edu/doi/full/10.1080/00461520.2019.1611432

Slavit, D., & Roth McDuffie, A. (2013). Self-directed teacher learning in collaborative contexts. *School Science and Mathematics, 113*, 94–105.

Snow, C. E. (2015). 2014 Wallace Foundation Distinguished Lecture: Rigor and realism – Doing educational science in the real world. *Educational Researcher, 44*, 460–466.

Stephens, N. M., Hamedani, M. G., & Destin, M. (2014). Closing the social-class achievement gap: A difference-education intervention improves first-generation students' academic performance and all students' college transition. *Psychological Science, 25*, 1–11.

Strickland-Cohen, M. K., Kennedy, P. C., Berg, T. A., Bateman, L. J., & Horner, R. H. (2016). Building school district capacity to conduct functional behavioral assessment. *Journal of Emotional and Behavioral Disorders, 24*, 235–246.

Stroul, B., & Friedman, R. M. (1986). *A system of care for children and adolescents with severe emotional disturbances.* Washington, DC: Georgetown University Child Development Center, National Technical Assistance Center for Children's Mental Health.

Sutherland, K. S., Conroy, M. A., McLeod, B. D., Kunemund, R., & McNight, K. (2019). Common practice elements for improving social, emotional, and behavioral outcomes of young elementary school students. *Journal of Emotional and Behavioral Disorders, 27*, 76–85.

Sutherland, K. S., Farmer, T. W., Kunemund, R. L., & Sterrett, B. I. (2018). Learning, behavioral, and social difficulties within MTSS: A dynamic perspective of intervention intensification. In N. D. Young, K. Bonanno-Sotiropoulos, & T. A. Citro (Eds.), *Paving the pathway for educational success: Effective classroom interventions for students with learning disabilities* (pp. 15–32). New York, NY: Rowman & Littlefield.

Sutherland, K. S., & Wehby, J. H. (2001). Exploring the relationship between increased opportunities to respond to academic requests and the academic and behavioral outcomes of students with EBD: A review. *Remedial and Special Education, 22*(2), 113–121.

Teachers Pay Teachers. (n.d.). Retrieved from https://schools.teacherspayteachers.com/ (accessed on February 21, 2019).

Walton, G. M. (2014). The new science of wise psychological interventions. *Current Directions in Psychological Science, 23*, 73–82.

Walton, G. M., & Cohen, G. L. (2011). A brief social-belonging intervention improves academic and health outcomes of minority students. *Science, 331*, 1447–1451.

Walton, G. M., & Wilson, T. D. (2018). Wise interventions: Psychological remedies for social and personal problems. *Psychological Review, 125*, 617–655.

Wei, R. C., Darling-Hammond, L., & Adamson, F. (2010). *Professional development in the United States: Trends and challenges* (Vol. 28). Dallas, TX: National Staff Development Council.

Wei, R. C., Darling-Hammond, L., Andree, A., Richardson, N., & Orphanos, S. (2009). *Professional learning in the learning profession: A status report on teacher development in the United States and abroad.* Dallas, TX: National Staff Development Council.

Wiley, A. L., Tankersley, M., & Simms, A. (2012). Teachers' causal attributions for student problem behavior: Implications for school-based behavioral interventions and research. In B. Cook, M. Tankersley & T. Landrum (Eds.), *Classroom behavior, contexts, and interventions* (pp. 279–300). Bingley: West Yorkshire, England. Emerald Group Publishing Limited.

Wilson, T. D. (2011). *Redirect: The surprising new science of psychological change.* New York, NY: Little Brown.

Yeager, D. S., Romero, C., Paunesku, D., Hulleman, C. S., Schneider, B., Hinojosa, C., & Trott, J. (2016). Using design thinking to improve psychological interventions: The case of the growth mindset during the transition to high school. *Journal of Educational Psychology, 108*, 374–391.

Yeager, D. S., & Walton, G. M. (2011). Social-psychological interventions in education: They're not magic. *Review of Educational Research, 81*, 267–301.

Index

Page numbers in italic denote figures, and page numbers in bold denote tables.

abstract thinking 65

academic achievement: antisocial behavior 276; ASPs and 170–171; behavior-specific praise and 204; classroom management and 402; early caregiving quality 111; HOPS 367; language skills and 83; parent engagement 103, 263; peer culture 239; and problem behavior 84; successful transitions and 191; teacher-child relationships and 60, 87; Tier 1 SEL 246, *see also* underachievement

academic coaches 72

academic engagement: ASPs and 171; BASE model 239; behavior-specific praise 204; challenging behaviors and 59; childhood adversity 38; classroom management and 86; FCU and improvements in 191; language skills 89; MST-EA and 74; multi-component interventions 267, 268, 269; negative impact of EBD on 463; pacing instruction to promote 235; same-race teacher–child matching 435; UDL and increased 440

academic engagement enhancement (AEE) 148, 229, **230**

academic failure 5, 35, 141, 186, 200, 215, 236

academic outcomes: coaching and 464; DRC 381; early adjustment and 191; EBD and 5, 400; the FCU and 118–119, 193; HOPS 366; ICPs and 236; parent engagement 99, 103; PCs and 105; peer influence and 54; peer support for families and focus on 107; same-race teacher–child matching 435; SEL delays and 35; success of intervention 17; UDL and 441

academic performance/functioning: executive functioning 169; FCU and improvements in 119, 191; interventions 170, 237, 255, 392; measurement of intervention effectiveness 407; multiple contexts and 372; negative peer experiences and 246; observation/screening 236, 238; OTMP deficits and 356; primary domains of 227–228

acceptability of intervention 72, 73, 373–374, 381, **421**

accommodations 404–405

accountability 170, 281, 309, 374, 375, 409

accreditation: residential programs 309

Achieve My Plan (AMP) 73

Achievement for All 408

acknowledgement of behavior 204

ACROSS: Advancing Collaborative Research in Out-of-School Settings 176

action-oriented interventions 279–280

active learning 464

activities: engaging, relevant and interactive 171, **172**

adaptation: behavioral 7, 11; development as a process of 5; human capacity for 57; "ordinary magic" of 8, 17, *see also* system reorganization

adaptation of interventions: BASE model 233–237; Care Process 326–329; CICO 207; context and 423, 427; criticality 463; DRCs 371; and effectiveness 428; FCU 119–120; MST model 287–288; SEL programs 40–42; TFC 296–297

adaptive expertise 451–452, 453–454

adaptive intervention specialists 450–452; preparation 454–457

adaptive learning engagement 255

adaptive support *see* Tiered Systems of Adaptive Support (TSAS) Framework

ADHD 9, 23; alternative classroom formats 403; core symptoms 356; data sharing 452; functional impairment severity **28**; interventions/ treatments 342, 348, 349, 350, 367, 368, 373, 381, 401; OTMP deficits 356–357; peer attitudes 128, 129; prevalence 25, **27**, 29; recognition of socially valued strengths of children with 135; targeting parental behaviors 10; treatment use 30

480 *Index*

adherence to medication 348
adherence to program 312, 428; BEST in CLASS 222, 223; DRC 374; HOPS 366; MST 281, 285, 286, 287, 288; teacher knowledge/skills and 44; trauma and adversity and 156
adjustment difficulties: developmental system and 7, 12; EBD and 59, 125, 186; ecological contexts 4; intervention 227
adolescence 50, 50–60; as an opportunity for change 50; changes to external factors 53–55; changes to internal factors 51–53; considering changes and tasks in combination 56–57; developmental tasks 55–56; FCU 190–191; treatment and service use 30–31; using developmental processes in system reorganization 59–60, *see also* middle and high school years; youth with color; youth with EBD
adoption of interventions 394, **421**, 424–425, 426
adoption/preparation phase 424
adult learning: awareness of principles of 457–458
adult linguistic input: and language development 88–89
adult mental health disorders 23
adult mentors/mentoring 262–263, 264, 269, 271, 296
adult outcomes 17, 54, 256
adverse childhood experiences (ACES) 153; research 154; screening for 158–159, *see also* trauma and adversity
adverse effects *see* side effects
advocacy 99, *see also* self-advocacy
affect (teacher) 131–133
affective education 73
African American students 405–406
After-School Environment Scale 171–173
afterschool programs (ASP) 167–177; applications of theory and empirical evidence 174–176; conclusions and recommendations for future research 176–177; elements of effective 170–174; free or low-cost 177n2; high quality 167, 168, 169, 170, 171–174; importance 169–170; parent satisfaction 167; public health approaches 168; re-education 168
age: and childhood EBD 28, 29; likelihood of treatment use 30; psychotropic medication use 341, *342*
age-divide: child to adult services 70
age-tailored peer roles 72
Agency Supervisor (AS) 335, 336
aggregated case data 324
aggression 141; in adolescence 52, 53; and antisocial behavior 112; classroom hierarchy 129; classroom norms 130, 131, 133; disabilities and engagement in 142; EBD and engagement in 463; EBD and experience of 58; interventions 252, 253, 254, 255, 256, 388, 390, 391; of peer buddies 136; peer cultures 133; peer influence 54, 128; teacher acceptance 132; teacher-student conflict and 132; in tough and troubled students 126; triggers for 127

aggression replacement training (ART) 313
agoraphobia **27**, **28**
Alexander, Q. 437
Algina, J. 221
alternative classrooms 403
alternative environments 10
alternative placements 442
Alternatives for Families: A Cognitive Behavioral Therapy (AF-CBT) **156**, 157
ambivalence: in FCU Feedback Session 117
American Academy of Child and Adolescent Psychiatry (AACAP) 344, 350
American Association for Children's Residential Centers (ACRC) 309
American Psychiatric Association (APA) 23
amygdala 66
analytical process (MST) 282–285
Anger Coping Program 391
anger management 267, 388, 389, 390
answer phase (CARE process) 326, *327*
anti-bullying programs 144, 173, 402, *see also* KiVa program; Olweus Bullying Prevention Program (OBPP); Steps to Respect
antidepressants 342
antisocial behavior: during adolescence 53; interventions 253, 292; and MST *see* Multisystemic Therapy (MST); peer influence 54, 128; predictors 111–112; risk factors 276
anxiety disorders 23; adolescence and 52; in caregivers 98; discontinuation of medication 349; functional impairment severity **28**; impact on social interactions 69; interventions/treatments 71, 155, 206, 251, 344, 350, 393, 456; median age of onset 29; prevalence 25, **27**, 29; sensitivity to facial cues 9; stable victims 148; treatment use 30, *see also* social phobias
appropriateness of intervention **421**, 423, 424
Arnold, D. 426
arrests/re-arrests: interventions reducing 253, 256, 286, 287, 296
assessment(s): of EBD, biases in 406; ecologically-based 400; FCU 114, 116–117, 188; of school ecology 238; for treatment, childhood trauma and adversity 154, *see also* fit analysis; functional behavioral assessment (FBA); medical assessment; psychiatric assessment; reassessment; risk assessment; self-assessment
Atkins, M. S. 452
attainment: of adolescent developmental tasks 55–56; EBD and poor educational/vocational 5, *see also* academic achievement
attention deficit/hyperactivity disorder *see* ADHD
attention problems 57, 83, 167, 245
attention-maintained behavior 266

attributional biases 10, 58, 128
Australia 408
autonomy 55, 60, 171, 190, 346, 405, 442
average students 125–126

Baker, A. J. 295
Baker, C. N. 426
Balas, E. A. 418
Ballentine, K. 309
Banking Time **36**, **37**, 43
BASE Model 134, 227–240; classroom
  management and student support 233–239;
  conceptual foundations and development of
  227–228; empirical support 239; future
  directions and support 239–240; intervention
  components 228–233
baseline data: problem analysis 376–377
Basic Plus (CCE) 270
Bauer, M. 420
Becker, S. P. 363
behavior(s) 11; correlated constraints model 7;
  disorders *see* EBD; distinguishing feelings
  from 249; drivers of 278, 279, 280; improvement
  in 17; interventions *see* interventions; rating
  scales 91; role in development 5, *see also* desired
  behavior; problem behavior(s); prosocial
  behavior(s)
behavior change 7; during adolescence 52–53;
  feedback 377; Wise Interventions 470–471
Behavior Education Program *see* Check In–Check
  out (CICO)
behavior management: professional development
  469–472, *see also interventions*
behavior momentum 234
behavior-related content: use of social media
  for 468
behavior-specific praise 204, **219**, 220
Behavioral, Academic and Social Engagement
  (BASE) model *see* BASE Model
behavioral consultation support 40
behavioral contract *see* Daily Report Card (DRC)
Behavioral and Emotional Screening System
  263–264
behavioral health: co-location within pediatrics
  121; family involvement 312; and MST 288;
  placement changes and 310; residential
  programs 307
behavioral kernels 168, 177
behavioral skills 250
behavioral theory 217, 277, 371
belief change mechanism 472
belonging 13, 100, 171, 239
benchmarking 378, 382
Beretvas, S. N. 41
BEST in CLASS **36**, **37**, 41, 42, 214, 217;
  conclusion 223; empirical support for 220–221;
  overview of practices 219–220; practice-based

coaching 218–219; study findings and
  implications for practice 221–223; teacher
  resource manual 218; teacher workshop
  217–218; theoretical framework 217, *218*;
  value-added nature 217, 222
BEST in CLASS – E 217; empirical support 221;
  practices 220
BEST in CLASS – PK 217; empirical support
  220–221; practices 219–220
best practices: child development and family
  functioning 111, 112, 114, 117, 121; cultural
  competence and use of 436; professional
  learning communities 408; psychotropic
  medications 341–353
biases: in assessment of EBD 406, *see also*
  attributional biases; cognitive biases; racial bias;
  reputation bias
bidirectional influences: adult-child
  communication 89; classroom peer ecologies
  127, 131; in development 4, 6, 7, 11, 14,
  53, 56, 112
biological factors 8, 38
biopsychosocial formulation 344
bipolar disorder 23, **27**, **28**, 344, 348
birth to adulthood: patterns and pathways
  from 5–8
Bishop-Fitzpatrick, L. 298
black students *see* youth of color
black teachers *see* teacher(s), of color
Blackwell, L. S. 471
blame 97, 106, 279, 281
Blueprints for Healthy Youth Development 42
Blueprints for Preventing Violence 292
boarding school environment 315
body acceptance 55
Bogen, D. 120
Boren, S. A. 419
Bounce Back 392–393, 394
boundary-setting 314
boys: ASPs and improved social skills 173; and
  childhood EBD 28–29; classroom hierarchy and
  aggression 129; EBD and peer affiliation
  127–128
Boys Town 298, 309
brain development 10, 65–66, 111, 343
Bransford, J. 453
Breaux, R. P. 364, 365, 367
Breeden, N. C. 468
Breland-Noble, A. M. 295
brief research articles 471
Brody, D. 28
Bronfenbrenner, U. 5, 53, 217, 276
Brookman-Frazee, L. 336, 337
Brownson, R. C. 457
Bruhn, A. L. 264
Bryan, R. L. 457
Building Bridges 316

482 *Index*

bullying 53, 54, 126, 141, 261, *see also* anti-bullying programs
Burns, B. J. 309, 311

Cabell, S. Q. 88
California: Department of Social Services 314; Map system 322, *see also* Los Angeles County (LAC) Department of Mental Health
California Institute for Mental Health (CIMH) 336
"can-do" attitude 281
Canadian DRC.O study 380
capacity-building 176, 440, 462
Capps, R. E. 406
care coordinators (Wraparound) 73
CARE process (MAP) 326–329, 334
career development (HYPE) 74
career preparation 55
caregiver strain 97, 100–101, 103
Caregiver Teacher Report Form (C-TRF) 221
Caring School Community 256
Carter, J. F. 388
Carver-Thomas, D. **437**, 438
cascades model *see* developmental cascades
"cascading dissemination" model of TFC 297
case conceptualization: FCU Feedback Session 115
case data 324, 334
Casey Family Programs 314, 316
Census of Juveniles in Residential Placement (2015) 307
certified teachers: lack of 59
challenging behaviors 87, 440; and academic engagement 59; home–school communication 271; interventions reducing 173, 205
Chamberlain, P. 292, 293, 296
Chang, L. 130, 132
Check & Connect (C&C) 267–268, 271; research 268–269
Check, Connect & Expect (CCE) 269–270, 271; research 270
Check In–Check out (CICO) 205, 207, 263, 264–265, 271, 392, 450; research 265–267
Chen, C. C. 126
child abuse/maltreatment 9, 38, 153, 157, 159, 160
Child and Adolescent Mental Health Division (CAMHD) 322
Child and Adolescent Needs and Strengths (CANS) 310
Child and Adolescent Service Systems Program (CASSP) 291, 292
child characteristics: and language support 90
child development *see* development
Child and Family Assessment (FCU) 114, 188
Child and Family Feedback Form (FCU) 115, *116*
child language: elicitation of 89–90
Child Parent Psychotherapy (CPP) **156**
child welfare 107, 299, 307
Child Welfare League of America 309

child well-being: policies promoting 160, *see also* Family Check-Up (FCU), for child well-being
childhood EBD: common 23; diagnoses 23, 29, 30; national epidemiological studies and ongoing surveillance efforts 24; prevalence 24, 25–29; treatment use 29–31; trends in prevalence 29; trends in treatment 31–32; underestimation of language skills 90; untreated 23, *see also* youth with EBD
choice-making 442
Chorpita, B. F. 330, 335
Chow, J. C. 84
Cicchetti, D. 111
classmates: efficacy of Fast Track Program for non-targeted 253–254
classroom: disruptions, EBD and 58; hierarchical structure 129, 131; norms 129–131, 133
Classroom Assessment Scoring System 221
classroom ecologies 125–136, 229
classroom management: adaptive, correlated constraints model *see* BASE model; consultation techniques 409; evidence-based interventions 133–136; as fundamental to student support 227; language-rich environments 84; PATHS curriculum 249; positive outcomes 402–403; teacher–child relationships 86; use of social media for 468
classroom social dynamics 229–233; EBPs targeting teachers' management of 133–136; peer relationships 125, 127–131; teacher effectiveness 148; teacher influence 125; undermining of teacher intentions 131
classroom-based interventions: SEL delays 35, **36–37**, 41, 42–43, *see also* BEST in CLASS
clinic-based mental health care 401
clinical dashboard (MAP) 333–334, 337
clinical theory: EBS system model 323, 325
Closeness Scale 221
closing phase (session planner) 325
co-location model 403
co-regulation 175
coaches/coaching: ADHD interventions 401; ASPs 175, 176; BEST in CLASS 218–219; Fast Track Friendship Group 250, 251; models 465; MST-EA 74; PASS approach 72; of PCs 104–105; program implementation 427; SEL programs 40, 42, 44; TFC programs 294, 298; to promote EBD supports 463–465, *see also* directed consultation (DC)
coaching 473
coercive family systems 5, 9, 13
cognitive behavioral interventions (CBIs) 386–395; characteristics 388; conclusion 393–394; efficiency and effectiveness 387–388; in schools 389–393; strength of 388; teaching strategies 388
cognitive behavioral therapy (CBT) 73, 155, 206, 277, 290–291, 313, 329, 344, 350, 456

Index 483

cognitive biases 248, 276
cognitive change/development 51–52, 65–66
cognitive control 53, 66
cognitive functioning 111
cognitive impairment 68
cognitive internal indicators 267
cognitive mediation techniques 388, 392
cognitive processing interventions 155
cognitive reframing 468
cognitive restructuring 337, 393
cognitive supports 267
cohabitation 66
Cohen, G. L. 470
coherence: coaching and 464
collaboration: in context of special education 456; and cultural understanding 442; in FCU 113, 115; FFTA standards and focus on 291; in professional development 465; with SISPs 438; in SMH services 403, 407; Wraparound 73, *see also* home–school collaboration
Collaborative for Academic, Social and Emotional Learning (CASEL) 42, 245, 256
collective participation: in PD 465
collegial support: implementation of EBPs 394
color *see* teacher(s), of color; youth of color
combination treatments 341, 344, 347–348, 350
communication: delays 35; facilitation behaviors 87; FCU assessment 114; inter-organizational 427; interventions 146, 175, 190; PCs and 106; in relation to psychotropic medication use 345, 347; TFC 293, *see also* home–school communication; language
communication skills 250, 439
community: -based interventions *see* Link to Learning; Multisystemic Therapy (MST); Treatment Foster Care (TFC); Wraparound; -partnered participatory research 425; EBP design and adoption in 424–425; ecologies, and youth violence 145; and intervention implementation 425; prioritization of SMH services 406
comparison of interventions 70
competence engagement behavior management 148
Competence Enhancement Behavior Management (CEBM) 229, **231**
competencies: in SEL model 143, 245, *see also* social competence
competent-aggressive students 128
complexity: and adoption of intervention 425
comprehension (language) 89
comprehensive SMH programming 402
comprehensive supports: SEL delays 43
conditions for learning (CFL) 440–441
conduct disorder 23, 25, **27**, **28**, 29, 30, 119
Conduct Problems Prevention Research Group (CPRG) 253

conflict: management 251; parent–child 54, 190; peer group 391; teacher–child 39–40, 59, 87, 132
Conflict Scale 221
confluence model of development 5
Connect-Cultivate-Consolidate 326
connections (social-ecological) 13
Conroy, M. A. 221
consent: medication and 346–347, 349
consequences: anticipating 249; TFC and implementation of 293
consider phase (CARE process) 326, *327*, 328
Consolidated Framework for Implementation Research (CIFR) 423
consolidation phase (treatment planner) 326
consultation techniques: classroom management 409
content-focused coaching 464
contextual adaptation (program) 427
contextual approach: to understanding behavior 39
contextual fit (program) 202
contextual influence: and implementation 423
contingent associations 9
contingent response 87
continuous effort/practice 281
conversational support 88, 89–90
Cook, C. 246
Cook, C. R. 263, 469
cooperation 171, 293
cooperative game 175
Coordinated Specialty Care (CSC) 71
coordinated universal and targeted SEL programs 247, *see also* Fast Track Program
coordination: developmental task attainment 55; FFTA standards and focus on 291; sustained CBI use 394; TFC 291, 293; trauma-informed care 158
coordination models (MAP) 323–329
Coping Cat 206, 401
Coping Power Program (CPP) 256, 391–392
coping skills 347, 388, 393, 439, 468
coping strategies 155, 387, 388, 390, 392, 393
Cornerstone 73
corrective feedback **219**, 220, 264
correlated constraints model 6–7, 10, 14, 17, 56–57, 59–60, *see also* BASE Model
cost effectiveness 160, 286, 296, 359
cost of intervention **421**, 424
Council for Exceptional Children Standards for Evidence-Based Practices in Special Education 266, 456
counseling 30, 31, 104, 403, 438, 439, 456, 468
covert aggression 53
Crew, S. 246
criminal behavior: EBD and 5; interventions 73, 253, 287, 298; multi-risk ICPs and 236; parental, and youth violence 141

484   *Index*

criminal justice: age divide between juvenile justice and 70; residential education and lower rates of involvement 315
Crowley, M. 256
cultivate phase (treatment planner) 326
cultural awareness 435
cultural competence 435–436
cultural diversity 189, 437, 440
cultural sensitivity 43–44, 293
culture: and acceptability of interventions 426; collaboration and understanding of 442; implications for SMH services 405–406; organizational 426
Curran, G. M. 420
curriculum-based measure (CBM) for SEL programs 147–148
Curtis, P. A. 298

daily activities of living: and meaningful treatment 168
daily planners (HOPS) 359
daily progress reports (DPRs) 205, 207, 264, 265, 270, 271
Daily Report Card (DRC) 371–383, 401, 403; adaptability 371; conclusion 382–383; description and theoretical underpinnings 371–372; empirical evidence supporting prioritization of 373–374; implementation 409; maximizing effectiveness 374–381; recommendations for future research 381–383; sample *377*
Daily Report Card Online (DRC.O) 379–380
Daleiden, E. L. 330, 335, 336
Darling-Hammond, L. 453
data collection: ASPs 175, 176; DRCs 381, 382; FCU 114; implementation planning 425; intervention specialists 451, 456; medical history taking 345; MST 281; problem analysis 376; scouting reports 238, *see also* directed consultation (DC)
data-based decision-making 205, 263–264, 269, 347, 452
De Los Reyes, A. 38
decision-making: benchmarks 378; brain development 65–66; clinical *see* Managing and Adapting Practice (MAP) system; data-based 205, 263–264, 269, 347, 452; discontinuation of medication 349; family-driven care 98; inclusion of adolescents in 190; intervention 146; residential care 310, *see also* responsible decision-making; shared decision-making
deep thinking: and expertise 454
delinquency 167; EBD and risk of 438; interventions reducing 253, 296, 298, 392
deprescribing 341, 348–352
depression 23; ACES and 154; adolescence and 52; attainment of developmental tasks 55; in

caregivers 98; discontinuation of medication 349; EBD and 438; impact on social interactions 69; interventions/treatments 155, 206, 255, 344, 393, 456; maltreatment history and poorer course of 157; parental monitoring and reduced 191; peer attitudes 128, 129; peer influence 54; prevalence **27**; PWEBS search **330**, **331**; sensitivity to facial cues 9; of stable victims 148; trauma and risk of 153; treatment use 30, *see also* major depressive episodes (MDE); maternal depression; postpartum depression
descriptive norms 130
desired behavior: acknowledging 204; reinforcement 9, 235
development 4; best practices in promoting 111, 112; teacher-child relationships and overall 87; trajectories 187, *see also* developmental systems
developmental cascades 5–6, 7, 13–14, 17, 111–112, 169, 236
developmental considerations: adaptation of EBPs 428; SEL programs and adaptations 39, 40–42; SMH services 406–407
developmental delay 68, 245
developmental leverage points 236, 237
developmental processes: and EBD during middle and high school years 50–60; and intervention 3, 12–13, 18; using in system reorganization 59–60
developmental science perspective 56–57, 58, 60, 142
developmental subsystems: behavioral factors 11; focus of correlated constraints model 14; importance in coordinating multi-factored interventions 17; internal 7, 8–10, 14; interplay between 5, *6*, 7, 11–12; social ecological factors 11
developmental systems 187; birth to adulthood 5–8; framework 4–5; intervention in the context of natural developmental factors and processes 8; need for workforce training and preparation 18; parts and interplay *see* developmental subsystems; reorganization *see* system reorganization
developmental tasks (adolescent) 55–56, 57, 60
developmental transitions 12, 50, 187, 188, 191
developmental turning points 8
developmentally appropriate interventions 73, 281
deviancy training 12, 13, 128, 251
Diagnostic and Statistical Manual (APA) 23
direct appeal 471
direct instruction 41, 391
directed consultation (DC) 237–238, 465–466
disability: race and identification of 435
discipline *see* harsh discipline; school(s), discipline
disengagement 97, 246, 267, 268
Dishion, T. J. 111, 119, 128
disliked students 127, 128, 131, 132, 134, 235
disruptive behavior 9–10; classroom norms 130; EBD and engagement in 463; ecological

Index 485

frameworks 372; interventions 119, 388; peer liking 128; social-emotional skill deficits and 245; treatment engagement 156

dissemination and implementation (D&I) science 321

distractibility 141

Dodge, K. A. 253

dominance over peers 126, 130

Domitrovich, C. E. 394, 425

dopamine deficits 9

Double ABCX Model of Family Stress 100–101, 103

Durlak, J. A. 246

dynamic systems perspective 4, 5, 6–7, 10, 11, 17, 39, 227

dynamic systems theory 455

dysthymia 23, **27**, **28**, 30

early childhood outcomes: the FCU and 119

early intervention 17; in the FCU 119

Early Intervention Foster Care (EIFC) 296

early/late onset model 5–6

eating disorders **27**, **28**, 29

EBD: considerations for the future 17–18; developmental systems and 4–8; during middle and high school years 50–60; ecological and individual risk factors 142; emotion recognition 9; epidemiology 23–32; interventions *see* interventions; language skills and 83–85; terminology 3, 23, 67; trauma and risk of 153; workforce *see* workforce professionals; in young adulthood 67–68; young people with *see* youth with EBD, *see also* social-emotional learning (SEL) delays

ecological approaches: ASPs 167–177; assessments 400; developmental research 66; DRC 372; language skills and problem behavior 84, 85; TFC 293; to addressing SEL skills 39; to treatment, child, environment and 5, *see also* Family Check-Up (FCU)

ecologies: of youth with EBD 3–4, 112, 141, 142, 237, *see also* classroom ecologies; environmental ecologies; multiple ecologies; social ecology(ies)

economic changes: affecting young adulthood 67

education: about interventions and implementation **421**; residential 315; in SMH 402, *see also* psychoeducation; re-education; special education

educational consultants (ECs) 249, 251

Edwall, G. 322

effectiveness of interventions: CBIs 387–388; DRC 373; increasing 4; lack of, in young adulthood 70; MST 281, 286–288, 288; residential programs 308–310; SEL 41; TFC 296, 298; violence prevention 146; Wise Interventions 471

efficacy of interventions: BEST in CLASS 220, 221; CBIs 391; Fast Track Program 249, 252–254; HOPS 361–366; MST 286, 288; psychotropic medications 341; SEALS 134; SEL

43, 44, 145–146, 256; violence prevention 146, 147–148, 149; young adulthood 70–71

egalitarian classrooms 129, 131

elementary schools: CBIs 392–393; as critical point of access for mental health services 31; Fast Track program 252–253; the FCU for 191–192; prevention and intervention in 35–45; SHM therapy in 407

elicitation of child language 89–90

embracing diversity model 328

emergency certification status 59

emotion: awareness 251, 392; changes, during adolescence 52; coaching 250, 251; coping 251, 252; development *see* social-emotional development; distress, adolescence and 52; dysregulation 9, 112, 141, 168, 171, 381; literacy 175, 388; management 391; reactivity 9, 10, 248; recognition 9, 254; resiliency 72

emotion regulation: adolescence and expectations of improved 52; classroom management 86; content shared on Pinterest 468; early caregiving quality 111; EBD and 50; interventions 41, 43, 119, 146, 155, 173, 250; successful transitions 191

emotional and behavioral disorders *see* EBD

emotional support 99; through Parent Connectors 103, 104

emotional understanding 248, 249

empathy 9, 144, 146, 251, 255, 390, 435, 470

employment 69, 71, *see also* Integrated Supported Employment and Supported Education; under employment; unemployment

engagement: of teachers 375; in treatment, trauma and 156–157, *see also* academic engagement; parent engagement

engaging activities 171, **172**

Engels, M. C. 132

environmental ecologies: antisocial behavior 112; EBD and experience of 4; emotion recognition and reactivity 9; and language research 91; SEL delays 38, 42

epidemiology of childhood EBD 23–32

episode level model (MAP) 326

Epstein, J. N. 363

escape-motivated behavior 266, 463

Espelage, D. L. 391

ethnicity *see* race and ethnicity

evaluate phase (CARE process) 326, *327*

evaluation: of intervention effectiveness 281, 381–382

event level model (MAP) 325

Every Student Succeeds Act (ESSA, 2015) 99, 394, 425, 438–439, 439

Everyday Parenting (EDP) 118, 120, 189–190

evidence-based programs and practices (EBP) 60, 112, 261; development 3; disproportionate representation of youth of color in 433;

486 *Index*

implementation *see* implementation science; lack of teacher knowledge/skills 59; leveraging opportunities to maximize impact 216–217; linking to developmental processes 18; mental health 292, 321, 402; rich residential environment 313–314; SEL delays 42; targeting teachers' management of classroom social dynamics 133–136; for trauma and adversity 154–157, 159; young adulthood 70–74, *see also individual interventions and programs*

evidence-based services (EBS) system model 323–325

executive functioning: academic behaviors 169; ADHD and deficits in 356–357; during adolescence 51–52, 65; poverty and 39; psychiatric conditions and 68

exosystem 53

expectations: defining and teaching behavioral 203–204; establishing prescribed 456; setting, TFC 293

experiential learning 393, 456–457

expertise 44, 408, 451–452

exploration phase 424, 427

Exploration, Preparation, Implementation, and Sustainment (EPIS) Framework 423–424, 426

expulsions 35, 58, 59, 236, 400, 442

externalizing disorders 23, 85, 125; interventions/treatments 135, 146, 155, 173, 221, 249, 253, 392; language ability and 83; likelihood of treatment 30; prevalence 25; SEL delays categorized as 38; student typology 126; trauma and risk of 153; untreated 386

Eye Movement Desensitization and Reprocessing (EMDR) 155

Fabiano, G. A. 374, 376

facial expressions: sensitivity to 9

fading strategies 265

family(ies): -based care, hybridization of residential care and 314; -driven care 98; as a barrier to deprescribing 352; children with EBD and marital discord among 97; empowerment 96, 98; involvement 41, 271, 312; management skills 186, 189; organization 247; peer to peer support 96–107; provision of resources and prevention of trauma and adversity 160, *see also* parent(s)

Family Check-Up (FCU), for child well-being 111–121; considerations for application and implementation 119–121; feedback sessions 115–118; next steps and conclusions 121; outcomes and empirical support 118–119; process 113–115; theoretical underpinnings 111–113

Family Check-Up (FCU) Kindergarten study 192

Family Check-Up (FCU), for youth and families with EBD 185–195; for adolescents and young adults 190–191; conclusions 194–195; ecological

model 187–188; for elementary school 191–192; empirical support 191; Everyday Parenting Curriculum 189–190; history of research 185; intervention 188–189; next steps and future directions 192–194; overall objective 187

Family Check-Up Online (FCU Online) 120, 193–194

Family Connections: A Treatment Foster Care Manual 292

Family Contact Log 104, 105

family ecologies: and antisocial behavior 111, 276; as countervailing impact on negative developmental cascades 112; during adolescence 54; for EBD 57–58; experiences for youth with EBD 57–58; and SEL delays 38; youth violence 141, 142, 145

Family First Prevention Services Act (FFPSA, 2018) 308

Family Focused Treatment Association (FFTA) 291, 294

family movement 96–98

Family Peer Advocates 99

family relationships 13, 54, 67

family stress model 100–101, 103

Farmer, E. M. Z. 168, 293, 295, 297, 309, 311

Farmer, T. W. 127, 168, 428

Fast Track Program 247–248; efficacy 252–254; Friendship Group 250–252, 254, 255; multi-component design 247–248; PATHS curriculum 248–249, 251, 252, 254–255, 256

feasibility of interventions 72, 73, 147, 337, 357, 374, **421**, 425

Federation of Families for Children's Mental Health (FFCMH) 96, 97, 98, 106

feedback 394; behavior change 377; BEST in CLASS 218–219, **219**, 220; in CBIs 388; CICO 264; in DC process 466; DRC 372; from prescribers, psychotropic medication use 346; providing supportive and engaging 235; SWPBIS 207, *see also* negative feedback; positive feedback

feedback learning 9, 10

feedback loop: adult-child communication 88, 89

Feedback Session (FCU) 114, 115–118, 188–189

"Feeling face" cards 249

feelings: distinguishing from behaviors 249

Feelings Dictionary 249

fidelity to program 40, 238, **421**, 462; BEST in CLASS 223; HOPS 366; Parent Connectors 104, 105; residential programs 311, 313; SWPBIS 205

Finkelhor, D. 159

Fisher, P. A. 296

fit: intervention-setting 425, 427, 428; student/environment 433

fit analysis 278–279, 282, 284

fit factors 278, 280, 282, 284

Fit2Play 174

Index 487

fixed mindsets 235, 470
flexibility 223, 440, 452
focus-interference framework (treatment planner) 326
follow-up services (FCU) 118
Forman, S. G. 426
Forness, S. F. 463
Forness, S. R. 57
foster care: education 315; outcomes 308; psychotropic medication 343, 349; separate child and adult services 70; young adults with EBD 68, 69, *see also* Treatment Foster Care (TFC)
Frazier, S. L. 174, 175
Freeman, S. F. 463
Friendship Group 250–252, 254, 255
Friendship Tips 250
friendships 55, 58, 60, 86, 246
functional behavioral assessment (FBA) 41, 208, 266, 455
funding **421**; community-based SMH providers 409; implementation facilitation 425; mental health services, California 322; peer support for families 106; residential programs 315

Galvan, A. 130
game-like activities 41
Garandeau, C. F. 148
Gatzke-Kopp, L. 428
gender: ASPs and improved social skills 173; and childhood EBD 28–29; identity 65, 68; psychotropic medication use 341–342; roles 55, *see also* boys; girls
general knowledge: EBS system model 323–324, 325
generalist special educators 450, 451, 454
generalization: MST treatment 281–282
generalization programming 250
generalized anxiety disorder 23, **27**, **28**, 30, 153
Gersten, R. 266
Girio, E. L. 373
Girio-Herrera, E. 363
girls: and childhood EBD 29
Gleason, B. 467
Gleason, S. 454
global level SMH 408–409
goal-setting 52, 207, 249, 378, 387, 388, 392, 442, 468
goals: adolescent social 52; DRC 371–372; FCU Feedback Session 118; MAP system 325; MST 279–280, 282, 284; progress monitoring and modification of 378; psychotropic medication 345; trauma-informed care 158
Goesling, D. **437**, 438
Gonsoulin, S. 440
Good Behavior Game (GBG) 145, 146, 270, 450, 455

Good Shepherd Services 176
Great Smoky Mountains Study of Youth (GSMS) 24, 25, **26**, **27**
Greenberg, M. 256
Greenhow, C. 467
Gresham, F. M. 246
Grissom, J. A. 435
group care 298, *see also* residential programs
group CBT 155
group-level social processes 127–129
grouping 170
growth: human capacity for 57
growth mindsets 235, 470

Hadley, P. A. 88
Hall, C. M. 467
halo effect 132
Hammerness, K. 453
Hans, S. S. 394
Harrison, J. 405
harsh discipline 5, 38, 59, 142, 440
Hatano, G. 451, 453
Havighurst, R. J. 55
Hawai'i Empirical Basis to Services Task Force 322
Hawken, L. S. 265
Hayden, H: E. 454
He, J. P. 28
Head Start 38–39, 41, 119
health care: separate child and adult services 70
Healthy Families America 159
Helping Youth on the Path to Employment (HYPE) 74
Henggeler, S. W. 286
hierarchical classrooms 129, 131
high quality ASPs 167, 168, 169, 170, 171–174
high-risk youth: efficacy of Fast Track Program 252–253; FCU 191; MST 276–288
Hirn, R. G. 59
Hoagwood, K. E. 99
Hobbs, N. J. 5, 168
Holdaway, A. S. 378
Hollowell, J. L. 127
home environments: alternative environments as compensating for chaotic 10; EBD and removal from 58
home visiting programs 113, 159
"home-grown" models of TFC 293
home–school collaboration 271, 373, 456
home–school communication 263, 269, 271, 372
home–school partnership 220
homelessness 69, 315
Homework Completion Cycle 367
Homework, Organization and Planning Skills (HOPS): conclusion 368; development of 357–358; evidence supporting efficacy of 361–366; implementation 366; implications for schools 367–368; main outcomes 366; predictors

of treatment response 366–367; Tier 1 – school-wide intervention 358–359; Tier 2 – small group intervention 359; Tier 3 – individual implementation 359–361
hope 72, 100
hormonal changes 10
Horner, R. H. 266
hostile attribution bias 58
Houchins, D. E. 270
houseparent model 312
huddles 175, 454
Huffstutter, K. J. 97
Hug, R. W. 309
Hughes, J. N. 132
humour 190
Hunter, L. J. 467
hybrid effectiveness-implementation designs 420
hybrid model of TFC 293, 297
hybrid residential and family-based care 314
Hymel, S. 148
hyperactivity: classroom norms 130; interventions 176, 388, 391; peer ecologies 129; peer exclusion 128, 130; youth violence 141, *see also* ADHD
hypervigilance 9
hypotheses generation 208, 282, 344

iatrogenic effects: ACE screening 159
identity 55, 65, 68
Im, M. 132
implementation determinants 422, 427
implementation mechanisms 422
implementation outcomes **421**, 422
implementation phase 424
implementation science 417–428; conceptual model 419, *420*; conclusions 428; defined 418–419; definitions 419–422; frameworks 423–424; future directions 426–428; goal 418, 422; objectives 419; for youth with EBD 424–426
implementation strategies 421–422
improvement science 473
impulse control 390
impulsivity 52, 53, 57, 141, 356, 388
Inagaki, K. 451, 453
inclusion: class rules for 135; classroom norms 130; peer groups 12; screening for 248; TFC and attention to 291
Incredible Years Classroom Management Training (TCM) for Teachers **36**, **37**, 41, 42
independence 54, 67, 73, 86, 190, 407
independent transportability trials: of MST 287
indirect appeal 471
individual case data (MAP) 324, 334
individual CBT 155, 329
Individual Educational Plans (IEPs) 97, 103, 186, 372, 402
individual model of HOPS 359–361

Individual Placement and Supports (IPS) 71
individual risk factors: antisocial behavior 276; for EBD 142, 143; interventions 140; youth violence 141
individualized interventions 40, 41, 291, 292, 358, 371, 403, 456
Individuals with Disability Education Act (IDEA) 15, 50, 140, 263, 322, 434
Individuals with Disability Education Improvement Act (IDEIA) 99
induction strategies 250, 251
inertia: as a barrier to deprescribing 352
infancy: emotion recognition 9; SEL delays 38
inferential language 89
inferential talk 89–90
information: peer support for families 99, 100, 103, 106; sharing 41–42, 114, 452, *see also* case data; data collection; data-based decision-making
informed consent 346–347
Ingersoll, R. **437**, 438
inhibitory control 52, 119
Initial Interview (FCU) 113–114, 115, 188
inpatient services: age and use 30
Institute of Education Sciences 42
instruction: pacing to promote engagement 235
instructional approach to discipline 202, 204
instructional feedback 456
instructional flexibility 440
instructional think-alouds 388
instructional transitions 12
instructive feedback 43, **219**, 220
instrumental mentoring 267
instrumental support 67, 100, 103
integrated interventions 401–402
Integrated Supported Employment and Supported Education 71, 74, 75
integrity of intervention 424, 425
intensity of intervention 60, 378, 394; C&C 268; FCU 121; MST 281, 283; peer-support services 106; school-based MTSS 378; TFC 298, 301; Tier 2 programs 206
interaction-centred model of language and behavioral development 83–91; associations between language skills and behavior problems 83–85; concluding remarks 91; effective classroom management 86; language-rich instructional environments 86–90; next steps for research 90–91; problematic behavior and classroom success 85–86
interactive activities 171, **172**
interdependence 67
interference problems 326
internal subsystem 7, 8–10, 14
internalizing disorders 23, 85; evaluation of DRC 381; interventions 173, 249, 253, 263, 266–267, 267; language ability and 83; likelihood of treatment 30; prevalence 25; rising number of

students with 271; SEL delays categorized as 38; student typology 126; trauma and risk of 153; unnoticed during adolescence 52; untreated 386, *see also* anxiety disorders; mood disorders
internet usage 193
interpersonal challenges 125
interpersonal competence patterns (ICPs) 236
interpersonal problem-solving skills 248, 249
interpersonal relationships 440; SEL 245, 256; sense of belonging 171; youth violence 142, 144, *see also* peer relationships
interpersonal therapy 329
intervention(s): behavioral frameworks 11; characteristics 424–425; in the context of natural development 8; developmental timing 4; effectiveness *see* effectiveness of interventions; efficacy *see* efficacy of interventions; implementation science definition 419–420; individualized 40, 41, 291, 292, 358, 371, 403, 456; leveraging development in 12–14; models and goals of support 15–17; need for careful coordination of 7; in preschool and early elementary school years 35–45; preventive *see* prevention; prioritizing 404–405, 409–410; success of 15–17, *see also* evidence-based programs and practices (EBPs); *individual interventions and programs*; treatment
intervention specialist coordinators *451*, 452–453; preparation 457–458
intervention specialists 449–458; knowledge and skills *451*, 455–456; need for 237; pre-intervention observations and interviews 465; preparation of 453–458; professional development support 466; roles 450–453; school-based collaborative care model 449–450; scouting report process 238–239
intervention-setting fit 427
invisible hand 131
IRIS Center 454
Iznardo, M. 373

James, S. 311, 313
Jameson, J. 406
job instability 442
Jones, D. E. 256
Just Do You (Young Adult Engagement Project) 72
Justice, L. M. 87, 88
juvenile justice 107; age divide between criminal justice and 70; MultifunC 313; placement of youth in residential programs 307; youth involvement 58, 69, 440, *see also* arrests/re-arrests; criminal behavior
Juvonen, J. 130

Kalberg, J. R. 266
Kaplan, J. S. 388
Kazdin, A. E. 38, 472, 473

KEEP 293, 297, 300
Kellam, S. G. 128
Kern, E. C. 435
Kern, L. 246
"kernels of influence" 175
Kim, E. M. 41
KiVa program 144, 148, 149
Knitzer, J. 96, 292
knowledge: EBS system model 323–325; intervention specialists *451*, 455–456, 457; program delivery, and teachers' lack of 59
knowledge sharing 467
Koerner, K. 427
Kotch-Jester, S. 454
Kreuter, M. W. 457
Kupersmidt, J. B. 426

labeling 40, 208, 281, 377
Ladwig, C. 221
Lane, K. L. 266
Langberg, J. M. 362, 363
Langley, A. K. 393
language: use in altering cognitions 388
language development: early caregiving quality and 111; poverty and 39, *see also* interaction-centred model of language and behavioral development
language skills: academic achievement and social development 83; and behavior problems 83–85; EBD and underestimation of 90; and engagement 89; and literacy skills 86
language support 90
language-rich instructional environments 84, 86–90
large-scale studies: ASPs 169, 177, *see also* national studies
Latendresse, S. 428
Latent Profile Analysis (LPA) 255
Lau, A. S. 336
leadership: ASPs and opportunities for 171, *see also* school leadership
learner-centred environment 453–454
learning environments 39, 85, 86, 87, 91, 215, 440, 441
learning opportunities 35, 39, 42, 59, 86, 91, 394, 442, 454, 457, 464
Lee, B. R. 298
Lee, I. A. 148
Lee, M. 148
LEGACY Together 175–176
legislative policies 425
lesbian, gay, bisexual and transgender (LGBT) 68, 69
licensing: residential programs 309
Life Course Model (LCM) 404–405
Light, J. M. 128
limit setting 114, 189–190

490 *Index*

Link to Learning 408–409
listening skills 190
literacy skills 86, 191
literal talk 89
Lloyd, B. P. 271
local control: public schools 408
local knowledge: EBS system model 323, 324, 325
lock-step interventions 60
"locus of control": psychotropic medication use 346
logistical barriers: to treatment engagement 156
loneliness 246
longitudinal studies: ASPs 170, 171, 177; Fast Track program 253; peer victimization 54; school discipline 59
LOOK **36**, **37**, 41, 42, 43
Los Angeles County (LAC) Department of Mental Health 322–323, 336–337
Loucks-Horsley, S. 465
Lourie, I. S. 309
Low, S. 391
low-income: mental health problems 68; psychotropic medication use 342; and SEL delays 38, 39; time spent in ASPs 176, *see also* poverty
Lyon, A. R. 427, 449

McCart, M. R. 288
McComas, J. J. 146
McDaniel, S. C. 270
McGinty, A. S. 88
McLeod, B. D. 43
McMillen, J. C. 309
macro factors: and implementation 425
macrosystem 53
major depressive episodes (MDE) 23, **27**, **28**, 29, 30, 31, 67–68
Making Socially Accepting Inclusive Classrooms (MOSAIC) 135
maladaptive classroom behavior 83
maladaptive mindsets 471
Managing and Adapting Practice (MAP) system 321–338; brief history 322–323; conclusion 338; in context of children's mental health services 321–322; coordination models 323–329; empirical studies 335–337; Professional Development Program (PDP) 334–335; tools 329–334
MAP Instructors 335
MAP Therapists 335
marginalization by peers 129
marriage 66
Masten, A. S. 111
maternal depression 38, 111, 119
Maternal, Infant and Early Childhood Home Visiting Program 159
"maximum feasible participation" 41

measurement approaches 418–419
measurement of language and behavior 90–91
mediators: identifying and targeting 14
Medicaid 307, 342, 343, 409
medical assessment: prior to prescribing 345
Medical Expenditure Panel Survey (MEPS) 24, 29, 31, 32
medical history: taking prior to prescribing 345
Mendlesohn, A. 120
"mental disorders" 23
mental health: EBPs 292, 321, 402; language ability and 83; SISP responsibilities 438–439; social class and 68; TFC and 299; treatment receipt 31; young adult peers and improved 72
mental health conditions: adult 23; caregivers 98; focus on discrete 321; interventions/treatments 292; low-income youth 68; percentage of young people experiencing 400, 463; schools and identification of 31; severe functional impairment 29; trauma and adversity and 68, 154, 158; unnoticed during adolescence 52
mental health services: age divide 70; ASPs as gateway to 175; counseling 438; failure 96; Fast Track Program and reduced use of 253; integrating successful interventions into 32; MAP in context of 321–322; need for training of local providers 256; in residential treatment centers 307; service use 3, 30–31; settings 30; systemic barriers, young adulthood 75; unmet need 472, *see also* outpatient services; school mental health (SMH) services; specialty mental health services
Mental Health Services Act (MHSA, 2004) 322
mentoring 72, 75, 207, 262–263, 264, 267, 269, 271, 296, 440
menu of service options (FCU) 118
Merikangas, K. R. 28, 30
mesosystem 53
messaging 471
meta-analyses: ASPs 170; CBIs 387–388, 389; developmental tasks 55–56; DRC 373; family school interventions 41; parent involvement and academic outcomes 99, 263; residential programs 308; SEL 246–247; social skills training 251–252; TF-CBT 155
metacognitive skills 452
Methods for the Epidemiology of Child and Adolescent Mental Disorders (MECA) 24
Michael, K. 406
Michel, J. J. 452
microsystem 53
middle and high school years: DRC intervention 382, *see also* adolescence
"millennial" generation 66
Milton Hershey School 315
mindful parenting 189
Mindmatters Program 408

Minnesota: Map system 322
Mittman, B. 420
Mixon, C. S. 380
model students 125
modeling 88, 103, 144, 175, 218, 248, 250, 277, 372, 388, 389, 390, 392, 394, 456, 464
models of care: residential programs 311–312
models for SMH services 404–405
modules (professional development) 466
Mojtabai, R. 29, 31
"mom and pop" programs (TFC) 294
monitoring: outcomes, MST 281; parental 189, 190, 191, 193; psychotropic medication use 345–346, *see also* mood monitoring; progress monitoring; self-monitoring
Mood Cup 175
mood disorders 23, 25, **27**, 28, 29, 52
mood monitoring 175
Morbidity and Mortality Weekly Report 29
Morris, P. 120
motivation: parental 188; youth 54, 171, 435
motivational interviewing (MI) 70–71, 73, 187, 188, 290, 313, 470
MST Services 286
Mufson, L. H. 329
multi-component interventions 72–73, 247–248, 264–270
multi-component support plans 208
multi-risk ICPs 236
Multi-Tiered Social-Emotional Learning 245–246; coordinated universal and targeted programs 247; summary and conclusions 256–257; targeted SEL programs (Tier 2) 246–247; universal SEL programs (Tier 1) 246, *see also* Fast Track Program
Multi-Tiered Systems of Support (MTSS) 200–201; assessment of risk factors for EBD 142; central tenet of 215; classroom management 133; framework 15; integration of PFS 120; intervention intensity 378; leadership *see* intervention specialists; linking SMH, systems of care and 17; rationale 200; SMH services 3, 404, 407, *see also* school-wide positive behavioral interventions and supports (SWPBIS); Tier 1 interventions; Tier 2 interventions; Tier 3 interventions
Multidimensional Treatment Foster Care (MTFC) **156**, 292, 308
Multidimensional Treatment Foster Care Program for Preschoolers (MTFC-P) 296–297
Multifunctional Treatment in Residential and Community Settings (MultifunC) 313, 314
multiple contexts: and student functioning 372
multiple ecologies: difficulties in 237; effectiveness of interventions and targeting of 276
multiple intervention strategies 421
multiple risk factors 6, 7, 50

Multisystemic Therapy for Child Abuse and Neglect (MST-CAN) **156**
Multisystemic Therapy for Emerging Adults (MST-EA) 73–74, 288
Multisystemic Therapy (MST) 276–288; adaptations to 287–288; characteristics 277; conclusions 288; empirical support 285–287; quality assurance (QA) system 285, 286, 287; residential programs and parental engagement 313; theoretical and empirical bases 276–277; treatment principles and process 277–285
Multisystemic Therapy for Problem Sexual Behavior (MST-BSP) 288
Murray, M. 309, 311

National Alliance for Mental Illness (NAMI) 96, 97, 106
National Association of School Psychologists (NASP) 467–468
National Center for Children in Poverty 38
National Center for Education Research 42
National Center for Health Statistics (NCHS) 341, 342
National Center for Intensive Intervention 206
National Center on Quality Teaching and Learning 42
National Center for Special Education Research 42
National Comorbidity Survey Adolescent Cohort (NCS-A) 24, 25, **26**, **27**, 28, 29–30
National Health Interview Survey (NHIS) 24
National Health and Nutrition Examination Survey (NHANES) 24, 25, **26**, **27**, 29, 30, 342
National Institutes of Health (NIH) 276, 418
National Longitudinal Transition Study-2 (NLTS2) 59
National Registry of Evidence-based Practices and Programs (NREPP) 42, 206, 292
national studies: ASPs 171; childhood EBD 24, 25, **26**, **27**, 28, 29–30, 32; residential programs 308
National Survey of Children's Exposure to Violence 153
National Survey of Children's Health (NSCH) 24, 29, 30
National Survey on Drug Use and Health (NSDUH) 24, 29, 31, 32, 307
National Trainer (NT) 336
NCS-A school sample 24
Negash, S. 309
negative emotional states 52
negative feedback 59, 239
negative outcomes 35, 40, 54, 58, 261, 288
negative peer responses 246
negative reinforcement 5, 215
neglect 38, 157, 159
Netherlands: psychotropic medication use 342
networking 190
neurotransmitters 343–344

492 *Index*

No Child Left Behind 425
no-risk ICPs 236
non-instruction 463
"non-traditional undergraduate" students 66
Norway: MST study 287; Multifunctional
 Treatment in Residential and Community
 Settings (MultifunC) 313
Nurse–Family Partnership 159
Nutritional Supplement Program for Women,
 Infants and Children (WIC) 119
Nygaard, P. 322

obesity 119, 154
objectives section: MAP practitioner guides 332
observation of impact: importance for
 parents 117
obsessive compulsive disorder (OCD) 23, **27**
off-label prescribing 343
Office of Civil Rights 435
office discipline referrals (ODRs) 263, 264, 267
Ogden 287
Okonofua, J. A. 471
Olfson, M. 31
Olweus Bullying Prevention Program (OBPP) 144,
 145, 146, 149
ongoing meetings: with intervention specialists 466
online newspapers 467
online professional development 335, 466
online support: technology and 468–469
online versions: of the DC 379–380; of the FCU
 120, 193–194; Huddles and Mood Cups 175
open-access learning materials 468
opening phase (session planner) 325
opportunities to respond 43, 217, **219**, 220,
 234, 456
oppositional-defiant disorder (ODD) 23, 25, **27**,
 28, 30, 112, 153
organization, time management and planning
 (OTMP) skills 356–357, 358; intervention *see*
 Homework, Organization and Planning Skills
 (HOPS)
organizational factors 426
organizations: trauma-informed 157, 158
Osher, T. W. 98
out-of-home placements 58, 187, 286, 287, *see also*
 foster care; residential treatment centers (RTCs)
outcomes *see* adult outcomes; implementation outcomes; youth outcomes
outpatient services: age and use 30; treatment
 attrition, young adulthood 69, 70; trends in
 receipt of 31
over-discipline 406
Owens, J. S. 373, 374, 378, 409

panic disorder 23, **27**, **28**, 30
paraprofessionals 297

parent(s): -reported child diagnoses 29, 30;
 behaviors, targeting 10; communication (CICO)
 207; discipline 5, 38, 141; drug abuse, and youth
 violence 141; education, and children's
 responses to psychosocial education 405;
 empowerment 99, 100, 279, 281; importance in
 youth behavior change 277; involvement/
 participation *see* parent engagement; linguistic
 input, and child language 88–89; monitoring
 189, 190, 191, 193; satisfaction with programs
 167, 374, *see also* family(ies); peer to peer support;
 treatment foster parents
Parent Child Interaction Therapy (PCIT) **156**
Parent Connector Coach 104–105
Parent Connectors 97, 100–106; core components
 101, 103; ease of customization 107; objectives
 100; randomized studies of 105–106;
 recruitment and training 104, 107; supervision
 104–105; theoretical foundations 100–103;
 topics and strategies used during calls 104
parent engagement: academic outcomes 103, 263;
 in Bounce Back 393; in education 97, 99–100; in
 interventions 41, 145; interventions addressing
 103, 188, 191, 391–392; low levels, and youth
 violence 141; residential programs 313
Parent Engagement and Empowerment Program
 model 99
Parent Management Therapy 313
parent outcomes: peer to peer support 98, 99, 103,
 105, 106, 107
Parent Self-Assessment (FCU) 116–117, 118
parent-adolescent relationships 67
parenting: and antisocial behavior 111; ineffective
 responses 5; positive 190, 192, 194, 247, 391;
 and risk of EBD 142; SEL delays 38; skills 73,
 118, 186, 187, 189, 191, 192, 194, 314; tools,
 TFC and effective use of 293
Parents as Agents of Change 99
parent–child interactions 114, 189
parent–child relationships 190, 191, 247
parent–teacher relationship 375
Park, S. 41
participant role approaches 144
participation *see* engagement
partnerships: home–school 220; residential and
 family-based care 314, *see also* research-practice
 partnerships (RPPs)
passive students 126
PATHS curriculum 41, 146, *see also* Fast Track
 Program
PATHS to Success program 251, 254–255
Patient Health Questionnaire-9 (PHQ-9) 336
Pavkov, T. W. 309
PAX Good Behavior Game (PAXGBG) 174,
 175, 176
pedagogical knowledge 451, 453, 456

pediatrics: co-location of behavioral health in 121; embedding of the FCU in 120–121; trauma prevention program 159–160

peer: acceptance 58, 130, 135; advocates 99; affiliation 5, 12, 13, 127, 128, 129, 132, 134, 135, 148, 239; alienation 246; buddies 135–136; conflict 391; culture(s) 127, 129, 131, 133, 134, 136, 229, 235, 239; exclusion 12, 128, 130–131; influence 9, 10, 54, 128, 129, 134, 276, 279; instructors 207; integration 55, 60; interaction 170, 252; liking/disliking 127, 128, 131, 132, 134, 235, 252, 257; mentors/mentoring 72, 75, 207, 440; mindset 235; pairing 251; partners 251; presence 10; providers 71; rejection 5, 9, 10, 35, 58, 125, 129, 130, 132, 133, 134, 246; roles 71–72; socialization 54; support 233, 440; victimization 54–55, 58, 126, 142, 146, 149, 157

Peer Academic Support for Success (PASS) 72

peer ecologies: during adolescence 54–55, 56; and youth with EBD 58, 125–136; youth violence 141, 142, 143–145

peer network intervention 176

peer relationships: classroom dynamics 125, 127–131; during adolescence and young adulthood 54–55, 65; in elementary school and impact in adulthood 125; interventions 388; participation in peer ecologies 127; peer cultures 131; social skills deficits 126; teacher attunement 60, 132, 134; teacher influence 131; youth with EBD and research on 58; youth violence 141, 143

peer support for families 96–107; the Family Movement 96–98; parent-to-parent approaches 98–100; pressing issues and new directions 106–107, *see also* Parent Connectors

Pelham, W. 405

penetration of intervention **421**

Pennington, B. 146

Pentimonti, J. M. 89

perceptual barriers: to treatment engagement 156

Performance Standards for Residential Care 309

person-in-context 228, 465

person-oriented analysis 7–8, 125, 236, 240

person-oriented research 473

personnel *see* staffing issues

perspective taking 10, 52, 387, 392

persuasive writings 472

Pew Research Center 193

Pfeiffer, J. P. 55

phase model (treatment planner) 326

phased approach: to trauma treatment 155

phases of implementation 424

physical assault 141, 153

physical environment 203

physical health 154, 345, 438–439

physical violence 157

physiological factors 8

Piasta, S. B. 88

Pinquart, M. 55

Pinterest 467, 468

PK-PATHS **36**, **37**, 42

placement transitions 12

placement-matching 310

plans/planning strategies **421**, 424

policies: prevention of trauma and adversity 160

policy context, attendance to **421**, 425

polypharmacy 341, 343, 347–348

polyvictimization 153

poor conditions for learning 440

poor outcomes: cognitive impairment and 68; configurations of problems and predicted 8; SEL delay and 35; youth with EBD 5

popular-aggressive students 126, 128, 130, 136

Positive Action 256

positive attitudes: parental self-efficacy 103

positive behavior support 86, 112, 114, 186, 189, 246, 377, 404

Positive Behavioral Interventions and Supports (PBIS) 15, 120, 263, 264

positive behavioral management plans 249

positive engagement 13, 239

Positive Family Support (PFS) 120

positive feedback 86, 239, 278

positive fit analysis 278–279

positive mindsets 229, 235

positive outcomes: classroom management and 402–403; early adjustment and 191; early caregiving quality 111; ensuring 4; the FCU and 118–119; MST and 286; parents perceived as key to 279; residential programs 311–312, 315; therapist adherence to MST and 285

positive parenting 190, 192, 194, 247, 391

positive reinforcement 204, 297, 392

positive relationships 13, 251, 262, 456; during adolescence 54; PATHS curriculum 248; with teachers, and prosocial behavior 144

positive self-esteem 248

positive and supportive classroom context 247

positive teacher attention 215

post discharge TFC: and sustained change 300

post-game (NAFASI) 175

post-program surveys: Parent Connectors 106

post-traumatic stress disorder (PTSD) 23; CBIs 393; discontinuation of medication 349; evidence-based treatment 155; functional impairment severity **28**; prevalence 25, **27**; risk of 154; treatment use 30

postpartum depression 71

poverty: and antisocial behavior 276; EBD and maladaptive outcomes 169; psychotropic medication use 342; and SEL delays 38, 39; serious mental illness 68; SMH services 408–409; treatment engagement 156; and youth violence 141

494   *Index*

Powell, B. J. 421
power imbalances: aggression and 129
practice elements: EBPs 216; linking to
    developmental processes 18; PWEBS 330; SEL
    programs 42–43
Practice Parameter (AACAP) 344–348
PRACTICE (TF-CBT) 155
practice-based coaching 40
practice-based research 473
Practitioner Guides (MAP) 331–333
"pragmatic" research 418–419
praise 43, 204, **219**, 220
pre-frontal cortex 53, 65–66
pre-game (NAFASI) 175
pre-intervention assessment 238
pre-intervention observations and interviews
    465–466
precorrection 219–220, 223
premack schedules 235
preschool age: SEL prevention and intervention
    35–45
present-focused interventions 279–280
Pressley Ridge-TFC 298
prevention: cascade model and focus on 13–14;
    CCE 270; of childhood trauma and adversity
    159–160; in preschool and early elementary
    school years 35–45; strong need for 17
prevention science 112
prevention windows 50
primary interventions *see* Tier 1 interventions
Principles of Parent Support 99
prioritizing interventions 404–405, 409–410
privacy 452
proactive aggression 53
proactive behavior management 297, 469
proactive parenting 189
proactive positive behavior support 86
problem behavior(s) 235; and academic
    achievement 84; adolescence and increase in
    190; baseline data and analysis 376–377; context
    and identification of 39; correlated constraints
    model 14; FBA 208; identification 375–376;
    impact on teacher–child relationships 215;
    interference with classroom success 85;
    interventions 205, 221, 297, 314; language
    delay 84; manifestation across contexts 9;
    mechanisms to prevent 85–86; in middle
    childhood 186; peer affiliation 5; percentage
    of children exhibiting 214; preschool-age
    children 38; student typology 126, *see also*
    antisocial behavior; challenging behaviors;
    disruptive behavior
problem-solving: in C&C 268; classroom
    instruction 86; consultation 375; difficulties 10,
    35; interventions 41, 114, 146, 155, 175, 189,
    190, 247, 248, 249, 250, 251, 252, 372, 389, 390,
    393; models 202, 390–391; peer support for

families 106; shared content on Pinterest 468;
    strength-based 466; UDL framework 442
procedural knowledge 451
process guides (MAP) 333
process quality: of ASPs 171–174
Proctor, E. 422
prodigal analysis 8
professional development (PD) 462–473; for BEST
    in CLASS practices 223; coaching 463–465;
    directed consultation 465–466; DRC
    intervention 380–381, 382; duration 465; future
    directions 472–473; need for 463; program
    implementation 40–41, 43, 426, 427; receptivity
    to 457; research 473; SEALS 134; tendency
    towards "train and hope" sessions 421; use of
    technology 466–469; "Wise" approaches
    469–472, *see also* coaches/coaching; training
Professional Development Program (PDP)
    334–335
professional issues: use of social media 468
professional learning communities 408
professional purposes: use of social media for 467
Program Standards for Treatment Foster Care
    290, 291, 295
progress monitoring 148, 334, 378–379, 406,
    407, 456
Project Alliance *185*, 186, 191
Project NAFASI 174–175
Project Re-Ed 314
Promise Neighbourhood 315
Promising Practices Rating Scale (PPRS) 171
Promoting Alternative Thinking Strategies *see*
    PATHS curriculum
"proof of concept" 168, 177, 313
prosocial behavior(s) 86, 135, 144, 173, 388, 391
prosocial engagement 250
protective factors/mechanisms 87, 223
psychiatric assessment: prior to deprescribing
    348–349; prior to prescribing 344
psycho-biological risk factors: youth violence 141
psychoeducation 155, 159, 326, 393
psychological changes: during adolescence 52
psychology research 417
psychology-related content: use of social media
    for 468
psychopathology 52, 154
psychosis 71
psychosocial interventions 155, 404, 405
psychotherapy 154, 350
psychotic disorders 344, 349
psychotropic medications 341–353; conclusion
    352–353; deprescribing 341, 348–352; dosage
    347; increase in children's use of 31; rates of
    children's use in the U.S. 341–343;
    recommended practices 344–348; unmet need
    29–30; what is known and unknown about use of
    343–344

Index 495

public charter schools 315
public health approaches 168, 169, 402
public schools: local control 408
puppet play 41
pursuit processes 52
PWEBS database 329–330, **331**
Pyne, J. M. 420
Pyramid Model for Supporting Social Emotional
Competence in Infants and Young Children **36**,
37, 41, 42, 43, 44

Qualified Residential Treatment Programs
(QRTP) 308
quality assurance (QA) 285, 286, 287, 309
quality childcare 10, 97, 111
quality control: online resources 467
Quality Indicators for Residential Treatment 309
quality management **421**, 424
quality residential care 309–310, 316

race and ethnicity: EBD in young adulthood 68;
and identification of disability 435; implications
for SMH services 405–406; psychotropic
medication use 342; treatment engagement 156;
treatment patterns, young adulthood 69; and
workforce professionals 434–435, *see also*
teacher(s), of color; youth of color
racial bias 433, 435
randomized controlled trials (RCTs) and
studies: ASPs 170; BASE Model 239; BEST in
CLASS 221; CBIs 391; FCU 118, 119, 121, 185,
191, 192, 193, 194; HOPS 366; HYPE 74;
impact of intervening in teacher beliefs 470;
MAP 335; mental health treatments 321; MST
285–286, 287, 288; MST-EA 74; Parent
Connectors 105–106; SEALS model 134; SEEK
160; SEL programs 247, 256, 257; SWPBIS 206;
TF-CBT 155; TFC 292, 296, 297, 298;
Wraparound 73
rapport 188, 326
rating scales 91, 171–173, 221, 336, 344, 401
Rauktis, M. E. 309
re-education 168
reactive aggression 53
reading: ASPs and improved 170, 171
reassessment: psychotropic medication use
347, 349
recruitment: of a diverse EBD workforce 436–438;
of Parent Connectors 104
referrals: to special education 43, 405, 435
reflection: and expertise 454
reflective writing exercises 472
reinforcement 5, 9, 11, 144, 204, 235, 250, 297,
388, 391, 392, 443
relationship building 99, 168, 262, 263, 267, 268,
293, 312, 314
relationship skills 143, 146, 248

relationships: adverse experiences and risk for 154;
cognitive impairment and poor outcomes 68;
during adolescence 53–55; mentoring 262;
parental *see* parent(s); supportive **219**, 220;
trusting 13, 171, 312, *see also* family relationships;
interpersonal relationships; positive relationships; student–teacher relationships; therapeutic
relationships
relaxation/training 155, 175, 325, 337, 392, 393,
456, 468
relevant activities 171, **172**
reputation bias 128, 129, 135
research-practice partnerships (RPPs) 168,
174–176
residential programs 306–316; changing role 306,
308; conclusions 316; creating positive outcomes
311–312; defining 306–307; effectiveness
308–310; the future of 312–315; prevalence 307;
psychotropic medication use 343
residential treatment centers (RTCs) 307, 310, 313
Residentially-Based Services (RBS) reform
project 314
resilience 17, 72, 175
Resolving Conflicts Creatively Program 256
respond phase (CARE process) 326, *327*
respond to unwanted behavior 204
Response to Intervention (RtI) 15, 120, 200, 358
responsible behavior 55, 250, 279, 280
responsible decision-making 143
Responsive Classroom 256
responsive interventions 270
responsiveness (teacher): to child communication
87, 88, 89
restructuring **421**
retention: of a diverse EBD workforce 436–438
reward systems 10, 367
reward-seeking behavior 53
Rice, C. I. **437**, 438
Ringeisen, H. 3, 30, 463
risk: generating information about 17; for
involvement in peer victimization 55; of peer
victimization 126; processes, developmental
systems and accumulation of 5–6, 7
risk assessment: suicide 406
risk factors: antisocial behavior 276; for EBD 50,
57–58, 68, 142; MTSS identification of 140,
142–143; multiple 6, 7, 50; teacher-child
interactions 223; youth violence 141, 143–145;
youth violence exposure 142, *see also* family risk
factors
risk-taking 53, 56, 66, 167
risky behaviors 56, 154, 191, 246, 402
risky decisions 10
Robinson, C. 270
Rodriguez, L. A. 435
role descriptions (MAP) 334–335
role transitions 65, 66

496 *Index*

role-play 103, 104, 118, 144, 148, 190, 218, 248, 251, 279, 285, 388, 390, 394
romantic relationships 55, 56
Rose, C. A. 58, 142
Rosenzweig, J. M. 97
routine expertise 451, 453
routines 234
rules 43; BEST in CLASS 219, 220, 223; establishing prescribed 456; for inclusion 135
Rundell, T. D. 454
rural youth 406

SAFE 174
safe learning environment 440
safe and organized environment 171, **172**
Salmivalli, C. 148
same-race teacher–child matching 435
Sameroff, A. J. 217
sample size: of interventions 70
San Pasqual Academy (California) 315
SANE guidelines 189
Santiago, C. D. 393
"saying is believing" process 472
scaffolding 89, 107, 189, 390, 404
scaling up interventions 44–45
Scantlebury, K. 454
scheduling: SMH services 407
schizophrenia 71
school(s): adjustment 125, 245; administrators 380, 382, 426, 436; behavior policies and procedures 204; cognitive behavioral interventions in 386–395; completion 59, 269, 400; discipline 58, 202, 204, 205, 405–406, 436, 440; disengagement 246, 267, 268; dropout 5, 59, 69, 236, 246, 269, 442; engagement *see* academic engagement; HOPS 358, 367–368; mentoring programs 262–263; rates of EBD as concern for 186; readiness 10, 35, 192, 254–255; SEL programs 169–170; transitions 12; unsuccessful implementation of interventions due to lack of resources 192–193; violence prevention programs 143, *see also* elementary schools; middle and high school years; secondary schools
school ecologies: adolescent development 55; and EBD 58–59, 142; pre-intervention assessment 238; and youth violence 141, 143–145
school entry: as effective point of intervention 192
school environment interventions: youth violence 144, 145, 146, 147, 148, 149
school leadership: intervention facilitation 426; and SMH services 408, 409, *see also* intervention specialists
school mental health providers (SMHP) 400, 401, 402, 403–404; HOPS implementation 357–358, 366, 367
school mental health (SMH) services 3, 400–410; advantages 400–402; age and service use 30;

conclusions 409–410; developmental considerations 406–407; dissemination and implementation 407–409; early identification of problems 31; implications of culture, race, SES and community 405–406; intervention specialists 457; lack of coordination and fragmentation of 255; linking MTSS, systems of care and 17; models for 404–405; parental support and student receipt of 105; school staff model 403; treatment receipt 31; types 402–404
school-age children: application of FCU 120
school-based collaborative care model 449–450
school-based consultation 462
school-to-school prison pipeline 440
school-wide positive behavioral interventions and supports (SWPBIS) 209; basis 201; foundational aspects 202; framework 201; history of evolution 201; implementation issues 208–209; problem-solving model 202; research base 202; research gaps and future directions 209; SMH 404, 407; summary 209–210; system of implementation 202; Tier 1 system 202–205, 209; Tier 2 system 205–207, 209; Tier 3 system 207–208; underlying premise 200
Scott, I. A. 348
Scott, L. A. 437
Scott, T. M. 59
scouting reports 237, 238–239, 465–466
screening: for adverse and traumatic experiences 158–159; for difficulties 236; for inclusion 248; tools 263–264, 267, 344; for youth with EBD 406
scripted stories 41
seating charts 135, 136
second generation antipsychotics (SGAs) 343, 344, 348
Second Step 145–146, 256, 390–391
secondary interventions *see* Tier 2 interventions
secondary schools: SHM therapy in 406, 407, *see also* middle and high school years
SEED Foundation Schools 315
SEEK 159–160
Seifert, H. 311
selected supports and adaptations *see* Tier 2 interventions
self-advocacy 69, 72, 439
self-assessment: parent 116–117, 118; teacher 382, 454
self-awareness 65, 143, 245, 250, 439
self-concept 52, 468
self-control 146, 248, 249, 250, 256, 390
self-determination 65, 72, 73, 267, 439, 441, 442
self-efficacy: family/parental 98, 103, 105, 191; teacher 221, 239, 394; young people 71, 216, 235, 257
self-harm 52, 352, 386, 406
self-management 143, 206, 207, 245, 358, 359, 403

self-monitoring 207, 250, 264, 269–270
self-reflection 65, 249
self-regulation 14, 192; difficulties 5, 186, 248, 387; during adolescence 53; the FCU and improvements in 119, 191; interventions 41, 119, 175, 250, 251, 253, 390, 391, 441; poverty and 39; in young adulthood 66
self-talk 388, 394
sensitive and responsive instruction **172**, 173
sentence diversity 88
separation anxiety disorder 25, **27**, **28**
serious emotional disturbance (SED) 23–24, 67
serious mental health condition (SMHC) 67
serious mental illness (SMI) 67, 68, 69
service learning 457
session planners (MAP) 325
setting events 11, 127, 130, 131, 133, 136
severe functional impairment **28**, 29, 31–32
sexual behaviors 154, 167, 191, 288
sexual relationships 56
sexual victimization 157
sexuality 65, 68
shared decision-making 71, 98, 349, 427
Shaw, D. 120
Sheidow, A. J. 288
Shepcaro, J. C. 266
Sheridan, S. M. 41
short-term residential treatment as intensive EBP Lab 313–314
side effects: accommodations 405; psychotropic medication 341, 343, 344, 345, 346, 347, 349, 350, 352
single risk ICPs 236
skill acquisition 73, 103, 147, 148, 250, 347, 367
skill-building/development 73, 99, 155, 171, 174, 189, 245, 250, 326, 377, 388, 404, 462
skills: intervention specialists *451*, 455–456, 458; program delivery, and teachers' lack of 59
small group HOPS 359, 366
Smith, E. P. 175
Smith, T. E. 41
Smyntek-Gworek, S. 454
social alienation 246
social awareness 143, 245, 250, 387
social class: health and mental health 68
social cognition 10, 141, 388
social competence 10, 58, 125, 130, 146, 171, 249, 254, 391, 442
Social Decision Making/Problem Solving Program 256
social development *see* social-emotional development
social dynamics: intervention design 12–13; management 148, 229–233, **232**, *see also* classroom social dynamics
social ecology(ies) 11, 227; connections 13; EBD and experience of 4; model (Bronfenbrenner's)

53, 84–85, 217, 261–262, 276–277; social cognitive difficulties 10; young adulthood 66–67; young adults with EBD 68–69, *see also* classroom ecologies; family ecologies; peer ecologies; school ecologies
Social Emotional Preschool Curriculum Consumer Report 42
social functioning: cognitive impairment and 68; FCU assessment 114; intervention specialists and 450, 458; interventions addressing 253; measurement of intervention effectiveness 407; need for dynamic systems perspective 58; young adulthood 66
social goals (adolescent) 52
social information processing 57, 58, 141
social integration 55, 60, 176, 246
social interaction(s) 41, 50, 60, 69, 127, 130, 135, 145, 148, 174, 175, 251, 263, 372
social isolation 13, 69, 97, 100, 106, 126, 128, 141
social learning theory 277
social media 467–468
social networks 73, 128
social phobias (anxiety) 25, **27**, **28**, 71, 83, 246, 251, 257
social processes: influence on development 171; strengthening 167–177, *see also* social dynamics
social skills: ASPs and improved 173; deficits 5, 125, 126, 276; early caregiving quality 111; peer context experiences 58; schools and the limiting of opportunities for enhancement of 170; shared content on Pinterest 468; teacher–child relationships 87; tough students perceived as having 126
Social Skills Improvement System – Rating Scale (SSIS-RS) 221
social skills training 13, 270, 313, 392; management of group processes 250; peer context 58; peer instructors 207; SISP 439; in small groups 206, *see also* BEST in CLASS; social-emotional learning (SEL) programs
social status: peer ecologies 126, 127, 129, 131, 133, 134, 135, 136
social ties: egalitarian classrooms 129
social work training study 337
social-emotional content: use of social media for 468
social-emotional development: classroom management and 402; internal factors 8–9; lack of cultural awareness 435; language skills and 83; young adulthood 65
social-emotional learning (SEL) 169, 245; ASPs and promotion of 170; failure in capacity building 440
social-emotional learning (SEL) delays 35; behavior and teacher–child relationship 39–40; conclusion 45; considerations and future directions 43–45; context and identification of

498   *Index*

problem behavior 39; overview of 35–38; predictors 38; prevalence 38–39, 40

social-emotional learning (SEL) programs 174, 394; adaptations and developmental considerations 40–42; classroom-based 35, **36–37**, 42–43; quality and effect sizes 216; scaling up 44–45; schools as primary context for 169–170; violence prevention 143, 144, 145, 146, 147–148, *see also* Multi-Tiered Social-Emotional Learning

social-emotional skills: and adult outcomes 256; deficits 169, 245, 246

socially responsible behavior 55, 250

socio-demography *see* age; gender

socioeconomic status: prevalence of SEL delays 38–39

Sorensen, L. C. 253

Soslau, E. 454

Southam-Gerow, M. A. 336

SPARKS 174

Spatzier, A. 130

special education: alternative classrooms 403; collaboration in context of 456; percentage of students receiving 3, 187, 261; referrals 43, 405, 435; separate child and adult services 70, *see also* intervention specialists

special education teachers (SETs) 434–435, 437, 438

specialized instructional support personnel (SISP) 438; responsibilities 438–439; serving youth with EBD 439; UDT and 442; use of UDL 439

specialty mental health services 30, 31, 71

specific phobias 25, **27, 28**

Sprott Brooks, D. 168

S.S.Grin program 256–257

stability: psychotropic medication 349, 350

stable victims: school environment interventions and 148

staffing issues: residential programs 312, 314; SMH services 408; TFC 300

stakeholders: implementation of EBPs 426

Stambaugh, L. 287

standardization of interventions 70, 75

"standards aligned resources" 467

Standards of Excellence for Residential Services 309

"step down" placement: TFC portrayed as 295

steps section: MAP practitioner guides 332

Steps to Respect 144, 256

Stetler, C. 420

stigma 97, 106

Stolz, S. 135, 136

Stop Now and Plan (SNAP) program 256

Stop and Think curriculum 270

Stormshak, E. A. 120

strategic formulations 277

stratium 66

strength-focused approaches 187, 278–279, 281, 466

Strengths and Difficulties Questionnaire 263, 379, 380

stress 192; management 72, 250, *see also* caregiver strain; family stress model

structural formulations 277

student(s): characteristics as predictor of response to intervention 209; with EBD *see* youth with EBD; intervention intensity 378; managing classroom contexts and adapting strategies to 233–237; pre-intervention assessment 238; self-monitoring 207, 250, 264, 269–270; testimonials 471–472; typologies 125–126

Student-Teacher Relationship Scale 91, 221

student-teacher relationships: adolescence 55; BEST in Class and improvement in 221; developing positive 456; and development 87; effective classroom management and 86; importance of 215; SEL delay 35, 39–40, 43, 44; social-emotional skill deficits and 246; student comfort in reporting violence 149; with youth with EBD 59, 60, 144; and youth violence 143–144

sub-goals (MST) 280

substance abuse 29, 141, 253

Substance Abuse and Mental Health Services Association (SAMSHA) 42, 157, 206, 292

substance use 5, 71, 167; ACES and risk of 154; disorders 52, 153; interventions 73, 119, 286, 287, 392; multi-risk ICPs and 236; parental monitoring and reduced 191; young adults with EBD 69

success of interventions 15–17

suicide 29, 52, 68, 154, 386, 406

supervision: development of adaptive expertise 454; and improved TFC outcomes 296; of PCs 104–105; treatment foster parents 294, 297, *see also* monitoring

support personnel *see* specialized instructional support personnel (SISP)

Supporting Early Adolescent Learning and Social Success (SEALS) program 134, 148

supportive beliefs intervention 469–470

supportive relationships **219**, 220

surveillance efforts: childhood EBD, United States 24, 29, 32

suspensions 35, 58, 59, 105, 236, 400, 442

sustainability of EBPs 44, 463

sustainability of skill development 277

sustained attention 191, 192

sustainment of intervention **421**, 422, 424

sustainment phase (EPIS) 424

Sutherland, K. S. 147, 221, 223

sympathy: classroom norms 130

synchrony 11, 127, 128, 227

syntax development 88

system reorganization 4, 6, 11, 57, 59–60, 237
Systematic Screening for Behavior Disorders (SSBD) 264
systems: trauma-informed 157, 158
systems of care 17, 43, 96–97, 98, 294–295, 301
systems theory 53, 169, 171, 262, 455

Talbert-Johnson, C. **437**, 438
Target Behavior Interview 375–376
targeted supports and interventions *see* Tier 3 interventions
targeting sequences: in MST 280
targets/goals *see* goals
teacher(s): attunement to peer affiliation 134; classroom social dynamics 125, 148; of color 434, 435, 437, 438; delivery of interventions 40–41, 42; and delivery of interventions 223; EBPs targeting management of classroom dynamics 133–136; engagement 375; language and child language development 89; need for caregiver input 41; and peer ecologies 131–133; perceptions of child skill and language support 90; professional development *see* professional development (PD); screening youth for EBD 406; social media 467, *see also* certified teachers; special education teachers; student-teacher relationships
Teacher Efficacy Beliefs Scale 221
teacher language-based practices 84–85
teacher resource manual (BEST in CLASS) 218
Teacher Self-Efficacy Scale 221
TeachersPayTeachers 467
teacher–child interactions: importance 215; need for flexibility of practices 216; negative 215, 463, *see also* BEST in CLASS; interaction-centred model of language and behavioral development
Teacher–Child Interactions Direct Observation System 221
Teaching Family 311, 312
team approaches: CSC 71; development of adaptive expertise 454; SWPBIS 208; TFC 291, 293
technology: DRC implementation 379–380, 382; and peer support for families 107; use in professional development 466–469
teen parenthood 5, 236
tertiary interventions *see* Tier 3 interventions
testimonials 471–472
theoretical knowledge 455
Theory of Planned Behavior (TPB) 101–102, 103, 469
therapeutic alliance 312, 346
therapeutic relationships (FCU) 188
Therapeutic Residential Care (TRC) 306
therapeutic strategies: FCU Friendship Group 251

Therapy Process Observational Coding System for Psychotherapy, Revised Strategies Scale (TPOCS-RS) 337
thinking skills 250, 251
Thoma, C. A. 441
Thompson, R. 298
Tier 1 interventions 14; BASE Model 234–235, 238, 239; classroom management 134; HOPS 358; SEL 43, 246; SWPBIS 200–201, 202–205, 209; TSAS Framework **16**, *see also* Fast Track Program
Tier 2 interventions 14; BASE Model 235–237, 238, 239; EBD and need for 214–215; HOPS 359; SEL 43, 246–247, 256; SWPBIS 201, 205–207, 209; TSAS Framework **16**, *see also* BEST in CLASS; Check & Connect (C&C)
Tier 3 interventions 14, 215; BASE Model 237, 238, 239; HOPS 359–361; SWPBIS 201, 207–208; TSAS Framework **16**
Tiered Systems of Adaptive Support (TSAS) Framework 15, **16**, 17, 228, 473
time after school: unstructured/unsupervised 167
time management 72, *see also* organization, time management and planning (OTMP) skills
timing (developmental): emergence of EBD 7; of interventions 4
Timmons-Mitchell 287
toddlers: SEL delays 38
Together Facing the Challenge (TFTC) 290, 293, 294, 297–298, 300
Tools for Getting Along (TFGA) 389–390
Total Problems for the Child Behavior Check List (CBCL) 295
tough students 126, 128, 130, 136
Trach, J. 148
tracking child behavior 189
tracking child progress 252
traditional undergraduate" students 66
"train-the-trainer" model of TFC 297–298
training: academic engagement enhancement 148; CBIs 394; developmental systems framework 18; for EBD students' transition needs 441–443; parental *see* Everyday Parenting (EDP); PATHS curriculum 249; of PCs 102, 104, 107; program implementation 427; of SISPs 439; TFC 297–298; trauma-informed 157–158, *see also* professional development
transactional framework (ecological): language skills and problem behavior 84, 85
transactional interplay: child and environment 4, 5; developmental subsystems 6, 7, 11–12
transactional model: problem behavior 39
transactional theory 217
transition(s): impact of OTMP deficits 357; intervention design 12; and long-term outcomes 191; preparing youth for 293; skills 439; to adulthood 65–75, *see also* developmental

500 *Index*

transitions; Universal Design for Transition (UDT)
Transition to Independence Process (TIP) Model 73
transitioning-age youth: discontinuation of medication 349
trauma and adversity: early exposure to 249; EBD and experience of 13; increasing the awareness of 157–158; and poor mental health 68; and SEL delays 38; US policies creating 160, *see also* adverse childhood experiences (ACES); post-traumatic stress disorder (PTSD); youth who experience trauma and adversity
trauma reminders: exposure to 155
Trauma-Focused Cognitive Behavior Therapy (TF-CBT) 155, 157
trauma-focused intervention 393
trauma-informed care 157–158
treatment: research, EBS system model 324, 325; trends in 31–32; unmet need 23, 29–30, 69, 472, 473; use, prevalence of 29–31; for youth who experience trauma and adversity 154–157, *see also* psychotropic medications
treatment family (PWEBS) 329
Treatment Foster Care Oregon (TFCO) 292, 293, 300; effectiveness 296; variations derived from 296–297
Treatment Foster Care (TFC) 290–302; challenges and future directions 299–301; conclusions 301–302; current directions and dilemmas 299; current state of knowledge 294–298; empirical support 290; evidence of effectiveness 308; history and key components 291–294
treatment foster parents 291, 293, 294, 297
treatment history: prior to prescribing 344
treatment planners (MAP) 326
treatment plans 345, 346
"treatment receipt" 30, 31
Triple-P Online intervention 193
troubled students 126
"truce of non-instruction" 463
trusting relationships 13, 171, 312
Tseng, V. 176

Unclaimed Children 96, 292
underachievement 169, 246
underemployment 71, 169, 247, 417, 442
understanding: stressed over performance 453; of student needs, lack of 436
unemployment 442
Unified Theory of Behavior Change 99
United Nations Convention on the Rights of the Child 160
United States: BASE Model 228; childhood EBD 23, 24; co-location of behavioral health within pediatrics 121; Fast Track Program 247; low priority of child-wellbeing policies 160; Map

system 322; need for recognition and treatment of EBD 30; rates of psychotropic medication use by children 341–343; residential programs 307, 314, 315; urban schools and use of online tools 467
Universal Design for Learning (UDL) 439–441; benefits 440–441; defined 439; empirical support 441
Universal Design for Transition (UDT) 441–442; preparing and supporting specialists from diverse backgrounds 442; translating to meet academic and transition goals 442–443
universal prevention programs: classroom management 133–134; effective ASPs 174; SEL 169, 174; youth violence *see* violence prevention programs, *see also* Tier 1 interventions
unmet needs 23, 29–30, 69, 472, 473
unwanted behavior: responding to 204–205
Upshur, C. C. 391
User-Centered Design 427
"usual care" TFC 297, 298, 299

value systems 55
value-added: BEST in CLASS 217, 222
Van den Berg, Y. H. M. 135, 136
Vaughn, A. J. 363
victimization: interventions addressing 173; youth with disabilities and higher rates of 142, *see also* peer, victimization; polyvictimization
Video Interaction Project (VIP) 119, 121
videotaped observation: FCU 114, 192
violence prevention programs: assessing efficacy, in real time 147–148; conclusion 149; implementation considerations 147–149; relevance for youth with EBD 149; research needs 145–147; school-based 143–145; selection 147; teachers' effectiveness in managing classroom social dynamics 148
visual cues 41
vocabulary development 87, 88, 89
Voegler-Lee, M. E. 426
Volpe, R. J. 376

Wagner, H. R. 311
wait time 87–88
Walton, G. M. 470
warm social climate 171–173, **172**
Web 2.0 technology 467
Weiss, B. 394
well-defined interventions 279–280
Werch, B. 221
what works: comprehensive supports 43; need for experimental control trials 473; person-oriented analysis 7; residential programs 309–310, 313, 315; TFC 299, 301

Index 501

What Works Clearinghouse (WWC) 42, 205, 206, 208, 265, 268
Whittaker, J. 307
Willoughby, M. T. 426
Wise Interventions 469–470, 473; achieving PD buy-in 470–471; content and activities 471–472
Wolfe, K. 266
workforce professionals 433–443; conclusion 443; culturally competent 435–436; diversification 433, 434, 442; professional development *see* professional development (PD); recruitment and retention 436–438; research on related services providers 438–439; special education teachers (SETs) 434–435; training for and preparing for transition needs 441–443; Universal Design for Learning (UDL) 439–443, *see also* intervention specialists; school mental health providers (SMHP); staffing issues; teachers
working phase (session planner) 325
workshops (professional development) 466
Wraparound 72–73, 75, 287

Yeager, D. W. 471
Young Adult Engagement Project (Just Do You) 72
young adult peers 71–72, 75
young adulthood 65–75; brain development 65–66; cognitive development 65; conclusion and future directions 74–75; EBD and developmental and social-contextual considerations 68–69; EBD in 67–68; evidence-based, promising practices 70–74, 74–75; FCU 190–191; role transitions 65, 66; service and system considerations 69–70; social functioning 66; social-contextual landscapes 66–67; social-emotional development 65
youth of color: ASPs and academic achievement/engagement 171; disproportionate representation in EBD programs 433; EBD and maladaptive outcomes 169; need for diverse

workforce 433; percentage served under IDEA 434; psychotropic medication use 342; referrals to special education 435; serious mental illness 68
youth with EBD: challenges in multiple domains 50; characteristics, considering in implementing innovative services 427; classroom peer ecologies and cultures 125–136; during middle and high school years 50–60; ecological contexts 3–4; interventions *see* interventions; language skills and engagement 89; middle and high school years for 57–59; outcomes *see* youth outcomes; parent participation/attendance, IEP meetings 97; percentage with 57; perception of houseparents 312; prevalence 3, 186; risk of trauma and adversity 157; social and emotional aspects 246; victimization and aggression among 142, *see also* high-risk youth
Youth Outcome Questionnaire 336
youth outcomes: EBD and long-term 140, 400; group care 308; implementation science definition 422; MST and identification of desired 284, *see also* academic outcomes; early childhood outcomes; poor outcomes; positive outcomes; negative outcomes
"youth as partner" mentality 173
youth violence: negative consequences 141; prevalence and risk factors 141; prevention *see* violence prevention programmes, *see also* aggression; bullying; physical assault
youth who experience trauma and adversity 153–160; prevalence and consequences 153–154; prevention 159–160; summary and conclusions 160; transforming systems to address 157–159; treatment for 154–157
YouTube 467, 468

Zucker, T. 88